TRADEMARKS AND UNFAIR COMPETITION

Beverly W. Pattishall

David Craig Hilliard

Joseph Nye Welch II

Members of the Chicago Bar
Adjunct Professors, Northwestern University School of Law

CONTEMPORARY CASEBOOK SERIES

Matthew Bender
IRWIN

1995 Reprint

Library of Congress Cataloging-in-Publication Data

Pattishall, Beverly W.
    Trademarks and unfair competition / Beverly W. Pattishall, David Craig Hilliard, Joseph Nye Welch II.
        p.   cm. — (Contemporary Casebook Series)
    Includes index.
    ISBN # 0-256-16475-4 (hardcover)
    1. Trademarks—United States—Cases. 2. Competition, Unfair—United States—Cases. I. Hilliard, David Craig. II. Welch, Joseph Nye, 1954- . III. Title. IV. Series: Cases and materials.
KF3179.P373   1994
346.7304'88—dc20   94-21711
[347.306488]   CIP

MATTHEW BENDER & CO., INC.
EDITORIAL OFFICES
11 PENN PLAZA, NEW YORK, NY 10001-2006 (212) 967-7707
2101 WEBSTER ST., OAKLAND, CA 94612-3027 (510) 446-7100

LEGAL EDUCATION PUBLICATIONS

FOREWORD

Nearly every practicing lawyer today encounters the fields of trademark and unfair competition law. We believe the focus of this text upon these fields will facilitate an in-depth understanding of an area too often thought technical and difficult.

We have sought in this volume to provide for both students and practitioners of trademark and unfair competition law an organized guide to the opinions, treatises, and commentary; a delineation of the principal questions and problems to be expected; and a synthesis of the current and developing law under each of the subdivisions of our Table of Contents. Like most similar efforts, this book was initially prepared to meet the needs of teaching a law school course. It has evolved to its present state with the enlightening benefit of criticism from Northwestern University law students and many practicing lawyers to whom it has been exposed. As a consequence, much that went in has later come out, and much that was not included originally, either because it had been overlooked or did not exist, has now gone in. The authors hope that those who may assay the yield from this crucible will find it now containing a maximum of the legally valuable and only a minimum of dross.

Acknowledgement is most appreciatively expressed to our colleagues, Raymond I. Geraldson, Jr., for his most helpful contributions to this work, and Kimberly W. Alcantara, for her scholarly contribution to our analysis of government regulation of unfair competition. We are also especially anxious to express our thanks to Mary Beth Sutton for her preeminent work in readying the manuscript for publication.

B.W.P.
D.C.H.
J.N.W.

April, 1994

TABLE OF CONTENTS

Page

Chapter 1

Principles of Trademark Law

Chapter 2

Creation and Maintenance of Trademark Rights

Page

Chapter 3

Trademark Registration and Administrative Proceedings

Chapter 4

Loss of Rights

Chapter 5

Infringement of Trademark Rights

Chapter 6

Proof of Infringement

Chapter 7

Special Defenses and Limitations

Page

Chapter 8

Trade Identity Law

Page

Page

Chapter 9

Jurisdiction and Remedies

Page

Chapter 10

Governmental Regulation

Page

CHAPTER 1

PRINCIPLES OF TRADEMARK AND UNFAIR COMPETITION LAW

§ 1.01 Historical Development

The origins of trademarks and commercial identification trace back into antiquity well prior to recorded history. The identifying marks of the makers frequently have been found on prehistoric implements, weapons, pottery and other articles of commerce. Much later, during the development period of our common law in England, those who sold goods, wares and produce that were the fruit of their own labor or craftsmanship likewise identified those products, or their places of business such as shops, inns or pubs, with their own means for trade identity. Sometimes it was their name, sometimes something more fanciful, but there soon developed problems and controversies arising out of uses by others of the same or similar names and marks for the same or similar goods or services. Because of the basic need in such controversies for writs of prohibition or injunctions, they usually were brought to the Chancellor.

The London shoemaker could not suffer such damage from another's use of a mark as would call for intervention of the law until the mark he employed to identify his own wares had come to signify their source through his own use. Likewise, that shoemaker needed little from the law beyond preventing continuation of a nearby competitor's use of the same or a similar mark likely to deceive the earlier user's customers and divert his trade. Accordingly, the law grew and unconsciously developed around the use fundamental that became its basic rationale. It evolved in sophistication, case by case, as was needed to cope with the increasing complexities of commerce and the artfulness of poachers, but it remained rooted in and logically dependent upon the proposition that the results of prior use are all that need or deserve the law's protection.

The issues of the controversies were, of course, ones of deceit, or the likelihood of deceit, arising out of a latecomer's use of a name or mark. Eventually, a small body of law developed for coping with these problems of name and mark confusion and likelihood of confusion in trade. In some areas of commercial activity, precedent was derived from the activities of the guilds and the law merchant, but all was directed pragmatically toward the needs of fair resolution of the problems which came before them, and they were problems essentially sounding in deceit.[1] It came

---

1 *See generally* F. I. Schecter, *The Historical Foundations of Trademark Law* (1925); E. S. Rogers, *Good Will, Trademarks and Unfair Trading* (1914); Rogers, *Some Historical*

to pass, therefore, that the common law, and later the statutory law, on the subject of trademarks and other means for identifying the source of goods and services was structured upon the proposition of prohibiting commercial confusion as to the source of goods or services.

The recorded development of this area of the law is surprisingly recent. The first written reference to a trademark case has been described as "an irrelevant reminiscent dictum"[2] appearing in a non-trademark case decision entitled *Southern v. How*, Popham 143, 79 Eng. Reprint 1243, first reported in 1656. English courts ever since have relied upon *Southern v. How* for their ancient jurisdiction to prevent trademark piracy. The basic proposition of protecting against deceitful use of names and marks is that the prior user is entitled to be protected because presumably some identity has been achieved by his or her use and that identity can be the subject of deception by a subsequent confusingly similar use. It is plain that governmental grants of limited monopoly to encourage invention or the literary arts have nothing to do with the subject.

The United States took the law of England as its own. Indeed, even as recently as fifty years ago, some British decisions often were cited to our courts as persuasive authority in trademark cases. It is intriguing that an early reference to trademark law in America is a notation in the court records of Fairfax County, Virginia disclosing that in 1772 George Washington, a resident of the County and then only a farmer and businessman, went to the Court to record a trademark for his flour which he proposed to name simply "G. Washington."

Not until the 1825 decision in *Snowden v. Noah*, Hopk. Ch. 347 (N.Y. Ch.) does there appear a reported decision in anything really resembling a trademark case, and it was hardly a step forward in our law. It was an action by the recent purchaser of a New York newspaper called THE NATIONAL ADVOCATE. He sought to enjoin the seller from publishing in New York a paper entitled THE NEW YORK NATIONAL ADVOCATE. The court refused on the ground that the names were sufficiently distinct to prevent deception. The first trademark statute was that of the State of New York, passed in 1845. No federal trademark statute existed until the Act of 1870, but by then eleven additional state trademark statutes had been passed. At that time, there were only 62 reported American trademark cases. Although scanty in number, many of the earlier American trademark/trade identity cases are intriguing and they uniformly disclose the basic rationale of protection against deceit respecting a prior use.

The first American treatise writer on trademark law, Francis H. Upton, states in his 1860 work, *Treatise on the Law of Trademarks*, that the peculiar phraseology of our Patent Act of 1842 may have led to the erroneous practice by some "of availing of its provisions to secure what is supposed to be an equivalent to trademark property." Upton also states quite correctly that: "The right of property in trademarks does not partake in any degree of the nature and character of a patent or copyright,

---

Matter Concerning Trademarks, 9 Mich. L. Rev. 29 (1910); B. G. Paster, *Trademarks —
Ancient Lineage of Trademarks*, 33 J. Pat. Off. Soc'y 876 (1951); L. E. Daniels, *The History
of the Trademark*, 7 Trademark Rep. 239 (1911).

[2] F. I. Schecter, *supra*, note 1, at 6 (1925).

to which it has sometimes been referred — nor is it safe to reason from any supposed analogies existing between them."

Originally, intent to defraud was conceived to be a legal necessity for any trademark cause of action, but it was soon recognized that the absence of intent to trade upon another's good will was neither cure nor comfort for the aggrieved party. Thus, the prerequisite of proof of intent to defraud in trade identity cases was gradually relaxed and eventually disappeared, and the simple test of likelihood of deception as to the source of goods or services of a prior user became the criterion for relief.

The United States trademark statutes have had a substantial effect upon the evolution of the law of trademarks and trade identity unfair competition by liberalizing the interpretation of what is needed for a cause of action. The first federal trademark statute, the Act of 1870, was held unconstitutional because Congress made the mistake, which judges, lawyers and businessmen are still regularly making, of confusing trade identity rights with patent rights. *Trade-Mark Cases*, 100 U.S. 82 (1879). Congress erroneously based the original trademark statute upon the patent and copyright clause of the United States Constitution, instead of the commerce clause. That statute was followed by the Act of 1881 and then by the Act under which much of our trademark law developed, the Act of 1905. The Act of 1920 was supplementary to the Act of 1905 and was adopted primarily to establish a form of limited rights registration so that United States enterprises whose marks were not registrable under the 1905 Act (e.g., surnames) could obtain a domestic trademark registration as a basis for obtaining foreign registrations in countries where domestic registration was a prerequisite (see Chapter 3, *infra*). In 1946, Congress passed the Lanham Act which, as amended, is currently in force (see Appendix).

The Act of 1905 especially encouraged the disappearance of both the earlier requirement of intent to deceive and the earlier confinement of causes of action to those involving essentially the same goods and the same names. The Lanham Act (1946) further liberalized and expanded the concept of infringement. It also introduced a statutory prohibition of unfair competition in its Section 43(a) (§ 8.02, *infra*). Perhaps its most significant innovations, however, were its provisions that federal registration of a trademark constitutes "constructive notice of the registrant's claim of ownership thereof" and for incontestability (Chapter 3, *infra*).

The Lanham Act has been amended several times since its passage. In 1984, provisions were added to combat the burgeoning problem of trademark counterfeiting (P.L. 98-473). In 1988, the Trademark Law Revision Act of 1988 (the "Revision Act") was passed by Congress. The Act of November 16, 1988, Pub. L. 100-667, Title I Section 132, 102 Stat. 3935, amending 15 U.S.C. § 1051 *et. seq.* The most notable change the Revision Act brought about was the provision for an "intent to use" federal registration system. U.S. applicants may now apply for federal trademark registration based on a "bona fide intention to use the mark in commerce," as an alternative to basing the application on actual use, which was the only valid basis for application prior to the Revision Act. An intent-based application confers upon the applicant nationwide "constructive use" rights as of the date of application, which become viable once the applicant actually begins use of the mark and the registration issues.

§ 1.02 The Nature of Trademark and Unfair Competition Law

Species

Unfair competition is the genus of which trademark infringement is one of the species. All trademark cases are in fact cases of unfair competition. (*Hanover Star Milling Co. v. Metcalf*, 240 U.S. 403, 413 (1916).) The principle of law has been reduced to a single sentence — No one has any right to represent his goods as the goods of another, and this is merely the duty to abstain from fraud. Whether any particular contrivance is calculated to result in the sale of one person's goods as those of another is a question of fact in each case. If it can be shown as a fact that a trader's goods are known on the market and distinguished from others by any name, whether descriptive, geographical or personal, or by any device, whatever its nature, or by color of label or style of dress, then this element, whatever it may be, represents goodwill which should be protected against use or imitation by another in any way likely to deceive the public as to the origin of the product or enable the sale of the defendant's article as and for complainant's. The extent of the restraint imposed on another's use of the particular element varies, depending on the facts in a particular case, from use coupled with such announcements as will effectually prevent mistake, to prohibition of all use in cases where no amount or attempted distinction will be effective.

The inaptness of the term "unfair competition law" has been described in 1 Nims, *The Law of Unfair Competition and Trademarks* * (4th ed. 1947) at pp. 2–3:

> *Play fair!*
>
> This action is the embodiment in law of the ancient rule of the playground — "Play fair!" For generations the law has enforced justice. In this action the basis is fairness — quite a different ethical principle. Many decisions have been approved as just which were most unfair. The maxim *caveat emptor* is founded on justice; the more modern rule which compels the use of truth in selling goods is founded on fairness. The rule of fairness conflicts with the rule of *caveat emptor*.
>
> It is unfortunate that the body of law termed unfair competition was christened with that title. It is a misnomer. It is misleading because . . . these rules also cover cases where there is no competition between the parties. To describe it with any accuracy is very difficult; for, though the common law of unfair competition may be a "limited concept," the acts to which these rules have been found to apply are ever changing in character as social and business conditions change. It applies to misappropriation as well as misrepresentation; to the selling of another's goods as one's own, to misappropriation of what equitably belongs to a competitor; to acts which lie outside the ordinary course of business and are tainted by fraud, coercion, or conduct otherwise prohibited by law. Most courts continue to confine it to acts which result in the passing off of the goods of one man for those of another, but this limitation is not universally accepted. The English term, "Passing Off," or its equivalent, "Palming Off," is hardly more satisfactory than our name "Unfair Competition."

There is a distinction which is often unnoted but which is basic in the law of unfair competition. On the one hand, there is the group of unfair acts referred to as trade identity unfair competition. On the other hand, there are a great many acts which are lumped together into the area of unfair competition law and classified as unfair competition but which do not generally relate to confusion as to the source of products or services. This latter group better may be called unfair trade practices.

Trade identity unfair competition is anything in the nature of deceiving as to source. It may take the form of trademark infringement, copying of trade names, labels, commercial dress or the like. If the torts are in fact ones of deception as to source or sponsorship of goods or services, they are all to be approached with the same legal philosophy and reasoning.

Unfair Trade – Tortious

Unfair trade practices are tortious acts often referred to broadly as unfair competition but ordinarily not comprising deception as to source. Usually, they are regulated by government agencies or actionable by private parties. False descriptions of goods, for example, really have nothing to do with deception as to source or sponsorship and are a different kind of tort than is trade identity unfair competition. The same is true of misrepresentation, trade disparagement, or false and deceptive advertising claims generally. Some degree of falsity in advertising claims commonly exists, but when the claims may materially deceive the public or damage competitors, unfair trade practices exist. Likewise, the acts prohibited by the antitrust laws fall within the general category of unfair competition as does trade secret law. In fact, an almost limitless variety of competitive "dirty tricks" falls within the unfair trade practice area of unfair competition.

At common law, such competitive dirty tricks usually were not actionable, because there was no injury for which there was a known remedy. As stated by Judge Learned Hand in *Ely-Norris Safe Co. v. Mosler Safe Co.*, 7 F.2d 603, 604 (2d Cir. 1925):

CL Competitive were not actionable

> The reason, as we think, why such deceits have not been regarded as actionable by a competitor, depends only upon his inability to show any injury for which there is a known remedy. In an open market it is generally impossible to prove that a customer, whom the defendant has secured by falsely describing his goods, would have bought off the plaintiff, if the defendant had been truthful. Without that, the plaintiff, though aggrieved in company with other honest traders, cannot show any ascertainable loss. He may not recover at law, and the equitable remedy is concurrent. The law does not allow him to sue as a vicarious avenger of the defendant's customer.

Same as consumer

Moreover, the common law principle of *caveat emptor* similarly discouraged or barred action by the consumer. As stated by Justice Holmes in *Deming v. Darling*, 20 N.E. 107 (Mass. 1889):

> [S]ome cases suggest that bad faith might make a seller liable for what are known as seller's statements, apart from any other conduct by which the buyer is fraudulently induced to forebear inquiries. *Pike v. Fay*, 101 Mass. 134. But this is a mistake. It is settled that the law does not exact good faith from a seller in those vague commendations of his wares which manifestly are open to

difference of opinion, which do not imply untrue assertions concerning matters of direct observation, (*Teague v. Irwin*, 127 Mass. 217), and as to which it always has been "understood, the world over, that such statements are to be distrusted."

Gradually, there developed in the law a primarily statutory basis for business and consumer protection against such unfair trade practices. These statutory changes and more innovative private causes of action have afforded a more effective way of curbing trademark infringement and other kinds of trade identity unfair competition.

§ 1.03 Protection of the Private Interest

As a part of the developing law of trademarks, and particularly with the advent of the registration statutes, there appeared the dubious notion that the right in a trademark is an actual property right. In 1879, the United States Supreme Court stated that the right to adopt and use a symbol or a device to identify one's merchandise with oneself and distinguish it from that of others was a property right long recognized by the common law. *Trade-Mark Cases*, 100 U.S. 82, 92 (1879). The notion that trade identity rights are property rights remains strong, 3 Callmann, *The Law Of Unfair Competition, Trademarks & Monopolies*, § 17.07 (Altman, ed. 1993), perhaps because of a fallacious equation of them with patent rights. The "property" concept, nevertheless, is logically incompatible and irreconcilable with the historic deception as to source rationale for trade identity, trademark and unfair competition law. There has developed, however, along with twentieth century national mass marketing, an obvious and demanding commercial need to protect what Justice Frankfurter called "the commercial magnetism" or "drawing power of a commercial symbol."

Trademark as Property no however yes to protectable

MISHAWAKA RUBBER & WOOLEN MFG. CO. v. S. S. KRESGE CO.

United States Supreme Court
316 U.S. 203 (1942)

FRANKFURTER, JUSTICE.

The petitioner, which manufactures and sells shoes and rubber heels, employs a trade-mark, registered under the Trade-Mark Act of 1905, 33 Stat. 724, 15 U.S.C. § 81 *et seq.*, consisting of a red circular plug embedded in the center of a heel. The heels were not sold separately, but were attached to shoes made by the petitioner. It has spent considerable sums of money in seeking to gain the favor of the consuming public by promoting the mark as assurance of a desirable product. The respondent sold heels not made by the petitioner but bearing a mark described by the District Court as "a circular plug of red or reddish color so closely resembling that of the plaintiff [petitioner] that it is difficult to distinguish the products sold by the defendant from the plaintiff's products." The heels sold by the respondent were inferior in quality to those made by the petitioner, and "this tended to destroy the good will created by the plaintiff in the manufacture of its superior product." Although there was no evidence that particular purchasers were actually deceived into believing that the heels sold by the respondent were manufactured by the petitioner, the District Court found that there was a "reasonable likelihood" that some purchases might have been induced by the purchaser's belief that he was obtaining the petitioner's product. "The ordinary purchaser, having become familiar with the plaintiff's trademark, would naturally be led to believe that the heels marketed by the defendant were the product of the plaintiff company."

. . . .

The protection of trade-marks is the law's recognition of the psychological function of symbols. If it is true that we live by symbols, it is no less true that we purchase goods by them. A trade-mark is a merchandising short-cut which induces a purchaser to select what he wants, or what he has been led to believe he wants. The owner of a mark exploits this human propensity by making every effort to impregnate the atmosphere of the market with the drawing power of a congenial symbol. Whatever the means employed, the aim is the same—to convey through the mark, in the minds of potential customers, the desirability of the commodity upon which it appears. Once this is attained, the trademark owner has something of value. If another poaches upon the commercial magnetism of the symbol he has created, the owner can obtain legal redress.

. . . .

"Commercial magnetism"

Reversed.

Notwithstanding the soundness of the *Mishawaka* decision, one problem with applying a property concept to the trade identity field is that trademarks comprised of ordinary words or names such as "Chicago," "Supreme" or "Jones" may acquire strong source-indicating significances but can hardly be characterized legally as any particular party's "property." The same sort of impediment is encountered in cases involving unfair competition claims based upon the similarity of the color or design of labeling or packaging, and this is so even though deception results. Thus, if only a property right exists, deceptive acts which do not involve a unique, fanciful or coined trademark are not readily prohibited since the existence of actual proprietary rights must first be established. Moreover, the property concept often relies in practice upon the support afforded by trademark registration certificates, a "proof of ownership" ordinarily unavailable in unfair competition cases.

As a result of the contradictions and limitations imposed by the property rationale, evolving trademark doctrine tended to merge somewhat illogically the concept of invasion of a property right with the fundamental tort concept logically and correctly based upon a merchant's interest in being protected from deceptions as to source or identity.

HANOVER STAR MILLING CO. v. METCALF

United States Supreme Court
240 U.S. 403 (1916)

PITNEY, JUSTICE.

Common-law trade-marks, and the right to their exclusive use, are of course to be classed among property rights, *Trade-Mark Cases*, 100 U.S. 82, 92, 93; but only in the sense that a man's right to the continued enjoyment of his trade reputation and the good-will that flows from it, free from unwarranted interference by others, is a property right, for the protection of which a trademark is an instrumentality. As was said in the same case (p. 94), the right grows out of use, not mere adoption. In the English courts it often has been said that there is no property whatever in a trademark, as such. *Per* Ld. Langdale, M.R. in *Perry v. Truefitt,* 6 Beav. 73; *per* Vice Chancellor Sir. Wm. Page Wood (afterwards Ld. Hatherly), in *Collins Co. v. Brown,* 3 Kay & J. 423, 426; 3 Jur. N.S. 930; *per* Ld. Herschell in *Reddaway v. Banham,* A.C. 1896, 199, 209. But since in the same cases the courts recognized the right of the party to the exclusive use of marks adopted to indicate goods of his manufacture, upon the ground that "a man is not to sell his own goods under the pretense that they are the goods of another man; he cannot be permitted to practice such a deception, nor to use the means which contribute to that end. He cannot therefore be allowed to use names, marks, letters, or other *indicia,* by which he may induce purchasers to believe, that the goods which he is selling are the manufacture of another person" (6 Beav. 73); it is plain that in denying the right of property in a trade-mark it was intended only to deny such property right except as appurtenant to an established business or trade in connection with which the mark is used. This is evident from the expressions used in these and other English cases. Thus, in *Ainsworth v. Walmsley,* L.R. 1 Eq. Cas. 518, 524, Vice Chancellor Sir Wm. Page Wood said:

> This court has taken upon itself to protect a man in the use of a certain trade-mark as applied to a particular description of article. He has no property in that mark *per se,* any more than in any other fanciful denomination he may assume for his own private use, otherwise than with reference to his trade. If he does not carry on a trade in iron, but carries on a trade in linen, and stamps a lion on his linen, another person may stamp a lion on iron; but when he has appropriated a mark to a particular species of goods, and caused his goods to circulate with this mark upon them, the court has said that no one shall be at liberty to defraud that man by using that mark, and passing off goods of his manufacture as being the goods of the owner of that mark.

. . . .

. . . . We agree with the court below (208 Fed. Rep. 519) that "Since it is the trade, and not the mark, that is to be protected, a trade-mark acknowledges no territorial boundaries of municipalities or states or nations, but extends to every market where the trader's goods have become known and identified by his use of the mark. But the mark, of itself, cannot travel to markets where there is no article to wear the badge and no trader to offer the article."

Affirmed.

The *Hanover* decision merged the property right concept with the tort rationale of protection against deception, stating that "it is the trade, and not the mark, that is to be protected." Later the reliance upon a property theory in trade identity cases was further eroded by Justice Holmes in *DuPont v. Masland*, 244 U.S. 100, 102 (1917), as follows: "The word property as applied to trade-marks and trade secrets is an unanalyzed expression of certain secondary consequences of the primary fact that the law makes some rudimentary requirements of good faith." This recognition of commercial integrity as the basis for trade identity protection was also voiced by the eminent trade identity law practitioner and authority, Edward S. Rogers:

> It was soon realized that trade could be stolen without resort to infringement of technical trade-marks, without violation of any then recognized property right. All manner of contrivances were employed — labels, packages and the like, were imitated, which resulted in public deception and private injury without, it was thought, subjecting the perpetrator to legal liability. The lawyers and courts at once found that their property theory was unworkable. Certainly no property could be claimed in the color of a label, or in the arrangement of the printed matter upon it, or in the shape of a bottle, or in any of the numberless things which help to identify a particular man's goods and which were being imitated for the purpose of stealing away his customers and appropriating his good will.
>
> It was perfectly clear that a man's trade could be taken away from him unlawfully and his customers deceived into purchasing a spurious article, in other ways than by imitation of his technical trademark, and it was a reproach to the law and courts of justice if they would sit idly by and see this go on. To meet this situation there has lately developed a considerable body of law dealing with this class of cases which, in this country, for want of a better name, are called cases of "unfair competition" or "unfair trading"; in Great Britain "passing off"; in France "concurrence deloyale"; and in Germany "unlauter wettbewerb".

Good Will, Trademarks and Unfair Trading, 126–127 (1914).

Thus, as commerce became increasingly complex and commercial pirates became more sophisticated, it was recognized that there are many aspects of trade identity which should be protected from many and perhaps unending varieties of deceptively tortious conduct.

Judge Learned Hand's famous statement in *Yale Electric Corp. v. Robertson,* 26 F.2d 972, 973–974 (2d Cir. 1928), makes clear that the fundamental element of trade identity law is protection against deception:

> The law of unfair trade comes down very nearly to this — as judges have repeated again and again — that one merchant shall not divert customers from

another by representing what he sells as emanating from the second. This has been, and perhaps even more now is, the whole Law and the Prophets on the subject, though it assumes many guises. Therefore it was at first a debatable point whether a merchant's good will, indicated by his mark, could extend beyond such goods as he sold. How could he lose bargains which he had no means to fill? What harm did it do a chewing gum maker to have an ironmonger use his trade-mark? The law often ignores the nicer sensibilities.

However, it has of recent years been recognized that a merchant may have a sufficient economic interest in the use of his mark outside the field of his own exploitation to justify interposition by a court. His mark is his authentic seal; by it he vouches for the goods which bear it; it carries his name for good or ill. If another uses it, he borrows the owner's reputation, whose quality no longer lies within his own control. This is an injury, even though the borrower does not tarnish it, or divert any sales by its use; for a reputation, like a face, is the symbol of its possessor and creator, and another can use it only as a mask. And so it has come to be recognized that, unless the borrower's use is so foreign to the owner's as to insure against any identification of the two, it is unlawful.

§ 1.04 Protection of the Public Interest

The public interest against deception is necessarily a fundamental consideration in trade identity unfair competition cases, yet the treatment of that interest is ordinarily residual to what is primarily a private complaint. *Scandinavia Belting Co. v. Asbestos & Rubber Works of America Inc.*, 257 F. 937, 941–942 (2d Cir. 1919); *Jenkins Bros. v. Kelly & Jones Co.*, 227 F. 211, 214 (3d Cir. 1915). *See generally* Diamond, *Public Interest and the Trademark System*, 62 J.P.O.S. 528 (1980); *Developments In The Law — Trade-Marks And Unfair Competition*, 68 Harv. L. Rev. 814, 885–893 (1955). The *Cross* case, *infra*, turns on protection of the public interest. *See also Stahly v. M. H. Jacobs Co.*, 183 F.2d 914 (7th Cir. 1950); *Marshak v. Green*, 746 F.2d 927 (2d Cir. 1984). *See generally* Chapter 7, *infra*.

T & T MANUFACTURING CO. v. A.T. CROSS CO.

United States Court of Appeals, First Circuit
587 F.2d 533 (1978), cert. denied, 441 U.S. 908 (1979)

KUNZIG, JUDGE.

The sole issue presented for review in this trademark infringement appeal is the validity and enforceability of a Settlement Agreement entered into by the defendant A.T. Cross Company (Cross) and The Quill Company (First Quill) [and later assigned to T & T Mfg. Co. (Second Quill)] for the manufacture and sale of certain pens and pencils. Chief Judge Raymond J. Pettine of the United States District Court for the District of Rhode Island held, *inter alia,* the Agreement was valid and enforceable and hence estopped Cross from asserting trademark infringement and unfair competition claims as outlined *infra.* Because we agree with the district court, we affirm.

. . . .

The principal contention of Cross [is] that the Settlement Agreement should not be enforced on grounds of public policy. Cross contends that an agreement settling a trademark dispute is to be enforced, but with one proviso, namely, that if such an agreement is likely to cause public confusion as to the respective products, then it should not be enforced.

At the outset, we note that the decisional, as well as the statutory law dealing with the area of trademarks is vitally concerned with the protection of the public interest. As was stated by this court in *General Baking Co. v. Gorman,* 3 F.2d 891 (1st Cir. 1925):

> It should never be overlooked that trade-mark and unfair competition cases are affected with a public interest. A dealer's good will is protected, not merely for his profit, but in order that the purchasing public may not be enticed into buying A's product when it wants B's product. *Id.* at 893.

Against this backdrop, Cross maintains that since the district court held that there was a likelihood of public confusion between the products of Second Quill and Cross, it follows that the Settlement Agreement allowing Second Quill to manufacture and sell such products may not be enforced.

We cannot agree with Cross that merely because the district court made a finding of likelihood of public confusion that *ipso facto* the Settlement Agreement should now not be enforced according to its terms. Rather, we agree with the district court's approach that the *degree* or *extent* of public confusion must be examined in order to ascertain whether there is any significant harm to the public by decreeing enforcement of the Settlement Agreement. Additionally, there are other considerations, most notably the policy, vital to the law of contracts, of holding people to the terms of agreements knowingly and wilfully entered into. These must also be considered in resolving the question of enforcement of the Settlement Agreement.

Courts have traditionally, in disputes similar to the present case, weighed the public interest concerning trademarks against the interest in contract enforcement. *Beer Nuts, Inc. v. King Nut Co.,* 477 F.2d 326, 328–29 (6th Cir. 1973), *cert denied,* 414 U.S. 858, *rehearing denied,* 414 U.S. 1033 (1973). In *Beer Nuts,* the court concluded that a party could not challenge a trademark as a descriptive word because by contract it had lost that defense. In deciding this, the court balanced the interest in "guarding against the depletion of the general vocabulary" of descriptive words against the contract interest that "a person should be held to his undertakings." *Id.* at 329.

Similarly, in *Peyrat v. L. N. Renault & Sons, Inc.,* 247 F. Supp. 1009 (S.D.N.Y. 1965), the court reviewed a contract permitting the importation of brandy under the same name as that used by the defendant in selling its wines. Therein the court stated, "The parties to a trademark controversy may contract between themselves for any legal purpose. The agreement is for a legal purpose and is valid and enforceable so long as no injury is caused to the public." *Id.* at 1014. The court, while noting that confusion as to the source of a consumer product is the type of public injury to be prevented, concluded that any such likelihood of confusion was sufficiently abrogated by the differing channels of commerce through which the two products traveled.

In the present case, the district court, following the spirit of previous cases, correctly evaluated the competing interests of contract enforcement with any harm the public might experience due to confusion arising between the products of Second Quill and Cross.

We observe that there was no allegation that the products of First Quill were inferior to Cross, nor was the Settlement Agreement entered into with any intent to deceive the public. Moreover, the Settlement Agreement specifically consented to the manufacture of only those pens which bore a *Quill* insignia as a distinguishing characteristic. Based upon the foregoing, it is clear, as the district court found, that any harm to the public as the result of a likelihood of confusion would not be significant.

The ascertainment of what is or is not in the public interest is often a difficult and nebulous task for a court to undertake. As the court stated in *Application of E. I. Dupont DeNemours & Co.*, 476 F.2d 1357, 1362, (Cust. & Pat. App. 1973):

> Reasonable men may differ as to the *weight* to give specific evidentiary elements in a particular case. In one case it will indicate that confusion is unlikely; in the next it will not. In neither case is it helpful or necessary to inject broad maxims or references to "the public interest" which do not aid in deciding. Only the facts can do that.

On the basis of the facts of the present case, we hold that the Settlement Agreement should be enforced according to its terms. Since we find that any harm to the public is not significant as the result of a likelihood of confusion between Second Quill's and Cross' products, the policy of holding a party to its contractual undertakings becomes dominant. Added into this balance is the judicial policy of encouraging extra-judicial settlement of trademark litigation. In the words of Chief Judge Pettine:

> Insisting that a court review a settlement to assure that no public confusion will result would make such agreements of little value to the parties. *T&T Mfg. Co., supra* at 827.

Moreover, to do so would undermine the policy of giving deference to the contractual agreements of reputable businessmen-users of valuable trademarks. *See, Application of E. I. Dupont DeNemours & Co., supra.*

As a final observation, we note that Cross originally entered into the Settlement Agreement with full knowledge of a potential for immediate public confusion between its products and those of First Quill. Now, some eleven years later, Cross seeks to disaffirm the Agreement on the basis of public confusion — the same basis it was instrumental in bringing about in the first place. It appears at best incongruous that a party should be permitted to disaffirm a contract as against public policy when such grounds are the very grounds that the party itself knowingly and wilfully helped to create. We decline so to do.

. . . .

Accordingly, we hold upon careful consideration of all briefs and submissions and after oral argument that the judgment of the district court sustaining the validity and enforceability of the Settlement Agreement is

Affirmed.

§ 1.05   The Monopoly Phobia

A competitive economy requires clear-cut source identification for goods and services, yet the right to exclude others from any deceptive use of a mark is a form of monopoly. That right, however, is only a qualified right to exclude, extending only to the limits of likelihood of deception. Of course, antitrust problems may arise because of ancillary restraints of trade (Chapter 7, *infra*), but occasionally it has been incorrectly suggested that the objectives of trade identity law and antitrust law are in conflict rather than complementary. *See United States v. Timken Roller Bearing Co.*, 83 F. Supp. 284, 315 (D. Ohio 1949); McCarthy, *Trademarks and Unfair Competition,* §§ 1:14, 1:16 (3d ed. 1992); Gilson, *Trademark Protection and Practice*, § 1.03[5] (1984 ed.); Schechter, *The Rational Basis of Trademark Protection*, 40 Harv. L. Rev. 813 (1927). *Compare* Papandreou, *The Economic Effect of Trademarks*, 44 Cal. L. Rev. 503 (1956); Craswell Report (1979) (FTC Policy Planning Issues Paper: Trademarks, Consumer Information and Barriers to Competition).

During the 1930's and continuing for thirty years, a period of retrogression in the development of our trademark case law occurred which has been referred to as the period of "monopoly phobia." *See* Pattishall, *Trademarks and the Monopoly Phobia,* 50 Mich. L. Rev. 967 (1952). This phobia seems to have been directly incident to the anti-business philosophy that grew out of the Great Depression years and was largely fostered by the courts whose judges were appointed during the New Deal era. While the Lanham Act's protectionist philosophy and provisions were notably antithetical to such political and legal tenets, the monopoly phobia continues to the present where, fueled in part by the early cases, it is frequently raised as a defense in trademark litigation. The *Standard Brands* and *Dwinell-Wright* cases, *infra*, contrast the thinking of two great jurists on this subject.

(Matthew Bender & Co., Inc.)

STANDARD BRANDS, INC. v. SMIDLER

United States Court of Appeals, Second Circuit
151 F.2d 34 (1945)

FRANK, CIRCUIT JUDGE (concurring).

. . . .

Before plaintiff used the symbol "V–8," it had been used by divers others — in selling automobile engines, a shaving-cream and an aftershave lotion. Then plaintiff used it in selling its vegetable-juice, marketed through food-stores and restaurants. Subsequently defendant sold its vitamin tablets, labeled "V–8," marketing them through drugstores. Meanwhile plaintiff has been selling its own vitamin tablets labeled "Stam," but never "V–8." The record contains no evidence that buyers of defendant's tablets believed that those tablets were manufactured by the maker of "V–8" vegetable-juice. On these facts, has plaintiff acquired so extensive a legal monopoly in the symbol "V–8" that defendant's conduct is unlawful?

With considerable doubt, I agree with my colleagues, in holding that plaintiff has such monopoly. I shall canvass in some detail the reasons for my doubts because they touch the trunk nerve of the trade-name doctrine, a doctrine which, I think, has been left in much obscurity.

I use the word "monopoly" advisedly, because basic in the consideration of cases like this is the fact that judicial protection of any trade name necessarily involves a legalized monopoly which does not — like patents, copyrights or public utility monopolies — rest upon any statute but is entirely judge-made. In the inception of the trade-name doctrine, the fact went largely unobserved. . . .

. . . .

Fundamental in laissez-faire theory were these assumptions, which were generally accepted by the courts: (1) The economic well-being of consumers is the paramount end of economic activity. (2) Competition will further that end far better than governmental protection. Because of those assumptions, the courts held, as Mr. Justice Holmes pointed out, that "a man has a right to set up a shop in a small village which can support but one of the kind, although he expects and intends to ruin a deserving widow who is established there already." (Significantly, such a man would be held liable if his purpose was not even partially to engage in business competition but solely to damage his rival.) In other words, usually where the economic interest of consumers conflicted with the economic interest of the competitor, only the consumer interest was judicially considered.

Yet, in intervening in the "unfair competition" cases, the courts at first seemed to have directed their attention primarily to the adverse effects of unethical business activities on business competitors and to have paid relatively little heed to the interest of consumers. For it does not follow that because conduct is unfair to a business rival it will harm consumers: By practices which are unethical when viewed from the angle of his competitors, a businessman is frequently able to undersell them; the resultant prices ease the strain on his customers' pocketbooks fully as much as if he had acted "fairly."

"Poaching" on a business rival's trade-name was an outstanding type of unfair competition with which the courts interfered. Inescapably, in protecting the first business users of such names, the judges created exclusive privileges monopolies. But in the early cases of that kind the judges scarcely perceived that they were not adhering to the rule that consumer welfare is paramount. This fact was concealed by calling a trade-name a "property right"; for, as previously observed, an exclusive "property right" was an exception to the laissez-faire theory of completely unrestrained free enterprise. Of course, in saying that a trade-name was a "property right," the courts begged the question: The question was whether, as a matter of policy, the courts should regard the first user of a name as the "owner" of a new kind of exclusive property right — and so possessed of a monopoly.

But, seemingly, before long the neglect of the consumer in the trade-name cases aroused the judicial conscience. This aroused conscience seemed to have prompted statements in the opinions that the courts' major purpose in granting injunctions against the unfair use of trade-names was to protect customers (consumers) from deception; that deception, it was said, inflicted economic injury on the customers. Such statements (perhaps because they were something of an afterthought) the judges did not verify. No one bothered to ascertain whether, in fact, when articles made by Jones are so labeled that the buyers think they were manufactured by Smith, the buyers invariably or usually suffer monetary loss as a result of the deception. Had suits been brought by the deceived buyers, the courts would have required proof of such actual economic detriment to the buyers; for it has never been held that an action will lie for deceit entailing no financial disadvantage; but the trade-name suits were not brought by buyers; they were brought by merchants asking protection from unfair competition. Nevertheless, for years the courts, when granting such protection, justified their decisions on the ostensible but unverified ground that the customers were being guarded against financial harm.

To be sure, the courts also referred to the injury to the first user of the name. But they did not stop to ask whether there was any conflict between the objective of (a) aiding consumers and (b) that of preventing loss to the businessman who first used the trade-name. They failed to see that the doctrine of so-called "unfair competition" is really a doctrine of "unfair intrusion on a monopoly." Had they done so, they would squarely have faced the question of the value to consumers of such a judge-made monopoly.

But reiteration of the consumer-benefit argument was bound, sooner or later, to evoke doubts such as this: If Alert & Co. sells a laundry soap, under the name "Quick Clean," at 75¢ a cake, and a competitor, Wiseacre, Inc., then begins to sell the identical soap under the same name at 50¢ a cake, Alert & Co. loses customers, and therefore money, if it maintains its price; but the purchasers are misled to their financial benefit. If the sole purpose were to protect consumers from direct financial loss, the second name-user in such a case would have a complete defense if he showed that he sold, at a lower price, precisely the same article (compounded of exactly the same ingredients) as the first user.

There are other reasons assigned for judicially safeguarding trade names. The public interest involved is primarily in the preservation of honesty and fair dealing in business and in procuring "the security of the fruits of individual enterprise." However, there is also the factor that the possibility of obtaining such monopolies as a reward for their enterprise may have the effect of inducing businessmen to bring out new products which may indirectly benefit the consuming public.

[*Eastern Wine Corp. v Winslow-Warren, Ltd.*, 137 F.2d 955 at 958 (2d Cir).]

. . . .

. . . Those who, oversimplifying economic problems, thoughtlessly urge the elimination of virtually all monopolies, not only disregard the unavoidable existence of monopolistic elements in almost all kinds of competition but dangerously invite a program which, by neglecting socially valuable aspects of some industrial integrations ("oligopolies") in some mass production industries, might tragically reduce our living standards. Monopoly-phobia, like most phobias, is both a symptom and a cause of a neurotic tendency which, in refusing bravely to face facts, cannot yield intelligent guidance.

NATIONAL FRUIT PRODUCT CO. v. DWINELL-WRIGHT CO.

United States District Court, District of Massachusetts
47 F. Supp. 499 (1942)

WYZANSKI, DISTRICT JUDGE.

Defendant or its predecessors have used the words White House together with a representation of the Executive Mansion as a trademark for the sale of coffee since January 1, 1888, for tea since 1907, for roasted peanuts since 1940 and for a blend of orange and grapefruit juice since 1941. . . .

Plaintiff or its predecessors have used the same mark on cider vinegar since 1907, sweet cider since about 1908, . . . prune juice since 1936, canned sauerkraut and sauerkraut juice since 1937, and apple juice since 1938. . . .

The immediate cause for this litigation was defendant's beginning in 1941 to market a blend of orange and grapefruit juice under the mark. . . .

. . . .

. . . The principle extending the protection of a mark to products different from those to which it was attached by the originator, has been attacked by some philosophical jurists, by some economists and by some students of the consumer movement. The jurists point out the fallacy in the theory that protection is necessary to safeguard a value created by the originator of the mark. That theory, it is said, "purports to base legal protection upon economic value, when, as a matter of actual fact, the economic value of a sales device depends upon the extent to which it will be legally protected." Felix S. Cohen, *Transcendental Nonsense and The Functional Approach*, 35 Col[um]. L. Rev. 809, 815. They add that it tends to promote undesirable monopolies since the "stock of available trade-marks presenting psychological advantages in certain classes of products is seriously restricted today." Stephen Ladas, *Trademarks and Names, Encyc. Soc. Sciences*, vol. XV, 57, 59; F.S. Cohen, *supra*, p. 817. Some economists assert that extension of trade-marks is undesirable because it prevents the lowering of prices which would otherwise occur, both on branded and even on competing unbranded merchandise. Twentieth Century Fund, *Does Distribution Cost Too Much?* (1939) p. 304; Robert S. Lynd, *The People As Consumers, Report of President Hoover's Research Committee on Recent Social Trends In The United States*, vol. II, ch. XXII, p. 875, n. 35; Sidney and Beatrice Webb, *Industrial Democracy* (1920 Ed.) pp. 683, 684. They say it also tends to diminish the role which merchants formerly performed as expert advisers to the consuming public. *Ibid*, p. 683. Furthermore, advocates of the consumers' interest often oppose legal tendencies to expand the coverage of a brand mark because their belief is that it tends to restrict reliance upon grade marks carefully describing exact quantity and quality, which these advocates champion. Lyon, Watkins & Abramson, *Government and Economic Life* (Brookings Institution 1939) vol. l, pp. 229–233; M.G Reid, *Consumers and The Market* (1938) pp. 362–378; A.T. Poffenburger, *Psychology In Advertising* (2nd Ed., 1932), pp. 312–321; Twentieth Century Fund, *supra*, p. 302. *Cf*. Temporary National Economic Committee, Monograph No. 24, *Consumer Standards* (1941), pp. 44, 348.

Perhaps most of this attack is launched not merely at the extension, but at the very existence, of trade-mark protection. However that may be, there remains much to be said for the hitherto prevailing principles protecting a trade-mark against use on kindred products as well as on the identical product. Regardless of how clearly philosophers now show the fallacy of asserting that trade-marks have a value apart from judicial protection, businessmen previously have been willing to place as high a value as forty-two million dollars upon a single trade-mark, undoubtedly partly because they thought it could not be used by others on the same or related goods. *Ibid*, p. 348; Robert S. Lynd, *The People As Consumers, Report of President Hoover's Research Committee on Recent Social Trends In The United States*, vol. II, ch. XXII, p. 876. Courts should hesitate, by reversing the trend of their decisions, to destroy the economic values which those very decisions created. If the abuse is great, Congress can amend the statute.

The asserted dangers of monopolies are undeniably not so great in trade-marks as in patents or certain other fields. As to marks derived from coined words, the establishment of what is loosely called a monopoly presents no possible threat to competitors or to the public. And as to marks taken from an existing vocabulary, the courts can create safeguards. Indeed they already have guarded against the threat. *Cf. Restatement, Torts*, § 731(f); see cases cited though not completely followed in *Landers, Frary & Clark v. Universal Cooler Corp.*, 2 Cir. 85 F.2d 46, 48, col. 2. As to prices, it may be that there are public advantages as well as disadvantages in trade-marked articles. While in times of stable or declining prices branded goods may be over-priced, in times of rising prices branded goods, contrary to the market as a whole, may maintain rigidity of prices since to the consumer their price is as familiar a standard as is their name. As to the argument that the effect of manufacturer's brands is to diminish the role of merchants there are several answers.

Merchants themselves, as the testimony at bar showed, develop their own brands for their own protection. P.D. Converse, *Essentials of Distribution* (1936), p. 119. And in the resulting Tower of Babel it may well turn out, as the consumer groups hope, that many customers will make their final selection not by brand, but on the basis of more informative labeling — though a few gourmets may retain faith in the brand name as the only dependable clue to style, taste and like subtleties that tickle their palates.

. . . .

Plaintiff's prayer for injunction granted.

Rather than a restraint on trade, trade identity rights are more appropriately viewed as a benefit to consumers, reducing consumer search costs and giving firms the incentive to maintain consistent product quality so as to make the investment of resources in developing and maintaining a strong trade identity worthwhile. This principle was stated by Judge Kozinski, in dissent, in *New Kids on the Block v. New America Publishing*, 971 F.2d 302, 305 n.2, 306 n.3 (9th Cir. 1992), as follows:

> In economic terms, trademarks reduce consumer search costs by informing people that trademarked products come from the same source. . . . Trademark protection . . . guards against the overuse of resources while also providing incentives for the creation of new combinations of resources.

See also G.S. Rasmussen & Assoc. v. Kalitta Flying Service, 958 F.2d 896, 900 (9th Cir. 1992). As stated in Landes and Posner, *Trademark Law: An Economic Perspective*, 30 J.L. & Econ. 265, 270 (1987):

> Creating [a trademark] reputation requires expenditures on product quality, service, advertising, and so on. Once the reputation is created, the firm will obtain greater profits because repeat purchases and word-of-mouth references will generate higher sales and because consumers will be willing to pay higher prices for lower search costs and greater assurances of consistent quality. . . . The free-riding competitor will, at little cost, capture some of the profits associated with a strong trademark because some consumers will assume (at least in the short run) that the free holder's brands are identical. If the law does not prevent it, free riding will eventually destroy the information capital embodied in a trademark, and the prospect of free riding may therefore eliminate the incentive to develop a valuable trademark in the first place.

CHAPTER 2

CREATION AND MAINTENANCE
OF TRADE IDENTITY RIGHTS

§ 2.01 Introduction

Trademarks, and in fact all trade identity rights in the United States, traditionally have been based upon first and continuous use in commerce in connection with one's goods or services. The rationale is that (1) use of indicia of source engenders marketplace awareness; (2) awareness results in symbolized goodwill; and (3) use of and indicia by others should be restricted to the extent it may be likely to result in a deceptive diversion of that symbolized goodwill. As stated in E. Rogers, *Good Will, Trade-Marks And Unfair Trading,* 54 (1914):

> [A trademark] is not a grant from the government or from a governmental bureau. It is not dependent upon invention or discovery, or evidenced by imposing documents embellished with red seals and red tape. It depends upon one thing only, priority of adoption and use, and continuous occupancy of the market with goods bearing the mark.

While first and continuous use of a trademark in connection with goods and services remains a valid basis for establishing trademark rights in this country, the Revision Act, which became effective November 16, 1989, provides an alternative means. It rewards the first to apply to register a mark based on a bona fide intent to use with an inchoate ownership right as of the application date that will become viable when the registration issues. Nonetheless, the registration will not issue until actual use has begun, and a non-registrant prior user will still have rights superior to the registrant in its geographical area of use established prior to the registrant's filing date. See the discussion on Concurrent Rights in Chapter 7, *infra.*

The sections in this chapter disclose the major criteria in establishing trademark rights. Set forth below are definitions of the basic terms in this field as codified in the Lanham Act (15 U.S.C. § 1127):

Trade Name; Commercial Name. The terms "trade name" and "commercial name" mean any name used by a person to identify his or her business or vocation.

Trademark. The term "trademark" includes any word, name, symbol, or device, or any combination thereof—

  (1) used by a person, or

(2) which a person has a bona fide intention to use in commerce and applies to register on the principal register established by this Act, to identify and distinguish his or her goods, including a unique product, from those manufactured or sold by others and to indicate the source of the goods, even if that source is unknown.

Service Mark. The term "service mark" means any combination thereof—

(1) used by a person, or

(2) which a person has a bona fide intention to use in commerce and applies to register on the principal register established by this Act, to identify and distinguish the services of one person, including a unique service, from the services of others and to indicate the source of the services, even if that source is unknown. Titles, character names and other distinctive features of radio or television programs may be registered as service marks notwithstanding that they, or the programs, may advertise the goods of the sponsor.

Certification Mark. The term "certification mark" means any word, name, symbol, or device, or any combination thereof—

(1) used by a person other than its owner, or

(2) which its owner has a bona fide intention to permit a person other than the owner to use in commerce and files an application to register on the principal register established by this Act, to certify regional or other origin, material, mode of manufacture, quality, accuracy, or other characteristics of such person's goods or services or that the work or labor on the goods or services was performed by members of a union or other organization.

Collective Mark. The term "collective mark" means a trademark or service mark—

(1) used by the members of a cooperative, an association, or other collective group or organization, or

(2) which such cooperative, association, or other collective group or organization has a bona fide intention to use in commerce and applies to register on the principal register established by this Act, and includes marks indicating membership in a union, an association, or other organization.

Mark. The term "mark" includes any trademark, service mark, collective mark, or certification mark.

Three noteworthy treatises on the law of trademarks are: McCarthy, *Trademarks and Unfair Competition* (3d ed. 1992); Gilson, *Trademark Protection and Practice* (1993 ed.); and Callman, *Unfair Competition, Trademarks and Monopolies* (Altman, 4th Ed. 1993).

§ 2.02 Adoption and Use

Adoption of Trademark

BLUE BELL, INC. v. FARAH MFG. CO.

United States Court of Appeals, Fifth Circuit
508 F.2d 1260 (1975)

Use

GEWIN, CIRCUIT JUDGE.

In the spring and summer of 1973 two prominent manufacturers of men's clothing created identical trademarks for goods substantially identical in appearance. Though the record offers no indication of bad faith in the design and adoption of the labels, both Farah Manufacturing Company (Farah) and Blue Bell, Inc. (Blue Bell) devised the mark "Time Out" for new lines of men's slacks and shirts. Both parties market their goods on a national scale, so they agree that joint utilization of the same trademark would confuse the buying public. Thus, the only question presented for our review is which party established prior use of the mark in trade. A response to *Issue* that seemingly innocuous inquiry, however, requires us to define the chameleonic term "use" as it has developed in trademark law.

Define "Use"

. . . .

Farah conceived the Time Out mark on May 16, after screening several possible *Conceive* titles for its new stretch menswear. Two days later, the firm adopted an hourglass logo and authorized an extensive advertising campaign bearing the new insignia. Farah presented its fall line of clothing, including Time Out slacks, to sales personnel on June 5. In the meantime, patent counsel had given clearance for use of the mark after scrutiny of current federal registrations then on file. One of Farah's top executives demonstrated samples of the Time Out garments to large customers in Washington, D. C. and New York, though labels were not attached to the slacks *Tags* at that time. Tags containing the new design were completed June 27. With favorable evaluations of marketing potential from all sides, Farah sent one pair of slacks bearing the Time Out mark to each of its twelve regional sales managers on July *— Sent to retailer* 3. Sales personnel paid for the pants, and the garments became their property in case of loss.

Following the July 3 shipment, regional managers showed the goods to customers *Customers* the following week. Farah received several orders and production began. Further *next week* shipments of sample garments were mailed to the rest of the sales force on July 11 *(July 5??)* and 14. Merchandising efforts were fully operative by the end of the month. The first shipments to customers, however, occurred in September.

Blue Bell, on the other hand, was concerned with creating an entire new division of men's clothing, as an avenue to reaching the "upstairs" market. Though initially to be housed at the Hicks-Ponder plant in El Paso, the new division would eventually enjoy separate headquarters. On June 18 Blue Bell management arrived at the name *Conceive* Time Out to identify both its new division and its new line of men's sportswear. Like Farah, it received clearance for use of the mark from counsel. Like Farah, it inaugurated an advertising campaign. Unlike Farah, however, Blue Bell did not ship a dozen marked articles of the new line to its sales personnel. Instead, Blue Bell authorized the manufacture of several hundred labels bearing the words Time Out and its logo shaped like a referee's hands forming a T. When the labels were completed on June 29, the head of the embryonic division flew them to El Paso. He instructed shipping personnel to affix the new Time Out labels to slacks that already bore the "Mr. Hicks" trademark. The new tags, of varying sizes and colors, were randomly attached to the left hip pocket button of slacks and the left hip pocket of jeans. Thus, although no change occurred in the design or manufacture of the pants, on July 5 several hundred pair left El Paso with two tags.

. . . .

The exclusive right to trademark belongs to one who first uses it in connection with specified goods. *McClean v. Fleming,* 96 U.S. 245 (1877); 3 R. Callman, *Unfair Competition, Trademarks and Monopolies* § 76.2(c) (3d ed. 1969). Such use need not have gained wide public recognition, and even a single use in trade may sustain trademark rights if followed by continuous commercial utilization. *Ritz Cycle Car Co. v. Driggs-Seabury Ordinance Corp.,* 237 F. 125 (S.D.N.Y. 1916).

The initial question presented for review is whether Farah's sale and shipment of slacks to twelve regional managers constitutes a valid first use of the Time Out mark. Blue Bell claims the July 3 sale was merely an internal transaction insufficiently public to secure trademark ownership. After consideration of pertinent authorities, we agree.

Secret, undisclosed internal shipments are generally inadequate to support the denomination "use." Trademark claims based upon shipments from a producer's plant to its sales office, and vice versa, have often been disallowed.

Though none of the cited cases dealt with *sales* to intra-corporate personnel, we perceive that fact to be a distinction without a difference. The sales were not made to customers, but served as an accounting device to charge the salesmen with their cost in case of loss. The fact that some sales managers actively solicited accounts bolsters the good faith of Farah's intended use, but does not meet our essential objection: that the "sales" were not made to the public.

The primary, perhaps singular purpose of a trademark is to provide a means for the consumer to separate or distinguish one manufacturer's goods from those of another. Personnel within a corporation can identify an item by style number or other unique code. A trademark aids the public in selecting particular goods. As stated by the First Circuit:

> But to hold that a sale or sales are the *sine qua non* of a use sufficient to amount to an appropriation would be to read an unwarranted limitation into the statute, for so construed registration would have to be denied to any manufacturer who adopted a mark to distinguish or identify his product, and perhaps applied it thereon for years, if he should in practice lease his goods rather than sell them, as many manufacturers of machinery do. It seems to us that although evidence of sales is highly persuasive, the question of use adequate to establish appropriation remains one to be decided on the facts of each case, and that evidence showing, first, adoption, and, second, *use in a way sufficiently public to identify or distinguish the marked goods in an appropriate segment of the*

public mind as those of the adopter of the mark, is competent to establish ownership. . . .

New England Duplicating Co. v. Mendes, 190 F.2d 415, 418 (1st Cir. 1951) (Emphasis added). Similarly, the Trademark Trial and Appeal Board has reasoned:

> To acquire trademark rights there has to be an open use, that is to say, a use has to be made to the relevant class of purchasers or prospective purchasers since a trademark is intended to identify goods and distinguish those goods from those manufactured or sold by others. There was no such "open" use rather the use can be said to be an "internal" use, which cannot give rise to trademark rights.

Sterling Drug, Inc. v. Knoll A. G. Chemische Fabriken, 159 U.S.P.Q. 628 (TTAB 1968)] at 631.

Farah nonetheless contends that a recent decision of the Board so undermines all prior cases relating to internal use that they should be ignored. In *Standard Pressed Steel Co. v. Midwest Chrome Process Co.,* 183 U.S.P.Q. 758 (T.T.A.B. 1974) the agency held that internal shipment of marked goods from a producer's manufacturing plant to its sales office constitutes a valid "use in commerce" for registration purposes.

An axiom of trademark law has been that the right to register a mark is conditioned upon its actual use in trade. . . . Theoretically, then, common law use in trade should precede the use in commerce upon which Lanham Act registration is predicated. Arguably, since only a trademark owner can apply for registration, any activity adequate to create registrable rights must perforce also create trademark rights. A close examination of the Board's decision, however, dispels so mechanical a view. The tribunal took meticulous care to point out that its conclusion related solely to registration use rather than ownership use.

> It has been recognized, and especially so in the last few years, that, in view of the expenditures involved in introducing a new product on the market generally and the attendant risk involved therein prior to the screening process involved in resorting to the federal registration system and in the absence of an "intent to use" statute, a token sale or a single shipment in commerce *may be sufficient to support an application to register a trademark* in the Patent Office notwithstanding that the evidence may not show what disposition was made of the product so shipped. That is, the fact that a sale or a shipment of goods bearing a trademark was *designed primarily to lay a foundation for the filing of an application for registration* does not, per se, invalidate any such application or subsequent registration issued thereon.

> . . . .

> . . . Inasmuch as it is our belief that a most liberal policy should be followed in a situation of this kind [*in which dispute as to priority of use and ownership of a mark is not involved*], applicant's initial shipment of fasteners, although an intra-company transaction in that it was to a company sales representative, was a bona fide shipment.

Standard Pressed Steel Co. v. Midwest Chrome Process Co., [183 U.S.P.Q. 758 (TTAB 1974)], at 764–65 (Emphasis added).

Priority of use and ownership of the Time Out mark are the only issues before this court. The language fashioned by the Board clearly indicates a desire to leave the common law of trademark ownership intact. The decision may demonstrate a reversal of the presumption that ownership rights precede registration rights, but it does not affect our analysis of common law use in trade. Farah had undertaken substantial preliminary steps toward marketing the Time Out garments, but it did not establish ownership of the mark by means of the July 3 shipment to its sales managers. The gist of trademark rights is actual use in trade.

Blue Bell's July 5 shipment similarly failed to satisfy the prerequisites of a bona fide use in trade. Elementary tenets of trademark law require that labels or designs be affixed to the merchandise actually intended to bear the mark in commercial transactions. *Persha v. Armour & Co.,* 239 F.2d 628 (5th Cir. 1957). Furthermore, courts have recognized that the usefulness of a mark derives not only from its capacity to identify a certain manufacturer, but also from its ability to differentiate between different classes of goods produced by a single manufacturer. *Western Stove Co. v. George D. Roper Corp.,* 82 F. Supp. 206 (S.D.Cal. 1949). Here customers had ordered slacks of the Mr. Hicks species, and Mr. Hicks was the fanciful mark distinguishing these slacks from all others. Blue Bell intended to use the Time Out mark on an entirely new line of men's sportswear, unique in style and cut, though none of the garments had yet been produced.

. . . In the instant case Blue Bell's attachment of a secondary label to an older line of goods manifests a bad faith attempt to reserve a mark. We cannot countenance such activities as a valid use in trade. Blue Bell therefore did not acquire trademark rights by virtue of its July 5 shipment. . . .

Careful examination of the record discloses that Farah shipped its first order of Time Out clothing to customers in September of 1973. Blue Bell, approximately one month behind its competitor at other relevant stages of development, did not mail its Time Out garments until at least October. Though sales to customers are not the *sine qua non* of trademark use, *see New England Duplicating Co. v. Mendes, supra* they are determinative in the instant case. These sales constituted the first point at which the public had a chance to associate Time Out with a particular line of sportswear. Therefore, Farah established priority of trademark use; it is entitled to a decree permanently enjoining Blue Bell from utilization of the Time Out trademark on men's garments.

The judgment of the trial court is affirmed.

ZAZÚ DESIGNS v. L'ORÉAL, S.A.

United States Court of Appeals, Seventh Circuit
979 F.2d 499 (1992)

EASTERBROOK, CIRCUIT JUDGE.

In 1985 Cosmair, Inc., concluded that young women craved pink and blue hair. To meet the anticipated demand, Cosmair developed a line of "hair cosmetics" — hair coloring that is easily washed out. These inexpensive products, under the name ZAZÚ, were sold in cosmetic sections of mass merchandise stores. Apparently the teenagers of the late 1980s had better taste than Cosmair's marketing staff thought. The product flopped, but its name gave rise to this trademark suit. Cosmair is the United States licensee of L'Oréal, S.A., a French firm specializing in perfumes, beauty aids and related products. Cosmair placed L'Oréal marks on the bottles and ads. For reasons the parties have not explained, L'Oréal rather than Cosmair is the defendant even though the events that led to the litigation were orchestrated in New York rather than Paris. L'Oréal does not protest, so for simplicity we refer to Cosmair and L'Oréal collectively as "L'Oréal."

L'Oréal hired Wordmark, a consulting firm, to help it find a name for the new line of hair cosmetics. After checking the United States Trademark Register for conflicts, Wordmark suggested 250 names. L'Oréal narrowed this field to three, including ZAZÚ, and investigated their availability. This investigation turned up one federal registration of ZAZÚ as a mark for clothing and two state service mark registrations including that word. One of these is Zazú Hair Designs; the other was defunct.

Zazú Hair Designs is a hair salon in Hinsdale, Illinois, a suburb of Chicago. We call it "ZHD" to avoid confusion with the ZAZÚ mark. (ZHD employs an acute accent and L'Oréal did not; no one makes anything of the difference.) The salon is a partnership between Raymond R. Koubek and Salvatore J. Segretto, hairstylists who joined forces in 1979. ZHD registered ZAZÚ with Illinois in 1980 as a trade name for its salon. L'Oréal called the salon to find out if ZHD was selling its own products. The employee who answered reported that the salon was not but added, "we're working on it." L'Oréal called again; this time it was told that ZHD had no products available under the name ZAZÚ.

L'Oréal took the sole federal registration, held by Riviera Slacks, Inc., as a serious obstacle. Some apparel makers have migrated to cosmetics, and if Riviera were about to follow Ralph Lauren (which makes perfumes in addition to shirts and skirts) it might have a legitimate complaint against a competing use of the mark. *Sands, Taylor & Wood Co. v. Quaker Oats Co.*, 24 U.S.P.Q.2d 1001, 1011 (7th Cir. 1992). Riviera charged L'Oréal $125,000 for a covenant not to sue if L'Oréal used the ZAZÚ mark on cosmetics. In April 1986, covenant in hand and satisfied that ZHD's state trade name did not prevent the introduction of a national product, L'Oréal made a small interstate shipment as the basis of an application for federal registration, filed on June 12, 1986. By August L'Oréal had advertised and sold its products nationally.

Unknown to L'Oréal, Koubek and Segretto had for some time aspired to emulate Vidal Sassoon by marketing shampoos and conditioners under their salon's trade name. In 1985 Koubek began meeting with chemists to develop ZHD's products. Early efforts were unsuccessful; no one offered a product that satisfied ZHD. Eventually ZHD received acceptable samples from Gift Cosmetics, some of which Segretto sold to customers of the salon in plain bottles to which he taped the salon's business card. Between November 1985 and February 1986 ZHD made a few other sales. Koubek shipped two bottles to a friend in Texas, who paid $13. He also made two shipments to a hair stylist friend in Florida — 40 bottles of shampoo for $78.58. These were designed to interest the Floridian in the future marketing of the product line. These bottles could not have been sold to the public, because they lacked labels listing the ingredients and weight. *See* 21 U.S.C. § 362(b); 15 U.S.C. §§ 1452, 1453(a); 21 C.F.R. §§ 701.3, 701.13(a). After L'Oréal's national marketing was under way, its representatives thrice visited ZHD and found that the salon still had no products for sale under the ZAZÚ name. Which is not to say that ZHD was supine. Late in 1985 ZHD had ordered 25,000 bottles silk-screened with the name ZAZÚ. Later it ordered stick-on labels listing the ingredients of its products. In September 1986 ZHD began to sell small quantities of shampoo in bottles filled (and labeled) by hand in the salon. After the turn of the year ZHD directed the supplier of the shampoo and conditioner to fill some bottles; the record does not reveal how many. 9/86 sold to public [Service Mark ZaZu]

After a bench trial the district court held that ZHD's sales gave it an exclusive right to use the ZAZÚ name nationally for hair products. 9 U.S.P.Q.2d 1972 (N.D. Ill. 1988). The court enjoined L'Oréal from using the mark (a gesture, since the product had bombed and L'Oréal disclaimed any interest in using ZAZÚ again). It also awarded ZHD $100,000 in damages on account of lost profits and $1 million more to pay for corrective advertising to restore luster to the ZAZÚ mark. Finding that L'Oréal had infringed ZHD's mark intentionally and used "oppressive and deceitful" tactics in the litigation, the court awarded an additional $1 million in punitive damages, topped off with $76,000 to cover ZHD's legal expenses. (L'Oréal has changed law firms for the appeal; its current counsel did not participate in the events that the district judge found to be unethical.)

. . . .

Federal law permits the registration of trademarks and the enforcement of registered marks. Through § 43(a) of the Lanham Act, 15 U.S.C. § 1125(a), a provision addressed to deceit, it also indirectly allows the enforcement of unregistered marks. But until 1988 federal law did not specify how one acquired the rights that could be registered or enforced without registration.* That subject fell into the domain of state law, plus federal common law elaborating on the word "use" in § 43(a). *Two*

---

* The Trademark Law Revision Act of 1988 added provisions allowing for registration of a mark on a showing that the applicant has a "bona fide intention . . . to use a trademark in commerce." 15 U.S.C. § 1051(b). Filing such an intent-to-use application establishes priority as of the date of filing (except as against those already using the mark), but a statement of actual use must be filed within 6 months, which may be extended to 24. 15 U.S.C. § 1051(d). At the same time the statute was revised to provide that " 'use in commerce' means the bona fide use of a mark in the ordinary course of trade, and not made merely to reserve a right in a mark." 15 U.S.C. § 1127.

(Matthew Bender & Co., Inc.) (Pub. 725)

'88 revision allowed for reg. w/ intent to use,

State & Fed Law re: "Use" required

Pesos, Inc. v. Taco Cabana, Inc., 112 S. Ct. 2753, 2757 (1992); *id.* 112 S. Ct. at 2766–67 (Thomas J., concurring). *See also* 15 U.S.C. § 1127 (" 'trademark' includes any word . . . used by a person"). At common law, "use" meant sales to the public of a product with the mark attached. *Trade-Mark Cases*, 100 U.S. 82, 94–95 (1879); *Menendez v. Holt*, 128 U.S. 514, 520–21 (1888). *See also Hanover Star Milling Co. v. Metcalf*, 240 U.S. 403, 414 (1916); *United Drug Co. v. Theodore Rectanus Co.*, 248 U.S. 90, 97 (1918).

"Use" is neither a glitch in the Lanham Act nor a historical relic. By insisting that firms use marks to obtain rights in them, the law prevents entrepreneurs from reserving brand names in order to make their rivals' marketing more costly. Public sales let others know that they should not invest resources to develop a mark similar to one already used in the trade. *Blue Bell, Inc. v. Farah Manufacturing Co.*, 508 F.2d 1260, 1264–65 (5th Cir. 1975); *see also* William M. Landes and Richard A. Posner, *Trademark Law: An Economic Perspective*, 30 J.L. & Econ. 265, 281–84 (1987). Only active use allows consumers to associate a mark with particular goods and notifies other firms that the mark is so associated.

Active use required!

Under the common law, one must win the race to the marketplace to establish the exclusive right to a mark. *Blue Bell v. Farah; La Societe Anonyme des Parfums LeGalion v. Jean Patou, Inc.*, 495 F.2d 1265, 1271–74 (2d Cir. 1974). Registration modifies this system slightly, allowing slight sales plus notice in the register to substitute for substantial sales without notice. 15 U.S.C. § 1051(a). (The legislation in 1988 modifies the use requirement further, but we disregard this.) ZHD's sales of its product are insufficient use to establish priority over L'Oréal. A few bottles sold over the counter in Hinsdale, and a few more mailed to friends in Texas and Florida, neither link the ZAZÚ mark with ZHD's product in the minds of consumers nor put other producers on notice. As a practical matter ZHD had no product, period, until months after L'Oréal had embarked on its doomed campaign.

Slight sales & w/ registration

ZHD, not enough sales

Distinguish Cases

In finding that ZHD's few sales secured rights against the world, the district court relied on cases such as *Department of Justice v. Calspan Corp.*, 578 F.2d 295 (C.C.P.A. 1978), which hold that a single sale, combined with proof of intent to go on selling, permit the vendor to register the mark. *See also Axton-Fisher Tobacco Co. v. Fortune Tobacco Co.*, 82 F.2d 295 (C.C.P.A. 1936); *Maternally Yours, Inc. v. Your Maternity Shop, Inc.*, 234 F.2d 538, 542 (2d Cir. 1956); *Community of Roquefort v. Santo*, 443 F.2d 1196 (C.C.P.A. 1971). But use sufficient to register a mark that soon is widely distributed is not necessarily enough to acquire rights in the absence of registration. The Lanham Act allows only trademarks "used in commerce" to be registered. 15 U.S.C. § 1051(a). Courts have read "used" in a way that allows firms to seek protection for a mark before investing substantial sums in promotion. *See Fort Howard Paper Co. v. Kimberly-Clark Corp.*, 390 F.2d 1015 (C.C.P.A. 1972) (party may rely on advertising to show superior registration rights); *but see Weight Watchers International, Inc. v. I. Rokeach & Sons, Inc.*, 211 U.S.P.Q. 700, 709 (T.M.T.A.B. 1981) (more than minimal use is required to register because the statute allows only "owner[s]" to register, and ownership of a mark depends on commercial use). Liberality in registering marks is not problematic, because the registration gives notice to latecomers, which token use alone does not. Firms need

Use sufficient to register is not enough to acquire rights doesn't = registration

only search the register before embarking on development. Had ZHD registered ZAZÚ, the parties could have negotiated before L'Oréal committed large sums to marketing.

ZHD applied for registration of ZAZÚ after L'Oréal not only had applied to register the mark but also had put its product on the market nationwide. Efforts to register came too late. At oral argument ZHD suggested that L'Oréal's knowledge of ZHD's plan to enter the hair care market using ZAZÚ establishes ZHD's superior right to the name. Such an argument is unavailing. Intent to use a mark, like a naked registration, establishes no rights at all. *Hydro-Dynamics, Inc. v. George Putnam & Co.*, 811 F.2d 1470, 1472 (Fed. Cir. 1987). Even under the 1988 amendments (see note *), which allow registration in advance of contemplated use, an unregistered *plan* to use a mark creates no rights. Just as an intent to buy a choice parcel of land does not prevent a rival from closing the deal first, so an intent to use a mark creates no rights a competitor is bound to respect. A statute granting no rights in bare registrations cannot plausibly be understood to grant rights in "intents" divorced from either sales or registrations. Registration itself establishes only a rebuttable presumption of use as of the filing date. *Roley, Inc. v. Younghusband*, 204 F.2d 209, 211 (9th Cir. 1953). ZHD made first use of ZAZ in connection with hair *services* in Illinois, but this does not translate to a protectable right to market hair *products* nationally. The district court construed L'Oréal's knowledge of ZHD's use of ZAZÚ for salon services as knowledge "of [ZHD's] superior rights in the mark." 9 U.S.P.Q.2d at 1978. ZHD did not, however, have superior rights in the mark as applied to hair products, because it neither marketed such nor registered the mark before L'Oréal's use. Because the mark was not registered for use in conjunction with hair products, any knowledge L'Oréal may have had of ZHD's plans is irrelevant. *Cf. Weiner King, Inc. v. Wiener King Corp.*, 615 F.2d 512 (C.C.P.A. 1980).

Imagine the consequences of ZHD's approach. Businesses that knew of an intended use would not be entitled to the mark even if they made the first significant use of it. Businesses with their heads in the sand, however, could stand on the actual date they introduced their products, and so would have priority over firms that intended to use a mark but had not done so. Ignorance would be rewarded — and knowledgeable firms might back off even though the rivals' "plans" or "intent" were unlikely to come to fruition. Yet investigations of the sort L'Oréal undertook prevent costly duplication in the development of trademarks and protect consumers from the confusion resulting from two products being sold under the same mark. *See Natural Footwear Ltd. v. Hart, Shaffner & Marx*, 760 F.2d 1383, 1395 (3d Cir. 1985). L'Oréal should not be worse off because it made inquiries and found that, although no one had yet sued the mark for hair products, ZHD intended to do so. Nor should a potential user have to bide its time until it learns whether other firms are serious about marketing a product. The use requirement rewards those who act quickly in getting new products in the hands of consumers. Had L'Oréal discovered that ZHD had a product on the market under the ZAZÚ mark or that ZHD had registered ZAZÚ for hair products, L'Oréal could have chosen another mark before committing extensive marketing resources. Knowledge that ZHD planned to use the

ZAZÚ mark in the future does not present an obstacle to L'Oréal's adopting it today. *Selfway, Inc. v. Travelers Petroleum, Inc.*, 579 F.2d 75, 79 (C.C.P.A. 1978).

. . . .

The district court erred in equating a use sufficient to support registration with a use sufficient to generate nationwide rights in the absence of registration. Although whether ZHD's use is sufficient to grant it rights in the ZAZÚ mark is a question of fact on which appellate review is deferential, *California Cedar Products*, 724 F.2d at 830; *cf. Scandia Down Corp. v. Euroquilt, Inc.*, 772 F.2d 1423, 1428-29 (7th Cir. 1985), the extent to which ZHD used the mark is not disputed. ZHD's sales of hair care products were insufficient as a matter of law to establish national trademark rights at the time L'Oréal put its electric hair colors on the market.

. . . .

Reversed and remanded.

———————

IN RE CANADIAN PACIFIC LIMITED

United States Court of Appeals, Federal Circuit
754 F.2d 992 (1985)

DAVIS, CIRCUIT JUDGE.

[Appeal from a decision of the Trademark Trial and Appeal Board refusing to register CANADIAN PACIFIC ENTERPRISES LIMITED, LES ENTREPRISES CANADIEN PACIFIQUE LIMITEE for a shareholder dividend reinvestment plan.]

. . . .

This appeal raises a question of first impression in the elusive quest to find an appropriate definition of "services" under the Lanham Act. The Act defines "service mark," but fails to define "services." A further difficulty is that the legislative history reveals little bearing on the definition of "services." Our predecessor court has reasoned that "no attempt was made to define 'services' simply because of the plethora of services that the human mind is capable of conceiving." *American International Reinsurance Co. v. Airco, Inc.*, 570 F.2d 941, 943, 197 U.S.P.Q. 69, 71 (C.C.P.A.), *cert. denied*, 439 U.S. 866 (1978). Under that principle, appellant points out, the statute is entitled to a liberal interpretation.

In the absence of persuasive reasons to the contrary, words in a statute are to be given their ordinary and common meaning. *Banks v. Chicago Grain Trimmers Assn., Inc.*, 390 U.S. 459, 465, *reh. denied*, 391 U.S. 929 (1968). Appellant states that the accepted dictionary definition of "services" is "the performance of labor for the benefit of *another*." (Citing *Webster's Collegiate Dictionary (5th Ed.)*) (emphasis added). We do not take exception to this definition. On the contrary, that definition is consistent with the Trademark Manual of Examining Procedure § 1301.01, which, in suggesting certain criteria for determining what constitutes a service, states that

Definition of Service

"a service must be performed to the order of or for the *benefit of others* than the applicant." (Emphasis added). Hence, our concern here lies in who is to be considered "other" or "another," consonant with the policies of trademark law. When the Lanham Trademark Act was enacted, Congress was concerned with protecting the purchasers of a service or product. The Committee on Patents stated its belief that the Bill accomplished two purposes:

Meant to protect public & company's good will of public

> One is to protect the *public* so it may be confident that, in purchasing a product bearing a particular trade-mark which it favorably knows, it will get the product which it asks for and wants to get. Secondly, where the owner of a trade-mark has spent energy, time, and money in presenting to the *public* the product, he is protected in his investment from its misappropriation. . . . [Emphasis added.]

S.Rep. No. 1333, 79th Cong., 2d Sess. 3, *reprinted in* 1946 U.S.Code Cong.Service 1274. Thus, it is this goodwill, established in the minds of the relevant buying public, which is protected by the registration of a service mark. *See* 1 McCarthy, *Trademarks and Unfair Competition*, § 2.7 (3d ed. 1992). Since it is a segment of the public which "purchases" and "benefits" from a service provided by the owner of the mark, then it is from the viewpoint of a "public" to which we direct our inquiry. The question then becomes whether the shareholders under the Plan are to be considered as members of a "public" for purposes of registrability of these marks.

What is considered the public

Because the Plan is available *only* to Enterprises' own stockholders in connection with their further investment or participation in Enterprises' own activities, we think that no person or entity "other" than Enterprises (and its 75% parent Canadian Pacific, which has made the applications) is at all involved, and therefore that there is no "public" — which by definition must consist of at least some group of the greater public that is separate from the applicant — to which (or to whom) the asserted service mark can be directed and be useful. Enterprises' shareholders are, in fact and in law, its owners, *i.e.,* all together they *are* Enterprises, and there is no other such owner.

Shareholders aren't the public they are Co.

In support of the contrary proposition that Enterprises' shareholders are the "other" in the definition of "services," and therefore members of a "public," appellant directs our attention to *American International Reinsurance Co. v. Airco, Inc., supra.* In that case, the applicant, whose principal business was the manufacture of sundry products, offered its *employees* a Retirement Income Plan. It was for this latter service that the applicant sought to register a service mark. In holding that such an activity constituted a "service" within the meaning of the Act, the CCPA stated that the "fact that the services in question are offered only to applicant's employees . . . is of no moment; the Act does not preclude registration simply because the services are offered only to a limited segment of the public." 570 F.2d at 943, 197 USPQ at 71. The court added that being employed by the applicant did not strip the employees of their status as members of the public. Appellant contends that by analogy its shareholders are the same as employees, and therefore that its marks are registrable.

Distinguish Case

A . . . critical distinction between *American International* and this case is that, unlike an employee, a shareholder has the right to participate proportionately in all profits, management, and the distribution of net assets on liquidation. *Freese v. United States*, 323 F. Supp. 1194, 1197 (N.D. Okla. 1971), *aff'd,* 455 F.2d 1146 (10th Cir.), *cert. denied,* 409 U.S. 879 (1972). A shareholder has an ongoing, fractional, equitable and proprietary interest in the property and assets of a corporation. 11 *Fletcher Cyc. Corp.* § 5100 (Perm.Ed.). In a word, he or she is the owner of an undivided portion of the corporation. *Id.* It follows, of course, that the "owner" of a corporation is the body of shareholders as a whole.

[handwritten: Shareholder is the public]

Appellant says that reinvestment, which in turn increases capitalization, benefits the shareholder and not just the corporation. The answer is that in this particular respect shareholders and corporations are inseparably tied together. The Plan's offer to the shareholders, as a whole, to increase their ownership in Enterprises is akin to an offer to *the* owner of the corporation, and thus is equivalent to an offer of a service to the corporation itself. The increased capitalization inures not only to the benefit of the corporate entity, but also to *all* the shareholders, who, as we have said, are the equitable owners of the corporation. Such a plan is analogous to a sole proprietor's, or a partnership's, offering a plan of reinvestment to himself or itself. There is no benefit or service conferred upon "another," and no benefit to be conferred on any member of the relevant buying "public." Instead, every service is rigidly limited to further ownership by the very family of owners of the marks sought to be registered. The Lanham Act does not afford this kind of intramural or internal protection.

Appellant has failed to convince us that its shareholders should be considered as members of the public, apart from appellant itself. Consequently, the Trademark Act does not apply to their activities, and we agree with the Board's decision that the applicant's marks are not registrable as service marks.

Affirmed.

THE COCA-COLA CO. v. BUSCH

United States District Court, Eastern District of Pennsylvania
44 F. Supp. 405 (1942)

GANEY, DISTRICT JUDGE.

. . . .

After alleging the required jurisdictional qualifications, the plaintiff's bill avers that it is engaged and has been for many years in the manufacture of a soft drink syrup under the trade mark "Coca-Cola"; that a considerable portion of the public abbreviate the trade mark to "koke (coke)", and call for it as "koke (coke)"; that when offered as a soft drink "Koke (coke)" means "Coca-Cola"; that the defendants have adopted as a name to be used on a soft drink the words "Koke-Up" and have caused the same to be copyrighted in the United States Patent Office; that the defendants threaten to manufacture, advertise, offer for sale and sell a soft drink,

[handwritten: 'Koke up' soft drink]

using the name "Koke-Up"; that unless enjoined by the court the defendants will carry out their threat and put on the market a soft drink named "Koke-Up"; that these threatened acts will constitute unfair competition; that the application of the word "koke" to a soft drink is a representation that it is Coca-Cola. The answer inter alia denies that a considerable number of the public abbreviate the trade mark "Coca-Cola" to "koke (coke)," or call for "Coca-Cola" as "koke (coke)," but that the public refers to and calls the plaintiff's product Coca-Cola; it is admitted that the defendants intend to manufacture, offer for sale and sell for soft drinks and use thereon the name "Koke-Up"; it is further denied that the acts averred in the complaint constitute unfair competition in the use of the name "Koke-Up" as a soft drink, and that in nowise is it a representation that it is "Coca-Cola."

. . . .

The purpose of a trade mark is to . . . identify the business in connection with which it is used and accordingly it will be protected only when used in connection with a business, for trade marks and the right to their exclusive use are property rights, in the sense that the right to one's trade, and the good will that follows from it, free from unwarranted interference from others is a property right. The trade mark is the instrumentality by which this property right is protected and the right grows out of its use in trade not merely out of its adoption. *Hanover Star Milling Co. v. Metcalf*, 240 U.S. 403; *United Drug Co. v. Theodore Rectanus Co.*, 248 U.S. 90; *Carthage Tobacco Works v. Barlow-Moore Tobacco Company*, 296 F. 142; *Amoskeag Co. v. Trainer*, 101 U.S. 51; *Consumers' Co. v. Hydrox Chemical Co.*, 40 App. D.C. 284. Accordingly, here the plaintiff company did not use the word "koke (coke)" or identify its product with the word by sale, advertisement or otherwise and so a strict construction of the authorities on common law trade mark infringement would seem to hold that there could be no infringement and accordingly it is to the broader field of unfair competition that we must look to for redress, if any. Strict interp. — no sale under 'Coke' no CL infringement

. . . . So broader "Unfair Competition" looked @

The word "koke (coke)" is simply an abbreviation which the public has made of the trade mark "Coca-Cola" since it is commonplace in our daily endeavor to shorten and abbreviate anything which is capable of being shortened or abbreviated, and I think it is also common knowledge that there is a marked tendency among American youth, usually to shorten and abbreviate, and it is therefore quite natural, that the purchasing public rather than use the full trade mark "Coca-Cola," make resort to the more abbreviated form "koke (coke)." Further, the testimony shows conclusively that soft drinks such as "Coca-Cola" are purchased by spoken word in a vast number of instances and when a "Coca-Cola" is wanted, resort is made to the abbreviation "koke (coke)" which has come to be the nickname for "Coca-Cola."

. . . . ① Coke is the nickname [Ct]

The American cases are few in number and some while seemingly opposed to the view here adopted, upon careful examination reveal no inconsistency with the position here taken. In *Bayuk Cigars, Inc. v. Schwartz*, 1 F. Supp. 283 [14 U.S.P.Q.

132], the court held that the term "Phillies" as applied to the plaintiff's cigars by the purchasing public, though never attached to or used by way of advertising in connection with the sale of the product, was not subject to the protection of a court of equity as against the defendant who later used the term "Phillies" in connection with his brand of cigars. However, the court says [14 USPQ at 135]: "This result is partly based upon the idea of the court that the plaintiff has not established, by a preponderance of evidence such a use of the word as would entitle it to the exclusive use of the same, as against the defendant who registered this word and marketed products thereunder prior to the time the word in question was actually applied to the packages containing the plaintiff's cigars." In the instant case there can be no question of the fact that the plaintiff has established by a preponderance of evidence that the word "coke" is used solely in designation of the plaintiff's product, as the record will show that almost every witness so testified. In *Berghoff Brewing Ass'n. v. Popel-Giller Co. Inc.*, 273 F. 328, which was solely a trade mark infringement case, the court held that the use of the word "Burg" in conversation, or in written orders for goods, by the customer of the plaintiff without proof that the owner of the trade mark ever applied the abbreviation to its goods, does not establish the adoption of the abbreviation as a trade mark, and hence no protection would be afforded by a court of equity. The factual situation in this case differs from that of the instant case inasmuch as the court noted: "It appears that customers occasionally order 'Burgmeister' beer by the abbreviated name of 'Burg'. Here, there is no such casual or occasional use, but the record discloses that "Coca-Cola" is almost generally designated as "coke" as above indicated and that it has been so designated for at least ten years, and in addition no unfair competition is averred. In *Coca-Cola Co. v. Branham et al.*, 216 F. 264, where the defendant's product was designated simply as "Koke" the court refused to permit redress by way of injunction for alleged trade mark infringement and unfair business competition in which it was alleged that the use of the word "Koke" was an infringement of the trade mark, "Coca-Cola," a case very similar to the instant case. However, the court said in this case: "If the use of the name had been observed by the defendants, and it was afterwards adopted by them with the purpose and intention of taking advantage of that fact and to engage in the manufacture and sale of a beverage and call it 'Koke', and sell it 'as and for Coca-Cola', then a case of unfair competition would undoubtedly be made out." In the instant case it is to be noted, and it is so found as a fact, that the defendant did observe the name of "Coca-Cola," realizing the value of the reputation and good will which the plaintiff company had built up, and he admittedly chose the name "Koke-Up" in order to take advantage of the reputation of the plaintiff's product.

. . . .

The better view it seems to me is that adopted in *Denver Chemical Mfg. Co. v. Lilley, et al.*, 216 F.869, wherein the court says: "It being conceded, as it must be, that while appellant adopted the name antiphlogistine for its product, since if for some reason the general public has given to the product another and different name, by which it alone is known to the trade, the appellant becomes entitled to protection by injunction against one who thereafter endeavors through the adoption of such term as the public employs as synonymous for or as a secondary designation of such product, for in so doing the purchasing public may be deceived as to the article purchased, and the appellant is deprived of that trade which its industry and money have built up." I am constrained to adopt this theory of the law as applicable to the instant case. . . .

. . . .

NOTES ON ADOPTION AND USE

Must use a mark to establish rights

(1) As a general rule, one must use a mark in order to acquire trademark rights. *Hanover Star Milling Co. v. Metcalf*, 240 U.S. 403 (1916). Unlike patent rights, trade-mark and other trade identity rights result from actual use and not from invention and registration. *Trade-Mark Cases*, 100 U.S. 82 (1879). The common-law rationale for this prescription stems from the very nature of trademarks themselves. The value of a trademark is no greater than what it symbolizes. With each sale of goods or services, goodwill, or what Mr. Justice Frankfurter called "commercial magnetism" (*Mishawaka Rubber*, § 1.03 *supra*), may be built up; in the absence of such use, nothing is symbolized and nothing exists which calls for legal protection. *See United Drug Co. v. Theodore Rectanus Co.*, 248 U.S. 90, 97 (1918) ("There is no such thing as property in a trade-mark except as a right appurtenant to an established business or trade in connection with which the mark is employed.")

(2) Courts generally find trademark use on goods only where goods are sold with the trademark clearly affixed thereto, *Persha v. Armour & Co.*, 239 F.2d 628 (5th Cir. 1957), or displayed with the goods, packages or containers so that the mark can be seen by purchasers in close proximity to the product. *See* § 45 of the Lanham Act (15 U.S.C. § 1127):

> *Use in Commerce.* The term "use in commerce" means a bona fide use of a mark in the ordinary course of trade, and not made merely to reserve a right in a mark. For purposes of this Act, a mark shall be deemed to be in use in commerce —
>
> (1) on goods when —
>
> > (A) it is placed in any manner on the goods or their containers or the displays associated therewith or on the tags or labels affixed thereto, or if the nature of the goods makes such placement impracticable, then on documents associated with the goods or their sale, and
> >
> > (B) the goods are sold or transported in commerce, and
>
> (2) on services when it is used or displayed in the sale or advertising of services and the services are rendered in commerce, or the services are rendered in more than one State or in the United States and a foreign country and the person rendering the services is engaged in commerce in connection with the services.

Should a trademark used solely *intrastate* be registrable on the federal register if its use *affects* interstate or foreign commerce? For a court that answered "yes," see *In re Silenus Wine*, 557 F.2d 506 (C.C.P.A. 1977). *See also* 1 Gilson, *Trademark Protection and Practice*, § 3.02[7], Note 53 (1993 ed.); Calhoun, *Use in Commerce After Silenus: What Does It Mean?* 70 Trademark Rep. 47 (1980). *See generally* Hellwig, *Acquisition of Trademark Rights Under the Trademark Law Revision Act of 1988*, 80 Trademark Rep. 311 (1990); Sacoff, *The Trademark Use Requirement In Trademark Registration, Opposition and Cancellation Proceedings*, 76 Trademark Rep. 99 (1986).

Affect interstate commerce, allowed to register

(3) A nickname for a product or service may acquire trademark significance when the public has come to know and use it as such. In addition to the *Coca-Cola* case, *supra, see, e.g., National Cable Television Association v. American Cinema Editors, Inc.*, 937 F.2d 1572 (Fed. Cir. 1991) (ACE used by the public as an acronym for the name of an association of film editors); *Anheuser-Busch, Inc. v. Power City Brewery, Inc.* 28 F. Supp. 740 (W.D.N.Y. 1939) ("BUD"); *Volkswagenwerk A.G. v. Advanced Welding & Mfg. Co.*, 193 U.S.P.Q. 673 (T.T.A.B. 1976) ("BUG"). These cases are generally regarded as exceptions to the general rules regarding adoption and use, in that there is no affixation and sale, *see, e.g., Digicom, Inc. v. Digicon, Inc.*, 328 F. Supp. 631, 634 (S.D. Tex. 1971). Can one reconcile this "exception" with the purpose of the adoption and use rule? What role should public usage play in this area of the law? Does this really fall within the ambit of trade identity unfair competition protection rather than strict trademark law protection? *See* McCarthy, *Trademarks and Unfair Competition*, § 7:4 (3d ed. 1992); 1 Gilson, *Trademark Protection and Practice*, § 2.06 (1993 ed.).

(4) In many countries registration of a trade-mark, irrespective of use, is the act which creates trademark rights, whereas in the United States registration for many years constituted governmental recognition of rights which have previously been acquired by use. *See* Pattishall, *The Use Rationale and the Trademark Registration Treaty*, 11 A.P.L.A.J. 97 (1974). As stated above, intent-to-use applications for federal registration in the United States now establish inchoate trademark rights as of the date of application, which become viable once actual use is made and the registration issues.

§ 2.03   Priority

WESTERN STOVE CO. v. GEORGE D. ROPER CORP.

United States District Court, Southern District of California
82 F. Supp. 206 (1949)

O'CONNOR, DISTRICT JUDGE.

. . . .

Gas range 1941 — 1 range

Plaintiff's factual chronology:

In 1941, plaintiff planned to manufacture and sell a large gas range, and actually did manufacture one in the year 1941, placing one in the home of Henry Honer,

President of plaintiff corporation, without any trade-mark thereon except the trade-mark "Western Holly." Plaintiff did not go forward with plans for manufacture and sale of stoves of this type and size because of war conditions, but, on or about November 1, 1946, Western Stove Company, Inc., commenced the manufacture of a large stove similar to that which it had manufactured in 1941.

Began Mfr. & advertising

On or about November 1, 1946 certain advertising agencies began the preparation of advertising material for use in connection with an advertising campaign for this stove, and Henry Honer and Mr. Roderick A. Mays, of one of the advertising agencies, had several discussions relative to the use of a suitable trade-mark for this range as "Town & Country."

On November 27, 1946 a wire was sent to Bacon & Thomas, Washington, D.C., requesting a search on "Town & Country," and a reply was received on November 29, 1946, indicating that "Town & Country" was available as a trademark.

Advertised Dec '46

Advertisements of this range as "Town & Country" by the plaintiff were first printed in December of 1946 and a quantity printed and sent to various customers of Western Stove Company, Inc., ...

In addition to the advertising in newspapers, the "Town & Country" range of Western Stove Company Inc. was made known to the public by means of radio advertising, in spot announcements. Commencing with January 19, 1947, and continuing on January 21st and January 23rd, 1947, spot announcements were given over the radio, and, commencing on December 1946, pamphlets were prepared giving the specifications and features of the "Town & Country" range of Western Stove Company Inc.

Distrib Jan '47 30

Sold March '47 [Interstate]

The first stoves which had the trade-mark "Town & Country" thereon by the use of the silk screen obtained from Process Arts Company were delivered to May Company, Los Angeles, California, and to Barker Bros., Los Angeles, California, on January 30, 1947, and, subsequent to January 30, 1947 all of the large stoves manufactured by Western Stove Company, Inc., have had the trademark, "Town & Country", thereon when delivered to customers; and the said stoves were first sold in interstate commerce in March, 1947, with trade-mark "Town & Country" thereon. [Emphasis in opinion.]

Neither Western Stove Company, Inc., nor any of its officers or those in authorit[y] or its attorneys had any knowledge of the adoption or contemplated use of the trade-mark, "Town & Country" by the defendant and/or intervener, prior to the receipt of a telegram from Geo. D. Roper Corporation on January 24, 1947, advising of the adoption of the trade-mark "Town & Country" by Geo. D. Roper Corporation.

Defendant's and/or the intervener's factual chronology:

On October 7th to the 11th, 1946, Roper exhibited at the 28th Annual Convention of the American Gas Association, at Atlantic City, New Jersey, a certain gas range which it featured as the "ultimate in automatic gas cookery", and this range was commonly referred to by the trade individuals attending this Convention as "The Roper $1,000.00 beauty." It was not until January, 1947, however, that the first of these ranges made under production manufacture was ready for delivery, although several pilot models were produced in December 1946, and, for the purpose of factory and manufacturing identification, this range was designated model 9310; and following the Atlantic City Convention, Roper promptly proceeded with plans for advertising and selling model 9310 range nationally, and sought a distinctive trade-mark for the same. At a meeting in November 1946, at the Roper plant attended by Cy. Edwards, advertising manager for Roper, residing at Rockford, Ill. and by E. "L." Jeanmaire, of the advertising agency of Hollingsworth & Collin, Rockford, Ill., the name of "Town & Country" was selected as a trade-mark.

. . . .

On or about December 16, 1946, one of Roper's sales representatives made an interstate sale of a Roper model 9310 gas range, and photographs of the "Town & Country" label on said model were taken for the purpose of providing prints to be used as facsimiles in an application by Roper to register its said trade-mark in the United States Patent Office. . . .

. . . .

On January 23, 1947, and again on March 2, 1947, Roper, after receiving notice on January 20, 1947, of plaintiff's advertisements, exemplified by plaintiff's Exhibit 17, gave notice by telegram to Western Stove Company of Roper's claimed trade-mark rights to the words "Town & Country" for gas ranges, and requested said Western Stove Company to discontinue the use of these words in the sale of gas ranges.

Subsequent to receiving notice of plaintiff's designation of the trademark, "Town & Country", in its advertising, defendant and/or the intervener caused labels to be made with the trade-mark thereon and attached same to a stove which was delivered to the Illinois Central Railway at Rockford, Ill. on January 24, 1947, for shipment to Tampa, Florida. This label was made January 23, 1947. It is shown by the Stipulated Statement of Facts that subsequent to January 24, 1947, defendant and the intervener sold numerous stoves and ranges with the trade-mark, "Town & Country", thereon throughout the United States including California.

. . . .

Plaintiff contends that, because, commencing with the latter part of November, 1946, and substantially continuously thereafter, it was active in bringing to the notice of its salesmen, dealers, and the public, the fact that its larger stoves and particularly model D-472-GLC were designated as "Town & Country", all of which activities were done by plaintiff without any knowledge of defendant's and/or intervener's selection or designation of the trade-mark, "Town & Country", for use on Roper stoves and ranges (it was not until January 23, 1947, that plaintiff became aware of selection of this trade-mark by defendant and/or intervener), it, plaintiff, acquired the prior right to use this trade-mark.

. . . In *Waldes v. International Manufacturers Agency,* D.C.N.Y., 237 F. 502, 505, decided in 1916, Judge Learned Hand said:

> . . . it is the priority of user alone that controls, even though, when the defendant comes into the field, it may not be fully established, or may not even

be enough established to have become associated largely in the public mind with the plaintiff's make. . . . Were it not so, it would be of extreme difficulty to show at just what point in time the mark became associated with the maker in enough of his customers' minds to justify the inference that the defendant's use might become confusing. Therefore, once his use begins, the rest of the public must avoid his fanciful mark.

. . . .

Furthermore, the right to a trade-mark does not depend upon any particular period of use, but once it is adopted in good faith and used, the right thereto inures, and will prevail against any subsequent user. *Walter Baker & Co. v. Delapenha,* C.C.N.J., 160 F. 746, 748; *Wallace & Co. v. Repetti, Inc.,* 2 Cir., 266 F. 307, 308. *Use in advertising and the like is not trade-mark use* . . . .

In the case of *Bayuk Cigars, Inc. v. Schwartz,* D.C.N.J., 1 F. Supp., 283, the plaintiff conducted a campaign of advertising using the word "Phillies", and its jobbers and purchasers were accustomed to use the word, "Phillies", as designating its cigar, but the plaintiff did not use the word, "Phillies", on its product until November 8, 1929, after which time the mark was stamped on the box with a rubber stamp, until January 1, 1930, and after that date the cigar boxes were labeled with the word "Phillies". This was subsequent to defendant's use of October 18th, 1929, at which time he commenced to market cigars labeled "Philadelphia Phillies". The court, in holding that defendant established the right to the mark, "Phillies", said, 1 F. Supp. at page 286:

> The cases seem to be uniform in holding that the right arises out of the actual application of the mark to vendible goods.

In the "Phillies" case, defendant's use preceded plaintiff's use by about twenty-one days, from October 18, 1929, to November 8, 1929. *See also Gemex Co. v. J. & K. Sales Co., Inc.,* D.C., 76 F. Supp. 150, *affirmed,* 1 Cir., 166 F.2d 569, and *DeLong Hook & Eye Co. v. Hump Hairpin Mfg. Co.,* 1921, 297 Ill. 359, 130 N.E. 765. *See also Consumers Co. v. Hydrox Chemical Co.,* 1913, 40 App.D.C. 284, 192 O.G. 744.

Furthermore, a single instance of use, coupled with continued use, is sufficient proof of ownership, *Worden v. Cannaliato,* 1923, 52 App. D.C. 254, 285 F. 988, 990; *Rit Cycle Car Co. v. Driggs-Seabury Ordinance Corp.,* D.C.N.Y. 237 F. 125, 128; *California Spray-Chemical Corp. v. Ansbacher Siegle Corp.,* 55 U.S.P.Q. 298, 300; *J.C. Penny Co. v. B. Lowenstein & Bros., Inc.,* 67 U.S.P.Q. 231, 232.

While it is true that the use of this phrase, "Town & Country", by the defendant and/or the intervener occurred after intervener's knowledge of the Barker Bros. newspaper advertisement of the plaintiff's product, this, in the court's opinion, is not material. The record shows that the defendant and/or the intervener were or was the first to affix this trade-mark, "Town & Country" to certain of its ranges, and this is the controlling factor; and, after learning that the plaintiff had commenced using this trade-mark to its product, the intervener promptly notified the plaintiff, by telegram dated January 23, 1947, of its (the intervener's) rights.

. . . .

The prayer of the defendant for a dismissal of the complaint will be granted, and the intervener will be given a perpetual and final injunction restraining the plaintiff from using the trade-mark, "Town & Country" or "Town and Country" on any of its stoves and gas ranges.

MANHATTAN INDUSTRIES, INC. v. SWEATER BEE BY BANFF, LTD.

United States Court of Appeals, Second Circuit
627 F.2d 628 (1980)

LUMBARD, CIRCUIT JUDGE.

. . . .

The "Kimberly" mark was owned as a registered trademark and used to identify high quality women's clothing by General Mills, Inc., until May 7, 1979. On that day, General Mills formally abandoned the mark. In response to rumors circulating within the trade in March and April 1979 that General Mills intended to discontinue using the mark, executives at Don Sophisticates and at Sweater Bee sought to acquire this valuable mark directly from General Mills, but neither succeeded because General Mills, for reasons unimportant here, decided to abandon rather than sell the mark.

Upon the mark's abandonment, a free-for-all ensued. The district court found that Don Sophisticates began shipping merchandise with labels bearing a "Kimberly" mark on May 9. Even before May 9, Don Sophisticates had displayed to customers "Kimberly" clothing which it had purchased from a supplier in anticipation of General Mills' discontinuance of the mark. From May 7 until October, when the complaint was filed, Don Sophisticates shipped over $10,000 worth of merchandise bearing the "Kimberly" mark.

Sweater Bee began shipping merchandise with labels bearing a "Kimberly" mark on May 10, the day the mark's abandonment was reported in the trade newspaper, *Women's Wear Daily*. Sweater Bee's four shipments on that day went to four states and since then Sweater Bee has shipped over $130,000 worth of merchandise with labels bearing a "Kimberly" mark. Bayard Shirt entered the race on May 11. By an assignment executed on June 29, Bayard Shirt and its parent company, Manhattan Industries, received all of Don Sophisticates' rights to the mark. By mid-September, Bayard Shirt had shipped over $45,000 worth of merchandise with labels bearing a "Kimberly" mark, and had spent over $9,000 in advertising and promoting its "Kimberly" line. Don Sophisticates, Sweater Bee and Bayard Shirt all applied to the United States Patent and Trademark Office for the registration of the mark.

Appellees brought this action under the Lanham Act, 15 U.S.C. § 1125(a), claiming the trademark right to the mark by virtue of prior and continuous use and seeking, in addition to an injunction against Sweater Bee's further use of the mark, an accounting of profits derived from the alleged infringement, damages, and costs. Sweater Bee counterclaimed on similar grounds and sought similar relief. Both parties claimed an exclusive, nationwide right to use the mark. The district court, after receiving the parties' affidavits and documents and hearing arguments, concluded that Don Sophisticates, and by assignment Bayard Shirt and Manhattan Industries had acquired the sole right to the mark by virtue of its prior use.

. . . .

When General Mills abandoned its mark Don Sophisticates and Sweater Bee "were equally free to attempt to capture the mark to their own use." *Sutton Cosmetics (P.R.) v. Lander Co.*, 455 F.2d 285, 288 (2d Cir. 1972). Don Sophisticates won the race, for it was the first to ship merchandise with labels bearing a "Kimberly" mark after the abandonment, and it did so with the intent of acquiring the mark. Accordingly, Don Sophisticates would ordinarily have "the right to use the mark unadorned," *id.*, and Bayard Shirt and Manhattan Industries, as its assignees, would receive that right, *id.*, *Glamorene Products Corp. v. Procter & Gamble Co.*, 538 F.2d 894, 895 (C.C.P.A. 1976). However, in light of the significant shipments and investment by Sweater Bee, we do not believe that Don Sophisticates' slight priority in time justifies awarding to the appellees the exclusive, nationwide right to the "Kimberly" mark. We have previously stated that "the concept of priority in the law of trademarks is applied 'not in its calendar sense' but on the basis of 'the equities involved.' " *Chandon Champagne Corp. v. San Marino Wine Corp.*, 335 F.2d 531, 534 (2d Cir. 1964). *See also* 3 Callmann, *Unfair Competition, Trademarks and Monopolies*, § 76.3(a), at 302 (3d ed.) ("Although adherence to the principle of priority has the advantage of temporal consistency, if it is applied as the dispositive test to resolve a trademark conflict, it might often result in injustice"). Given the evenly balanced equities in this case, it would be inequitable to allow only the appellees to use the "Kimberly" mark. Sweater Bee has proved "that it entered the market sufficiently early to be equally entitled with [appellees] to the use of the ['Kimberly'] mark. In such case, to protect the public, each company [will] have to differentiate its product from that of the other company and perhaps also from the original ['Kimberly'] mark." *P. Daussa Corp. v. Sutton Cosmetics (P.R.), Inc.*, 462 F.2d 134, 136 (2d Cir. 1972).

One of the purposes of the Lanham Act is to prevent confusion among the public as to the source of goods. . . . No doubt the parties can create and present to the district court sufficiently distinct labels bearing the "Kimberly" mark so that the purchasers of high quality women's clothing can distinguish appellees' "Kimberly" goods from appellant's. We therefore remand to the district court for the fashioning of an appropriate order not inconsistent with this opinion.

Reversed and remanded.

CALIFORNIA CEDAR PRODUCTS CO. v. PINE MOUNTAIN CORP.

United States Court of Appeals, Ninth Circuit
724 F.2d 827 (1984)

TANG, CIRCUIT JUDGE.

. . . .

. . . In July 1978, the Kingsford Company (Kingsford-Clorox), a Clorox subsidiary, bought all of the stock of Old Duraflame, Inc., including the "Duraflame" trademark. . . .

. . . On April 21, 1982, Kingsford-Clorox formally decided to terminate its artificial firelog business, authorizing its vice-president, Bolingbroke, to abandon the "Duraflame" trademark on a date that he was to determine. On June 8, 1982, Kingsford-Clorox agreed to sell back over $3 million of its extant inventory to California Cedar and granted California Cedar a right of first refusal regarding sale of the trademark.

On June 26, 1982, Bolingbroke apparently attempted to phone California Cedar and Pine Mountain in order to inform them that he was planning to announce the abandonment of the trademark effective June 28, 1982. He reached Pine Mountain on June 26, 1982 but did not reach California Cedar until June 28, 1982.

On June 28, 1982, Kingsford-Clorox published a notice in the Wall Street Journal announcing the abandonment of the "Duraflame" trademark, effective that date. Also on June 28, 1982, Kingsford-Clorox's attorneys filed documents in the United States Patent and Trademark Office abandoning its registered "Duraflame" trademark.

Immediately after the phone-call on June 26, 1982, Pine Mountain inserted some of its firelogs in a Duraflame wrapper, pasted its name under the word "Duraflame" on the wrapper, and shipped the firelogs to Utah. On June 28, 1982, California Cedar began selling Duraflame firelogs in California and interstate commerce, in wrappers bearing the "Duraflame" trademark but identifying California Cedar as the source. On June 30, 1982, Consumer Chemical shipped firelogs from Canada to New York, in wrappers bearing the name "Duraflame" but identifying the manufacturer as Polysolve Corporation, an affiliate of Consumer Chemical with interlocking proprietors, owners and directors. California Cedar's first post-abandonment Canadian sales occurred on August 10, 1982, and its first post-abandonment European sales occurred October 7, 1982.

Claiming that it had appropriated the abandoned "Duraflame" trademark by first post-abandonment use, California Cedar brought actions in district court under § 43(a) of the Lanham Trademark Act, 15 U.S.C. § 1125(a) (1982), seeking to enjoin Pine Mountain and Consumer Chemical's use of the trademark. The district court found that California Cedar sold the first "Duraflame" firelogs in the United States and in Europe subsequent to Kingsford-Clorox's formal abandonment of the trademark, and that Consumer Chemical made the initial use of the abandoned trademark in Canada. After consolidating the two cases, the district court enjoined: (1) Pine Mountain from using the "Duraflame" trademark and trade dress in the United

States, Europe and Canada; (2) Consumer Chemical from using the "Duraflame" trademark and trade dress in the United States and Europe; and (3) California Cedar from using the "Duraflame" trademark and trade dress in Canada. Pine Mountain and Consumer Chemical appealed.

All parties concur with the district court's conclusion that the first party to use an abandoned trademark in a commercially meaningful way after its abandonment, is entitled to exclusive ownership and use of that trademark and trade dress. Appellants argue, however, that the district court applied an erroneous legal standard in determining that June 28, 1982, the date on which Kingsford-Clorox intended the abandonment to become effective, was the date that the abandonment actually occurred. Consumer Chemical argues that the trademark was abandoned as early as March 31, 1982 when Kingsford-Clorox wrote off the good will associated with the trademark for accounting purposes. Pine Mountain argues that abandonment was effective on June 26, 1982 when Kingsford-Clorox notified Pine Mountain of the impending abandonment. These arguments are not persuasive.

The district court's finding of abandonment was not made solely on the expression of intent of Kingsford-Clorox, but upon the totality of the circumstances including the express intent that abandonment be effective on June 28, 1982. All indications are that Kingsford-Clorox intended to continue use of the trademark through June 28, 1982, and maintained sufficient control over it until that date. For example, Kingsford-Clorox continued to negotiate a possible sale of the trademark almost until the moment abandonment was announced. Because Bolingbroke testified that Kingsford-Clorox intended to give up the trademark on June 28, because Kingsford-Clorox's attorneys filed notice of abandonment in the United States Patent and Trademark Office on June 28, and because Kingsford-Clorox published a formal announcement in the Wall Street Journal declaring abandonment as of June 28, the district court properly concluded that the abandonment was effective on that date.

Pine Mountain claims that even if abandonment occurred on June 28, 1982, it established the first post-abandonment use because its goods were then in commerce. Because this claim conflicts with the district court's finding that Pine Mountain's putative trademark use did not resume until June 29, 1982, we apply a clearly erroneous standard of review. Fed.R.Civ.P. 52(a). Pine Mountain's "use in commerce" was a June 28 shipment of firelogs sold on June 26; this sale was both premature and in bad faith. The district court resolved complicated factual issues in determining which parties established the first post-abandonment uses in the American, Canadian and European markets, and its findings are not clearly erroneous.

. . . .

The decision of the district court is affirmed.

NOTES ON PRIORITY

(1) The "first to affix" rule discussed in this section may sometimes appear to achieve arbitrary results. It has been defended, however, on the grounds of necessity and definitiveness, and because it affords a high degree of predictability. Should the equities in individual cases be afforded greater recognition? Is the rule in keeping with modern advertising methods where media advertising may make a greater impression on buyers than symbols physically imprinted on the product or where such advertising has actually preceded sale of the goods? *See* McCarthy, *Trademarks and Unfair Competition,* § 16.8 (3d ed. 1992).

It is possible through advertising and promotion to associate a particular mark with a particular product in the mind of the public *before* any actual sale takes place. During the gap between the created association and actual sale, another company may enter the market with the same product bearing the same trademark, intentionally or unintentionally taking advantage of the promotional efforts of the first advertiser. Which company should receive ownership rights to the trademark? The Ninth and First Circuits now favor the first adopter and *advertiser,* the one who first created the association. ". . . [U]se in a way sufficiently public to identify or distinguish the marked goods in an appropriate segment of the public mind as those of the adopter of the mark, is competent to establish ownership, even without evidence of actual sales." *New West Corp. v. NYM Co. of Cal., Inc.,* 595 F.2d 1194, 1200 (9th Cir. 1979) (quoting *New England Duplicating Co. v. Mendes,* 190 F.2d 415, 418 (1st Cir. 1951)), cited in *Walt Disney v. Kusan Inc.,* 204 U.S.P.Q. 284, 287 (C.D. Cal. 1979).

Prior use of a mark in advertising or catalogues, although insufficient to fulfill the requirements of first use in commerce for registration, may prevent a subsequent user from obtaining a federal registration. *See, e.g., Sears, Roebuck & Co. v. Mannington Mills, Inc.,* 38 U.S.P.Q. 261 (T.T.A.B. 1963), in which Sears' prior use of VINYL-THRIFT for floor coverings in catalogs and newspaper advertisements was held to constitute "use at least analogous to trademark use serving to indicate origin thereof in Sears" and preclude registration of THRIFT-VINYL for floor coverings. Section 2(d) of the Lanham Act bars federal registration of any mark which is confusingly similar to a mark or trade name previously used by another. (15 U.S.C. § 1052(d)). *See Alfred Electronics v. Alford Mfg. Co.,* 333 F.2d 912 (C.C.P.A. 1964); *Missouri Silver Pages Directory v. Southwestern Bell Media,* 6 U.S.P.Q.2d 1028 (T.T.A.B. 1988) (solicitation of "listees" for directory might constitute sufficient usage). Is this result consistent with the general purposes of the creation and protection of trademark rights? *See* McCarthy, *Trademarks and Unfair Competition,* § 20:4 (3d ed. 1992); Sacoff, *The Trademark Use Requirement In Trademark Registration, Opposition and Cancellation Proceedings,* 76 Trademark Rep. 99 (1986); Callmann, *Trademarks: The Right to Use v. The Right to Register: The Dunhill Case,* 51 Trademark Rep. 1209 (1961); Lunsford, *The Right to Use and the Right to Register — The Trade-Mark Anomaly,* 43 Trademark Rep. 1 (1953).

(2) Corporations may expend months or years and many thousands of dollars in developing a new product only to discover that another company had begun to use

their intended trademark. *Ginseng-Up Corporation v. American Ginseng Co., Inc.,* 215 U.S.P.Q. 471 (S.D. N.Y. 1981) ("A gap between the initial foray into the market and the resumption of sales of the product has been recognized as a fact of life in marketing"). To avoid such problems, some companies have relied upon elaborate and expensive "token-use" programs. These programs commonly involved the special printing of a few labels bearing the proposed trademark, which were then affixed to a prototype of the product or substituted as labels for similar products and sent to cooperating retailers for sale to the public. Some token-use programs involved dozens of marks with periodic shipments to cooperating retailers in every state. Such programs resulted in considerable litigation, and strong doubt was cast on their validity. *See La Sociétée Anonyme des Parfums Le Galion v. Jean Patou, Inc.,* 495 F.2d 1265 (2d Cir. 1974) (sales of 89 bottles of SNOB perfume over a twenty-year period held insufficient to maintain trademark rights, despite the commonness of such maintenance programs in the industry); *Proctor & Gamble Co. v. Johnson & Johnson, Inc.,* 205 U.S.P.Q. 697 (S.D.N.Y. 1979) (Proctor & Gamble's "Minor Brands" program, in which a case of each product annually was shipped interstate to cooperating retailers and sold for a nominal price, held not to be bona fide commercial use which would sustain rights in its registered and minor brand trademarks). In *Clairol, Inc. v. Holland Hall Products, Inc.,* 165 U.S.P.Q. 214 (T.T.A.B. 1970), the Board ruled that "Trademark rights are not created by sporadic, casual and nominal shipments of goods bearing a mark. There must be a trade in the goods sold under the mark or at least an active and public attempt to establish such a trade." In *Ralston Purina v. On-Cor Frozen Foods, Inc.,* 223 U.S.P.Q. 979 (Fed. Cir. 1984), however, the court effectively held that where the "inherent and identifiable character" of the developed product intended to be marketed under the mark was not changed from that of the product used in a token shipment, the token use would be considered bona fide. The decisions in the token use area often have turned upon the presence or absence of a good faith continuing effort to actually bring the trademark-bearing product, in its developed form, to market. *See also Blue Bell, Inc. v. Jaymar-Ruby, Inc.,* 497 F.2d 433 (2d Cir. 1974); *DeMert & Dougherty, Inc. v. Chesebrough-Pond's Inc.,* 348 F. Supp. 1194 (N.D. Ill. 1972). *See* 1 Gilson, *Trademark Protection and Practice,* § 3.02[5] (1993 ed.); McCarthy, *Trademarks and Unfair Competition* § 19.37 (3d ed. 1992); Fletcher, *"Time Out," "Snob," "Wipe Out" and "Chicken of the Sea": The Death Knell of "Token Use"?,* 65 Trademark Rep. 336 (1975).

(3) The disjunction between the federal trademark registration system and the commercial realities of developing a product for the market, which caused many applicants to resort to questionable token use in an effort to establish rights, provided much of the impetus for the 1988 revision of the Lanham Act which included intent to use registration provisions. For some of the historical debate which led up to that change, see Pattishall, *The Use Rationale and the Trademark Registration Treaty,* 61 A.B.A. J. 83, 84 (1975). For further discussion of the intent to use federal registration system, see Chapter 3, *infra,* and Smith, *Intent-To-Use Practice* (1992 ed.).

(4) Prior use of a mark may establish prior rights in an abbreviation of that mark. In *Forum Corp. of North America v. Forum, Ltd.,* 903 F.2d 434 (7th Cir. 1990),

plaintiff had superior rights in the abbreviation FORUM for business training program services based on its past use of THE FORUM CORPORATION OF NORTH AMERICA and THE FORUM CORPORATION, even though defendant alleged that it was the first to use FORUM as a mark for similar services.

(5) Should the right of the prior user of a mark be foreclosed by bad faith adoption and use? What factors should be considered in determining bad faith on the part of the prior user? See the discussion on Intent in Chapter 5, *infra*; *Stern Electronics, Inc. v. Kaufman*, 523 F. Supp. 635 (E.D.N.Y. 1981) (defendants first used the mark SCRAMBLE in bad faith to preempt plaintiff's rights). *Cf. Selfway, Inc. v. Traveler's Petroleum, Inc.*, 579 F.2d 75, 79 (C.C.P.A. 1978) (no cognizable equities arise from a party's preemptive use after knowledge of another's intent to use). In the absence of an application that matures to registration, an intent to use a mark is not protectable. *Zazú Designs v. L'Oréal, S.A.*, 979 F.2d 499, 504 (7th Cir. 1992).

(6) Prior use in a foreign country, even if well known, may not establish prior rights in the United States. In *Person's Co. v. Christman*, 9 U.S.P.Q.2d 1477 (T.T.A.B. 1988), *aff'd*, 900 F.2d 1565 (Fed. Cir. 1990), on a trip to Japan the registrant had become aware of the cancellation petitioner's use there of the mark PERSON'S for clothing, and subsequently the registrant began using mark in the United States for clothing. Because the petitioner's foreign use did not have an "effect on U.S. commerce," however, the registrant was held to have superior rights here and the petition was dismissed.

(7) When a trademark is formally abandoned, a race to acquire rights to it may develop between competitors. In *Manhattan Industries, Inc. v. Sweater Bee by Banff, Ltd.*, *supra*, the court elected not to follow the priority of use principle in resolving such a contest. Using a "balancing of equities" test instead, the court found that significant shipments and investment by the latecomer weighed evenly as against the first user's priority in time, and that in the interests of equity both parties should be allowed to use the mark. The case was remanded to the district court for the fashioning of an order which would sufficiently distinguish the labels of the parties. Are any problems created by such an approach? In a subsequent decision, the defendant was held in contempt for failing to use the mark in the manner ordered, *Manhattan Industries, Inc. v. Sweater Bee by Banff, Ltd.*, 885 F.2d 1 (2d Cir. 1989). Compare *California Cedar Products v. Pine Mountain Corp.*, *supra*.

§ 2.04 Distinctive, Suggestive and Descriptive Terms

INTRODUCTION

The cases in this section demonstrate the problems of maintaining rights in trademarks that are inherently nondistinctive, generally because they are descriptive in some way of the goods or services which they are supposed to identify as to source. Note the discussion in the opinions of secondary meaning and trademarks referred to as "narrow" or "weak."

"Narrow and weak" trademarks are those which, by virtue of their primary significance or connotation, the relevant public does not ordinarily associate with any particular, albeit anonymous, source. Secondary meaning is the term applied to the source-indicating significance of a mark (or other means for trade identity) as contrasted with its *primary* or language significance. Thus, IVORY has acquired a *secondary* meaning signifying a particular manufacturer's soap, whereas its *primary* meaning is the substance of an elephant's tusk. The Lanham Trademark Act substituted the word "distinctive" for the common-law phrase "secondary meaning" (15 U.S.C. § 1052(f)) as being more readily understandable, but the term of art "secondary meaning" retains its legal vitality. A mark which would not have been registrable under the 1905 Trademark Act because it was essentially descriptive, laudatory, geographically descriptive, or primarily merely a surname (15 U.S.C. § 85) became registrable under the present Act upon a showing that it had acquired distinctiveness through use as a trademark (15 U.S.C. § 1052(f)), i.e., had become distinctive of the source of the goods or services to which it was applied. See Chapter 3, *infra*.

UNION CARBIDE CORP. v. EVER-READY, INC.

United States Court of Appeals, Seventh Circuit
531 F.2d 366 (1976)

WILBUR F. PELL, JR., CIRCUIT JUDGE.

[After an initial treatment of the issue of incontestability (see discussion in Chapter 3, *infra*), the Court analyzed the source indicating significance of plaintiff's trademark EVEREADY for electrical products, the district court having declared the trademark invalid.]

. . . .

A mark is invalid if it is merely descriptive of the ingredients, qualities, or characteristics of an article of trade, *Warner & Co. v. Lilly & Co.*, 265 U.S. 526, 528 (1924). Suggestive marks, however, have long been distinguished from descriptive ones. *Watkins Products, Inc. v. Sunway Fruit Products Inc.*, 311 F.2d 496 (7th Cir. 1962), *cert. denied*, 373 U.S. 904 (1963); *Independent Nail & Packing Co., Inc. v. Stronghold Screw Products, Inc.*, 205 F.2d 921 (7th Cir. 1953), *cert. denied*, 346 U.S. 886; Restatement of the Law of Torts § 721 Comment(a) (1938). They may be thought of as a middle ground between arbitrary or fanciful names and descriptive names. *E.g., General Shoe Corporation v. Rosen*, 111 F.2d 95, 98 (4th Cir. 1940). The line between descriptive and suggestive marks is scarcely "pikestaff plain." Various tests have been used by courts to make the distinction. The district court, citing *General Shoe Corporation v. Rosen, supra; WG. Reardon Laboratories, Inc. v. B & B Exterminators*, 71 F.2d 515 (4th Cir. 1934); and *Stewart Paint Manufacturing Co. v. United Hardware Distributing Co.*, 253 F.2d 568 (8th Cir. 1958), stated:

> Suggestive terms "suggest," but do not describe the qualities of a particular product. The distinction threatens to be one without a difference. Essentially,

however, the common and ordinary meaning of the term to the public and the incongruous use of it as it relates to the product determine whether a term is suggestive.

392 F. Supp. at 286. Another test which has been used and which was footnoted by the district court is whether competitors would be likely to need the terms used in the trademark in describing their products. *See* McCarthy, *supra,* § 11:21 at 391–92 (1973); Restatement of the Law of Torts § 721 Comment (a) (1938).

This court has not adopted a particular test for distinguishing between suggestive and descriptive marks. We disagree with the district court that it is a distinction without a difference, although it is often a difficult distinction to draw and is, undoubtedly, often made on an intuitive basis rather than as the result of a logical analysis susceptible of articulation. This only emphasizes the need to give due respect to the determination of the patent office if the distinction is to be drawn in a consistent manner. Perhaps the best statement of the distinction appears in A. Seidel, S. Dalroff, and E. Gonda, *Trademark Law and Practice* § 4.06 at 77 (1963):

> Generally speaking, if the mark imparts information directly, it is descriptive. If it stands for an idea which requires some operation of the imagination to connect it with the goods, it is suggestive.

The information imparted may concern a characteristic, quality, or ingredient of the product. . . . Incongruity is not essential for a mark to be suggestive, rather than descriptive; but incongruity is a strong indication of non-descriptiveness, and it is probably the unusual case where a mark will be suggestive but not descriptive where there is no incongruity. The more imagination that is required to associate a mark with a product the less likely the words used will be needed by competitors to describe their products.

In analyzing Carbide's mark, the district court noted the dictionary definitions of "ever" and "ready" and concluded: "Thus, the combination of 'ever' and 'ready' means constantly prepared or available for service." Dissecting marks often leads to error. Words which could not individually become a trademark may become one when taken together. . . .

. . . The mark EVEREADY . . . suggests the quality of long life, but no one in our society would be deceived into thinking that this type of battery would never wear out or that its shelf life was infinite. There is less incongruity with regard to flashlight bodies. Nevertheless, we need not decide whether the mark's reference is too direct for the mark to be considered nondescriptive or whether the district court's holding to that effect should be overruled because of what we consider overwhelming evidence in the record of secondary meaning.

Secondary meaning need only be shown if a mark sought to be registered or sustained is found to be or is conceded to be descriptive.

. . . .

. . . To establish secondary meaning it is not necessary for the public to be aware of the name of the manufacturer from which a product emanates. It is sufficient if the public is aware that the product comes from a single, though anonymous, source. . . .

We agree with the district court's summary of the factors relevant on the issue of secondary meaning: "The amount and manner of advertising, volume of sales, the length and manner of use, direct consumer testimony and consumer surveys." The district court also summarized the evidence in this case relating these factors to Carbide:

> The evidence shows that Carbide and its predecessors have distributed and sold electrical products under the EVEREADY mark since 1909; that in 1915 10 million dry cell batteries marked EVEREADY alone were sold with an advertising cost of approximately $225,000; that Carbide's sales of electrical products under the EVEREADY mark from 1963 to 1973 exceeded $100,000,000 each year; that during the 1963-1973 period Carbide advertised in magazines and trade journals, on radio and television and through point of sale displays and that the cost of the 1963-67 advertising was $50,000,000.

392 F. Supp. at 288.

Advertising expenditures, of course, are a measure of the input by which a company attempts to establish a secondary meaning. In issue is the success of this effort. The chief inquiry is directed toward purchasers' attitudes toward a mark. *Carter-Wallace Inc. v. Procter & Gamble Co.*, 434 F.2d 794, 802 (9th Cir. 1970). The public's attitude is more directly indicated by remarks of counsel for Ever-Ready. In his opening statement he said, "All right. We don't sell batteries, and that's what everybody thinks of when you mention the name EVEREADY." Later during the trial he made a similar remark.

Two surveys were taken in anticipation of this litigation. . . . In each of the surveys an insignificant number of persons named Carbide as the maker of defendants' products, but in excess of 50% of those interviewed associated Carbide products, such as batteries and flashlights, with defendants' mark. The only conclusion that can be drawn from these results is that an extremely significant portion of the population associates Carbide's products with a single anonymous source. The survey questions were not designed to establish secondary meaning: but once the issue of descriptiveness was improperly considered, the survey results could not be ignored.

Additionally, we find it difficult to believe that anyone living in our society, which has daily familiarity with hundreds of battery-operated products, can be other than thoroughly acquainted with the EVEREADY mark. While perhaps not many know that Carbide is the manufacturer of EVEREADY products, few would have any doubt that the term was being utilized other than to indicate the single, though anonymous, source. A court should not play the ostrich with regard to such general public knowledge.

We hold that the district court's determination that there was inadequate evidence to find that EVEREADY had acquired a secondary meaning is clearly erroneous.

[The Court went on to hold that the district court was also clearly erroneous in its finding of no likelihood of confusion, and directed the lower court to enter an appropriate injunction against defendants should the defendants fail to sustain their antitrust affirmative defenses upon remand.]

FRANCE MILLING CO. v. WASHBURN-CROSBY CO.

United States Court of Appeals, Second Circuit
7 F.2d 304 (1925)

. . . .

The plaintiff, hereinafter called France, sued to protect its trade-mark "Gold Medal" as applied to prepared "pancake" and buckwheat flour. The first of these products is composed of wheat and corn flours, leavened and seasoned, and the second is a mixture of wheat and buckwheat flours, similarly treated; and both have hitherto been sold by France in packages, usually rather small, for purposes of distribution. Plaintiff is a corporation doing business at Cobleskill, N.Y.; and has been putting out its flours since 1904, in which year it obtained a gold medal for the same at the Louisiana Purchase Exposition at St. Louis. In the following year it adopted, and has since continuously used, the words "Gold Medal" as its trade-mark for the goods that won the prize, accompanied by a representation of the obverse and reverse of a medal. . . .

. . . .

Washburn, by its predecessors, and in a continuous and extending business, has used "Gold Medal" as a trade-mark for wheat flour since 1880, selling the same in barrels and bags; but until the end of 1923 or thereabouts it never made nor sold pancake flour, and had nothing to do with buckwheat so far as shown. For many years it has had a branch establishment at Buffalo, N. Y., in charge of a vice president, and from that branch France bought some of the wheat flour it required, giving orders and conducting correspondence on paper prominently announcing its trade-mark and the character of its products. This began at least as early as 1912.

. . . .

. . . During the 44 years that Washburn has used "Gold Medal" as a trade-mark, the phrase has been registered upwards of 60 times in the Patent Office, and applied to articles as diverse as fishing rods and finishing wax, kidney medicine, and beer, and almost every kind of food product.

[The District Court enjoined defendant's use of "Gold Medal" on pancake and buckwheat flour and denied defendant's counterclaim.]

. . . .

HOUGH, CIRCUIT JUDGE (after stating the facts as above).

There was a good deal said at bar about fraud and wrongdoing, which we lay entirely aside. The reason for France's assumption of Gold Medal in 1905 was pardonable pride in his prize; there was no intent on his part to trade on Washburn's fame, nor is there any evidence that he ever did so trade.

We likewise lay aside all arguments based on registration of marks; these litigants must both stand on what are usually (and not very accurately) called their "common-law" rights, aided by such equities derived from conduct and lapse of time as may serve them.

France and Washburn, now that the latter has gone into the business of selling prepared flours, are competitors, something they never were before 1924. It may be true that a competent cook can mix Washburn's Gold Medal flour with corn meal, leaven and appetizing flavors, and make perhaps the best "pancakes"; but the parties hereto do not make nor sell cakes — they sell the cook something out of which she can evolve the edible product without thought or much labor. This something Washburn neither made nor sold before 1924; France did and had for 20 years.

Thus at the time this suit began the situation in one view was exactly "the ordinary case of parties competing under the same mark, [and] it is correct to say that prior appropriation settles the question" between them. *Hanover, etc., Co. v. Metcalf*, 240 U.S. 403.

. . . .

To take another view of the matter, the degree or exclusiveness of appropriation accorded to the originator of a trade-name often varies with the kind of name he originates. If the name or mark be truly arbitrary, strange, and fanciful, it is more specially and peculiarly significant and suggestive of one man's goods, than when it is frequently used by many and in many differing kinds of business. Of this "Kodak" is a famous example, and the English courts have prevented one from putting forth Kodak bicycles, at the suit of the originator of the name for a totally different article. *Eastman v. Kodak Cycle Co.*, 15 R. P. C. 105; *cf. Re Dunn's Trade-Mark*, 7 R. P. C. 311, and *Dunlop v. Dunlop*, 16 R. P. C. 12. In this court the same influence is seen in *Aunt Jemima Mills Co. v. Rigney*, 247 F. 407, 159 C. C. A. 461, L. R. A. 1918C, 1039, where the above line of cases is quoted and relied on.

The phrase "Gold Medal" is distinctly not in the same class of original, arbitrary, or fanciful words, as "Kodak" and "Aunt Jemima." It is a laudatory phrase, suggestive of merit, recognized by some organization of authority awarding a prize. It is only allied to some particular business or person by insistent, persistent advertising. Washburn's flour has been so advertised, and the proof is ample that publicity efforts have borne fruit, so that Gold Medal flour means among purchasers Washburn's flour. Yet it must always be remembered that there is nothing original about the name per se; it is exactly like the phrase "Blue Ribbon," and has been as extensively and variously applied. (One who devises a new, strange, "catching" word to describe his wares may and often has by timely suit prevented others from taking his word or set of words to gild the repute of even wholly different goods (cases *supra*); but one who takes a phrase which is the commonplace of self-praise like "Blue Ribbon" or "Gold Medal" must be content with that special field which he labels with so undistinctive a name.) Of this *Pabst, etc., Co. v. Decatur, etc., Co.* (C. C. A.) 284 F. 110, and *Anheuser, etc., Co. v. Budweiser, etc., Co.* (C. C. A.) 295 F. 306, constitute a perfect illustration. In the first decision Blue Ribbon was restricted to the single product with which plaintiff had associated it, while in the second Budweiser was given a wider sphere of influence. In the present case, Washburn has made known by advertising Gold Medal not a line of products, nor any product of a varied business, but one separate, well-known commodity, pure wheat flour, and with that he must be content.

[handwritten: Washburn gets pure wheat flour that is all.]

Taking still another view of the evidence, Washburn's claim is not timely; the laches, indeed the acquiescence, of so many years, while France was building up a noncompetitive business, must be given weight. *Carroll v. McIlvaine,* 183 F. 22, 105 C. C. A. 314, affirming 171 F. 125, is conclusive against the award of any injunction against France, and the inequity of granting such relief is too manifest for discussion. *[handwritten: — Washburn is not timely.]*

Result is: Washburn, by persistent and pushing use of a well-known and nondistinctive name has on this record made it a good trade-mark for just what it was applied to, pure or straight wheat flour; to that commodity France never applied the name, but did apply it to a commercially distinct article as he had good right to do.

Both parties are entitled to be protected in their several businesses. France has not attacked Washburn; therefore the latter needs no relief. Washburn has deliberately attacked France; therefore the decree below was right, and is affirmed with costs.

MARILYN MIGLIN MODEL MAKEUP, INC. v. JOVAN, INC.

United States District Court, Northern District of Illinois
224 U.S.P.Q. 178 (1984)

[handwritten: "Pheromone"]

McGARR, DISTRICT JUDGE.

Plaintiff Marilyn Miglin Model Makeup, Inc. ("Miglin") brought an action against defendant Jovan, Inc. ("Jovan") for trademark infringement and false advertisement arising out of Jovan's use of the word "pheromone" in connection with one of its fragrance lines. In a memorandum opinion and order dated September 28, 1983, this court granted Jovan's motion for summary judgment as to all counts of the complaint. The action is currently before the court on Jovan's motion for summary judgment on its counterclaim which seeks a declaratory judgment that Miglin does not have any trademark rights in the word "pheromone" and cancellation of Miglin's federal trademark registration. . . .

. . . .

[handwritten: "Pheromone" is not generic for perfume]

Jovan does not allege that the term "pheromone" is generic, which would preclude trademark registration regardless of secondary meaning; while this court has found "pheromone" to be generic for "an organic substance used for communication between individuals of the same species," see Mem. Op. & Order, Sept. 28, 1983, at 3, it cannot be seriously claimed to be generic for perfume, as it is used by Miglin. Rather, Jovan claims that if Miglin's product is a pheromone or contains a pheromone, the mark "Pheromone" is merely descriptive; if it is not a pheromone

[handwritten: But Jovan claims 'pheromone' is merely descriptive.]

or does not contain a pheromone, the mark is deceptively misdescriptive.[2] In either event, proper trademark registration would be dependent on the acquisition of secondary meaning. *Thus Miglin could have to have given a 2nd meaning*

The court will accept as true Miglin's own statements that, in effect, it does not know or care whether "Pheromone" perfume contains pheromones, and thus will assume that "Pheromone" perfume does not contain pheromones and does not purport to be a pheromone itself. That assumption disposes of the argument that the mark is merely descriptive and moves the court on to a determination of whether the mark is deceptively misdescriptive.

Misdescription

Unlike the category of deceptive marks, see note 2 *supra,* which deceive consumers into purchasing a product based on a misrepresentation of the product's ingredients, a deceptively misdescriptive mark is one in which customer confusion as to ingredients, rather than mistaken reliance, is at issue. A classic example of a deceptively misdescriptive mark is "Glass Wax" for a glass and metal cleaning product containing no wax. See *Gold Seal Co. v. Weeks,* 129 F. Supp. 928, 105 U.S.P.Q. 407 (D.D.C. 1955), *aff'd per curiam sub nom. S.C. Johnson & Son v. Gold Seal Co.,* 230 F.2d 832, 108 U.S.P.Q. 400 (D.C. Cir.), *cert. denied,* 352 U.S. 829 (1956). In *Gold Seal,* the district court rejected the contention that the mark was deceptive, finding that customers were satisfied with the product whether it contained wax or not. 129 F. Supp. at 934 & n.10, 105 U.S.P.Q. at 411 & n.10. Nevertheless, the court found it to be deceptively misdescriptive, stating, inter alia, "that customers might justifiably believe it does contain the element wax, whether or not it was significant to them in purchasing the product." *Id.* at 935, 105 U.S.P.Q. at 411–12 (footnote omitted).

Yes, Pheromone is misdescriptive

The court is persuaded by that reasoning to find that the name "Pheromone" for a fragrance which does not purport to be a pheromone or to contain pheromones is deceptively misdescriptive, particularly in light of the fact that fragrance products, such as Jovan's "Andron," *do* exist and *do* purport to contain pheromones. In further support of this finding are instances of consumer and industry confusion, raised in the Miglin depositions, as to whether "Pheromone" perfume contains pheromones.

Miglin falls back on its contention that, were it not for Jovan's efforts to educate the public as to the scientific meaning of the term "pheromone," consumer confusion would not exist; consumers would know the word "pheromone" only as the source

---

[2] In its counterclaim, Jovan raises only the grounds of merely descriptive and deceptively misdescriptive, while in its memoranda, it also contends that Miglin's use of the mark is deceptive which, under 15 U.S.C. § 1052(a), would preclude trademark registration regardless of secondary meaning. "[D]eception is found when an essential and material element is misrepresented, is distinctly false, and is the very element upon which the customer reasonably relies in purchasing one product over another." *Gold Seal Co. v. Weeks,* 129 F. Supp. 928, 934, 105 U.S.P.Q. 407 (D.D.C. 1955), *aff'd per curiam sub nom. S.C. Johnson & Son v.* Gold Seal Co., 230 F.2d 832, 108 U.S.P.Q. 400 (D.C. Cir.), *cert. denied,* 352 U.S. 829 (1956). At the very least, a question of fact exists as to whether customers purchased Miglin's "Pheromone" perfume in reliance on a mistaken belief that it contains pheromones. For that reason, to the extent the court feels compelled to address a ground not raised in the counterclaim, the ground of deception is not susceptible at this time to summary judgment.

designation of Miglin's fragrance products. This argument merely begs the question. In this age when "sex sells," it was only a matter of time before a recently-coined term with sexual connotations, tailor-made for a product in the "romantic field" of fragrances, would make its way into the common vocabulary.

Having determined that Miglin's "Pheromone" mark for perfume is deceptively misdescriptive, the court must now address the question of secondary meaning, which, if determined to exist, would save Miglin's trademark registration from cancellation. "In other words, although the term's 'primary' meaning was [deceptively misdescriptive], if through use the public had come to identify the terms with plaintiff's product in particular, the [term] would have become a valid trademark." *Gimix, Inc. v. JS&A Group, Inc.*, 699 F.2d 901, 907, 217 U.S.P.Q. 677, 682–83 (7th Cir. 1983).

The ultimate issue regarding secondary meaning — what impact has the term had on the public consciousness? — can be determined by considering the following factors: the amount and manner of advertising, volume of sales, length and manner of use, direct consumer testimony and consumer surveys. *Union Carbide Corp. v. Ever-Ready, Inc.*, 531 F.2d 366, 380, 188 U.S.P.Q. 623, 635–36 (7th Cir.), *cert. denied*, 429 U.S. 830, 191 U.S.P.Q. 416 (1976). The owner of the challenged trademark bears "the burden of establishing a genuine issue of material fact as to whether its mark has attained secondary meaning in the mind of the public." *Gimix*, 699 F.2d at 908, 217 U.S.P.Q. at 683–84.

. . . .

In the instant case, the most telling factor to be considered is the length of Miglin's use of the mark. Although the court can envision extraordinary circumstances under which a mark could obtain secondary meaning within a short period of time, nothing of that magnitude is evident in this case. The Seventh Circuit has placed considerable emphasis on length of use; in its recent decision in *Gimix, Inc. v. JS&A Group, Inc.*, 699 F.2d 901, 217 U.S.P.Q. 677 (7th Cir. 1983), the court stated:

> [T]he period of time involved here, from the introduction of plaintiff's product in 1975 until the introduction of [defendant's] similar product in 1980, is so brief as to cast serious doubt upon the very possibility of having established a strong secondary meaning; by way of contrast, the Ever-Ready [sic] battery, for example, had been marketed under that name for over fifty years.

Id. at 907, 217 U.S.P.Q. at 682–83 (citing *Union Carbide Corp. v. Ever-Ready Inc.*, 531 F.2d 366, 380, 188 U.S.P.Q. 623, 635-36 (7th Cir.), *cert. denied,* 429 U.S. 830, 191 U.S.P.Q. 416 (1976)). In the instant case, even less time elapsed between Miglin's first use of the mark and Jovan's introduction of its "Andron" fragrance using the term "pheromone-based."

In light of the above discussion, Miglin has failed to establish a genuine issue of material fact as to whether its "Pheromone" mark has attained secondary meaning.

For the foregoing reasons, defendant-counterplaintiff Jovan's motion for summary judgment on its counterclaim is granted.

NOTES ON DISTINCTIVE, SUGGESTIVE AND DESCRIPTIVE TERMS

(1) The court in *Big O Tire Dealers, Inc. v. The Goodyear Tire & Rubber Company*, 408 F. Supp. 1219 (D. Col. 1976), *aff'd*, 561 F.2d 1365 (10th Cir. 1977), gave the following explanatory jury instruction for the various classifications of words used in trademark law:

In trademark usage, words can be classified according to the degree of their distinctiveness. A "coined" word is an artificial word which has no language meaning except as a trademark.

EXXON is a coined word used by an oil company.

A fanciful word is like a coined word in that it is invented for the sole purpose of functioning as a trademark and it differs from the coined word only in that it may bear a relationship to another word or it may be an obsolete word.

FAB is a shortened version for fabulous and is a fanciful word used for detergent.

An "arbitrary" word is one which is in common linguistic use but when used with the goods in issue it neither suggests nor describes any ingredient, quality or characteristic of those goods.

OLD CROW for whiskey is an example of an arbitrary word.

A "suggestive" word is one which suggests what the product is without actually being descriptive of it.

STRONGHOLD for threaded nails is suggestive of their superior holding power.

A merely "descriptive" word is one which draws attention to the ingredients, quality or nature of the product.

TENDER VITTLES as applied to cat food is descriptive.

A "generic" word is one which is the language name for the product.

BUTTER is the language word for butter. There can be no trademark rights in a generic term. They remain in the public domain as a part of our language.

The right to protection of a trademark comes from its use to identify the product.

We speak of strong and weak marks in terms of the amount of use necessary to create protected rights. Words which are coined, fanciful or arbitrary are distinctive almost from their first use. Suggestive words are also protected as trademarks when used distinctively for particular products.

Words which are merely descriptive do not obtain protection solely from their use as a trademark. Such words must first acquire distinctiveness from the effect of the owner's efforts in the market place. This is what is called the development of secondary meaning; that is a merely descriptive term used as a trademark must have been so used that its primary significance in the minds of the consuming public is not the product itself but the identification of it with a single source. . . .

Note that no secondary meaning need be shown for a "suggestive" term as, in the particular use made of it, it is not perceived by the public according to its ordinary meaning, i.e. as simply describing the product in some way. Because secondary meaning need not be proved for suggestive marks and such marks are considered entitled to a broader scope of protection, that line of distinction is often the focus of much attention in trademark litigation. In many instances, however, the attempt to pigeonhole the term in issue and to determine the presence or absence of secondary meaning unnecessarily distracts from the basic test of likelihood of confusion. *But see* discussion of the *Taco Cabana* decision in Chapter 8, *infra*.

(2) Descriptive marks are those which describe to potential customers the characteristics, nature, qualities, or ingredients of goods or services. They have generally been denied trademark protection, in the absence of proven source-indicating significance (secondary meaning or distinctiveness), in the equitable belief that the number of such appropriate terms is limited and that all merchants should equally be allowed to describe (or praise) their own goods while competing for customers. *Canal Co. v. Clark*, 80 U.S. 311 (1871); *Telechron, Inc. v. Telicon Corp.*, 198 F.2d 903 (3d Cir. 1952). "Suggestive" marks are said to fall into a category between those that are merely descriptive and those that are fanciful and arbitrary. Thus, it is said that trademark protection may be afforded to suggestive terms which shed some light upon the qualities or characteristics of goods but which are not descriptive of such goods in that "an effort of the imagination on the part of the observer" would be required to know their nature. *General Shoe Corp. v. Rosen*, 111 F.2d 95, 98 (4th Cir. 1940). *See Q-Tips, Inc. v. Johnson & Johnson*, 206 F.2d 144, 146 (3d Cir. 1953), *cert. denied*, 346 U.S. 867 (1953) (Q-TIPS held suggestive as a combination of an arbitrary first syllable and a somewhat descriptive second syllable "[used] in an unusual way"). *Compare 20th Century Wear, Inc. v. Sanmark-Stardust, Inc.*, 747 F.2d 81, 88 (2d Cir. 1984) (what might have taken a "step of the imagination" in 1973 or 1975 no longer did in more energy conservation conscious 1981 for "Cozy Warm ENERGY-SAVERS" women's pajamas). This distinction arose at common law partly because the courts strained to find trademark infringement where marks were neither fanciful nor descriptive in a strict sense. Fueling these metaphysical exercises was the 1905 Trademark Act which, unlike the Lanham Act, prohibited the registration of any descriptive marks, including those which had acquired secondary meanings. Does this "suggestive" mark test aid the objectivity of the courts or predictability in the law in this area? *See* McCarthy, *Trademarks and Unfair Competition*, § 11:6 (3d ed. 1992); Irani, *The Importance of Record Evidence to Categorize Marks as Generic, Descriptive or Suggestive*, 83 Trademark Rep. 571 (1993); Treece & Stephenson, *Another Look at Descriptive and Generic Terms in American Trademark Law*, 66 Trademark Rep. 452 (1976).

(3) Is a better test one which inquires whether competitors need the term to describe their goods? *See Minnesota Mining & Mfg. Co. v. Johnson & Johnson*, 454 F.2d 1179, 1180 (C.C.P.A. 1972) ("[T]hey have been able to describe that product

and advertise it without the use of the term coined by their competitor.") *Cf. Murphy v. Provident Mutual Life Insurance Company*, 923 F.2d 923, 927 (2d Cir. 1990), *cert. denied*, 112 S. Ct. 65 (1991) (advertising use of "hot" and thermometer graphic held descriptive; "If Ford Motor Company advertised its car as 'hot' and used a thermometer in its advertisements, would the thermometer be protected absent a showing of secondary meaning. We think not.") Is this test entirely fair? Is it more objective and predictable? Does it have any inherent drawbacks? Is it a valid criterion to determine whether a term is commercially needed to describe goods to inquire whether it is in fact being used by competitors? *See Shoe Corp. of America v. Juvenile Shoe Corp.*, 266 F.2d 793 (C.C.P.A. 1959); *Security Center, Ltd. v. First National Security Centers,* 750 F.2d 1295, 1299 (5th Cir. 1985). *Cf. Chapin-Sacks Mfg. Co. v. Hendler Creamery Co.*, 231 Fed. 550 (D.C. Md. 1916), *modified,* 254 Fed. 553 (4th Cir. 1918), where general usage in the trade caused an originally suggestive mark to become descriptive. *See also Bernard v. Commerce Drug Co.,* 964 F.2d 1338 (2d Cir. 1992) (ARTHRITICARE merely descriptive for gel that relieves arthritis pain); *Investacorp, Inc. v. Arabian Investment Banking Corp.*, 931 F.2d 1519 (11th Cir.), *cert. denied*, 112 S. Ct. 639 (1991) (INVESTACORP merely descriptive for financial services).

(4) What criteria should a court apply in determining whether a term is being used in a trademark sense, i.e., to identify as to source? *See Venetianaire Corp. v. A&P Import Co.,* 429 F.2d 1079, 1082 (2d Cir. 1970) ("[D]efendant obviously used the term 'as a symbol to attract public attention.' "); Garner, *A Display Theory of Trademarks,* 47 Trademark Rep. 303 (1957). *Cf. Pacific Indus., Inc. v. Minnesota Mining & Mfg. Co.,* 425 F.2d 1265 (C.C.P.A. 1970); *Levi Strauss & Co. v. Blue Bell, Inc.*, 216 U.S.P.Q. 606 (N.D. Cal. 1982). The mere presence of a word on a product label does not necessarily constitute a trademark use. In *Minnesota Mining & Mfg. Co. v. Minnesota Linseed Oil Paint Co.,* 229 F.2d 448 (C.C.P.A. 1956), the paint company's registered mark "Minnesota" was ordered cancelled when found to be used on the product labels only as part of the company's name, rather than as a name for the product.

(5) Should the courts simply employ the basic test of trade identity unfair competition, *i.e.*, likelihood of confusion? *See Transgo, Inc. v. Ajac Transmission Corp.*, 768 F.2d 1001, 1015 (9th Cir. 1985) ("secondary meaning can also be established by evidence of likelihood of confusion"); *Interpace Corp. v. Lapp, Inc.*, 721 F.3d 460 (3d Cir. 1983) (the tests for secondary meaning and likelihood of confusion are "indistinguishable in practice"). How would you prove that an alleged trademark has source-indicating significance? *See* 1 Gilson, *Trademark Protection and Practice* § 2.09 (1993 ed.); McCarthy, *Trademarks and Unfair Competition* § 15:10 (3d ed. 1992). In *Pabst Blue Ribbon v. Decatur Brewing Co., 284 F. 110 (7th Cir. 1922),* plaintiff, the manufacturer of Pabst Blue Ribbon beer, was unsuccessful in its attempt to prevent the defendant from selling packages of ingredients for home brewed beer under the name "Blue Ribbon." The court observed that "Blue Ribbon" was a term signifying "high merit," which was used at the time on over sixty widely varying products, and that it was therefore only entitled to limited protection. Should we automatically assume that the public gives such marks little significance as indicators of source? In *In re Wileswood, Inc., 201 U.S.P.Q. 400 (T.T.A.B. 1978)*

the Trademark Trial and Appeal Board rejected applications to register "America's Best Popcorn" and "America's Favorite Popcorn," stating that "the phrases in question are only self-awarded laudations of applicant's product, which others might be equally entitled to use, for whatever they are worth, for the same product."

(6) Does proof of actual confusion as to source implicitly and necessarily also constitute proof of secondary meaning or distinctiveness? *See International Kennel Club, Inc. v. Mighty Star, Inc.*, 846 F.2d 1079, 1086–87 (7th Cir. 1988); *American Scientific Chemical, Inc. v. American Hospital Corp.*, 690 F.2d 791, 793 (9th Cir. 1982) ("actual confusion is an indicium of secondary meaning"); McCarthy, *Trademarks and Unfair Competition*, § 15.3 (3d ed. 1992); *The Trademark Confusion Test — Good or Bad; Weak or Strong?* 1964 B.C. Indus. & Com. L. Rev. 401; Pattishall, *Secondary Meaning in Trade Identity Cases; Some Questions and Suggested Answers*, 45 Trademark Rep. 1261 (1955); Garner, *Narrow and Weak Trade Marks*, 22 Geo. Wash. L. Rev. 40 (1953). Should bad faith copying by a defendant raise a presumption that secondary meaning exists? *Osem Food Industries Ltd. v. Sherwood Foods Inc.*, 917 F.2d 161, 164 (4th Cir. 1990). See the discussion on Intent, *infra*.

(7) Can an informative slogan acquire trademark significance through extensive advertising and use? *See, e.g., Roux Laboratories, Inc. v. Clairol, Inc.*, 427 F.2d 823 (C.C.P.A. 1970) (HAIR COLOR SO NATURAL ONLY HER HAIR DRESSER KNOWS FOR SURE); *Bristol-Myers Co. v. Approved Pharmaceutical Corp.*, 149 U.S.P.Q. 869 (N.Y. 1966) (EXTRA STRENGTH PAIN RELIEVER). Need a slogan be "distinctive" to be given trademark protection? *See In re Joseph Bancroft & Sons Co.*, 129 U.S.P.Q. 329 (T.T.A.B. 1961); *Reed v. Amoco Oil*, 611 F. Supp. 9 (M.D. Tenn. 1984); Cf. *M.B.H. Enterprises, Inc. v. WOKY Inc.*, 633 F.2d 50 (7th Cir. 1980); *In re O.F Mosberg & Sons, Inc.*, 175 U.S.P.Q. 191 (T.T.A.B. 1972); *Maidenform, Inc. v. Munsingwear, Inc.*, 195 U.S.P.Q. 297 (S.D.N.Y. 1977) (UNDERNEATH IT ALL). *See generally* 1 Gilson, *Trademark Protection and Practice*, § 2.10 (1993 ed.); McCarthy, *Trademarks and Unfair Competition*, § 7.5 (3d ed. 1992); Helget, *Slogans — Protectable Marketing Tools?* 74 J. Pat. & Trademark Off. Soc'y 551 (1992).

(8) Some New York district courts had protected nascent goodwill under an equitable theory of "secondary meaning in the making." *See, e.g., National Lampoon, Inc. v. American Broadcasting Cos.*, 376 F. Supp. 733 (S.D.N.Y. 1974), *aff'd per curiam*, 497 F.2d 1343 (2d Cir. 1974); *Orion Picture Co. v. Dell Publishing Co.*, 471 F. Supp. 392 (S.D.N.Y. 1979); *Metro Kane Imports, Ltd. v. Federated Department Stores, Inc.*, 625 F. Supp. 313, 317 (S.D.N.Y. 1985) (a claim of interference with plaintiff's attempt to develop secondary meaning presented "a viable federal question"). The theory had been criticized as unclear and unnecessary, *see* McCarthy, *Trademarks and Unfair Competition*, § 15.21 (3d ed. 1992), and for focusing upon the intent of the seller while neglecting the response to the symbol by the consuming public, *Black & Decker Mfg. Co. v. Ever-Ready Appliance Mfg. Co.*, 684 F.2d 546 (8th Cir. 1982); *A.J. Canfield Co. v. Concord Beverage Co.*, 228 U.S.P.Q. 479, 487 (E.D. Pa. 1985). *See* Scagnelli, *Dawn of a New Doctrine? — Trademark Protection for Incipient Secondary Meaning*, 71 Trademark Rep. 527

(1981). After considering the theory in *Laureyssens v. Idea Group, Inc.*, 964 F.2d 131, 137 (2d Cir. 1992), the Second Circuit rejected it, stating, "Where there is no actual secondary meaning in a trade dress, the purchasing public simply does not associate the trade dress with a particular producer. Therefore a subsequent producer who adopts an imitating trade dress will not cause confusion." *See also Cicena Ltd. v. Columbia Telecommunications Group*, 900 F.2d 1546, 1550 (Fed. Cir. 1990) (the Federal Circuit holding that the Second Circuit would reject the doctrine of secondary meaning in the making); *Lang v. Retirement Living Publishing Co., Inc.*, 949 F.2d 576 (2d Cir. 1991) (declining to adopt the doctrine). Is it fair, however, to permit a competitor to preempt developing secondary meaning?

§ 2.05 Geographical Terms

INTRODUCTION

Geographical terms, such as Scotch, American, California and Allegheny, may be broadly considered as being "descriptive" trademarks, although they fall within a particular category of that designation. Because of the threshold impression that such terms are or should be universally available to all residents of the locality involved, because the number of such terms applicable to a locality is limited, and because their use for trade identity purposes is generally so common, the problems of defining rights and the scope of exclusivity are particularly difficult.

AMERICAN WALTHAM WATCH CO. v. UNITED STATES WATCH CO.

Massachusetts Supreme Judicial Court
173 Mass. 85, 53 N.E. 141 (1899)

HOLMES, JUSTICE.

This is a bill brought to enjoin the defendant from advertising its watches as the "Waltham Watch" or "Waltham Watches," and from marking its watches in such a way that the word "Waltham" is conspicuous. The plaintiff was the first manufacturer of watches in Waltham, and had acquired a great reputation before the defendant began to do business. It was found at the hearing that the word "Waltham," which originally was used by the plaintiff in a merely geographical sense, now, by long use in connection with the plaintiff's watches, has come to have a secondary meaning as a designation of the watches which the public has become accustomed to associate with the name. This is recognized by the defendant so far that it agrees that the preliminary injunction, granted in 1890, against using the combined words "Waltham Watch" or "Waltham Watches" in advertising its watches, shall stand, and shall be embodied in the final decree.

The question raised at the hearing, and now before us, is <u>whether the defendant shall be enjoined further against using the words "Waltham" or "Waltham, Mass.,"</u> upon plates of its watches, without some accompanying statement which shall distinguish clearly its watches from those made by the plaintiff. The judge who heard the case found that it is of considerable commercial importance to indicate where the defendant's business of manufacturing is carried on, as it is the custom of watch manufacturers so to mark their watches, but, nevertheless, found that such an injunction ought to issue. He also found that the use of the word "Waltham," in its geographical sense, upon the dial, is not important, and should be enjoined.

The defendant's position is that, whatever its intent and whatever the effect in diverting a part of the plaintiff's business, it has a right to put its name and address upon its watches; that to require it to add words which will distinguish its watches from the plaintiff's in the mind of the general public is to require it to discredit them in advance; and that if the plaintiff, by its method of advertisement, has associated the fame of its merits with the city where it makes its wares, instead of with its own name, that is the plaintiff's folly, and cannot give it a monopoly of a geographical name, or entitle it to increase the defendant's burden in advertising the place of its works.

In cases of this sort, as in so many others, what ultimately is to be worked out is a point or line between conflicting claims, each of which has meritorious grounds, and would be extended further were it not for the other. *Ferrule Co. v. Hills,* 159 Mass. 147, 149, 150, 34 N.E. 85. It is desirable that the plaintiff should not lose custom by reason of the public mistaking another manufacturer for it. It is desirable that the defendant should be free to manufacture watches at Waltham, and to tell the world that it does so. The two desiderata cannot both be had to their full extent, and we have to fix the boundaries as best we can. On the one hand, the defendant must be allowed to accomplish its desideratum in some way, whatever the loss to the plaintiff. On the other, we think, the cases show that the defendant fairly may be required to avoid deceiving the public to the plaintiff's harm, so far as is practicable in a commercial sense. It is true that a man cannot appropriate a geographical name; but neither can he a color, or any part of the English language, or even a proper name to the exclusion of others whose names are like his. Yet a color in connection with a sufficiently complex combination of other things may be recognized as saying so circumstantially that the defendant's goods are the plaintiff's as to pass the injunction line. *New England Awl & Needle Co. v. Marlborough Awl & Needle Co.,* 168 Mass. 154, 156, 46 N.E. 386. So, although the plaintiff has no copyright on the dictionary, or any part of it, he can exclude a defendant from a part of the free field of the English language, even from the mere use of generic words, unqualified and unexplained, when they would mislead the plaintiff's customers to another shop. *Reddaway v. Banham* [1896] App. Cas. 199. So, the name of a person may become so associated with his goods that one of the same name coming into the business later will not be allowed to use even his own name without distinguishing his wares. *Brinsmead v. Brinsmead,* 13 Times Law R. 3; *Reddaway v. Bonham* [1896] App. Cas. 199, 210. *See Singer Mfg. Co. v. June Mfg. Co.,* 163 U.S. 169, 204, 16 Sup. Ct. 1002; *Cream Co. v. Keller,* 85 Fed. 643.

And so, we doubt not, may a geographical name acquire a similar association with a similar effect. *Montgomery v. Thompson* [1891] App. Cas. 217.

Whatever might have been the doubts some years ago, we think that now it is pretty well settled that the plaintiff, merely on the strength of having been first in the field, may put later comers to the trouble of taking such reasonable precautions as are commercially practicable to prevent their lawful names and advertisements from deceitfully diverting the plaintiff's custom.

We cannot go behind the finding that such a deceitful diversion is the effect, and intended effect, of the marks in question. We cannot go behind the finding that it is practicable to distinguish the defendant's watches from those of the plaintiff, and that it ought to be done.

Decree for plaintiff.

COMMUNITY OF ROQUEFORT v. WILLIAM FAEHNDRICH, INC.

United States Court of Appeals, Second Circuit
303 F.2d 494 (1962)

KAUFMAN, CIRCUIT JUDGE.

The Community of Roquefort (hereafter sometimes referred to as Community), a municipality in France, is the holder of a certification mark "Roquefort" for cheese, which is registered in the United States Patent Office under Section 4 of the Lanham Trade-Mark Act of 1946, 15 U.S.C.A. § 1054. Together with a French cheese exporter, another French agent, and an American cheese packaging concern, the Community filed a complaint against William Faehndrich, Inc. (hereafter referred to as Faehndrich), a New York cheese importer. The complaint alleged, *inter alia,* that Faehndrich was infringing the Community's "Roquefort" certification mark; and, in general, it sought to enjoin Faehndrich from selling cheese not produced in accordance with that mark but labeled or represented as "Imported Roquefort Cheese." Plaintiffs moved for summary judgment. At the same time they announced that if relief were granted on the Community's cause of action for infringement, the other claims would be withdrawn. The defendant denied infringement, and filed a cross motion for summary judgment. From a judgment in favor of the Community of Roquefort, and the issuance of a permanent injunction against continued infringement of the certification mark, the defendant Faehndrich appeals.

It appears that for centuries there has been produced and cured in the natural limestone caves in and about the municipality of Roquefort a sheep's milk blue-mold cheese, which has been marketed in this country for many years as "Roquefort Cheese." In an effort to protect themselves against unfair competition, producers of such French "Roquefort Cheese" frequently have asked our courts to prevent misleading use of the "Roquefort" designation. *See, e.g., Douglas v. Mod-Urn Cheese Packing Co., Inc.,* 161 Misc. 21, 290 N.Y.S. 368 (Sup. Ct. 1936); *Douglas v. Newark*

Cheese Co., Inc., 153 Misc. 85, 274 N.Y.S. 406 (Sup. Ct. 1934). For similar reasons the Community of Roquefort, in 1953, obtained a certification mark so that the term "Roquefort," as applied to cheese, would be used exclusively:

> . . . to indicate that the same has been manufactured from sheep's milk only, and has been cured in the natural caves of the Community of Roquefort, Department of Aveyron, France, in accordance with the historic methods and usages of production, curing and development which have been in vogue there for a long period of years.

Since that time the Community has been diligent in protecting the mark.

Nevertheless, in 1960, Faehndrich imported into the United States a quantity of sheep's milk blue-mold cheese, labeled "Imported Roquefort Cheese" (at Faehndrich's direction), which had been produced in Hungary and Italy. Of course, it was not (and could not be) produced by authority of the Community of Roquefort under its mark. When imported, Faehndrich's cheese was packaged in a manner clearly indicating the countries of origin. On the other hand, when Faehndrich prepared the cheese for re-sale, the labels prominently displaying the words "Product of Italy" and "Product of Hungary" were replaced with new wrappers printed "Imported Roquefort Cheese" and "Made from Pure Sheep's Milk Only," *without any indication of origin.* Hence, there was nothing on the wrappers which would suggest to the retail-buying public that Faehndrich's cheese came from Hungary or Italy.

In order to clarify our discussion of the single question presented by this appeal, i.e., whether Judge Metzner was correct in granting the Community of Roquefort's motion for summary judgment, it will be helpful to summarize the law applicable to certification marks such as the mark involved in this case, and by way of explanation, to point out certain distinctions between *trade-marks* on the one hand, and *certification marks* on the other.

Until the Lanham Act of 1946, a geographical name could not be registered as a *trade-mark.* This prohibition operated to prevent a single producer from appropriating the name of a particular place or area in which he was located to the exclusion of other and similarly situated producers. *Canal Co. v. Clark*, 80 U.S. 311 581 (1872). "If the name was to be found in an atlas . . . , that was sufficient to preclude registration." Robert, *Commentary on the Lanham Trade-Mark Act, 15 U.S.C.A. following § 1024*, 265, 271 (1948). Nevertheless, if a geographical name which had become distinctive of certain goods was registered by oversight, it was protected against infringement, *Baglin v. Cusenier Co.*, 221 U.S. 580, 591-593 (1911); moreover, if the name acquired such new significance as an indication of origin of goods, i.e., a secondary meaning, its use was protected from unfair competition even though it could not be registered as a trademark. *Elgin National Watch Co. v. Illinois Watch Case Co.*, 179 U.S. 665 (1901); Vandenburgh, *Trademark Law and Procedure* §§ 4.60, 4.70 (1959).

Section 2(e) of the Lanham Act continued to prohibit registration of a geographical name as a trade-mark, if "when applied to the goods of the applicant [it] is primarily geographically descriptive . . . ," 15 U.S.C.A. § 1052(e)(2), *unless* such a name "has become distinctive of the applicant's goods . . . ," 15 U.S.C.A.

§ 1052(f). Under the Lanham Act, therefore, if a geographical name acquires a secondary meaning, it can be registered as a trade-mark. Vandenburgh, op. cit. *supra.*

In addition to this extension of trade-mark law, the Lanham Act created an entirely new registered mark which was denominated a "certification mark." 15 U.S.C.A. § 1054; Robert, op. cit. *supra,* at p. 270.

> The term "certification mark" means a mark used upon or in connection with the products . . . of one or more persons other than the owner of the mark to certify regional or other origin, material, mode of manufacture, quality, accuracy or other characteristics of such goods . . . 15 U.S.C.A. § 1127.

A geographical name does not require a secondary meaning in order to qualify for registration as a certification mark. It is true that section 1054 provides that certification marks are "subject to the provisions relating to the registration of trademarks, so far as they are applicable. . .." But Section 1052(e)(2), which prohibits registration of names primarily geographically descriptive, specifically excepts "indications of regional origin" registrable under section 1054. Therefore, a geographical name may be registered as a certification mark even though it is primarily geographically descriptive. This distinction, i.e., that a geographical name cannot be registered as a *trademark* unless it has secondary meaning, but can be registered as a *certification mark* without secondary meaning, has significance. A trade-mark gives a producer exclusive rights; but a certification mark, owned by a municipality, such as Roquefort, must be made available without discrimination "to certify the goods . . . of *any* person who maintains the standards or conditions which such mark certifies." (Italics added.) 15 U.S.C.A. § 1064(d)(4). *See* 4 Callmann, *Unfair Competition and Trade Marks* § 98.4(c)(2 ed. 1950).

On the other hand, a geographical name registered as a certification mark must continue to indicate the regional origin, mode of manufacture, etc. of the goods upon which it is used, just as a trade-mark must continue to identify a producer.

> When the meaning of a mark that had previously served as an indication of origin changes so that its principal significance to purchasers is that of indicating the nature or class of goods and its function as an indication of origin is subservient thereto, it is no longer a mark but rather is a generic term. Vandenburgh, op. cit. *supra,* § 9.20.

Therefore, if a geographical name which has been registered as a certification mark, identifying certain goods, acquires principal significance as a description of those goods, the rights cease to be incontestable, 15 U.S.C.A. § 1065(4), and the mark is subject to cancellation, 15 U.S.C.A. § 1064(c); Robert, op. cit. *supra,* at pp. 280-281.

In the present case Faehndrich does not contest the validity of the mark's registration, as to which the Community's certificate of registration is prima facie proof. 15 U.S.C.A. § 1057(b). Instead, Faehndrich argues that there is a genuine issue of fact concerning the existence of generic meaning, i.e., whether the term "Roquefort" has acquired principal significance as a description of blue-mold sheep's milk cheese, regardless of its origin and without reference to the method of curing employed in the limestone caves of Roquefort, France. The difficulty with Faehndrich's position, however, is that nowhere in the affidavits submitted below on the motion for summary judgment is there any allegation of facts which suggests that such a genuine issue exists; nor does Faehndrich make any allegation that it could prove such facts at a trial. The affidavits are barren of any allegations or facts that consumers understand the word "Roquefort" to mean nothing more than blue-mold cheese made with sheep's milk. Indeed, the Community's affidavits indicate the contrary. They allege that the only other cheese of this nature commercially sold in the United States, a product of Israel, is marketed as "Garden of Eden — Heavenly Cheese — Sheep's Milk Blue-Mold Cheese"; that a similar Tunisian product is marketed abroad as "Bleu de Brebis"; and that the same cheese which Faehndrich imports from Hungary and sells with the label "Imported Roquefort Cheese" is sold in Belgium as "Merinofort." Moreover, we have already noted that producers of French Roquefort cheese have diligently protected the name from unfair competition in this country.

The purpose of summary judgment is to dispose of cases in which "there is no genuine issue as to any material fact and . . . the moving party is entitled to a judgment as a matter of law." Rule 56(c), Fed.R.Civ.P., 28 U.S.C.A.; *see* 6 Moore, *Federal Practice*, ¶ 56.04 (2 ed. 1953). Since the object is to discover whether one side has no real support for its version of the facts, the Rule specifically states that affidavits shall "set forth such facts as would be admissible in evidence." Rule 56(e), Fed.R.Civ.P. In view of this, we agree with Judge Metzner that Faehndrich "has failed to show . . . that there is any possibility on a trial that he can raise an issue of fact" in regard to generic meaning.

Moreover, since Faehndrich's wrappers indisputably bore the inscription "Imported Roquefort Cheese," we believe that the District Court was justified in finding, as a matter of law, that appellant's use of an identical mark on substantially identical goods was "likely to cause confusion or mistake or to deceive purchasers as to the source of the origin of the goods." 15 U.S.C.A. § 1114. *Accord Triumph Hosiery Mills, Inc. v. Triumph International Corp.,* 191 F. Supp. 937, 940 (S.D.N.Y. 1961).

We are well aware of the dangers involved in haphazard use of summary judgment procedures. However, summary judgment cannot be defeated where there is no indication that a genuine issue of fact exists; to permit that would be to render this valuable procedure wholly inoperative and to place a "devastating gloss" on the rule. *See* Clark, *Clarifying Amendments to the Federal Rules?*, 14 Ohio St. L.J. 241, 249-250 (1953).

Affirmed.

IN RE NANTUCKET, INC.

United States Court of Customs and Patent Appeals
677 F.2d 95 (1982)

MARKEY, CHIEF JUDGE.

Nantucket, Inc. (Nantucket) appeals from a decision of the Trademark Trial and Appeal Board (board) affirming a refusal to register the mark NANTUCKET for men's shirts on the ground that it is "primarily geographically deceptively misdescriptive." *In re Nantucket, Inc.*, 209 U.S.P.Q. 868 (T.T.A.B. 1981). We reverse.

. . . .

The board correctly notes that its test for registrability of geographic terms is "easy to administer" and "*minimizes* subjective determinations by eliminating any need to make unnecessary inquiry into the nebulous question of whether the public associates particular goods with a particular geographical area in applying Section 2(e)(2)." [Emphasis in original.] Ease-of-administration considerations aside, the board's approach does raise the question of whether public association of goods with an area must be considered in applying § 2(e)(2). That question is one of first impression in this court. We answer in the affirmative.

The board's test rests mechanistically on the one question of whether the mark is recognizable, at least to some large segment of the public, as the name of a geographical area. NANTUCKET is such. That ends the board's test. Once it is found that the mark is the name of a known place, i.e., that it has "a readily recognizable geographic meaning," the next question, whether applicant's goods do or do not come from that place, becomes irrelevant under the board's test, for if they do, the mark is "primarily geographically descriptive"; if they don't, the mark is "primarily geographically deceptively misdescriptive." Either way, the result is the same, for the mark must be denied registration on the principal register unless resort can be had to § 2(f).[3]

. . . .

Geographic terms are merely a specific kind of potential trademark, subject to characterization as having a particular kind of descriptiveness or misdescriptiveness. Registration of marks that would be perceived by potential purchasers as describing or deceptively misdescribing the goods themselves may be denied under § 2(e)(1). Registration of marks that would be perceived by potential purchasers as describing or deceptively misdescribing the geographic origin of the goods may be denied under

---

[3] Section 2(f) provides:

> Except as expressly excluded in paragraphs (a), (b), (c), and (d) of this section, nothing in this chapter shall prevent the registration of a mark used by the applicant which has become distinctive of the applicant's goods in commerce. The Commissioner may accept as prima facie evidence that the mark has become distinctive, as applied to the applicant's goods in commerce, proof of substantially exclusive and continuous use thereof as a mark by the applicant in commerce for the five years next preceding the date of the filing of the application for its registration.

§ 2(e)(2). In either case, the mark must be judged on the basis of its role in the marketplace.

As the courts have made plain, geographically deceptive misdescriptiveness cannot be determined without considering whether the public associates the goods with the place which the mark names. If the goods do not come from the place named, and the public makes no goods-place association, the public is not deceived and the mark is accordingly not geographically deceptively misdescriptive.

In *World Carpets, Inc. v. Dick Littrell's New World Carpets*, 438 F.2d 482, 486, 168 U.S.P.Q. 609, 612-13 (CA 5 1971), the court said: "[T]he wording of the statute makes it plain that not all terms which are geographically suggestive are unregistrable. . . .. Indeed, the statutory language declares nonregistrable only those words which are 'primarily geographically descriptive.' The word 'primarily' should not be overlooked, for it is not the intent of the federal statute to refuse registration of a mark where the geographic meaning is minor, obscure, remote, *or unconnected with the goods.*" [Emphasis added.] Thus, if there be no connection of the geographical meaning of the mark with the goods in the public mind, that is, if the mark is arbitrary when applied to the goods, registration should not be refused under § 2(e)(2).

In *National Lead Co. v. Wolfe*, 223 F.2d 195, 199, 105 U.S.P.Q. 462, 465 (CA 9), *cert. denied*, 350 U.S. 883, 107 U.S.P.Q. 362 (1955), the court held that neither DUTCH, nor DUTCH BOY, as applied to paint, was used "otherwise than in a fictitious, arbitrary and fanciful manner," and noted that "there is no likelihood that the use of the name 'Dutch' or 'Dutch Boy' in connection with the appellant's goods would be understood by purchasers as representing that the goods or their constituent materials were produced or processed in Holland or that they are of the same distinctive kind or quality as those produced, processed or used in that place."

. . . .

Section 2(e)(2) provides that registration shall not be refused *unless* the mark is primarily geographically deceptively misdescriptive of the goods. The only indication of record that NANTUCKET is primarily a geographical term resides in dictionary listings referring to Nantucket Island as a summer resort and former whaling center. There is no evidence of record to support a holding that the mark NANTUCKET as applied to men's shirts is "deceptively misdescriptive." There is no indication that the purchasing public would expect men's shirts to have their origin in Nantucket when seen in the market place with NANTUCKET on them. Hence buyers are not likely to be deceived, and registration cannot be refused on the ground that the mark is "primarily geographically deceptively misdescriptive."

Accordingly, the decision of the board is *reversed.*

NIES, JUDGE, concurring.

I join the court's holding that there must be an indication that "the purchasing public would expect men's shirts to have their origin in Nantucket when seen in the marketplace with NANTUCKET on them." Moreover, I agree that on the present record the board's decision holding that NANTUCKET for men's shirts is "primarily geographically deceptively misdescriptive" must be reversed. I choose to concur, however, because I reach the same conclusion from a different direction, and because the court leaves open what the PTO must show to make a prima facie case under § 2(e)(2) with respect to this application.

Appellant had urged that the court adopt the rule that a goods/place association can be established under § 2(e)(2) only if the place identified by the geographic name claimed as a mark was "noted for" the goods, like IDAHO for potatoes or PARIS for perfume. The standard of registrability enunciated by the court has not been restricted to such a stringent test. To have done so would have created as rigid a rule in favor of registration as the board had used to deny registration. If a geographic name were arbitrary in the absence of a reputation for the goods, any trader who is the *first* to use any geographic name for particular goods would, thereby, appropriate it to his exclusive use. Moreover, the rationale advanced by appellant is not limited to geographic names of places where the likelihood of future commercial exploitation by others is small but would be equally applicable if the claimed mark for shirts were CHICAGO. The answer to the basic question of public association of goods with a place, i.e., geographic descriptiveness, cannot be decided on this simplistic basis.

. . . .

Concerning the authority cited by the appellant, it is apparent that the issue of whether the public is likely to believe a particular geographic name is informational when it appears on a product has been lost sight of in some decisions, which have applied mechanical rules wholly inappropriate to trademark cases. A geographic name is not unprotectible or unregistrable because it can be labelled a geographic name, but because it tells the public something about the product or the producer about which his competitor also has a right to inform the public. Thus, the names of places devoid of commercial activity are arbitrary usage.

In this category are names of places such as ANTARCTICA, MOUNT EVER-EST, or GALAPAGOS, at least when used for ordinary commercial products, such as beer and shoes. Names such as SUN, WORLD, GLOBE, MARS, or MILKY WAY are also arbitrary, not informational; competitors do not need to use the terms to compete effectively. *Sun Banks of Florida, Inc. v. Sun Federal Savings & Loan Association,* 651 F.2d 311, 211 U.S.P.Q. 844, *reh'g denied,* 659 F.2d 1079 (CA 5 1981); *World Carpets, Inc. v. Dick Littrell's New World Carpets,* 438 F.2d 482, 486, 168 U.S.P.Q. 609, 612-13 (CA 5 1971). If the pertinent issue is kept in mind, the question of geographic descriptiveness or its corollary, deceptive misdescriptiveness, can more easily be resolved.

It is also apparent that some opinions fail to grasp that the defense of geographic descriptiveness, put forth by an alleged infringer, should be available only to one with a legitimate personal interest in use of the name. When raised by others, the defense can only be characterized as contrived. In this respect, a geographic name is comparable to a surname in protectibility: one of the same name may have a defense of inherent right to use; one with a different name should not be heard to demand that secondary meaning must be established by a prior user. The issue in such a case is which of the two parties has superior rights and whether the public interest is served by enjoining use by the latecomer. The first of the two users in such litigation need not prove rights against the world to prevail. *National Lead Co. v. Wolfe*, 223 F.2d 195, 200, 105 U.S.P.Q. 462, 465–66 (CA 9), *cert. denied*, 350 U.S. 883 (1955).

. . . .

. . . In my view it is incumbent on the PTO to put forth evidence that other businesses have or are likely to have legitimate interests in use of the geographic name claimed by the applicant. The solicitor suggests that this court may take judicial notice that Nantucket has a lively summer tourist trade and that men's shirts are generally available in summer resorts and locations frequented by tourists. I do not believe it is appropriate to take such judicial notice at the appellate level as to do so would deprive an applicant of the opportunity to respond. *In re Water Gremlin Co.*, 635 F.2d 841, 845, 208 U.S.P.Q. 89, 92 (C.C.P.A. 1980). Moreover, as pointed out by appellant, the solicitor's position is not the board's position. Were the application for NANTUCKET for steam turbines, the board's test would preclude registration.

The PTO frequently makes use of telephone directories in connection with proving surname significance. The same type of evidence could be made of record to show that businesses dealing in the same or related goods exist in the named area. This would, in my view, make a prima facie case. With a name such as CHICAGO, such a prima facie case in all likelihood could be made regardless of goods and an applicant would have a difficult task to overcome it. With a name such as NANTUCKET, one would expect that there are at least some goods for which the term is arbitrary. If the PTO makes a prima facie case which the applicant is unable to overcome, the applicant must resort to proof of distinctiveness in accordance with § 2(f) to secure registration.

Can be arbitrary

NOTES ON GEOGRAPHICAL TERMS

Law

(1) Geographical terms are protectable as trademarks if they have acquired secondary meaning. They are not protectable if they are deceptive or primarily descriptive or are deceptively misdescriptive of the geographical origin of the goods or services. *See Elgin National Watch Co. v. Illinois Watch Case Co.*, 179 U.S. 665 (1901); McCarthy & Devitt, *Protection of Geographic Denominations: Domestic and International*, 69 Trademark Rep. 199 (1979); Merchant, *Deceptive and Descriptive Marks*, 56 Trademark Rep. 141 (1966). The Lanham Act provides in § 2(a) that a "deceptive" and in § 2(e)(2) that a "primarily geographically descriptive or deceptively misdescriptive" mark may not be registered, but § 2(f) provides that a mark which originally was geographically descriptive may be registered if it has become distinctive of the goods or services in commerce. What is the purpose of this difference? Why is CAMBRIDGE a potentially protectable trademark for Florida oranges while CALIFORNIA is not? In *Scotch Whisky Association v. United States Distilled Products Co.*, 952 F.2d 1317 (Fed. Cir. 1991), the dismissal of an

opposition under § 2(a) was reversed because the Scottish surname McADAMS for whisky might deceptively suggest Scottish origin for applicant's Canadian whisky.

Following the United States' entry into the North American Free Trade Agreement with Canada and Mexico, President Clinton in December 1993 signed implementing legislation, HR3450, which amended §§ 2(f) and 23(a) to preclude registration of "primarily geographically deceptively misdescriptive" marks. Such a mark previously was registrable under § 2(f) if it had become distinctive. A grandfather clause permits registration on the principal register if the mark became distinctive prior to the date of the bill's enactment. What effect would it have on Judge Nies' analysis in the *Nantucket* case if applicant had begun use after the date of the bill's enactment?

(2) In *In re Nantucket, Inc., supra*, the Court of Customs and Patent Appeals reversed a refusal to register because people would not expect shirts bearing the trademark NANTUCKET to have been made there. Judge Nies emphasized in her concurring opinion that the lack of commercial activity on Nantucket was what made the trademark arbitrary and registrable without proof of secondary meaning. She pointed out that the use of a trademark like CHICAGO would have presented a much different problem. This concurrence was cited, and its reasoning followed in *In re Handler Fenton Westerns, Inc.*, 214 U.S.P.Q. 848 (T.T.A.B. 1982), in refusing registration of DENVER WESTERNS for western-style shirts.

> . . . [Applicant's] shirts have their geographic origin in Denver, one of the largest and best-known cities of the American west, and applicant cannot reasonably expect that its mark is used in an arbitrary manner with respect to its goods or that purchasers would not believe its western-style shirts marked "DENVER WESTERNS" have their geographic origin in Denver.

See also In re Charles S. Loeb Pipes, Inc., 190 U.S.P.Q. 238 (T.T.A.B. 1976) (OLD DOMINION held unregistrable for pipe tobacco of unspecified origin). *Cf. Institut National Des Appellations D'Origine v. Vinters Int'l Co.*, 958 F.2d 1574 (Fed. Cir. 1992), in which the Federal Circuit affirmed that CHABLIS WITH A TWIST did not deceptively suggest French origin because "Chablis" is generic in this country, and *In re Jacques Berniere, Inc.*, 13 U.S.P.Q.2d 1725 (Fed. Cir. 1990), reversing a refusal to register RODEO DRIVE for perfume, the Federal Circuit finding no evidence that people would believe applicant's perfume originated on Rodeo Drive in Beverly Hills.

(3) What factors should be considered in determining whether the following marks are descriptive, or deceptively misdescriptive? IRISH SPRING for Soap; DUTCH CLEANSER; ENGLISH LEATHER for after-shave lotion; ITALIAN MAIDE for canned vegetables? How would you determine whether these marks are entitled to trademark protection? *See Hamilton-Brown Shoe Co. v. Wolf Bros. & Co.*, 240 U.S. 251 (1916) (AMERICAN GIRL for shoes). In *Singer Mfg. Co. v. Birginal-Bigsby Corp.*, 319 F.2d 273 (C.C.P.A. 1963), Singer's opposition to registration of AMERICAN BEAUTY for Japanese made sewing machines was sustained on the ground that such a mark would be primarily geographically deceptively misdescriptive under § 2(e)(2) of the Lanham Act. Although Singer did not use AMERICAN as a trademark itself, it was the principal domestic manufacturer of sewing machines

and had emphasized in its advertising that its sewing machines were made in America by American craftsmen. It was on this basis that the court granted Singer standing to oppose. The court stated that "the continuing use of AMERICAN BEAUTY by appellee in the manner disclosed by the record is very likely to damage Singer by bringing about the sale of Japanese made machines to those who, if not deceived as to their origin, would, instead, purchase a Singer machine." *See also Scotch Whisky Ass'n v. Consolidated Distilled Products, Inc.*, 210 U.S.P.Q. 639 (N.D. Ill. 1981), in which the court enjoined use of LOCH-A-MOOR as a trademark for American-made liqueur because potential purchasers would be misled to believe that the liqueur was a product of Scotland, endowing it, unjustifiably, with added prestige and salability.

(4) The Lanham Act specifically provides that collective and certification marks "including indications of regional origin used in commerce" are registrable. (15 U.S.C. § 1054). *See generally* Bengedkey & Mead, *International Protection of Appellations of Origin and Other Geographic Designations*, 82 Trademark Rep. 765 (1992); Pollack, *"Roquefort" — An Example of Multiple Protection for a Designation of Regional Origin Under the Lanham Act*, 52 Trademark Rep. 755 (1962). 15 U.S.C. § 1127 defines a certification mark as "a mark used upon or in connection with the products or services of one or more persons *other than the owner of the mark* to certify regional or other origin. . . ." One court has interpreted this to mean that a producer of the goods in question cannot own a certification mark. *See Black Hills Jewelry Manufacturing Co. v. Gold Rush, Inc.*, 633 F.2d 746, 750 (8th Cir. 1980). Defendant in that case was nonetheless enjoined from using the trademark BLACK HILLS GOLD, as their jewelry was not manufactured in South Dakota, and the court found that purchasers would be misled as to origin. *See also Underwriters Laboratories, Inc. v. United Laboratories, Inc.*, 203 U.S.P.Q. 180 (N.D. Ill. 1978).

§ 2.06   Surnames

INTRODUCTION

Like geographical terms, yet differently, surnames as trademarks or as identifying portions of trademarks pose special problems of protectibility. The notion that every one should be able to use his name to identify his goods or business is deeply rooted in American mores even though perhaps unconsciously. Should everyone born with the name Ford be entitled to manufacture and sell automobiles under that name? The courts have historically revealed a distaste for unqualifiedly prohibiting the use of one's own name in commerce, but when pressed with hard cases, they have generally relied upon the basic test of likelihood of confusion. The cases that follow delineate some of the problems and their judicial treatment.

Cts Don't unqualifiedly prohibit Use of one's own name -

HAT CORPORATION OF AMERICA v. D. L. DAVIS CORP.

United States District Court, District of Connecticut
4 F. Supp. 613 (1933)

HINCKS, DISTRICT JUDGE,

[Defendant shared its earnings with William H. Dobbs for the apparent purpose of using his name on its products. The defendant corporation subordinated its own name on its products, and conspicuously imprinted the name "Wm. H. Dobbs" on the sweatband of hats and on the hat boxes.]

. . . .

The facts of the case at bar are such that Wm. H. Dobbs himself could not use the name "Dobbs" in the marking of hats publicly offered for sale or in advertising hats for sale, without deceiving and confusing the public to the plaintiff's damage. That such deceit and damage have resulted from his operations as heretofore conducted in conjunction with Bert Pope, Inc., and the defendant, is only too clear on the evidence. More doubtful, perhaps, is the task of determining now whether any explanatory suffix to the name, such as "not connected with the original Dobbs," would suffice to avoid the confusion.

The efficacy of such prefixes [sic] obviously is affected by psychological considerations, a surer understanding of which is much to be desired. The field seems not to have been yet cultivated by the scientific psychologist. Cf. Isaac on Traffic in Trade-Symbols, 44 Harv. L. Rev. 1210. But surely a reading of the long and widespread litigation that has grown out of the use of such names as "Baker" and "Rogers" (for a convenient review of which see Nims on Trade Marks, p. 125 et seq.) leads one to question the efficacy of such limitations. And, obviously, halfway limitations inadequate to prevent confusion, propagate litigation, devastating uncertainty in business, and a cynical reaction to the administration of law. Such results cannot be justified by a false tenderness for the rights of the individual. To be sure, he is entitled to protection in all proper use of his name, but not to a use which, though true to the few fully informed, is false to the many who are only partially informed.

Since the only purpose of an explanatory suffix is to prevent confusion between the impressions conveyed by the defendant's use of the name and those conveyed by the plaintiff's use of the name, the efficacy of such a suffix will largely depend upon the connotations which the public has become habituated to attach to the plaintiff's use of the name. Since this name has acquired its secondary meaning largely by advertising, that fact and the content of such advertising will indicate the association of ideas which attaches in the public mind to the name. The evidence shows that the plaintiff's advertising has emphasized the surname only. It is a fair inference that the public has long since forgotten, if it ever knew, De Witt Dobbs, the man, and Dobbs & Co., the plaintiff's predecessor of which he was the president. The surname alone remains in the public mind as an identification mark about which cluster associated ideas such as quality and style in headgear. The name has become a purely impersonal symbol. It no longer signifies anything as to the place of manufacture, or the personal identity of the manufacturer.

This, the evidence fairly indicates, is the meaning of "Dobbs" to the public. Precisely the same images are evoked by the sight or sound of "Wm. H. Dobbs," and the effect is no different if followed by such a phrase as "not connected with the original Dobbs." For the eye of the purchaser, long taught to identify the product by the name Dobbs alone, promptly registers the identity as complete upon catching the surname without noticing and pondering the significance of initials or suffix. And even the occasional purchaser who notices the suffix is not enlightened. For one who has known of one Dobbs only, suddenly confronted with the suggestion that there are in existence varieties of the species, is not informed which Dobbs is "his" Dobbs. Confusion is created by the very explanation intended to avert confusion. The purchaser whose impressions have been gradually acquired through continuous advertising cannot himself mentally locate the origin of his impressions as to time or place. And it is not to be expected that a hat clerk who chances to wait on him can accurately trace his impressions.

And so here, I conclude, Wm. H. Dobbs was precluded by the combination of the public interest and the plaintiff's right from using even his own name on the product or in advertising or elsewhere as the designation or as a part of the designation of the product. This conclusion has equal application to the use of the name on the hat box. For the public knows the product by the name, not by the box. Subject to these limitations, however, he had the right to manufacture and sell hats under his own name. He could lease or buy factories or stores, he could hire help, and could carry on a thousand other incidents of business under his own name, without causing any confusion.

. . . .

Now, obviously, a court cannot pass upon the misleading propensities of advertising matter not yet formulated. And especially since the fairness of the impression conveyed by advertising depends on such delicate factors as stress of voice, emphasis, and arrangement of type, as well as subject-matter, it is not practicable to lay down any rule more definite than that the advertising matter must be truthful, both in fact and in the impression conveyed, in view of the existing background. Any injunction, therefore, which would issue on the facts of this case against Wm. H. Dobbs if he were a party, should wholly enjoin all use of the word "Dobbs" on the product and its containers, and in the designation of the product, and should further prevent use of the name in advertising any product so as to cause confusion between the product of Wm. H. Dobbs and of the plaintiff, or otherwise to mislead the public to the plaintiff's hurt. Such a decree would, I think, be effective to prevent such a spread of litigation as attended the use of the Baker name, for example. And if by the generality of the provisions last above set forth, uncertainty should result, at least it would be such as could promptly be settled by application of the one party to amend the decree so as to authorize the use of a specific advertisement, or by the other party on a motion for contempt. Indeed, quite possibly many such details could be satisfactorily settled by conference in chambers without the need for formal motion and ruling.

And further, as against Wm. H. Dobbs, any injunction to which the plaintiff would be entitled, would need to be carefully restricted in its scope to the territory in which the plaintiff had clearly proved the currency of its name in its secondary meaning.

(Matthew Bender & Co., Inc.)

Such then, as I see it, are the mutual rights and liabilities between Wm. H. Dobbs and the plaintiff. If I felt that these rights of Wm. H. Dobbs were transferable by Exhibit R, or otherwise, I should grant an injunction against the defendant transferee along the lines indicated above. But, holding as I have above indicated, that under the particular facts as shown in this case, such rights as Wm. H. Dobbs had were wholly personal to him, and transferable neither to the defendant nor any one else, I hold that an injunction may issue against this defendant, without the limitations to which Wm. H. Dobbs would be entitled, wholly restraining it from all use whatsoever of the name "Dobbs," whether prefixed by initials or given names, or suffixed by explanations, either imprinted on any hats which it manufactures or sells or offers for sale, or on the containers thereof, or in advertising the same or otherwise in connection with its operations in the manufacture, distribution, and sale of hats.

I should perhaps make it plain that my reason for attempting to define the rights of Wm. H. Dobbs, notwithstanding my holding that his rights were not transferable, was to facilitate a final settlement of this troublesome and important litigation by a single appeal — in any case my own efforts prove unavailing to compose the peace between the parties.

The plaintiff is entitled to a decree, with costs, providing for the ascertainment of damages, and an injunction which, in the absence of defendant's consent as to form, may be settled in chambers in New Haven on five days' notice, or otherwise by agreement.

WYATT EARP ENTERPRISES, INC. v. SACKMAN, INC.

United States District Court, Southern District of New York
157 F. Supp. 621 (1958)

EDELSTEIN, DISTRICT JUDGE

. . . .

Plaintiff is a producer of motion pictures for television and is the proprietor of a very successful series entitled "The Life and Legend of Wyatt Earp," nationally and internationally televised over the facilities of the American Broadcasting Company. The defendant has been in the business of manufacturing children's playsuits for many years, and, after the commencement of the "Wyatt Earp" television program by the plaintiff, entered into a license agreement with it purporting to grant the right to defendant to use "the name and likeness of Hugh O'Brian in the characterization of Wyatt Earp," O'Brian being the star of the program, portraying the title character. The agreement was not renewed by the plaintiff upon its expiration, another manufacturer having been licensed in place of defendant. The defendant has, after the expiration of its rights under the agreement, continued to manufacture and market children's playsuits under the name, mark and symbol of "Wyatt Earp," although without using the name and likeness of Hugh O'Brian and without specific reference to "ABC-TV."

(Matthew Bender & Co., Inc.) (Pub. 725)

The plaintiff seeks to enjoin the defendant's use of the name, mark and symbol "Wyatt Earp" on its playsuits on the ground that, by plaintiff's efforts, the name has come to have a secondary meaning indicative of origin, relationship and association with the television program; and that the public is likely to attribute the use of the name "Wyatt Earp" by the defendant to the plaintiff as a source of sponsorship and buy defendant's merchandise in this erroneous belief. The defendant denies the possibility of secondary meaning attaching to the name, arguing that it belonged to a living person out of the nation's history, and hence has become a part of the public domain not subject to commercial monopolization by anyone. Such a contention, I believe, overstates the law. Certainly the defendant, along with the plaintiff and everyone else, has some interest in a name out of history, as they have in words of common speech. "The only protected private interest in words of common speech is after they have come to connote, in addition to their colloquial meaning, provenience from some single source of the goods to which they are applied." *Adolph Kastor & Bros. v. Federal Trade Commission*, (2 Cir.) 138 F.2d 824, 825, 60 U.S.P.Q. 154, 155. The question is, in determining whether there is a protected private interest, whether the name "Wyatt Earp" has come to have such a connotation of provenience. If it has, the plaintiff has a cognizable interest in preventing the likelihood of consumer confusion, and it is such an interest as the law will protect against an opposing interest no greater than that of all persons in the use of the names in history. It is true that where a symbol is not fanciful but merely descriptive, the plaintiff bears a very heavy burden of proving confusion is likely. *See* dissenting opinion of Judge Frank in *Triangle Publications v. Rohrlich*, (2 Cir.) 167 F.2d 969, 974, 976, 77 U.S.P.Q. 196, 200, 201. Or it may be that a nonfanciful, real name is such a part of the national fabric that all have a measurable interest in its use, to the extent that it acquires no secondary meaning extending into a defendant's field so as to cause a likelihood of confusion. *Durable Toy & Novelty Corp. v. J. Chein & Co.*, (2 Cir.) 133 F.2d 853, 56 U.S.P.Q. 339, *cert. denied*, 320 U.S. 211, 57 U.S.P.Q. 568. ". . . [E]ach case presents a unique problem which must be answered by weighing the conflicting interests against each other." *Id.* at 855, 56 U.S.P.Q. at 341. Although "Wyatt Earp" is the name of an historical person, the defendant's interest in it is, I feel, not so strong as was the defendant's interest in the name "Uncle Sam" in the toy case, nor is the possibility of a secondary meaning attaching to "Wyatt Earp" so unlikely. If the plaintiff can show that it is likely to succeed, at trial, in proving that it invested the name of Wyatt Earp with a commercial significance and good will that is attributable to itself and that is likely to be appropriated by the defendant by way of consumer confusion, it will be entitled to the relief it seeks.

It is perhaps not too much to say, even at this preliminary stage of the proceedings, that the name of Wyatt Earp has been battered into the public consciousness by the television program to an extent far beyond any fame or notoriety ever previously attached to the marshall's name. Between September of 1955 and the end of November 1957, 102 motion picture films have been produced under the general title, "The Life and Legend of Wyatt Earp," which is also a service mark owned by the plaintiff and registered in the United States Patent Office. The firms have been televised each week, 52 weeks a year, on the transcontinental release facilities of the American Broadcasting Company. More than $3,000,000 has been spent by the plaintiff in producing the films, and more than $3,500,000 has been received by the television network for its time and facility charges during the two year period commencing in September of 1955 and ending in August of 1957. Such charges continue to be made and received at the rate of more than $2,000,000 per year. By reason of the popularity of the production, enormous publicity has been generated in other media of mass communication. Popularly known as the "Wyatt Earp Program," it has from its inception been among the most popular television entertainments in the nation, viewed weekly on millions of television receivers by additional millions of persons. As an indication of the public acceptance of the program, there has been a great and increasing nationwide demand for articles and products sponsored by the plaintiff and bearing the name, mark and symbol of "Wyatt Earp." It has been asserted without denial or other comment that goods and merchandise marketed under the name of "Wyatt Earp" were unheard of prior to the first telecast of the show. The finding is nearly inescapable that the commercial value now enjoyed by the name is attributable almost entirely to the program. The plaintiff, as a result, has entered into the business of licensing merchandise rights in connection with the program under agreements controlling the nature and quality of the goods licensed so as to maintain high standards and to preserve the integrity of its good will. Under these agreements the royalties to be received for the year 1957 will exceed $100,000. The merchandise so promoted, in no way unique aside from its program identification, obviously sells much more readily than the same merchandise would sell without the program identification, as borne out by the fact that manufacturers pay substantial sums of money for the privilege of sponsorship, by way of licensing agreements. It can be found preliminarily, therefore, that the name and characterization of "Wyatt Earp" as televised by the plaintiff has become identified in the mind of the consumer public with merchandise upon which the name had been imprinted; that this identification and good will has extended to the field of children's playsuits sold and distributed under the name, mark and symbol "Wyatt Earp"; and that defendant is merchandising "Wyatt Earp" playsuits because of a popular demand for merchandise identified with the program and the plaintiff.

Since the expiration of its privileges under the licensing agreement with the plaintiff, the defendant has marketed its play clothes without the names and likeness of the star of the television program and without specific reference to "ABC-TV." It further has made certain modifications in the design of its suits. Samples of suits made by the defendant under its license and made after the expiration of its license, as well as a sample made by the current licensee, together with their boxes were handed up to the court as exhibits. Defendant's present outfit, despite the changes, appears to bear a striking resemblance to the outfit it previously made under license and to the one made by the present licensee; and these costumes, approximating the one worn by the television "Wyatt Earp," indeed seem to be markedly different from other "western" costumes. The defendant continues to mark on its boxes the name "Wyatt Earp" together with the legend "official outfit." Moreover, in its catalogue, the Wyatt Earp outfit is advertised in a context with three "TV personality" western outfits, all of them being characterized as "official," but with the "TV personality" designation omitted from the Wyatt Earp display. The text and layout are presented in such a manner as to convey the impression of an identification of defendant's Wyatt Earp playsuit with the Wyatt Earp television program. Indeed, it is so difficult to understand how any other impression could be conveyed that the finding of an intent to convey an erroneous notion of association with the program is highly probable. Unless the word "official" is passed over as sheer gibberish, the idea of sponsorship is inescapably implied.

The "critical question" in a case of secondary meaning "always is whether the public is moved in any degree to buy the article because of its source and what are the features by which it distinguishes that source." *Charles D. Briddell, Inc. v. Alglobe Trading Corp.,* (2 Cir.) 194 F.2d 416, 419, 92 U.S.P.Q. 100, 102. For under the common law of unfair competition, as well as under the Lanham Act, the likelihood of consumer confusion is the test of secondary meaning. *Id.* at p. 421, 92 U.S.P.Q. at 104. I find that, for the purposes of preliminary injunctive relief, plaintiff has met the burden of proving the likelihood of consumer-confusion. The public is moved to buy merchandise because of an identification with the name "Wyatt Earp" as developed by the plaintiff's television program. The defendant's use of the name created a likelihood that the public would believe, erroneously, that its playsuits were licensed or sponsored by the plaintiff, to the injury of the plaintiff's good will and to the hazard of its reputation. There is a high probability that, upon the trial of the issues, plaintiff will be able to establish that the name, mark and symbol "Wyatt Earp" has acquired a secondary meaning in the minds of the public as identified and associated with the television program and the plaintiff, and extending into the field of children's playsuits.

It is true that the plaintiff and defendant are not direct competitors in the same field of endeavor. The plaintiff does not manufacture children's playsuits. But where secondary meaning and consumer confusion are established, use of a trade name even upon noncompeting goods may be enjoined. *See Triangle Publications v. Rohrlich,* (2 Cir.) 167 F.2d 969, 972, 77 U.S.P.Q. 196, 198. And as held by the Court of Appeals in that case, the same principle applies to the situation of confusion about sponsorship. "In either case, the wrong of the defendant consisted in imposing upon the plaintiff a risk that the defendant's goods would be associated by the public with the plaintiff, and it can make no difference whether that association is based upon attributing defendant's goods to plaintiff or to a sponsorship by the latter when it has been determined that plaintiff had a right to protection of its trade name." *Id.* at p. 973, 77 U.S.P.Q. at 199. *See also Hanson v. Triangle Publications,* (8 Cir.) 163 F.2d 74, 74 U.S.P.Q. 280, *cert. denied,* 332 U.S. 855, 76 U.S.P.Q. 621; *Adolph Kastor & Bros v. Federal Trade Commission, supra; Esquire, Inc. v. Esquire Bar,* 37 F. Supp. 875, 49 U.S.P.Q. 592. Furthermore, in the case at bar, it would seem that something more than mere sponsorship is involved, something that very closely approaches direct competition. The plaintiff does not manufacture children's playsuits, but it licenses another to do so on a royalty basis. Any customers purchasing from the defendant on the strength of the "Wyatt Earp" name are customers diverted from plaintiff's licensee, to its direct pecuniary injury, in addition to any danger to its reputation.

While there is little doubt that the violation of plaintiff's rights by a diversion of purchasers to the defendant could readily be compensated for in a judgment for money damages, it also appears that a denial of preliminary injunctive relief would work irreparable and serious injury to the plaintiff by jeopardizing the entire licensing system it has built at great effort and expense. On a balance of the harms, the plaintiff stands to suffer much greater injury by a denial of injunctive relief than any which can befall defendant by granting such relief. Accordingly, the motion for a preliminary injunction will be granted.

. . . .

IN RE ETABLISSEMENTS DARTY ET FILS

United States Court of Appeals, Federal Circuit
759 F.2d 15 (1985)

NIES, CIRCUIT JUDGE.

This appeal from the decision of the U.S. Patent and Trademark Office (PTO) Trademark Trial and Appeal Board (TTAB or board), reported at 220 U.S.P.Q. 260 (1984), affirming the examiner's refusal to register DARTY as a service mark on the Principal Register. Refusal is based on the ground that DARTY is "primarily merely a surname within the meaning of Section 2(e)(3) of the Lanham Act (15 U.S.C. § 1051 *et seq.*), and, thus, is not registrable on the Principal Register in the absence of evidence that the name has become distinctive of the applicants' goods in commerce, as specified in Section 2(f).

The board correctly recognized that the PTO had the burden of establishing a *prima facie* case that DARTY is "primarily merely a surname.". . .

. . . .

The statute in Section 2(e)(3) (15 U.S.C. § 1052(e)(3)) reflects the common law that exclusive rights in a surname *per se* can not be established without evidence of long and exclusive use which changes its significance to the public from a surname of an individual to a mark for particular goods or services. The common law also recognizes that surnames are shared by more than one individual, each of whom may have an interest in using his surname in business, and by the requirement for evidence of distinctiveness, in effect, delays appropriation of exclusive rights in the name. See 1 J. Gilson, *Trademark Protection and Practice* § 2.08 (1982). The statute, thus, provides a period of time, as under the common law, to accommodate the competing interests of others. An analysis of similar considerations in connection with geographic terms can be found in *In re Nantucket, Inc.,* 677 F.2d 95, 102-04, 213 U.S.P.Q. 889, 895-96 (C.C.P.A. 1982) (Nies, J., concurring).

The question of whether a word sought to be registered is primarily merely a surname within the meaning of the statute can be resolved only on a case by case basis. Even though a mark may have been adopted because it is the surname of one connected with the business, it may not be primarily merely a surname under the statute because it is also a word having ordinary language meaning. The language meaning is likely to be the primary meaning to the public. *See Fisher Radio Corp. v. Bird Electronic Corp.*, 162 U.S.P.Q. 265, 266-67 (T.T.A.B. 1969) (BIRD not primarily merely a surname). On the other hand, where no common word meaning can be shown, a more difficult question must be answered concerning whether the mark presented for registration would be perceived as a surname or as an arbitrary term.

In this case, the subject mark is not only the surname of a principal of the business, but also is used in the company name in a manner which reveals its surname significance, at least to those with a modicum of familiarity with the French language. (Darty et Fils translates as Darty and Son). This, in itself, is highly persuasive that the public would perceive DARTY as a surname. In addition, the examiner made of record evidence that others in a number of cities in this country bear the surname DARTY. Thus, as a surname, DARTY is not so unusual that such significance would not be recognized by a substantial number of persons. Nor can the interests of those having the surname DARTY be discounted as *de minimis.* Under these circumstances, the statutory policy against immediate registration on the Principal Register appropriately should be applied.

Appellant has attempted to convince us that this case is the same as *In re Kahan & Weisz*, 508 F.2d at 832-33, 184 U.S.P.Q. at 421-22, in which DUCHARME for watches was held not to be primarily merely a surname. However, in that case it is apparent that the PTO initially refused registration without any evidence that DUCHARME was a surname. As indicated therein, the PTO sought to buttress its position by resort to the applicant's submissions. Not only was the refusal to register without the examiner having made a *prima facie* case improper, but also, as one might expect, the applicant's evidence was insufficient to establish a case for the PTO.

. . . .

We conclude that in view of the uncontrovertable evidence of surname usage of record, and the unpersuasiveness of appellant's argument that DARTY would be understood as a play on the word "dart," the board's finding that DARTY is primarily merely a surname is not clearly erroneous.

. . . .

Affirmed.

_____

NOTES ON SURNAMES

(1) It is now generally recognized that there is no paramount "right" to use a surname in business where it is likely to be confused with a name that has already acquired source-indicating significance. *See Ford Motor Co. v. Ford d/b/a Ford Records*, 462 F.2d 1405 (C.C.P.A. 1972), *cert. denied*, 409 U.S. 1109 (1973); Mandell, *Personal Name Trademarks — Your Name May Not Be Your Own*, 70

Trademark Rep. 326 (1980); McCarthy, *Trademarks and Unfair Competition*, § 13:2 (3d ed. 1992); 1 Gilson, *Trademark Protection and Practice*, § 2.08 (1993 ed.). When a surname has become strongly connected in the public mind with a certain product (e.g., STETSON hats), and a latecomer bearing the surname attempts to use the name in selling a competing product, the courts will sometimes allow the latecomer use of the name so long as it is accompanied by a prefix, suffix or disclaimer designed to allow the public to distinguish between sources. *See Taylor Wine Co. v. Bully Hill Vineyards*, 569 F.2d 731 (2d Cir. 1978) (Walter J. Taylor permitted to use his signature on his wines or in advertising but only with a disclaimer so as to avoid confusion with TAYLOR wines); *Caesar's World, Inc. v. Caesar's Palace*, 490 F. Supp. 818 (D.N.J. 1980) (New Jersey beauty salon owner enjoined from trademark use of "Palace" and from such use of his first name "Caesar," unless in conjunction with his last name, to avoid confusion with the Las Vegas hotel "CAESAR'S PALACE").

(2) In *Sullivan v. Ed Sullivan Radio & TV, Inc.*, 152 N.Y.S.2d 227 (App. Div. 1956), the strength of the general public's identification of the then popular television variety show host with radio and television convinced the court that the defendant must be enjoined from using his own name, Ed Sullivan, in that form, for his business of selling and repairing radio and television sets. A lack of competition between plaintiff and defendant and the fact that defendant only owned an isolated store in Buffalo, New York did not deter the court from its holding.

> . . . The state of facts may so change as to encompass a situation where there may be a series or a chain of similar stores throughout the country, in which case indeed, unless appellant had taken this present, prompt, action, he might at a later date encounter great difficulty in obtaining an injunction because of his own laches.

The court further noted the possibility that defendant might sell his store to a corporation in more direct competition with the television host. Plaintiff's use of "Sullivan," "E.J. Sullivan," or "Edward J. Sullivan," however, specifically was not enjoined.

(3) Section 2(e) of the Lanham Act (15 U.S.C. § 1502(e)) precludes registration of a trademark which "is primarily merely a surname" unless it "has become distinctive of the applicant's goods in commerce." *See In re Darty, supra; Societe Civile Des Domaines Dourthe Freres v. S.A. Consortium Vinicole De Bordeaux Et De La Garonde*, 6 U.S.P.Q.2d 1205 (TTAB 1988) (DOURTHE for wine refused registration). *Cf. In re Hutchinson Technology*, 825 F.2d 552 (Fed. Cir. 1988) (HUTCHINSON TECHNOLOGY for computer components in its entirety held registrable, even though part of the mark was primarily merely a surname). Why should a surname be treated any differently from an arbitrary mark which is registrable upon adoption and use? What is primarily merely a surname? Should a common surname be treated differently from an uncommon one? *See* Smith, *Primarily Merely*, 63 Trademark Rep. 24 (1973). Note that § 2(a) of the Lanham Act prohibits registration of a mark "which may disparage or falsely suggest a connection with persons living or dead" and § 2(c) prohibits registration of a mark "identifying a particular living individual except by his written consent." *See*

Gordon, *Right of Property in Name, Likeness, Personality and History*, 55 Nw. U. L. Rev. 553 (1960).

(4) The courts ordinarily enjoin any surname use by the junior user where such use is not in good faith. *Société Vinicole de Champagne v. Mumm*, 143 F.2d 240 (2d Cir. 1944) (change of name); *R. W. Rogers Co. v. William Rogers Mfg. Co.*, 70 F. 1017 (2d Cir. 1895) (corporate use of a shareholder's name). Absent intent, many courts have simply required the addition of a prefix, suffix, initials or first name, or the use of color, type style, or further clarifying language. *See* the discussion on disclaimers in the Remedies section of Chapter 9, *infra*, and *Unfair Competition: Injunctive Relief and the Personal Name Exemption*, 51 Minn. L. Rev. 782 (1967). Why should the courts seek such compromise solutions respecting surnames? Do such additions really avoid the basic problem of consumer deception? How can a court insure that the consumer will know "which Dobbs is 'his' Dobbs?" *See John B. Stetson Co. v. Stephen L. Stetson Co.*, 128 F.2d 981 (2d Cir. 1942), where the defendant had been ordered to place notices on his hat labels that he was NEVER CONNECTED IN ANY WAY with the famous manufacturer of Stetson hats. Defendant's response over time was progressively to shrink the disclaimer on the labels until its impact on purchasers was negligible. The court responded to defendant's claim of literal compliance by stating that it had plainly violated the spirit of the injunction and enjoined all use of STETSON except in the notice of differentiation. What other devices or sanctions might be utilized to balance the interest of the parties and the public? *See* Jacoby & Raskopf, *Disclaimers in Trademark Infringement Litigation: More Trouble Than They're Worth?*, 76 Trademark Rep. 35 (1986); Radin, *Disclaimers as Remedies for Trademark Infringement: Inadequacies and Alternatives*, 76 Trademark Rep. 59 (1986).

(5) When a business enterprise makes authorized trademark use of a person's surname, should it be able to prevent subsequent trademark use of the name by that person in connection with a separate but similar enterprise? In *Holiday Inns, Inc. v. Trump*, 617 F. Supp. 1443 (D.N.J. 1985), defendant had contracted for plaintiff to use defendant's surname "Trump" in connection with plaintiff's casino hotels. Defendant then began using his surname in connection with his own casino hotel. Despite a finding of "substantial evidence in the record of actual confusion" (617 F. Supp. at 1474), the court denied plaintiff relief, citing plaintiff's failure to contractually reserve exclusive rights, defendant's long-standing practice of using his name in connection with his business projects, the public's association of his name with high quality services, and the public's consequent interest in defendant's continued use of that name. In *John Curry Skating Co. v. John Curry Skating Co.*, 626 F. Supp. 611 (D.D.C. 1985), renowned ice skater John Curry and his new marketing corporation as defendants obtained summary judgment against his former marketing corporation when the plaintiff failed to demonstrate that the public associated the mark with plaintiff rather than defendants. *Compare Levitt Corp. v. Levitt*, 593 F.2d 463 (2d Cir. 1979), where defendant was enjoined after having sold his name and accompanying good will with his business.

(6) Surnames that are primarily historical are said to be inherently distinctive arbitrary marks not requiring proof of secondary meaning, thus making them

different from the general category of surnames. What is the rationale for this distinction? Why should the use of RAMESES or ROBIN HOOD have trademark significance upon adoption and use, while use of O'REILLY is not protectable until secondary meaning is shown? *See Lucien Piccard Watch Corp. v. Since 1868 Crescent Corp.*, 314 F. Supp. 329, 331 (S.D.N.Y. 1970) (DA VINCI); McCarthy, *Trademarks and Unfair Competition*, § 13:10 (3d ed. 1992).

§ 2.07 Colors

INTRODUCTION

Despite the considerable pragmatic role that color plays in trade identity matters, the protection to be accorded it often poses judicial dilemmas. It may be perfectly clear and demonstrable that color similarities result in confusion and likelihood of confusion, but it cannot be ignored that the spectrum is exceedingly limited. The following cases disclose some of the difficulties the law has encountered in this area. Consider the consumer products well known to you because of color or combinations of color of packaging or labeling (e.g., Campbell's Soup). How much protection should be given such identifying features?

———————

CAMPBELL SOUP CO. v. ARMOUR & CO.

United States Court of Appeals, Third Circuit
175 F.2d 795 (1949)

GOODRICH, CIRCUIT JUDGE.

Campbell Soup Company and Carnation Company joined as plaintiffs against Armour and Company. They sought an injunction to stop the use by Armour of a red and white label used on some of its food products; likewise, an accounting. The District Court denied relief and the plaintiffs appeal.

. . . .

. . . We find no difference between state and federal decisions and we are not, therefore, driven to the microscopic examination of state decisions for the last dictum which will assist us to find and apply state law.

It is worth the space involved to call attention to just what it is the plaintiffs claim. Their suit here is based solely upon their claimed exclusive right to the use of red and white in packaging their food products. While their registration describes the red over white as a rectangular design, when the colors appear on their packages they appear in the form of an endless band which runs around the entire container. The Campbell red is not the same as the Carnation red. Indeed, the Carnation red is not the same on all of its products, according to the sample labels offered in the plaintiffs' exhibits. The red used by Armour is a specially blended color. The usual

Armour label is white over red instead of red over white, as the plaintiffs use the colors, but in some cases Armour uses the red and white bands vertically.

What the plaintiffs are really asking for, then, is a right to the exclusive use of labels which are half red and half white for food products. If they may thus monopolize red in all of its shades the next manufacturer may monopolize orange in all its shades and the next yellow in the same way. Obviously, the list of colors will soon run out.

That a man cannot acquire a trade-mark by color alone has been stated a good many times in decisions and textbooks. *Can't use color as trademark.*

The rule is well stated in *James Heddon's Sons v. Millsite Steel & Wire Works,* 6 Cir., 1942, 128 F.2d 6, 9:

> Color, except in connection with some definite, arbitrary symbol or in association with some characteristics which serve to distinguish the article as made or sold by a particular person is not subject to trade-mark monopoly.

In *Diamond Match Co. v. Saginaw Match Co.,* 6 Cir., 1906, 142 F. 727, 729, the following language appears which is particularly appropriate here:

> Sometimes a color, taken in connection with other characteristics, may serve to distinguish one's goods, and thus be protected by the courts . . .; but, as a rule, a color cannot be monopolized to distinguish a product. . . .

> The primary colors, even adding black and white, are but few. If two of these colors can be appropriated for one brand of tipped matches, it will not take long to appropriate the rest.

And in an earlier suit by Carnation's predecessor, the Washington Supreme Court said, *Pacific Coast Condensed Milk Co. v. Frye & Co.,* 1915, 85 Wash. 133, 147 P. 865, 869:

> The primary colors are few, and as the evidence shows those suitable for light products, such as milk, are even more limited. To allow them to be appropriated as distinguishing marks would foster monopoly by foreclosing the use by others of any tasty dress.

Plaintiffs cite to us a number of cases, however, in which various color combinations as trade-marks have been upheld. Here, too, the law is well settled. Color is a perfectly satisfactory element of a trade-mark if it is used in combination with a design in the form, for example, of a picture or a geometrical figure. The *Barbasol* [*v. Jacobs,* 160 F.2d 336 (7th Cir. 1947)] case is typical. Here was a package using several colors but in a distinct and arbitrary design. The mere division of a label into two background colors, as in this case, is not, however, distinct or arbitrary, and the District Court so found. *Color combined w/ a design is Ok.*

When we say that plaintiffs cannot have exclusive right to a trademark of a red and white label, we are by no means denying their right to acquire a trademark when the color is combined with other things in a distinctive design. As a matter of fact, the distinctiveness of plaintiffs' packages does not depend upon color alone, although each has been granted registration of a trade-mark described in terms of color. Each has its name in one of the color bands in a uniform and specified type of script. Each has a very distinctive design on its label. Carnation has a small bouquet of carnation flowers. Campbell has a medallion of individual design. Armour, too, does not depend upon color alone. It uses different colors with different products and each has the Armour name in an individual type of script accompanied by the star which it says has been the mark of its good over many years. In denying the plaintiffs the exclusive use of color alone we are not passing upon the question whether they have acquired trade-marks entitled to protection in the sum total of the combinations which make up their respective labels for their goods. Finally, there was no unfair competition. Certainly there was not the slightest evidence that Armour passed off its goods as those of the plaintiffs. The Trial Judge found as a matter of fact that "no intelligent purchaser using reasonable care would be confused as between the goods of either plaintiff." There was considerable evidence on this point of confusion and the record is full of reports of a series of tests conducted in different retail stores. We are satisfied with the fact conclusion of the Trial Judge on this point.

A number of other points have been raised in the presentation of this appeal. We do not deem it necessary to go into them and our failure to do so is not an indication that we disagree with the District Court upon them. We think that what is said above is sufficient to show that the decision below was correct.

The judgment of the District Court will be affirmed.

AMERICAN CHICLE CO. v. TOPPS CHEWING GUM, INC.

United States Court of Appeals, Second Circuit
208 F.2d 560 (1953)

L. HAND, CIRCUIT JUDGE.

The defendant appeals from a final judgment, permanently enjoining it from infringing the plaintiff's trade-mark, used in the sale of small nuggets of candy covered chewing gum of various flavors; and dismissing the defendant's counter-claim, for the cancellation of the mark. The registration described the mark as follows: "The trademark consists of an O shaped figure colored red having a parallelogram of light shade, usually white, extending horizontally from the central right portion of such figure, together with parallel bands, over and under such figure and parallelogram, of a dark color contrasting with that of the parallelogram, as shown in the drawing. The lining on the O shaped figure denotes the red color, and the lining on the bands indicates shading only. No claim is made to the representation of a carton apart from the other features of the mark shown on the drawing. . . ."

Since 1939, the plaintiff has used the trade-mark in suit on cardboard boxes (three and five eighths inches by one and three quarters), holding ten or twelve nuggets, the nuggets in each box being of a single flavor. There are a number of different flavors, each flavor being in a box of a different color. One box is for peppermint nuggets, and on it the color of the "parallel bands over and under" the O "figure and parallelogram" is yellow. The "O shaped figure colored red" appears at the left on all the boxes, its opening being cut through the cardboard so as to show some of the nuggets within. The "parallelogram of light shade" — in practice always white — bears the word "Chiclets," written in large black letters, and is the most arresting feature of the "make-up" as a whole. In later boxes the "parallelogram of light shade" has been extended far enough to the left to break the circle of the "O shaped figure," and change it into a sort of "C." Up to 1949 the defendant had been selling similar chewing gum nuggets of peppermint flavor in packages, each containing about two nuggets, several packages being inclosed in, and sold from, a containing canister. The "make-up" of these packages was altogether unlike the plaintiff's; but in 1949 it began to market its peppermint nuggets by the dozen in boxes (four inches by two), that have at their left end a broken "O," the upper half of which is colored green, the lower half red. From the broken "O" a white "parallelogram" extends to the right end of the box, flanked above and below by "parallel bands" of yellow, giving the box a predominant tone of the same shade of that color as the plaintiff's. Upon the white "parallelogram" appears in large letters the word, "Topps," in place of "Chiclets" on the plaintiff's boxes; but there is no other substantial difference between the "make-up" of the box except for the defendant's break in the "O" and its upper green half.

. . . .

Upon this dispute we accept the finding that "the similarity in appearance . . . is likely to cause confusion . . . of an appreciable number of ordinarily prudent purchasers," in spite of the word "Topps" replacing "Chiclets." The situation is therefore one where, although "the majority of people" do not suppose that the word "Chiclets" is generic, there is a "tendency" to read it so; and it follows that to these buyers, who are numerous enough to become "a problem for many years to our company," the word has ceased to denote any definite "source of origin." How far this may have affected the validity of the trade-mark, "Chiclets" (for that too is registered), is not important here. What is important is that to those buyers, who think "Chiclets" to be a descriptive term, the "make-up" that accompanies it may well be what assures them that they were getting the "Chiclets" that they have become used to; and the word, "Topps," would not in that event tell them of any new "source of origin." It is reasonable to believe that the fabulous sum — $11,000,000 — that has been spent in "publicizing" the plaintiff's nuggets as "Chiclets" has fixed the word in the minds of many buyers as meaning no more than a candy coated gum nugget; and to some degree destroyed it as a trade-mark. That is a peril to which all such advertising is subject; its very success may prove its failure.

We may properly assume, therefore, that, although the defendant's "make-up" is not "likely to cause confusion" among attentive buyers, there is a substantial minority, "likely" to be misled. If we were to read the statute literally, such a minority would be enough, for the text does not limit infringement by the number of those who may be misled. However, we do not read this statute as *tabula rasa*;

we construe it in the background of the law as it stood in 1946; and that law defined the issue of infringement less literally. On all but the most extreme occasions it involved a balance of two conflicting interests: that of the "owner" of the mark to prevent the diversion of prospective customers as opposed to that of the putative infringer to be free to compete for them. In the case at bar this becomes a balance between the plaintiff's prospective loss of a not insignificant number of customers — i.e., the more careless ones — and the defendant's interest in continuing the use of a "make-up" that in itself has no conceivable value. For the defendant has not suggested even the most diaphanous reason for selecting for its peppermint box out of all possible permutations of color and design, just the plaintiff's — or at least almost the plaintiff's — combination, except for the substitution of "Topps" for "Chiclets." It would be absurd to see in this anything but a hope to bring to its own net just those buyers who are on the fringe of the plaintiff's possible customers. In the language of Judge Byer, the imitation "revealed an apparent purpose to come as close to the plaintiff's package as the law might close its eyes to, so long as Topps is used instead of Chiclets." What we said in *Miles Shoes, Inc. v. R.H. Macy & Co.*, 2 Cir., 199 F.2d 602, 603, applies to the letter, *mutatis mutandis*: "Why it should have chosen a mark that had long been employed by Macy and had become known to the trade instead of adopting some other means to identify its goods is hard to see unless there was a deliberate purpose to obtain some advantage from the trade which Macy had built up." Indeed, it is generally true that, as soon as we see that a second comer in the market has, for no reason that he can assign, plagiarized the "make-up" of an earlier comer, we need no more; for he at any rate thinks that any differentia he adds will not, or at least may not, prevent the diversion and we are content to accept his forecast that he is "likely" to succeed. Then we feel bound to compel him to exercise his ingenuity in quarters further afield.

The defendant relies upon *Life Savers Corp. v. Curtiss Candy Co.*, 7 Cir., 182 F.2d 4; and it is true that in that case there was evidence that, in spite of the defendant's name, "Curtiss," plainly appearing on its wrapper, there were customers, who bought the defendant's goods, thinking them to be the plaintiff's; moreover, the court, 182 F.2d at page 8, cited a number of decisions to the effect that a new competitor "is not obligated to protect the negligent and inattentive purchaser from confusion resulting from indifference." It cannot be denied that courts have at times reasoned as though a second comer were free to divert a first comer's customers, if he confined himself to those who were unduly careless. If the issue were whether such buyers could complain that they did not get what they wanted, it might be an answer in the second comer's mouth that they had themselves to thank for their failure to look more closely at the "make-up"; though even that is a doubtful answer. Be that as it may, the issue becomes altogether different when it is between a first, and a second comer, for the first comer's careless customers are as valuable to him as any others; and their carelessness can hardly be charged to him. Why they should be deemed more legitimate game for a poacher than his careful buyers, it is hard to see, unless it be on the ground that he should have made his mark so conspicuous that it would serve to hold even the most heedless. Surely that is an adequate defence. We are not committed to the doctrine in this circuit, and we know of no decision of the Supreme Court that precludes our following our own judgment. We do indeed distinguish the question how far a second comer is to be charged *ab initio* with the duty of anticipating that there will be careless buyers whom his "make-up" may divert. That is one thing; we are speaking of a patent effort to catch such buyers, even though the effort be limited to them. The following excerpts from the *Restatement of Torts* seem to us, at least by implication, to bear us out. Section 729, Comment f: "But if he" (the second comer) "adopts his designation with the intent of deriving benefit from the trade-mark or trade name his intent may be sufficient to justify the inference that there is confusing similarity . . . his judgment manifested prior to the controversy is highly persuasive. His denial that his conduct was likely to achieve the result intended by him will ordinarily carry little weight." Again, § 729, Comment g: "The buying habits of the purchasers of the particular goods in question are also significant. If the goods are bought by purchasers who exercise considerable attention and inspect fairly closely, the likelihood of confusion is smaller than when the goods are bought by purchasers who make little or no inspection." We are by no means sure that *Life Savers Corp. v. Curtiss Candy Co.*, *supra*, 182 F.2d 4, is to the contrary; but, if it must be so construed, with great deference we must leave the last word to the Supreme Court.

Judgment affirmed.

IN RE OWENS-CORNING FIBERGLAS CORP.

United States Court of Appeals, Federal Circuit
774 F.2d 116 (1985)

NEWMAN, CIRCUIT JUDGE.

Owens-Corning Fiberglas Corporation (OCF) appeals from the decision of the United States Patent and Trademark Office's Trademark Trial and Appeal Board (the Board) affirming the examining attorney's denial of registration of the color "pink" as a trademark for fibrous glass residential insulation. We reverse.

I.

Alleging use in commerce since 1956, OCF applied on January 25, 1980, application Serial No. 247,707, for registration on the Principal Register of the color "pink" as uniformly applied to OCF's fibrous glass residential insulation. The Board held that the overall color of goods is capable of functioning as a trademark, but affirmed the examiner's denial of registration on the ground that OCF had not adequately demonstrated that the color "pink" is distinctive of OCF's goods. *In re Owens Corning Fiberglas Corp.*, 221 U.S.P.Q. 1195 (T.T.A.B. 1984).

The Board's conclusion that there is no inherent bar to trademark registration of the color of goods, when the color is an overall color rather than in the form of a design, is in harmony with modern trademark theory and jurisprudence. Prior to passage of the Trademark Act of 1946, 15 U.S.C. § 1051 *et seq.* (the Lanham Act), color alone could not be registered as a trademark. In 1906 the Supreme Court wrote:

Whether mere color can constitute a valid trade-mark may admit of doubt. Doubtless it may, if it be impressed in a particular design, as a circle, square, triangle, a cross, or a star. But the authorities do not go farther than this.

A. Leschen & Sons Rope Co. v. Broderick & Bascom Rope Co., 201 U.S. 166, 171 (1906). The Patent Office and the courts followed this view. For example, applications were rejected to register the color violet for gasoline, *In re General Petroleum Corp. of California*, 49 F.2d 966, 9 U.S.P.Q. 511 (C.C.P.A. 1931); and a blue-and-aluminum color for oil well reamers, *In re Security Engineering Co., Inc.*, 113 F.2d 494, 46 U.S.P.Q. 219 (C.C.P.A. 1940).

. . . .

Under the Lanham Act trademark registration became available to many types of previously excluded indicia. Change was gradual and evolutionary, as the Patent and Trademark Office and the courts were presented with new concepts. Registration has been granted, for example, for containers, product configurations; and packaging, even if subject to design patent protection; for tabs having a particular location on a garment; slogans; sounds; ornamental labels; and goods which take the form of the mark itself.

The jurisprudence under the Lanham Act developed in accordance with the statutory principle that if a mark is capable of being or becoming distinctive of applicant's goods in commerce, then it is capable of serving as a trademark.

Color marks, as other indicia, were no longer barred from registration. As for all marks, compliance with the legal requirements for registration depends on the particular mark and its circumstances of use. In determining registrability of color marks, courts have considered factors such as the nature of the goods, how the color is used, the number of colors or color combinations available, the number of competitors, and customary marketing practices. In the case of *Campbell Soup Co. v. Armour & Co.*, 175 F.2d 795, 798, 81 U.S.P.Q. 430, 432 (3d Cir.), *cert. denied*, 338 U.S. 847, 83 U.S.P.Q. 543 (1949), the court refused to protect the red and white colors of Campbell's labels on the ground that if Campbell were to "monopolize red in all of its shades" competition would be affected in an industry where colored labels were customary.

The court in *Campbell Soup* referred to the color depletion theory: that there are a limited number of colors in the palette, and that it is not wise policy to foster further limitation by permitting trademark registrants to deplete the reservoir. *See, e.g., Diamond Match Co. v. Saginaw Match Co.*, 142 F. 727 (6th Cir.), *cert. denied*, 203 U.S. 589 (1906); *International Braid Co. v. Thomas French & Sons, Ltd.*, 150 F.2d 142, 66 U.S.P.Q. 109 (C.C.P.A. 1945). This theory is not faulted for appropriate application, but following passage of the Lanham Act courts have declined to perpetuate its *per se* prohibition which is in conflict with the liberating purposes of the Act.

. . . .

As with utilitarian features in general, when the color applied to goods serves a primarily utilitarian purpose it is not subject to protection as a trademark. *See, e.g., In re Pollak Steel Co.*, 314 F.2d 566, 136 U.S.P.Q. 651 (C.C.P.A. 1963) (registration of reflective fence post coating refused despite *de facto* secondary meaning), and *Sylvania Electric Products, Inc. v. Dura Electric Lamp Co.*, 247 F.2d 730, 114 U.S.P.Q. 434 (3d Cir. 1957) (blue dot on flashbulb not a valid trademark because functional, whether or not a *de facto* secondary meaning had been acquired). In *William R. Warner & Co. v. Eli Lilly & Co.*, 265 U.S. 526 (1924), the Supreme Court refused to authorize exclusive rights in the brown color of a quinine preparation which was due to the presence of chocolate as a masking agent and suspension medium. The Court carefully distinguished that situation from one where the ingredient was "non-essential," "a mere matter of dress," or one where it "merely serve[s] the incidental use of identifying the respondent's preparation." 265 U.S. at 531. In *Deere & Co. v. Farmhand, Inc.*, 560 F. Supp. 85, 217 U.S.P.Q. 252, 261, 262 (S.D. Iowa 1982), *aff'd*, 721 F.2d 253 (8th Cir. 1983), the court refused to enforce the color "John Deere green" as a common law trademark for front end loaders on the bases that the color green was "aesthetically functional" in that purchasers wanted their farm equipment to match, and that secondary meaning had not been established. Such conditions limit an applicant's right to register a color for its goods, in order to prevent the appropriation of functional product features from the public domain. We thus consider whether the color "pink" may be so characterized.

The Supreme Court has stated "a product feature is functional if it is essential to the use or purpose of the article or if it affects the cost or quality of the article." *Inwood Laboratories, Inc. v. Ives Laboratories, Inc.*, 456 U.S. 844, 850 n. 10, 214 U.S.P.Q. 1, 4 n.10 (1983), *citing Sears, Roebuck & Co. v. Stiffel Co.*, 376 U.S. 225, 238, 140 U.S.P.Q. 524, 530–31 (1964). In *In re Morton-Norwich Products, Inc.*, 671 F.2d 1332, 1340–41, 213 U.S.P.Q. 9, 15–16 (C.C.P.A. 1982), the court looked at the following factors to determine functionality: (1) whether a particular design yields a utilitarian advantage, (2) whether alternative designs are available in order to avoid hindering competition, and (3) whether the design achieves economies in manufacture or use.

No argument has been raised that the color "pink" for OCF's fibrous glass residential insulation violates any of these factors, or that alternative, equally arbitrary designs are not available to other producers of fibrous glass insulation. To the contrary, when the arbitrary color arrangement distinguishes the goods from other sources of the same product, as in *In re AFA Corp.*, 196 U.S.P.Q. 772 (T.T.A.B. 1977), or where a variety of color designs has been utilized by other producers, courts have viewed this as evidence that such design features are primarily non-functional in nature. *See In re Tec Torch Co., Inc.*, 143 U.S.P.Q. 124 (T.T.A.B. 1964) (colors of cables for welding torch serve as trademark); *Ex parte Ohio Knife Co.*, 117 U.S.P.Q. 449 (Comm'r Pat. 1958) (color markings on knife handles may serve as indications of origin).

. . . .

As the Board observed, there is no overriding public policy which requires that the color "pink" applied to residential fibrous glass insulation be excluded from the statutory definition of a trademark. It appears from the record that OCF is the only manufacturer that colors this insulation, and that there are only a small number of producers. Applying these considerations the Board found:

Thus, in a case where there is no competitive need (whether characterized as "aesthetic" or otherwise) for colors to remain available to all competitors, the color depletion argument is an unreasonable restriction on the acquisition of trademark rights. We are confronted with such a case. The record indicates that fibrous glass insulation ordinarily has a light yellow-white coloring. Moreover, there is no evidence in this record of widespread industry practice of dyeing fibrous glass insulation a color different from that which it has as a result of the manufacturing process, nor is there anything in the record suggesting a need to do so.

In re Owens-Corning Fiberglas Corp., 221 U.S.P.Q. at 1198.

We agree with the Board that the color "pink" has no utilitarian purpose, does not deprive competitors of any reasonable right or competitive need, and is not barred from registration on the basis of functionality.

We agree with the Board that "[d]eciding likelihood of confusion among color shades. . .is no more difficult or subtle than deciding likelihood of confusion where word marks are involved." 221 U.S.P.Q. at 1198. The Board has engaged in such "shade confusion" analysis in the past without apparent difficulty. *See, e.g., Wire Rope Corp. of America, Inc. v. Secalt S.A.*, 196 U.S.P.Q. 312 (T.T.A.B. 1977) (red and yellow strand wire versus red strand wire); *Youngstown Sheet and Tube Co. v. Armco Steel Corp.*, 170 U.S.P.Q. 162 (T.T.A.B. 1971) (Board "can make its own comparison" of grey and orange banded fence post versus orange banded pipe); *In re Hodes-Lange Corp.*, 167 U.S.P.Q. 255 (T.T.A.B. 1970) (registration of yellow banded ampul allowed despite prior registration of bronzy gold banded ampul; it is "of no consequence" that the PTO color designating lines are the same for yellow and gold).

We conclude that OCF's use of the color "pink" performs no non-trademark function, and is consistent with the commercial and public purposes of trademarks. A pink color mark registered for fibrous glass insulation does not confer a "monopoly" or act as a barrier to entry in the market. It has no relationship to production of fibrous glass insulation. It serves the classical trademark function of indicating the origin of the goods, and thereby protects the public.

. . . .

II.

The Board, having established the potential trademark character of the color "pink" for fibrous glass residential insulation, nonetheless refused registration on the ground that OCF had not met its burden of proving "that pink functions as a trademark for that insulation." *In re Owens-Corning Fiberglas Corp.*, 221 U.S.P.Q. at 1199.

OCF argues that the color "pink" has become distinctive of its insulation by virtue of exclusive and continuous use since 1956, and has acquired a secondary meaning in the marketplace. OCF had taken the position before the examiner and the Board that its mark was registrable under section 2(f) of the Lanham Act (15 U.S.C.

§ 1052(f)), and had submitted extensive evidence in support of acquired distinctiveness.

. . . .

The Board stated that color is "really nothing other than a type of product ornamentation." *In re Owens-Corning Fiberglas Corp.*, 221 U.S.P.Q. at 1198. We agree that color is usually perceived as ornamentation. While ornamentation is not incompatible with trademark function, "unless the design is of such nature that its distinctiveness is obvious, convincing evidence must be forthcoming to prove that in fact the purchasing public does recognize the design as a trademark which identifies the source of the goods." *In re David Crystal, Inc.*, 296 F.2d 771, 773, 132 U.S.P.Q. 1, 2 (C.C.P.A. 1961) (registration denied for red and blue bands on white socks).

must identify mark w/ product

. . . .

An evidentiary showing of secondary meaning, adequate to show that a mark has acquired distinctiveness indicating the origin of the goods, includes evidence of the trademark owner's method of using the mark, supplemented by evidence of the effectiveness of such use to cause the purchasing public to identify the mark with the source of the product. The statute is silent as to the weight of evidence required for a showing under section 2(f) "except for the suggestion that substantially exclusive use for a period of five years immediately preceding filing of an application may be considered prima facie evidence." *Hehr*, 279 F.2d at 528, 126 U.S.P.Q. at 382–83.

. . . .

The Board found OCF's totality of evidence insufficient because it "does not indicate to what extent that advertising has emphasized 'pink' as a mark" and because it does not provide any "indication of the extent to which the sample advertising materials of record (which emphasize the 'pink' mark) have been used." *In re Owens-Corning Fiberglas Corp.*, 221 U.S.P.Q. at 1199. We have reviewed the showing in light of the Board's criticisms.

Board! OCF didn't emphasize pink as a mark

. . . .

OCF submitted to the Examiner and to the Board its network television advertising schedule for the period August 17, 1980 through March 30, 1981. This schedule shows that OCF purchased nearly two hundred separate blocks of network time during broadcasts of major sporting events such as the Super Bowl, the Rose Bowl, the U.S. Tennis Open, and the World Series; prime time network series including "Sixty Minutes," "M*A*S*H," and "Magnum, P.I."; and network showing of theatrical movies; all to advertise its "pink" insulation. The breadth of this exposure was not challenged by the Board, unlike the submissions in *In re Soccer Sport Supply Co.*, 507 F.2d at 1403, 184 U.S.P.Q. at 348, where "the evidence fail[ed] to disclose information from which the number of people exposed to the design could be estimated".

Cf: baloney! they do too assoc. it.

The record contains detailed storyboards for two different commercials aired during this time period featuring the "Pink Panther," a pink cartoon character promoting the use of "pink" Owens-Corning Fiberglas insulation. The narration for these commercials discusses how homeowners can cut the high cost of fuel if they would only "[a]dd another layer of pink" in their attics. The scenes emphasize the distinctive "pink " color of OCF's product and reinforce the image with the slogan "Put your house in the pink."

Narration from another television commercial of record told consumers that "[b]lankets of pink Fiberglas insulation around your house could cut your air conditioning bills year after year." The photographic stills for this commercial show an Eskimo in Death Valley staying cool in an igloo encased in a "pink" blanket of OCF's insulation.

OCF's advertising was discussed in an article of record entitled "Mfr. Promotions Boost Insulation Traffic" in the January 5, 1981 issue of *National Home Center News*. The article states that "Owens-Corning's Pink Panther television campaign made the biggest splash" of any manufacturer promotion that year, and describes a nationwide "February Pink Sale" event planned by OCF to include "more network TV Pink Panther commercials, point-of-sale materials and newspaper advertising with dealer listings." It also notes that "O-C has increased its consumer ad budget by several million dollars over last year." The article states that "Forest City buyer, John Ogden reported the powerful impact of the O-C ad campaign at store level. He said some shoppers will no longer buy fiberglass insulation unless it is pink."

Further evidence of promotion of "pink" was submitted in the form of a transcript of a radio commercial. The text included:

> If you'd like to keep your house warmer in winter, cooler in summer . . . you'll love that "pink." Because now you can wrap your home in the comfort of pink Owens-Corning Fiberglas insulation . . . And, right now, in stores where you buy pink Owens-Corning Fiberglas insulation, you can take advantage of our best ever sales event. . . . You'll never have a better opportunity to "think pink" . . . buy "pink" . . . install "pink" in time for the severe weather ahead. So, look for the special Pink Panther displays — with complete details — see how easy it is to "put your house in the pink" at [your local dealer].

The record states that OCF advertised in popular consumer magazines including House & Garden, Better Homes and Gardens, Mechanix Illustrated, Popular Mechanics, Popular Science, Changing Times, Home Energy Digest, and House Beautiful; these ads also featured the Pink Panther character. Applicant's submissions show the use of slogans in its advertising, *e.g.*, "Pink of Perfection"; "The Pink Cooler"; "Big Pink"; "Love that Pink"; "Pink Power"; "America's Favorite Pink Product"; "Tickled Pink"; "Put your House in the Pink"; "Up with Pink"; "Prime Time Pink"; "Think Pink"; "Think More Pink"; "Beat the Cold with Pink"; "All that Pink"; and "Plant Some Pink Insulation in your Attic".

OCF's early advertising efforts introduced the "pink" product to its dealers with the explanation that it was "colored pink so your customers will recognize it as the latest and the best!" OCF also submitted evidence of point-of-sale advertising materials that it has supplied to its dealers through the years, many of which were coordinated with OCF's television campaigns. The Board objected that this evidence did not show the extent to which these advertising materials had actually been used by dealers. We conclude that this objection does not outweigh the total evidence of broad distribution and sales efforts in this case.

* They did prove association of pink

. . . .

In addition, the record contains consumer survey evidence. This survey was conducted to enable OCF to evaluate an advertising program, but its data are pertinent to the issue. In June 1980 male homeowners were asked the question "To the best of your knowledge, what manufacturer makes pink insulation?". Forty-one percent responded with applicant's name and 14% responded with the name of some other insulation manufacturer. A similar survey in January 1981, after the first Pink Panther television commercial blitz, showed that applicant's recognition rate had increased to 50%.

Plus Consumer survey

The Board held that this evidence was not convincing because it did not "establish that those respondents associate pink insulation with a single source." *In re Owens-Corning Fiberglas Corp.*, 221 U.S.P.Q. at 1198. The Solicitor further criticized the survey on the basis that the way the question was presented inhibited plural responses from persons who might have believed that more than one manufacturer makes "pink" insulation. We do not agree that such criticism requires outright rejection of survey data showing that 50% of the respondents named OCF, the only manufacturer to color its insulation pink. Whether or not this survey alone is conclusive, the results show a syndetic relationship between the color "pink" and Owens-Corning Fiberglas in the minds of a significant part of the purchasing public.

By their nature color marks carry a difficult burden in demonstrating distinctiveness and trademark character. Each case must be considered on its merits. OCF's evidence shows advertising expenditures exceeding $42,000,000; in *Hehr* [279 F.2d 526 (C.C.P.A. 1960)], the advertising expenditures that were deemed adequate to show secondary meaning were about $112,000. Consumer recognition in 1981 as to the source of "pink" insulation was 50%, a percentage considerably greater than that held sufficient in many cases. See, e.g., *Zatarains, Inc. v. Oak Grove Smokehouse, Inc.*, 698 F.2d 786, 217 U.S.P.Q. 988 (5th Cir. 1983), where 23–28% correct responses were held sufficient to establish secondary meaning. We conclude that the Board placed an inappropriately heavy evidentiary burden on OCF. As stated in *In re Hollywood Brands, Inc.*, 214 F.2d 139, 141, 102 U.S.P.Q. 294, 296 (C.C.P.A. 1954), there is nothing in the statute "which expressly or impliedly imposes an unreasonable burden of proof upon an applicant for registration thereunder, nor is it within our province to read such rigid provisions into it."

On the totality of the evidence, the Board's finding that the color "pink" does not function as a trademark for OCF's fibrous glass residential insulation is clearly erroneous.

The requirements of the statute having been met, OCF is entitled to register its mark under 15 U.S.C. § 1052(f).

Reversed.

NOTES ON COLORS

Old:
color only when design
part of

(1) The general rule used to be that color was accorded trademark protection only when it was employed as an element of a distinctive design. *A. Leschen & Sons Rope Co. v. Broderick & Bascom Rope Co.*, 201 U.S. 166 (1906); 1 Gilson, *Trademark Protection and Practice* § 2.11 (1993 ed.); McCarthy, *Trademarks and Unfair Competition* § 7:16 (3d ed. 1992); 3 Callmann, *The Law of Unfair Competition, Trademarks and Monopolies* § 18.13 (Altman, 4th ed. 1993). *But see Luxor Cab Mfg. Corp. v. Leading Cab Co.*, 125 Misc. 764, 211 N.Y.S. 866 (1925), *aff'd*, 215 A.D. 798, 213 N.Y.S. 847 (1925), where the color of taxicabs was held entitled to trademark protection.

(2) The reason often stated for the general rule that color alone should not have trademark significance was the limited number of colors available. It was said that if color *per se* could be appropriated, all primary colors would soon be subject to monopoly (see the *Campbell Soup* case, *supra*). Is it necessarily undesirable if colors *per se* are protected where confusion is likely? *See Owens-Corning, supra.* How does the requirement of a distinctive design affect the test of likelihood of confusion? Compare the *Campbell Soup* case, *supra,* with *Barbasol Co. v. Jacobs*, 160 F.2d 336 (7th Cir. 1947), where the court held that a shaving cream box having diagonal blue, white, and red stripes forming a border for a blue panel was a distinctive design. *See also* Samuels & Samuels, *Color Trademarks: Shades of Confusion,* 83 Trademark Rep. 554 (1991); *Application of Esso Standard Oil Co.,* 305 F.2d 495 (C.C.P.A. 1962); *Application of Data Packaging Corp.*, 453 F.2d 1300 (C.C.P.A. 1972).

Reject color depletion rule (revived old)

(3) At least one court in recent years has relied on the old general rule that color alone is not protectable. In *NutraSweet Co. v. Stadt Corp.*, 917 F.2d 1024 (7th Cir. 1990), *cert. denied*, 111 S. Ct. 1640 (1991), the Seventh Circuit affirmed summary judgment that defendant's use of a blue packet for its SWEET ONE sugar substitute did not infringe plaintiff's rights in its blue packet for its EQUAL sugar substitute. The court followed the traditional rule in holding that plaintiff could protect its "overall trade dress," but not "the mere color of its packet." The court was concerned that if color alone were protected "infringement actions could soon degenerate into questions of shade confusion," and that protecting the color blue in this case "might create a barrier to otherwise lawful competition in the tabletop sweetener market." *Id.*, at 1027–28. Are these concerns valid or warranted? *Compare Qualitex Co. v. Jacobson Products Co.*, 13 F.3d 1297 (9th Cir. 1994) (holding that color cannot be registered) with *Master Distributors, Inc. v. Pako Corp.*, 986 F.2d 219 (8th Cir. 1993) (endorsing the *Owens-Corning* decision and rejecting the color depletion theory as applied to plaintiff's shade of blue for splicing tape), and *Keds Corp. v. Renee International Trading Corp.*, 888 F.2d 215 (1st Cir. 1989) (preliminary injunction upheld for incontestably registered blue rectangle label for sneakers, the court opining that the "color depletion theory" was somewhat out of date). *See generally* Schmidt, *Creating Protectable Color Trademarks*, 81 Trademark Rep. 285

(1991); Coleman, *Color as Trademarks: Breaking Down The Barriers of the Mere Color Rule*, 74 J. Pat. & Trademark Office Soc'y 345 (1992).

(4) What weight should be given to the "functional" significance of colors? In *Life Savers Corp. v. Curtiss Candy Co.*, 182 F.2d 4 (7th Cir. 1950), the court held "the use of color, including colored stripes, as background on labels is functional and indicates the color and flavor of candy the package contains." In *North Shore Laboratories Corp. v. Cohen*, 721 F.2d 514, 523 (5th Cir. 1983), the court found that tire repair products at issue were necessarily brown in color and that "plaintiff occupies the same position as a cola manufacturer attempting to prohibit other cola manufacturers from selling brown cola." Should color's "ornamental" qualities be given significance? *See American Basketball Ass'n v. AMF Voit, Inc.*, 358 F. Supp. 981 (S.D.N.Y. 1973), *aff'd*, 487 F.2d 1393 (2d Cir. 1974), *cert. denied*, 416 U.S. 986 (1974), where the court held that "mere coloration of the various panels of the ordinary basketball is not sufficiently distinctive to be the subject of a statutory trademark. . . . I find that the colors are merely a decoration or embellishment." 358 F. Supp. at 985. *But see Ideal Toy Corp. v. Plawner Toy Mfg. Corp.*, 685 F.2d 78 (3d Cir. 1982) (where an imitator using an arrangement of color patches similar to that on a Rubik's Cube was preliminarily enjoined).

For an example of how far courts have gone to find a color functional, see *Norwich Pharmacal Co. v. Sterling Drug, Inc.*, 271 F.2d 569 (2d Cir. 1959), *cert. denied*, 362 U.S. 919 (1960), wherein the court inferred that the color pink used in a stomach upset remedy (PEPTO-BISMOL) served as a psychosomatic soothing element characterized as "functional."

(5) In both the *Life Savers* and *American Chicle* cases, *supra,* the court attempted to strike a balance between the plaintiff's interest in loss of careless customers and the defendant's interest in continued use of its package design and colors. Can the two cases be reconciled? Should the question of whether "Life Savers" or "Chiclets" had become generic have influenced either decision? (See the discussion on Generic Terms in Chapter 4, *infra*.)

(6) While color per se is generally not accorded trademark protection, a rival dealer may not appropriate another's mark by merely changing its color. Why not? *See National Ass'n of Blue Shield Plans v. United Bankers Life Ins. Co.*, 362 F.2d 374 (5th Cir. 1966), where two distinctive designs (Blue and Red Shields) differed only as to the color used. The court held that the use of different colors could not prevent a likelihood of confusion with respect to the public.

CHAPTER **3**

TRADEMARK REGISTRATION
AND ADMINISTRATIVE PROCEEDINGS

§ 3.01 Introduction

The federal law of trademarks is governed by the Trademark Act of 1946, 15 U.S.C. § 1050 *et seq.,* popularly known as the Lanham Act. The intent of the Act is stated in § 45, as follows: ~~*labor*~~

> The intent of this Act is to regulate commerce within the control of Congress by making actionable the deceptive and misleading use of marks in such commerce; to protect registered marks used in such commerce from interference by State, or territorial legislation; to protect persons engaged in such commerce against unfair competition; to prevent fraud and deception in such commerce by the use of reproductions, copies, counterfeits, or colorable imitations of registered marks; and to provide rights and remedies stipulated by treaties and conventions respecting trademarks, trade names, and unfair competition entered into between the United States and foreign nations.

(15 U.S.C. § 1127.) This intent is primarily implemented by a federal registration system through which marks, when registered, are entitled to the various benefits of the Act. Although federal registration was provided for in both the Acts of 1881 and 1905, the Lanham Act broadened registrability and strengthened its effect in an effort to respond to the needs of commerce.

(See Chapter 1, *supra*; the Lanham Act is reproduced in its entirety in the Appendix).

§ 3.02 The Benefits of Federal Registration

The right to registration flows from use in commerce. Federal registration of a mark cannot be had until it is in use; federal registration generally does not enlarge the common-law right to its protection. There are, however, substantial benefits which accrue from federal registration, including: (a) constructive notice of the registrant's claim of ownership of the mark, 15 U.S.C. § 1072; (b) nationwide constructive use as of the date of application, 15 U.S.C. § 1057(c); (c) prima facie evidence of the registration's validity, of the registrant's ownership of the mark, and of the registrant's exclusive right to use the mark in commerce in connection with the goods or services specified in the registration certificate, 15 U.S.C. § 1057(b); (d) the right to institute a trademark action in the federal courts without regard to diversity of citizenship or the amount in controversy, 15 U.S.C. § 1121; (e) the right to request Customs officials to bar the importation of goods bearing infringing trademarks, 15 U.S.C. § 1124; (f) provision for treble damages, attorneys' fees and other remedies in civil actions for infringement, 15 U.S.C. §§ 1116–1120; and (g) the right, after continuous use of the mark for five years after registration, to have the registration become incontestable and thereby constitute conclusive evidence of registrant's exclusive right to use the mark in commerce for the identified goods or services, 15 U.S.C. § 1065, subject to certain defenses, including fraud, abandonment, misrepresentation, prior use, use in violation of antitrust laws, fair use, and equitable defenses, such as laches, 15 U.S.C. § 1115(b). *See, e.g., Orient Express Trading Co. v. Federated Department Stores, Inc.*, 842 F.2d 650 (2d Cir. 1988) (incontestable registrations cancelled because plaintiff had committed fraud on the Patent and Trademark Office by greatly exaggerating its claims of use in its §§ 8 and 15 affidavits).

The most important of the Lanham Act's benefits in pragmatic impact are constructive use and constructive notice, incontestability, and the right to a federal cause of action, the last being discussed in Chapter 9, Jurisdiction and Remedies, *infra*. Upon registration, the public is charged with constructive notice of the claim of ownership of the trademark, and non-owner use of it subsequent to that registration cannot be justified or defended by claim of innocence, good faith or lack of knowledge. Thus, a principal registration has nationwide effect, preserving the registrant's right to expand at a later date without fear of having that right usurped by a newcomer. *Dawn Donut Co. v. Hart's Food Stores, Inc.*, 267 F.2d 358 (2d Cir. 1959); *Sterling Brewing, Inc. v. Cold Spring Brewing Corp.*, 100 F. Supp. 412 (D. Mass. 1951). Under the Revision Act, this nationwide priority right will date back to the time of application. 15 U.S.C. § 1057(c). In *United States Jaycees v. Chicago Junior Ass'n of Commerce & Industry*, 505 F. Supp. 998 (N.D. Ill. 1981), the court observed that "the effect of incontestability is to foreclose *all* defenses [in infringement suits] except the seven defenses specifically enumerated in the statute." *See Park 'N Fly, infra*, at footnote 3, setting out these defenses.

STERLING BREWING, INC. v. COLD SPRING BREWING CORP.

United States District Court, District of Massachusetts
100 F. Supp. 412 (1951)

McCarthy, District Judge

. . . .

With respect to [15 U.S.C. § 1072 (Constructive Notice)] the commentary on the Act by Daphne Robert, to be found in 15 U.S.C.A., introductory to Chapter 22, is illuminating . . . .

The greatest single advantage of a principal registration is that it is constructive notice of the registrant's claim of ownership of the mark. This means simply that so long as a mark remains on the principal register, everyone is charged with notice of the claim of ownership. . .. It means that such use is an unlawful use and cannot be justified by a claim of innocence, good faith or lack of knowledge. Its practical effect is to give *nation-wide effect* to a principal registration, providing notice to intrastate users as well as others, and thereby eliminating one of the weaknesses inherent in prior statutes.

The same author in the "New Trade Mark Manual," 1947, sums up the situation as follows:

. . . This answers the question so often asked: "What does my registration give me?" Up to now, there was good reason for asking the question, and lawyers and judges were frequently hard put to find a satisfactory answer. . . . Its practical effect is to give nationwide coverage to a Federal registration. . . . It provides a sense of security to the registrant by preserving for him the right to expand his market at a later date without fear of having had it usurped by a newcomer. The prior laws did not enlarge the common law, but the common law to this extent is now supplanted by the statute.

Pp. 129, 130.

. . . .

PARK 'N FLY, INC. v. DOLLAR PARK AND FLY, INC.

United States Supreme Court
469 U.S. 189 (1985)

JUSTICE O'CONNOR delivered the opinion of the Court.

. . . .

I

Petitioner operates long-term parking lots near airports. After starting business in St. Louis in 1967, petitioner subsequently opened facilities in Cleveland, Houston, Boston, Memphis, and San Francisco. Petitioner applied in 1969 to the United States Patent and Trademark Office (Patent Office) to register a service mark consisting of the logo of an airplane and the words "Park 'N Fly." The registration issued in August 1971. Nearly six years later, petitioner filed an affidavit with the Patent Office to establish the incontestable status of the mark. As required by § 15 of the Trademark Act of 1946 (Lanham Act), 60 Stat. 433, as amended, 15 U.S.C. § 1065, the affidavit stated that the mark had been registered and in continuous use for five consecutive years, that there had been no final adverse decision to petitioner's claim of ownership or right to registration, and that no proceedings involving such rights were pending. Incontestable status provides, subject to the provisions of § 15 and § 33(b) of the Lanham Act, "conclusive evidence of the registrant's exclusive right to use the registered mark . . ." § 33(b), 15 U.S.C. § 1115(b).

Respondent also provides long-term airport parking services, but only has operations in Portland, Oregon. Respondent calls its business "Dollar Park and Fly." Petitioner filed this infringement action in 1978 in the United States District Court for the District of Oregon and requested the court permanently to enjoin respondent from using the words "Park and Fly" in connection with its business. Respondent counterclaimed and sought cancellation of petitioner's mark on the grounds that it is a generic term. *See* § 14(c), 15 U.S.C. § 1064(c). Respondent also argued that petitioner's mark is unenforceable because it is merely descriptive. *See* § 2(e), 15 U.S.C. § 1052(e). . . .

After a bench trial, the District Court found that petitioner's mark is not generic and observed that an incontestable mark cannot be challenged on the grounds that it is merely descriptive. . . .. The District Court permanently enjoined respondent from using the words "Park and Fly" and any other mark confusingly similar to "Park 'N Fly."

The Court of Appeals for the Ninth Circuit reversed. 718 F.2d 327 (1983). The District Court did not err, the Court of Appeals held, in refusing to invalidate petitioner's mark. *Id.,* at 331. The Court of Appeals noted, however, that it previously had held that incontestability provides a defense against the cancellation of a mark, but it may not be used offensively to enjoin another's use. *Ibid.* Petitioner, under this analysis, could obtain an injunction only if its mark would be entitled to continued registration without regard to its incontestable status. Thus, respondent could defend the infringement action by showing that the mark was merely descriptive. Based on its own examination of the record, the Court of Appeals then determined that petitioner's mark is in fact merely descriptive, and therefore respondent should not be enjoined from using the name "Park and Fly." *Ibid.*

The decision below is in direct conflict with the decision of the Court of Appeals for the Seventh Circuit in *Union Carbide Corp. v. Ever-Ready Inc.,* 531 F.2d 366, *cert. denied,* 429 U.S. 830 (1976). We granted certiorari to resolve this conflict, 465 U.S. —, 104 S. Ct. 1438 (1984), and we now reverse.

. . . .

This case requires us to consider the effect of the incontestability provisions of the Lanham Act in the context of an infringement action defended on the grounds that the mark is merely descriptive. Statutory construction must begin with the language employed by Congress and the assumption that the ordinary meaning of that language accurately expresses the legislative purpose. *See American Tobacco Co. v. Patterson,* 456 U.S. 63, 68 (1982). With respect to incontestable trade or service marks, § 33(b) of the Lanham Act states that "registration shall be conclusive evidence of the registrant's exclusive right to use the registered mark" subject to the conditions of § 15 and certain enumerated defenses.[3] Section 15 incorporates

---

[3] Section 33(b) of the Lanham Act, as set forth in 15 U.S.C. § 1115(b), provides:

If the right to use the registered mark has become incontestable under section 1065 of this title, the registration shall be conclusive evidence of the registrant's exclusive right to use the registered mark in commerce or in connection with the goods or services specified in the affidavit filed under the provisions of said section 1065 subject to any conditions or limitations stated therein except when one of the following defenses or defects is established:

(1) That the registration or the incontestable right to use the mark was obtained fraudulently; or

by reference subsections (c) and (e) of § 14, 15 U.S.C. § 1064. An incontestable mark that becomes generic may be cancelled at any time pursuant to § 14(c). That section also allows cancellation of an incontestable mark at any time if it has been abandoned, if it is being used to misrepresent the source of the goods or services in connection with which it is used, or if it was obtained fraudulently or contrary to the provisions of § 4, 15 U.S.C. § 1054, or §§ 2(a)–(c), 15 U.S.C. §§ 1052(a)–(c).[4]

One searches the language of the Lanham Act in vain to find any support for the offensive/defensive distinction applied by the Court of Appeals. The statute nowhere distinguishes between a registrant's offensive and defensive use of an incontestable mark. On the contrary, § 33(b)'s declaration that the registrant has an "exclusive right" to use the mark indicates that incontestable status may be used to enjoin infringement by others. A conclusion that such infringement cannot be enjoined renders meaningless the "exclusive right" recognized by the statute. Moreover, the language in three of the defenses enumerated in § 33(b) clearly contemplates the use of incontestability in infringement actions by plaintiffs. *See* §§ 33(b)(4)–(6), 15 U.S.C. §§ 1115(b)(4)–(6).

The language of the Lanham Act also refutes any conclusion that an incontestable mark may be challenged as merely descriptive. A mark that is merely descriptive of an applicant's goods or services is not registrable unless the mark has secondary meaning. Before a mark achieves incontestable status, registration provides prima facie evidence of the registrant's exclusive right to use the mark in commerce.

---

(2) That the mark has been abandoned by the registrant; or

(3) That the registered mark is being used, by or with the permission of the registrant or a person in privity with the registrant, so as to misrepresent the source of the goods or services in connection with which the mark is used; or

(4) That the use of the name, term, or device charged to be an infringement is a use, otherwise than as a trade or service mark, of the party's individual name in his own business, or of the individual name of anyone in privity with such party, or of a term or device which is descriptive of and used fairly and in good faith only to describe to users the goods or services of such party, or their geographic origin; or

(5) That the mark whose use by a party is charged as an infringement was adopted without knowledge of the registrant's prior use and has been continuously used by such party or those in privity with him from a date prior to registration of the mark under this chapter or publication of the registered mark under subsection (c) of section 1062 of this title: *Provided, however,* That this defense or defect shall apply only for the area in which such continuous prior use is proved; or

(6) That the mark whose use is charged as an infringement was registered and used prior to the registration under this chapter or publication under subsection (c) of section 1062 of this title of the registered mark of the registrant, and not abandoned: *Provided, however,* That this defense or defect shall apply only for the area in which the mark was used prior to such registration or such publication of the registrant's mark; or

(7) That the mark has been or is being used to violate the antitrust laws of the United States.

[4] Sections 2(a)–(c) prohibit registration of marks containing specified subject matter, *e.g.*, the flag of the United States. Sections 4 and 14(e) concern certification marks and are inapplicable to this case.

§ 33(a), 15 U.S.C. § 1115(a). The Lanham Act expressly provides that before a mark becomes incontestable an opposing party may prove any legal or equitable defense which might have been asserted if the mark had not been registered. *Ibid.* Thus, § 33(a) would have allowed respondent to challenge petitioner's mark as merely descriptive if the mark had not become incontestable. With respect to incontestable marks, however, § 33(b) provides that registration is *conclusive* evidence of the registrant's exclusive right to use the mark, subject to the conditions of § 15 and the seven defenses enumerated in § 33(b) itself. Mere descriptiveness is not recognized by either § 15 or § 33(b) as a basis for challenging an incontestable mark.

. . . .

III

Nothing in the legislative history of the Lanham Act supports a departure from the plain language of the Statutory provisions concerning incontestability. Indeed, a conclusion that incontestable status can provide the basis for enforcement of the registrant's exclusive right to use a trade or service mark promotes the goals of the statute. The Lanham Act provides national protection of trademarks in order to secure to the owner of the mark the good will of his business and to protect the ability of consumers to distinguish among competing producers. *See* S. Rep. No. 1333, at 3, 5. National protection of trademarks is desirable, Congress concluded, because trademarks foster competition and the maintenance of quality by securing to the producer the benefits of good reputation. *Id.,* at 4. The incontestability provisions, as the proponents of the Lanham Act emphasized, provide a means for the registrant to quiet title in the ownership of his mark. . . . The opportunity to obtain incontestable status by satisfying the requirements of § 15 thus encourages producers to cultivate the good will associated with a particular mark. This function of the incontestability provisions would be utterly frustrated if the holder of an incontestable mark could not enjoin infringement by others so long as they established that the mark would not be registrable but for its incontestable status.

. . . .

The dissent echoes arguments made by opponents of the Lanham Act that the incontestable status of a descriptive mark might take from the public domain language that is merely descriptive. As we have explained, Congress has already addressed concerns to prevent the "commercial monopolization," of descriptive language. The Lanham Act allows a mark to be challenged at any time if it becomes generic, and, under certain circumstances, permits the non-trademark use of descriptive terms contained in an incontestable mark. Finally, if "monopolization" of an incontestable mark threatens economic competition, § 33(b)(7), 15 U.S.C. § 1115(b)(7), provides a defense on the grounds that the mark is being used to violate federal antitrust laws. At bottom, the dissent simply disagrees with the balance struck by Congress in determining the protection to be given to incontestable marks.

. . . .

We conclude that the holder of a registered mark may rely on incontestability to enjoin infringement and that such an action may not be defended on the grounds that the mark is merely descriptive. . . .

[Reversed and remanded.]

JUSTICE STEVENS, dissenting.

. . . .

If the registrant of a merely descriptive mark complies with the statutory requirement that prima-facie evidence of secondary meaning must be submitted to the Patent and Trademark Office, it is entirely consistent with the policy of the Act to accord the mark incontestable status after an additional five years of continued use. For if no rival contests the registration in that period, it is reasonable to presume that the initial prima-facie showing of distinctiveness could not be rebutted. But if no proof of secondary meaning is ever presented, either to the Patent and Trademark Office or to a court, there is simply no rational basis for leaping to the conclusion that the passage of time has transformed an inherently defective mark into an incontestable mark.

No matter how dedicated and how competent administrators may be, the possibility of error is always present, especially in nonadversary proceedings. . . .

On the basis of the record in this case, it is reasonable to infer that the operators of parking lots in the vicinity of airports may make use of the words "park and fly" simply because those words provide a ready description of their businesses, rather than because of any desire to exploit petitioner's good will. There is a well-recognized public interest in prohibiting the commercial monopolization of phrases such as "park and fly." When a business claims the exclusive right to use words or phrases that are a part of our common vocabulary, this Court should not depart from the statutorily mandated authority to "rectify the register," 15 U.S.C. § 1119, absent a clear congressional mandate. Language, even in a commercial context, properly belongs to the public unless Congress instructs otherwise. In this case we have no such instruction; in fact, the opposite command guides our actions: Congress' clear insistence that a merely descriptive mark, such as "Park 'N Fly" in the context of airport parking, remain in the public domain unless secondary meaning is proved.

. . . .

The Court suggests that my reading of the Act "effectively emasculates § 33(b) under the circumstances of this case." But my reading would simply require the owner of a merely descriptive mark to prove secondary meaning before obtaining any benefit from incontestability. If a mark is in fact "distinctive of the applicant's goods in commerce" as § 2(f) requires, that burden should not be onerous. If the mark does not have any such secondary meaning, the burden of course could not be met. But if that be the case, the purposes of the Act are served, not frustrated, by requiring adherence to the statutory procedure mandated by Congress.

. . . .

The Revision Act has resolved a conflict among the courts by providing that, in addition to the previously identified § 1115(b) defenses, equitable defenses (such as laches and estoppel) may be raised in actions involving incontestable registrations. The Revision Act also revised 15 U.S.C. § 1115(b) expressly to confirm that protection of an incontestably registered mark is still "subject to proof of infringement." In other words, as stated by the Tenth Circuit in *Coherent, Inc. v. Coherent Technologies, Inc.*, 935 F.2d 1122 (10th Cir. 1991), the incontestable status of a plaintiff's registration does not mean "any use by another party automatically constitutes infringement."

Some courts have recognized, significantly, that although under *Park 'N Fly* the *validity* of an incontestably registered trademark cannot be challenged on descriptiveness grounds, the *strength* of the mark, which may involve its descriptiveness, may be considered in assessing likelihood of confusion. *See, e.g., Munters Corp. v. Matsui America, Inc.*, 909 F.2d 250, 252 (7th Cir.), *cert. denied*, 111 S. Ct. 591 (1990) (assessing descriptiveness of incontestably registered mark for strength and likelihood of confusion purposes "is correct practice in the Seventh Circuit"); *Miss World (UK), Ltd. v. Mrs. America Pageant, Inc.*, 856 F.2d 1445, 1449 (9th Cir. 1988) ("incontestable status does not alone establish a strong mark"); *Oreck Corp. v. U.S. Floor Systems, Inc.*, 803 F.2d 166, 171 (5th Cir.) ("[i]ncontestable status does not make a weak mark strong"), *cert. denied*, 107 S. Ct. 2462 (1987). *But see Dieter v. B&H Industries*, 880 F.2d 322, 329 (11th Cir. 1989) (incontestably registered mark "presumed to be at least descriptive with secondary meaning," and thus "relatively strong"), *cert. denied*, 111 S. Ct. 369 (1990). *See* Razzano, *Incontestability: Should It Be Given Any Effect In A Likelihood Of Confusion Determination*, 82 Trademark Rep. 409 (1992).

See also Institute for Scientific Information, Inc. v. Gordon and Breach, Science Publishers, Inc., 931 F.2d 1002 (3d Cir.), *cert. denied*, 112 S. Ct. 302 (1991) (descriptiveness of plaintiff's incontestably registered mark may be considered in context of defendant's § 33(b) fair use defense).

§ 3.03 Acquisition and Maintenance of Federal Registrations

The right to registration flows from use in commerce. Section 45 of the Lanham Act, 15 U.S.C. § 1127, provides that use of a mark on goods sufficient to obtain federal registration occurs when the mark "is placed in any manner on the goods or their containers or the displays associated therewith or on the tags or labels affixed thereto and the goods are sold or transported in commerce." *See* Chapter 2, *supra*. When the claimed use on goods is based on display rather than affixation, it is generally required that the display be point-of-purchase material designed to attract the attention of prospective purchasers. *In re ITT Rayonier, Inc.*, 208 U.S.P.Q. 86, 87 (T.T.A.B. 1980). Brochures, catalogs, package inserts, leaflets, etc. accordingly have been held insufficient as specimens of use. *In re Bright of America, Inc.*, 205 U.S.P.Q. 63, 71 (T.T.A.B. 1979) and decisions cited therein. *But see In re Ultraflight, Inc.*, 221 U.S.P.Q. 903, 906 (T.T.A.B. 1984), where the Board noted that in some instances inserts may be part of the goods themselves, and held that use of the mark in issue on an instruction manual inserted in a powered hand-glider assembly kit was affixation adequate for registration purposes.

The sufficiency of use of a claimed service mark requires a different analysis since there is nothing physical to which the mark can be affixed. "Service" has been defined as "the performance of labor for the benefit of another," *In re Canadian Pacific Ltd.*, 754 F.2d 992, 994 (Fed. Cir. 1985) (the court noting the term is not defined in the Lanham Act). Valid use of a service mark requires that it be "used or displayed in the sale or advertising of services" rendered in commerce. 15 U.S.C. §§ 1127, 1052, 1053. Therefore, acceptable service mark use under § 45

> extends beyond the narrow concept of trademark use of a mark in the accepted manner of affixation to the goods . . . and encompasses a broad spectrum of use including business cards, stationery, circulars, direct mailing pieces, advertisements in the various media including radio and television commercials, store signs, and any other method that may be employed in promoting one's service . . . [S]uch use must be an open and notorious public use directed to the segment of the purchasing public for whom the services are intended . . . and [must] inform or apprise prospective purchasers of the present or future availability of the adopter's service under the mark.

Computer Food Stores, Inc. v. Corner Store Franchises, Inc., 176 U.S.P.Q. 535, 538 (T.T.A.B. 1973). For example, use in a newspaper advertisement to identify real estate services was sufficient in *Hovnanian Estates, Inc. v. Covered Bridge Estates, Inc.*, 195 U.S.P.Q. 658 (T.T.A.B. 1977), as was use on handbills to identify entertainment in *In re Florida Cypress Gardens, Inc.*, 208 U.S.P.Q. 288 (T.T.A.B. 1980).

A trade name, as defined in § 45, can be registered under the Act, but only if used as a trademark to identify the source of goods or services, and not merely as a company or organizational name. "[T]rade names qua trade names do not qualify for registration," and where an asserted mark is a trade name, "there is a presumption that the present usage is also that of a trade name" and not a trademark. *Application of Pennsylvania Fashion Factory, Inc.*, 588 F.2d 1343, 1345 (C.C.P.A. 1978) (use of retail store name on shopping bags held insufficient).

A mark used to identify a collective group, e.g., a union label, is registrable as a "collective mark" when properly used in a like manner to a trademark or service mark. *See, e.g., Schroeder v. Lotito*, 221 U.S.P.Q. 812, 819 (D.R.I. 1983) (holding that suit for infringement may be brought by the collective mark owner organization on behalf of its members). A certification mark, or a mark used in connection with goods or services to certify, inter alia, region of origin, or quality, or characteristics of the goods or services, is also registrable under the Lanham Act. The Underwriters Laboratories "UL" mark and the Good Housekeeping seal of approval are examples of certification marks. *See also Community of Roquefort*, in Chapter 2, *supra* (ROQUEFORT for cheese). Registration of collective and certification marks is authorized by 15 U.S.C. § 1054.

[A]   The Principal Register   + Supplemental

The Lanham Act provides for two Registers, the Principal (15 U.S.C. § 1051) and the Supplemental (15 U.S.C. § 1091). A mark is not registrable on either the Principal Register or Supplemental Register if it consists or is comprised of (1) immoral, deceptive, scandalous, or disparaging matter; (2) the flag or insignia of any nation, state, or municipality or any simulation thereof; (3) a name, portrait, or signature identifying any living individual or deceased President without written consent; or (4) a mark likely to be confused with a previously used or registered mark. A mark which is merely descriptive, deceptively misdescriptive, primarily geographically descriptive, or primarily merely a surname is not registrable on the Principal Register unless it "has become distinctive of the applicant's goods in commerce," that is, if it has acquired secondary meaning, but such a mark may be registrable on the Supplemental Register without such showing. 15 U.S.C. §§ 1052, 1091.

Can't be registered

A trademark "search" is usually desirable to determine whether a proposed mark has been anticipated by a previously used or registered one. Ordinarily, a search for confusingly similar marks should examine (1) federal registrations and applications; (2) state registrations; and (3) common-law usage disclosed by trade directories and the like. Complete records of federal registrations and applications are maintained at the United States Patent and Trademark Office in Arlington, Va. In addition, private trademark search services provide computerized searches for federal and state registrations and most common-law uses. If no confusingly similar prior registrations or uses are found, the mark must then be used in interstate commerce prior to obtaining federal registration. 15 U.S.C. § 1051. *Larry Harmon Pictures Corp. v. Williams Restaurant Corp.,* 929 F.2d 662 (Fed. Cir. 1992) (use in interstate commerce required).

Federal registration of a trademark on the Principal Register is obtained by filing a verified written application with the Trademark Division of the United States Patent and Trademark Office accompanied by a drawing of the mark, three specimen labels or facsimiles of the mark as actually used, and the statutory filing fee. The application can be based on either actual use or intent to use. The application confers upon the applicant a nationwide right of priority, as of the filing date of the application, against all competing claimants except prior users, prior applicants, and foreign treaty applicants with an earlier priority filing date. (As to the last, see the discussion in the Foreign Registration section, below). That nationwide right of priority is contingent upon use being made and the registration issuing. 15 U.S.C. § 1057(c).

Descriptive marks are registrable if they have acquired secondary meaning (or "distinctiveness"). Secondary meaning may be shown by circumstantial proof, such as proof of substantial sales and advertising and by direct evidence, such as surveys. Until 1989, the law allowed the Commissioner to accept as prima facie evidence of distinctiveness proof (*e.g.,* an affidavit) of substantially exclusive and continuous use in commerce of the mark during the five years preceding the filing of the application. In 1989, the Revision Act changed the law to allow the proof of acquired distinctiveness to be based on the five-year period preceding the date on which the *claim* of distinctiveness is made. This is important because such claims are often made during the sometimes lengthy post-filing period after a finding of descriptiveness by the examining attorney.

If the Trademark Division determines that no prior registrations of marks exist that are likely to cause confusion and that the mark is otherwise entitled to registration, the mark and the other particulars specified in the application are published in the *Official Gazette* of the Patent and Trademark Office. This publication notifies the public of the application in order to enable possible opposition by any person who believes he or she would be damaged by the issuance of registration for that mark. 15 U.S.C. § 1062(a).

If no opposition proceeding is instituted against a use-based application within the time allowed after publication in the *Gazette*, a Certificate of Registration is issued. If no opposition is instituted within the time allowed after the publication in the *Gazette* against an intent-to-use application for which no amendment alleging use has been filed, the applicant receives a Notice of Allowance, and only after the applicant timely files a statement that use in interstate commerce has begun is a Certificate of Registration issued. The registrant is then entitled to use notice of such registration, including the symbol "®," in association with its mark so as to inform the public of its federal registration.

The intent-to-use applicant must commence use of the mark and file a statement of use, plus specimens, within six months of the date the Patent and Trademark Office issues the "Notice of Allowance" for the application. The initial six-month period will be extended for an additional six months upon written application reconfirming the bona fide intent to use, and payment of any applicable fees. Additional six-month extensions may be obtained, not to exceed a total of three years from the notice of allowance, upon similar applications and fee payments plus showings of good cause. Failure to file a timely statement of use will result in a ruling of abandonment of the application.

Registration of a trademark on the Principal Register remains in force under the Revision Act for ten years provided that the registrant files an affidavit or declaration of use "within one year next preceding the expiration of . . . six years" from the date of registration. 15 U.S.C. § 1058(a). The affidavit must show, with support by specimens, that the mark is still in use in connection with all the specified goods or services, or that nonuse is due to special circumstances and not due to any intention to abandon the mark. *Id.* If the affidavit is not filed, the registration will be cancelled by the Patent and Trademark Office. Each registration may be renewed for periods of ten years (twenty years under pre-Revision Act law) upon application duly filed. 15 U.S.C. § 1059. *See generally* Hawes, *Trademark Registration Practice* (1993 ed.); Smith, *Intent-to-Use Trademark Practice* (1992 ed.).

[B]   The Supplemental Register

The Supplemental Register had its origins in the Act of 1920 which provided for the registration of marks not registrable under the 1905 Act (e.g., surnames). Among the intentions of the 1920 Act was enabling the users of such marks to obtain registrations in those foreign countries whose laws required as a prerequisite registration in the applicant's country of origin. The Lanham Act in effect continued this Register as a means of registering "marks capable of distinguishing applicant's goods or services and not registrable on the principal register." 15 U.S.C. § 1091.

A registration on the Supplemental Register confers none of the presumptions or prima facie evidence benefits afforded by a registration on the Principal Register. It does, however, afford the right to a federal cause of action and to the possibility of treble damages for infringement. In addition, it entitles the registrant to use notice of registration in association with the mark and meets the need for a registration in the applicant's country of origin in most foreign countries where that is a prerequisite for registration. Intent-to-use applications to register on the Supplemental Register are not permitted.

§ 3.04 State Registrations

Every state provides for the registration of trademarks, and many have adopted the Model State Trademark Bill. When use of a mark is not "in commerce," such registration may be all that is available. Generally, the state statutes specify what may be registered, what constitutes infringement (likelihood of confusion), and remedies. Their actual substantive legal effect in addition to the common law is limited in most circumstances. United States Trademark Association, *State Trademark and Unfair Competition Law* (1993 ed.); 1 Gilson, *Trademark Protection and Practice,* § 10.12 (1993 ed.); McCarthy, *Trademarks and Unfair Competition,* § 22:1 (3d ed. 1992); Sherman, *Registration of Trademarks Under State Law*, 59 A.B.A. J. 515 (1973); Seasonwein, *The Effect of State Trademark Registration*, 61 Trademark Rep. 457 (1971).

§ 3.05 Foreign Registrations

Almost every nation of the world provides for the registration of trademarks. Trade identity law, and the rules and regulations respecting registration differ markedly, however, from country to country. Most other countries do not require use of the mark as a prerequisite to registration. Several multicountry treaty arrangements exist which encompass trademark-trade identity rights, the principal ones being the Union of Paris (Callmann, *Unfair Competition, Trademarks and Monopolies,* App. XX) and the Madrid Arrangement (*Id.*, Apps. XXII and XXIII). The United States is a member of the former but not the latter. For general commentaries on trademark registration abroad, see Horwitz, *World Trademark Law and Practice*, (2d ed. 1993); 1 Gilson, *Trademark Protection and Practice,* § 9.01 (1993 ed.).

Section 44 of the Lanham Act, 15 U.S.C. § 1126, allows an applicant to register a mark in the United States based upon an application to register the mark in a foreign country which is a party to a trademark treaty with the United States. The United States application must be filed within six months of filing the foreign application for § 44(d) to apply. The Court of Appeals for the District of Columbia held in *SCM Corporation v. Langis Foods Ltd. ("Lemon Tree")*, 539 F.2d 196 (D.C.

Cir. 1976), that § 44(d) provided a foreign applicant a six-month priority right which could not be invalidated by an intervening use in the United States during that period. The foreign applicant had used the mark in Canada prior to applying in the United States. In *Crocker National Bank v. Canadian Imperial Bank of Commerce*, 223 U.S.P.Q. 909 (T.T.A.B. 1984), the Board, relying on *Lemon Tree*, held in a cancellation proceeding that a foreign applicant was entitled to registration based upon a foreign application, without alleging or demonstrating use anywhere. The Commissioner of Patents has changed positions several times on the requirement of use by foreign applicants. *See Ex Parte British Insulated Callender's Cables Ltd.*, 83 U.S.P.Q. 319 (Comm'r Pats. 1949) (holding there must be use somewhere, though not necessarily in the United States, prior to registration); *Ex parte Society Fromageries Bel*, 105 U.S.P.Q. 392 (Comm'r Pats. 1955) (holding there need not be use prior to registration); *In re Certain Incomplete Trademark Applications*, 137 U.S.P.Q. 69 (Comm'r Pats. 1963) (holding there must be use somewhere prior to registration). *See generally* Offner, *Requirements for Filing Trademark Applications by Foreigners in the United States of America*, 55 Trademark Rep. 1074 (1965); Zelnick, *Shaking the Lemon Tree: Use and The Paris Union Treaty*, 67 Trademark Rep. 329 (1977).

The implementation of an intent-to-use registration system in this country has decreased the advantage foreign applicants have over domestic applicants. Section 44 nonetheless provides a privilege to certain foreign applicants that is unavailable to domestic applicants, who must use a mark in commerce prior to obtaining a registration. A foreign registrant's continued failure to use the mark for a period of years *after* registration, however, may result in a finding of abandonment. *Imperial Tobacco v. Philip Morris, Inc.*, 899 F.2d 1575 (Fed. Cir. 1990) (registration cancelled for abandonment based on five years of non-use).

§ 3.06 Federal Administrative Proceedings

[A] Trademark Trial and Appeal Board — Registerable only [not infring.]

Inter partes proceedings may be brought before the Trademark Trial and Appeal Board (T.T.A.B.) of the United States Patent and Trademark Office and are concerned only with whether or not a mark is registrable, or, if registered, whether or not the registration should be cancelled. The four basic inter partes proceedings are opposition, cancellation, interference, and concurrent use. They are quasi-judicial proceedings and generally follow the format of a civil action as to pleadings, motion practice, discovery, record, argument, and decision. Following joinder of issue, periods are set for discovery, deposition testimony by the party in the position of plaintiff and then by the defending party, followed by rebuttal and briefing. Oral hearing may be had before the Board, corresponding to oral summation in a court action.

A final decision of the Trademark Trial and Appeal Board may be either appealed to the Court of Appeals for the Federal Circuit (until 1982, when its jurisdiction was enlarged, called the Court of Customs and Patent Appeals (C.C.P.A.)) or reviewed by a district court in a trial de novo. 15 U.S.C. § 1071. If the case is appealed to the Federal Circuit, however, the appellee may elect instead to have the case reviewed by a district court in a trial de novo 15 U.S.C. § 1071(a). On review by a district court, the decision of the Trademark Trial and Appeal Board is generally held to be controlling as to likelihood of confusion "unless the contrary is established by testimony which in character and amount carries thorough conviction." *Fleetwood Co. v. Hazel Bishop, Inc.*, 352 F.2d 841, 844 (7th Cir. 1965). On appeal, the Federal Circuit will not overrule a finding of fact unless it is "clearly erroneous" (Fed. R. Civ. P. 52(a)), and it has been held that the Federal Circuit's own determinations operate as a collateral estoppel in a subsequent trademark infringement action. *Flavor Corp. of America v. Kemin Indus. Inc.*, 493 F.2d 275 (8th Cir. 1974).

[1] Opposition Proceedings

A Notice of Opposition may be filed by "any person who believes that he would be damaged by the registration of a mark . . . ." If the registration is successful, the trademark will not be registered. 15 U.S.C. § 1063. The opposition must be filed within thirty (30) days of the application being published in the *Official Gazette*, although extensions of time to oppose, within limits, may be obtained. 15 U.S.C. § 1063(a).

The Trademark Rules of Practice (T.R.P.) specify that "The opposition must set forth a short and plain statement showing how the opposer would be damaged by the registration of the opposed mark and state the grounds for opposition." T.R.P. 2.104. An opposition may thus be initiated by a registrant opposing registration of a confusingly similar mark, *Specialty Brands, Inc. v. Coffee Bean Distributors, Inc.*, 748 F.2d 669 (Fed. Cir. 1984); by one who has prior use but not registration of a trademark for which registration is now sought by another, *Wilson v. Delaunay*, 245 F.2d 877 (C.C.P.A. 1957); or by one who uses, in a descriptive, generic, or geographic manner, and without claiming trademark rights thereto, a word or term now sought to be registered by another, *Quaker Oil Corp. v. Quaker State Oil Refining Corp.*, 161 U.S.P.Q. 547 (T.T.A.B. 1969), *aff'd*, 453 F.2d 1296 (C.C.P.A. 1972) (descriptive use); *R. Neumann & Co. v. Bon-Ton Auto Upholstery, Inc.*, 326 F.2d 799 (C.C.P.A. 1964) (deceptively misdescriptive use). Opposition may also be based on trade name or advertising use of a term or mark, *Knickerbocker Toy Co. v. Faultless Starch Co.*, 467 F.2d 501 (C.C.P.A. 1972). Thus, it is not necessary that the opposer show exclusive use or exclusive right to use a word or term. First use by an opposer *after* the filing of an intent-to-use application of an allegedly confusingly similar mark apparently is insufficient grounds for opposition under the Revision Act. In *Zirco v. American Telephone and Telegraph Co.*, 1991 T.T.A.B. LEXIS 43 (T.T.A.B. 1991), an opposition by a post-filing-date common law user against an intent-to-use applicant was dismissed, contingent upon registration issuing, the Board confirming that an intent-to-use applicant may successfully rely on its constructive use priority filing date in opposition proceedings.

Neither the rules nor the statute specify the nature or amount of the damage which must be shown by the opposer; however, "damage may be shown by proving that the registration will interfere with the free, normal, and lawful operation of the opposer's business, even though the mark sought to be registered does not conflict with any rights he may have in a mark." Robert, *The New Trademark Manual*, 85 (1947). Upon a showing of likelihood of confusion, damage will be presumed, *Daggett & Ramsdell v. Procter & Gamble Co.*, 275 F.2d 955 (C.C.P.A. 1960). Registrations on the Supplemental Register cannot be opposed but may be cancelled. *Kwik-Kopy Franchise Corp. v. Dimensional Lithographers, Inc.*, 165 U.S.P.Q. 397 (T.T.A.B. 1970).

The grounds generally relied upon for opposing the registration of a mark are those enumerated in § 2 of the Lanham Act, 15 U.S.C. § 1052. The most common basis for opposition is § 2(d), whereby the opposer claims that the applicant's mark resembles either opposer's registered or common-law trademark. In such cases the test is likelihood of confusion between the two marks.

It is important, however, to distinguish the likelihood of confusion test in an infringement action from that in an opposition proceeding. In an opposition, since the ultimate issue is not infringement but whether the applicant's mark qualifies for federal registration, the test is based on similarities of the marks as they appear in the application and as registered or used by opposer. In the past, such matters as label, package, or wrapper similarities were therefore neither material nor relevant in an opposition proceeding, although they ordinarily would be in an action for infringement. *Crown Zellerbach Corp. v. Martin*, 153 U.S.P.Q., 141 (T.T.A.B. 1967), *aff'd*, 422 F.2d 918 (C.C.P.A. 1970), *cert. denied*, 400 U.S. 911 (1970); *The Tas-T-Nut Co. v. Variety Nut & Date Co.*, 128 U.S.P.Q. 166 (T.T.A.B. 1961), *aff'd*, 304 F.2d 903 (C.C.P.A. 1962). *Compare, however, Kenner Parker Toys, Inc. v. Rose Art Indus., Inc.*, 963 F.2d 350 (Fed. Cir. 1992), in which the court found that "the trade dress of the marks enhances their inherently similar commercial impression" in holding that FUNDOUGH was confusingly similar to PLAY-DOH for modelling compounds. Trade dress has been considered in opposition proceedings to help determine the connotation a word mark imparts. *Specialty Brands, Inc. v. Coffee Bean Distributors, Inc.*, 748 F.2d 669 (Fed. Cir. 1984) (applicant's claim that its SPICE VALLEY mark for tea conveyed a country valley image was rebutted by square rigged sailing ship on its label; confusion held likely with SPICE ISLANDS for tea); *American Rice, Inc. v. H.I.T. Corp.*, 231 U.S.P.Q. 793 (T.T.A.B. 1986) (contrary to applicant's contentions, trade dress demonstrated its GOLDEN RIBBON mark imparted a "contest award" image like that of opposer's BLUE RIBBON mark; confusion held likely).

An opposition proceeding is governed by the Federal Rules of Civil Procedure and the Trademark Rules of Practice, T.R.P. 2.116(a). An answer is required of the applicant in response to a notice of opposition, and these two pleadings correspond to the complaint and answer in a court action. T.R.P. 2.116(c). In its answer to an opposition based on a prior registration, the applicant may not raise a defense attacking the validity of opposer's registration except by way of a counterclaim for cancellation which must be verified and be accompanied by the required fee. T.R.P. 2.106(b). The defenses of laches, estoppel or acquiescence normally will be considered "only if there is a reasonable doubt [that] likelihood of confusion exists." *White Heather Distillers, Ltd. v. American Distilling Co.*, 200 U.S.P.Q. 466, 469

(T.T.A.B. 1980). *Accord CBS, Inc. v. Man's Day Publishing Co.*, 205 U.S.P.Q. 470, 475 (T.T.A.B. 1980). The Federal Circuit has held, however, that in registration cases, laches begins to run from the time that the applicant's application to register the mark is published in the *Official Gazette*, since that is the point in time at which a party can object to the applicant's registration of the mark. *National Cable Television Ass'n v. America Cinema Editors, Inc.*, 937 F.2d 1572, 1581 (Fed Cir. 1991). Presumably that is true for acquiescence as well. *Cf. Coach House Restaurant v. Coach & Six Restaurants Inc.*, supra, 934 F.2d at 1563–64 (acquiescence as to use compared with acquiescence as to registration). Testimony is taken by deposition, and documentary evidence is authenticated and offered during periods set by the Board corresponding to the trial in court proceedings. Subsequent to the taking and filing of testimony and other evidence, the parties may submit briefs and be heard in final argument before the Board.

[2]   Cancellation Proceedings

A cancellation petition may be filed by "any person who believes that he is or will be damaged by the registration of a mark." 15 U.S.C. § 1064. The proceeding is essentially the same as an opposition and, with certain exceptions, must be brought within five years of the date of registration. Within that period, it may be based on the same grounds as would have supported an opposition. If a potential opposer misses the final date within which a notice of opposition must be filed, his attack must be by way of a cancellation. Although the issues are normally the same, the cancellation petitioner theoretically bears a heavier burden, since he must overcome the prima facie rights of the registrant evidenced by the registration certificate. 15 U.S.C. § 1057(b). If cancellation is sought after five years of registration, it then may be based only on the grounds specified in § 14 of the Lanham Act (15 U.S.C. § 1064), namely, that the mark has become the generic name of an article or substance, the mark has been abandoned, the registration was fraudulently obtained, the mark is being used so as to misrepresent the source of the goods or services, or the registration was obtained contrary to the provisions of §§ 4 and 2(a), (b), or (c) of the Act. Partial cancellation or modification of the registration by limitation of the goods and services specified also may be obtained under the proper circumstances. 15 U.S.C. §§ 1064, 1068.

As in an opposition proceeding, damage must be alleged by the cancellation petitioner (15 U.S.C. § 1064) and may be shown by proving likelihood of confusion or that the registration does or will interfere with the free operation of his business. Also as in an opposition proceeding, a cancellation proceeding is jurisdictionally confined to the continuing right of a party to the federal registration of his mark — not the right to use the mark. *Hammermill Paper Co. v. Gulf States Paper Corp.*, 337 F.2d 662 (C.C.P.A. 1964).

[3]   Interference Proceedings

Section 16 of the Lanham Act, 15 U.S.C. § 1066, provides:

> Whenever application is made for the registration of a mark which so resembles a mark previously registered by another, or for the registration of which another

has previously made application, as to be likely when applied to the goods or when used in connection with the services of the applicant to cause confusion or mistake or to deceive, the Commissioner may declare that an interference exists. No interference shall be declared between an application and the registration of a mark the right to use of which has become incontestable.

Prior to 1972, an interference proceeding was declared and instituted by the Commissioner of Patents and Trademarks when there were two applications pending for conflicting trademarks or, on petition by the applicant, when an application alleged priority of use of a mark which conflicted with a subsisting registration which had not become incontestable. In 1972, the Trademark Rules of Practice were changed, virtually eliminating interference proceedings. An interference will now be declared only on petition to the Commissioner of Patents and Trademarks and "only upon a showing of extraordinary circumstances which would result in a party being unduly prejudiced without an interference." T.R.P. 2.91(a). No undue prejudice will exist if an opposition or cancellation proceeding is available. See, however, *In re Family Inns of America, Inc.*, 180 U.S.P.Q. 332 (Comm'r 1974), where extraordinary circumstances were shown as multiple applications had been filed for similar marks which would have required successive opposition proceedings.

An interference will be declared only between marks which have been determined to be otherwise registrable by the Examiner. T.R.P. 2.92. The primary issue considered is priority of use, and, hence, the right to federal registration. The party whose application was filed last will be designated as the junior party and has the burden of proof as to priority. T.R.P. 2.96. The proceeding is before the Trademark Trial and Appeal Board, and the procedures are generally the same as in an opposition or cancellation proceeding.

[4]   Concurrent Use Proceedings

While the benefits of federal registration are national in scope, there are occasional innocent concurrent uses of the same or similar marks for the same or similar goods which, because they are used in different territories, do not give rise to a likelihood of confusion. In these situations, concurrent registrations may be obtained under § 2(d) of the Lanham Act by persons having made lawful use of the same or similar marks in commerce, provided such use is prior to the earliest filing date of any pending applications or subsisting registrations for conflicting marks. 15 U.S.C. § 1052(d). The Commissioner may also issue concurrent registrations when a court of competent jurisdiction finds more than one person entitled to use the same or similar mark in commerce. 15 U.S.C. § 1052(d).

One who believes that he is entitled to such a concurrent use registration may file an application which specifies, to the extent of his or her knowledge, the particulars and areas respecting the concurrent lawful use by others, and the area, goods and mode of use for which the applicant seeks registration. T.R.P. 2.42. The Patent and Trademark Office will then notify the other parties concerned and will institute a proceeding which generally follows the practice in an interference. T.R.P. 2.99(c). If concurrent registrations are issued, the Commissioner prescribes the conditions and limitations for the use of the mark thereunder by the respective parties. 15 U.S.C.§ 1052(d). *See generally* Rice, *Concurrent Use Applications and Proceedings*, 72 Trademark Rep. 403 (1982), and the discussion on Concurrent Rights in Chapter 7, *infra*.

[B] International Trade Commission   *ITC action for IP*

Under 15 U.S.C. § 1124 and 19 C.F.R. § 133.0 *et seq.*, federal registrants may record their registered trademark with the Bureau of Customs and thereby cause Customs to take steps to prohibit entry of infringing imports. *See* McCarthy, *Trademarks and Unfair Competition*, § 29:12 (3d ed. 1992). Owners of unregistered trademarks and trade dress may litigate before the International Trade Commission ("ITC") under 19 U.S.C. § 1337 ("§ 337") to obtain similar relief. Registrants in some instances may also find it advantageous to seek remedial orders from the ITC. *See, e.g., In re Certain Airtight Cast-Iron Stoves*, 215 U.S.P.Q. 963 (I.T.C. 1980).

The International Trade Commission is an administrative body authorized under § 337 to take action against unfair methods of competition and unfair acts in the importation of articles into the United States. Section 337(a) provides in pertinent part:

(1) Subject to paragraph (2), the following are unlawful, and when found by the Commission to exist shall be dealt with, in addition to any other provision of law, as provided in this section:

(A) Unfair methods of competition and unfair acts in the importation of articles (other than articles provided for in subparagraphs (B), (C), and (D)) into the United States, or in the sale of such articles by the owner, importer, or consignee, the threat or effect of which is -

(i) to destroy or substantially injure an industry in the United States;

(ii) to prevent the establishment of such an industry; or

(iii) to restrain or monopolize trade and commerce in the United States.

. . .

(C) The importation into the United States, the sale for importation, or the sale within the United States after importation by the owner, importer, or consignee, of articles that infringe a valid and enforceable United States trademark registered under the Trademark Act of 1946.

. . .

(2) Subparagraphs (B), (C), and (D) of paragraph (1) apply only if an industry in the United States, relating to the articles protected by the patent, copyright, trademark, or mask work concerned, exists or is in the process of being established.

(3) For purposes of paragraph (2), an industry in the United States shall be considered to exist if there is in the United States, with respect to the articles protected by the patent, copyright, trademark, or mask work concerned —

(A) Significant investment in plant and equipment;

(B) Significant employment of labor or capital; or

(C) Substantial investment in its exploitation, including engineering, research and development, or licensing.

(4) For the purposes of this section, the phrase "owner, importer, or consignee" includes any agent of the owner, importer, or consignee.

Complainants in an ITC proceeding are given a hearing before a Commission Administrative Law Judge (ALJ) who also exercises authority over discovery disputes and prehearing conferences. Prehearing and hearing procedures generally parallel pretrial and trial procedures of the federal courts, although they usually advance to and through trial more rapidly. The procedural rules are set forth in 19 C.F.R. Part 210. *See also* proposed changes to these procedural rules, set forth at 57 Fed. Reg. 52830 (1992). The ALJ's decision as to whether a violation has occurred and whether a remedy should be ordered is presented to the Commission as a recommendation. The Commission then makes a final determination and, if appropriate, issues a remedial order. Four of the Commission's six Commissioners must favor complainant for it to prevail.

A final determination of the Commission becomes effective immediately; however, the President of the United States has sixty days in which to disapprove the decision for policy reasons or to approve it by taking no action. The power to disapprove is rarely exercised. *But see In the Matter of Certain Alkaline Batteries*, 225 U.S.P.Q. 862 (Pres. Reagan, Jan. 4, 1985), *appeal dismissed*, 778 F.2d 1578 (Fed. Cir. 1985); *Young Engineers, Inc. v. ITC*, 721 F.2d 1305 (Fed. Cir. 1983). If the sixty days pass without action by the President, an appeal then may be taken to the Court of Appeals for the Federal Circuit.

An initial and important advantage to litigating before the ITC rather than in federal court is that a demonstration of personal jurisdiction over foreign manufacturers, which may not have the requisite "minimum contacts," is not required in § 337 actions. This is because the statute permits in rem orders, which act against goods, not parties, and therefore creates a separate subject matter jurisdiction independent of personal jurisdiction. *Sealed Air Corp. v. U.S. Int'l Trade Commission*, 645 F.2d 976, 986 (C.C.P.A. 1981).

The Commission is authorized to issue: (1) a general exclusion order directed against all infringing products; (2) a cease and desist order directed against a party; and (3) temporary relief during the pendency of an ITC proceeding in the form of an exclusion or cease and desist order. 19 U.S.C. §§ 1337(d), (e), (f). It cannot, however, award damages.

Section 337 is particularly useful to a complainant plagued by many infringers of a popular product. It affords the opportunity to stop all infringing imports in one action. A general exclusion order will cause their exclusion regardless of manufacturer, thereby providing relief even against unidentified infringers. The difficulties of enforcement encountered with federal court in personam decrees against foreign manufacturers are avoided to a large extent with ITC exclusion orders, which are enforced by the Customs Service at U.S. ports of entry. Cease and desist orders are effective against domestic importers of the infringing goods, and are enforceable in federal court. 19 U.S.C. § 1337(f).

Another advantage to ITC proceedings is the dispatch with which they are conducted. Section 337 requires completion of the proceedings within 12 months of publication of the notice of investigation in the Federal Register or, for more complicated cases, within 18 months. However, a complainant must be prepared for the concomitant extreme expedition of discovery and hearing schedules in prosecuting its case. Respondents who attempt to impede the discovery process risk sanctions and evidentiary presumptions against them. Respondents are allowed to raise "[a]ll legal and equitable defenses" under § 337(c) including, presumably, all defenses found in trademark law, *see, e.g.,* Ch. 7, *infra.* Respondent counterclaims, however, will not be considered in an ITC action.

For trade dress and unregistered marks, a successful complainant must prove (1) that it has a protectable trademark or trade dress (2) with which a likelihood of confusion among consumers is created by the trademark or trade dress of the imported goods at issue, and (3) that the effect or tendency of importation of the goods is to substantially injure or destroy (4) a domestic industry (5) that is efficiently and economically operated. Nos. (1) and (2) generally present typical trademark protection problems encountered in the federal courts. Since nationwide rights are being asserted under the statute, however, if the claimed mark or trade dress is not inherently distinctive, nationwide secondary meaning must be shown. *See In re Sneakers with Fabric Uppers & Rubber Soles,* 223 U.S.P.Q. 536, 539 (I.T.C. 1983). Domestic corporations with less than national areas of sale or reputation thus may be precluded from successfully bringing a complaint before the ITC.

The complainant also has the burden of demonstrating that the claimed trademark is not generic, *Sneakers with Fabric Uppers,* 223 U.S.P.Q. at 540, or that the claimed trade dress is not functional, *New England Butt Co. v. U.S. Int'l Trade Commission,* 756 F.2d 874 (Fed. Cir. 1985).

A domestic industry typically "consists of that part of complainant's business devoted to the manufacture, distribution and sale of the product bearing the allegedly infringed trademark," *Sneakers with Fabric Uppers,* 223 U.S.P.Q. at 543, but may consist of other domestic activities respecting the product bearing the trademark or trade dress at issue. *Compare Schaper Mfg. Co. v. U.S. Int'l Trade Commission,* 717 F.2d 1368, 1372-73 (Fed. Cir. 1983) (complainant's performance of some packaging, warehousing, distribution, advertising and quality control regarding toy trucks manufactured abroad held insufficient to constitute a domestic industry) with *In re Certain Cube Puzzles,* 219 U.S.P.Q. 322, 334-35 (I.T.C. 1982) (complainant's repair and packaging of, and extensive quality control over, cube puzzles manufactured abroad, which added value to them, held significant enough to constitute a domestic industry). *See also Bally/Midway Mfg. Co. v. ITC,* 714 F.2d 1117, 1120-23 (Fed. Cir. 1983), where the court reversed an ITC finding of no domestic industry, holding that complainant did have such an industry for its RALLY-X video games at the time the complaint was filed, if not subsequently as a result of respondent's acts, and that "there is nothing in the statute which requires that an industry must be of any particular size," citing *In re Von Clemm,* 229 F.2d 441, 444 (C.C.P.A. 1955).

Once the existence of a domestic industry has been established, the "efficiently and economically operated" statutory requirement is easily met. In *Sneakers with Fabric Uppers*, 223 U.S.P.Q. at 544, the ITC stated: "Indicia of efficient and economic operation include: Use of modern equipment, effective quality control programs, competitiveness, successful sales efforts, and profitability of the subject product." To date no respondent has ever successfully demonstrated "inefficient and uneconomic" operation of a domestic industry.

"Substantial injury" or "tendency to substantially injure" is proven by evidence of lost sales, lost profits or lost customers. *See, e.g., In re Certain Cube Puzzles*, 219 U.S.P.Q. 322, 336 (I.T.C. 1982) (lost accounts and profits established requisite injury; "it does not matter that [complainant] did not suffer a loss or had increasing profits, so long as it lost profits to the imported [products]"); *Sneakers with Fabric Uppers*, 223 U.S.P.Q. at 544 (complainant successfully relied on "declining sales and profits, a deteriorating cash flow situation, employee layoffs and production cutbacks").

In *Bally/Midway*, 714 F.2d at 1124, the court stated that "[w]here the unfair practice is the importation of products that infringe a domestic industry's copyright, trademark or patent right, even a relatively small loss of sales may establish, under Section 337(a), the requisite injury to the portion of the complainant's business devoted to the exploitation of those intellectual property rights." In a subsequent case, however, the same court rejected complainant's contention that injury should be inferred any time the ITC finds infringement, regardless of whether damage to the domestic industry is shown, stating, "Section 337 does not function merely as the international extension of our patent, trademark and copyright laws." *Textron, Inc. v. U.S. Int'l Trade Commission*, 224 U.S.P.Q. 625, 631 (Fed. Cir. 1985). Instead, "[e]ven in the context of patent, trademark or copyright infringement, the domestic industry must normally establish that the infringer holds, or threatens to hold, a significant share of the domestic market in the covered articles or has made a significant amount of sales of the articles." (*Id.* at 632).

The ITC also is statutorily obligated to consider the public interest in every case. Section 337(d) requires the Commission to consider "the effect of [the] exclusion [of imports] upon the public health and welfare, competitive conditions in the United States economy, the production of like or directly competitive articles in the United States and United States consumers. . . ." A staff attorney represents the public interest in all ITC proceedings, and even where the Commission finds a violation of § 337, the public's interest in an open economy may dictate that no remedy be ordered. *See, e.g., In re Certain Automatic Crankpin Grinders*, 205 U.S.P.Q. 71, 80 (I.T.C. 1979) (due to public interest considerations, no remedy ordered for violation of § 337 via patent infringement). An ITC finding that public interest considerations outweigh a complainant's need for relief is extremely rare.

As a result of the statutory public interest element, a complainant must establish the economic side of the case and prove infringement even when a respondent defaults:

> A finding of a violation of section 337 requires something more than a mere showing that a respondent has defaulted. The remedy of an exclusion order,

unlike the relief available in the federal courts, sometimes affects persons other than the named parties respondent. For that reason, a default does not per se establish complainant's right to relief. . . . [Instead] reasonable effort . . . to produce substantial, reliable and probative evidence to establish a prima facie case of violation [is required].

In re Certain Food Slicers, 219 U.S.P.Q. 176, 178-79 (I.T.C. 1981). *See also In re Sneakers with Fabric Uppers & Rubber Soles*, 223 U.S.P.Q. 536, 537-38 (I.T.C. 1983) (default proceeding).

In the past, the ITC has rarely issued temporary relief orders (similar to preliminary injunctions) because of the already expedited nature of its proceedings. This, coupled with the Commission's inability to award damages, led many respondents simply to default and sell off their inventory during the 12- or 18-month investigation period rather than incur the expense of defending themselves. A recent Second Circuit decision may discourage this practice among some future respondents. In *Union Mfg. Co., Inc. v. Hans Baek Trading Co.*, 763 F.2d 42, 45 (2d Cir. 1985), the court held that ITC trademark decisions have *res judicata* effect in federal court where the parties are the same and "when the issues raised and the procedures available in the ITC proceeding are in all important respects the same as those in District Court." Consequently, a respondent that defaults or loses before the ITC now may be deemed already to have lost on the infringement issue in a subsequent federal court action, with only the issue of damages remaining for trial.

Nonetheless, under some circumstances a complainant needing fast relief from the widespread infringing imports may prefer moving for preliminary injunctions in federal court against the major offenders while simultaneously seeking from the ITC a general exclusion order as well as cease and desist orders against domestic importers. *See, e.g., In re Certain Cube Puzzles*, 219 U.S.P.Q. 322, 325, 337 (I.T.C. 1982).

In 1988, the Tariff Act was amended to delete the requirements to prove injury to a domestic industry, and efficient and economic operation of the domestic industry, where the plaintiff seeks to protect a federally registered trademark. As a result, the owner of the registered trademark need only prove the validity of the registration and infringement, and that a domestic industry relating to the goods bearing the mark exists or "is in the process of being established." The period of determining whether to grant temporary relief also has been shortened.

See generally, Duvall, *Federal Unfair Competition Actions: Practice & Procedure Under Section 337 of the Tariff Act* (1991 ed.); 1a Gilson, *Trademark Protection and Practice*, § 8.15 (1993 ed.); McCarthy, *Trademarks and Unfair Competition*, § 29:23 (3d ed. 1992); Katz & Cohen, *Effective Remedies Against the Importation of Knock-offs: A Comparison of Remedies Available from the International Trade Commission, Customs and Federal Courts*, 66 J.P.O.S. 660 (1984).

CHAPTER **4**

LOSS OF RIGHTS

§ 4.01   Introduction

Trademark rights are lost when the mark no longer signifies the source of the *[Generic* goods or services. Section 45 of the Lanham Act, 15 U.S.C. § 1127, provides that *or* a mark shall be deemed to be abandoned "when its use has been discontinued with *abandoned]* intent not to resume such use" or "when any course of conduct of the registrant, including acts of omission as well as commission, causes the mark to become the generic name for the goods or services on or in connection with which it is used, or otherwise to lose its significance as a mark." Under this provision, therefore, rights in a mark are lost when it comes to signify or denominate the product itself or when, by acts of omission or commission, it is abandoned, assigned without goodwill or licensed in gross.

§ 4.02   Generic Terms

Diamond, TRADEMARK PROBLEMS AND HOW TO AVOID THEM

187–190 (1973) *

Brand names can be over-sold. If your product is way ahead of all its competitors, this may be the time to look around for danger signals and take preventive action if necessary. When a product is so successful that the public adopts the brand name as the name of the product itself — as distinguished from one particular manufacturer's version of that product — then the brand name has passed into the language and the manufacturer who originated it no longer has the exclusive right to use it.

Some horrible examples of valuable brand names actually lost in this way are: aspirin, cellophane, linoleum, milk of magnesia and shredded wheat. Each of these once represented the product of a single manufacturer, who obviously invested substantial sums in building up the brand. Each of them reached the point where it came to mean the product rather than merely a source for the product, and competitors won the right to use the name for their own versions of it. Technically, the brand name had become a generic term for the product, and generic terms are incapable of functioning as trademarks.

---

* Copyright ©1973 by Sidney A. Diamond. Copyright ©1955 through 1972 by Crain Communication, Inc. Reprinted by permission of National Textbook Company, Chicago, IL, publisher.

(Matthew Bender & Co., Inc.)   (Pub. 725)

There are ways of guarding against this result. Explanatory footnotes in advertising are a common technique for putting the public on notice that the manufacturer claims trademark rights in his brand name, and that it is not just the name of the product itself. Du Pont, for example, has used this: " 'Orlon' is Du Pont's registered trademark for its acrylic fiber." RCA Victor footnoted Victrola with the legend: "RCA Trademark for record players." Slogans can perform a similar function, perhaps even more effectively. The Eastman Kodak Company from time to time used: "If it isn't an Eastman, it isn't a Kodak." At a later period, its advertisements carried, underneath the Kodak logo, a line reading: " — a trade-mark since 1888." Another typical footnote reads: "TABASCO is the registered trademark for the brand of pepper sauce made by McIlhenny Co."

Some companies place advertisements devoted specifically to education for proper trademark usage in consumer and trade publications. Minnesota Mining (for Scotch), Du Pont (for Orlon) and the Technicolor Corporation have used such campaigns; Du Pont also issues instruction booklets on the correct manner of using its registered marks.

The appearance of a company's brand name editorially in lower case type is a specific danger signal. Many manufacturers react by sending a form letter to the editor pointing out the unfavorable implication that the brand name has become just a word in the language, and requesting initial caps and quotation marks in all future uses.

The problem discussed here is particularly acute when a new product is to be introduced. Care must be taken that the brand name coined for the new item is used in such a way that it identifies the source of the product and that it does not become the name by which the public identifies the product itself. This can be done by using the words "brand" or "trademark" to show the manufacturer's intention. But that is only a beginning, because the purchasing public may not keep such a fine point in mind.

A superior method is to use the brand name in association with the name of the general type of product involved. For example, the family medicine cabinet displays: "BISODOL Antacid Tablet" and "CORICIDIN Cold Relief Tablets." Legal commentators are fond of suggesting that if the Bayer Company had marked its famous product "ASPIRIN brand of acetylsalicylic acid" or even just "ASPIRIN headache pills" — instead of "BAYER ASPIRIN" — it probably never would have lost its trademark rights. Q-Tips, Inc., which was forced to defend its trademark in court and did so successfully against the claim that it had become generic, labels its packages: "QTIPS Cotton Swabs."

Another way to guard against public misuse or misunderstanding of a brand name is to apply it to more than a single item. Johnson & Johnson, for example, has a whole line of Band-Aid products. And Vaseline is a well-known brand of hair tonic as well as the trademark for various types of petroleum jelly.

. . . .

A special aspect of this question is the patented product. The existence of a patent means that the manufacturer has a legal monopoly for seventeen years; nobody else can make the product without his consent. If that manufacturer exercises his monopoly, his planning should include both a brand name for the product and some additional word or words by which the public can identify it. Otherwise, the brand name will be the only designation the product has; when the patent expires and competitors become free to make the product, they will automatically acquire the right to use the brand name too. This is precisely what happened in the case of shredded wheat, among others. The reason for this rule of law is that the original manufacturer would be able to get the effect of an illegal extension of his patent monopoly unless competitors were free to call the product by its name — otherwise they would be unable to identify it in the way the public had learned to call for it.

DUPONT CELLOPHANE CO. v. WAXED PRODUCTS CO.

United States Court of Appeals, Second Circuit
85 F.2d 75 (1936)

Augustus N. Hand, Circuit Judge.

This is a suit brought by the complainant, a wholly owned subsidiary of E. I. DuPont de Nemours & Co., for the infringement by the defendant of the alleged trademark "Cellophane" through using the same in connection with goods not of the complainant's manufacture.

. . . .

The trial judge having found that the complainant at one time had the right to prevent the use of the word "cellophane" by others concluded that this right could only cease, if voluntarily abandoned. Hence much of the opinion of the court below was devoted to showing that there was no abandonment. We do not differ with it in respect to the question of abandonment and think that it was fairly established that the complainant endeavored to retain its rights and that abandonment, which depends on a voluntary surrender of the trademark to the public, did not occur. *Hanover Milling Co. v. Metcalf,* 240 U.S. 403, 419; *Saxlehner v. Eisner & Mendelson Co.,* 179 U.S. 19

In our opinion this case does not properly turn on abandonment, nor does it even turn on the question whether the word cellophane was at one time more than a descriptive term. The real problem is what it meant to the buying public during the period covered by the present suit. In other words, did it simply mean a transparent glycerinated cellulose hydrate regenerated from viscose, and nothing more, or did it mean such an article of commerce manufactured by or originating with the complainant?

The court below made a finding that the name "characterizes a single thing coming from a single source, and is a valid trade-mark; even if it should be shown that the product is more emphasized than the producer or that the identity of the producer is unknown." This finding seems to us not only not warranted by the evidence but clearly disproved.

The product and use of cellophane in commerce is attributed to one Brandenberger, of Bezons, France, at about the year 1909. He coined the word "cellophane" as suggesting a product made of cellulose and transparent, and registered "La Cellophane" written in a fancy script as a trade-mark. It would have served as a useful trade-mark, at least in the beginning, if it had not almost immediately lost ground as such because it was employed to describe the article itself. Indeed, no other descriptive word was adopted. In answer to the question whether "Cellophane was the name by which that new product was christened by Mr. Brandenberger," Mr. Yerkes, the DuPont president, said: "I considered that Cellophane was the name which he gave to the product which he invented." That Brandenberger used the word cellophane in a generic sense is evident from his United States patents Nos. 1,226,897 and 1,406,148. In the first he said: "The invention relates to a label made of cellophane." And in the second he not only used the word generically in the specification, but he also had a claim reading thus: "4. A band, as claimed in Claim 2 in which the cellulosic material consists of cellophane."

. . . .

On December 28, 1923, DuPont applied for registration of the name "DuPont Cellophane" in an oval frame as a trade-mark and registration was granted on July 22, 1924. It never used "La Cellophane" or "Cellophane" in distinctive script, the old marks of the French company, until 1932, when it applied for re-registration of those marks in which it claimed rights by assignment. In January, 1924, Yerkes wrote a letter to the Patent Office, in support of the application to register the mark "DuPont Cellophane" in an oval frame, and argued that cellophane should be entered in Class 50 as "Merchandise not otherwise classified." With his letter he sent the department a copy of the article of December, 1923, in the *DuPont Magazine* from which we have already quoted. He used the word "cellophane" throughout his letter in a generic sense, spelling it with a small "c. "

In August, 1924, the DuPont Company began to advertise to the candy trade and published a double page advertisement in the "Manufacturing Confectioner" with the heading: "Cellophane — the new superwrap is now available for your holiday line," and below it the new mark "DuPont Cellophane" in an oval frame. In December, 1924, there was an article entitled: "Selling with Cellophane." "How manufacturers and others are using this material to speed up sales." It described the development of the product in France and in this country and its many uses for enclosing delicate fabrics on display at dress-goods counters, for making artificial flowers, and beads, for trimming hats and for wrapping fruits, nuts, cakes, candies, soaps, perfumes, cigarette packages, and cigars.

. . . .

To the question whether "cellophane" is a trade-mark, directed at the instigation of the DuPont Company to 17,000 selected subscribers of the *Delineator, Good Housekeeping, Saturday Evening Post*, and *Ladies Home Journal*, 72 per cent of the subscribers answered that it was. This left 28 per cent to whom the word gave no indication of origin. The answers did not show that the source was DuPont, but only that the goods were manufactured by one concern. Moreover, as they were induced by flattering letters from the magazines and by offers of prizes in return for prompt replies, they might well have stimulated a search for a registered trademark that theretofore had been unknown. Such proofs have no great weight.

The course of conduct of the complainant and its predecessors, and especially complainant's advertising campaign, tended to make cellophane a generic term descriptive of the product rather than of its origin and, in our opinion, made it so to at least a very large part of the trade.

The expiration in 1928 of United States patents No 991,267 and No. 1,002,634 to Brandenberger for processes for manufacturing and drying films terminated any right the complainant had to the exclusive use of the name cellophane so far as it had become merely descriptive of the product itself. *Singer Mfg. Co. v. June Mfg. Co.*, 163 U.S. 169; *Linoleum Manufacturing Company v. Nairn*, L.R. 7 Ch. Div. 834. The fact that it had registered "Cellophane" as a trade-mark would give it no right to monopolize a term useful to designate a commercial article. Others might employ it to designate their goods but should guard against misleading any customer who might intend to buy cellophane manufactured by the DuPont Company. . . .

. . . .

But neither the absence of a patent nor its complete invalidity will prevent a word from obtaining a generic meaning. As Justice Bradley said in *Celluloid Mfg. Co. v. Cellonite Mfg. Co.*, (C.C.) 32 F. 94, 98, about the word "celluloid":

> As a common appellative, the public has a right to use the word for all purposes of designating the article or product, except one, — it cannot use it as a trademark, or in the way that a trade-mark is used, by applying it to and stamping it upon the articles. The complainant alone can do this, and any other person doing it will infringe the complainant's right. Perhaps the defendant would have a right to advertise that it manufactures celluloid. But this use of the word is very different from using it as a trade-mark stamped upon its goods.

In the case at bar the defendant has never used either the words "cellophane" or "DuPont Cellophane," with or without the oval, on its goods. It has merely filled orders for cellophane with its own product.

The District Court erred in concluding that "the trade-mark cellophane does not depend upon what was in the customer's mind" and in deciding the case on the theory that the public understanding as to the meaning of the word was immaterial. Such a theory is out of accord with the essence of the law of trade-marks. The rights of the complainant must be based upon a wrong which the defendant has done to it by misleading customers as to the origin of the goods sold and thus taking away its trade. Such rights are not founded on a bare title to a word or symbol but on a cause of action to prevent deception. It, therefore, makes no difference what efforts or money the DuPont Company expended in order to persuade the public that "cellophane" means an article of DuPont manufacture. So far as it did not succeed in actually converting the world to its gospel it can have no relief.

Some people still think of Du Pont

. . . .

In the present case the word "cellophane" ordinarily signifies the cellulose product we have been discussing and nothing more, but to certain persons it is probable that it means the complainant's goods. The situation, therefore, somewhat resembles that in *Singer Mfg. Co. v. June Mfg. Co.*, 163 U.S. 169, *Bayer Co. v. United Drug Co.*, (D.C.) 272 F. 505, and *Ford v. Foster*, (1872) L.R. 7 Ch. App. 611, so often found in litigations involving infringement of trade-marks and unfair competition where the decree should adjust the somewhat conflicting rights of the parties. The defendant should be allowed to use the word cellophane unconditionally in dealing with those to whom it means no more than the product and should be able to fill orders for cellophane received from such persons either with Sylvania cellophane or any other cellophane. But as the complainant's use of the word "cellophane" has had a wide publicity, there may be some persons who desire DuPont cellophane. Accordingly, it seems to us in the interest of justice that, when filling orders for cellophane, the defendant should state that the product sold is Sylvania cellophane or the cellophane of whomsoever may be the maker, and need state nothing more. The defendant may likewise use the word cellophane in its advertisements provided it shall prefix the maker's name as a possessive.

Most prefix this with name when selling cellophane

. . . .

Decree modified as above without costs upon this appeal to either party.

KELLOGG CO. v. NATIONAL BISCUIT CO.

Unfair competition

United States Supreme Court
305 U.S. 111 (1938)

MR. JUSTICE BRANDEIS delivered the opinion of the Court.

This suit was brought in the federal court for Delaware by National Biscuit Company against Kellogg Company to enjoin alleged unfair competition by the manufacture and sale of the breakfast food commonly known as shredded wheat. The competition was alleged to be unfair mainly because Kellogg Company uses, like the plaintiff, the name shredded wheat and, like the plaintiff, produces its biscuit in pillow-shaped form.

Kellog did shredded wheat, enjoined in D.C.

. . . .

The plaintiff concedes that is does not possess the exclusive right to make shredded wheat. But it claims the exclusive right to the trade name "Shredded Wheat" and the exclusive right to make shredded wheat biscuits pillow-shaped. It charges that the defendant, by using the name and shape, and otherwise, is passing off, or enabling others to pass off, Kellogg goods for those of the plaintiff. Kellogg Company denies that the plaintiff is entitled to the exclusive use of the name or of the pillow-shape; denies any passing off; asserts that it has used every reasonable effort to distinguish its product from that of the plaintiff; and contends that in honestly competing for a part of the market for shredded wheat it is exercising the common right freely to manufacture and sell an article of commerce unprotected by patent.   — *Kellog 2nies P has exclusive right.*

Ct: Generic

First. The plaintiff has no exclusive right to the use of the term "Shredded Wheat" as a trade name. For that is the generic term of the article, which describes it with a fair degree of accuracy; and is the term by which the biscuit in pillow-shaped form is generally known by the public. Since the term is generic, the original maker of the product acquired no exclusive right to use it. As Kellogg Company had the right to make the article, it had, also, the right to use the term by which the public knows it. *Compare Saxlehner v. Wagner,* 216 U.S. 375; *Holzapfel's Compositions Co. v. Rahtien's American Composition Co.,* 183 U.S. 1. Ever since 1894 the article has been known to the public as shredded wheat. For many years, there was no attempt to use the term "Shredded Wheat" as a trade-mark. When in 1905 plaintiff's predecessor, Natural Food Company, applied for registration of the words "Shredded Whole Wheat" as a trademark under the so-called "ten year clause" of the Act of February 20, 1905, c. 592, § 5, 33 Stat. 725, William E. Williams gave notice of opposition. Upon the hearing it appeared that Williams had, as early as 1894, built a machine for making shredded wheat, and that he made and sold its product as "Shredded Whole Wheat." The Commissioner of Patents refused registration. The Court of Appeals of the District of Columbia affirmed his decision, holding that "these words accurately and aptly describe an article of food which . . . has been produced . . . for more than ten years. . . ." *Natural Food Co. v. Williams,* 30 App. D.C. 348.

1905 – determined generic

Moreover, the name "Shredded Wheat," as well as the product, the process and the machinery employed in making it, has been dedicated to the public. The basic patent for the product and for the process of making it, and many other patents for special machinery to be used in making the article, issued. . . . In those patents the term "shredded" is repeatedly used as descriptive of the product. The basic patent expired October 15, 1912; the others soon after. Since during the life of the patents "Shredded Wheat" was the general designation of the patented product, there passed to the public upon the expiration of the patent, not only the right to make the article as it was made during the patent period, but also the right to apply thereto the name by which it had become known. . . .

When Patent expired so did trademark

It is contended that the plaintiff has the exclusive right to the name "Shredded Wheat," because those words acquired the "secondary meaning" of shredded wheat made at Niagara Falls by the plaintiff's predecessor. There is no basis here for applying the doctrine of secondary meaning. The evidence shows only that due to the long period in which the plaintiff or its predecessor was the only manufacturer of the product, many people have come to associate the product, and as a consequence the name by which the product is generally known, with the plaintiff's factory at Niagara Falls. But to establish a trade name in the term "shredded wheat" the plaintiff must show more than a subordinate meaning which applies to it. It must show that the primary significance of the term in the minds of the consuming public is not the product but the producer. This it has not done. The showing which it has made does not entitle it to the exclusive use of the term shredded wheat but merely

2ndary meaning
no good.
Can't be primary meaning of good

entitles it to require that the defendant use reasonable care to inform the public of the source of its product.

The plaintiff seems to contend that even if Kellogg Company acquired upon the expiration of the patents the right to use the name shredded wheat, the right was lost by delay. The argument is that Kellogg Company, although the largest producer of breakfast cereals in the country, did not seriously attempt to make shredded wheat or to challenge plaintiff's right to that name until 1927, and that meanwhile plaintiff's predecessor had expended more than $17,000,000 in making the name a household word and identifying the product with its manufacture. Those facts are without legal significance. Kellogg Company's right was not one dependent upon diligent exercise. Like every other member of the public, it was, and remained, free to make shredded wheat when it chose to do so; and to call the product by its generic name. The only obligation resting upon Kellogg Company was to identify its own product lest it be mistaken for that of the plaintiff.

Second. The plaintiff has not the exclusive right to sell shredded wheat in the form of a pillow-shaped biscuit — the form in which the article became known to the public. That is the form in which shredded wheat was made under the basic patent. The patented machines used were designed to produce only the pillow-shaped biscuits. And a design patent was taken out to cover the pillow-shaped form. Hence, upon expiration of the patents the form, as well as the name, was dedicated to the public. As was said in *Singer Mfg. Co. v. June Mfg. Co.,* [163 U.S. 169], p. 185:

> It is self evident that on the expiration of a patent the monopoly granted by it ceases to exist, and the right to make the thing formerly covered by the patent becomes public property. It is upon this condition that the patent is granted. It follows, as a matter of course, that on the termination of the patent there passes to the public the right to make the machine in the form in which it was constructed during the patent. We may, therefore, dismiss without further comment the complaint, as to the form in which the defendant made his machines.

Where an article may be manufactured by all, a particular manufacturer can no more assert exclusive rights in a form in which the public has become accustomed to see the article and which, in the minds of the public, is primarily associated with the article rather than a particular producer, than it can in the case of a name with similar connections in the public mind. Kellogg Company was free to use the pillow-shaped form, subject only to the obligation to identify its product lest it be mistaken for that of the plaintiff.

Third. The question remains whether Kellogg Company in exercising its right to use the name "Shredded Wheat" and the pillow-shaped biscuit, is doing so fairly. Fairness requires that it be done in a manner which reasonably distinguishes its product from that of plaintiff.

Each company sells its biscuits only in cartons. The standard Kellogg carton contains fifteen biscuits; the plaintiff's twelve. The Kellogg cartons are distinctive. They do not resemble those used by the plaintiff either in size, form, or color. And the difference in the labels is striking. The Kellogg cartons bear in bold script the names "Kellogg's Whole Wheat Biscuit" or "Kellogg's Shredded Whole Wheat Biscuit" so sized and spaced as to strike the eye as being a Kellogg product. It is true that on some of its cartons it had a picture of two shredded wheat biscuits in a bowl of milk which was quite similar to one of the plaintiff's registered trademarks. But the name Kellogg was so prominent on all of the defendant's cartons as to minimize the possibility of confusion.

Some hotels, restaurants, and lunchrooms serve biscuits not in cartons and guests so served may conceivably suppose that a Kellogg biscuit served is one of the plaintiff's make. But no person familiar with plaintiff's product would be misled. The Kellogg biscuit is about two thirds the size of plaintiff's; and differs from it in appearance. Moreover, the field in which deception could be practiced is negligibly small. Only 2½ per cent of the Kellogg biscuits are sold to hotels, restaurants and lunchrooms. Of those so sold 98 per cent are sold in individual cartons containing two biscuits. These cartons are distinctive and bear prominently the Kellogg name. To put upon the individual biscuit some mark which would identify it as the Kellogg product is not commercially possible. Relatively few biscuits will be removed from the individual cartons before they reach the consumer. The obligation resting upon Kellogg Company is not to insure that every purchaser will know it to be the maker but to use every reasonable means to prevent confusion.

It is urged that all possibility of deception or confusion would be removed if Kellogg Company should refrain from using the name "Shredded Wheat" and adopt some form other than the pillow-shape. But the name and form are integral parts of the goodwill of the article. To share fully in the goodwill, it must use the name and the pillow-shape. And in the goodwill Kellogg Company is as free to share as the plaintiff. *Compare William R. Warner & Co. v. Eli Lilly & Co.*, 265 U.S. 526, 528, 530. Moreover, the pillow-shape must be used for another reason. The evidence is persuasive that this form is functional — that the cost of the biscuit would be increased and its high quality lessened if some other form were substituted for the pillow-shape.

Kellogg Company is undoubtedly sharing in the goodwill of the article known as "Shredded Wheat"; and thus is sharing in a market which was created by the skill and judgment of plaintiff's predecessor and has been widely extended by vast expenditures in advertising persistently made. But that is not unfair. Sharing in the goodwill of an article unprotected by patent or trade-mark is the exercise of a right possessed by all and in the free exercise of which the consuming public is deeply interested. There is no evidence of passing off or deception on the part of the Kellogg Company; and it has taken every reasonable precaution to prevent confusion or the practice of deception in the sale of its product.

Fourth. By its "clarifying" decree, the Circuit Court of Appeals enjoined Kellogg Company from using the picture of the two shredded wheat biscuits in the bowl only in connection with an injunction against manufacturing the pillow-shaped biscuits and the use of the term shredded wheat, on the grounds of unfair competition. The use of this picture was not enjoined on the independent ground of trade-mark infringement. Since the National Biscuit Company did not petition for certiorari, the question whether use of the picture is a violation of that trade-mark although Kellogg Company is free to use the name and the pillow-shaped biscuit is not here for review.

Decrees reversed with direction to dismiss the bill.

NOTES ON GENERIC TERMS

(1) A term is generic when its principal significance to the public is to indicate the product or service itself, rather than its source. *Feathercombs, Inc. v. Sole Products Corp.*, 306 F.2d 251 (2d Cir. 1962), *cert. denied,* 371 U.S. 910 (1962). As stated by Judge Friendly in *Abercrombie & Fitch Co. v. Hunting World, Inc.*, 537 F.2d 4, 9 (2d Cir. 1976), "[a] generic term is one that refers, or has come to be understood as referring, to the genus of which the particular product is a species." It is the *public's* perception of the trademark which determines the extent of the rights possessed by its owner. What effect on a determination of genericness should the availability of other generic terms for the product have? In *Bayer Co. v. United Drug Co.*, 272 F. 505 (S.D.N.Y. 1921), the issue was whether Bayer's originally coined trademark "Aspirin" had become a generic term for the chemical compound "acetyl salicylic [sic] acid." Judge Learned Hand stated the test as follows:

> The single question, as I view it, in all these cases, is merely one of fact: What do these buyers understand by the word for whose use the parties are contending? If they understand by it only the kind of goods sold, then, I take it, makes no difference whatever efforts the plaintiff has made to get them to understand more.

Bayer's own generic use of the term on its labels stating "Bayer Tablets of Aspirin" was instrumental in causing Judge Hand to hold that "Aspirin" indeed had become generic to consumers. However, Judge Hand did find that manufacturing chemists, physicians and retail druggists recognized "Aspirin" as plaintiff's trademark, and that for them "acetyl salicylic acid" was the generic term. As a result, defendant was enjoined from selling the drug to this group under the name "Aspirin," except in small packages (50 tablets or less) for resale to consumers.

(2) Courts often examine the usage of a term in print media as evidence of its significance to the public. In *S.S. Kresge v. United Factory Outlet*, 598 F.2d 694, 696 (1st Cir. 1979), the court noted, "A survey of well-known dictionaries reveals that the term 'mart' is generic since it is another word for store or market"; preliminary injunctive relief sought by the operator of stores named "The Mart" against advertising use of that word by operator of "K-Mart" stores accordingly was denied. *See also In re Minnetonka*, 212 U.S.P.Q. 772 (T.T.A.B. 1981), in which the many references to "soft soap" in dictionaries and historical sources constituted convincing evidence that "softsoap" for soap product is generic and not registrable; *Eastern Airlines, Inc. v. New York Airlines, Inc.*, 218 U.S.P.Q. 71 (S.D.N.Y. 1983), in which dictionaries, Shakespeare and Walt Whitman were cited in support of the court's finding that "Air Shuttle" is generic, and *Team Central, Inc. v. Xerox Corp.*, 606 F. Supp. 1408 (D. Minn. 1985), where the court relied on the dictionary definition in finding the use of "Team" in "Team Xerox" generic, stating "once a

term is proven to be generic, evidence of purported buyer association of the term with a single source will not change the result," quoting McCarthy, *supra*. Expert witnesses also may be successfully utilized in establishing that a term is generic. In *WSM, Inc. v. Hilton*, 724 F.2d 1320 (8th Cir. 1984), for example, an expert in the field of regional English helped establish that "opry" was a dialectical variation of "opera" used as a generic term for a show consisting of country music, dancing and comedy routines.

(3) Could a trademark which became generic ever regain its source-indicating significance? In *Singer Mfg. Co. v. June Mfg. Co.*, 163 U.S. 169, 203 (1886), the Supreme Court held SINGER for sewing machines generic, stating that the word "had become public property, and the defendant had a right to use it." Years later in *Singer Mfg. Co. v. Briley*, 207 F.2d 519, 521 n. 3 (5th Cir. 1953), the court held that the Singer Company had "recaptured from the public domain the name 'Singer' . . . [and it] has thus become a valid trademark." 207 F.2d at 521 n. 3. *See also Singer Mfg. Co. v. Redlich*, 109 F. Supp. 623, 624 (S.D. Cal. 1952), where the court held SINGER a valid trademark and declined to distinguish *Singer v. June*, relying instead on the company's long history of extensive use of the mark and subsequent unreported lower court decisions recognizing its rights. Could a term which is generic ab initio, e.g. "chair," ever gain source-indicating significance? *See Kellogg Co. v. National Biscuit Co., supra*; Derenberg, *Shredded Wheat — The Still-Born Trade Marks*, 16 N.Y.U. L.Q. Rev. 376 (1939).

(4) Judge Friendly once observed that "no matter how much money and effort the user of a generic term has poured into promoting the sale of its merchandise and what success it has achieved in securing public identification, it cannot deprive competing manufacturers of the right to call an article by its name." *Abercrombie & Fitch Co. v. Hunting World, Inc., supra* Note (1). In *Miller Brewing Co. v. G. Heilemann Brewing Co.*, 561 F.2d 75 (7th Cir. 1977), the court found that the term "lite" or "light" as applied to a low calorie beer was generic and therefore could not be appropriated as a trademark. It reasoned that:

> other brewers whose beers have qualities that make them "light" as that word has commonly been used remain free to call their beer "light." Otherwise a manufacturer could remove a common descriptive word from the public domain by investing his goods with an additional quality, thus gaining the exclusive right to call his wine "rose," his whiskey "blended," or his bread "white."

Compare Anheuser-Busch, Inc. v. The Stroh Brewery Co., 750 F.2d 631 (8th Cir. 1984) ("LA" for reduced or low alcohol beer). *See also In re Miller Brewing Co.*, 226 U.S.P.Q. 666 (T.T.A.B. 1985) (Applicant's distinctive display of LITE for low calorie beer granted registration).

But there is nothing immutable about words. Their meanings change not infrequently. If a word is generic, then it does not signify source; confusion as to source cannot result from its use by another, and such use will not be prohibited. *See also Loglan Institute, Inc. v. The Logical Language Group, Inc.*, 962 F.2d 1038 (Fed. Cir. 1992) (LOGLAN generic for an invented logical language); *Best Buy Warehouse v. Best Buy Co.*, 920 F.2d 536 (8th Cir. 1990) (BEST BUY generic as used in the names BEST BUY WAREHOUSE, BEST BUY OFFICE FURNITURE and BEST BUY OFFICE WAREHOUSE), *cert. denied*, 111 S. Ct. 2893 (1991); *A.J. Canfield Co. v. Vess Beverages, Inc.*, 859 F.2d 36 (7th Cir. 1988) (CHOCO-LATE FUDGE generic for diet chocolate sodas); *Murphy Door Bed Co. v. Interior Sleep Systems, Inc.*, 874 F.2d 95 (2d Cir. 1989) (MURPHY BED generic for wall beds); *National Conference of Bar Examiners v. Multistate Legal Studies*, 692 F.2d 478 (7th Cir. 1982), *cert. denied*, 104 S. Ct. 69 (1983) ("Multistate Bar Examina-tion"); *Reese Publishing Co. v. Hampton Int'l Communications*, 620 F.2d 7 (2d Cir. 1980) ("Video Buyer's Guide" for a magazine); *cf. Texas Pig Stands, Inc. v. Hard Rock Cafe Int'l, Inc.*, 951 F.2d 684 (5th Cir. 1992) (PIG SANDWICH not generic for barbecued pork sandwich); *H. Marvin Ginn Corp. v. International Assn. of Fire Chiefs*, 228 U.S.P.Q. 528 (Fed. Cir. 1986) ("Fire Chief" not generic for fire-fighting magazine). *See* Note, *Trademarks and Generic Words: An Effect-On-Competition Test*, 51 U. Chi. L. Rev. 868 (1984). However, measures may be taken to help prevent a distinctive term from becoming generic. *See, e.g., E.I. DuPont de Nemours & Co. v. Yoshida International, Inc.*, 393 F. Supp. 502, 507 (E.D.N.Y. 1975), in which the court cited the plaintiff's successful and "vigilant trademark education and protection program" for TEFLON for a non-stick finish included instruction of salespeople, industrial buyers and others as to correct usage in advertising and business correspondence; a publication on correct usage distributed to customers; "extensive surveillance by its legal and advertising departments as well as the outside advertising agency," with misuses promptly responded to; and "protective trademark advertising to impart to the general public the understanding that TEFLON symbolizes DuPont's non-stick finish"; and *Selchow & Righter Co. v. McGraw Hill Book Co.*, 580 F.2d 25, 27 (2d Cir. 1978), where the court granted a preliminary injunction "at least in part" because defendant's book entitled THE COMPLETE SCRABBLE DICTIONARY might render generic plaintiff's mark SCRABBLE for a word game. *See also Nestle Co., Inc. v. Chester's Market, Inc.*, 571 F. Supp. 763 (D. Conn. 1983), in which "Toll House" for chocolate chip cookies was held generic. That holding was subsequently vacated pursuant to a settlement agreement between the parties. *Nestle Co., Inc. v. Chester's Market, Inc.*, 756 F.2d 280 (2d Cir. 1985). In what ways might the public be educated as to the intended trademark significance of a term in advertising and on labels?

(5) In *King-Seeley Thermos Co. v. Aladdin Industries, Inc.*, 321 F.2d 577 (2d Cir. 1963), King-Seeley's belated attempts to educate the public and rescue its registered THERMOS trademark from the public domain were unsuccessful. King-Seeley argued that the availability of an easily used generic name, vacuum bottle, distinguished its case from the *Aspirin* and *Cellophane* cases, *supra*. The Court rejected this argument, stating, "the test is not what is available as an alternative to the public, but what the public's understanding is of the word it uses." Despite its finding that "Thermos" was a generic term, the Court allowed King-Seeley to use "Thermos" as it had in the past, with a capital "T" and the federal registration symbol, while defendant was ordered to always use the lower case "t," preceded by defendant's company name, and also to refrain from using "original" and "genuine" in conjunction with "thermos." Similarly, in *Windsurfing International v. Fred Ostermann GmbH*, 613 F. Supp. 933 (S.D.N.Y. 1985), *modified*, 782 F.2d

995 (Fed. Cir. 1986), the owner of patent rights realized too late that "windsurfer" had become a generic term for sailboards. Subsequent efforts to educate the public and police the mark were held unsuccessful. Furthermore, a patent license provision restraining anyone but WSI from producing any product using the term "Windsurfer" was held unlawful trademark misuse, being an attempt to inhibit competition beyond the scope of WSI's patent monopoly. See the discussion on Antitrust law in Chapter 7, *infra*.

(6) Is the following from the *Thermos* opinion an overstatement: "Of course, it is obvious that the fact that there was no suitable descriptive word for either aspirin or cellophane made it difficult, if not impossible, for the original manufacturers to prevent their trademark from becoming generic." Would the decisions in the *Aspirin* and *Cellophane* cases have been the same had the manufacturers themselves not used their trademarks generically or acquiesced in such use by others? *See* Porter, *Trade-Marks Publici Juris Through Generic Use*, 8 Intr. L. Rev. N.Y.U. 48 (1952-53). For a discussion of practices which lead to a trademark's becoming generic and those which help to prevent it, see Zivin, *Understanding Generic Words*, 63 Trademark Rep. 173 (1973). *Cf.* Oddi, *Assessing "Genericness": Another View*, 78 Trademark Rep. 560 (1988); McLeod, *The Status of So Highly Descriptive And Acquired Distinctiveness*, 82 Trademark Rep. 607 (1992); Folsom & Teply, *Trademarked Generic Words*, 89 Yale L.J. 1323 (1980); Swann, *The Economic Approach to Genericism: A Reply to Folsom and Teply*, 70 Trademark Rep. 43 (1980).

(7) In 1978 it was held that the Federal Trade Commission had jurisdiction to bring, in the public interest, a petition to cancel the federal registration for the allegedly generic trademark FORMICA. 15 U.S.C. § 1064; *FTC v. Formica Corp.*, 200 U.S.P.Q. 182 (T.T.A.B. 1978). *See also Formica Corp. v. Lefkowitz*, 200 U.S.P.Q. 641 (C.C.P.A. 1979), *cert. denied*, 442 U.S. 917 (1979). In 1980, however, in response to criticism that the FTC was overreaching in this area as well as others, Congress passed the Federal Trade Commission Improvements Act which, *inter alia*, limited the FTC's powers in this area. Pub. L. No. 96-252, 94 Stat. 374. *See generally* Chapter 10, *infra*.

(8) There is no type of word or term immune to becoming generic. The issue is entirely one of the state of the public mind. Thus, the problem for the trademark user is one of educating the public. Trademarks consisting of arbitrary terms, *Saxlehner v. Wagner*, 216 U.S. 375 (1910) (HUNYADI for bitter water), surnames, *Ludlow Valve Mfg. Co. v. Pittsburgh Mfg Co.*, 166 F. 26 (3d Cir. 1908) (LUDLOW for valves), and geographic names, *French Republic v. Saratoga Vichy Spring Co.*, 191 U.S. 427 (1903) (VICHY for water), have become generic. *See Keebler Co. v. Rovira Biscuit Corp.*, 624 F.2d 366, 375 (1st Cir. 1980). In *Dan Robbins & Associates, Inc. v. Questor Corp.*, 599 F.2d 1009, 1014 (C.C.P.A. 1979), the court stated: "Whether the relevant purchasing public regards a term as a common descriptive [i.e., generic] name is a question of fact to be resolved on the evidence (citation omitted). Purchaser testimony, consumer surveys, and listings in dictionaries, trade journals, newspapers and other publications, are useful evidence." A foreign word can also be generic, if it translates into English as the generic word for a product or even if it has no English translation. *See Selchow & Righter Co. v.*

Western Printing & Lithographing Co., 47 F. Supp. 322 (E.D. Wis. 1942), *aff'd*, 142 F.2d 707 (7th Cir. 1944), *cert. denied*, 323 U.S. 735 (1944) (PARCHEESI, similar to Hindustani word "pachisi," a name of a game); *Weiss Noodle Co. v. Golden Cracknel & Specialty Co.*, 290 F.2d 845 (C.C.P.A. 1961) (HA-LUSH-KA phonetically spelled Hungarian word "haluska," for egg noodles); *In re Northland Aluminum Products, Inc.*, 777 F.2d 1556 (Fed. Cir. 1985) (BUNDT, German word for a type of ring cake).

(9) A word can be generic in one country while retaining its source-indicating significance in others. ASPIRIN is not protectible in the United States, but remains a valid trademark in Canada and a number of other countries. *See Keebler Co.*, *supra* (EXPORT SODAS is a generic term for crackers in Puerto Rico); *Carcione v. The Greengrocers, Inc.*, 205 U.S.P.Q. 1075 (E.D. Cal. 1979) (GREENGROCER is a generic term in Britain for retailers of fresh vegetables and fruit, but may not be in the United States). Similarly, a term may be generic for some products but not others. In *Abercrombie & Fitch, supra* Note (1), "safari" was found to be generic for the well-known hat and bushjacket, but not for such clothing items as bermuda shorts, swim trunks and scarves. Similarly, "polo" was found to be generic with regard to polo shirts and coats, but descriptive or fanciful as applied to other clothing items. *Polo Fashions, Inc. v. Extra Special Products, Inc.*, 451 F. Supp. 555 (S.D.N.Y. 1978). "Rugger" was given similar treatment by the Court for bold striped knit shirts versus night shirts, tennis clothes, and other items. *Anvil Brand, Inc. v. Consolidated Foods Corp.*, 464 F. Supp. 474 (S.D.N.Y. 1978).

(10) In 1982 the Ninth Circuit held that "Monopoly" is a generic term for board games which have the creation of a monopoly as the winner's goal. *Anti-Monopoly, Inc. v. General Mills Fun Group, Inc.*, 684 F.2d 1316 (9th Cir. 1982), *cert, denied,* 459 U.S. 1227 (1983). Despite impressive evidence of the public's association of "Monopoly" with a board game manufactured by Parker Brothers, the Court was persuaded that the mark was generic by survey evidence indicating that consumers were not *motivated* to buy the game *because* it was made by Parker Brothers. How would other well-known products fare under such a test? How does this "motivation test" compare with Learned Hand's test for trademark significance in the "Aspirin" case, *supra*, i.e., that buyers understand the word to mean that the product came from the same single, though perhaps anonymous, source with which they are familiar? The *Anti-Monopoly* decision has been much criticized. Interestingly, a shortly subsequent Ninth Circuit decision made no reference to it in holding that the Coca-Cola Company's trademark "Coke" had not become generic. *Coca-Cola Co. v. Overland, Inc.*, 692 F.2d 1250 (9th Cir. 1982). *See* Zeisel, *The Surveys That Broke Monopoly*, 50 U. Chi. L. Rev. 896 (1983). In 1984, Congress amended the Lanham Act to prevent a recurrence of the motivation test enunciated in the *Anti-Monopoly* case. 15 U.S.C. § 1064(c); 15 U.S.C. § 1127.

§ 4.03 Abandonment

INTRODUCTION

Abandonment of trade identity rights occurs when nonuse is coupled with the absence of an intention to continue or resume the use of a previously used name or mark. For example, if it can be proved that a claimant at some period has in fact discontinued use without the intention to resume, he will be held to have abandoned and forfeited to the public domain, as of the date of his intended discontinuance, all his prior rights to exclusivity. Any rights he may subsequently possess will be newly acquired and their priority will run only from the new date when use is resumed with intention to continue such use. *See generally* 1 Gilson, *Trademark Protection and Practice*, § 3.06 (1993 ed.); McCarthy, *Trademarks and Unfair Competition*, § 17:3 (3d ed. 1992); Callmann, *Unfair Competition, Trademarks and Monopolies*, § 19.65 (4th ed. 1993). Section 45 of the Lanham Act provides that two years nonuse of a registered mark constitutes prima facie abandonment, but that presumption is frequently rebutted merely by a convincing demonstration of a state of mind to resume use. *See Guiding Eyes For Blind Inc. v. Guide Dog Foundation For Blind*, 384 F.2d 1016 (C.C.P.A. 1967).

The dubious legal and logical propriety of resolving the important questions of whether trade identity rights exist on the basis of the subjective state of mind of the claimant is discussed in Pattishall, *The Impact of Intent In Trade Identity Cases*, 65 Nw. U. L. Rev. 421, 434–438 (1970).

GOLD SEAL ASSOCIATES, INC. v. GOLD SEAL ASSOCIATES, INC.

United States District Court, Southern District of New York
56 F.2d 452 (1932)

PATTERSON, DISTRICT JUDGE.

The suit is for unfair competition. In March, 1930, the plaintiff was organized as a New York corporation to engage in the advertising business. The plan was to assemble a large number of retail merchants who should be known as "Gold Seal Associate Merchants" and who were to receive plaques bearing that title for display in their stores. The plaintiff was to arrange programs for radio broadcasting in the course of which the reliability of merchants with that sign was to be brought to the attention of the public. The plaintiff's profit was to come from the fees to be paid by the merchants. The business was operated by McClure, Brooks, and Weiss, McClure advancing the capital. Salesmen were sent out to sign up merchants and over 200 contracts were obtained. Plaques were distributed to these merchants. Two radio broadcasts were given in June, 1930, and then funds gave out. In December, 1930, the plaintiff had to relinquish its office.

Meanwhile those interested turned their attention toward raising new money to continue the enterprise. In January, 1931, McClure met Leighton and three others and tried to interest them in the matter. Negotiations with this group continued until March and then broke down. The idea evidently appealed to the Leighton group, however, for a month later it organized the defendant corporation, in name identical to that of the plaintiff. The defendant is a Delaware corporation, formed to engage in the same kind of business that the plaintiff had been conducting. It proceeded to sign up retail merchants and distributed plaques practically identical to those that had been distributed by the plaintiff. Radio broadcasting programs were begun in December, 1931. The plaintiff then brought this suit in which it asks for an injunction and damages.

Certain further facts bearing upon the defense of abandonment were brought out at the trial. In December, 1930, McClure had discussed the refinancing of the plaintiff's business with two young men, Dwyer and Doing. The following February Dwyer and Doing formed Honor Crest Associates, Inc., to engage in a wider and more ambitious advertising business. Part of their plan was to take over the plaintiff's business in case financing could be secured. McClure was cognizant of this project and invested money in it. The Honor Crest could not raise the necessary funds and discontinued business in the summer of 1931.

While it appears that the plaintiff now owes over $20,000 to creditors and has no money or tangible assets, the efforts made by McClure and Brooks to refinance continued down to the fall of 1931. This was shown by undisputed oral testimony, some of it from disinterested witnesses, and is corroborated by written evidence of an incontrovertible character. Weiss, now connected with the defendant, had retired from active association with the plaintiff in September, 1930, but had retained his stock interest. In December, 1930, he gave the plaintiff or McClure an option to buy his stock for $2,000, the option reciting that the stock might be used in bringing about a reorganization. In June, 1931, this option was extended until October 1, 1931. It was further shown that the plaintiff or McClure paid the New York franchise tax for the year ending October 31, 1931, payment having been made as late as August, 1931.

Upon the foregoing facts the plaintiff is manifestly entitled to relief unless there is merit in the contention that it had abandoned its business and good will by the time the defendant entered the field. The men behind the defendant company, after negotiating with those interested in the plaintiff, took a corporate name identical to that of the plaintiff and caused their company to engage in the same line of business. The plaques sent out to merchants are nearly the same. Confusion was bound to result. The only defense interposed is that of abandonment by the plaintiff.

To constitute an abandonment of a trade-mark or trade-name, there must be, not only nonuse, but also an intent to abandon. *Baglin v. Cusenier Co.*, 221 U.S. 580; *Hanover Star Milling Co. v. Metcalf*, 240 U.S. 403; *Beech-Nut Packing Co. v. Lorillard Co.*, 273 U.S. 629. Lapse of time without use may be evidence from which an intent to abandon may be inferred, the strength of such inference being dependent upon the period of discontinuance, the cause of it, and other factors. *Rockowitz Corset & Brassiere Corporation v. Madame X Co., Inc.*, 248 N.Y. 272, 162 N.E. 76. But the fact remains that an intent to relinquish must be shown.

Here no intent on the plaintiff's part to abandon its business forever was made [*Intent to eliquish the business not shown.*]
to appear. It had been forced by lack of funds to suspend the active prosecution of
the business, and such suspension had continued for about a year. But the proof
already referred to shows convincingly that honest efforts were being made all along
to revive the plaintiff and to resume the business. Taxes were being paid and attempts
at reorganization were kept up. It cannot be said that the company had thrown away
its name and whatever good will still clung to it. The fact that the defendant took
the same name and the same insignia is a fair indication that those behind it thought
they still had value. If the fact of suspension of business because of financial
misfortunes should be held to justify outsiders straightway in helping themselves
to a corporate name and insignia, then the chance of resuscitation would be killed,
and on winding up the creditors of the concern would find themselves deprived of
an asset of possible value.

The fact that McClure had formed a connection of some sort with another concern
endeavoring to enter the same line of business under another title is urged by the
defendant as proof of abandonment. But McClure at the same time was continuing
his efforts to put new life into the plaintiff. Moreover, an abandonment by McClure [*McClure not the only part of the corp.*]
would not be an abandonment by the plaintiff. The latter was apparently insolvent,
and its creditors had rights in its assets that McClure could not destroy.

It follows that the plaintiff is entitled to an injunction restraining the defendant
from using its present corporate title and its plaques. The plaintiff may submit a
decree.

AMERICAN PHOTOGRAPHIC PUBLISHING CO. v. ZIFF-DAVIS PUBLISHING CO.

United States Court of Appeals, Seventh Circuit
135 F.2d 569 (1943)

[*Held. (no more than 1 mag)*]
[*No 'Commercial Use' Existed.*]
[*4 Actions show Intent*]
[*Expressions of intent to abandon are evident*]

KERNER, CIRCUIT JUDGE.

Plaintiff, American Photographic Publishing Company, appeals from a decree [*Appeal from decree dismissing infring. of CL trademark*]
dismissing, for want of equity, its complaint alleging infringement of its common
law trade-mark and unfair competition. Jurisdiction rested on diversity of citizenship
and the requisite jurisdictional amount.

The facts are not in dispute. On October 27, 1914, plaintiff, a Massachusetts
corporation, purchased from Frank R. Fraprie a magazine entitled "Popular Photography." Thereafter and until May, 1916, plaintiff's magazines, "Popular Photography incorporating The Photographic Times," designed to appeal primarily to the
amateur photographer, and "American Photography," designed to appeal to the
expert photographer, were published as separate periodicals. At that time plaintiff
consolidated both publications in "American Photography," which was aimed to
please readers and advertisers of both its predecessors. For six months the magazine

carried on its cover the "American Photography incorporating Popular Photography and The Photographic Times." Thereafter, only the name "American Photography" appeared on the cover. From the date of consolidation, the masthead of plaintiff's magazine has carried the title "American Photography" in large letters, followed by the word "incorporating" and a list of the names of former publications, including Popular Photography in smaller type. This list rose from eight in 1916 to thirteen prior to defendant's first use of the title "Popular Photography."

On January 19, 1937, upon application theretofore made by the defendant, the title "Popular Photography including Amateur Cinematography" was registered by the defendant in the United States Patent Office as Trade Mark No. 342,417. After defendant's magazine entitled "Popular Photography" was published, plaintiff, on April 7, 1937, notified defendant that the name "Popular Photography" belonged to it, that it intended to defend its rights therein, and thereafter plaintiff filed its complaint in the instant case and began cancellation proceedings against the defendant in the United States Patent Office. An Examiner of Interferences found plaintiff had abandoned "Popular Photography" as a title and as a trade-mark, that Popular Photography as used by plaintiff was not a trade-mark and dismissed plaintiff's petition. The Commissioner of Patents affirmed the decision of the Examiner of Interferences, and upon appeal that decision was affirmed, 127 F.2d 308.

Since May, 1937, defendant's magazine "Popular Photography" has appeared monthly. Its size, style, dress, composition and content differ from plaintiff's publication, and the typographical make-up of the titles of the two magazines is different. The title Popular Photography, claimed by plaintiff, did not appear in the advertising manual "Standard Rate and Data Service" at the time defendant adopted it, nor has it appeared there since under plaintiff's name. No subscriptions were lost by plaintiff when defendant's magazine appeared, and plaintiff's newsstand sales increased afterwards. From its very first issue defendant's periodical has had a very much greater circulation than plaintiff's ever had or than its "American Photography" has.

The principal issue presented here is whether plaintiff's carrying the title Popular Photography on the masthead of its publication, "American Photography," was such a trade-mark use as to prevent abandonment of its right to the exclusive use of that title.

. . . .

The term "masthead" is a technical term of the printing trade, referring to the page in a publication which shows the title of the publication, the titles of publications which have been merged or consolidated under the name of the publication, the names of publishers and editors, the place where published, the subscription rates, the date of issue, and the frequency of publication. The relevant part of plaintiff's masthead read as follows:

AMERICAN
PHOTOGRAPHY

ANTHONY'S PHOTOGRAPHIC BULLETIN, ESTABLISHED 1870

THE PHOTOGRAPHIC TIMES, ESTABLISHED 1871

THE AMERICAN PHOTOGRAPHY, ESTABLISHED 1879

THE AMERICAN JOURNAL OF PHOTOGRAPHY, EST. 1879

THE PHOTO BEACON, ESTABLISHED 1883

AMERICAN AMATEUR PHOTOGRAPHER, ESTABLISHED 1889

CAMERA NOTES, ESTABLISHED 1897

PHOTO ERA, ESTABLISHED 1898

CAMERA AND DARK ROOM, ESTABLISHED 1898

PHOTOGRAPHIC TOPICS, ESTABLISHED 1902

THE AMATEUR PHOTOGRAPHER'S WEEKLY, EST. 1912

POPULAR PHOTOGRAPHY, ESTABLISHED 1912

PHOTO CRAFT, ESTABLISHED 1897

Plaintiff contends that by keeping Popular Photography on its masthead it retained the exclusive right to use it. The names of the periodicals listed under American Photography do not even purport, however, to represent existing publications. Commercially they are dead, and they are, at most, names of the ancestors of the present magazine. Like epitaphs on the tombstones in the family burial plot, they reflect an honored past; but their present function is merely to describe the history and back ground of "American Photography."

. . . .

Although trade-mark rights are property, they are not protected per se; it is only the good will in connection with which the mark is used that is protected. *Hanover Star Mill. Co. v. Metcalf*, 240 U.S. 403, 412–414. As its name indicates, the function of a trade-mark is to serve as a distinctive mark showing the origin or ownership of the particular article to which it is affixed. *Elgin Nat. Watch Co. v. Illinois Watch-Case Co.*, 179 U.S. 665, 673. Whether a mark identifies an article, then, should be considered in ascertaining whether it should be protected against alleged infringement. Here, plaintiff's use of Popular Photography was not a tag for its article; indeed, the masthead is a perfunctory matter which interests readers little, if at all. The patent office tribunals found that plaintiff's subscribers were not even aware that the notation Popular Photography appeared in the masthead of "American Photography." Because it is not a commercial signature and is very inconspicuous, a masthead use is not the same as use on the cover, on a banner head, news head, or feature head. Since the title in question, Popular Photography, was not used in such a way as to identify the publication "American Photography," its appearance in the masthead was not a trade-mark use, i.e., the mark did not signify the individuality of source, and the authorities cited by plaintiff are distinguishable for the reason that the name or title in dispute in them was identified with the article. Since exclusive right arises only from distinctive use, *Lawyers Title Ins. Co. v.*

Lawyer's Title Ins. Corp., 71 App. D.C. 120, 109 F.2d 35, 44, and since the owner of a trade-mark may not make a negative and merely prohibitive use of it as a monopoly, *United Drug Co. v. Theodore Rectanus Co.*, 248 U.S. 90, plaintiff could not prevent defendant from adopting the title Popular Photography.

We do not wish to be understood as holding that the day after the owner of a trade-mark ceases to publish a periodical under one title and begins to publish it under another, carrying the former title on the masthead, some person could appropriate it with impunity, for he could not. *Cf. Powell v. Valentine*, 106 Kan. 645, 189 P. 163. We are passing only on the situation here presented, where there has been discontinuance of the former publication for more than twenty years, coupled with evidence to show abandonment. Although plaintiff contends there has been no abandonment, we think that the record clearly discloses that plaintiff abandoned the name Popular Photography as its trade-mark.

Express indications of abandonment are not wanting. The masthead of "American Photography" has listed the name Popular Photography along with the other discontinued publications. In the last issue of plaintiff's "Popular Photography" as a separate publication, in April, 1916, plaintiff printed the following: "We are therefore able to announce to our readers that the April issue of Popular Photography will be the last published, and that with the May issue of American Photography, Popular Photography will be merged in this magazine." Moreover, when plaintiff registered its trade-mark in 1938, it registered not American Photography Including Popular Photography, but simply American Photography. Furthermore, Fraprie, the editor of "American Photography" and former editor of plaintiff's "Popular Photography," stated in a letter that "Popular Photography" had not been published for several years. On being questioned, he stated that he hoped to start a new magazine by that name, which shows that there was no magazine entitled Popular Photography extant when defendant commenced publishing its magazine.

Plaintiff contends, however, that since Fraprie (who was director, treasurer, and editor, as well as a very large stockholder, and thus well qualified to speak for plaintiff) stated that he never intended to abandon the mark Popular Photography, it was not lost because intent is an essential of abandonment. But actions frequently speak louder than words. The facts and circumstances shown by this record outweigh this contention. Twenty years of non-use plus statements and actions showing intent to discontinue a publication are cogent indications that the one-time owner had given up its rights therein. In reaching this conclusion, we are not unaware of the decisions holding that intention is necessary to abandonment. But the purely subjective intention in the abandoner's mind to re-engage in a former enterprise at some indefinite future time is not sufficient to avoid abandonment where an objective analysis of the situation furnishes ample evidence to warrant the inference of abandonment. *Golenpaul v. Rosett*, 174 Misc. 114, 18 N.Y.S.2d 889; *American Photographic Pub. Co. v. Ziff-Davis Pub. Co.*, Cust. & Pat. App., 127 F.2d 308. Rather, we think the recognitive sense of the public, i.e. the present associative identity of the mark in the public mind with its employer's goods, is the basis for trade-mark rights. *Cf. Hanover Star Mill. Co. v. Metcalf*, 240 U.S. 403, 412–413. Many of the opinions which discuss intent reveal a fact situation where there has

[handwritten margin notes: "disuse doesn't mean abandonment if 2ndary meaning still exists"]

been obvious survival of the associative significance of the mark. Hence, if the mark still means the first appropriator in the public mind, disuse will not be abandonment, *Ansehl v. Williams*, 8 Cir., 267 F.9; *Gold Seal Associates v. Gold Seal Associates*, D.C., 56 F.2d 452, but if the good will built up by the use of a mark has perished so that it no longer has any associative significance in the public mind, it may be re-appropriated. (Citations omitted).

We do not believe that when defendant commenced to use the title Popular Photography (May, 1937) the public had in mind that it meant plaintiff's magazine, which had ceased to exist twenty years before. To us it seems that the vitality of any stimulus given by the name had been so diluted by the passage of time as to have no potency. Neither is there any evidence indicating that the defendant expected to, or obtained the slightest advantage from the one-time reputation of plaintiff's former magazine.

. . . .

. . . We think that the meager instances of confusion to which plaintiff points are more properly attributable to carelessness on the part of the inquirers than to the conduct of the defendant. Cf. *Cridlebaugh v. Rudolph*, 3 Cir., 131 F.2d 795, 801; *Pulitzer Pub. Co. v. Houston Printing Co.*, [4 F.2d 924, *aff'd* 11 F.2d 834]. Hence we have concluded that there was no unfair competition.

The judgment of the District Court is affirmed.

———————

EXXON CORP. v. HUMBLE EXPLORATION CO.

United States Court of Appeals, Fifth Circuit,
695 F.2d 96 (1983)

HIGGINBOTHAM, CIRCUIT JUDGE.

[handwritten margin notes: "Difference between intent to relinquish + intent not to resume." "Different intent to resume required under 1127 not here." "Issue" "5th Cir. Abandonment b/c of limited sales. [under 1127]"]

Humble Exploration Company, Inc. appeals from an order of the district court, 524 F. Supp. 450, enjoining its use of "Humble" as a trade name. The main issue on appeal is whether the district court erred in finding that Exxon Company, U.S.A. had not abandoned the use of the trademark HUMBLE. Because we find that the limited arranged sales of HUMBLE products as part of Exxon's trademark mainte- nance program are insufficient uses to avoid prima facie abandonment under 15 U.S.C. § 1127, we reverse and remand to the district court for a determination of Exxon's intent to resume use of the trademark.

Humble Oil and Refining Company was founded as a Texas corporation in 1917. Its activities included oil exploration, refining and marketing. In 1959, that company and the other regional affiliated oil companies owned by Standard Oil Company of New Jersey merged to form a larger Humble Oil & Refining Company, a Delaware corporation.

In the early 1960's, the newly expanded Humble Oil & Refining Company introduced a new branding system for its products and service stations. Throughout the country, large HUMBLE signs were erected on the company's service stations, totalling over 20,000 by 1972. At each station, a second sign in an oval located at the roadside carried a regional house mark: ENCO in Texas and other western states,

ESSO in the eastern states and HUMBLE in the state of Ohio. From the early 1960's through 1972, the Humble Oil & Refining Company name appeared on all of the Company's packaged products, sometimes accompanied by the trademark ESSO, ENCO or HUMBLE, depending on the intended area of sale.

Because its management concluded that the use of three trade names, HUMBLE, ESSO and ENCO, was confusing to customers, in late 1972 Humble Oil & Refining Company adopted the name EXXON as its sole primary brand name and on January 1, 1973, Humble Oil & Refining Company became Exxon Company, U.S.A. Exxon spent in excess of twelve million dollars in advertising its name change in television and print media. EXXON signs replaced the three regional signs and all packaged products were relabeled with EXXON labels before distribution. Except for inventory at the service station level, the changeover was complete by mid-1973.

On April 12, 1972, the Board of Directors of Humble Oil & Refining Company passed a resolution calling for continued use of HUMBLE after the changeover to EXXON "in ways other than as a primary brand name." Company publications expressed the intention to protect the name HUMBLE. To do so, Exxon instituted a trademark maintenance program for the mark.

. . . .

The district court framed the abandonment issue thus: "Is the limited use of a famous trademark solely for protective purposes a use sufficient to preclude abandonment under the common law and the Lanham Act?" It answered the question in the affirmative. Plaintiff-Appellee withdrew its Texas and common law claims in the district court, so the resolution of the abandonment issue must focus on the federal standards for abandonment set forth in the Lanham Act.

Under the Act,

A mark shall be deemed to be abandoned—

(a) When its use has been discontinued with intent not to resume use. Intent not to resume may be inferred from circumstances. Nonuse for two consecutive years shall be prima facie abandonment.

15 U.S.C. § 1127 (1982). The burden of proof is on the party claiming abandonment, but when a prima facie case of trademark abandonment exists because of nonuse of the mark for over two consecutive years, the owner of the mark has the burden to demonstrate that circumstances do not justify the inference of intent not to resume use. *See Sterling Brewers, Inc. v. Schenley Industries, Inc.*, 441 F.2d 675, 679 (Cust. & Pat. App. 1971).

Appellant argues that Exxon has not used the HUMBLE mark since its changeover program. Since that time, Exxon has 1) sold existing inventory of packaged products bearing the name "Humble Oil and Refining Company"; 2) made periodic sales of nominal amounts of Exxon gasoline, motor oil and grease in pails bearing the names HUMBLE and EXXON; 3) sold Exxon bulk gasoline and diesel fuel to selected customers, who received HUMBLE invoices, through three corporations organized for that purpose; and 4) sold 55-gallon drum products from the Baytown, Texas refinery, all bearing a stencil with the names HUMBLE and EXXON.

The existing inventory was depleted by mid-1974; the sale of 55-gallon drums began in 1977. Whether or not these sales are "uses" for the purposes of 15 U.S.C. § 1127, the period between those sales was longer than two years, and under the Lanham Act, "nonuse for two consecutive years is prima facie abandonment." 15 U.S.C. § 1127. During that period between sales of inventory and sales of 55-gallon-drum products, Exxon can point to only two types of sales as possible uses. As earlier described, Exxon made limited sales of packaged products with both EXXON and HUMBLE on the labels to targeted customers in these amounts: $9.28 in 1973, $.0 in 1974, $140.12 in 1975 and $42.05 in 1976. Second, products in bulk form and not bearing a trade name or mark were sold to selected customers who received the explanation that they were receiving Exxon products. The only use of HUMBLE in connection with these sales was on the invoices sent to the customers. The issue, thus, is whether these two categories of arranged sales through the trademark protection program during that period constitute "use" sufficient to avoid prima facie abandonment.

Appellant relies primarily on *La Societe Anonyme des Parfums LeGalion v. Jean Patou, Inc.*, 495 F.2d 1265 (2d Cir. 1974), and *Procter and Gamble v. Johnson & Johnson, Inc.*, 485 F. Supp. 1185 (S.D.N.Y. 1979), *aff'd without opinion*, 636 F.2d 1203 (2d Cir. 1980), to support its argument that arranged sales are nonuse. In *Jean Patou*, the plaintiff LeGalion, a French perfume manufacturer, had sold its perfume under the trademark SNOB in a number of foreign countries but was unable to sell its product in the United States because of Patou's registration for the mark in this country. Claiming that Patou had not established rights in the mark, LeGalion filed suit. The facts revealed that Patou had made 89 sales of perfume over a 20-year period and engaged in no advertising. The court found that Patou's real purpose in making the 89 sales was to keep a competitor at bay and that this "purely defensive" token use was insufficient to obtain enforceable rights in the mark. *Id.* at 1273–74. The court observed: "The token sales program engaged in here is by its very nature inconsistent with a present plan of commercial exploitation." *Id.* at 1273. It continued: "A trade mark maintenance program obviously cannot in itself justify a minimal sales effort, or the requirement of good faith commercial use would be read out of the trademark law altogether." *Id.* at 1273 n. 10.

In *Procter and Gamble*, the plaintiff maintained a "Minor Brands Program" for the purpose of protecting its ownership rights in brand names not being actively used in commerce on its products. Employees not normally involved in Procter and Gamble's (P & G's) merchandising operation took an active P & G product, labeled it with a minor brand, and shipped it to customers. For example, P & G's Prell shampoo was bottled under thirteen different minor brand labels. Fifty units of each were shipped annually to at least ten states. The court held that the plaintiff had no enforceable rights in the mark SURE for tampons on the basis of its inclusion in this minor brands program.

The district court below distinguished these cases because they treat the acquisition or adoption of a trademark that has not developed goodwill. According to the court, Exxon's use of the HUMBLE mark "in commerce for protective purposes is a good faith use" because of the residual goodwill built up in the mark. Despite the trial court's distinction, § 1127 of the Lanham Act, without mentioning goodwill, requires continued use of a mark or intent to resume use to avoid a finding of abandonment. The first requirement is not present on this record. The limited sales of packaged products to targeted customers and the arranged sales of bulk products through the three shell corporations were not sufficient uses to avoid prima facie proof of abandonment under the statute. The HUMBLE trademark was not used to identify the source of the goods. The packaged products were Exxon products with HUMBLE used as a secondary name. Of course, "the fact that a product bears more than one mark does not mean that each cannot be a valid trademark." *Old Dutch Foods, Inc. v. Dan Dee Pretzel & Potato Chip Co.*, 477 F.2d 150, 154 (6th Cir.1973). For example, in *Old Dutch* the defendant had used concurrent marks, OLD DUTCH and DAN DEE, on all his products for over thirty years. Each mark must, however, be a bona fide mark. *See Blue Bell, Inc. v. Farah Manufacturing Company, Inc.*, 508 F.2d 1260, 1267 (5th Cir.1975).

In this case, the mark HUMBLE was used only on isolated products or selected invoices sent to selected customers. No sales were made that depended upon the HUMBLE mark for identification of source. To the contrary, purchasers were informed that the selected shipments would bear the HUMBLE name or be accompanied by an HUMBLE invoice but were the desired Exxon products. That is, the HUMBLE mark did not with these sales play the role of a mark. That casting, however, is central to the plot that the Lanham Act rests on the idea of registration of marks otherwise born of use rather than the creation of marks by the act of registration. That precept finds expression in the Lanham Act requirement that to maintain a mark in the absence of use there must be an intent to resume use. That expression is plain. The Act does not allow the preservation of a mark solely to prevent its use by others. Yet the trial court's reasoning allows precisely that warehousing so long as there is residual good will associated with the mark. Exxon makes the same argument here. While that may be good policy, we cannot square it with the language of the statute. In sum, these arranged sales in which the mark was not allowed to play its basic role of identifying source were not "use" in the sense of § 1127 of the Lanham Act.

. . . .

This court recognizes that the goodwill associated with the mark HUMBLE has immense value to Exxon. That fact, coupled with the efforts under the trademark maintenance program, could suggest Exxon's intent to resume use of the mark, but the trial court did not make that finding. The court found that the trademark protection program evidenced "an intent not to relinquish HUMBLE" and "an intent not to abandon HUMBLE," but it did not specifically address Exxon's intent to resume use as required by § 1127 the Lanham Act. . . . There is a difference between intent not to abandon or relinquish and intent to resume use in that an owner may not wish to abandon its mark but may have no intent to resume its use.

. . . In the context of a challenge strictly under the Lanham Act to an alleged warehousing program, as the facts of this case present, the application of the statutory language is critical. That is, this court having found that the two types of uses under the trademark maintenance program were not sufficient uses to avoid prima facie proof of abandonment, the district court must specifically address Exxon's intent to resume use of the HUMBLE trademark. An "intent to resume" requires the trademark owner to have plans to resume commercial use of the mark. Stopping at an "intent not to abandon" tolerates an owner's protecting a mark with neither commercial use nor plans to resume commercial use. Such a license is not permitted by the Lanham Act.

Requires plans to resume

The judgment is reversed and the case is remanded for further proceedings consistent with this opinion. In doing so, we emphasize that we do not decide here whether the present record would support a finding that Exxon had sufficient intent to resume use of the Humble mark so as to avoid its loss, nor do we here address Exxon's rights under the common law to block any present use of the mark in a confusing manner. Finally, we leave to the trial court the decision whether additional evidence on the issue of intent to resume use ought to be heard.

Remanded to find if Exxon had sufficient intent to resume.

NOTES ON ABANDONMENT

(1) Trademark rights may survive even a substantial period of nonuse of the mark if the failure to use is involuntary. In 1903 the Congregation of the Chartreuser, an order of monks in France, was held to be dissolved by operation of law and its properties were seized and liquidated. The liquidator then began manufacturing a liqueur, intended to match the flavor and appeal of that made by the monks, under their famous trademark CHARTREUSE.

Forced to set up new facilities in Spain and barred from using their old marks and symbols in France, the monks imported the necessary French herbs and resumed manufacture of the liqueur under a new designation, "Liqueur des Peres Chartreux." The labels for the liqueur also stated that it was the only one identical to the liqueur previously manufactured by secret process in France. In a subsequent infringement suit by the monks against a New York corporation importing French "chartreuse" the defendant claimed abandonment. *Baglin, Superior General of the Order of Carthusian Monks v. Cusenier Co.*, 221 U.S. 580 (1911). In the opinion authored by Justice Hughes, the Supreme Court quoted *Saxlehner v. Eisner & Mendelsohn Co.*, 179 U.S. 19, 31 (1900), observing, "Acts which unexplained would be sufficient to establish an abandonment may be answered by showing that there never was an intention to give up and relinquish the right claimed." Finding that they had acted reasonably under the circumstances, and that their efforts to prevent use of the old mark in France and other countries clearly demonstrated that there was no intent to abandon, the Court concluded that the monks retained their trademark ownership rights. *See Kardex Systems, Inc. v. Sistenco N.V.*, 583 F. Supp. 803 (D. Me. 1984) (financial difficulties); *Cuban Cigar Brands N.V. v. Upmann International, Inc.*, 199 U.S.P.Q. 193 (S.D.N.Y. 1978) (government action); *Merry Hull & Co. v. Hi-Line Co.*, 243 F. Supp. 45 (S.D.N.Y. 1965) (bankruptcy); *The General Tire & Rubber Co. v. Greenwold*, 127 U.S.P.Q. 240 (S.D. Cal. 1960) (production difficulties); *Lawyers Title Ins. Co. v. Lawyers Title Ins. Corp.*, 109 F.2d 35, 45 n. 47 (D.C. Cir. 1939), *cert. denied*, 309 U.S. 684 (1940) (business reorganization); *Miller Brewing Co. v. Oland's Breweries, Ltd.*, 548 F.2d 349 (C.C.P.A. 1976) (business reorganization); *Nettie Rosenstein, Inc. v. Princess Pat, Ltd.*, 220 F.2d 444, 453 (C.C.P.A.

No intent to give up mark

1955) (war). *See also Chandon Champagne Corp. v. San Marino Wine Corp.,* 335 F.2d 531 (2d Cir. 1964).

(2) If rights in a mark are held for a period by a trustee in bankruptcy who is simply liquidating the assets of a dormant business, does the mark become abandoned because the trustee has no intent to resume its use but only to sell the rights in it? *See Merry Hull, supra; Johanna Farms, Inc. v. Citrus Bowl, Inc.,* 199 U.S.P.Q. 16 (E.D.N.Y. 1978). *Compare Hough Manufacturing Corp. v. Virginia Metal Industries, Inc.,* 203 U.S.P.Q. 436 (E.D. Va. 1978); *Haymaker Sports, Inc. v. Turian,* 581 F.2d 257 (C.C.P.A. 1978). Might protectable goodwill in a mark persist even after use of the mark has ceased? *See Ferrari S.p.A. Esercizio Fabbriche Automobili E Corse v. McBurnie,* 11 U.S.P.Q.2d 1843 (S.D. Cal. 1989) (despite 13 years non-use of FERRARI DAYTONA SPIDER automobile body style and no intention to resume use, proof of persisting goodwill and ongoing parts support sufficiently demonstrated no abandonment of trade dress rights); *Seidelmann Yachts, Inc. v. Pace Yacht Corp.,* 14 U.S.P.Q.2d 1497 (D. Md. 1989), *aff'd without publ. op.,* 13 U.S.P.Q.2d 2025 (4th Cir. 1990) (persisting goodwill after use ends may be weighed in considering abandonment); *Defiance Button Machine Co. v. C & C Metal Products Corp.,* 759 F.2d 1053 (2d Cir.), *cert. denied,* 474 U.S. 844 (1985) (the question is whether the goodwill symbolized by the mark dissipated during the period of non-use); Bowker, *The Song Is Over But The Melody Lingers On: Persistence Of Goodwill And The Intent Factor In Trademark Abandonment,* 56 Fordham L. Rev. 1003, 1022 (1988).

(3) What factors should a manufacturer consider before modernizing a mark used successfully for years? Abandonment may result if the modernized mark is too different from the old mark, and priority will then be measured from first use of the new mark. The key in trademark modernization is maintaining the continuity of the commercial impression between the old and new marks. *In re Nuclear Research Corp.,* 16 U.S.P.Q.2d 1316, 1317 (T.T.A.B. 1990); *Hess's of Allentown, Inc. v. National Bellas Hess, Inc.,* 169 U.S.P.Q. 673 (T.T.A.B. 1971). *See* Radin, *Selected Issues Arising Under the Doctrine of Trademark Abandonment,* 79 Trademark Rep. 433 (1989); Pattishall, *The Goose and the Golden Egg — Some Comments About Trademark Modernization,* 47 Trademark Rep. 801 (1957). *Compare Ilco Corp. v. Ideal Security Hardware Corp.,* 527 F.2d 1221 (C.C.P.A. 1976) (HOME PROTECTION CENTER found not to create the same continuous commercial impression as HOME PROTECTION HARDWARE, causing defendant to lose priority of use, resulting in cancellation of registration) *with Drexel Enterprises, Inc. v. J.R. Richardson,* 312 F.2d 525 (10th Cir. 1962) (trademark rights in HERITAGE for furniture not abandoned when slant script changed to block letters and mark combined with "Henredon").

(4) Should trademark rights be held abandoned if the use is changed from one product to another? Should it make any difference whether the products are closely related? *See Lucien Piccard Watch Corp. v. Since 1868 Crescent Corp.,* 314 F. Supp. 329 (S.D.N.Y. 1970); *Robinson Co. v. Plastics Research & Dev. Corp.,* 264 F. Supp. 852 (W.D. Ark. 1967); *Mishawaka Rubber & Woolen Mfg. Co. v. Bata Narodni Podnik,* 222 F.2d 279 (C.C.P.A. 1955).

(5) In *Beech-NutPacking Co. v. P. Lorillard Co.*, 273 U.S. 629 (1926), plaintiff sought to enjoin defendant's use of BEECHNUT for tobacco. Plaintiff had continuously used the trademark BEECH-NUT for chewing gum, peanut butter, and other foods since before 1900. Mr. Justice Holmes wrote as follows:

[handwritten: Old Case]

> The defendant claims the mark "Beechnut" for tobacco through successive assignments from the Harry Weissinger Tobacco Company, of Louisville, Kentucky, which used it from and after 1897. The plaintiff does not contest the original validity of this mark or suggest any distinction on the ground that it originated in a different State, but says that the right has been lost by abandonment. It appears that brands of tobacco have their rise and fall in popular flavor, and that the Beechnut had so declined that in 1910 only twenty-five pounds were sold, and the trade-mark was left dormant until after the dissolution of the American Tobacco Company which then held it. This was in 1911, and the Lorillard Company took over the mark with many others. Then, in connection with an effort to get a new brand that would hit the present taste, this mark was picked out, some of the adjuncts were changed, and in 1915 the new tobacco was put upon the market. Nothing had happened in the meantime to make the defendant's position worse than if it had acted more promptly, and we see no reason to disturb the finding of two Courts that the right to use the mark had not been lost. The mere lapse of time was not such that it could be said to have destroyed the right as matter of law. A trade-mark is not only a symbol of an existing good will, although it commonly is thought of only as that. Primarily it is a distinguishable token devised or picked out with the intent to appropriate it to a particular class of goods and with the hope that it will come to symbolize good will. Apart from nice and exceptional cases, and within the limits of our jurisdiction, a trade-mark and a business may start together, and in a qualified sense the mark is property, protected and alienable, although as with other property its outline is shown only by the law of torts, of which the right is a prophetic summary. Therefore the fact that the good will once associated with it has vanished does not end at once the preferential right of the proprietor to try it again upon goods of the same class with improvements that renew the proprietor's hopes.

[handwritten margin note: Stopped selling Beechnut tobacco, then resumed.]

[handwritten margin note: Goodwill that has departed doesn't recur.]

Has the law as disclosed in the subsequent cases of this section followed or departed from such a rule?

(6) Trademarks cannot be reserved or "hoarded" without trademark use or genuine intent to resume such use. *Imperial Tobacco, Ltd. v. Philip Morris, Inc.*, 899 F.2d 1575, 1581 (Fed. Cir. 1990) ("the Lanham Act was not intended to provide a warehouse for unused marks"); *Silverman v. CBS, Inc.*, 870 F.2d 40 (2d Cir.), *cert. denied*, 492 U.S. 907 (1989) (AMOS N ANDY abandoned for TV show characters). *Accord: E. Remy Martin & Co. v. Shaw-Ross International Imports, Inc.*, 756 F.2d 1525 (11th Cir. 1985); *Highland Potato Chip Co. v. Culbro Snack Foods*, 720 F.2d 981 (8th Cir. 1983). *Compare P.A.B. Produits v. Santinine Societa*, 570 F.2d 328 (C.C.P.A. 1978), where the registrant's shipments of cosmetics under the trademark PAB were also claimed to be token use. There the court stated that, "the balance of equities plays an important role in determining whether registrant's use is

[handwritten margin note: Must have intent to reuse]

sufficient to preserve registration" and prevent abandonment, and found that cancellation petitioner's failure to demonstrate that it "stands in the wings ready to utilize the mark commercially" defeated any assertion that registrant was only maintaining the mark to bar a competitor from marketing its product. *See also Stetson v. Howard D. Wolf & Associates*, 955 F.2d 847, 850 (2d Cir. 1992) (the lower court erred in applying a "no intent to abandon" test; the correct test was whether there was "no intent . . . to resume use in the reasonably foreseeable future"); *Roulo v. Russ Berrie & Co.*, 886 F.2d 931, 939 (7th Cir. 1989), *cert. denied*, 493 U.S. 1075 (1990) (it was within jury's prerogative to credit plaintiff's testimony that she intended to resume use of mark after three years of non-use); *Cerveceria Centroamericana, S.A. v. Cerveceria India, Inc.*, 892 F.2d 1021 (Fed. Cir. 1989) (discussing parties' burdens of proof respecting abandonment); *AmBrit, Inc. v. Kraft, Inc.*, 805 F.2d 974 (11th Cir. 1986) (registration cancelled for abandonment; "[t]hat Kraft used the mark in 1980 does not mean that Kraft intended to use the mark in 1978").

§ 4.04 Assignment Without Goodwill

INTRODUCTION

Trade identity rights are "assignable with the goodwill of the business in which the mark is used, or with that part of the goodwill of the business connected with the use of and symbolized by the mark." This statement of existing common law was codified in the Lanham Act (15 U.S.C. § 1060). "[F]ollowing a proper assignment, the assignee steps into the shoes of the assignor," and may assert the same rights the assignor could have. *Premier Dental Products Co. v. Darby Dental Supply Co.*, 794 F.2d 850 (3d Cir.), *cert. denied*, 479 U.S. 950 (1986).

The concept of assigning trade identity rights appurtenant to the business which they represent is derived quite logically and consistently from the rationale of trade identity protection which limits that protection to the source-indicating function. Historically, in Anglo-American law, the concept was rigidly applied to the extent of requiring that the mark could only be transferred with the entire physical business with which it was associated. Some commentators have noted that the physical transfer of machines, customer lists, of factories and plants may be required. *See* Nims, *Unfair Competition and Trademarks*, § 17 (4th ed. 1947). *Compare* McCarthy, *Trademarks and Unfair Competition*, § 18:2 (3d ed. 1992).

This logical rule was followed in the United Kingdom with little flexibility until recent times. In the United States, however, the practical needs of commerce for more freedom of alienability for trademarks resulted in considerable relaxation of the logical doctrine in actual practice and in permitting an element of legal fiction for assignments of marks so long as the assignment instrument included the approved formal (or fictional) language: "with the goodwill of the business . . . symbolized by the mark." (15 U.S.C. § 1060.)

PEPSICO, INC. v. GRAPETTE CO.

United States Court of Appeals, Eighth Circuit
416 F.2d 285 (1969)

Lay, Circuit Judge.

PepsiCo, Inc., a holding company of several subsidiaries including Pepsi Cola Co., a national soft drink bottler, sought an injunction against Grapette-Aristocrat, Inc. and its holding company Grapette Co. (hereinafter referred collectively as Grapette) on the alleged infringement of its trademark "Pepsi." In 1965 Grapette purchased the mark "Peppy" and intended to bottle a soft "pepper" drink with that name. The district court found that the mark "Peppy" was confusingly similar to "Pepsi" and as such would constitute infringement under 15 U.S.C. § 1114 (1964). However, not withstanding this finding of infringement, the court denied the plaintiff injunctive relief on the ground that it was guilty of laches. 288 F. Supp. at 937, 159 U.S.P.Q. at 410. PepsiCo., Inc. appeals. We reverse.

The evidence shows that Pepsi Cola Co. has bottled beverages duly registered under trademarks "Pepsi Cola," "Pepsi" and "Pep-Kola" for many years. *See* 15 U.S.C. § 1065. Grapette is a national bottler and distributor of soft drinks, concentrates and syrups. In 1965 it developed a formula for a new syrup to be used in a pepper type bottled beverage as opposed to a cola beverage. In searching for a name to market the new product, defendant discovered the 1926 registration of the mark "Peppy" by H. Fox and Co., a partnership. The mark had been renewed by Fox in 1946 and 1966. Sometime between 1932 and 1937 Fox began to use the mark "Peppy" in conjunction with a cola flavored syrup which was distributed on a local basis, confined mostly to the Eastern states of New York, New Jersey and Connecticut. The cola distribution was sold exclusively as syrup. Since 1958, Fox's syrup has been sold only to jobbers in 28 ounce consumer size bottles. Some ten to twelve years prior to this time it was sold also to the fountain trade as a syrup in gallon containers.

In 1965, Grapette Co. entered into an agreement with Fox Corp. in which the trademark "Peppy" was assigned to defendant for a consideration of $7,500. At this time Fox Corp. was in a Chapter 11 bankruptcy proceeding. Although Fox Corp. made a formal assignment of "goodwill," it is conceded by defendant that none of Fox Corp.'s physical assets or plant were transferred with the trademark; no inventory, customer lists, formulas, etc. Upon acquisition of the "Peppy" mark, Grapette began arrangements to have this mark placed upon its new pepper flavored soft drink. Fox Corp. continued to sell its cola syrup under the mark "Fox Brand" as well as agreeing to act as a distributor of defendant's "Peppy." In 1965, plaintiff warned the defendant of possible litigation if it did not stop the use of its mark. On April 21, 1966, this action was begun.

Plaintiff contends (1) that the transfer of the trademark "Peppy" by Fox Corp. was invalid because it was an assignment in "gross" and that therefore, Grapette cannot stand in the shoes of its predecessor in order to assert the defense of laches; and (2) that the defense of laches is not supported by sufficient evidence.

It is not disputed that Grapette must stand in the place of Fox Corp. Without a valid assignment, Grapette's rights to the use of "Peppy" accrue only as of November 1965 and it could not assert the defense of laches. PepsiCo, Inc. asserts that the 1965 assignment of the trademark by Fox Corp. to Grapette was a legal nullity in that the trademark was transferred totally disconnected from any business of goodwill of the assignor. We must agree.

Section 1060 of the Lanham Act provides:

> A registered mark or a mark for which application to register has been filed shall be assignable with the goodwill of the business in which the mark is used, or with that part of the goodwill of the business connected with the use of and symbolized by the mark, and in any such assignment it shall not be necessary to include the goodwill of the business connected with the use of and symbolized by any other mark used in the business or by the name or style under which the business is conducted. . . .

15 U.S.C. § 1060.

The early common law rule that a trademark could not be assigned "in gross" was recognized in this circuit in *Macmahan Pharmacal Co. v. Denver Chem. Mfg. Co.*, 113 F. 468 (8 Cir. 1901), and in *Carroll v. Duluth Superior Milling Co.*, 232 F. 675 (8 Cir. 1916). This court in *Carroll* observed that a trademark could only be transferred "in connection with the assignment of the particular business in which it has been used, with its goodwill, and for continued use upon the same articles or class of articles." *Id.* at 680. We later explained "that there is no property in a trademark except as a right appurtenant to an established business or trade, when it becomes an element of goodwill." *Atlas Beverage Co. v. Minneapolis Brewing Co.*, 113 F.2d 672, 674–675, 46 U.S.P.Q. 395, 397–398 (8 Cir. 1940). The rule found derivation in *Kidd v. Johnson*, 100 U.S. 617 (1879). The necessity to assign more than the naked mark was premised upon the primary object of the trademark "to indicate by its meaning or association the *origin* of the article to which it is affixed." (Emphasis ours.) 100 U.S. at 620. This court recently observed in *Sweetarts v. Sunline, Inc.*, 380 F.2d 923, 926, 154 U.S.P.Q. 459, 462 (8 Cir. 1967): "A trademark is generally any name, sign, or mark which one adopts to denominate commercial goods originating from him."

As pointed out in the *Restatement (Second) of Torts*, § 756, comment a at 136 (Tent. Draft No. 8, 1963):

> A trademark or trade name is not itself an independent object of property, nor is the right to use such mark or name. The designation is only a means of identifying particular goods, services, or a business associated with a particular commercial source, whether known or anonymous . . . . Goodwill is property, and since it is transferable the symbol of the property is transferable along with it.

Strict adherence to this rule has been vigorously criticized as impractical and legalistic. Schecter, *The Rational Bases of Trademark Protection*, 40 Harv. L. Rev. 813 (1926); Grismore, *The Assignment of Trademarks and Trade Names*, 30 Mich. L. Rev. 489 (1932); Callmann, *Unfair Competition, Trademarks and Monopolies*,

§ 78 (3d ed. 19.); Note, *Trademark Protection Following Ineffective Assignment*, 88 U. Pa. L. Rev. 863 (1940). According to these commentators, the continuum of the rule fails to comprehend the modern image of the trademark to the consuming public. Strict application of the rule undoubtedly fails to recognize the function of the trademark as representing as well (1) a guaranty of the product and (2) the inherent advertising value of the mark itself. *Id.*

Some recent cases have given recognition that in certain situations a naked assignment might be approved. Grapette emphasizes the case of *Hy-Cross Hatchery v. Osborne*, 303 F.2d 947, 133 U.S.P.Q. 687 (C.C.P.A. 1962), as being controlling.

There the plaintiff sought cancellation of the trademark "Hy-Cross" solely on the basis that the assignee of the original registrant took nothing but the naked mark. The evidence showed that all the assignee received was the mark itself. Osborne, the assignor, did not continue in the same business of raising chickens. The court in discussing the issue of naked assignment stated the following [133 U.S.P.Q. at 689–690]:

> Unlike the cases relied on, Osborne, so far as the record shows, was using the mark at the time he executed the assignment of it. He had a valid registration which he also assigned. With these two legal properties he also assigned, in the very words of the statute, "that part of the goodwill of the business connected with the use of and symbolized by the mark. . . ." He was selling chicks which his advertising of record shows were designated as "No. 111 HY-CROSS (Trade Mark) AMERICAN WHITES." As part of his assignment, by assigning the goodwill, he gave up the right to sell "HY-CROSS" chicks. This had been a part of his "business." By the assignment, Welp, the assignee, acquired that right. The record shows that he began selling "Hy-Cross Hatching Eggs" and chicks designated as "HY-CROSS 501," "HY-CROSS 610," and "HY-CROSS 656." Thus, what had once been Osborne's business in "HY-CROSS" chicks became Welp's business. We do not see what legal difference it would have made if a crate of eggs had been included in the assignment, or a flock of chickens destined to be eaten.

> As for the argument that the transfer should have been held illegal because Osborne sold one kind of chick and Welp sold another under the mark, whereby the public would be deceived, we think the record does not support this. The *type* of chick appears to have been otherwise indicated than by the trademark, as by the numbers above quoted as well as by name. Osborne, moreover, was not under any obligation to the public not to change the breed of chicks he sold under the mark from time to time.

In the instant case we need not decide whether the strict common law rule must apply or whether the approach, as suggested by Hy-Cross, should prevail. Inherent in the rules involving the assignment of a trademark is the recognition of protection against consumer deception. Basic to this concept is the proposition that any assignment of a trademark and its goodwill (with or without tangibles or intangibles assigned) requires the mark itself be used by the assignee on a product having substantially the same characteristics. *See e.g., Independent Baking Powder Co. v. Boorman*, 175 F. 448 (C.C.D.N.J. 1910) (alum baking powder is distinctive from phosphate baking powder); *Atlas Beverage Co. v. Minneapolis Brewing Co.*, 113 F.2d 672, 46 U.S.P.Q. 395 (8 Cir. 1940) (whiskey is a different product than beer); *H.H. Scott, Inc. v. Annapolis Electroacoustic Corp.*, 195 F. Supp. 208, 130 U.S.P.Q. 48 (D. Md. 1961) (audio reproduction equipment is distinctive from hi-fidelity consoles). *Cf. W.T. Wagner's Sons Co. v. Orange Snap Co.*, 18 F.2d 554 (5 Cir. 1927) (No infringement: ginger ale is in a different class than fruit flavored soft drinks).

Historically, this requirement is founded in the early case of *Filkins v. Blackman*, 9 Fed. Case 50 (No. 4786) (C.C.D. Conn. 1876), wherein the court observed:

> If the assignee should make a different article, he would not derive, by purchase from Jonas Blackman, a right which a court of equity would enforce, to use the name which the inventor had given to his own article, because such a use of the name would deceive the public. The right to the use of a trademark cannot be so enjoyed by an assignee that he shall have the right to affix the mark to goods differing in character or species from the article to which it was originally attached.

Id. at 52.

. . . .

Where a transferred trademark is to be used on a new and different product, any goodwill which the mark itself might represent cannot legally be assigned. "The trademark owner does not have the right to a particular word but to the use of the word as the symbol of particular goods." Callmann, § 78.1(a) at 426. To hold otherwise would be to condone public deceit. The consumer might buy a product thinking it to be of one quality or having certain characteristics and could find it only too late to be another. To say that this would be remedied by the public soon losing faith in the product fails to give the consumer the protection it initially deserves.

It is here that Grapette's use of the mark "Peppy" meets terminal difficulty. Grapette's intended use of the mark is one to simply describe its new pepper beverage.[4] The evidence is clear that Grapette did not intend to adopt or exploit any "goodwill" from the name "Peppy" and Fox's long association and use of it *with a cola syrup*. When one considers that Grapette did not acquire any of the assets of Fox, did not acquire any formula or process by which the Fox syrup was made, *cf. Mulhens & Kropff Inc. v. Fred Muelhens, Inc.*, 38 F.2d 287 (2 Cir. 1929), *rev'd*, 43 F.2d 937, 6 U.S.P.Q. 144 (2 Cir. 1930), *mandate clarified*, 48 F.2d 206, 9 U.S.P.Q. 182 (2 Cir. 1931), and then changed the type of beverage altogether, the assignment on its face must be considered void. It seems fundamental that either the defendant did not acquire any "goodwill" as required by law or if it did, assuming as defendant argues the mark itself possesses "goodwill," by use of the mark on a

[4]Mr. Fooks, Chairman of the Board of Grapette, testified:

> We went into his office (Mr. Fox's) office and I told him just frankly my situation, and I had this product ready for the market with no name, and I thought his name was a very suitable name, and if it wasn't too valuable I would like to purchase it.

Record at 176a–177a.

totally different product, Grapette intended to deceive the public. Either ground is untenable to the validity of the assignment.

We hold that the assignment to Grapette of the trademark "Peppy" is void and that Grapette possesses no standing to raise the equitable defense of laches.

Judgment reversed and remanded for further relief to be determined by the district court.

BLACKMUN, CIRCUIT JUDGE, concurring.

I concur, but on the ground that *Hy-Cross Hatchery, Inc. v. Osborne*, 303 F.2d 947, 133 U.S.P.Q. 687 (C.C.P.A. 1962), the case relied upon by the district court here, is not, or should not be, helpful authority for Grapette. *Hy-Cross* is a peculiar case factually in that, among other aspects, live baby chicks were the product of both assignor and assignee. The court did place some reliance on what it seemed to regard as a genuine transfer of goodwill, 303 F.2d at 950, 133 U.S.P.Q. at 689–690, and, accordingly, saw little legal significance in the absence of an assignment of tangible chicks themselves. *See J. C. Hall Co. v. Hallmark Cards, Inc.*, 340 F.2d 960, 963, 144 U.S.P.Q. 435, 437–438 (C.C.P.A. 1965), where the same court apparently relates the significance of *Hy-Cross* to the absence of a transfer of tangible assets.

But if, as Grapette urges, the *Hy-Cross* holding has greater import than its peculiar facts suggest for me, then I would regard it as aberrational to settled authority. I prefer to stay with the usual rule, long established I thought, that a trademark may not validly be assigned in gross. And product difference is only an aspect of this traditional rule. A naked assignment is all that Fox and Grapette attempted and effected. It is not enough.

MERRY HULL & CO. v. HI-LINE CO.

United States District Court, Southern District of New York
243 F. Supp. 45 (1965)

RYAN, CHIEF JUDGE.

. . . .

. . . In 1947, plaintiff through Gladys Geissmann (Merry Hull) designed a line of infants' and young children's wear called "Merry Mites by Merry Hull" which was received with great enthusiasm by fashion editors and department store representatives and buyers. In order to sell its designs plaintiff leased and began operation of two factories in Pennsylvania to manufacture these garments. To secure capital and finance this enterprise a corporation was formed on February 3, 1948 under the name of Merry Hull, Inc., which acquired all the assets of the plaintiff's Infant's Wear Division, the division which had been set up for the Merry Mites wardrobe, excepting the glove division. In need of additional capital after almost a year of manufacturing and selling Merry Hull, Inc., in November, 1948 was merged into a newly formed Ohio corporation, Merry Mites, Inc., which continued the business of its predecessor. Plagued by financial difficulties in the spring of 1950, Merry Mites, Inc. (Ohio) filed a Chapter X proceeding in Ohio and later, on July

14, 1950 was adjudged a bankrupt, and the reorganization trustee became the bankruptcy trustee. By order of a Referee in Bankruptcy, all the assets of the bankrupt were sold to one Rudolph, an auctioneer, and on November 30, 1950 at a public auction in New York defendant Hi-Line purchased from the auctioneer the bankrupt's name Merry Mites, Inc., as well as some of its assets. Defendant Merry Mites, Inc., was organized in New York on December 27, 1950 to take title to these assets and the name; it did so and commenced the manufacture and sale of boyswear under that name in spring of 1951, which it continued for the next six years and was engaged in at the time this suit was instituted. Defendants' claim of right to the use of the mark "Merry Mites" flows from the purchase by Hi-Line from the auctioneer.

In October, 1950, plaintiff commenced to make a few sales of children's garments and continued to do so sporadically through the next six years. Plaintiff's claim of right to the use of the mark derives from these sales, although it is not disputed that during these years 1950-57 it was not listed in the New York City Telephone Directory, that it made no attempt to sell and did not sell any of the large department stores, that it had no facilities to fill orders, and that its income tax returns during these years showed no gross or net income from the sale of children's garments, or from any business.

. . . .

Since the corporation had title to the trademark upon its bankruptcy the trustee was vested with the same, which he could sell, assign and transfer. And this brings us to plaintiff's second point which is that since there was no going business at the time of the sale by the trustee to Rudolph, the auctioneer, to which the mark could attach the transfer, it was legally ineffective to give Rudolph the right to the exclusive use of the mark.

Since the purpose of a mark is to protect the goodwill of a business, a right in the mark is created by its adoption and use in connection with that business, and if there is no business there is no goodwill and therefore nothing to protect. This is not to say, however, that goodwill can exist only in connection with an active going business and that at the moment business is suspended the goodwill ceases to exist for if this were so there would be few instances where a mark could be transferred in a bankruptcy sale, and little need for the Bankruptcy Act to provide for the vesting of title to trademarks in the Trustee (*May v. Goodyear Tire & Rubber Co.*, D.C., 10 F. Supp. 249). Goodwill is an asset of a bankrupt like any other asset, and to hold that upon the bankruptcy of the business, the goodwill vanishes would be to deprive the creditors of the bankrupt of what might be a substantial asset (*Hammond v. Bunker*, 9 R.P.C. 301; *Woodward v. White Satin Mills Corp.*, 8 Cir., 42 F.2d 987). Of course it does not follow that a trustee could not so deal with a mark as to effect its abandonment or its demise, and thus have nothing to transfer (*R. F. C. v. J. G. Menihan Corp.*, D.C., 28 F. Supp. 920). But, this was not the case here.

For the two months following the Chapter X petition, the trustee was authorized to and did continue the business of manufacturing and selling children's garments under the "Merry Mites" label; and following the adjudication he continued to do so from the bankrupt's two factories and its New York office — filling orders and completing unfinished garments for them; although now these operations were in order to liquidate the estate for the creditors rather than to keep the business going. Operations came to an end about one month before the Trustee was authorized by the Referee to accept Rudolph's offer to purchase the entire estate. The trustee's use of the mark kept it alive during this time.   *Intent*

In Rudolph's offer, which the Trustee was directed to accept, it was expressly stated that "it was understood that the trustee will deliver all of the assets of the bankrupt corporation including all rights the trustee may have in the corporate name, free and clear of any and all encumbrances." And it was clear at the hearing before the Referee to approve the acceptance of this offer that Rudolph in purchasing the corporate name was acquiring "the good will and everything else," for which he was paying $80,000. In fact it was at this very hearing that plaintiff through Mrs. Geissmann and counsel unsuccessfully objected to the sale of the trade name, the designs, patterns, trademark, tags, label, etc. claiming that title to them had reverted to plaintiff.

On October 4, 1950, the Referee directed the trustee to accept the offer of Rudolph and authorized and directed the trustee to deliver

> all the assets of the bankrupt corporation, including all rights the Trustee may have in the corporate name, free and clear of any and all encumbrances.

The only property of the bankrupt excluded from the sale was cash which the bankrupt had in a bank. The trustee executed and delivered to Rudolph a bill of sale, incorporating the above language, dated December 11, 1950.

The two newspaper notices which Rudolph ran to advertise the auction at which he hoped to dispose of what he had purchased, listed for sale "tradename, trademarks and patterns" of the bankrupt. On or about November 30, 1950, in New York City, he held an auction sale of the bankrupt stock of Merry Mites, Inc., which he had purchased. Defendants Sheldon and Weinreb attended the auction and, in competitive bidding, Sheldon, on behalf of defendant Hi-Line Co., Inc., purchased for $1,900 the name *"Merry Mites" and other assets of the bankrupt*, including patterns, piece goods, swatches, samples, and wire mannequins. In addition to receiving the personal property and merchandise, Hi-Line Co., Inc., received written *assignment* *& received* *of Rudolph's right, title and interest in and to the corporate name "Merry Mites, Inc."* A large quantity of finished and unfinished garments and furniture and the other assets listed in the Trustee's inventory were disposed of to other buyers. On December 27, 1950, the present defendant Merry Mites, Inc., was formed. The bill of sale from Hi-Line Co., Inc., to defendant dated March 29, 1951, transferred all its interest in the corporate name as well as all the chattels it had purchased from Rudolph — these as we have seen included samples, patterns, piece goods, swatches and wire mannequins. Between December 27, 1950 and March, 1951, defendant Merry Mites, Inc. set up manufacturing facilities to produce children's garments. In the spring of 1951, it began marketing children's garments, using its corporate name "Merry Mites, Inc." in connection with the manufacture and sale of children's garments in intrastate and interstate commerce. Since 1951, it has marketed its children's garments under the name "Merry Mites, Inc." and has sold them in the

151
Hi Line
sells
Merry Mites

better stores throughout the country, and has widely advertised them under this name with commercial success. The patterns and samples purchased from Rudolph and Hi-Line Co., Inc., have been used by defendant as primary samples for the manufacture of the garments although they had to be altered and reworked for commercial use. It is undisputed, and in fact forms part of plaintiff's claim for unfair competition, that the garments produced by defendant are substantially the same style as those formerly produced by the bankrupt.

So much for the intent of the parties, — we now consider the last question, whether as a matter of law the goodwill of the business passed with the corporate name so as to constitute it a legally protected trademark.

Because Hi-Line Co., Inc., did not purchase all or substantially all the assets of the estate as listed in the Trustee's inventory, plaintiff argues that it did not acquire the goodwill of the bankrupt. But it is not the volume that is the test — at least in this type of purchase where the sale is not that of reorganized going business, rather one in liquidation (*cf. American Dirigold Corp. v. Dirigold Metals Corp.*, 6 Cir., 125 F.2d 446; *United States Ozone Co. v. United States Ozone Co.*, 7 Cir., 62 F.2d 881; *S. F. Myers Co. v. Tuttle*, 2 Cir., 183 F. 235). Rather the test is whether the assets which are purchased with the name are sufficient to enable the purchaser to "go in real continuity with its past" (*Mutual Life Ins. Co. v. Menin*, 2 Cir., 115 F.2d 975). The importance of these assets to the continuity of the bankrupt's business as a manufacturer of children's distinctive garments, is obvious. As a matter of everyday business sense, patterns and samples of a garment claimed to be so distinctive as to be entitled to patent protection would seem to be necessary to the manufacture of the garments (*R. F C. v. J. G. Menihan Corp.*, *supra*). They were the unique feature of the business, as evidenced not only by their transfer to the Merry Mites, Inc. (Ohio) on the merger, but by the employment of Mrs. Geissmann as designer and her release of all claim to the name "Merry Mites," and to the designs — which were to become and remain the property of the corporation. Plaintiff recognized this, when after its unsuccessful attempts to obtain an assignment of the name first from the Trustee in Bankruptcy and then from Rudolph, it attempted to obtain these designs and patterns from defendant Hi-Line Co., Inc., in order to go into the business under the "Merry Mites" label.

We conclude that defendant obtained good title to the mark through Hi-Line's purchase at the bankruptcy sale, that it began to exploit it as soon as practicable, and that as a consequence any attempted use by plaintiff was unlawful, and assuming it sufficient, incapable of establishing it as the owner of the mark.

. . . .

[*Judgment for defendant.*]

NOTES ON ASSIGNMENT WITHOUT GOODWILL

(1) The requirement that the assignment must include the goodwill of the business *tangible* represented by the mark has been construed even in recent years by some courts *assets* to mean that the assignee must also acquire tangible assets to establish the transfer *required.* of goodwill. *PepsiCo, Inc. v. Grapette Co., supra; Mister Donut of America, Inc. v. Mr. Donut, Inc.*, 418 F.2d 838, 841–842 (9th Cir. 1969); *Uncas Mfg. Co. v. Clark & Coombs Co.*, 200 F. Supp. 831, 835–836 (D.R.I. 1962), *aff'd*, 309 F.2d 818 (1st Cir. 1962); *G's Bottom's Up Social Club v. F.P.M. Industries, Inc.*, 574 F. Supp. 1490 (S.D.N.Y. 1983). *See also Hough Manufacturing Corp. v. Virginia Metal Industries, Inc.*, 203 U.S.P.Q. 436 (E.D. Va. 1978) (separate earlier sale of defunct business's tangible assets rendered later sale of trademark and goodwill invalid as *Purpose:* an assignment in gross). Recognizing that the central purpose of the assignment rules *don't mislead* is to prevent consumers from being misled as to the source of the product, many *the public.* courts have accepted a mere recitation of transfer of goodwill as sufficient without *similarity* any transfer of tangible assets, so long as a substantial similarity exists between the *of products* products or services of the assignor and assignee. *VISA, U.S.A., Inc. v. Birmingham* *must exist.* *Trust National Bank*, 696 F.2d 1371 (Fed. Cir. 1982); *Money Store v. Harriscorp Finance, Inc.*, 689 F.2d 666 (7th Cir. 1982); *Glamorene Products Corp. v. Procter & Gamble Co.*, 538 F.2d 894 (C.C.P.A. 1976); *Sterling Brewers, Inc. v. Schenley Industries, Inc.*, 441 F.2d 675, 680 (C.C.P.A. 1971); *J.C. Hall Co. v. Hallmark Cards, Inc.*, 340 F.2d 960, 963 (C.C.P.A. 1965); *Hy-Cross Hatchery, Inc. v. Osborne*, 303 F.2d 947, 950 (C.C.P.A. 1962).

Compare Berni v. International Gourmet Restaurants, Inc., 838 F.2d 642, 646–47 (2d Cir. 1988), holding the assignment invalid where there was no evidence goodwill was transferred and operations did not resume within a reasonable time; *and Marshak v. Green*, 746 F.2d 927 (2d Cir. 1984), where the court reversed an order forcing sale of a musical group's service mark to satisfy a debt, finding "entertainment services are unique to the performers. Moreover, there is neither continuity of management nor quality and style of music," and concluding that the public would be confused if another group used the mark; *and Haymaker Sports, Inc. v. Turian*, 581 F.2d 257 (C.C.P.A. 1978), where the assignment was held invalid since assignee-escrowee never used the mark itself and never acquired any tangible assets or goodwill of assignor.

(2) An assignment of rights with a license back to the assignor has become an *License* accepted means of resolving disputes and quieting title. *E. & J. Gallo Winery v.* *back to assignor* *Gallo Cattle Co.*, 967 F.2d 1280, 1290 (9th Cir. 1992) ("a simultaneous assignment and license back of a mark is valid where . . . it does not disrupt continuity of the products or services associated with a given mark"); *Sands, Taylor & Wood Co. v. The Quaker Oats Co.*, 978 F.2d 947, 956–57 (7th Cir. 1992), *cert. denied*, 113 S. Ct. 1879 (1993); *VISA U.S.A., Inc. v. Birmingham Trust Nat'l Bank*, 696 F.2d 1371, 1377 (Fed. Cir. 1982) ("well-settled commercial practice"), *cert. denied*, 464 U.S. 826 (1983). In *E. & J. Gallo*, the Court reasoned that the requisite goodwill had been assigned in settlement of an infringement suit because the goodwill the plaintiff believed the defendant wrongfully appropriated was returned (assigned) to the plaintiff. *Compare Greenlon, Inc. of Cincinnati v. Greenlawn, Inc.*, 542 F. Supp.

895 (S.D. Ohio 1982), where the court found that while "no tangible assets must be transferred to the assignee to validate the assignment of a mark," the assignment at issue was invalid where assignor transferred no part of his business in effecting assignment and receiving license back.

(3) The Court in the *PepsiCo* case discusses legal recognition of the "advertising" and "guarantee" functions of trademarks. Are these consistent with the rationale of the Anglo-American system of trade identity protection which limits that protection to the source-indicating function? *See* Greenfield, *Good Will as a Factor in Trademark Assignments — A Comparative Study*, 60 Trademark Rep. 173 (1970). Would legal recognition of "advertising" or "guarantee" functions — permitting in-gross assignment of trade marks — result in a more commercially viable assignment law? If the law permitted assignment in entire disregard or derogation of the source-indicating function of trademarks, would new problems of trademark protection based upon confusion as to source be created? Assuming the correctness of the propositions that a trademark is a guarantee and a symbol of goodwill, is there, nevertheless, a fraud on, or deception of, the public or purchasers incident to entirely uninhibited alienability of marks?

(4) Respecting the assignment of federal trademark registrations, note that § 10 of the Lanham Act, 15 U.S.C. § 1060, provides that a trademark assignment document may be recorded and that such recordation " . . . shall be prima facie evidence of execution." The section further provides, "An assignment shall be void as against any subsequent purchaser for a valuable consideration without notice, unless it is recorded in the Patent Office within three months after the date thereof or prior to such subsequent purchase."

(5) In the *Merry Hull* case, trademark assets were held to have been validly transferred in a bankruptcy sale. How long should goodwill survive the cessation of business? *See Defiance Button Machine Co. v. C. & C. Metal Products Corp.*, 759 F.2d 1053 (2d Cir. 1985); *Hough Manufacturing Corp., supra* Note (1); *Johanna Farms, Inc. v. Citrus Bowl, Inc.*, 199 U.S.P.Q. 16 (E.D.N.Y. 1978); *Hot Shoppes, Inc. v. Hot Shoppe, Inc.*, 203 F. Supp. 777 (M.D.N.C. 1962); *Atlantic Brewing Co. v. Warsaw Brewing Co.*, 77 U.S.P.Q. 392 (Comm'r 1948). Is the new user obligated to maintain a character or quality of goods equivalent to those previously produced? Is the new user burdened to employ some means to distinguish his product so as to avoid misleading the public into the belief that the goods still emanate from the original source? *Compare Manhattan Medicine Co. v. Wood*, 108 U.S. 218, 223 (1883) *with* the cases in this section.

(6) Can trademark rights be "split" where confusion is likely? For example, where a trademark is used by a manufacturer for two related products, can the manufacturer assign to another the mark and goodwill as to one of the products? *See Gentry Canning Co. v. Blue Ribbon Growers, Inc.*, 138 U.S.P.Q. 536 (T.T.A.B. 1963); *McCane v. Mims*, 187 F.2d 163, 167 (C.C.P.A. 1951) ("we know of no law which prevents a seller from reserving from a sale of a business a line or lines of merchandise that he wishes to continue to exploit himself."); *Gould Engineering Co. v. Goebel*, 68 N.E. 702 (Mass. 1946). What consideration should be given to the public's interest in not being deceived? *See California Fruit Growers Exchange v.*

Sunkist Baking Co., Chapter 5, *infra*, wherein two plaintiffs agreed not to dispute each other's rights in the trademarks SUNKIST and SUN-KIST for fruits and vegetables respectively and then sued to enjoin a third party's use of SUNKIST for bread. The court felt the plaintiffs' agreement between themselves was inconsistent with and tarnished their claim that there was a likelihood of confusion caused by a third party's use of the same mark. Does this "Sunkist Doctrine" conflict with the general policy of courts favoring settlement of disputes through agreement? *Cf. American Chicle Co. v. Topps Chewing Gum Inc.*, 112 F. Supp. 848 (E.D.N.Y. 1953), *aff'd*, 210 F.2d 680 (2d Cir. 1954).

§ 4.05 Licensing and Franchising

INTRODUCTION

A trademark may be licensed for use by another where the licensor controls the nature and quality of the goods or services in connection with which it is used. The concept of licensing is simply that the licensee is an arm of the licensor. Thus, use by the licensee does not violate the source-indicating function of the trademark. Licensing without such control is called licensing in gross. In the absence of real and effective control by the licensor the trademark will no longer symbolize a particular source and the licensor may no longer have a protectable interest in the trademark. The principle of valid trademark licensing is frequently unknown to, and overlooked by, businesspeople and even their counsel. They are inclined to treat the trade identity rights as ordinary property rights, and particularly as patent rights, which they are not.

DAWN DONUT CO. v. HART'S FOOD STORES, INC.

United States Court of Appeals, Second Circuit
267 F.2d 358 (1959)

LUMBARD, CIRCUIT JUDGE.

. . . .

The final issue presented is raised by defendant's appeal from the dismissal of its counterclaim for cancellation of plaintiff's registration on the ground that the plaintiff failed to exercise the control required by the Lanham Act over the nature and quality of the goods sold by its licensees.

We are all agreed that the Lanham Act places an affirmative duty upon a licensor of a registered trademark to take reasonable measures to detect and prevent misleading uses of his mark by his licensees or suffer cancellation of his federal registration. The Act, 15 U.S.C.A. § 1064, provides that a trademark registration may be cancelled because the trademark has been "abandoned." And "abandoned" is defined in 15 U.S.C.A. § 1127 to include any act or omission by the registrant which causes the trademark to lose its significance as an indication of origin.

Prior to the passage of the Lanham Act many courts took the position that the licensing of a trademark separately from the business in connection with which it had been used worked an abandonment. *Reddy Kilowatt, Inc. v. Mid-Carolina Electric Cooperative, Inc.*, 4 Cir., 1957, 240 F.2d 282, 289; *American Broadcasting Co. v. Wahl Co.*, 2 Cir., 1941, 121 F.2d 412, 413; *Everett O. Fisk & Co. v. Fisk Teachers' Agency, Inc.*, 8 Cir., 1924, 3 F.2d 7, 9. The theory of these cases was that:

> A trade-mark is intended to identify the goods of the owner and to safeguard his good will. The designation if employed by a person other than the one whose business it serves to identify would be misleading. Consequently, "a right to the use of a trade-mark or a trade-name cannot be transferred in gross." *American Broadcasting Co. v. Wahl Co.*, *supra*, 121 F.2d at page 413.

Other courts were somewhat more liberal and held that a trade-mark could be licensed separately from the business in connection with which it had been used provided that the licensor retained control over the quality of the goods produced by the licensee. *E. I. DuPont de Nemours & Co. v. Celanese Corporation of America*, 1948, 167 F.2d 484, 35 C.C.P.A. 1061, 3 A.L.R.2d 1213; *see also* 3 A.L.R.2d 1226, 1277–1282 (1949) and cases there cited. But even in the *DuPont* case the court was careful to point out that naked licensing, viz. the grant of licenses without the retention of control, was invalid. *E. I. DuPont de Nemours & Co. v. Celanese Corporation of America*, *supra*, 167 F.2d at page 489.

The Lanham Act clearly carries forward the view of these latter cases that controlled licensing does not work an abandonment of the licensor's registration, while a system of naked licensing does. 15 U.S.C.A. § 1055 provides:

> Where a registered mark or a mark sought to be registered is or may be used legitimately by related companies, such use shall inure to the benefit of the registrant or applicant for registration, and such use shall not affect the validity of such mark or of its registration, provided such mark is not used in such manner as to deceive the public.

And 15 U.S.C.A. § 1127 defines "related company" to mean "any person who legitimately controls or is controlled by the registrant or applicant for registration in respect to the nature and quality of the goods or services in connection with which the mark is used."

Without the requirement of control, the right of a trademark owner to license his mark separately from the business in connection with which it has been used would create the danger that products bearing the same trademark might be of diverse qualities. *See American Broadcasting Co. v. Wahl Co.*, *supra*; *Everett O. Fisk & Co. v. Fisk Teachers' Agency, Inc.*, *supra*. If the licensor is not compelled to take some reasonable steps to prevent misuses of his trademark in the hands of others the public will be deprived of its most effective protection against misleading uses of a trademark. The public is hardly in a position to uncover deceptive uses of a trademark before they occur and will be at best slow to detect them after they happen. Thus, unless the licensor exercises supervision and control over the operations of its licensees the risk that the public will be unwittingly deceived will be increased and this is precisely what the Act is in part designed to prevent. *See* Sen. Report No. 1333, 79th Cong. 2d Sess. (1946). Clearly the only effective way to protect the public where a trademark is used by licensees is to place on the licensor the affirmative duty of policing in a reasonable manner the activities of his licensees.

Dissent argues for more finding of facts, and @ least limit dismissal of trademark only for finished goods —

I dissent [Note, author of opinion is disagreeing with part of the majority opinion] from the conclusion of the majority that the district court's findings are not clearly erroneous because while it is true that the trial judge must be given some discretion in determining what constitutes reasonable supervision of licensees under the Lanham Act, it is also true that an appellate court ought not to accept the conclusions of the district court unless they are supported by findings of sufficient facts. It seems to me that the only findings of the district judge regarding supervision are in such general and conclusory terms as to be meaningless. . . .

disagree w/ D.C. findings of facts

Plaintiff's licensees fall into two classes: (1) those bakers with whom it made written contracts providing that the baker purchase exclusively plaintiff's mixes and requiring him to adhere to plaintiff's directions in using the mixes; and (2) those bakers whom plaintiff permitted to sell at retail under the "Dawn" label doughnuts and other baked goods made from its mixes although there was no written agreement governing the quality of the food sold under the Dawn mark.

The contracts that plaintiff did conclude, although they provided that the purchaser use the mix as directed and without adulteration, failed to provide for any system of inspection and control. Without such a system plaintiff could not know whether these bakers were adhering to its standards in using the mix or indeed whether they were selling only products made from Dawn mixes under the trademark "Dawn."

The absence, however, of an express contract right to inspect and supervise a licensee's operations does not mean that the plaintiff's method of licensing failed to comply with the requirements of the Lanham Act. Plaintiff may in fact have exercised control in spite of the absence of any express grant by licensees of the right to inspect and supervise.

The question then, with respect to both plaintiff's contract and non-contract licensees, is whether the plaintiff in fact exercised sufficient control.

Here the only evidence in the record relating to the actual supervision of licensees by plaintiff consists of the testimony of two of plaintiff's local sales representatives that they regularly visited their particular customers and the further testimony of one of them, Jesse Cohn, the plaintiff's New York representative, that "in many cases" he did have an opportunity to inspect and observe the operations of his customers. The record does not indicate whether plaintiff's other sales representatives made any similar efforts to observe the operations of licensees.

Moreover, Cohn's testimony fails to make clear the nature of the inspection he made or how often he made one. His testimony indicates that his opportunity to observe a licensee's operations was limited to "those cases where I am able to get into the shop" and even casts some doubt on whether he actually had sufficient technical knowledge in the use of plaintiff's mix to make an adequate inspection of a licensee's operations.

The fact that it was Cohn who failed to report the defendant's use of the mark "Dawn" to the plaintiff casts still further doubt about the extent of the supervision Cohn exercised over the operations of plaintiff's New York licensees.

Thus I do not believe that we can fairly determine on this record whether plaintiff subjected its licensees to periodic and thorough inspections by trained personnel or whether its policing consisted only of chance, cursory examinations of licensees by technically untrained salesmen. The latter system of inspection hardly constitutes a sufficient program of supervision to satisfy the requirements of the Act.

Therefore it is appropriate to remand the counterclaim for more extensive findings on the relevant issues rather than hazard a determination on this incomplete and uncertain record. I would direct the district court to order the cancellation of plaintiff's registrations if it should find that the plaintiff did not adequately police the operations of its licensees.

But unless the district court finds some evidence of misuse of the mark by plaintiff in its sales of mixes to bakers at the wholesale level, the cancellation of plaintiff's registration should be limited to the use of the mark in connection with sale of the finished food products to the consuming public. Such a limited cancellation is within the power of the court. Section 1119 of 15 U.S.C.A. specifically provides that "In any action involving a registered mark the court may . . . order the cancellation of registrations, in whole or in part, . . ." Moreover, partial cancellation is consistent with § 1051(a)(1) of 15 U.S.C.A., governing the initial registration of trademarks which requires the applicant to specify "the goods in connection with which the mark is used and the mode or manner in which the mark is used in connection with such goods. . . ."

The district court's denial of an injunction restraining defendant's use of the mark "Dawn" on baked and fried goods and its dismissal of defendant's counterclaim are affirmed.

ALLIGATOR CO. v. ROBERT BRUCE, INC.

United States District Court, Eastern District of Pennsylvania
176 F. Supp. 377 (1959)

KIRKPATRICK, DISTRICT JUDGE.

These are motions by the defendants to dismiss and for summary judgment.

It appears from the complaint that The Alligator Company has been engaged since 1908 in the manufacture and sale of clothing, principally coats and raincoats. It is the owner of two registered trademarks, one of 1909 consisting of a picture of an alligator together with the words "Alligator Brand" in block capitals and the other, registered in 1929, consisting of the word "Alligator," in script. The latter is registered for various garments including "work shirts." There is nothing before the Court to indicate that The Alligator Company is or has been manufacturing shirts.

The plaintiff Crystal has been since October 1951 the sole distributor in this country for a rather widely known type of sport shirt manufactured in France and called the "Lacoste" shirt — a garment bearing an emblem embroidered on the breast and appearing also on the neck band and hang-tag, consisting of the representation of a scaly reptile which is intended for a crocodile but could just as well be an alligator. It further appears that in September 1958 The Alligator Company granted

[handwritten margin note at top: Company doesn't necessarily have to be in control of quality of goods to be related, however, this isn't determinative, however it does go towards proving "related"]

to Crystal the right to use the word "crocodile" and "the pictorial representations of a lizard-like reptile" in connection with the latter's sale of the Lacoste shirt as well as a number of other articles of men's clothing specified in the license.

It is not at the present time disputed that the defendants are selling shirts advertised *[handwritten: Robert Bruce]* as "Alligator" shirts and bearing labels affixed to the breasts thereof consisting of the representation of an alligator or crocodile. The main question raised by these motions, and the only one which requires discussion, arises from the defendant's contention that, inasmuch as The Alligator Company has given Crystal the right to use its trademarks in connection with the sale of goods not manufactured by The Alligator Company, the trademarks no longer identify the goods with the maker, have lost their significance as an indication of origin and, consequently, must be held to have been abandoned. *[handwritten: Δ - trademark no longer identifies good w/ the maker.]*

. . . .

Alligator's license agreement with Crystal has been brought before the Court by affidavit and a study of it, particularly Section 2(b) and (c), shows that Crystal agrees to maintain the quality of its trademarked product in "the same relative quality *[handwritten: System of inspection]* position in the apparel market" as samples submitted with the agreement. An adequate system of inspection is provided for by which Alligator is in a position to learn at any time whether such quality is being maintained and, upon a determination that it is not, to terminate the agreement.

This, it seems to me, constitutes Crystal, on paper at least, a related company *[handwritten: on paper it is "related"]* within the meaning of the statute. However, I do not think that the issue is one which can be decided for either party on a motion to dismiss or for summary judgment. The mere fact that one company has the legal right to control the quality of the goods sold under the trademark is not finally and conclusively determinative of the question whether the companies are "related." The statute does not refer to a person whom the registrant has the right to control." The language is "any person who . . . *is controlled by the registrant."* What the parties actually do in carrying out the agreement is necessarily a question of fact and presents an issue which precludes the entry of judgment at this time.

The defendants cite an opinion of the Commissioner of Patents in *Ex parte C. B. Donald Co.*, 117 U.S.P.Q. 485. That case is distinguishable upon its facts in that *[handwritten: Ex Parte Decision]* it deals with an application for registration by a person, admittedly not the owner of the mark nor the manufacturer of the goods. The Commissioner at the beginning of his opinion states that Section 5 of the Lanham Act was not intended to create *[handwritten: A not intended to create new rights]* any new rights, something which it would be doing if interpreted to give a right of registration to one who does not own the mark, has never used it or made the goods. It is pointed out that Section 5 recognizes the rights of the owner of a mark but does not create any right of ownership which did not theretofore exist. If, in view of some language in the latter part of the opinion, the Commissioner is to be understood as denying the right of a trademark owner to license a related company to use the mark, it seems to me that such statement would be in direct conflict with the Act and would have to be disregarded. Section 5 of the Lanham Act by expressly excepting cases where an element of deceit is involved impliedly recognizes that, if goods sold under a trademark have to be in conformity with the trademark owner's standards of quality, there is no deception of the public.

The defendants' motions are denied.

THE ORIGINAL GREAT AMERICAN CHOCOLATE CHIP COOKIE COMPANY v. RIVER VALLEY COOKIES, LIMITED

United States Court of Appeals, Seventh Circuit
970 F.2d 273 (1992)

POSNER, CIRCUIT JUDGE.

. . . .

This case arises from a squabble between a franchisor that we shall call the "Cookie Company" and the Sigels, who had a franchise to operate a Cookie Company store in a shopping mall in Aurora, Illinois. The company terminated the Sigels' franchise but they continued to sell cookies under the company's trademark, using batter purchased elsewhere after their supply of Cookie Company batter ran out. So the company sued them (and their corporate entity) to enjoin their violating the Trademark Act, 15 U.S.C. §§ 1051 *et seq.*, and moved for a preliminary injunction. The Sigels counterclaimed, charging that their franchise agreement had been terminated in violation both of the franchise agreement and of the Illinois Franchise Disclosure Act, Ill. Rev. Stat. ch. 121, ¶ 1719, and moving for preliminary injunction directing the Cookie Company to restore their franchise. (Both parties had additional grounds for their motions, but these need not be discussed.) The district court granted the Sigels' motion and denied that of the Cookie Company.

The Sigels received the franchise in 1985. Between 1987 and the issuance of the preliminary injunction last year, they committed a number of material breaches. They repeatedly failed to furnish insurance certificates indicating that the Cookie Company was an additional insured on the Sigels' liability insurance policy. They paid four invoices (aggregating either $13,000 or $30,000 — the record is unclear) more than 10 days after they were due, which meant more than 20 or more than 40 days after billing, because the agreement gave the Sigels either 10 or 30 days to pay their bills, depending on what kind of bill it was. (The average delay beyond the due date was either 28 days or 31 days; again the record is unclear.) They made five other late payments. Seven times they sent the Cookie Company checks that bounced. They flunked several inspections by the company's representatives, who found oozing cheesecake, undercooked and misshapen cookies, runny brownies, chewing gum stuck to counters, and ignorant and improperly dressed employees. An independent auditor found that in a three-year period the Sigels had underreported their gross sales by more than $40,000 (a nontrivial 2.8 percent of the total — almost three times the allowed margin of error); the result was to deprive the Cookie Company of almost $3,000 in royalties. After the company terminated the franchise, the Sigels pretended it was still in effect, refused to vacate the premises, and violated the franchise agreement by selling unauthorized products — cookies made with batter not supplied by the Cookie Company.

[Handwritten annotations at top:] Using trademark in violation of franchise. No sign of inequitable conduct by company. Inspections to verify std of goods were performed + ____ were legal.

After most of these violations the company sent the Sigels a notice of default and the violations were then cured, though not always within 5 days as required by the franchise agreement. The company relies on the alternative ground for termination — three or more violations within a 12-month period, a ground that does not require notice or an opportunity to cure. By the Sigels' own account, most of the violations occurred within an even shorter period in 1989 and 1990 when the store was being mismanaged by the person whom the Sigels (who live in St. Louis) had hired to run it.

The fact that the Cookie Company may, as the Sigels argue, have treated other franchisees more leniently is no more a defense to a breach of contract than laxity in enforcing the speed limit is a defense to a speeding ticket. The fact particularly pressed by the Sigels that their violations may have been the fault not of the Sigels themselves but of their manager and that they ceased when the manager was replaced is similarly irrelevant. Liability for breach of contract is strict. *Patton v. Mid-Continent Systems, Inc.*, 841 F.2d 742, 750 (7th Cir. 1988). It does not require proof of inexcusable neglect or deliberate wrongdoing. Even if it did, the Sigels would lose because the misconduct of a manager within the scope of his employment is attributed to the owner even in a negligence case. The case must be treated as if they had managed the store in person. We do not share the popular prejudice against absentee ownership but the Sigels cannot be allowed to obtain a legal advantage by virtue of being absentee owners.

. . .

[Handwritten annotation:] good faith req'd to contract

That does not end our inquiry. Illinois like other states requires, as a matter of common law, that each party to a contract act with good faith, and some Illinois cases say that the test for good faith "seems to center on a determination of commercial reasonability." *Dayton v. McDonald's Corp.*, 466 N.E.2d 958, 973 (Ill. App. 1984); *Kawasaki Shop of Aurora, Inc. v. Kawasaki Motors Corp.*, 544 N.E.2d 457, 463 (Ill. App. 1989); *see also Lippo v. Mobil Oil Corp.*, 776 F.2d 706, 714 n. 14 (7th Cir. 1985). The equation, tentative though it is ("seems to center on") makes it sound as if, contrary to our earlier suggestion, the judges have carte blanche to declare contractual provisions negotiated by competent adults unreasonable and to refuse to enforce them. We understand the duty of good faith in contract law differently. There is no blanket duty of good faith; nor is reasonableness the test of good faith.

Contract law does not require parties to behave altruistically toward each other; it does not proceed on the philosophy that I am my brother's keeper. That philosophy may animate the law of fiduciary obligations but parties to a contract are not each other's fiduciaries, *Continental Bank, N.A. v. Everett*, 964 F.2d 701, 704–06 (7th Cir. 1992); *Dyna-Tel, Inc. v. Lakewood Engineering & Mfg. Co.*, 946 F.2d 539, 543 (7th Cir. 1991); *Market Street Associates Limited Partnership v. Frey*, 941 F.2d 588, 593-95 (7th Cir. 1991); *Kham & Nate's Shoes No. 2, Inc. v. First Bank of Whiting*, 908 F.2d 1351, 1357 (7th Cir. 1990) — even if the contract is a franchise. *Murphy v. White Hen Pantry*, 691 F.2d 350, 354 (7th Cir. 1982). Contract law imposes a duty, not to "be reasonable," but to avoid taking advantage of gaps in a contract in order to exploit the vulnerabilities that arise when contractual performance is

[Handwritten annotation at bottom:] provision invoked dishonestly = "bad faith"

sequential rather than simultaneous. *Market Street Associates Limited Partnership v. Frey, supra,* 941 F.2d at 593–96. Suppose A hires B to paint his portrait to his satisfaction and B paints it and A in fact is satisfied but says he is not in the hope of chivvying down the agreed-upon price because the portrait may be unsaleable to anyone else. This, as we noted in *Morin Building Products Co. v. Baystone Construction, Inc.,* 717 F.2d 413, 415 (7th Cir. 1983), would be bad faith, not because any provision of the contract was unreasonable and had to be reformed but because a provision had been invoked dishonestly to achieve a purpose contrary to that for which the contract had been made. The same would be true here, we may assume, if the Sigels had through their efforts built the Aurora cookie store into an immensely successful franchise and the Cookie Company had tried to appropriate the value they had created by canceling the franchise on a pretext: three (or four, or five or for that matter a dozen) utterly trivial violations of the contract that the company would have overlooked but for its desire to take advantage of the Sigels' vulnerable position. *Wright-Moore Corp. v. Ricoh Corp.,* 908 F.2d 128, 136–37 (7th Cir. 1990). This has not been shown. Not only were many of the violations not trivial, but there is no suggestion of exceptional performance by the Sigels. True, it was a new franchise, and it has been doing well ever since the incompetent manager was booted out; but it is in a prime location, and the company in negotiating the terms of the franchise rated it a "good" franchise — one very likely to do well.

. . .

The preliminary injunction should have been denied for the additional reason that the Sigels had infringed the Cookie Company's trademarks, in violation of the Trademark Act. (The Sigels do not, and cannot, *S & R Corp. v. Jiffy Lube Int'l, Inc.,* 968 F.2d 371, 374–75, 376, 377–78 (3d Cir. 1992), deny the violation.) Unclean hands is a traditional defense to an action for equitable relief. The purpose is to discourage unlawful activity, and is as relevant to preliminary as to final relief. *Shondel v. McDermott,* 775 F.2d 859, 868 (7th Cir. 1985). It is true that a modern chancellor unlike his medieval forbears does not have uncabined discretion to punish moral shortcomings by withholding equitable relief. *Polk Bros., Inc. v. Forest City Enterprises, Inc.,* 776 F.2d 185, 193 (7th Cir. 1985); *Proimos v. Fair Automotive Repair, Inc.,* 808 F.2d at 1275. Modern equity is a system of entitlements. But equitable relief is costly to the judicial system, especially in a case such as this where the relief sought would cast the court in a continuing supervisory role. It would make no sense to incur that cost on behalf of someone who was trying to defraud the person against whom he was seeking the court's assistance. "One who has defrauded his adversary to his injury in the subject matter of the action will not be heard to assert a right in equity." *Fruhling v. County of Champaign,* 420 N.E.2d 1066, 1071 (Ill. App. 1981), quoted in *Polk Bros., Inc. v. Forest City Enterprises, Inc., supra,* 776 F.2d at 193; *see also id.* at 194.

The Sigels argue that they had no choice but to infringe the Cookie Company's trademarks surreptitiously, because, had they stopped selling cookies under the company's trademarks after the company stopped shipping batter to them, they would have been forced to default on their promissory note. They are wrong. They had a choice. They could have sued the company for breach of contract and violation

[handwritten margin note: By acting fraudulently there should not be granted equitable relief] of the disclosure law and moved for a preliminary injunction in that action. Instead of following that route, the open and honorable one, they infringed the company's trademarks covertly and did not move for an injunction until they were discovered and sued for infringement. They should not be rewarded with a preliminary injunction for their putting their franchisor to the expense of suing them for trademark infringement. Although, as we explained in *Polk Bros.*, the course of decisions in Illinois (it is Illinois' version of the doctrine of unclean hands that we must apply in this diversity case) has not run entirely true, 776 F.2d at 194, we think an Illinois court would deny an injunction to a firm that by its fraudulent conduct had precipitated the very suit in which it was seeking the injunction. "If the plaintiff creates or contributes to the situation on which it relies, the court denies equitable relief in order to deter the wrongful conduct." *Id.* at 193.

In pooh-poohing their misconduct the Sigels place too much weight on our decision in *Lippo*. That decision held that the particular franchise agreement, which did not have the terms as the one here, made the sale of misbranded product a curable violation. The decision, interpreted narrowly in *Beermart, Inc. v. Stroh Brewery Co.*, 804 F.2d 409, 412 (7th Cir. 1986), should not be understood to stand for the broader proposition that trademark infringement by a franchisee is a trivial offense that should never entitle the franchisor to cancel the franchise, or for the still broader proposition that in a dispute between franchisee and franchisor the judicial thumb should be on the franchisee's pan of the balance. All other objections to one side (for example, the judicial oath, which, echoing Deuteronomy, requires judges to judge "without respect to persons"), such a tilt is hardly likely to help franchisees as a group. James A. Brickley, Federick H. Dark & Michael S. Weisbach, *The Economic Effects of Franchise Termination Laws*, 34 J. Law & Econ. 101 (1991). The more difficult it is to cancel a franchise, the higher the price that franchisors will charge for franchises. So in the end the franchisees will pay for judicial liberality and everyone will pay for the loss of legal certainty that ensues when legal principles are bent however futilely to redistributive ends.

The idea that favoring one side or the other in a class of contract disputes can redistribute wealth is one of the most persistent illusions of judicial power. It comes from failing to consider the full consequences of legal decisions. Courts deciding contract cases cannot durably shift the balance of advantages to the weaker side of the market; they can only make contracts more costly to that side in the future, because franchisors will demand compensation for bearing onerous terms. *Amoco Oil Co. v. Ashcraft, supra*, 791 F.2d at 522.

The Cookie Company appealed not only from the grant of the Sigels' motion for a preliminary injunction but also from the denial of its motion for a preliminary injunction against the Sigels' violation of its trademarks. To this part of the company's appeal the Sigels do not deign to reply. We take this to be a concession that they have no defense to the motion. The Cookie Company is entitled to the injunction that it sought, and we remand for its entry.

Reversed and remanded, with directions.

NOTES ON LICENSING AND FRANCHISING

(1) Originally, at common law, the licensing of a trademark to another ordinarily worked an abandonment of trademark rights. *See, e.g., MacMahan Pharmacal Co. v. Denver Chem. Mfg. Co.*, 113 F. 468 (8th Cir. 1901); Rogers, *Good Will, Trade Marks and Unfair Trading*, 106 (1914). It gradually developed, however, that trade identity rights could be licensed for use by another as long as the licensor controlled the nature and quality of the goods and services with which they are used. *See* Shniderman, *Trade-Mark Licensing — A Saga of Fantasy And Fact*, 14 Law & Contemp. Probs. 248 (1949). In 1946, the Lanham Act codified the existing common law by providing that a registration is not invalidated where a mark is used by a "related company" (15 U.S.C. § 1055). As amended in 1988, the Lanham Act defines a related company as "any person whose use of a mark is controlled by the owner of the mark with respect to the nature and quality of the goods or services on or in connection with which the mark is used" (15 U.S.C. § 1127).

(2) While a license can be oral, a separate written license agreement is an important foundation for proof of the licensor's control of the nature and quality of the goods or services in connection with which the licensed trademark is used. Such agreements, together with the actual exercise of control, are an essential requirement for any effective licensing program. *See* Diamond, *Requirements of a Trademark Licensing Program*, Bus. Law. 295 (Jan. 1962); *Tandy Corp. v. Marymac Industries, Inc.*, 213 U.S.P.Q. 702 (S.D. Tex. 1981) (licensee's use of mark for mail order services violated license agreement and was enjoined under § 43(a) of the Lanham Act). The License agreement should describe (a) the mark or other means for trade identity involved; (b) the goods or services in connection with which it is to be used; (c) the standards of quality for the goods or services; (d) the methods of supervision and control (regular submission of samples, rights of inspection, maintenance of test re cords, etc.); (e) any limitations on territory, sublicensing, or the sale of competing goods (*but see* the section on Antitrust Law in Chapter 7, *infra*); (f) the time period or duration of the license and reversion of all rights after termination; and (g) the termination of rights of both parties for breach of the license agreement.

(3) Failure of a licensor or franchisor to take reasonable measures to control the activities of a licensee or franchisee with respect to the nature and quality of the goods or services bearing the mark can result in the loss of trademark rights. 15 U.S.C. §§ 1055, 1127. In *Universal City Studios, Inc. v. Nintendo Co.*, 578 F. Supp. 911, 929 (S.D.N.Y. 1983), *aff'd*, 746 F.2d 112 (2d Cir. 1984), the Court held that the plaintiff's rights were forfeited and denied any relief by virtue of uncontrolled licensing:

> Uncontrolled licensing of a mark results in abandonment of the mark by the licensor. [citations omitted] "The critical question . . . is whether the plaintiff sufficiently policed and inspected its licensees' operations to guarantee the quality of the products they sold under its trademarks to the public." [Citations omitted].

To the same effect is *First Interstate Bancorp v. Stenquist*, 16 U.S.P.Q.2d 1704 (N.D. Cal. 1990), in which plaintiff, owner of the registered mark FIRST INTER-STATE for banking services, sued defendant, who used the same mark for real estate services. The Court granted plaintiff summary judgment on defendant's infringement counterclaim. The Court found that: "[D]efendant's grant of a license to use his trademark without any significant control over the quality of the services provided by the licensee constituted a naked license, and resulted in abandonment of the rights to the trademark." Informal contacts and a seven-year professional and social relationship between the licensor and licensee were not enough to establish control over the quality of the licensee's work. *informal contacts not enough*

(4) There is variation as to what constitutes "adequate" control. It is clear, *What's Control* however, that it is the exercise of control, not merely the right to exercise control, which will be evaluated by the courts to determine whether the franchisor has lost its trademark rights. *See General Motors Corp. v. Gibson Chemical & Oil Corp.*, 786 F.2d 105, 110 (2d Cir. 1986). The traditional rule is that no relief ordinarily can be had if the franchisor fails to exercise control over both the nature of the goods and their quality. It has been held that a license which gives a licensee *carte blanche* to manufacture any kind of product under the licensed mark is void as against public policy. *Cartier, Inc. v. Three Sheaves Co.*, 465 F. Supp. 123, 129 (S.D.N.Y. 1979). The licensor may itself perform the necessary inspection and testing to determine compliance with its quality standards, or it may delegate such authority to a third party. *Accurate Merchandising, Inc. v. American Pacific*, 186 U.S.P.Q. 197, 200 (S.D.N.Y. 1975). In either case, the quality standards must be prescribed by the licensor.

(5) In some situations, if there is a sufficiently close relationship between the licensor and licensee, *e.g.*, where they share the same officers, sufficient quality control may result from that relationship alone. *Taco Cabana Int'l, Inc. v. Two Pesos, Inc.*, 932 F.2d 1113, 1121 (5th Cir. 1991), *aff'd*, 113 S. Ct. 20 (1992); *Hurricane Fence Co. v. A-1 Hurricane Fence Co.*, 468 F. Supp. 975 (S.D. Ala. 1979); *Accurate Merchandising, Inc. v. American Pacific*, 186 U.S.P.Q. 197 (S.D.N.Y. 1975). In *In re Raven Marine, Inc.*, 217 U.S.P.Q. 68 (T.T.A.B. 1983), however, the Trademark Trial and Appeal Board held that merely having the same stockholders, directors or officers, without proof of effective licensing controls, did not constitute a valid licensing arrangement. In a few cases, courts have held that a licensor properly relied on the efforts of a licensee to protect the quality of the goods. *See, e.g., Syntex Laboratories, Inc. v. Norwich Pharmacal Co.*, 315 F. Supp. 45, 56 (S.D.N.Y. 1970), *aff'd*, 437 F.2d 566 (2d Cir. 1971); *Land O'Lakes Creameries, Inc. v. Oconomowoc Canning Co.*, 221 F. Supp. 576, 581 (E.D. Wis. 1963), *aff'd*, 330 F.2d 667, 670 (7th Cir. 1964); *Embedded Moments, Inc. v. International Silver Co.*, 648 F. Supp. 187 (E.D.N.Y. 1986). To maintain the validity of its mark, however, a licensor should not rely on the licensee's efforts to insure compliance with the licensor's standards. McCarthy, *Trademarks and Unfair Competition*, § 18:17 (3d ed. 1992).

(6) Notwithstanding the strong language in the decisions requiring supervision and control, some courts have been reluctant to hold that valuable trade identity

rights have been lost unless the failure to exercise control has in fact resulted in deception or injury. *Taco Cabana Int'l, Inc. v. Two Pesos, Inc.*, 932 F.2d 1113, 1121 (5th Cir. 1991), *aff'd on other grounds*, 112 S. Ct. 2753 (1992) (holding there need not be formal quality control where "the particular circumstances of the licensing arrangement indicate the public will not be deceived"); *Transgo, Inc. v. Ajac Transmission Parts Corp.*, 768 F.2d 1001, 1017–18 (9th Cir. 1985); *United States Jaycees v. Philadelphia Jaycees*, 639 F.2d 134 (3d Cir. 1981); *Heaton Distributing Co. v. Union Tank Car Co.*, 387 F.2d 477 (8th Cir. 1967); *Dawn Donut, supra*; *Purity Cheese Co. v. Frank Ryser Co.*, 153 F.2d 88 (7th Cir. 1946). *But see Yamamoto & Co. (America) v. Victor United, Inc.*, 219 U.S.P.Q. 968, 980 (C.D. Cal. 1982); *Sheila's Shine Products, Inc. v. Sheila Shine, Inc.*, 486 F.2d 114 (5th Cir. 1973); *Checker Cab Mfg. Corp. v. Green Cab Co.*, 35 F.2d 631 (6th Cir. 1929); *First Interstate Bancorp. v. Stenquist*, 16 U.S.P.Q.2d 1704, 1707, *summary judgment granted*, 18 U.S.P.Q.2d 1159 (N.D. Cal. 1990) (naked license); *Universal City Studios v. Nintendo Co.*, 578 F. Supp. 911, 929 (S.D.N.Y. 1983), *aff'd*, 746 F.2d 112 (2d Cir. 1984). *See also* Borchard, *Trademark Sublicensing and Quality Control*, 70 Trademark Rep. 99 (1980). *Cf.* Park, *"Naked" Licensing Is Not A Four Letter Word: Debunking The Myth of the Quality Control Requirement in Trademark Licensing*, 82 Trademark Rep. 531 (1992).

(7) Can a licensor authorize a licensee to extend use of a trademark to new or different products or services? *See* the *Alligator* case, *supra*; *Yamamoto & Co. (America) v. Victor United, Inc.*, *supra* Note (6). Must a licensor use the trademark before licensing its use by others? The Revision Act confirmed that use by a licensee is adequate to bestow rights on a licensor. 15 U.S.C. § 1056.

Note that the licensee will normally be estopped to deny the licensor's exclusive rights in the mark where there is a valid license agreement. *Smith v. Dental Prod. Co.*, 140 F.2d 140 (7th Cir. 1944), *cert. denied*, 322 U.S. 743 (1944); *E.F Prichard Co. v. Consumers Brewing Co.*, 136 F.2d 512 (6th Cir. 1943), *cert. denied*, 321 U.S. 763 (1944). And use of the mark by an ex-licensee after license termination normally will constitute infringement. *Church of Scientology International v. Elmira Mission of The Church of Scientology*, 794 F.2d 38 (2d Cir. 1986).

Should a licensee be estopped as well from contesting the validity of the trademark during the course of the licensing agreement? *See Seven-Up Bottling Co. v. The Seven Up Co.*, 192 U.S.P.Q. 121 (E.D.Mo. 1976). In *Edwin K. Williams & Co. v. Williams*, 542 F.2d 1053 (9th Cir. 1976), the Court held that a licensee who resisted any supervision of quality control "should not be permitted" to assert abandonment of the mark by licensor due to lack of sufficient control. *Compare Professional Golfers Assn. v. Banker's Life Co.*, 186 U.S.P.Q. 447 (5th Cir. 1975), in which the Court adopted the "intermediate view" that "after expiration of the license, a former trademark licensee may challenge the licensor's title on facts which arose after the contract has expired."

(8) Under 15 U.S.C. § 1114(1), the owner of a registered mark, including a licensor, has standing to sue for infringement of that mark. There has been a split of authority, however, as to whether a *licensee* should have such standing. *Compare DEP Corp. v. Interstate Cigar Corp. Inc.*, 622 F.2d 621, 623–624 (2d Cir. 1980),

reasoning that a licensee should not, with *Wynn Oil Co. v. Thomas*, 839 F.2d 1183, 1189–1190 (6th Cir. 1988), where the court concluded, without discussion, that an exclusive licensee has standing to sue for infringement of a registered mark.

Some courts have found standing for exclusive and nonexclusive licensees under the broader language of § 43(a) of the Lanham Act, 15 U.S.C. § 1125(a), which provides that an infringer "shall be liable in a civil action by any person who believes that he or she is or is likely to be damaged by such act." *See, e.g., Frisch's Restaurants, Inc. v. Elby's Big Boy, Inc.*, 670 F.2d 642, 649 (6th Cir. 1982) (exclusive licensee-franchisee had standing to sue under § 43(a)); *Quabaug Rubber Co. v. Fabiano Shoe Co.*, 567 F.2d 154, 159–160 (1st Cir. 1977) (non-exclusive U.S. distributor had no standing to sue for infringement under § 32, but did have standing under § 43(a)); *Ferrero U.S.A., Inc. v. Ozark Trading, Inc.*, 753 F. Supp. 1240, 1245 (D.N.J. 1991), *aff'd*, 19 U.S.P.Q.2d 1468 (3d Cir. 1991) (exclusive U.S. distributor had standing under § 43(a) to sue parallel importer; "use of the broad phraseology 'any person' in the Lanham Act . . . denotes an intent not to limit enforcement to merely the trademark owner"). It still may be necessary, however, under some circumstances to join the licensor as a party. *JTG of Nashville, Inc. v. Rhythm Band, Inc.*, 693 F. Supp. 623, 627 (M.D. Tenn. 1988) (ordering joinder of licensor in action by licensee).

(9) Characterization of a transfer of trademark rights can have tax consequences as well. If the transfer is characterized as an assignment, the money made from the assignment by the assignor will be considered a capital gain; if the transfer is found to be a license, the money made will be treated as ordinary income. *See Consolidated Foods Corp. v. United States*, 196 U.S.P.Q. 664 (7th Cir. 1978) (royalty arrangement found to be inconsistent with the characteristics of an assignment). The 1986 tax law eliminated the preferential corporate capital gains rate, but the concept of capital gains remains important in that corporate capital losses are still only deductible to the extent of corporate capital gains. *See generally* Bell, Smith & Simensky, *A State Tax Strategy for Trademarks*, 81 Trademark Rep. 445 (1991); Reed, *Trademarks In the Sale of Part of a Business: Concurrent Use and Licensing*, 80 Trademark Rep. 514 (1990).

(10) In the 1960's, the concept of licensing became the basis for a new industry for exploiting goodwill: franchising. In the early stages of this franchising boom, some enterprises and their promoters were primarily concerned with the sale of franchises rather than their successful operation. For this and other reasons, the franchisee was often left with few rights under the franchise agreement, which led to federal and state regulation of the industry. *See generally* Glickman, *Business Organizations: Franchising* (1994).

In the 1970's, various state franchising laws were enacted and the Federal Trade Commission's Trade Regulation Rule on Franchising was adopted as a new means to protect prospective franchisees. Bus. Franchise Guide (CCH) ¶¶ 3000–4530.03; 16 C.F.R. § 436 (1979). The FTC and most states seek to enhance franchisee rights through disclosure of specific categories of information which may bear upon the desirability of a franchise. Enforcement to date has been largely limited to cases involving affirmative, false and fraudulent disclosures. Bus. Franchise Guide (CCH)

¶¶ 8354, 8807. Private remedies are not available under the FTC Rule but can be had under several of the state statutes. 1981 — Trade Cas. (CCH) ¶ 64,031; *Freedman v. Meldy's, Inc.*, 587 F. Supp. 658 (E.D. Pa. 1984); Bus. Franchise Guide (CCH), *supra.* In addition, the Uniform Franchise and Business Opportunities Act, which was promulgated in 1987 and has still not been adopted in any state, provides for administrative enforcement of minimum standards of "good faith" derived from the Restatement (Second) of Contracts § 205 and the Uniform Commercial Code § 2-103. Bus. Franchise Guide (CCH) ¶¶ 6080–6193.

(11) In litigation, the tension is often between the franchisor's claim of a right to protection under the trademark laws and the franchisee's claim of rights under the franchise agreement and federal and state compliance laws. Ordinarily, courts give precedence to the need for protection under the trademarks laws, and use of a mark by an ex-franchisee after termination of the franchise will constitute infringement. This result comports with the fundamental trademark principle that such unlicensed use is likely to confuse and irreparably harm the public. 15 U.S.C. § 1127; *Church of Scientology Int'l v. Elmira Mission of The Church of Scientology*, 794 F.2d 38, 44 (2d Cir. 1986) ("the public interest is especially served by issuing a preliminary injunction against a former licensee as the licensee's status increases the probability of consumer confusion"); *S&R Corp. v. Jiffy Lube Int'l, Inc.*, 968 F.2d 371, 374–378 (3d Cir. 1992) (preliminary injunction granted); *The Original Great American Chocolate Chip Cookies Co. v. River Valley Cookies Ltd.*, 970 F.2d 273 (7th Cir. 1992), *rehearing en banc denied*, 1992 U.S. App. LEXIS 20894; *Downtowner Passport Int'l Hotel Corp. v. Norlew, Inc.*, 841 F.2d 214, 219 (8th Cir. 1988) (the quantum of proof of likelihood of confusion needed is less in actions against a terminated franchisee); *Century 21 Real Estate Corp. v. Sandlin*, 846 F.2d 1175 (9th Cir. 1988) (permanent injunction granted on summary judgment motion); *Ramada Inns, Inc. v. Gadsden Motel Co.*, 804 F.2d 1562 (11th Cir. 1986) (consequential damages awarded under Lanham Act).

(12) Franchisees may make a wide range of contract claims after termination directed to such issues as wrongful termination and such remedies as recission and the reallocation of any wrongful gains by the franchisor. Fundamental to many of these claims is the implied covenant of good faith and fair dealing, a talisman often invoked by terminated franchisees.

Ordinarily, however, no obligation should be implied which will obliterate a right expressly given under a written contract. In *Hubbard Chevrolet Co. v. General Motors Corp.*, 873 F.2d 873 (5th Cir.), *cert. denied*, 493 U.S. 978 (1989), for example, the Fifth Circuit refused to apply an "implied" covenant of good faith and fair dealing to the actions taken by General Motors in a dispute regarding the relocation of an automobile dealership and held that the District Court erred when it instructed the jury on that implied covenant. The Court noted that it would not imply the good faith covenant where the parties have unmistakably expressed their respective rights. *Hubbard*, 873 F.2d at 877. *See also The Original Great American Chocolate Chip Cookie Co. v. River Valley Cookies, Ltd., supra.*

(13) Courts favoring implied covenants of good faith and fair dealing do so in part because the concept evokes ethical principles of fair play. Strong support exists

in state and federal compliance laws. Bus. Franchise Guide (CCH) ¶¶ 8354, 8807; 16 CFR § 436 (1979), and the requirements of good faith under the Uniform Commercial Code § 2-103 and the Restatement of Contracts § 205. *See also* § Williston, *A Treatise on the Law of Contracts* §§ 1301, 1335 (3d ed. 1968). In *Dayan v. McDonald's Corp.*, 466 N.E.2d 958 (Ill. App. Ct. 1984), for example, the Court ruled that:

> a party vested with contractual discretion must exercise that discretion reasonably and with proper motive, and may not do so arbitrarily, capriciously or in a manner inconsistent with the reasonable expectations of the parties.

Id. at 972. *See also Carvel Corp. v. Diversified Management Group, Inc.*, 930 F.2d 228 (2d Cir. 1991) (holding that the jury was inadequately instructed on the implied good faith obligation in the performance of an area development agreement); *Beraha v. Baxter Health Care Corp.*, 956 F.2d 1436, 1443–45 (7th Cir. 1992) (not a duty "to be nice or to behave decently — but requiring exercise of its discretion" consistent with reasonable expectations of the parties).

(14) Trademark franchisors have been held liable for personal injuries and property damage resulting from defective products and services supplied by franchisees. In *Kosters v. Seven-Up Co.*, 595 F.2d 347, 353 (6th Cir. 1979), the Sixth Circuit stated the principle in dicta as follows: "Liability is based on the franchisor's control and the public's assumption, induced by the franchisor's conduct, that it does in fact control and vouch for the product." *See Oberlin v. Marlin American Corp.*, 596 F.2d 1322 (7th Cir. 1979). *Compare Taylor v. Checkrite, Ltd.*, 627 F. Supp. 415 (S.D. Ohio 1986) (liability found where the franchisor maintained common types of controls over its franchisees) *with* the following cases holding that traditional franchisor controls do not constitute an agency agreement: *Hayman v. Ramada Inn, Inc.*, Bus. Franchise Guide (CCH) ¶ 893 (N.C. Ct. App. 1987) *and Robert Broock v. Nutri/System, Inc.*, 654 F. Supp. 7 (S.D. Ohio 1986). Vicarious liability may also exist, moreover, where there is apparent authority of the franchisor over the franchisee. In *Gizzi v. Texaco, Inc.*, 437 F.2d 308, 310 (3d Cir.), *cert. denied*, 404 U.S. 829 (1971), the Court ruled the "apparent authority" of Texaco over its franchisee was a question for the jury. *See also Crinkley v. Holiday Inns, Inc.* 844 F.2d 156 (4th Cir. 1988) (franchisor held vicariously liable under apparent agency theory for failure to provide adequate security). *Compare Case v. Holiday Inns, Inc.*, 851 F.2d 356 (4th Cir. 1988); *Giger v. Mobil Oil Corp.*, 823 F.2d 181 (7th Cir. 1987). These developments in the case law increase the risks to the franchisor of vicarious liability where the ex-franchisees retain for any period of time the trade identity of the franchisor. Customarily, franchisors require indemnification by franchisees, but such protection might well be ineffective against an ex-franchisee, so that the franchisor would need its own insurance and other liability protection. *See* Laufer & Gurnick, *Minimizing Vicarious Liability of Franchisors for Acts of Their Franchisees*, 6 Franchise L.J. 3 (1987); Hawes, *Trademark Licensing Can Lead To Product Liability*, 34 Prac. Law. 23 (1988).

CHAPTER **5**

INFRINGEMENT OF TRADEMARK RIGHTS

§ 5.01 Likelihood of Confusion, Mistake or Deception

Under the 1905 Act the test for trademark infringement required that the marks be both "confusingly similar" and used on goods "of the same descriptive properties." Under the 1946 Act, the test originally required that a mark be "likely to cause confusion or mistake or to deceive *purchasers* as to the source of origin of such goods or services." In 1962 the Act was amended to delete the word "purchasers." The evolution of the test demonstrates the emergence of a better understanding of the commercial realities of trademark use. Consider the purposes for each step in this evolution.

1962 deceive as to source of origin.

The concept of prior use and the resultant development of an identifying significance deserving of protection against a likelihood of confusion are the touchstones upon which Anglo-American trade identity law was built, the former providing the basis for rights, and the latter the scope within which they may be asserted. Deceptively simple, the test of likelihood of confusion is the essential statement of what trade identity unfair competition is all about under the common law and the federal statute. Often, however, it is obscured by nonessential and secondary considerations. What relationship among goods is relevant to the test? What persons are relevant to the test? What weight should be given to similarities of appearance? To oral similarities? To meaning similarities? Is the issue one of fact or law? Is it a mixed issue of fact and law?

Likihood of confusion

The first three sections that follow demonstrate application of the likelihood of confusion test of infringement to individual cases. Similarity of the obvious factors of appearance, sound, connotation, goods, and marketing environment is involved. Consider the interplay and varying relative importance of these considerations in each of the cases. Note that this framework, while generally applicable, does not encompass many considerations which may arise in individual cases, e.g., intentional infringement, use of a family of marks, use of several marks on a product or natural expansion of a business into related product areas. Some of these additional factors, however, are considered in the immediately following decisions and others in subsequent sections. Note also the tendency of the courts to reach their conclusions as to likelihood of confusion, and thus infringement, subjectively and based upon their own reactions as to similarity rather than objectively and based upon evidence. Is this deficiency one of the court, or of counsel, or does it simply reflect the circumstances of these cases?

Usually a subjective interpretation

§ 5.02 Similarity of Appearance, Sound or Connotation

INTRODUCTION

Similarity of appearance has always been the paramount criterion in determining likelihood of confusion. If anything, its importance has been augmented in recent decades by the impact of television, mass media advertising and self-service marketing. Generally, similarity of sound has been accorded less weight by the courts and less attention by the infringers. Even in a visual and graphic age, however, it remains a principal trade identity consideration. Assume that the only appreciable similarity between two marks lies in how they sound. Might infringement result? The problem of similarity of connotation also raises difficult and subtle semantic questions. As with questions of appearance and pronunciation, however, the issue in cases of similar connotation remains not what is the dictionary definition but what is likely to be the understanding of an appreciable number of those who may encounter the marks.

GORDON'S DRY GIN CO. v. EDDY & FISCHER CO.

United States District Court, District of Rhode Island
246 F. 954 (1917)

BROWN, DISTRICT JUDGE.

The bill charges unlawful imitation of plaintiff's trade-marks and labels and unfair competition.

Upon a comparison of the respective labels of plaintiff and defendant there appears a general resemblance, which, on a casual observation, might lead to a confusion of goods. This general resemblance is not destroyed by the points of difference upon which the defendant insists.

At the hearing the plaintiff introduced in evidence, without objection from the defendant certificate of registration No. 21,734 of trade-mark for spirituous liquors and cordials, consisting of the representation of "a boar's head resting on a roll," and also certificate of registration No. 68,640 of trade-mark for gin, showing in the drawing a complete label having a similar boar's head as a central feature. While the bill is somewhat indefinite, in that the "boar's head" as a registered trade-mark is not therein described, but merely appears in exhibits attached to the bill, yet as the defendant's answer specifically denies that its labels and trade-marks are in imitation of the labels and trade-marks of the plaintiff, and as the case was tried upon evidence as to the registered trade-mark of a "boar's head," as well as upon evidence of general imitation of labels including with a boar's head other features, the case made at final hearing properly may be considered as presenting questions both of infringement of trade-mark and of unfair competition. The defendant uses upon its labels the representation of a boar's head. Upon comparison there is considerable difference in the drawings, and it is probable that one familiar with the plaintiff's drawing would at once perceive the difference. This, however, is not a sufficient justification for the use of a boar's head by the defendant. The defendant's trade-mark answers the general description of plaintiff's in that it is a boar's head.

Δ's trademark is a boar's head good enough

A trade-mark is a sign which may become known to the public by name as well as by sight. Thus "The Bull Dog Bottling," with a bulldog's head, became known as "Dog's Head" beer; and its proprietors were granted an injunction against the use of a "rough terrier's head." *Read v. Richardson*, 45 Law T. (N.S.) 54.

The actual physical resemblance of the two marks is not the sole question for the court; for if the plaintiff's goods have, from his trade-mark, become known in the market by a particular name, the adoption by the defendant of a mark or name which will cause his goods to bear the same name in the market is as much a violation of the plaintiff's rights as an actual copy of his mark. *Seixo v. Provezende*, L. R. 1 Ch. 192; *De Voe Snuff Co. v. Wolff*, 206 Fed. 420, 124 C.C.A. 302.

Though the plaintiff offered no evidence to show that its gin was called by the name "Boar's Head," and no evidence of actual deception of customers, it offered evidence that the gin had been sold in large quantities for many years (since 1769) associated with the representation of a boar's head, and had been extensively advertised at a large expense.

Where a trade-mark consists of printed words, it may be infringed by the same words in different form, type, or writing; and it would seem also to follow that the oral use of the same words as descriptive of goods other than those of the proprietor of the original trade-mark might constitute infringement. The written word and the spoken word have the same meaning, and as goods are bought and sold by oral as well as by written description, pictorial trade-marks which are sufficiently alike to have the same name are likely to lead to confusion in oral description of goods. Thus one who tries and likes beer with a bulldog trade-mark may remember it as "Dog's Head," and extol its qualities under that name to one who calls for "Dog's Head" and is satisfied when given a bottle with a dog's head, though it be a rough terrier's head. *See Read v. Richardson*, 45 Law T. (N.S.) 54.

Rule of a picture oral description which is the same can infringe

Upon comparison of the labels considered as a whole I am of the opinion that the plaintiff has established such imitation as might prove deceptive. I am not satisfied, however, that the defendant is guilty of a fraudulent intention of palming his goods off as the goods of the plaintiff, or that actual deception has resulted. The correspondence shows that the defendant, after notice, though denying imitation, was willing to concede the plaintiff's view and to eliminate the boar's head. He afterwards concluded to stand upon his rights. . . .

Not ruling of fraudulent intent or actual deception. (damages)

While I am not satisfied that the plaintiff has made out a case entitling it to an account of profits (*see Straus v. Notaseme Co.*, 240 U.S. 179, 183), that question may be further heard upon the settlement of a decree.

I am of the opinion that the plaintiff is entitled to an injunction restraining the defendant's use of a boar's head as a trade-mark for gin, and also the use of its present labels.

A draft decree may be presented accordingly.

AMERICAN CYANAMID CO. v. UNITED STATES RUBBER CO.

United States Court of Customs and Patent Appeals
356 F.2d 1008 (1966)

RICH, JUDGE.

This appeal is from the decision of the Trademark Trial and Appeal Board (142 U.S.P.Q. 359) sustaining appellee's opposition to registration on the Principal Register of the word mark CYGON on application serial No. 107,307, filed October 28, 1960, by appellant. The mark is sought to be registered for "an insecticide" and the claimed date of first use is September 15, 1960.

Opposition is based in part on prior use and registration of PHYGON for "fungicides. . . ."

Both products fall into the class of agricultural chemicals and they are both pesticides. They are sold through the same channels of trade to the same consumers, namely, farmers.

The board felt that "it is clear that the products of the parties are of such a nature that they would be attributed to a single producer if sold under the same or similar mark." While that might be true in the case of the same mark, we cannot agree that the similar marks here, under the circumstances of this case, would likely lead to confusion *as to source*. The evidence shows that, with a single exception on the part of appellant, the producers' names are prominently associated with the marks on labels in such a way as to preclude mistake as to the origin of the goods. As to the exception, the evidence is that the distributor's name appears in place of that of the producer.

However, the similarity in sound and spelling, particularly the former, is sufficient, we think, to create a likelihood of various kinds of confusion and mistake, considering the close relationship of the goods in use. They are both for use on the farm and would, we presume, be used by workers of divers degrees of intelligence, experience, and carefulness. While a farm manager planning a spraying program would no doubt exercise such a degree of care in selecting and compounding his spray as to preclude mistake on his part, we see merit in appellee's argument that the sale, purchase, and handling of CYGON and PHYGON products at the verbal level, possibly under noisy conditions, might result in confusion or mistake and even damage to crops through a confused worker applying the wrong material.

. . . .

We do not see error in the decision of the board to sustain the opposition on the ground of likelihood of confusion or mistake and it is therefore affirmed.

HANCOCK v. AMERICAN STEEL & WIRE CO. OF NEW JERSEY

United States Court of Customs and Patent Appeals
203 F.2d 737 (1953)

JOHNSON, JUDGE.

This is an appeal from the decision of the Commissioner of Patents, speaking through the Assistant Commissioner, 91 U.S.P.Q. 350, affirming the decision of the Examiner of Trade-Mark Interferences sustaining appellee's opposition to registration of the mark sought by appellant.

On May 5, 1948, appellant, Paul P. Hancock, filed his application, serial No. 556,262, in the Patent Office for registration, under the Trade-Mark Act of 1946, 15 U.S.C.A. § 1051 et seq., of the mark "Tornado" in association with a pictorial representation of a whirlwind for use upon "wire fencing." Continuous use of the mark since April 9, 1948, was alleged in the application.

August 5, 1949, appellee filed notice of opposition to the registration so sought, alleging prior use of the trade-mark "Cyclone" as applied to "wire fencing, fence posts and gates, etc." Opposer alleged in its notice of ownership of Registration No. 212,792 for the mark "Cyclone" was applied to "wire fencing, etc.," issued May 11, 1926, to its predecessor in title and duly renewed by the opposer under the Act of 1946. As grounds of opposition, appellee alleged that the mark sought by appellant is applied to identical goods and so nearly resembles its own mark that confusion or mistake or deception of purchasers is likely.

Both parties filed stipulated facts in lieu of testimony.

It is stipulated by the parties that the goods involved are identical, namely, wire fencing of the heavy chain link type which is used largely for enclosing industrial plants, playgrounds and the like, and to some extent by home owners. The opposer's prior use of its mark "Cyclone" for these products is established by the stipulated facts and conceded by appellant.

Essentially, the position taken by the opposer before the examiner and the commissioner, and before this court, is that appellant's mark "Tornado" has an identical or substantially identical popular meaning as "Cyclone," particularly in view of the pictorial representation of a whirlwind in the former mark; and that simultaneous use of these marks on wire fencing is therefore likely to cause confusion as to origin, especially since the marks are arbitrary as applied to this type of goods. To support his position, appellee has relied upon certain dictionary definitions which he has called to the attention of the Patent Office tribunals and this court.

In Webster's New International Dictionary, 2nd Ed., we find the following:

> cyclone . . . 1.a) A wind blowing circularly, esp. in a storm. b) *Popularly, a tornado.* See Tornado, 2b. [Italics supplied.]. . . .

Other definitions of similar import are called to our attention by appellee's counsel in his brief.

The examiner sustained appellee's opposition holding the marks were likely to cause confusion for the following reasons:

> Irrespective of what meteorological differences there might be between a tornado and cyclone, they are commonly understood by most people to be circulatory windstorms of violent proportions, and to them they are synonymous in meaning and convey the same mental impression. As applied to fencing the notations "Tornado" and "Cyclone" are obviously arbitrary terms, with a possible remote suggestiveness of strength, and while these terms are unlike in appearance and sound they are nevertheless deemed to be so nearly identical in meaning as to be clearly likely to give rise to confusion, or mistake, or deception of purchasers as to the origin thereof when applied contemporaneously thereto.

. . . .

The meaning of these two words is the crux of the case. Courts take judicial notice of the meaning of words, *Nix v. Hedden*, 149 U.S. 304, and the court may always refer to standard dictionaries or other recognized authorities to refresh its memory and understanding as to the common meaning of language. *United States v. Doragon Co.*, 12 Cust. App. 524, T.D. 40732, *modified on other grounds*, 13 Cust. App. 182. This court has often resorted to dictionary definitions to determine the ordinary significance and meaning of words in issue. *See Lever Brothers Company v. Babson Brothers Company*, 197 F.2d 531, 39 C.C.P.A. Patents, 1021; *Eureka Williams Corp. v. Willoughby Machine & Tool Co.*, 194 F.2d 543, 39 C.C.P.A., Patents, 832; *also Cheek-Neal Coffee Co. v. Hal Dick Mfg. Co.*, F.2d 106, 17 C.C.P.A., Patents, 1103. It is our opinion, therefore, that when opposer called to the attention of the examiner and the commissioner the above-quoted definitions in such recognized authorities as the Webster's and Funk & Wagnall's dictionaries referred to *supra*, those tribunals might properly rely upon these dictionary definitions as indicating the popular meaning of the terms in issue, in the absence of any sufficient reason why they should not do so. If appellant is of the opinion that these dictionary definitions are in error, he should have introduced pertinent recognized authorities, or other suitable evidence, for the consideration of the Patent Office tribunals and this court. Accordingly, we regard this contention as being without merit.

We turn now to appellant's first contention. In determining likelihood of confusion between marks on identical goods, it is proper to consider their appearance, sound and meaning. *Firestone Tire & Rubber Co. v. Montgomery Ward & Co.*, 150 F.2d 439, 32 C.C.P.A., Patents, 1074. Clearly the involved marks "Tornado" and "Cyclone" do not look or sound alike. But a combination of all three factors need not necessarily exist, and an opposition to registration may be sustained if the marks are identical or so similar in meaning that confusion as to origin is deemed likely. *See Norris, Inc., v. Charms Co.*, 111 F.2d 479, 27 C.C.P.A., Patents, 1174.

On the basis of the dictionary definitions and similar authorities called to our attention, we think that the examiner and commissioner properly held that the marks were identical, or substantially so, in ordinary meaning. We concur also with those officials in the opinion that the mark "Cyclone" is essentially an arbitrary mark as

[handwritten: arbitrary mark, not descriptive]

applied to wire mesh fencing of the type here involved, although we think it is remotely suggestive of strength, as pointed out by the examiner. In view of this, we think that contemporaneous use of appellant's and appellee's marks on wire fencing is likely to result in confusion or mistake in trade, notwithstanding that there is a distinction between the technical meteorological meanings of the two terms. We are primarily concerned with the meaning of the marks to members of the public at large who are prospective purchasers of such wire, and not to meteorological experts.

[handwritten: Reasoning, holding]

. . . .

The most pertinent case cited by appellant is *Lever Bros. Co. v. Babson Bros. Co., supra.* In that case the question before us was whether confusion in trade was likely if applicant's mark "Surge" and opposer's mark "Surf" were both applied to cleaning detergents. Opposer relied considerably on the fact that one of six dictionary definitions of "surge" was similar to the dictionary definition of "surf." We affirmed the concurrent holdings of the Patent Office tribunals that the marks were simple, well-known words which do not look or sound alike when considered in their entireties. We also agreed with their concurrent holdings that the two words do not have the same ordinary connotation or meaning to the average person, notwithstanding that one of the six dictionary definitions of "surge" is similar to the definition of "surf." Our holding in this case that confusion is likely is based on our belief that the popular or ordinary meanings of "Tornado" and "Cyclone" are identical, although there are certain technical distinctions between the two terms. We see no inconsistency between this holding and our decision in the *Lever Bros.* case, and we do not regard that case as determinative in appellant's favor.

Affirmed.

NOTES ON SIMILARITY OF APPEARANCE, SOUND OR CONNOTATION

Similarity of Appearance

(1) In deciding whether the appearance of two marks is likely to result in confusion, consideration must be given to the visual impression created by each mark as a whole in the marketplace. It is not a question of similarity or dissimilarity of the various parts considered in a vacuum. At issue is whether or not consumers or potential consumers are likely to be confused in their general recollection of the marks, rather than the resemblance, or lack of it, disclosed by a side-by-side comparison by the court. *See* Chapter 6, *infra*; *Beer Nuts, Inc. v. Clover Club Foods Company*, 805 F.2d 920 (10th Cir. 1986); *Beer Nuts, Inc. v. Clover Club Foods Company*, 711 F.2d 934, 941 (10th Cir. 1983); *Johann Maria Farine Gegenuber Dem Julichs-Plat v. Chesebrough-Pond's, Inc.*, 470 F.2d 1385 (C.C.P.A. 1972); *Columbian Steel Tank Co. v. Union Tank and Supply Co.*, 277 F.2d 192, 196 (C.C.P.A. 1960). Is a side-by-side comparison more or less likely to encourage

objectivity and discourage subjective, "visceral" judicial reactions to marks? *See Miss Universe, Inc. v. Patricelli*, 408 F.2d 506 (2d Cir. 1969).

(2) Since rights in trademarks arise out of use, they necessarily exist in the entire mark as used, and not as segmented or dissected. *Joseph Schlitz Brewing Co. v. Houston Ice & Brewing Co.*, 250 U.S. 28, 29 (1919) (Holmes, J.: "It is a fallacy to break the fagot stick by stick"); *Beckwith v. Commissioner of Patents*, 252 U.S. 538, 545–546 (1920); *Sleeper Lounge Co. v. Bell Mfg. Co.*, 253 F.2d 720, 722 (9th Cir. 1958). As stated in *Grandpa Pidgeon's of Missouri, Inc. v. Borgsmiller*, 477 F.2d 586, 587 (C.C.P.A. 1973), "Legal surgery, in which trademarks have parts enhanced or discarded, is of little aid in determining the effect of design marks on purchasers who merely recollect."

(3) Should predominant or salient features of a mark be entitled to extra weight in determining likelihood of confusion? Are consumers or potential consumers more likely to have a general recollection of the principal feature than the mark as a whole? *See Henri's Food Products Co. v. Kraft, Inc.*, 717 F.2d 352, 356 (7th Cir. 1983); *Burger Chef Systems, Inc. v. Sandwich Chef Inc.*, 608 F.2d 875 (C.C.P.A. 1979); 1 Gilson, *Trademark Protection and Practice*, § 5.03 (1993 ed.); McCarthy, *Trademarks and Unfair Competition*, § 23:15 (3d ed. 1992).

(4) The mere repositioning or substitution of one letter in a well-known trademark does not avoid a likelihood of confusion and a determination of infringement. *See Squirt Co. v. Seven-Up Co.*, 207 U.S.P.Q. 12, 20, 480 F. Supp. 789 (E.D. Mo. 1979), *aff'd on infringement finding*, 628 F.2d 1086 (8th Cir. 1980) (QUIRST infringes SQUIRT for soft drinks); *Cartier, Inc. v. Three Sheaves Co., Inc.*, 465 F. Supp. 123 (S.D.N.Y. 1979) (CATTIER infringes CARTIER for cosmetics).

(5) In *Vornado, Inc. v. Breuer Electrical Mfg. Co.*, 390 F.2d 724 (C.C.P.A. 1968), the manufacturer of TORNADO vacuum cleaners and other electrical machines opposed an application for registration of VORNADO for electrical appliances. Despite the fact that TORNADO is a common well-known word and VORNADO was a coined mark, the court found confusion likely based upon the striking similarity in sound and appearance of the two marks, and affirmed the denial of registration. Applicant had contended that the differing styles of presentation would adequately distinguish the two, but the court held that "the display of a mark is of no material significance since the display may be changed at any time as may be dictated by the fancy of the applicant or the owner of the mark."

In dissent, Judge Rich argued that the public was likely to remember the marks as different, and distinguish their sources, because VORNADO is "an irritating trade mark."

> . . . I will amplify my meaning by saying that my first impulse was to call it an "itchy" mark, that word denoting a "mild stimulation of pain receptors." This *may* be a personal reaction to the mark which I have to many marks which are just enough different from common words to make one brood about them and their possible origins. The one thing I am certain about with respect to such marks is that they are *not* the words they resemble. That is why I hold the opinion I do in this case that confusion is unlikely. . . .

Similarity of Sound

(6) Two marks, hardly similar in appearance or meaning, may be so similar in sound as to result in a likelihood of confusion, particularly where the products are ordinarily purchased by spoken word. *Kimberly-Clark Corp. v. H. Douglas Enterprises*, 774 F.2d 1144 (Fed. Cir. 1985) (HUGGIES v. DOUGIES for disposable diapers); *Crown Radio Corp. v. Soundscriber Corp.*, 506 F.2d 1392 (C.C.P.A. 1974) (CROWNSCRIBER v. SOUNDSCRIBER for tape recorders); *Grotrian, Helfferich, Schulz, etc. v. Steinway & Sons*, 523 F.2d 1331 (2d Cir. 1975) (GROTRIAN-STEINWEG v. STEINWAY for German-made pianos); *Dr. Ing H.F.C. Porsche Ag. v. Zin*, 481 F. Supp. 1247 (N.D. Tex. 1979) (PORSHA for automobile sales and repair of PORSCHE cars v. PORSCHE for automobile manufacture); *J.B. Williams Co. v. Le Conte Cosmetics, Inc.*, 523 F.2d 187 (9th Cir. 1975), *cert. denied*, 424 U.S. 913 (1976) (LE CONTE v. CONTI for hair care products.)

(7) Where correct pronunciation of a mark results in no similarity in sound, what weight should be given evidence that the mark is often mispronounced thereby resulting in similarity? What evidence would be probative? Can there be "correct" pronunciation of trademarks so far as the issue of infringement is concerned? *See J.B. Williams, supra* Note (6); *Plough, Inc. v. Kreis Laboratories*, 314 F.2d 635 (9th Cir. 1963); *National Distillers and Chemical Corp. v. Wm. Grant & Sons, Inc.*, 505 F.2d 719, 721 (C.C.P.A. 1974); *Gaby, Inc. v. Irene Blake Cosmetics, Inc.*, 166 F.2d 164 (C.C.P.A. 1948); *Lebow Bros, Inc. v. Lebole Euroconf S.p.A.*, 503 F. Supp. 209, 212 (E.D. Pa. 1980).

(8) For an analysis of factors to consider in determining whether similarity in sound may result in a likelihood of confusion, see *G.D. Searle & Co. v. Chas. Pfizer & Co.*, 265 F.2d 385 (7th Cir. 1959), *cert. denied*, 361 U.S. 819 (1959) (BONAMINE found confusingly similar to DRAMAMINE). *Compare Standard Brands, Inc. v. Eastern Shore Canning Co.*, 172 F.2d 144 (4th Cir. 1949), *cert. denied*, 337 U.S. 925 (1949), where no likelihood of confusion was found between V-8 for vegetable juice and VA for tomato juice and lima beans.

Similarity of Connotation

(9) In one of the many legal disputes over the years following the historic order that the Standard Oil Trust be dissolved, *Standard Oil v. United States*, 221 U.S. 1 (1911), Humble Oil, a wholly owned subsidiary of Standard Oil of New Jersey, sought a declaratory judgment allowing it to use its ESSO mark in a five-state area historically inhabited by defendant Standard Oil of Kentucky. *Standard Oil Co. (Kentucky) v. Humble Oil & Refining Co.*, 363 F.2d 945 (5th Cir. 1966). The district court perceived dissimilarities in sound between the pronunciation of ESSO and S O and between the appearance of the party's signs, and held that there was no likelihood of confusion as to source. In reversing, the appellate court noted that other courts had found no dissimilarity in sound, and went on to state that:

> The test is not whether an ordinary buyer can on normal inspection tell that "ESSO" as shown on signs looks different from "Standard" or "Standard Oil" when shown on signs. Rather the test is whether some normally intelligent buyers think that "ESSO" is another name for Standard Oil or think it is in fact

a Standard Oil designation, and therefore, believe ESSO stations are Standard
Oil stations.

The long history of Standard Oil litigation and the many and varied instances of
confusion in the record led the appellate court to conclude that "the public believes
that all of the pseudonyms for Standard Oil [e.g. SOHIO] belong to the same or
related companies." *See also Standard Oil Co. v. Standard Oil Co.*, 252 F.2d 65
(10th Cir. 1958).

(10) Confusion as to source may arise solely as a result of the mental associations
evoked by two marks, usually words. *Apple Computer, Inc. v. Formula International, Inc.*, 725 F.2d 521 (9th Cir. 1984) (APPLE v. PINEAPPLE for computer
products); *AMF Inc. v. Sleekcraft Boats*, 599 F.2d 341 (9th Cir. 1979) (SLEEK-
CRAFT v. SLICKCRAFT for recreational boats); *American Home Products Corp.
v. Johnson Chemical Co.*, 589 F.2d 103 (2d Cir. 1978) (ROACH MOTEL v.
ROACH INN for insect traps); *S.C. Johnson v. Drop Dead Co.*, 326 F.2d 87 (9th
Cir. 1963) (PLEDGE v. PROMISE for furniture polish); *Playboy Enterprises, Inc.
v. Chuckleberry Publishing Inc.*, 486 F. Supp. 414 (S.D.N.Y. 1980) (PLAYBOY
v. PLAYMEN for magazines); *Thought Factory, Inc. v. Idea Factory, Inc.*, 203
U.S.P.Q. 331 (C.D. Cal. 1978) (THOUGHT FACTORY v. IDEA FACTORY for
greeting cards); *Londontown Manufacturing Co. v. Cable Raincoat Co.*, 371 F. Supp.
1114 (S.D.N.Y. 1974) (SMOG meaning smoky fog v. LONDON FOG for raincoats).
But see National Distiller's & Chemical Corp. v. William Grant & Sons, Inc., 505
F.2d 719 (C.C.P.A. 1974), where the court held DUET for prepared alcoholic cock-
tails not likely to be confused with DUVET for French brandy and stated, "The
familiar is readily distinguishable from the unfamiliar; DUET is a familiar word;
DUVET is not." *Accord: Jacobs v. International Multifoods Corp.*, 688 F.2d 1234
(C.C.P.A. 1982) (BOSTON TEA PARTY for tea not infringed by BOSTON SEA
PARTY for restaurant services). In affirming the dismissal of a petition to cancel
the registration of HUNGRY HOBO based on HOBO JOE'S, both for restaurant
services, the court in *Colony Foods, Inc. v. Sagemark, Ltd.*, 735 F.2d 1336, 1339
(Fed. Cir. 1984), approvingly cited the following analysis by the Trademark Trial
and Appeal Board:

Comparing them in their entireties we find petitioner's mark [HOBO JOE's]
to designate a particular person of the itinerant or vagrant persuasion while
respondent's mark [HUNGRY HOBO] gives the impression of an anonymous
person of that kind in need of a meal. Thus, customers would leave petitioner's
restaurants with an image of a particular individual hobo named Joe, as opposed
to the concept of an anonymous hobo whose distinguishing characteristic is that
he happens to be hungry, as would be the case with respondent's mark. Stated
otherwise, the fact that both marks play on the hobo theme is not enough to
make confusion likely, in light of the differences in the marks as a whole.

In this area courts correctly stress what the words mean to that particular segment
of the public allegedly confused (*see Hancock, supra.*) Why is this important?

(11) Word marks may cause a likelihood of confusion with marks that are pictorial
representations of the words. In *Beer Nuts, Inc. v. King Nut Co.*, 477 F.2d 326 (6th
Cir. 1973), *cert. denied*, 414 U.S. 858 (1974), the representation of a stein of beer

on a package of nuts infringed plaintiff's BEER NUTS trademark. In *Mobil Oil Corp. v. Pegasus Petroleum Corp.*, 229 U.S.P.Q. 890 (S.D.N.Y. 1986), the court found plaintiff's well-known "flying horse" design mark for petroleum products infringed by defendant's use of the trade name PEGASUS in the oil industry. What if the pictorial representation differs in some ways from the word mark? *See Izod, Ltd. v. Zip Hosiery Co.*, 405 F.2d 575 (C.C.P.A. 1969) (TIGER HEAD v. Representation of Tiger's Head); *Alligator Co. v. Ciarochi*, 141 F. Supp. 806 (E.D. Pa. 1956) (ALLIGATOR v. representation of alligator).

(12) How should a foreign word with a connotation similar to a registered American trademark be treated? In *In re Sarkil, Ltd.*, 721 F.2d 353 (Fed. Cir. 1983), the court held that the French word REPECHAGE, which has various meanings including "make-up examination," is not confusingly similar in connotation to registered mark SECOND CHANCE. In *Pizzeria Uno v. Temple*, 747 F.2d 1522 (4th Cir. 1984), the appellate court reversed a lower court holding that PIZZERIA UNO for restaurant services was the equivalent of "Number One [or Best] Pizzeria," a weak descriptive mark not infringed by TACO UNO for similar services. The correct translation, according to the appellate court, was "merely 'one' ", no more and no less, making plaintiff's mark suggestive and, ultimately, infringed. *Cf. In re American Safety Razor Co.*, 2 U.S.P.Q.2d 1459 (T.T.A.B. 1987) (GOOD MORNING for shaving cream confusingly similar to BUENOS DIAS for soap). *See generally* McCarthy, *Trademarks and Unfair Competition*, § 23:14 (3d ed. 1992).

(13) The connotations of words and symbols involve psychological and environmental as well as strictly semantic and communicative considerations. Just what mental images, understandings, and impressions are conveyed or evoked by the stimulus of a particular word or symbol, to whom, and how generally? Are the purchasers and potential purchasers those whose minds have been particularly conditioned by their experience to react in a particular pattern? Are they the general public and are the reactions of the general public to the stimulus involved likely to be uniform? These inquiries actually are relevant not only to trade identity cases involving connotation, but also to the entire gamut of unfair trade competition.

§ 5.03   Marketing Environment

#2

INTRODUCTION

It is unlikely you would assume that infant care products emanate from a manufacturer of automobile parts, or vice versa. This is so despite the use of the same or similar marks for such goods. Our experience in such matters conditions our conscious or subconscious thought process in concluding, either correctly or incorrectly, that products come from the same or a related source. All conceivable factors and circumstances affecting both the physical environment where particular goods are purchased, or the thought patterns of the people themselves who customarily make such purchases, are a part of the marketing environment. All of that environment bears upon the issue of likelihood of confusion.

Marketing Environment [handwritten]

CALIFORNIA FRUIT GROWERS EXCHANGE v. SUNKIST BAKING CO.

United States Court of Appeals, Seventh Circuit
166 F.2d 971 (1947)

MINTON, CIRCUIT JUDGE.

. . . .

. . . [T]he plaintiff Exchange is a non-profit co-operative marketing association incorporated under the laws of California and is engaged primarily in marketing and selling citrus fruits throughout the United States and in foreign countries. The plaintiff Corporation is a New York corporation engaged in the selection, preparing, padding, and marketing of canned and dried fruits and vegetables, including raisins, throughout the United States and in foreign countries. *[handwritten: P Sunkist raisins fruit]*

Exchange has employed the trade-mark "Sunkist" in the sale of over two billion dollars worth of goods and has expended over forty million dollars in advertising the trade-mark. Certificates of registration for the trade-mark "Sunkist" have been issued to Exchange by the United States Patent Office for oranges, lemons, citrus fruits, oils and acids, pectin, citrus-flavored non-alcoholic maltless beverages as soft drinks, and concentrates for making soft drinks. Corporation has employed the trade-mark "Sun-Kist" since 1907 and has sold approximately fifty million dollars worth of goods bearing such trade-mark and has expended in excess of $350,000 in advertising it. Certificates of registration for the trade-mark "Sun-Kist" have been issued by the Patent Office to Corporation for canned and dried fruits and vegetables, milk, butter, walnuts, catsup, pickles, olive oil, jams, jellies, olives, coffee, tea, beans, pineapple juice, grape juice, tomato juice, raisins, grapes, and various other products. The joint and concurrent use of the trade-marks "Sunkist" and "Sun-Kist" by both plaintiffs has eventuated under and by virtue of an agreement between them whereby each has granted the other the right to employ the mark on the goods aforesaid.

[handwritten left margin: 2 P's both agree Sun-Kist Sunkist]

The defendant Sunkist Baking Company is . . . engaged in baking and selling bread and buns, including white bread, whole-wheat bread, "Weet-Hart" bread and raisin bread, in interstate commerce, under the firm name and style of "Sunkist Baking Co.," in and about Rock Island and adjacent cities. Each loaf of bread sold by the defendants is enclosed in a wrapper bearing the name "Sunkist Baking Co." and also the words "Sunkist Bread. . . ."

[handwritten left margin: D Sunkist Baking]

The court found that the plaintiffs' and the defendants' goods are sold in the same channels and may be consumed together, and that the defendants have endeavored to appropriate and capitalize upon the plaintiffs' trade-marks. . . .

[handwritten left margin: D.C. infringement]

. . . .

Unless "Sunkist" covers everything edible under the sun, we cannot believe that anyone whose I.Q. is high enough to be regarded by the law would ever be confused or would be likely to be confused in the purchase of a loaf of bread branded as

[handwritten left margin: Appeal. No infringement]

"Sunkist" because someone else sold fruits and vegetables under that name. The purchaser is buying bread, not a name. If the plaintiffs sold bread under the name "Sunkist," that would present a different question; but the plaintiffs do not, and there is no finding that the plaintiffs ever applied the word "Sunkist" to bakery products.

. . . .

We do not think there is a finding that there is likelihood of confusion as to the source of origin of the products, as required by the Lanham Act.

The court made the following finding as a part of Finding 12: "Defendants' bread bearing the word 'Sunkist' as used by defendants would naturally or reasonably be supposed to come from plaintiffs."

Let us assume that this finding can be separated from its context in Finding 12, which we do not think it can be, and that it is a finding that there is likelihood of confusion among the public as to the source of origin. Then this finding is not sustained by substantial evidence. The only evidence to support this finding is the testimony of two so-called experts who testified on behalf of the plaintiffs, and the fact that bread is sold in the same class of stores and to the same class of customers as the plaintiffs' fruits and vegetables. Against this finding is the difference in the nature of the products themselves — they are not of the same descriptive properties. As to this difference, its weight and significance is as open to us as to the District Courts. Certainly the stores where the products of the parties are sold and the customers to whom they are sold are as well-known to us as to the District Court, and such subsidiary facts are of little or no significance, according to an eminent authority who says:

> However, it has been pointed out, with reason, that modern stores sell all sorts of commodities, and a rule that all goods sold in the same stores are to be considered related goods, would have the practical effect of creating universal trade-marks independent of the nature of the goods on which they are used.

Nims, *Unfair Competition and Trade-Marks, Fourth ed.*, 1947, Vol. I, p. 693.

There is another strange aspect about this confusion which the plaintiffs contend is likely to occur. It will be observed that the plaintiffs have launched into the market two classes of goods under the marks "Sunkist" and "Sun-Kist," which goods are much more nearly of the same class and descriptive properties than the defendants' bread is of the same class and descriptive properties as any of the products of the two plaintiffs; and this is all done without confusion because the parties have agreed, forsooth, there shall be no confusion. Granted the plaintiffs had a right to contract away the public's likelihood of confusion from their closely related products sold all over the United States and in foreign countries, their cry that there is a likelihood of confusion of the source of a loaf of bread put out by a local bakery at Rock Island, Illinois, with their products because they market fruits and vegetables under the same name, is hardly audible to us. When a customer bought a jar of jelly under the name "Sunkist," he could not be confused as to whether it came from California Fruit Growers Exchange or California Packing Corporation. The plaintiffs had taken care of that by contract. We are supposed to believe that when a customer bought fruits or vegetables under the name "Sunkist," he was not confused as to whether the fruit came from the California Fruit Growers Exchange or the vegetables from the California Packing Corporation; but if he bought a loaf of bread under the name "Sunkist," he was likely to think that he bought it from one or the other of the plaintiffs because they sold fruits and vegetables, but never bread. With the plaintiffs practicing such hocus-pocus with the trade-name "Sunkist," we shall ask to be excused when we are admonished by these dividers of confusion by contract to hear their vice president and advertising manager shout confusion on behalf of the purchasing public.

. . . .

For the reasons above set forth, the judgment of the District Court is reversed and the causes remanded, with directions to dismiss the complaint.

PURE FOODS, INC. v. MINUTE MAID CORP.

United States Court of Appeals, Fifth Circuit
214 F.2d 792 (1954)

RIVES, CIRCUIT JUDGE.

The defendant is appealing from a judgment in favor of the plaintiff in an action for infringement of a trade-mark registered under the Lanham Act, 15 U.S.C.A. § 1051 et seq. The complaint alleges the manufacture and sale by the plaintiff in interstate commerce to and from the State of Florida of frozen fruit juice concentrates under the trade-mark "Minute Maid," and also alleges the registration of said trade mark under the Lanham Act, and that the defendant has violated the plaintiff's rights in the trade-mark and has unfairly competed with the plaintiff by selling frozen meats under the designation "Minute Made."

. . . .

Coming to the merits, it is true that an applicant registers a trade-mark in connection with particular goods specified in the certificates of registration, 15 U.S.C.A. §§ 1051, 1057. Plaintiff's registered trade-mark is limited to frozen juice concentrates. The remedies of an owner of a registered trade-mark, however, are not limited to the goods specified in the certificate but extend to any goods on which the use of an infringing mark "is likely to cause confusion or mistake or to deceive purchasers as to the source of origin of such goods." 15 U.S.C.A. 1114(1). The Lanham Act thus adopts the principle stated in A.L.I. Restatement of the Law of Torts, Vol. III, § 730, pp. 597, 598, § 731.

> One's interest in a trade-mark or trade name came to be protected against simulation, . . . not only on competing goods, but on goods so related in the market to those on which the trade-mark or trade name is used that the good or ill repute of the one type of goods is likely to be visited upon the other. Thus one's interest in a trade-mark or trade name is protected against being subjected to the hazards of another's business.

A factual issue is necessarily presented as to what goods meet that description. *John Walker & Sons v. Tampa Cigar Co.*, 5 Cir., 197 F.2d 72, 74; *Chappell v. Goltsman*, 5 Cir., 197 F.2d 837, 838; A.L.I. Restatement of the Law of Torts, Vol. III, § 731,

p. 600. In the cases relied on by the defendant, that factual issue was determined in favor of the defendants while here it has been decided by the district court in favor of the plaintiff.

D.C. P prevails

The appellant-defendant insists, however, that there cannot be confusion or likelihood of confusion as to the origin of the products when the parties are not in competition and neither causes damage to the other. The district court did not find that there was no damage or likelihood of damage, but merely found that "There was no proof of actual monetary damage or injury as a result of defendant's actions to the good will or business of the plaintiff." For that reason, the district court did not order an accounting. The district court further found:

No proof of monetary damages

> Defendant's use of the words "Minute Made" has caused confusion and mistake on the part of purchasers as to the source of origin of defendant's products. The use of such words is likely to continue to cause confusion and mistake in the minds of the general public.

It is difficult for the owner of a trade-mark to prove the amount of his damage or how much of it is caused by the infringement. To authorize preventive relief through the issuance of an injunction proof of actual damage is not necessary, but the likelihood of damage is sufficient. *See* 15 U.S.C.A. § 1114(1); A.L.I. Restatement of the Law of Torts, Vol. III, § 744, p. 631; 28 Am. Jur., Injunctions, § 30. Without expressing any opinion on the cases from the Second Circuit establishing what the defendant refers to as the Learned Hand doctrine, that, though the public may be deceived, the plaintiff has no claim to be its vicarious champion, we think that in this case there was sufficient likelihood of damage to the plaintiff to justify enjoining the infringement. Both parties sell frozen food products. Some companies have expanded their businesses so as to include many such products. Plaintiff's frozen fruit juice concentrates and defendant's frozen meats are both purchased by common purchasers, housewives, through common outlets, retail stores, and are displayed in the frozen food departments in those stores, often in locations not far apart. A number of housewives testified to their actual confusion and mistake in buying the defendant's products on their faith in the plaintiff's reputation.

Likelihood of confusion *'frozen products.*

. . . .

Affirmed.

NOTES ON MARKETING ENVIRONMENT

Environment where encountered

(1) The environment in which marks are actually and usually encountered by the purchasing public is an important psychological conditioning factor that may contribute to or detract from a likelihood of confusion. *Star Watch Case Co. v. Junghans, A.G.*, 267 F.2d 950 (C.C.P.A. 1959); *Avon Shoe Co. v. David Crystal, Inc.*, 171 F. Supp. 293 (S.D.N.Y. 1959), *aff'd*, 279 F.2d 607 (2d Cir. 1960), *cert. denied*, 364 U.S. 909 (1960). Where goods are sold through the same channels of trade, or in the same store or specialty shop, likelihood of confusion is enhanced

because one is thereby mentally conditioned toward assuming a single source. *See Villager, Inc. v. Dial Shoe Co.*, 256 F. Supp. 694 (E.D. Pa. 1966) (women's clothes and women's shoes); *Rosenberg Bros. & Co. v. Elliott*, 7 F.2d 962 (3d Cir. 1925) (clothing and hats). *Compare H. Lubovsky, Inc. v. Esprit de Corp.*, 627 F. Supp. 483 (S.D.N.Y. 1986), in which the court found that shoes and sportswear are sold in different stores or departments. What is the effect if the products of both parties are sold in supermarkets or department stores? *See California Fruit Growers , supra*; *Canada Dry Corp. v. American Home Prods. Corp.*, 468 F.2d 207 (C.C.P.A. 1972); *Kraft-Phenix Cheese Corp. v. Consolidated Beverages*, 107 F.2d 1004 (C.C.P.A. 1939). *Compare Meat Indus. Suppliers, Inc. v. Kroger Co.*, 130 U.S.P.Q. 434, 439 (N.D. Ill. 1961) ("It has been asserted that the average purchaser undergoes, while in a supermarket, an experience not unlike that of hypnosis," referring to V. Packard, *The Hidden Persuaders*, 91–92 (Cardinal ed. 1958)); *American Sugar Refining Co. v. Andreassen*, 296 F.2d 783 (C.C.P.A. 1964). Should such stores be viewed as amalgams of separate and distinct product selling areas? In *Federated Foods, Inc. v. Fort Howard Paper Co.*, 544 F.2d 1098, 1103 (C.C.P.A. 1976), the court stated its views as follows:

> A wide variety of products, not only from different manufacturers within an industry but also from diverse industries, have been brought together in the modern supermarket for the convenience of the customers. The mere existence of such an environment should not foreclose further inquiry into the likelihood of confusion arising from the use of similar marks on any goods so displayed.

See also Pure Gold, Inc. v. Syntex (U.S.A.), Inc., 739 F.2d 624 (Fed. Cir. 1984), wherein FERMODYL PURE GOLD for hair treatment preparations was held not likely to be confused with PURE GOLD for citrus fruits and juices; *Scott Paper Co. v. Scott's Liquid Gold, Inc.*, 589 F.2d 1225 (3d Cir. 1978) (SCOTT'S LIQUID GOLD for household cleaner not likely to be confused with SCOTT for paper products). Some courts have made shelving location part of their analysis in such cases. In *Procter & Gamble Co. v. Johnson & Johnson, Inc.*, 485 F. Supp. 1185 (S.D.N.Y. 1979), the court found there was a "competitive distance" between the product whose trade marks were in issue; "while the two types of products are sold in the same outlets, they are not sold side by side or on the same shelf. In drug stores, supermarkets and discount houses, deodorants have one shelving section and women's menstrual protection products another." *See also Lever Brothers Co. v. American Bakeries Co.*, 693 F.2d 251 (2d Cir. 1982) (No side-by-side sales could possibly occur, since margarine must be kept in refrigeration compartments and bread is not). *Compare In re Martin's Famous Pastry Shoppe, Inc.*, 748 F.2d 1565, 1567 (Fed. Cir. 1984), in which the court found that although bread and cheese may be kept in different areas of market, often they are displayed in close proximity. In *Electronic Design & Sales, Inc. v. Electronic Data Systems Corp.*, 954 F.2d 713 (Fed. Cir. 1992), confusion was held unlikely between EDS and Design for battery chargers and power supplies and EDS for computer services despite the products being sold to many of the same corporate customers; the court found the products were sufficiently different and there was no demonstration that the same person within each corporation bought both parties' products.

(2) How important in determining likelihood of confusion is the fact that one party sells only at retail and the other only at wholesale? *See World Carpets, Inc. v. Dick Littrell's New World Carpets*, 438 F.2d 482 (5th Cir. 1971); *Pierce Foods Corp. v. Tyson Foods, Inc.*, 231 U.S.P.Q. 287 (D.N.J. 1986); *Blue Bell, Inc. v. Ruesman*, 335 F. Supp. 236 (N.D. Ga. 1971). *Compare Kaufman v. Matzak*, 33 Trademark Rep. 18 (Pa. Comm. Pl. 1942).

(3) What significance, if any, should be given to how the products in question are ordinarily purchased: Over the counter? By self-service? In busy stores without opportunity for visual comparison? At little expense? To be consumed in use? By telephone? On impulse? In haste? By the foreign-born? By children? By lip-movers? By illiterates? What if the products are ordinarily bought as a personal matter with great care? By experts? By purchasing agents? At great expense? After careful comparison? By prescription? *See* Leeds, *Confusion and Consumer Psychology*, 46 Trademark Rep. 1(1956). *See also Specialty Brands, Inc. v. Coffee Bean Distributors, Inc.*, 748 F.2d 669 (Fed. Cir. 1984), in which purchasers of relatively inexpensive products were held to a lesser standard of purchasing care; *Lindy Pen Co. v. Bic Pen Corp.*, 725 F.2d 1240, 1245 (9th Cir. 1984), wherein the court held there was no likelihood of confusion in the visual marketplace, but remanded the case on the issue of confusion created by telephone solicitations; *Fuji Photo Film v. Shinohara Shoji*, 754 F.2d 591, 595–96 (5th Cir. 1985), holding that confusion was likely despite the disparity in cost of the products and the sophistication of the purchasers; *Sleepmaster Prods. Co. v. American Auto-Felt Corp.*, 241 F.2d 738 (C.C.P.A. 1957); *L.J. Mueller Furnace Co. v. United Conditioning Corp.*, 222 F.2d 755 (C.C.P.A. 1955); *Pocket Books, Inc. v. Dell Publishing Co.*, 49 Misc. 2d 596, 368 N.Y.S.2d 46 (1966) (lip-movers). *Compare Whitehall Pharmacal Co. v. Denney*, 255 F.2d 693 (C.C.P.A. 1958).

(4) What is the effect of modern advertising, radio, and television on marketing environment? *See* 1 Gilson, *Trademark Protection and Practice* § 5.09[1] (1993 ed.); Brown, *Advertising and the Public Interest: Legal Protection of Trade Symbols*, 57 Yale L.J. 1165 (1948); Backman, *The Role Of Trademarks in our Competitive Economy*, 58 Trademark Rep. 219 (1968); Sorenson, *Trademarks, Technology and Social Change: Research Into Trademark Confusion*, 62 Trademark Rep. 43 (1972); Hartman, *Subliminal Confusion: The Misappropriation of Advertising Value*, 78 Trademark Rep. 506 (1988).

§ 5.04   Similarity of Goods and Services

INTRODUCTION

Where goods sold under the same or similar marks are themselves similar, the same, or in some way closely related, the likelihood that they may be attributed to the same or a related source is enhanced. This is so because from our experience we have learned that manufacturers and merchants usually tend to manufacture and market within one field. Thus, it seems reasonable and likely to us that if similar marks are applied to similar goods they probably come from the same, or a related, source.

AUNT JEMIMA MILLS CO. v. RIGNEY & CO.

United States Court of Appeals, Second Circuit
247 F. 407 (1917)

WARD, CIRCUIT JUDGE.

This is an appeal from a decree of the United States District Court for the Eastern District of New York dismissing the complainant's bill for infringement of trademark and for unfair competition on the ground that the goods manufactured by the parties respectively are different, viz, self-rising flour, by the complainant and pancake syrup by the defendants.

The Davis Milling Company, of St. Joseph, Mo., originated the trade-mark, which consists of the words "Aunt Jemima's," accompanying the picture of a negress laughing, in 1899, as we infer from the statement and declaration accompanying the registered trade-mark taken out in the United States Patent Office April 3, 1906, for self-rising flour. February 1, 1914, the Milling Company sold out its business, trademarks, and good will to the Aunt Jemima Mills Company, the complainant in this case.

Since February 15, 1908, Rigney & Co., the defendants, have used a trade-mark precisely like the complainant's, which was registered December 29, 1908, in the Patent Office on an application filed March 6, 1908, for certain syrups and sugar creams. March 14, 1908, as soon as the application came to its attention, the Milling Company wrote to Rigney & Co. as follows:

St. Joseph, Mo., March 14, 1908.

Rigney & Co., Brooklyn, N. Y. — Gentlemen: We have your letter of the 5th. We are surprised to have you use the name "Aunt Jemima," for your syrup, but presume you can do so without violating any law in the matter. Mr. Jackson wrote us about this, but we did not know that you were going to do it right "hot off the pan" as one might say. We thought you were going to wait to hear from us. We note you say you have copyrighted "Aunt Jemima." Were you able to obtain a copyright of "Aunt Jemima" for maple syrup, or did you simply register it as a trade-mark? The sample which you sent us has been received, and it is as far as we can see, a very fine article. The looks of the Aunt Jemima Pancake Cream, as you call it, is not as good as the taste. The looks we think could be improved perhaps. Do you make this in a syrup as well as in the cream? Do you work the trade entirely through brokers, or do you handle it with salesmen working the retail trade? Would you be interest (sic) in taking on a pancake flour proposition along with your maple syrup and other lines? If so, we might have something of interest for you. Yours truly, The Davis Milling Co.,

Robert R. Clark.

It is perfectly clear that Rigney & Co. adopted the trade-mark (though with full knowledge of the complainant's prior use) upon the advice of counsel and in full belief that they had a right to use it for their specific products. They brought it to the attention of the Milling Company, the complainant's predecessor, a little over two weeks after they had selected it, and one day before they filed their application for registration in the Patent Office.

The above letter is obviously no evidence of abandonment or of nonuser by the complainant, but the defendants say it is an acquiescence in their use of the trade mark for syrups. We do not so construe it. The complainant was speaking of a matter of law, and said it "presumed" that the defendants could do so without violating any law. But if, as matter of law, the defendants had no right to use the trade-mark, this expression of opinion by the complainant does not make the law other than it is, nor estop it from relying on the law as it really is. *Bigelow on Estoppel*, p. 634. Indeed, the complainant seems, in addition, to have been misled by the defendants as to the facts, because the letter goes on to say that the defendants had written they had copyrighted the trade-mark, and to ask whether they meant that they had registered it in the Patent Office. No reply to this letter was ever received. If the complainant had authorized the defendants to use the mark, or even had said it did not object to their doing so, mistake of law would not save it. When, however, it merely expressed a legal opinion, it did nothing to mislead the defendants, and they took the risk of acting on that opinion if it were erroneous. The bill was filed in December, 1915.

This brings us to inquire what the law on the subject really is. We find no case entirely like the present. In *Hanover Star Milling Co. v. Allen & Weeks*, 208 Fed. 513, 125 C.C.A. 515, L.R.A.. 1916D, 136, *affirmed, Hanover Star Milling Co. v. Metcalf*, 240 U.S. 403, which was also said by Mr. Justice Pitney to be a most unusual case, it was held that a trade-mark is not a subject of property, and that even a technical trade-mark like the one under consideration will be protected only in markets where it has been established; that is, where it has come to indicate the origin of ownership of the goods in marks. In that case the trade-mark was adopted without any knowledge whatever of the prior use. The right to a trademark, though strictly appurtenant to the trade, becomes a property right as soon as it identifies the trade. . . .

. . . .

It is said that even a technical trade-mark may be appropriated by any one in any market for goods not in competition with those of the prior user. This was the view of the court below in saying that no one wanting syrup could possibly be made to take flour. But we think that goods, though different, may be so related as to fall within the mischief which equity should prevent. Syrup and flour are both food products, and food products commonly used together. Obviously the public, or a large part of it, seeing this trade-mark on a syrup, would conclude that it was made by the complainant. Perhaps they might not do so, if it were used for flatirons. In this way the complainant's reputation is put in the hands of the defendants. It will enable them to get the benefit of the complainant's reputation and advertisement. These we think are property rights which should be protected in equity. We have held in *Florence v. Dowd*, 178 Fed. 73, 101 C.C.A. 565, that a manufacturer of hair brushes under the trade-mark "Keepclean," who did not make toothbrushes, is entitled to be protected against the unfair competition of one who manufactures toothbrushes under the trade-mark "Sta Kleen." So in *Collins Co. v. Oliver Ames Co.*, (C.C.), 18 Fed. 561, a manufacturer of metal articles, which had never made shovels, was granted an injunction preventing the defendant from putting the complainant's trade-mark on its shovels.

. . . . No one has a right to apply another's name to his own goods. If, for instance, one were to publish a book on banking under the name of a firm of bankers, it would be no answer to say that there was no competition between banking and publishing, or that the bankers had sustained no pecuniary damage, or that the book was a good book. The act would still be a trespass, for which the bankers would be entitled to at least nominal damages at law, and, that remedy being inadequate and the trespass being a continuing one, they would be entitled to relief in equity. Such is our decision in *British American Tobacco Co. v. British American Cigar Stores Co.*, 211 Fed. 933, 128 C.C.A. 431, Ann. Cas. 1915B, 363, in which a company engaged solely in the wholesale tobacco business was protected against the use of a similar corporate name by a retailer of cigars, although there was no competition between them.

There are many decisions of the English courts to the same effect. In *Eastman Company v. Kodak Cycle Co.*, 15 Reports Patent Cases, 105, the complainant was a manufacturer of cameras under the name Kodak. Defendant, under the name "Kodak Cycle Company," began the manufacture of bicycles, calling them "Kodak" cycles, and registered the name as a trade-mark for bicycles and other vehicles. The Eastman Company brought suit to restrain the use of the word "Kodak" and to rectify the register. The motion for injunction and the motion to rectify the register came on to be heard together. The motion to rectify was sustained, and the defendant's mark expunged, and an injunction was granted. Mr. Justice Romer said:

> Then I have to deal with the application for an injunction against the defendants in respect of what they are doing. They have just started business practically, and it appears to me that to allow them to use the word "Kodak" as part of the title of the Kodak Cycle Company, Limited, would be to give them the benefit of what, in my opinion, substantially amounts to an improper dealing on their part. It would be to allow this company certainly to cause confusion between it and the plaintiff company. I think it would injure the plaintiff company, and would cause the defendant company to be identified with the plaintiff company, or to be recognized by the public as being connected with it, and I think, accordingly, the defendant, the Kodak Cycle Company, Limited, ought to be restrained from carrying on business under that name
>
> . . . .

. . . .

As the defendants' conduct was wrongful, the complainant is entitled to an injunction, notwithstanding the delay of some eight years in asserting its rights (*McLean v. Fleming*, 96 U.S. 245), but is not entitled to an accounting for damages and profits.

The decree is reversed.

TRIANGLE PUBLICATIONS, INC. v. ROHRLICH

United States Court of Appeals, Second Circuit
167 F.2d 969 (1948)

AUGUSTUS N. HAND, CIRCUIT JUDGE.

The plaintiff, Triangle Publications, Inc., a Delaware corporation, has published since September 1944, a girls' magazine entitled "Seventeen," for which a trade-mark registration was granted to plaintiff on January 9, 1945, for a "monthly magazine devoted to the interests of girls." In February 1945, the defendants, citizens of New York, adopted "Miss Seventeen Foundations Co." as a partnership name under which to make and sell girdles, and "Miss Seventeen" as the trade-mark for those girdles. . . .

. . . .

The judge found that from September 1944, when the plaintiff first published its magazine "Seventeen" for girls thirteen to eighteen years of age, the magazine became an important medium for advertising teen-age apparel and accessories, and that by January 1945 a large proportion of the users of teenage apparel had acquired a belief that articles, including girdles, advertised in or mentioned editorially by the magazine had an added desirability. He found further that by January 1945 the use of "Seventeen" to describe any article of teen-age apparel, including girdles, was likely to create the belief in the mind of teen-age girls that the article was advertised in or commented upon editorially by the magazine. . . .

. . . .

It is settled law that a plaintiff who has established a right to a trade name which is fanciful or arbitrary or has acquired a secondary meaning is entitled to protection of his reputation against the use of that name by others even upon noncompeting goods, if the defendant's goods are likely to be thought to originate with the plaintiff. *Yale Electric Corporation v. Robertson*, 2 Cir., 26 F.2d 972; *L. E. Waterman Co. v. Gordon*, 2 Cir., 72 F.2d 272; *Standard Brands v. Smidler*, 2 Cir., 151 F.2d 34; *Bulova Watch Co. v. Stolzberg*, D.C. Mass., 69 F. Supp. 543; Restatement, Torts, § 730. We can see no reason why the principle laid down by the foregoing decisions does not apply to the situation of confusion as to sponsorship found by the district judge to exist in the record before us. In either case, the wrong of the defendant consisted in imposing upon the plaintiff a risk that the defendant's goods would be associated by the public with the plaintiff, and it can make no difference whether that association is based upon attributing defendant's goods to plaintiff or to a sponsorship by the latter when it has been determined that plaintiff had a right to protection of its trade name. In each case the plaintiff is likely to suffer injury to his reputation and his trade name. Indeed, we have already applied this principle in a case involving sponsorship or approval of goods by the Boy Scouts of America in *Adolph Kastor & Bros. v. Federal Trade Commission*, 2 Cir., 138 F.2d 824. *See also Esquire, Inc. v. Esquire Bar*, D.C.S.D. Fla., 37 F. Supp. 875, where the use of the name of the magazine "Esquire" was enjoined.

Two decisions upon which the defendants rely are *Durable Toy & Novelty Corp. v. J. Chein & Co.*, 2 Cir., 133 F.2d 853, and *Vogue Co. v. Thompson-Hudson Co.*, 6 Cir., 300 F. 509; *Vogue Co. v. Vogue Hat Co.*, 6 Cir., 6 F.2d 875, *certiorari denied*, *Thompson v. Vogue Co.*, 273 U.S. 706. In the first case we declined to enjoin the use of the name "Uncle Sam" in connection with toy banks. In weighing the conflicting interests there, it was thought that "Uncle Sam" represented a common name or symbol of national solidarity, was a part of the national mythology in the use of which all had a measurable interest and was therefore not subject to sole appropriation by an individual. It was also thought that the name was most unlikely to have acquired any secondary meaning to customers in stores. In the case at bar the name "Seventeen" as applied to plaintiff's magazine was not used in a descriptive sense and was properly held arbitrary and fanciful. The defendants made use of the word as referring to the magazine rather than for some legitimate purpose, as was done in *Durable Toy & Novelty Corp. v. J. Chein & Co., supra*. In the *Vogue* case, an injunction was at first denied as to use of the name of the magazine because the word "Vogue" was held to be descriptive and to have acquired no secondary meaning, though an injunction against the use of that name was later granted because of the fraud in defendant's appropriation of plaintiff's insignia, the use of which had been originally enjoined. We think the facts are thus plainly distinguishable from those in the case at bar. Similarly, a reading of the opinions in other cases cited by defendants shows that they invoke no different principle of law but are distinguishable on their facts, because they involve merely descriptive names or names which had acquired no secondary meaning that extended into defendant's field so as to cause a likelihood of confusion.

Defendants argue that plaintiff's use of the trade name "Seventeen" subsequent to the use of that term by a company named Juerelle, Inc., upon cosmetics tends to cause more confusion than does the word as applied to girdles, for the reason that the cosmetic field is larger and represents a more general interest on the part of teen-age girls. It may be that some confusion was caused in the cosmetic field in view of the protest by Juerelle, Inc., against the use of tags furnished by the plaintiff to cosmetic companies which advertised in plaintiff's magazine and competed with Juerelle, Inc. But the use of these tags was thereupon abandoned by the plaintiff and so far as the record indicates there was no subsequent objection by this company to the use by the plaintiff of the trade name "Seventeen." In any event, this prior use of "Seventeen" in the cosmetic field has no bearing on the issues before us and would not destroy the value of the name which the plaintiff has built up for its magazine in the apparel field or provide any defense for defendants' subsequent acts of unfair competition. . . .

. . . .

The judgment in the action by Triangle Publications, Inc. is modified so as to dispense with the direction for an accounting, but is otherwise affirmed. . . .

HYDE PARK CLOTHES, INC. v. HYDE PARK FASHIONS, INC.

United States Court of Appeals, Second Circuit
204 F.2d 233 (1953)

[The Court of Appeals affirmed a judgment dismissing a complaint on the merits after a trial in a suit charging likelihood of confusion between "Hyde Park" for men's clothes and "Hyde Park" for ladies suits and coats.]

CLARK, CIRCUIT JUDGE (dissenting).

Plaintiff-appellant has had the misfortune — so it seems to me — to come before a panel of this court allergic to the doctrine historically associated with us because of its nurture by our most illustrious judges of protecting trade names against competition which will create confusion as to the source of goods sold under such names. The change of the assignment calendar which has so operated against plaintiff might as easily have brought it success, to judge by the three most recent cases on this issue before us, the unanimous decision in each instance — two in fact reversing decisions below — of another panel. . . .

. . . .

The single question here seems to me to come down simply to this: Does the defendant's use of the name confusingly mislead purchasers as to the source of the goods?

This counterstatement of the case will show why I think the enactment of the Lanham Act affords the definite solution of our problem. So far as I can understand myself, I did not feel any particular bias originally in the premises; if anything, I felt equal repugnance for the excesses of American advertising as for the attempts at a "free ride" upon a business reputation built up by others. In other words, the situation was one where a declaration of public policy by the constitutional body having that responsibility should be welcome. And since the background of congressional action included not only the development of the "federal" rule in this and other circuits, but its very careful formulation in one of the most admired of all the restatements, 3 Restatement, Torts, Division 9, and notably §§ 715–740 (1938), I felt and still feel that we should accept the congressional mandates on the whole rather gratefully. The Act was under consideration for several years and by several Congresses. We have already quoted and relied — in the *Johnson* case, *supra* — the final statement of its purpose in the Report of the Senate Committee on Patents, No. 1333, May 14, 1946, U.S. Code Cong. Serv., 79th Cong., 2d Sess., 1946, pp: 1274, 1277, to establish a national law in the field. I think we should also take heed of its statement of "Basic Purposes" and particularly of the one it mentions first, "to protect the public so it may be confident that, in purchasing a product bearing a particular trademark which it favorably knows, it will get the product which it asks for and wants to get." I stress this particularly because the vital consumer interest, perhaps the most durable of any in the case, is significantly overlooked in the statement of interests to be protected approvingly adopted by my brethren from the *Federal Television* case. I think it important that women, when being led to buy the somewhat lower priced goods of defendant, should not be also led to think that they are getting goods backed up with the plaintiffs' long established reputation in the garment industry. And it is not without significance, too, that the Senate Committee thought to meet head on that specter of monopoly relied on to defeat trade-marks in some of the cases — though not here; this it does in a considerable section, citing, inter alia, decisions of Justice Holmes and Pitney, under the rubric, "Trade-Marks Defeat Monopoly by Stimulating Competition." U.S. Code Cong. Serv., *supra* at pages 1274, 1275.

As we have often pointed out, most recently in the *Admiral* case with appropriate citation of authorities, the test is the likelihood of confusion, not the number of specific instances of customer mistake which can be piled up. When we approach the case from this standpoint I submit the answer cannot really be in doubt. For here we have two competitors — the one with long established reputation, the other breaking in — manufacturing and selling in the same way in what seems to me the one industry, referred to in the opinion as "the garment trade." The connection seems to me much closer than, e.g., razor blades and fountain pens, *L. E. Waterman Co. v. Gordon*, 2 Cir., 72 F.2d 272, 273, or refrigerators and sewing machines, *Admiral Corp. v. Penco, Inc.*, *supra*, or other precedents therein cited. If we take the nine factors bearing on the issue of infringement and the "limitation of protection with reference to kind of goods" so carefully formulated in 3 Restatement, Torts § 731, I suggest that practically everyone argues against limitation here. I shall not take space to go through them *seriatim*, but might stress such highlights as the general likelihood that the goods of one will be mistaken for those of the other, the extent to which the goods are marketed through the same channels, the relation in function between them, the degree of distinctiveness of the trade-mark or trade name, the length of time of use, etc. I rather deprecate the seizing on small distinctions in the goods — of a kind not quickly occurring to a shopping customer — to justify this form of competition. By making ever finer distinctions between products, we could easily do away with all possibility of protection to an established trade reputation. For instance, I should take this decision for authority to sell any of the new and increasingly popular synthetic materials for summer and sport wear under the name of any of the older manufacturers of woolen suits. *But see Rosenberg Bros. & Co. v. Elliott*, 3 Cir., 7 F.2d 962; *Blek Co. v. Mishawaka Rubber & Woolen Mfg. Co.*, 57 App.D.C. 149, 18 F.2d 191; *Long's Hat Stores Corp. v. Long's Clothes*, 224 App. Div. 497, 231 N.Y.S. 107.

The majority's view of the statutory test seems to me to encourage an element of partiality in this field based on a wholly irrelevant consideration, namely, the trier's response to the apparent fairness or unfairness of the acts of a defendant considered from his own standpoint. This I fear is too subjective a reaction to be anything but a pitfall for the court. Under such a concept it will be comparatively easy for most competitors to shield themselves from any challenge by ostentatious ignorance of their own business and its ramifications until they have successfully appropriated another's title. Meanwhile the confusion of customers and the destruction of another's business can go on with impunity so long as the competitor can show a purity of his own purpose. Further he is aided by substantially a presumption in his favor; for if we believe in a considerable degree of free competition, we must consider his efforts praiseworthy unless carried to ill-defined predatory extremes. I cannot avoid wondering if the defendant is as innocent of what was so generally and so widely known as it is pictured in this record. Even more, I think this too untrustworthy a basis upon which to make decisions involving important business relations turn. We have rejected it as late as the other decisions in this term cited above and we should do the same here.

I think the plaintiff entitled to an injunction.

NOTES ON SIMILARITY OF GOODS AND SERVICES

(1) It is now well settled, and in fact codified in the Lanham Act, 15 U.S.C. § 1114, that trademark rights afford protection against not only the use of similar marks on similar goods or services, but also against use on other goods or services that might naturally be supposed to emanate from the same source. *Yale Elec. Corp. v. Robertson*, 26 F.2d 972, 973–974 (2d Cir. 1928); *Landers, Frary & Clark v. Universal Cooler Corp.*, 85 F.2d 46, 47–48 (2d Cir. 1936). For an excellent discussion of the development of the "related goods" rule, see Lunsford, *Trademark Infringement and Confusion of Source*, 35 Va. L. Rev. 214 (1949). In *Scarves by Vera, Inc. v. Todo Imports Ltd.*, 544 F.2d 1167 (2d Cir. 1976), the court noted that many if not most fashion designers sell perfumes and cosmetics under their own trademarks, indicating that such products are closely related. Similarly, in *Helene Curtis Industries v. Church & Dwight Co.*, 560 F.2d 1325 (7th Cir. 1977), the court viewed underarm deodorant and baking soda as related goods where plaintiff had long promoted its ARM & HAMMER baking soda for use as a deodorant. *Compare Federated Foods, Inc. v. Fort Howard Paper Co.*, 544 F.2d 1098 (C.C.P.A. 1976) (HY-TOP plastic bags, aluminum foil and sponges were held not so related to HY-TEX toilet tissue that confusion would be likely, the only link established being that they might be found in the same area of the supermarket) *with In re Martin's Famous Pastry Shoppe, Inc.*, 748 F.2d 1565 (Fed. Cir. 1984) (bread and cheese held related) *and In re Mars, Inc.*, 741 F.2d 395 (Fed. Cir. 1984) (candy bars and fresh citrus fruits held not related). In *Astra Pharmaceutical Products, Inc. v. Beckman Instruments, Inc.*, 718 F.2d 1201 (1st Cir. 1983), the court found that use of defendant's ASTRA blood analyzer laboratory instrument and plaintiff's ASTRA drugs in the health care field was not enough to make them related goods. *See also Alpha Industries, Inc. v. Alpha Steel Tube & Shapes, Inc.*, 616 F.2d 440 (9th Cir. 1980), in which ALPHA for steel tubes was held not to infringe ALPHA for steel-making machinery because the items were expensive, the purchasers sophisticated and from two distinct groups, and the mark weak. *See also* the discussion in Chapter 6, *infra*, of the multifactor tests applied by the federal courts in assessing likelihood of confusion.

(2) If goods or services are not competitive, how is it possible for the public to become confused? Even if the public is confused, how can the plaintiff be damaged?

Compare Hyde Park Clothes v. Hyde Park Fashions, supra, with the *Aunt Jemima* and *Triangle Publication* cases, *supra, and Tisch Hotels, Inc. v. Americana Inn, Inc.,* 350 F.2d 609 (7th Cir. 1965). *See also Spring Mills, Inc. v. Ultracashmere House, Ltd.,* 689 F.2d 1127 (2d Cir. 1982); *James Burrough Ltd. v. Sign of the Beefeaters, Inc.,* 572 F.2d 574 (7th Cir. 1978); in both, the courts found no direct diversion of customers but instead deception of the public (BEEFEATER'S) and loss of goodwill or tarnishment of reputation (ULTRACASHMERE).

(3) Some courts have recognized enforceable trademark rights for a trademark owner in a "natural area of expansion." In *Tiffany & Co. v. Parfums Lamborghini,* 214 U.S.P.Q. 77 (S.D.N.Y. 1981), the court held that a demonstrated intention to enter the perfume field and recent purchase of plaintiff by a cosmetics and perfume company entitled plaintiff to trademark protection in the noncompeting perfume field. Similarly, in *Exquisite Form Industries, Inc. v. Exquisite Fabrics of London,* 378 F. Supp. 403 (S.D.N.Y. 1974), the court stated that "if it is demonstrated that plaintiff has continuously expanded its product line in the past, and has further plans to expand into defendant's area, a court may be justified in finding a likelihood of confusion even between dissimilar products." In the Second Circuit this potential expansion has been described as a potential for "bridging the gap." *Lever Bros. v. American Bakeries Co.,* 693 F.2d 251, 258 (2d Cir. 1982). *Mushroom Makers, supra,* 580 F.2d at 49; *Lever Bros., supra,* 693 F.2d at 258; *Vitarroz, supra,* 644 F.2d at 969. Goods across the gap and goods in the natural area of expansion presumably are not related goods. If the court finds that the goods *are* related, is the natural area of expansion irrelevant? *Helene Curtis Industries, Inc., supra,* 560 F.2d at 1331.

(4) The Third Circuit has held that where a defendant-newcomer enters a field already occupied by the established business of a plaintiff, the standard should be "possibility of confusion," not likelihood of confusion. *Merchant & Evans, Inc. v. Roosevelt Building Products Co.,* 963 F.2d 628, 637–38 (3d Cir. 1992); *Country Floors, Inc. v. Gepner,* 930 F.2d 1056 (3d Cir. 1991). *Cf. Barre-National, Inc. v. Barr Laboratories, Inc.,* 773 F. Supp. 735, 740–41 (D.N.J. 1991) (declining to apply Third Circuit "possibility of confusion" standard where plaintiff's field was not truly separate and new to defendant). Why should a different standard apply?

(5) "Famous" or "celebrated" marks are sometimes afforded greater protection than those less well-known. Should they be? *See, e.g., Tuxedo Monopoly, Inc. v. General Mills Fun Group, Inc.,* 648 F.2d 1335 (C.C.P.A. 1981) (MONOPOLY for wearing apparel likely to cause confusion with MONOPOLY for real estate board game; "lack of present intent to expand use of one's mark is not an overriding consideration"); *Radio Corp. of Am. v. Rayon Corp. of Am.,* 139 F.2d 833 (C.C.P.A. 1943) (RCA fabric held to infringe RCA radios); *CPC International, Inc. v. Skippy, Inc.,* 231 U.S.P.Q. 811, 814 (E.D. Va. 1986) ("consumers in today's world will automatically connect any product bearing the mark 'SKIPPY' with SKIPPY peanut butter and the company that manufactures it"); *Hallmark Cards, Inc. v. Hallmark Dodge, Inc.,* 229 U.S.P.Q. 882 (W.D. Mo. 1986) (HALLMARK DODGE for automobile dealership infringes HALLMARK for greeting cards); *John Walker & Sons, Ltd. v. Bethea,* 305 F. Supp. 1302 (D.S.C. 1969) (JOHNNY WALKER Motel held to infringe JOHNNY WALKER Scotch Whiskey); *Miles Laboratories, Inc. v.*

Goodfriend, 106 U.S.P.Q. 336 (Comm'r 1955). *Compare Alligator Co. v. Larus & Brothers Co.*, 86 U.S.P.Q. 332 (Comm'r 1950). A "famous" or "celebrated" mark often will be protected regardless of dissimilarity of goods or services. What is the rationale, if any, for such disparate treatment? In *James Burrough Ltd. v. Sign of the Beefeater, Inc.*, 540 F.2d 266, 276 (7th Cir. 1976), the court stated: "A mark that is strong because of its fame or its uniqueness, is more likely to be remembered and more likely to be associated in the public mind with a greater breadth of products or services, than is a mark that is weak." *Compare B.V.D. Licensing Corp. v. Body Action Design, Inc.*, 846 F.2d 727 (Fed. Cir. 1988), where the court held confusion was unlikely between the famous mark B.V.D. for men's underwear and the mark B.A.D for clothing, including undergarments. It reasoned that the better known a mark is, the more readily the public becomes aware of even a small deviation from it. In *Kenner Parker Toys, Inc. v. Rose Art Industries, Inc.*, 963 F.2d 350 (Fed. Cir. 1992), the Federal Circuit distinguished *B.V.D.* and held that FUNDOUGH was confusingly similar to PLAY-DOH for modelling compounds. In doing so, it reemphasized the traditional rule that famous marks are entitled to greater protection, stating (at p. 1457):

> If investors forfeit legal protection by increasing a mark's fame, the law would then countenance a disincentive for investments in trademarks. The law is not so schizophrenic. In consonance with the purposes and origins of trademark protection, the Lanham Act provides a broader range of protection as a mark's fame grows.

Finding *B.V.D.* to be an unusual decision, it stated, "The holding of *B.V.D.*, to the extent it treats fame as a liability, is confined to the facts of that case." *Id.*, at 1457. *See generally* McCarthy, *Trademarks and Unfair Competition*, § 11:24 (3d ed. 1992).

(6) The existence of third-party uses of the same or a similar mark can weaken a trademark owner's rights and narrow the scope of its protection. As the Federal Circuit's predecessor court explained in *King Candy Co. v. Eunice King's Kitchen, Inc.*, 496 F.2d 1400, 1401 (C.C.P.A. 1974), this narrowed scope of protection simply means that when weak marks are at issue, confusion may be unlikely because the public easily distinguishes between the different uses:

> The expressions "weak" and "entitled to limited protection" are but other ways of saying . . . that confusion is unlikely because the marks are of such non-arbitrary nature or so widely used that the public easily distinguishes slight differences in the marks under consideration as well as differences in the goods to which they are applied, even though the goods of the parties may be considered "related."

The owner of a mark in such a "crowded field" therefore has a limited ability to prevent the use of similar marks. As stated by Professor McCarthy, "In such a crowd, customers will not likely be confused between any two of the crowd and may have learned to carefully pick out one from another." McCarthy, *Trademarks and Unfair Competition*, § 11:26 at p. 511 (3d ed. 1992).

In *Taj Mahal Enterprises, Ltd. v. Trump*, 742 F. Supp. 892 (D.N.J. 1990), *summary judgment gr.*, 745 F. Supp. 240 (D.N.J. 1990), for example, numerous third-party uses made plaintiff's TAJ MAHAL mark for its restaurant weak. Conversely, Donald Trump's TRUMP surname was very strong, and confusion was held unlikely with his TRUMP TAJ MAHAL casino and hotel. To similar effect are: *Plus Products v. Plus Discount Foods, Inc.*, 722 F.2d 999 (2d Cir. 1983) (weakness of mark PLUS makes confusion with noncompeting goods unlikely); *McKee Baking Company v. Interstate Brands Corporation*, 738 F. Supp. 1272 (E.D. Mo. 1990) (numerous third-party uses of "LITTLE" made confusion unlikely between plaintiff's LITTLE DEBBIE and defendant's LITTLE DOLLIES), *Warner Lambert Co. v. McCrory's Corp.*, 718 F. Supp. 389 (D.N.J. 1989) (third-party uses of similar trade dress; preliminary relief denied).

(7) What should be the result if consumers believe there is only a remote connection between the products or services of the plaintiff and the defendant, e.g., sponsorship? *See Fleishmann Distilling Corp. v. Maier Brewing Co.*, 314 F.2d 149, 155 (9th Cir. 1963), *cert. denied*, 374 U.S. 830 (1963) ("It is not material whether he would think that the makers of the Scotch whiskey were actually brewing and bottling this beer, or whether it was being produced under their supervision or pursuant to some other arrangement with them. He would probably not concern himself about any such detail."); *James Burrough, supra* Note (5). In *Dallas Cowboys Cheerleaders v. Pussycat Cinema, Ltd.*, 604 F.2d 200 (2d Cir. 1979), the defendant was preliminarily enjoined from distributing or exhibiting the "sexually depraved" movie "Debbie Does Dallas" because use of the plaintiff's cheerleader uniform would mislead the public into believing that plaintiff sponsored the movie. Similarly in *Gucci Shops, Inc. v. R.H. Macy & Co.*, 446 F. Supp. 838 (S.D.N.Y. 1977), the court found that use of GUCCI GOO on a diaper bag could mislead the public into believing plaintiff Gucci was somehow associated with the product's manufacture, promotion and sale, and in *Coca-Cola Co. v. Gemini Rising, Inc.*, 346 F. Supp. 1183 (E.D.N.Y. 1972), defendant was enjoined from use of ENJOY COCAINE in famous Coca-Cola script on its posters. Are there any reasons other than confusion that should entitle the trademark owner to protection against such uses? *See* the discussion on *Parody* in Chapter 7, *infra*. Should the court take into account general public knowledge that modern corporations are often widely diversified and market unrelated products? *See* 1 Gilson, *Trademark Protection and Practice*, § 5.05 [8] (1993 ed.); *Nationwide Mutual Insurance Co. v. First Nationwide Savings*, 221 U.S.P.Q. 686, 692–93 (S.D.N.Y. 1982); *Carling Brewing Co. v. Philip Morris Inc.*, 297 F. Supp. 1330, 1337–1338 (N.D. Ga. 1968).

(8) Should it make a difference whether noncompetitive goods are of a higher, equal or inferior quality compared to those of plaintiff at the time of suit? *See Lever Bros., supra*, Note (3), 693 F.2d at 258 ("Because the purpose of protecting a user's mark on non-competing goods is, in part, to guard against tarnishing the reputation of the mark . . . proof that [defendant's product] had proved highly successful with consumers weighs heavily against [plaintiff]"); *AMF, Inc. v. Sleekcraft Boats*, 599 F.2d 341, 353 (9th Cir. 1979) ("when the alleged infringer's goods are of equal quality, there is little harm to the reputation earned by the trademarked goods. Yet this is not assurance of continued quality. . . . The wrong inheres in involuntarily entrusting one's business reputation to another's business"); *Stork Restaurant, Inc. v. Sahati*, 166 F.2d 348 (9th Cir. 1948); *Yale Elec. Corp. v. Robertson*, Chapter 1,

supra, ("This is an injury even though the borrower does not tarnish it, or divert any sales by its use; for a reputation, like a face, is the symbol of its possessor and creator, and another can use it only as a mask"); *Cartier, Inc. v. Three Sheaves Co.,* 465 F. Supp. 123, 128, 129 (S.D.N.Y. 1979) ("Defendants products are inexpensive, and continued use of the mark CATTIER or PIERRE CATTIER . . . gives the consumer public the impression that Cartier is now the source of inexpensive rather than high priced and high quality merchandise thereby diluting plaintiff's mark").

§ 5.05   Intent

Pattishall, THE IMPACT OF INTENT IN TRADE IDENTITY CASES*

65 Nw. U. L. Rev. 421 (1970)

It has been said that "[t]he protection of trademarks is the law's recognition of the psychological function of symbols." The axiomatic depth of this statement by the late Mr. Justice Frankfurter soon becomes apparent in any encounters with the law of trade identity. The pragmatic impact of another judicial statement reveals itself much later. It was Judge Learned Hand who wrote of proven intent to compete unfairly in *My-T-Fine Corp. v. Samuels*:

> But when it appears, we think that it has an important procedural result; a late comer who deliberately copies the dress of his competitors already in the field, must at least prove that his effort has been futile. Prima facie the court will treat his opinion so disclosed as expert and will not assume that it was erroneous. He may indeed succeed in showing that it was; that, however bad his purpose, it will fail in execution; if he does, he will win. . . . But such an intent raises a presumption that customers will be deceived.

The essence of this reasoning had been expressed several decades earlier in more earthly language by Master of the Rolls Cozens-Hardy:

> If I find that a man, taking a particular name under which to trade, is a knave, I give him credit for not being also a fool, and I assume that there is a reasonable probability that his knavish purpose will succeed.

The presumption of infringement doctrine of the *My-T-Fine* case and of decisions which both preceded and followed it expressing the same rationale has long been familiar. The extraordinary impact which a showing of wrongful intent has exercised in the entire field of trade identity law, however, appears to have been inadequately recognized. Courts today frequently and correctly comment that the intent element is not legally requisite in either trademark infringement or unfair competition law. The body of decided cases reveals, nonetheless, that in an astonishingly high percentage of trade identity decisions in which relief was granted, the defendant was found guilty, either directly or circumstantially, of intended poaching if not outright

---

*Reprinted by special permission of Northwestern University School of Law, Volume 65, *Northwestern University Law Review*, pp. 421–422 (1970).

fraud. Indeed, empirical observation indicates that something in the nature of this form of *animus furandi* remains virtually an essential ingredient for a winning plaintiff's suit in the area of trade identity law.

MY-T-FINE CORPORATION v. SAMUELS

United States Court of Appeals, Second Circuit
69 F.2d 76 (1934)

L. HAND, CIRCUIT JUDGE.

The plaintiff is the manufacturer of a confection of chocolate and sugar, used in making a kind of pudding, and sold in small cardboard boxes. The suit, which is founded upon diversity of citizenship, is to protect its make-up which the defendant is alleged to have copied. . . .

. . . The suit is to protect the box of 1929. By 1933 the plaintiff's sales had grown to an enormous total, over 100,000,000 in all; it had spent more than a million and a half dollars in advertisement; its trade had spread very extensively through the Union. To some extent its product has become known as the "Red and Green package," but by far the greater number of customers ask for it by its name, "My-T-Fine."

The defendants sell a similar product under the name, "Velmo." Before July 1, 1931, when they first introduced it into New York City, the body of their box, which was of substantially the same size as the plaintiff's, was solidly of about the same shade of green, but had no red stripes along the edges. At the top of the front was a black, instead of a white, chevron on which in large red letters was the word, "Velmo." Below in black was the word, "Chocolate," and below that in red on a white stripe, "Dessert." The back was also of green, on which the direction for using were printed in black; these were in part a literal copy of the plaintiff's. In July, 1931, the defendants added red stripes around all the edges of this box, of substantially the same width as the plaintiff's, and a white tablet on the back to contain the printed matter. They sold it very generally throughout the city of New York, so generally that they insist it must have come to the plaintiff's notice very soon after it was first put on sale. The suit was filed on July 7, 1933, and the plaintiff at once moved for a preliminary injunction. The judge, thinking the similarity between the packages too little, and the delay too long, denied the motion.

It would be impossible on this record to say that any one who meant to buy the plaintiff's pudding has hitherto been misled into taking the defendants' by a mistake in the appearance of the box. Indeed such evidence is usually hard to get even after a trial, and upon this motion the affidavits are too hazy and unreliable, even if undisputed. The plaintiff has proved no more than that the boxes look a good deal alike, and that confusion may well arise; and were it not for the evidence of the defendants' intent to deceive and so to secure the plaintiff's customers, we would scarcely feel justified in interfering at this stage of the cause. We need not say whether that intent is always a necessary element in such causes of suit; probably it originally was in federal courts. *McLean v. Fleming*, 96 U.S. 245; *Lawrence Mfg. Co. v. Tennessee Mfg. Co.*, 138 U.S. 537; *Elgin National Watch Co. v. Illinois Watch*

Case Co., 179 U.S. 665. But when it appears, we think that it has an important procedural result; a late comer who deliberately copies the dress of his competitors already in the field, must at least prove that his effort has been futile. Prima facie the court will treat his opinion so disclosed as expert and will not assume that it was erroneous. *Fairbank Co. v. R. W. Bell Mfg. Co.*, 77 F. 869, 877 (C.C.A. 2); *Capewell Horse Nail Co. v. Green*, 188 F. 20, 24 (C.C.A. 2); *Wolf Bros. & Co. v. Hamilton*, 165 F. 413, 416 (C.C.A. 8); *Thum Co. v. Dickinson*, 245 F. 609, 621, 622 (C.C.A. 6); *Wesson v. Galef*, (D.C.) 286 F. 621, 626. He may indeed succeed in showing that it was; that, however bad his purpose, it will fail in execution; if he does, he will win. *Kann v. Diamond Steel Co.*, 89 F. 706, 713 (C.C.A. 8). But such an intent raises a presumption that customers will be deceived.

In the case at bar, it seems to us fairly demonstrated that the defendants have copied the plaintiff's make-up as far as they dared.

. . . At the very outset the directions were lifted bodily from the back of the plaintiff's box; and although the defendants were within their rights as to that, still the circumstance is relevant because it proves that the box had been before them when they designed their own make-up, and that it had been their point of departure. In addition they took solid green for the body, and put on a chevron; and while perhaps they did not choose a general combination of red and green, at least they adopted a red lettering. Whether or not they meant to get hold of the plaintiff's customers by that make-up, their next step was bolder, and put their intent beyond question; they added the red stripes at every edge; so that the real differences that remained were only in the name and the color of the chevron. As they had not the slightest original interest in the colors chosen and their distribution, they could only have meant to cause confusion, out of which they might profit by diverting the plaintiff's customers. This being the intent, the dissimilarities between the two do not in our judgment rebut the presumption.

The delay of two years before beginning suit does not seem to us of importance, even upon this application. There is indeed some question as to just when the plaintiff learned of the defendants' second box; but we see nothing in that to give us pause; we are ready to assume that it learned of its appearance at once. Again, were it not for the intent of trade unfairly, we might hesitate, but advantages built upon a deliberately plagiarized make-up do not seem to us to give the borrower any standing to complain that his vested interests will be disturbed. . . .

The decree is reversed; the plaintiff may take an injunction against the use of the second box, i.e., that with the red edges. For the present and until trial, the earlier box will not be enjoined.

HAROLD F. RITCHIE, INC. v. CHESEBROUGH-POND'S, INC.

United States Court of Appeals, Second Circuit
281 F.2d 755 (1960)

SWAN, CIRCUIT JUDGE.

On June 25, 1957 Harold F. Ritchie, Inc., a New Jersey corporation and owner of the registered trademark "Brylcreem," bought suit against Chesebrough-Pond's, Inc., a New York corporation, charging trademark infringement and unfair competition by appellee's use of the trademark "Valcream." The complaint sought injunctive relief pursuant to 15 U.S.C.A. § 1116, and an accounting of profits, treble damages and costs pursuant to 15 U.S.C.A. § 1117. Federal jurisdiction was based on the Lanham Act, 15 U.S.C.A. §§ 1114, 1121, with pendent jurisdiction of the claim of unfair competition, 28 U.S.C.A. § 1338(b), and also on diverse citizenship, 28 U.S.C.A. § 1332. The trademarks, Brylcreem and Valcream, were employed to designate cream hairdressing for men which is marketed in collapsible metal tubes packaged in paperboard cartons. The case was tried before Chief Judge Ryan without a jury. Pursuant to his opinion of September 14, 1959, reported in 176 F. Supp. 439, judgment was entered dismissing appellant's action. The court found no such similarity between "Valcream" and "Brylcreem" as to cause likelihood of confusion to purchasers, and concluded that appellant had not sustained the burden of proving either trademark infringement or unfair competition. Timely notice of appeal was duly filed. .

. . . .

Appellant points out that the two products are identical in the size and shape of the tubes and cartons, the prices identical, the colors similar, the orifice identical in size, and the advertising on the tubes and packages substantially the same. Moreover the contents of the tubes are indistinguishable. They look, feel and smell the same; and their ingredients are concededly virtually identical. As to each of these items appellant admits it had no monopoly, but it contends, and we agree, that the multiplicity of the similarities is objective evidence of defendant's conscious imitation of plaintiff's product.

Even of more significance than the so-called "objective" evidence of intent is the "subjective" evidence of which the proof was largely documentary. Having decided to market a cream style hairdressing in tubes, defendant asked an advertising agency to suggest names for this hair dressing "of the Brylcreem Type," emphasizing that need for a name was of "top priority." Exh. 65. The agency responded with a list of 25 names for "Bryl Cream Type." Exh. 58. From this list the appellee picked Valcreem, one of the two names on the list which most closely approximated appellant's trademark. Other exhibits (66, 67, 68, 69 and 70) show that up to January 5, 1956, defendant intended to use the suffix "creem." Why or when the determination was made to change "creem" to "cream" can only be surmised. A memorandum in November 1955 from appellee's files reveals that the successful market "pioneering" by "Brylcreem" was a compelling reason for appellee's choice of the name "Valcream." Exh. 94. The similarities between the original Brylcreem tube and the Valcream tube are accounted for by the fact that when the artist was summoned to design the Valcream tube, there was a tube of Brylcreem on the desk in front of him. Joint Appendix 125. When it came to devising the instructions for use and the statement of ingredients on the outside of defendant's carton, the advertising agency was sent a carton of "Brylcreem" as an aid in composing a "like panel on Valcream." Exh. 87. Even the color of the cap was made red, conforming with Brylcreem, when the question arose whether to make it red or white. Exh. 78. Before marketing Valcream, appellee ran a series of "blind product tests" by which it was learned that "34% . . . saw no difference between Brylcreem and Valcream. . . . While the sample was too small to be definitive in preferences this close, it would appear, at most, that any superiority of Brylcreem would probably be no more than 1% point over Valcream, if any." Exh. 86; see exhs. 89 and 90. In making such tests, defendant consumed five hundred and fifteen 1-3/4 ounce tubes of Brylcreem. Exh. 80.

In our opinion the above evidence of intentional imitation was not given adequate consideration by the court below. Doubtless the trial court's summary rejection of this evidence was due to the court's finding of no confusing similarity between the two trademarks standing alone. We think the District Court should have considered the names of the two products in conjunction with the similarity of the presentation of the products with respect to their design and general appearance, containers, tubes, price, size, perfume, and other non-functional aspects. . . .

Admittedly there is nothing to prevent a second comer from making and selling the identical product of the first comer, providing the second comer so names and dresses its product as to avoid all likely confusion. Clearly this test has not been met. This is true not only because of the conscious imitation referred to above, but also because as a result of the similarity of name and dress, actual confusion did occur.

The Gil Hodges television broadcast provided one source of evidence of confusion which is briefly summarized in the District Court opinion. Appellee made an offer by television in certain west coast cities to refund purchasers of the 59¢ size of Valcream with a check for that sum signed by the baseball player Gil Hodges. This evidence included thirteen instances in which Brylcreem cartons were mailed to appellant in response to appellee's television commercial. Appellee also received at least ten, and probably more Brylcreem cartons in response to its offer. There was no evidence of the receipt of cartons of any other competing hairdressing. Another source of evidence was the testimony of the department manager in charge of cosmetics in the Katz Drug Store in Des Moines, Iowa, and the depositions of two employees of Katz Drug Store in Kansas City, Missouri. Two additional instances of confusion were also proved. The Oklahoma Drug Sales Company of Lawton, Oklahoma, mistakenly invoiced appellant for Valcream advertising in a local paper; and Dakota Drug, Inc., of Minot, North Dakota, sent appellant a letter relating to a price reduction offer made by appellee for Valcream. Even Standard & Poor's somehow transposed the two names and attributed the product Brylcreem to the appellee corporation.

The court brushed aside this evidence with the statement: "The evidence of actual confusion introduced at the trial was hardly overwhelming. Most of the deposition and oral testimony, as we have observed, showed no confusion but carelessness and inattention on the part of the purchaser." In our opinion this statement by the trial judge is not a finding of fact based on testimony but is merely a characterization of the testimony embodying the judge's view as to what "confusion" is. In denying significance to the evidence of actual confusion we think the court erred. . . .

Actual confusion or deception of purchasers is not essential to a finding of trade-mark infringement or unfair competition, it being recognized that "reliable evidence of actual instances of confusion is practically almost impossible to secure." But where such proof has been adduced, weight should be given it. Here the evidence is impressive in view of its spontaneous character and difficulty of attainment.

. . . .

For the foregoing reasons we believe that the trial court erred in dismissing the action. Accordingly, the judgement is reversed and the case remanded for further proceedings not inconsistent with this opinion.

CLARK, CIRCUIT JUDGE (dissenting).

. . . .

. . . Remember defendant has been in the general cosmetic business longer than the plaintiff, and nothing could be more natural than its attempt to catch up with the plaintiff's advertising success. Much of what is now cited against it to my mind shows on the contrary very considerable concern to make its competition legal and proper. Of course it intended to compete; it would have been wholly disingenuous and dishonest to have claimed it was oblivious of the presently largest distributor in the business. So when it rejected its original word "Valcreem" to spell "cream" properly, I should think its action commendable, rather than the reverse. To say that defendant picked from a long list of possible names laid before it one of the two names which most closely approximated plaintiff's trade-mark is to accept blindly the plaintiff's self-serving asseveration, the truth of which is not apparent on inspection of the 250 or more names set forth. And so as to the much belabored "late-comer" argument, it of course is valid, namely, where there is real copying, not where the names are as dissimilar as here. I shall not pause to examine each tidbit of detail, but trust I have set forth enough to explain my own conviction that both the so-called "objective" and "subjective" evidence of intent of itself shows nothing illegal or improper in the competitive battle; on the contrary, it tends to indicate a scrupulous attempt to learn and to observe the proper legal limits.

. . . .

I would affirm.

O. & W. THUM CO. v. DICKINSON

United States Court of Appeals, Sixth Circuit
245 F. 609 (1917)

WARRINGTON, CIRCUIT JUDGE.

. . . .

[Both parties make fly paper in Grand Rapids, Michigan.] It will not do for a subsequent maker of a product like that of the first user to segregate the details of the earlier trade packages and dress, and then, on the theory that the first user does not possess an exclusive right to them separately, appropriate them in whole or in substantial part by piecemeal; and yet this is the theory on which the defendant Dickinson's claims are for the most part bottomed. This ignores the first user's grouping of parts; of details for the very purpose of denoting the origin of his product; it is through such distinctive characteristics, considered in a unitary way, that the first user and the public can be protected against confusion and deception as to his product. Wherever, then, the first user has through a particular trade dress, as here, so identified his product as to indicate that it is his, every principle of fair dealing, fair competition, forbids any subsequent user of the same product to adopt any part of the first user's dress without otherwise effectively distinguishing his dress from that of the first user. . . . It results that, by adopting and persisting in the use of plaintiff's sizes of packages and fly sheet, defendant Dickinson incurred and still rests under an obligation at least to avoid still further and material similarity through the dress applied to his packages. It is hard to see that defendants have observed any such rule.

Turning attention to the progressive course pursued by the defendant Dickinson, but few illustrations are necessary to make this clear. One is found in the external dress of his cases of 1914. Prior to that year the dress of defendant's cases, although changed from time to time, was not in either color or arrangement, as already pointed out, particularly objectionable; but a distinct change was made in the dress for that year. . . . [Defendant began using cases "of the same dimensions, seemingly of the same kind of wood, and made and enclosed in the same way; and some of these bear close resemblance also in (the color and language of) their external dress."] The plaintiff, it is true, made some changes in the dress of its case for 1914; but they are of minor character and do not operate to alter the striking resemblances of the dress whether the comparison be made with respect to plaintiff's dress of 1913 or 1914.

As to the cartons, apt illustration of defendant's encroachment by degrees upon plaintiff's carton is found in the identity of the language in terms already shown to be displayed on the edges of the carton lids. This identity could not have been the result of either accident or necessity; it must have come about through design. It was shown that before 1909 there was some difference between the words employed by the respective parties, as, for instance, plaintiff's directions were, "Do not stand on edge;" "Keep very dry;" but in the year named defendant changed his directions and made them exactly like plaintiff's. Defendant even changed his method of securing the corners of the carton lid from metal clasps to "paper corners," the same as plaintiff had used for years, and also changed to that of plaintiff the method of holding the carton lid in place.

An illuminating example of defendant's progression appears on both the outside and inside faces of the fly sheets. It will be borne in mind that in the infringement suit we described the figures and matter imprinted on these sheets. It appears that the defendant's first design for his fly sheet consisted of two full ellipses defined in red lines, with a red Maltese cross shown at the extremities of the major axes, but with the four flies disposed, two above and two below the ellipses, at points opposite their respective minor axes; this design also bore the words, in red letters within and without the ellipses, which are set out in the infringement suit. An important change, however, was made in this design. The two full ellipses were replaced by a single ellipse centrally located, with fractional ellipses at the ends of its major axis. This change brought the four flies into the same relation with the full ellipses and the fractional ellipses that the four circles bear to the complete and fractional ellipse of plaintiff's registered trade-mark. Defendant's final change came when he converted his red ellipse and fractional ellipses, with the matter displayed within them, into black. We have already in substance stated that the testimony to the effect that this change was necessary as a matter of expense is not convincing. It seems to us that the reason for the change is to be found in the purpose obviously to be inferred from the gradual encroachments made upon the plaintiff's mark rather than in the slightly increased cost shown.

What, then, is to be deduced from the resemblances described and the method of gradual change in bringing them about? This method cannot be misunderstood. The effect of every step in the process was more or less to imitate something theretofore existing in plaintiff's trade-mark or trade dress. This course consumed time and evidently involved deliberation; and in view of the sequel every step was toward a definite end. The course thus pursued appears to have avoided present opposition and contest and so to have secured the advantage of the use of the parts so taken; but it did not conceal the intent with which the encroachments were evidently made. . . .

. . . .

It must therefore be concluded that placing these goods on the market, whether by the producer or his selling agent, the Ackerman Company, imports an intent to have them mistaken for and confused with plaintiff's product; and in determining the effect of this, it is not enough to consider simply the jobber or the retailer, though of course their interests are entitled to protection. As we in effect said when passing on the question of infringement of plaintiff's trade-mark, jobbers and retailers are cautious buyers and have the means of identifying manufacturers when negotiating their purchases; but it is well known that all jobbers and retailers are not so considerate of either the interests or the choice of unsuspecting users. The subject, then, cannot be fully considered unless the interests of purchasing users are taken into account. It results that plaintiff is entitled to relief.

. . . .

It is urged further that through its laches and acquiescence plaintiff is estopped to claim any relief. It is true that it was not until 1914 that plaintiff took active measures to interfere with the course pursued by either of the defendants. This presents another effect of the progressive course of encroachment, already considered; such a course does not tend to arouse hostile action until it is fully developed; indeed, this happened; plaintiff does not appear to have regarded the situation as requiring active interference until near the opening of the fly paper season of 1914, when, as we have seen, radical and apparently permanent changes in the Dickinson trade-mark and trade dress were introduced. Plaintiff then took definite action, both through written notices and the institution of suits. In these circumstances we cannot think the defendants can shield themselves behind the charge of laches; this would be to ignore the fact that the true design of the partial encroachments, of the continuing trespass, did not develop until the culmination in 1914; permanent benefits in the good will and trade reputation of another cannot be acquired in this way. Still this is not to say that the full measure of relief sought should be granted. Even if laches and acquiescence could rightfully be imputed to plaintiff, it might well be denied an accounting of profits for a substantial portion of the encroachment period, and yet be granted relief by injunctions as to the future. *Hanover Milling Co. v. Metcalf*, 240 U.S. 403, 418, 419. Further, it is not necessary to the due protection of plaintiff's trade tokens that an injunction should go to all their minutiae; relief that will operate to prevent confusion and deceit as to the origin of the products of the respective parties, with a limited accounting, is all that should be granted; as nearly as may be, the decrees should be formulated so as to fix conditions that will admit of full and fair competition but destroy unfair competition.

. . . .

NOTES ON INTENT

(1) While the intent of an alleged infringer is a relevant consideration in determining likelihood of confusion, it is not requisite that a complainant establish wrongful intent in order to prevail in a trade identity action. *See Lois Sportswear, U.S.A., Inc. v. Levi Strauss & Co.*, 799 F.2d 867, 875 (2d Cir. 1986); *Tisch Hotels, Inc. v. Americana Inn, Inc.*, 350 F.2d 609 (7th Cir. 1965); *Fleischmann Distilling Corp. v. Maier Brewing Co.*, 314 F.2d 149 (9th Cir. 1963), *cert denied*, 375 U.S. 830 (1963). As a practical matter, however, courts more readily find a trade identity tort where evidence of wrongful intent is presented. *See* Pattishall, *The Impact of Intent, supra*. In *Perfect Fit Industries v. Acme Quilting Co.*, 618 F.2d 950 (2d Cir. 1980), the court noted that secondary meaning for plaintiff's mattress pad trade dress had not been shown, but confusing similarity could be presumed from defendant's intentional copying. Similarly, in *HMH Publishing Co. v. Brincat*, 504 F.2d 713 (9th Cir. 1974), the court stated it would have found no likelihood of confusion as to sponsorship by plaintiff publisher of Playboy magazine of defendant's automotive products and services sold under the mark PLAYBOY except for the "somewhat weak" evidence of defendant's intent. *See also Fuji Photo Film Co. v. Shinohara Shoji*, 754 F.2d 591, 596 (5th Cir. 1985), where the court stated, "Good faith is not a defense to trademark infringement . . . the reason for this is clear: if potential purchasers are confused, no amount of good faith can make them less so. Bad faith, however, may, without more, prove infringement."

(Matthew Bender & Co., Inc.)

(2) Generally, proof of intent is based upon circumstantial evidence, direct evidence rarely being available. Thus, in *Spring Mills, Inc. v. Ultracashmere House, Ltd.*, 689 F.2d 1127 (2d Cir. 1982), the court found: "No motive other than a desire for a free ride would appear to explain the slavish copying of the Ultrasuede hand tag by defendants." Courts often draw a presumption of bad faith merely from proof that defendant knew of plaintiff's mark at the time of adoption. *Nabisco Brands v. Kaye*, 760 F. Supp. 25, 27 (D. Conn. 1991) (confusion held likely where, while claiming non-infringement, defendant admitted his A-2 mark for steak sauce was designed to draw on the market recognition of plaintiff's A-1 mark); *Caesars World, Inc. v. Caesar's Palace*, 490 F. Supp. 818 (D.N.J. 1980) (Defendant's "innocent adoption" defense must fail in light of visit to plaintiff's resort hotel nine months before the opening of defendant's beauty salon with similar trade name). *Compare Century 21 Real Estate Corp. v. Magee*, 19 U.S.P.Q.2d 1530, 1534–35 (C.D. Cal. 1991) (defendant used CENTURY 31 for real estate brokerage services and claimed he had never heard of plaintiff's CENTURY 21 mark; the court nonetheless inferred an intent to benefit from plaintiff's goodwill and enjoined defendant); *Brooks Bros. v. Brooks Clothing of California Ltd.*, 60 F. Supp. 442 (S.D. Cal. 1945), *aff'd*, 158 F.2d 798 (9th Cir. 1947) (innocent adoption became wrongful intent when defendant began to advertise falsely in source-confusing manner). Is continuous use after protest from the plaintiff evidence of wrongful intent? *See Anheuser-Busch, Inc. v. Power City Brewery, Inc.*, 28 F. Supp. 740 (W.D.N.Y. 1939). *Compare Isador Straus v. Notaseme Hosiery Co.*, 240 U.S. 179 (1916) *with Johnson & Johnson v. Quality Pure Mfg., Inc.*, 484 F. Supp. 975 (D.N.J. 1979), wherein the court held, "once the similarity is brought to his attention a failure or refusal to alter the trade dress to avoid the confusion is equivalent to an original and actual intent." *Accord*: *Jockey International, Inc. v. Burkard*, 185 U.S.P.Q. 201 (S.D. Cal. 1975); *Fotomat Corp. v. Cochran*, 437 F. Supp. 1231 (D. Kan. 1977). *Compare H. Lubovsky, Inc. v. Esprit de Corp.*, 627 F. Supp. 483, 490–91 (S.D.N.Y. 1986), where the court found no bad faith in defendant's use of ESPRIT for clothes despite its knowledge of plaintiff's federal registration and use of ESPRIT for shoes and its previous unsuccessful attempt to purchase plaintiff's rights.

(3) Should a burden of proof of good faith be placed upon one who adopts a mark identical to the existing mark of another? *See Kiki Undies Corp. v. Promenade Hosiery Mills, Inc.*, 411 F.2d 1097 (2d Cir. 1969), *cert. dismissed*, 396 U.S. 1054 (1970). Does the constructive notice provision of the Lanham Act affect the defense of innocent adoption? Does constructive notice support a claim of wrongful intent or deliberate infringement? *See* Chapter 2, *supra*; *In re Beatrice Foods Co.*, 429 F.2d 466, 472–473 (C.C.P.A. 1970).

(4) Historically, the United States Patent and Trademark Office has not given great weight to the intent element on the premise that it does not have jurisdiction or power to adjudicate that issue. *See Scholl Mfg. Co. v. Principle Business Enterprises, Inc.*, 150 U.S.P.Q. 217, 219 (T.T.A.B. 1966); *Coca-Cola Co. v. Fanta*, 155 U.S.P.Q. 276, 278 (T.T.A.B. 1967). Is this position consistent with the *My-T-Fine* doctrine? Where the statutory issue is likelihood of confusion, should not all evidence relevant to that issue be examined? *Compare Standard Brands, Inc. v. Peters*, 191 U.S.P.Q. 168,

171 (T.T.A.B. 1975), wherein the Board stated that intent may be a factor in proceedings "to the extent that it can . . . resolve any doubt as to the question of likelihood of confusion." If the Board initially determines that confusion is likely, however, or that there is no reasonable likelihood of confusion, intent will not affect the decision. *Electronic Water Conditioners, Inc. v. Turbomag Corp.*, 221 U.S.P.Q. 162, 165 (T.T.A.B. 1984).

(5) It is often said that a second comer to a market has a duty to avoid all likelihood of consumers confusing his product with that of the first comer. Failure to do so will cause courts to "look with suspicion" on the second comer, *Chevron Chemical Co. v. Voluntary Purchasing Groups*, 659 F.2d 695, 704 (5th Cir. 1981), and may give rise to an inference of intentional copying, *Fotomat, supra*, Note (2). In *American Home Products v. Johnson Chemical Co.*, 589 F.2d 103, 107 (2d Cir. 1978), the court stated that

> the registrant is presumptively entitled to protection from a recent second comer's appropriation of the word mark by the use of a synonym on goods in direct competition. This is particularly true when no reasonable explanation is offered to show the second comer's need to come so close to the mark.

The implicit reasoning seems to be that "it is so easy for a business man . . . to select marks and packaging that cannot possibly be confused . . . " *Chevron, supra*, 659 F.2d at 704. *See also Londontown Manufacturing Co. v. Cable Raincoat Co.*, 371 F. Supp. 1114 (S.D.N.Y. 1974) ("it is hard to see why a second comer would come so close unless he wanted to obtain some advantage from the trade which [the plaintiff] had built up.") *But compare Thompson Medical Co. v. Pfizer, Inc.*, 753 F.2d 208, 218 (2d Cir. 1985), where error was found in the lower court stating, "we have invoked [the doctrine] only where there exists a highly distinctive mark of the senior user and proof of bad faith by the junior user." *Cf.* Clayton & Schlossberg, *Requiem for the Second Comer Doctrine*, 81 Trademark Rep. 465 (1991).

(6) Usually, sufficient evidence of intent is held to raise a rebuttable presumption of likelihood of confusion. *See RJR Foods, Inc. v. White Rocks Corp.*, 603 F.2d 1058 (2d Cir. 1979); *Processed Plastic Co. v. Warner Communications*, 675 F.2d 852 (7th Cir. 1982); *HMH Publishing Co., supra*, Note (1); *Beer Nuts, Inc. v. Clover Club Foods Co.*, 805 F.2d 920 (10th Cir. 1965); *National Football League Properties, Inc. v. New Jersey Giants, Inc.*, 229 U.S.P.Q. 785 (D.N.J. 1986). One court held that presumption to be rebutted when it found that, "Defendants, while acting with an improper intent, carried out their promotional scheme in such an inept fashion — whether deliberately or not — that plaintiff's rights were not disturbed." *Johnny Carson Apparel, Inc. v. Zeeman Manufacturing Co.*, 203 U.S.P.Q. 585, 595 (N.D. Ga. 1978). *See also Alberto Culver Co. v. Andrea Dumon, Inc.*, 466 F.2d 705, 709–710 (7th Cir. 1972).

(7) Non-distinctive marks must be shown to have acquired secondary meaning before their infringement may be found. Might proof of intentional copying constitute evidence of secondary meaning as well as evidence of likelihood of confusion? *See RJR Foods, supra* (defendant's intentional simulation supports plaintiff's claim of secondary meaning in its trade dress); *Osem Industries Ltd. v. Sherwood Foods, Inc.*, 917 F.2d 161 (4th Cir. 1990) (defendant's admission that it

copied the trade dress of plaintiff's soup packages created both a presumption of secondary meaning and of likely confusion which defendant failed to rebut); *Transgo, Inc. v. Ajac Transmission Parts Corp.*, 768 F.2d 1001, 1016 (9th Cir. 1986) ("Proof of exact copying, without any opposing proof, can be sufficient to establish a secondary meaning"); *M. Kramer Mfg. Co. v. Andrews*, 783 F.2d 421, 448 (4th Cir. 1985) ("evidence of intentional, direct copying establishes a prima facie case of secondary meaning"); *National Lampoon, Inc. v. American Broadcasting Cos.*, 376 F. Supp. 733, 747 (S.D.N.Y. 1974) ("Deliberate 'passing off' is not only evidence of likelihood of confusion, but of secondary meaning as well"); *E.R. Squibb & Sons, Inc. v. Permo Pharmaceutical Labs, Inc.*, 195 U.S.P.Q. 545, 547 (S.D.N.Y. 1977); *Polo Fashions, Inc. v. Extra Special Product, Inc.*, 451 F. Supp. 555, 563 (S.D.N.Y. 1978). Why? *Compare Co-Rect Products v. Marvy! Advertising Photography*, 780 F.2d 1324, 1332 (8th Cir. 1985), in which the court held that intent is a factor in determining secondary meaning but is not conclusive, and that secondary meaning had not been established despite defendant's copying.

(8) Some courts have distinguished between an intent to profit by confusion of consumers and an intent only to capitalize on plaintiff's mark, without creating such confusion. In affirming the dismissal of plaintiff's claim in *Toho Co. v. Sears, Roebuck & Co.*, 645 F.2d 788 (9th Cir. 1981), the court found that Sear's use of a BAGZILLA trademark and reptilian monster on its garbage bags was intended only as a "pun," one which did not create any consumer confusion as to sponsorship by creators of the GODZILLA movie character. In *American Footwear Corp. v. General Footwear Co.*, 609 F.2d 655 (2d Cir. 1979), the court found that the manufacturer of a BIONIC BOOT hiking boot had the intent to capitalize on the market or fad created by a television show featuring a BIONIC MAN, but not the intent to confuse the public into the belief that the manufacturer's product was a product of the show's creators, and accordingly found that no unfair competition had resulted. *See also Philip Morris, Inc. v. R.J. Reynolds Tobacco Co.*, 188 U.S.P.Q. 289 (S.D.N.Y. 1975) (one competitor may intentionally capitalize on another's advertising investment so long as he does not attempt to confuse the public as to source); *Brooks Shoe Mfg. Co. v. Suave Shoe Corp.*, 533 F. Supp. 75 (S.D. Fla. 1981), *aff'd*, 716 F.2d 854 (11th Cir. 1983) (defendant's intentional copying of plaintiff's V design and color scheme for running shoes did not indicate likelihood of confusion where evidence showed that the design and color scheme were "fashionable" in the industry and defendant only had "an intent to copy a fashion"). *Compare Universal City Studios, Inc. v. Montgomery Ward & Co.*, 207 U.S.P.Q. 852 (N.D. Ill. 1980), in which defendant's use of JAWS, JAWS TWO and JAWS POWER for trash compactors was held to infringe plaintiff's marks for motion pictures. The court stated that intentional misappropriation is evidence of secondary meaning and likelihood of confusion — "[t]he public need only believe there is some connection or association with or approval by the producer of the movie." Is the principal concern in such cases a diminishment of the distinctiveness of plaintiff's mark, rather than likelihood of confusion? *See* the discussion on dilution law in Chapter 8, *infra*.

In the Restatement (Third) of Unfair Competition (Tentative Draft No. 2, March 23, 1990), Section 22 on Intent provides:

(1) A likelihood of confusion may be inferred from proof that the actor used a designation resembling another's trademark, trade name, collective mark, or certification mark with the intent to cause confusion or to deceive.

(2) A likelihood of confusion may not be inferred from proof that the actor intentionally copied the other's designation if the actor acted in good faith in circumstances that do not otherwise indicate an intent to cause confusion or to deceive.

(9) Under the doctrine of progressive encroachment it is unlawful to appropriate piecemeal a means for trade identity that could not be taken as a whole. In addition to *O. & W. Thum Co.*, supra, see *Independent Nail & Packing Co. v. Stronghold Screw Products, Inc.*, 205 F.2d 921 (7th Cir. 1953). In *Independent Nail*, the plaintiff invented a ribbed nail which it named STRONGHOLD, registering that name as a trademark five years later. At the date of trial plaintiff controlled almost the entire market for "metal fasteners." Defendant began using STRONGHOLD as a trademark for screws slightly before plaintiff's registration, but became aware of plaintiff's registration soon thereafter. Nonetheless, defendant elected to use the mark on its letterheads, business forms and catalogs. A few years later defendant changed its name to Stronghold Screw Products, prompting the first protest from plaintiff. Independent Nail had not previously protested the use of the mark because defendant's prior name, Manufacturer's Screw Products, had always appeared prominently with any use of STRONGHOLD. The court found that defendant's incorporation of "Stronghold" into its business name constituted progressive encroachment, citing *O. & W. Thum Co.* It found plaintiff justifiably had not taken action until the encroachment was fully developed, and granted plaintiff injunctive relief.

(10) Progressive encroachment may simply be considered as evidence disclosing a planned or contrived intent to deceive. In *Commerce Foods, Inc. v. PLC Commerce Corp.*, 504 F. Supp. 190 (S.D.N.Y. 1980), over a three-year period defendant progressively changed the design on its tins for imported hard candy to imitate the lettering, language, visual design and bordering of plaintiff's candy tin design. This was viewed as evidence of intent to confuse consumers and accordingly raised the presumption of likelihood of confusion. *Compare My-T-Fine v. Samuels with* Clark, J., in *Harold F. Ritchie, Inc. v. Chesebrough-Pond's Inc.*, supra. Progressive encroachment also may be claimed by a trademark owner in response to a defendant's allegation of unreasonable delay in assertion of trademark rights. In *Prudential Insurance Co. v. Gibraltar Financial Corp.*, 694 F.2d 1150 (9th Cir. 1982), Prudential alleged two theories of encroachment: that over a 28-year period Gibraltar had progressively modified its "rock" design mark to resemble more closely Prudential's, and that Gibraltar had gradually expanded its business into direct competition in Prudential's market. The court rejected both allegations. As to the former, it held: "The marks of the two companies looked as similar twenty-eight years ago as they look today, probably because they represent the same rock, albeit with decreasing fidelity to the real thing." It rejected Prudential's second argument upon finding that the two parties still were not in direct competition despite Gibraltar's enormous growth. The court held that Prudential's claims therefore were

barred by gross laches. In *American Rice, Inc. v. Arkansas Rice Growers Co-Op*, 532 F. Supp. 1376, 1390 (S.D. Tex. 1982), the court stated "laches is inapposite where the evidence demonstrates a history of slow encroachment followed by increased direct competition"; defendant's change in trade dress "intensified" the likelihood of confusion which had developed. Should there be some point in time after which a progressive encroacher is allowed to enjoy the benefits of his own goodwill? Should such problems be handled purely on a case-by-case basis? *See* Kilmer, *Progressive Encroachment: Analysis Of A Counterdefense To Laches And Acquiescence In Trademark Infringement Litigation*, 74 Trademark Rep. 229 (1984).

(11) Some courts have extended the theory of progressive encroachment to include the gradual encroachment on a party's market, the theory again being that "such a course does not tend to arouse hostile action until it is fully developed." *O. & W. Thum, supra.* In *Parrot Jungle, Inc. v. Parrot Jungle, Inc.*, 512 F. Supp. 266 (S.D.N.Y. 1981), the court rejected defendant's claim of laches, stating:

> [t]here is a substantial difference between plaintiff's awareness of a pet store or stores in New York and its awareness of a national franchising effort. . . . A modest encroachment is one thing, a sudden proposed national exploitation of plaintiff's name is quite another, and plaintiff's failure to challenge the former will not entirely disable plaintiffs from preventing the latter. . . .

Likewise in *John Wright, Inc. v. Casper Corp.*, 419 F. Supp. 292, 323 (E.D. Pa. 1976), the court rejected a laches defense when the delay occurred during a time of progressive market encroachment culminating in "sudden promotional expansion aimed at the exploitation of [the] market created by the plaintiff," citing *Independent Nail, supra* Note (9). *See also Tandy Corp. v. Malone & Hyde, Inc.*, 769 F.2d 362, 367 (6th Cir. 1985), and the court's discussion of market encroachment in *Prudential Insurance Co., supra* Note (10) ("growth alone does not infringement make"), and *E-Systems, Inc. v. Monitek, Inc.*, 222 U.S.P.Q. 115, 117 (9th Cir. 1983) ("had defendant's encroachment been minimal, or its growth slow and steady, there would be no laches"); *University of Pittsburgh v. Champion Products, Inc.*, 686 F.2d 1040, 1046 (3d Cir. 1982), *cert. denied*, 459 U.S. 1087 (1982); *E. & J. Gallo Winery v. Gallo Cattle Co.*, 12 U.S.P.Q.2d 1657, 1676 (E.D. Cal. 1989) ("A senior user is not required to object to a junior user's practice until the respective marks have had substantial exposure in common channels of trade so as to pose a real threat of potential confusion"), *aff'd in relevant part*, 967 F.2d 1280 (9th Cir. 1992); *N. Hess & Sons, Inc. v. Hess Apparel*, 216 U.S.P.Q. 721, 725 (D. Md. 1982), *aff'd*, 730 F.2d 1412 (4th Cir. 1984).

§ 5.06 Counterfeiting

INTRODUCTION

A flourishing market has developed in the sale of imitative products bearing deliberately copied, or "counterfeit," trademarks. Often the imitative products are manufactured in countries where parts and labor are cheaper than elsewhere in the world. By use of the counterfeit trademark, traffickers in such products intentionally deceive purchasers into believing that the imitative product, made at less expense and often sold at a lower price, is the genuine item. Often thought of as an attempt to capitalize upon designer names such as Gucci or Christian Dior, the intentional counterfeiting of trademarks also encompasses such diverse items as computer hardware and software, drugs, medical devices, and parts for cars and airplanes. In addition to constituting blatant trademark infringement, the manufacture and sale of counterfeit merchandise may pose dangers to the public health and safety, as such merchandise is often of inferior quality. It may also result in serious damage to the business and reputation of the trademark owner, who is perceived as sponsoring inferior quality goods which fall apart or fail to function as advertised.

The "Trademark Counterfeiting Act of 1984" (P.L. 98–473, 15 U.S.C. § 1116, 18 U.S.C. § 2320) was enacted in response to this burgeoning illegal industry and provides both criminal and civil causes of action. *See generally* 73 Trademark Rep. 459 *et. seq.* (1983).

IN RE VUITTON ET FILS S.A.

United States Court of Appeals, Second Circuit
606 F.2d 1 (1979)

Per Curiam:

This is a petition by Vuitton et Fils S.A. ("Vuitton") for a writ of mandamus directed to the United States District Court for the Southern District of New York, Charles L. Brieant, Jr., Judge, instructing the court to issue *ex parte* a temporary restraining order in an action entitled *Vuitton et Fils S.A. v. Dame Belt & Bag Co., Inc., and Morty Edelstein*, 79 Civ. 0262. In our judgment, we are justified in asserting mandamus jurisdiction in this peculiar case, and we direct the district judge to issue an appropriate *ex parte* order under Fed. R. Civ. P. 65.

Vuitton is a French company, a *societé anonyme*, engaged in the sale and distribution of expensive leather goods, including a wide variety of luggage, handbags, wallets and jewelry cases, all under a trademark registered with the United States Patent Office in 1932. This trademark, a distinctive arrangement of initials and designs, has been extensively advertised over the years. Recently, Vuitton has had the misfortune of having to compete with New York area retailers who have been able to obtain counterfeit Vuitton merchandise from various sources and who sell that merchandise at prices considerably below those charged by Vuitton for the authentic items. This, of course, has not pleased Vuitton and, in response, it has commenced 84 actions nationwide and 53 actions in this Circuit charging trademark infringement and unfair competition. 15 U.S.C. §§ 1114, 1121, 1125; New York General Business Law § 368-d. This present dispute originated in one of these actions. *See also Vuitton et Fils S.A. v. Carousel Handbags*, 592 F.2d 126 (2d Cir. 1979).

On January 16, 1979, Vuitton filed a complaint in the district court seeking preliminary and permanent injunctions against the defendants, Dame Belt & Bag Co., Inc. and an individual named Morty Edelstein, and requesting damages. The gist of the complaint was that the defendants had infringed Vuitton's trademark and engaged in unfair competition by offering for sale luggage and handbags identical in appearance to those merchandised by Vuitton. Accompanying the complaint was an affidavit by Vuitton's attorney explaining why service of process had not been effected and requesting that an *ex parte* temporary restraining order be issued against the defendants under Fed. R. Civ. P. 65(b). Vuitton explains its need for an *ex parte* order in the following terms:

> Vuitton's experience, based upon the 84 actions it has brought and the hundreds of other investigations it has made . . . has led to the conclusion that there exist various closely-knit distribution networks for counterfeit Vuitton products. In other words, there does not exist but one or two manufacturers of counterfeit merchandise, but rather many more, but a few of which have been identified to date.

> Vuitton's experience in several of the earliest filed cases also taught it that once one member of this community of counterfeiters learned that he had been identified by Vuitton and was about to be enjoined from continuing his illegal enterprise, he would immediately transfer his inventory to another counterfeit seller, whose identity would be unknown to Vuitton.

> . . . [I]n most Vuitton cases defendants maintain few, if any, records. The now too familiar refrain from a "caught counterfeiter" is "I bought only a few pieces from a man I never saw before and whom I have never seen again. All my business was in cash. I do not know how to locate the man from whom I bought and I cannot remember the identity of the persons to whom I sold."

> . . . If after Vuitton has identified a counterfeiter with an inventory of fake merchandise, that counterfeiter is permitted to dispose of that merchandise with relative impunity *after* he learns of the imminence of litigation but *before* he is enjoined from doing so, Vuitton's trademark enforcement program will be stymied and the community of counterfeiters will be permitted to continue to play its "shell game" at great expense and damage to Vuitton.

A hearing on this application was held the next day, January 17, 1979, before Judge Brieant. Counsel for Vuitton explained: "All we seek this Court to do but for a few hours is to maintain the status quo, namely the defendants' inventory of counterfeit Vuitton merchandise." Vuitton also explained that, if notice of the pending litigation was required, "by the time this Court entered an order, most if not all of the merchandise would have been removed from the premises." Because Vuitton was capable of giving the defendants in this action notice, however, a matter readily conceded by Vuitton, the district court declined to grant the request. That decision is, of course, not appealable, *Austin v. Altman*, 332 F.2d 273, 275 (2d Cir. 1964). The district court denied certification of the question presented by this case under 28 U.S.C. § 1292(b), and this petition followed. For reasons that follow, we instruct the district court to grant an appropriate *ex parte* temporary restraining order pursuant to Fed. R. Civ. P. 65(b), narrow enough and of brief enough duration to protect the interests of the defendants, the precise terms of which shall be determined by the district court.

Rule 65(b) provides in relevant part as follows:

> A temporary restraining order may be granted without written or oral notice to the adverse party or his attorney only if (1) it clearly appears from specific facts shown by affidavit or by the verified complaint that immediate and irreparable injury, loss, or damage will result to the applicant before the adverse party or his attorney can be heard in opposition, and (2) the applicant's attorney certifies to the court in writing the efforts, if any, which have been made to give the notice and the reasons supporting his claim that notice should not be required.

As explained by the Supreme Court in *Granny Goose Foods, Inc. v. Teamsters*, 415 U.S. 423, 438–39 (1974), "[t]he stringent restrictions imposed . . . on the availability of *ex parte* temporary restraining orders reflect the fact that our entire jurisprudence runs counter to the notion of court action taken before reasonable notice and an opportunity to be heard has been granted both sides of a dispute. *Ex parte* temporary restraining orders are no doubt necessary in certain circumstances, . . . but under federal law they would be restricted to serving their underlying purpose of preserving the status quo and preventing irreparable harm just so long as is necessary to hold a hearing, and no longer." *See also Carroll v. Princess Anne*, 393 U.S. 175, 180 (1968) ("There is a place in our jurisprudence for *ex parte* issuance, without notice, of temporary restraining orders of short duration. . . "). *Cf. Fuentes v. Shevin*, 407 U.S. 67, 93 (1972) ("There may be cases in which a creditor could make a showing of immediate danger that a debtor will destroy or conceal disputed goods. But the statutes before us are not 'narrowly drawn to meet any such unusual condition.' ").

Assuming that all of the other requirements of Rule 65 are met, the rule by its very terms allows for the issuance of an *ex parte* temporary restraining order when (1) the failure to issue it would result in "immediate and irreparable injury, loss, or damage" and (2) the applicant sufficiently demonstrates the reason that notice "should not be required." In a trademark infringement case such as this, a substantial likelihood of confusion constitutes, in and of itself, irreparable injury sufficient to satisfy the requirements of Rule 65(b)(1). *See P. Daussa Corp. v. Sutton Cosmetics (P.R.), Inc.*, 462 F.2d 134, 136 (2d Cir. 1972); *Robert Stigwood Group Ltd. v. Sperber*, 457 F.2d 50, 55 (2d Cir. 1972); *Omega Importing Corp. v. Petri-Kine Camera Co.*, 451 F.2d 1190, 1195 (2d Cir. 1971); *Miller Brewing Co. v. Carling O'Keefe Breweries*, 452 F. Supp. 429, 437–38 (W.D.N.Y. 1978). Here, we believe that such a likelihood of product confusion exists. The allegedly counterfeit Vuitton merchandise is virtually identical to the genuine items. Indeed, the very purpose of the individuals marketing the cheaper items is to confuse the buying public into believing it is buying the true article.

We also believe that Vuitton has demonstrated sufficiently why notice should not be required in a case such as this one. If notice is required, that notice all too often appears to serve only to render fruitless further prosecution of the action. This is precisely contrary to the normal and intended role of "notice," and it is surely not what the authors of the rule either anticipated or intended.

Accordingly, we hold that, when a proper showing is made, such as was made in this case, and when the rule is otherwise complied with, a plaintiff is entitled to have issued an *ex parte* temporary restraining order. Such an order should be narrow in scope and brief in its duration. The petition is granted.

UNITED STATES v. INFURNARI

United States District Court, Western District of New York
647 F. Supp. 57 (1986)

Curtin, Chief Judge.

At the conclusion of jury selection in this case, both parties requested a pretrial ruling from the court as to the elements of the Trademark Counterfeiting Act, 18 U.S.C. § 2320. Counts I and II of the indictment charge defendant with trafficking or attempting to traffic in counterfeit Rolex and Piaget watches, in violation of § 2320. The parties have filed briefs in support of their respective interpretations of the statute.

Section 2320 authorizes criminal sanctions for certain activities involving the use of counterfeit marks. The statute was enacted less than two years ago, as part of the Comprehensive Crime Control Act of 1984. Section 2320 provides, in pertinent part:

> (a) Whoever intentionally traffics or attempts to traffic in goods or services and knowingly uses a counterfeit mark on or in connection with such goods or services shall, if an individual, be fined not more than $250,000 or imprisoned not more than five years, or both, and, if a person other than an individual, be fined not more than $1,000,000.

> . . . .

> (d) For the purposes of this section—

> (1) the term "counterfeit mark" means—

>> (A) a spurious mark—

>>> (i) that is used in connection with trafficking in goods or services;

>>> (ii) that is identical with, or substantially indistinguishable from, a mark registered for those goods or services on the principal register in the United States Patent and Trademark Office and in use, whether or not the defendant knew such mark was so registered; and

(iii) the use of which is likely to cause confusion, to cause mistake, or to deceive;

. . . .

(2) the term "traffic" means transport, transfer, or otherwise dispose of, to another, as consideration for anything of value, or make or obtain control of with intent so to transport, transfer, or dispose of. . . .

The parties agree that the elements of the crime are: 1) intentional trafficking or attempted trafficking in goods (§ 2320(a)); 2) use of a counterfeit mark that is (a) spurious; (b) used in connection with trafficking in goods; (c) identical to or substantially indistinguishable from a registered trademark; and (d) likely to cause confusion, mistake, or deception (§ 2320(d)(1)(A)); and 3) knowing use of a counterfeit mark (§ 2320(a)).

The parties disagree as to whether there is a knowledge or intent requirement associated with the second element, the definition of counterfeit mark. Defense counsel contends that a defendant must act either knowingly or intentionally as to each of the four subparts of the definition. The government maintains that this interpretation is contrary to both the language of the statute and its legislative history.

I find that the defendant must have knowledge as to each of the subparts of the second element. Section 2320(d)(1)(A) of the statute, which provides a definition of the term "counterfeit mark," does not explicitly require knowledge or intent. However, § 2320(a) requires "knowing use" of a counterfeit mark. "Counterfeit mark" has a technical definition under the Statute; a mark must meet the listed criteria to fall within the definition. An individual cannot be convicted under the statute unless he knows the mark is counterfeit, as defined in § 2320(d)(1)(A). For example, if a defendant did not know the mark was spurious, or that it was likely to cause confusion, he could not know the mark was counterfeit.

As noted in the legislative history:

[The bill] provides for stiff criminal penalties for those who intentionally traffic in goods or services *knowing them to be counterfeit.* . . . Of course, a person who trafficked in counterfeit goods or services without the mental state required by this bill might still be civilly liable under the Lanham Act or similar State statutes, which do not require proof of the defendant's state of mind.

S. Rep. No. 98-526, June 21, 1984, p.11, reprinted in 1984 U.S. Code Cong. & Ad. News, 3627, 3631 (emphasis added).

Furthermore, the definition of "counterfeit mark" contains an aspect for which knowledge is explicitly *not* required, implying that knowledge is necessary for the remaining parts of the definition. Under § 2320(d)(1)(A)(ii), the counterfeit mark must be identical with or substantially indistinguishable from another mark, one which is registered with the U.S. Patent and Trademark Office. The statute specifically provides that the defendant need not know whether the other mark is actually registered.

It is the court's view that in a prosecution under 18 U.S.C. § 2320, the government must prove that defendant knew the mark is counterfeit: that he knew that the mark is spurious, that it is used in connection with trafficking in goods or services, that it is identical to or virtually indistinguishable from another mark, and that it is likely to cause confusion, mistake, or to deceive. As noted above, while the legitimate mark must have been registered with the patent office, whether defendant was aware of that fact is immaterial.

The other issue raised by the parties is whether the likelihood of confusion is to the immediate purchaser or to the public at large. Defendant maintains that he must have known that there was a likelihood that his immediate purchaser would be confused or misled. The government believes it is sufficient that there is a likelihood of confusion, mistake, or deception to any member of the public, even a mere viewer of the article, whether or not there was any likelihood that the immediate purchaser would be confused. (See Proposed Charges, p. 8, ¶ 8 of the Government's Brief.)

It appears that this issue will not arise frequently in criminal prosecutions under statute since, for the most part, those who traffic in counterfeit goods seek to confuse or defraud the immediate buyer. 1184 U.S. Code Cong. & Ad. News at 3627. In the instant case, however, this point could be crucial. The court has been advised that the evidence may show that Mr. Infurnari told his customers that the watches were not actual Rolex or Piaget watches.

The operative language in the criminal statute, 18 U.S.C. § 2320, "the use of which is likely to cause confusion, to cause mistake, or to deceive," is the same as the language in the Lanham Act, 15 U.S.C. § 1114(1)(a). Case law has made clear that post-sale confusion as to the source of a product is actionable under the Lanham Act. *Lois Sportswear v. Levi Strauss & Co.*, 799 F.2d 867 (2d Cir. 1986); *Grotian v. Steinway & Sons*, 523 F.2d 1331, 1342 (2d Cir. 1975); and *Syntex Laboratories, Inc. v. Norwich Pharmacal Co.*, 437 F.2d 566 (2d Cir. 1971). There is no clear indication in section 2320 or its legislative history as to the intended scope of that phrase and whether it is to be the same as the civil statute.

Two recent cases have addressed this issue. In *United States v. Torkington*, Cr. 85-6168 (S.D. Fla. February 10, 1986), the court dismissed an indictment charging defendant with violating 18 U.S.C. § 1220 for selling two replica Rolex watches. The court found that the goods were not counterfeit under § 2320 because it was unlikely that a purchaser would be confused into believing that a watch which sold for $27 was a genuine Rolex watch, which sold for thousands of dollars. The court noted that although there may have been a possibility that those who viewed the watch *after* the sale would be confused, it was unlikely that the purchaser would be confused. This case is currently on appeal before the United States Court of Appeals for the Eleventh Circuit.

In *United States v. Gonzalez*, 630 F. Supp. 894 (S.D. Fla. 1986), the court declined to follow *Torkington*, noting that the criminal Trademark Counterfeiting Act and the civil Lanham Act seek to protect both consumers and manufacturers, to protect trademarks in and of themselves, and to prevent "the cheapening and dilution of the genuine product." *Id.* at 896.

The Trademark Counterfeiting Act subjects those who traffic in goods involving the knowing use of counterfeit marks to criminal sanctions. The purpose of the Act is to fight this "rapidly growing form of commercial fraud." 1984 *U.S Code Cong. & Ad. News,* at 3627, see 3627–32.

It appears that Congress did not have a case like Mr. Infurnari's in mind when it passed 18 U.S.C. § 2320. Nonetheless, Congress chose to use the same operative language in the criminal trademark act as in the Lanham Act. Both the Second and Ninth Circuits had already held that post-sale confusion was actionable when § 2320 was passed. *See Syntex Laboratories, supra,* and *Levi Strauss v. Blue Bell, Inc.,* 632 F.2d 817 (9th Cir. 1980). As was noted in *Gonzalez, supra,* the act is also intended to benefit manufacturers and the integrity of trademarks.

Requiring that the defendant had knowledge that goods bearing a counterfeit mark would cause confusion, mistake, or would deceive either the immediate purchaser or prospective purchasers who would later view the product is not inconsistent with Congress's goals in enacting § 2320.

The court will meet with counsel on October 30, 1986, at 9 a.m. to discuss plans for trial.

So ordered.

FENDI S.A.S. DI PAOLA FENDI E SORELLE v. COSMETIC WORLD, LTD.

United States District Court, Southern District of New York
642 F. Supp. 1143 (1986)

SAND, DISTRICT JUDGE.

Fendi is a limited partnership with its principal place of business in Italy. It is engaged in the manufacture and sale of a wide variety of fashion merchandise, including furs, pocketbooks and leather apparel. Most of the items in question here are women's handbags. Plaintiff's products are sold throughout the United States, but are distributed through only a limited number of carefully selected retail stores. The Fendi company has undertaken considerable effort to assure that genuine Fendi goods never travel outside of this exclusive retail network. Genuine Fendi products bear the registered trademark of the Fendi company, consisting of the word "FENDI" (Reg. No. 1,244,466), and a monogram comprised of two initial F's ("FF") (Reg. No. 1,214,472). Both the FENDI and FF monogram trademarks have been extensively advertised and now represent prestigious symbols in fashion.

On December 12 and 13, 1985, an ex parte seizure order was executed, and more than 1,000 items bearing counterfeit Fendi trademarks were seized at the Vincelli premises . . . .

On the uncontested facts here, we find plaintiff is entitled to summary judgment on the issue of liability. Plaintiff has established that defendants, in violation of 15 U.S.C. § 1051 *et seq.,* actively engaged in the sale of goods bearing counterfeit

FENDI and FF trademarks and attempted to pass off such goods as genuine Fendi products. Specifically, the deposition of Paolo Vincelli establishes that the Vincellis imported and distributed to numerous retailers merchandise bearing counterfeit Fendi trademarks. P. Vincelli Deposition at 57, 116. It also demonstrates that Paolo Vincelli travelled to Italy to find a source of imitation Fendi handbags so that he could sell them in the United States, and once there, had a source make merchandise specifically for him bearing the Fendi trademarks. *Id.* at 21. Moreover, the handbags themselves were designed in a deliberate attempt to duplicate genuine Fendi merchandise. *Id.* at 91–92. Vincelli told the retail merchants to whom he sold his products that the products were imitation Fendi merchandise and that the retailers' customers would likely be deceived into thinking that they were buying genuine Fendi products. *Id.* at 92, 118.

. . . .

. . . Section 1116(d), as amended, allows for an ex parte seizure order for "goods and counterfeit marks involved in [the] violation" of either 15 U.S.C. § 1114(1)(a) or 36 U.S.C. § 380. Plaintiff apparently reads § 1118's amended portion referring to the destruction of "articles" seized pursuant to amended § 1116(d), which in turn refers to the seizure of goods as well as trademarks, as "anticipat[ing] [the] destruction of seized counterfeit merchandise and condition[ing] the granting of such an order only upon plaintiff's giving the appropriate United States attorney 10 days notice of its application." Plaintiff's Memorandum in Support of Its Motion at 10.

We do not find the issue so simple. The point remains that Congress failed to amend section 1116 to explicitly provide for the destruction of anything other than infringing marks and the machinery used to produce them. Contrasted with this failure is Congress's affirmative amending of the Criminal Code to grant government prosecutors in criminal prosecutions for trademark counterfeiting the right to seek destruction of the goods themselves. This grant was also part of the 1984 amendments to the Lanham Act and is now codified at 18 U.S.C. § 2320, which reads in pertinent part:

> (b) Upon a determination by a preponderance of the evidence that any articles in the possession of a defendant in a prosecution under this section bear counterfeit marks, the United States may obtain an order for the destruction of such articles.

Despite Congress's failure to enact a civil provision analogous to the criminal provision authorizing destruction of goods, we find that such destruction was intended by Congress to be allowed in civil cases. Our finding is based upon the legislative history of the Act (although that history was cited by neither party). The Joint Explanatory Statement of both Houses of Congress, 130 Cong. Record H. 12,076, 12,077 (Oct. 10, 1984), after making clear that the criminal amendments provide for the destruction of actual goods, explained: "This provision gives the court the same options it has in ordering destructions under 15 U.S.C. 1118." Implicit in this statement is that the Court in civil cases may order the actual goods, as well as the infringing marks, destroyed.

The amount of Fendi's monetary recovery is governed by 15 U.S.C. § 1117, which provides for treble damages against an individual who intentionally uses a trademark

3x damgs expected

knowing it to be counterfeit. 15 U.S.C. § 1117(b). Under the amended statute, absent "extenuating circumstances," federal courts are expected, and not merely authorized to "enter judgment for three times such profits or damages, whichever is greater, together with reasonable attorney's fee." *Id.* What constitutes extenuating circumstances is determined on a case by case basis. Where the defendant is an "unsophisticated individual, operating on a small scale, for whom the imposition of treble damages would mean that he or she would be unable to support his or her family," treble damages may be inappropriate. Joint Explanatory Statement, 130 Cong. Record H. 12,076 at 12,083 (Oct. 10, 1984). However, Congress has indicated that "it will be a rare case in which a defendant who has trafficked in goods or services using a mark that he or she knows to be counterfeit can show that he or she should not be assessed treble damages." *Id.* at 12.

In this instance, we find no extenuating circumstances mitigating defendants' willful infringement of plaintiff's registered trademark. Indeed, we believe treble damages and attorneys' fees are particularly appropriate here in view of the undisputed evidence that defendants deliberately arranged to first obtain counterfeit goods and then sell them as genuine items to an innocent public. This seems as blatant a case of counterfeiting as there could be.

. . . .

Defendants are liable to plaintiff under the Lanham Act, 15 U.S.C. § 1051 *et seq.* and are permanently enjoined from counterfeiting plaintiff's registered trademarks. In addition, this case is referred to Magistrate Joel J. Tyler to report and recommend the appropriate damage award and attorneys' fees award.

NOTES ON COUNTERFEITING

(1) The Trademark Counterfeiting Act of 1984 provides criminal and civil penalties for anyone who "intentionally traffics or attempts to traffic in goods or services and knowingly uses a counterfeit mark on or in connection with such goods or services." A "counterfeit mark" is defined as:

> a spurious mark that is used in connection with trafficking in goods or services [and] that is identical with or substantially indistinguishable from a mark registered for those goods or services on the principal register . . . and in use, whether or not the defendant knew such mark was so registered.

(15 U.S.C. § 1116.) The Act subjects individuals engaged in trademark counterfeiting to criminal penalties of up to $250,000 and/or up to five years imprisonment. Heavier fines are provided for corporate violators and stiffer penalties for repeat offenders. In civil actions the Act provides for treble damages or profits (whichever is greater) and attorney's fees, unless the court finds that there are "extenuating circumstances."

(2) Seizure of counterfeit industrial parts and other merchandise before they are distributed in the market understandably has become an extremely important civil

remedy in this area of law. The 1984 Act authorizes federal courts to grant ex parte seizures of counterfeit goods and related materials in appropriate circumstances. The seized goods are taken into the custody of the court and the applicant for seizure must provide adequate security for payment for any damages suffered due to a wrongful seizure.

Under the Act, the applicant for a seizure order must, among other things, demonstrate the following under 15 U.S.C. § 1116(d)(4):

(1) that another order, such as a temporary restraining order, would not be adequate;

(2) the applicant has not publicized the requested seizure;

(3) a likelihood of success in proving that the mark in question is counterfeit, and was used "in connection with the sale, offering for sale, or distribution of goods";

(4) that "an immediate and irreparable injury" will occur without an *ex parte* seizure (this normally is satisfied by demonstrating that the counterfeit merchandise may be distributed);

(5) the matter to be seized will be at the location identified in the application;

(6) the harm to the applicant making the request for an order outweighs the possible harm to the defendant, (a relatively easy showing under most circumstances);

(7) the person against whom the order is granted would move, destroy, or conceal the counterfeit goods.

Other requirements under the Act include prior notice to the local U.S. Attorney before the seizure. 15 U.S.C. § 1116(d)(2). After the seizure, the court is bound to protect the accused party from publicity, § 1116(d)(6), and from disclosure of its trade secrets or confidential information, § 1116(d)(7). *See generally General Motors Corp. v. Gibson Chem. & Oil Corp.*, 786 F.2d 105 (2d Cir. 1986) (although seizure order is not subject to interlocutory appeal, defendant's interests protected by requiring security to be posted and conducting prompt post-seizure hearing); *Major League Baseball Promotion Corp. v. Crump*, 1988 U.S. Dist. LEXIS 14,692 (D. Minn. 1988) (§ 1116 provides protection to defendants in addition to that available under F. R. Civ. P. 65).

(3) The Act does have its limitations. It only applies to *federally registered* trademarks. Certain goods also are exempted from the Act. For example, gray market goods, *i.e.,* goods bearing an authentic trademark intended for sale abroad but imported for sale in a country where the trademark signifies a domestic source (discussed in Chapter 7, *infra*), are exempted because current Treasury Department regulations apply to their importation. Additionally, if a licensee manufactures too much of a product under a valid trademark licensing agreement, those "overruns" are not considered counterfeit goods because of the owner's initial approval. The overrun exception does not apply, however, if the licensee uses the mark for goods not covered by the licensing agreement. Finally, trade dress, that is, the color, shape or design of a product or its packaging, is not covered by the Act unless it is registered as a trademark.

CL authority may ____

When confronted with circumstances outside the Act's statutory authority, however, courts have relied upon common law authority in ordering civil seizures, as well as Rule 65 of the Federal Rules of Civil Procedure, and the All Writs Act, 28 U.S.C. § 1651, which empowers judges to issue all orders necessary in aid of their jurisdiction. *See, e.g., Pepe (U.K.), Ltd. v. Ocean View Factory Outlet Corp.,* 770 F. Supp. 754 (D.P.R. 1991). Prior to passage of the Counterfeiting Act, the courts had fashioned similar relief in a number of cases which remain important for the protection of unregistered marks against counterfeiters. *See* the *Vuitton* case, *supra; Polo Fashions, Inc. v. Dick Bruhn, Inc.,* 793 F.2d 1132 (9th Cir. 1986); *Ford Motor Co. v. B & H Auto Supply, Inc.,* 646 F. Supp. 975 (D. Minn. 1986). In *Reebok International Ltd. v. Marnatech Enterprises,* 970 F.2d 552, 560 (9th Cir. 1992), the district court issued a preliminary injunction order freezing the defendant's assets, concluding that the defendant counterfeiters might otherwise "hide their allegedly ill-gotten funds" and ultimately preclude monetary relief to plaintiff. In affirming, the Ninth Circuit held that because the Lanham Act authorizes an accounting of profits as a form of final equitable relief, the district court had the inherent power to freeze assets "to ensure the availability of that final relief." While concurring with the majority decision, Judge Fernandez described the order as a type "that could drive an opponent to the wall regardless of the ultimate merits of the action. It is a frightening example of the reach of the court's injunctive powers." 970 F.2d at 563.

The copyright laws also authorize seizures of counterfeits of copyrighted works. 17 U.S.C. § 503.

(4) To balance the strong remedies made available to plaintiffs, the Counterfeiting Act provides a cause of action against parties who wrongfully obtain seizure orders. 15 U.S.C. § 1116(d)(11). In *General Electric Co. v. Speicher,* 676 F. Supp. 1421 (N.D. Ind. 1988), *rev'd,* 877 F.2d 531 (7th Cir. 1988), the district court awarded defendant wrongful seizure damages after plaintiff's representatives took unauthorized photos and seized irrelevant items as well as non-counterfeit goods. The Seventh Circuit reversed in a strongly worded opinion by Judge Posner, observing that the broad seizure order issued by the district court encompassed non-counterfeit items, and holding that the unauthorized photographs were not unlawful since everything photographed could have been seized.

In *Electronic Laboratory Supply v. Cullen,* 977 F.2d 798 (3d Cir. 1992), the Third Circuit held that an attorney representing a party is not an "applicant" under § 1116(d)(11), and cannot be liable for wrongful seizure under that section.

(5) The legislative intent underlying the Counterfeiting Act and the concern over this burgeoning problem have spurred some strongly stated judicial decisions. *See, e.g., Louis Vuitton S. A. v. Lee,* 875 F.2d 584 (7th Cir. 1989), in which a district judge's refusal to award monetary relief against "two small, unsophisticated and unwary immigrants" in a counterfeiting case was reversed. In assigning the case to a new judge on remand, Judge Posner observed that "[t]he Lanham Act was not written by Robin Hood" and that the original trial judge "forgot that while the Lee's are human, so are the customers, employees, suppliers and owners of Louis Vuitton. A corporation is not a thing; it is a network of relations among human beings." 875 F.2d at 590.

In *Hard Rock Cafe Licensing Corp. v. Concessions Services, Inc.*, 955 F.2d 1143, 1148 (7th Cir. 1992), the court held that the owner of a flea market could be liable for the counterfeiting violations of a vendor "if it knew or had reason to know of them," citing the Supreme Court's test for contributory liability set forth in *Inwood Laboratories, Inc. v. Ives Laboratories, Inc.*, 456 U.S. 844 (1982). It also reconfirmed the Seventh Circuit's holding in *Louis Vuitton v. Lee, supra*, that "willful blindness is equivalent to actual knowledge," and further clarified that, "[t]o be willfully blind a person must suspect wrongdoing and deliberately fail to investigate." 955 F.2d at 1149.

In *Fendi S.A.S. di Paola Fendi e Sorelle v. Cosmetic World, Ltd.*, 642 F. Supp. 1143 (S.D.N.Y. 1986), the court held that in civil, as well as criminal, cases, a court may order destruction of the actual goods in addition to the infringing counterfeit marks.

See generally Bainton, *Reflections on The Trademark Counterfeiting Act of 1984: Score a Few for the Good Guys*, 82 Trademark Rep. 1 (1992).

(6) There are two state of mind elements of the criminal offense: intentional trafficking and knowing use of a counterfeit mark. The criminal sanctions apply to "[w]hoever intentionally traffics or attempts to traffic in goods or services and knowingly uses a counterfeit mark on or in connection with such goods or services." 18 U.S.C. § 2320(a). The purchase of counterfeit items for personal use is not penalized under the Act.

According to the sponsors of the Act, the government can prove the intentional trafficking element easily, since most people who sell goods do so "on purpose." The knowledge element is the more difficult to prove, as the prosecution must show that the defendant had "an awareness or a firm belief" that the mark was counterfeit. The burden of proof for this element, however, can also be met if the prosecution shows that the defendant was "willfully blind" to the counterfeit nature of the mark. However, "If a person has an honest, good faith belief that the mark in question is not counterfeit, he or she will not be liable." *Joint Statement on Trademark Counterfeiting Legislation*, 130 Cong. Rec. H12, 077 (daily ed. Oct. 10, 1984).

Criminal sentencing under the Act is discretionary. The legislative history of the Act stresses that an appropriate deterrent would include a combination of a prison term and fine. The drafters of the Act recognized, however, that the imposition of the maximum fines would be unlikely, except for the most egregious forms of counterfeiting. *See, e.g., United States v. Hon*, 904 F.2d 803 (2d Cir. 1990) (defendant, convicted of selling counterfeit watches, sentenced to thirty-six months probation and assessed a $6,000 fine). *Cf. United States v. Song*, 934 F.2d 105, 109 (7th Cir. 1991) (upholding defendant's five criminal convictions for trafficking in counterfeit goods bearing five trademarks belonging to five different trademark owners; "the correct unit of prosecution under Section 2320 is the counterfeit mark").

(7) Even if a defendant explains to the purchaser that the cheap ROLEX watch is actually a counterfeit, the defendant will still be liable under the Counterfeiting Act. *United States v. Gantos*, 817 F.2d 41, 43 (8th Cir.), *cert. denied*, 484 U.S. 860

(1987). One reason given is that while the direct purchaser may not be confused, those who observe the wearer of the counterfeit, or who receive the counterfeit as a gift, are likely to be confused into believing it is the real thing. This usually is referred to as "post-sale confusion." *See, e.g., United States v. Hon*, 904 F.2d 803 (2d Cir. 1990), *cert. denied*, 498 U.S. 1069 (1991) (jury could consider likelihood of confusion of general public, not just purchasing public); *United States v. Yamin*, 868 F.2d 130, 133 (5th Cir.), *cert. denied*, 492 U.S. 924 (1989) (no error where jury was instructed to find liability if general public, not just potential purchasers, likely to be confused); *United States v. Torkington*, 812 F.2d 1347, 1352–1353 (11th Cir. 1987) (likelihood of confusion encompasses post-sale confusion). The direct purchaser, furthermore, would be able to sell it to an unknowing third party without explaining it is counterfeit.

(8) Under § 526 of the Tariff Act of 1930, 19 U.S.C. § 1526, it is also possible for a trademark owner to alert the U.S. Customs Service to the anticipated import of goods bearing a particular counterfeit trademark. Compliance with the requirement of 19 C.F.R. 133.0 *et seq.*, promulgated under § 526, will result in the Service barring the entrance of any such goods which it discovers.

(9) A state anti-counterfeiting statute similar to the federal statute has been enacted in California (Cal. Bus. & Prof. Code § 14340).

CHAPTER **6**

PROOF OF INFRINGEMENT

§ 6.01 Introduction

The question of likelihood of confusion is not an ordinary question. It is one of the state of mind of numberless individuals under certain conditions. Rarely, if ever, can its resolution be utterly black or white. A determination must be made whether appreciable confusion of source will result from the use of an accused mark or other means for trade identity. This determination or prediction should be derived from evidence. Set forth below are various categories of evidence that are usually relevant and material to the question:

(a) *Evidence of Source-Indicating Significance.* Evidence of the source-indicating significance of the mark claimed to be infringed is usually of fundamental importance. Examples of such evidence include (1) a showing of prior and substantial continuous use, sales, and advertising of the mark to identify the product or service as coming from a single source; (2) registration certificates; and (3) the direct testimony, or other admissible evidence, of representative members of the general purchasing public demonstrating that the mark indicates to them a product or service from a single source.

(b) *Evidence of Actual Confusion.* Traditionally, and logically, this is thought to be the best and most nearly conclusive of all evidence bearing upon likelihood of confusion. Indeed, if confusion has actually arisen from the use of the mark in issue, can its likelihood be denied, and is it not the best possible evidence? Examples of such evidence include confused-purchaser testimony, and misdirected complaints, mail, telephone calls and the like. Ordinarily, such evidence is exceedingly difficult to obtain and, with some exceptions, it is usually accorded heavy weight.

(c) *The Conditions of the Trade.* The environment of the sale, the nature of the purchasers, the character of the purchase — i.e., impulse or studied, and similar circumstances — are important and significant evidentiary facts relevant to the ultimate question of likelihood of confusion.

(d) *Evidence of Intent.* While direct or circumstantial evidence of a wrongful intent is not a prerequisite to infringement or trade identity unfair competition, it is held to be strong evidence that the second user will succeed in his intention to profit from confusion with the goods or services of the prior user. Such evidence may be disclosed by the testimony of those who selected or devised the accused mark, device or label, by documents and otherwise. (*See* Chapter 5, *supra*).

(e) *Testimony of Dealers or Others Experienced in the Trade.* This evidence usually consists of dealers' and merchants' reactions to the mark and the reaction they would expect from those whose habits they have long observed in the sphere concerned (i.e., their customers). Testimony confined to the witness' own individual confusion reaction is probative and entitled to weight; but testimony that is a prediction of the reaction of others is opinion and its competence is limited to the extent that it may be expert.

(f) *Reaction Tests or Surveys.* These are psychologically and statistically scientific methods for determining the reaction of a relevant group of people (e.g., potential consumers) to the accused mark, label, etc. If scientifically valid and reliable, such a test should offer a legitimate basis for a finding of likelihood of confusion, secondary meaning, or both. (*See* § 6.03, *infra*.)

See generally 1 Gilson, *Trademark Protection and Practice*, § 2.09[1] (1984 ed.); McCarthy, *Trademarks and Unfair Competition*, §§ 15:1O–20 (3d ed. 1992); Lunsford, *The Mechanics of Proof of Secondary Meaning*, 60 Trademark Rep. 263 (1970).

§ 6.02   The Elements of Proof

BEER NUTS, INC, v. CLOVER CLUB FOODS CO.
[BEER NUTS I]

United States Court of Appeals, Tenth Circuit
711 F.2d 934 (1983)

SEYMOUR, CIRCUIT JUDGE.

Beer Nuts, Inc. (Beer Nuts) sued Clover Club Foods (Clover Club) alleging trademark infringement under 15 U.S.C. § 1114 (1976), unfair competition under 15 U.S.C. § 1125 (1976), and a pendent claim of state law trademark infringement. These claims arose from Clover Club's use of the words "Brew Nuts" with a picture of an overflowing stein on packages containing a sweetened, salted peanut product virtually identical to a product sold by Beer Nuts.

. . . .

Infringement of a trademark occurs when the use of the similar mark is likely to cause confusion in the marketplace concerning the source of the different products. *Vitek Systems, Inc. v. Abbott Laboratories*, 675 F.2d 190, 192 (8th Cir. 1982). "The resolution of this issue requires the court to consider numerous factors to determine whether, under all the circumstances, there is a likelihood of confusion." *Id.* In making this determination, this court has used the criteria set out in Restatement of Torts § 729 (1938):

(a) the degree of similarity between the designation and the trade-mark or trade name in

(i) appearance;

(ii) pronunciation of the words used;

(iii) verbal translation of the pictures or designs involved;

(iv) suggestion;

(b) the intent of the actor in adopting the designation;

(c) the relation in use and manner of marketing between the goods or services marketed by the actor and those marketed by the other;

(d) the degree of care likely to be exercised by purchasers.

See Drexel Enterprises v. Richardson, 312 F.2d 525, 528 (10th Cir. 1962). Other courts have used some formulation of this same test. *See, e.g., Soweco, Inc. v. Shell Oil Co.*, 617 F.2d at 1 178, 1185 (5th Cir. 1980); *McGregor-Doniger, Inc. v. Drizzle, Inc.*, 599 F.2d at 1126, 1130 (2d Cir. 1979); *AMF Inc. v. Sleekcraft Boats*, 599 F.2d 341, 348–49 (9th Cir. 1979); *Union Carbide Corp. v. Ever-Ready, Inc.*, 531 F.2d 366, 381–82 (7th Cir. 1976); *Fotomat Corp. v. Cochran*, 437 F. Supp. 1231, 1242 (D. Kan. 1977). The above list is not exhaustive and no one factor is determinative. The facts of a particular case may require consideration of other variables as well. *McGregor-Doniger*, 599 F.2d at 1130; *Polaroid Corp. v. Polarad Electronics Corp.*, 287 F.2d 492, 495 (2d Cir.), *cert. denied*, 368 U.S. 820 (1961).

As set forth above, "[s]imilarity of the marks is tested on three levels: sight, sound, and meaning . . . Each must be considered as [it] is encountered in the marketplace. Although similarity is measured by the marks as entities, similarities weigh more heavily than differences." *AMF Inc.*, 599 F.2d at 351; *Vitek Systems, Inc.*, 675 F.2d at 192.

It is not necessary for similarity to go only to the eye or the ear for there to be infringement. The use of a designation which causes confusion because it conveys the same idea, or stimulates the same mental reaction, or has the same meaning is enjoined on the same basis as where the similarity goes to the eye or the ear. Confusion of origin of goods may be caused alone by confusing similarity in the meaning of the designations employed. The whole background of the case must be considered.

Standard Oil Co. v. Standard Oil Co., 252 F.2d 65, 74 (10th Cir. 1958) (footnotes omitted).

In evaluating similarity, "[i]t is axiomatic in trademark law that 'side-by-side' comparison is not the test." *Levi Strauss & Co. v. Blue Bell, Inc.*, 632 F.2d 817, 822 (9th Cir. 1980); *American Home Products Corp. v. Johnson Chemical Co.*, 589 F.2d 103, 107 (2d Cir. 1978); *James Burrough Ltd. v. Sign of Beefeater, Inc.*, 540 F.2d 266, 275 (7th Cir. 1976); *Fotomat Corp.*, 437 F. Supp. at 1244. The marks "must be compared in the light of what occurs in the marketplace, not in the courtroom." *James Burrough Ltd.*, 540 F.2d at 275. "A prospective purchaser does not ordinarily carry a sample or specimen of the article he knows well enough to call by its trade name, he necessarily depends upon the mental picture of that which symbolizes origin and ownership of the thing desired." *Avrick v. Rockmont Envelope Co.*, 155 F.2d 568, 573 (10th Cir. 1946). Therefore, the court must determine whether the alleged infringing mark will be confusing to the public when singly presented. *Id.* at 572–73; *American Home Products*, 589 F.2d at 107; *James Burrough Ltd.*, 540 F.2d at 275; *Union Carbide*, 531 F.2d at 382.

"Intent on the part of the alleged infringer to pass off its goods as the product of another raises an inference of likelihood of confusion . . ." *Squirtco v. Seven-Up Co.*, 628 F.2d 1086, 1091 (8th Cir.1980); *Alpha Industries v. Alpha Steel Tube & Shapes, Inc.*, 616 F.2d 440, 446 (9th Cir.1980). "[P]roof that a defendant chose a mark with the intent of copying plaintiff's mark, standing alone, may justify an inference of confusing similarity." *Sun-Fun Products, Inc. v. Suntan Research & Development, Inc.*, 656 F.2d 186, 190 (5th Cir.1981). One who adopts a mark similar to another already established in the marketplace does so at his peril, *Fotomat Corp.*, 437 F. Supp. at 1243, because the court presumes that he "can accomplish his purpose: that is, that the public will be deceived." *AMF Inc.*, 599 F.2d at 354; *Fotomat Corp.*, 437 F. Supp. at 1243. All doubts must be resolved against him. *American Home Products*, 589 F.2d at 107.

Also relevant to likelihood of confusion are the means by which the products are marketed. "Converging marketing channels increase the likelihood of confusion." *AMF Inc.*, 599 F.2d at 353. The possibility of confusion is greatest when products reach the public by the same retail outlets. *See generally Exxon Corp. v. Texas Motor Exchange*, 628 F.2d 500, 505–06 (5th Cir. 1980); *Scott Paper Co. v. Scott's Liquid Gold, Inc.*, 589 F.2d 1225, 1229 (3d Cir.1978). Confusing similarity is most likely when the products themselves are very similar. *Exxon Corp.*, 628 F.2d at 505; *see Fotomat Corp.*, 437 F. Supp. at 1243–44.

Finally, the court must examine the degree of care with which the public will choose the products in the marketplace. " 'The general impression of the ordinary purchaser, buying under the normally prevalent conditions of the market and giving the attention such purchasers usually give in buying that class of goods, is the touchstone.' " *McGregor-Doniger*, 599 F.2d at 1137 (quoting 3 R. Callmann, *The Law of Unfair Competition, Trademarks and Monopolies* § 81.2, at 577 (3d ed. 1969) (footnote omitted)); *see Squirtco*, 628 F.2d at 1091. Buyers typically exercise little care in the selection of inexpensive items that may be purchased on impulse. Despite a lower degree of similarity, these items are more likely to be confused than expensive items which are chosen carefully. *Sun-Fun Products*, 656 F.2d at 191; *Fotomat Corp.*, 437 F. Supp. at 1244.

In this case, the district court's resolution of the infringement claim was improperly based solely on a side-by-side package comparison, although the parties presented evidence on other relevant factors, including Clover Club's intent in adopting the trademark "Brew Nuts," the manner in which Beer Nuts and Brew Nuts are marketed, and the degree of care purchasers exercise when buying the products. *See* Restatement of Torts, § 729(b), (c), (d). Moreover, the court erroneously equated likelihood of confusion with similarity. *See AMF Inc.*, 599 F.2d at 350. Similarity must be considered along with the other factors set out in the Restatement to determine whether, under all the circumstances of the marketplace, confusion is likely. The court's failure to weigh all of the relevant factors in determining likelihood of confusion constitutes reversible error. Although we offer no opinion regarding the merits of this case, we remand for a proper evaluation of similarity and a reconsideration of likelihood of confusion under the correct legal standards and the evidence presented.

Remand for review

. . . .

BEER NUTS, INC. v. CLOVER CLUB FOODS CO.
[BEER NUTS II]

United States Court of Appeals, Tenth Circuit
805 F.2d 920 (1986)

TACHA, CIRCUIT JUDGE.

In our prior opinion, we held that marks may be confusingly similar if, as entities, they look or sound similar or convey the same idea or meaning. We directed the district court to consider appearance, pronunciation of words used, verbal translation of the pictures or designs involved, and suggestion. These factors are not to be considered in isolation; they must be examined in the context of the marks as a whole as they are encountered by consumers in the marketplace. Similarities are to be weighed more heavily than differences, especially when the trademarks are used on virtually identical products packaged in the same manner. 711 F.2d at 940–41. The district court erred in focusing almost exclusively on the differences between the trademarks. The district court found that the BEER NUTS and BREW NUTS trademarks are not similar in appearance because the words do not look alike, the meaning of the word "brew" is broader than the word "beer," and the Clover Club trademark appears on the BREW NUTS package. The district court also found that the words in the trademarks are not similar in pronunciation and that Clover Club's use of the overflowing stein with the words BREW NUTS does not give rise to a verbal translation that equates BEER NUTS with BREW NUTS. 605 F. Supp. at 860.

Although there are clearly differences between the marks, the phonetic and semantic similarities outweigh these differences. The words "brew" and "beer" are not identical, but they have a similar sound. They are both one syllable words having four letters three of which are the same, and they both begin with the same letter. Moreover, the evidence shows that the word "brew" is a common synonym for "beer." Clover Club's marketing manager admitted at trial that the word "brew" in Clover Club's mark connotes "beer." Because Clover Club joined the term "brew" with a representation of a stein which has an overflowing head of foam, the word "brew" in Clover Club's trademark cannot reasonably be taken to mean coffee or tea or beverages in general; it can only be understood to mean beer. BREW NUTS thus necessarily conveys the same meaning or idea as BEER NUTS. The presence of the smaller Clover Club trademark is not enough to eliminate the likelihood of confusion in this case where the products and their marks are similar because consumers typically do not engage in side by side comparison of the products. 711 F.2d at 941. Moreover, a secondary trademark on a small, inexpensive item such as a package of nuts does not eliminate the possibility of confusion because consumers exercise little care in purchasing these products. *Id.*

We previously instructed the district court that similarities in the marketing of the products and the degree of care exercised by purchasers are factors to be weighed in light of the similarity of the marks. 711 F.2d at 940–41. Both Beer Nuts and Clover Club use their marks on sweetened salted peanuts. There is no dispute that the products are marketed in the same manner. The district court correctly understood the effect which we held those facts should have on its consideration of the issue of likelihood of confusion, stating:

> Accordingly, less similarity between the BREW NUTS package and the BEER NUTS trademark may lead to a likelihood of confusion than when the goods themselves are different or when the goods themselves are marketed differently. The court recognizes that "[t]he possibility of confusion is greatest when products reach the public by the same retail outlets," *Beer Nuts*, at 941, and that "[c]onfusing similarity is most likely when the products are themselves very similar." *Id.*

605 F. Supp. at 863. Nevertheless, the district court failed to give the virtual identity of the parties' products and marketing methods proper weight. Because the marks are very similar in many respects, the virtual identity of the products and marketing methods adds strength to the position that the products are likely to be confused.

Regarding the degree of care exercised by purchasers, this court stated that "[b]uyers typically exercise little care in the selection of inexpensive items that may be purchased on impulse. Despite a lower degree of similarity, these items are more likely to be confused than expensive items which are chosen carefully." 711 F.2d at 941 (citations omitted). The district court noted that BREW NUTS and BEER NUTS are both relatively inexpensive snack foods. 605 F. Supp. at 863. Furthermore, Clover Club's president admitted that Clover Club's BREW NUTS are purchased as impulse items in that they are not generally on a shopper's grocery list. According to this evidence and the law of this case, the district court should have concluded that the two products are purchased with little care and are thus likely to be confused. The district court failed to reach this conclusion and instead found that consumers exercise substantial care in purchasing the parties' products and are not likely to be confused.[6] 605 F. Supp. at 863–64. We find that the district court's conclusion is erroneous.

---

[6]In reaching its conclusion, the district court relied on testimony of Clover Club's president that consumers often exercise great care in purchasing potato chips. 605 F. Supp. at 863–64. The testimony concerned a study Clover Club had conducted fifteen years earlier. The study itself was not introduced into evidence. The witness testified that the study consisted of videotapes of customers selecting potato chips in the snack food aisle of a Salt Lake City grocery store. He further testified that from the study he concluded that many people carefully examined the packages and compared them with competitors' packages before they made a selection. Given the applicable law, this testimony cannot outweigh the uncontested fact that BEER NUTS and BREW NUTS are both inexpensive snack foods purchased as impulse items.

BEER NUTS contends that the testimony concerning the study is inadmissible. Since this testimony cannot overcome the other evidence in the case, we need not rule on BEER NUTS' contention.

Intent

    Clover Club's intent in adopting BREW NUTS with an overflowing stein as a trademark is also a factor in assessing likelihood of confusion. . . . We thus instructed the district court that deliberate adoption of a similar mark may lead to an inference of intent to pass off goods as those of another which in turn supports a finding of likelihood of confusion.

    The inference of intent is especially strong when the parties have had a prior relationship. Such a relationship provides evidence of the alleged infringer's intent to trade on the plaintiff's goodwill. *Sicilia Di R. Biebow & Co. v. Cox*, 732 F.2d 417, 432 (5th Cir. 1984). Beer Nuts' use of its trademark predated by two decades the use of the BREW NUTS trademark. Clover Club distributed BEER NUTS for many years prior to developing BREW NUTS. BEER NUTS is a very successful product. Clover Club cannot deny knowledge of the BEER NUTS trademark and the popularity of the product. Clover Club sells its product in the same markets as Beer Nuts. The names of the products are similar. The packages are similar. Clover Club's advertising agency advised against the use of the BREW NUTS trademark. The combination of these factors makes clear that Clover Club deliberately adopted a mark similar to the BEER NUTS mark.

    Notwithstanding this evidence, the district court refused to draw any inference of intent, stating that "Beer Nuts presented no direct evidence that Clover Club intended to pass BREW NUTS off as the product of another and thus derive benefit from another's reputation." 605 F. Supp. at 862. The district court concluded that no inference of intent could be drawn from the similarities between the trademarks because the marks are not similar. *Id.* However, as we have previously noted, the district court erred in concluding that the marks are not similar, and intent should have been inferred from that similarity.

    The district court also relied on Clover Club's assertion that Frito Lay, not Beer Nuts, is its competition. 605 F. Supp. at 863. However, the inference of intent which results from the deliberate adoption of a similar trademark is not rebutted by evidence as to who the infringer's competitors might be. The ultimate question is whether there is a likelihood of confusion between the trademarks; it does not matter who the infringer identifies as its chief competitor in the market.

    Because of the similarity of the marks and the inferences that should have been drawn therefrom, all doubts should have been resolved against the alleged infringer Clover Club. 711 F.2d at 941. We find no indication in the trial court opinion that this legal standard was applied to the factual inquiry.

    In deciding whether likelihood of confusion exists, the district court noted that Beer Nuts presented no evidence of actual confusion. The court stated that this absence of evidence "supports the conclusion that confusion about the source of BREW NUTS is unlikely." 605 F. Supp. at 864.

    While evidence of actual confusion supports a finding of likelihood of confusion, *Soweco*, 617 F.2d at 1186; *Union Carbide*, 531 F.2d at 383, absence of such evidence does *not* necessarily support a finding of *no* likelihood of confusion, especially when the products involved are inexpensive, *Sicilia Di R. Biebow & Co.*, 732 F.2d at 433. "It would be exceedingly difficult to detect instances of actual confusion when . . . the goods are relatively inexpensive and their actual properties are exactly identical. . . ." *Chevron Chem. Co. v. Voluntary Purchasing Groups*, 659 F.2d 695, 705 (5th Cir.1981), *cert. denied*, 457 U.S. 1126 (1982). Purchasers are unlikely to bother to inform the trademark owner when they are confused about an inexpensive product. *Union Carbide*, 531 F.2d at 383.

In the present case, it is undisputed that the products are inexpensive and virtually identical. Therefore, the district court erred in finding that the absence of evidence of actual confusion supports a conclusion that there is no likelihood of confusion.

. . . .

Reversed and remanded.

NOTES ON PROOF OF INFRINGEMENT

(1) All of the federal courts now apply multifactor tests as guidelines in assessing the likelihood of confusion occurring. One of the first to set forth such a test was the Second Circuit in *Polaroid Corp. v. Polarad Electronics Corp.*, 287 F.2d 492, 495 (2d Cir. 1961):

> . . . Where the products are different, the prior owner's chance of success is a function of many variables: the strength of his mark, the degree of similarity between the two marks, the proximity of the products, the likelihood that the prior owner will bridge the gap, actual confusion, and the reciprocal of defendant's good faith in adopting its own mark, the quality of defendant's product, and the sophistication of the buyers. Even this extensive catalogue does not exhaust the possibilities — the court may have to take still other variables into account.

The Second Circuit now applies that test in competing goods cases as well. *Thompson Medical Co. v. Pfizer, Inc.*, 753 F.2d 208, 214 (2d Cir. 1985).

The other circuits utilize similar factor tests, *see, e.g., Ford Motor Co. v. Summit Motor Products, Inc.*, 930 F.2d 277, 293 (3d Cir.), *cert. denied*, 112 S. Ct. 373 (1991) (listing ten relevant factors); *Schwinn Bicycle Co. v. Ross Bicycles, Inc.*, 870 F.2d 1176, 1185 (7th Cir. 1989) (referring to the factors as "digits" of confusion); *Boston Athletic Ass'n v. Sullivan*, 867 F.2d 22, 29 (1st Cir. 1989); *Conagra, Inc. v. Singleton*, 743 F.2d 1508, 1514 (11th Cir. 1984). Some courts use the factors listed in Section 729 of the Restatement of Torts (1938), *e.g., Beer Nuts, Inc. v. Clover Club Foods Co.*, 805 F.2d 920, 925 (10th Cir. 1986).

The most extensive list of factors is used in the Patent and Trademark Office, and was set forth in *In re E. I. Du Pont de Nemours & Co.*, 476 F.2d 1357, 1361 (C.C.P.A. 1973):

> In testing for likelihood of confusion under Sec. 2(d), therefore the following, when of record, must be considered:

(1) The similarity or dissimilarity of the marks in their entireties as to appearance, sound, connotation and commercial impression.

(2) The similarity of dissimilarity and nature of the goods or services as described in an application or registration or in connection with which a prior mark is in use.

(3) The similarity or dissimilarity of established, likely-to-continue trade channels.

(4) The conditions under which and buyers to whom sales are made, i.e. "impulse" vs. careful, sophisticated purchasing.

(5) The fame of the prior mark (sales, advertising, length of use).

(6) The number and nature of similar marks in use on similar goods.

(7) The nature and extent of any actual confusion.

(8) The length of time during and conditions under which there has been concurrent use without evidence of actual confusion.

(9) The variety of goods on which a mark is or is not used (house mark, "family" mark, product mark).

(10) The market interface between applicant and the owner of a prior mark:

   (a) a mere "consent" to register or use.

   (b) agreement provisions designed to preclude confusion, i.e. limitations on continued use of the marks by each party.

   (c) assignment of mark, application, registration and good will of the related business.

   (d) laches and estoppel attributable to owner of prior mark and indicative of lack of confusion.

(11) The extent to which applicant has a right to exclude others from use of its mark on its goods.

(12) The extent of potential confusion, i.e., whether de minimis or substantial.

(13) Any other established fact probative of the effect of use.

The *Du Pont* factors are used by that court's successor, the Federal Circuit, *see, e.g., Specialty Brands, Inc. v. Coffee Bean Distributors Inc.*, 748 F.2d 669, 671–72 (Fed. Cir. 1984).

Depending upon the circumstances of the case, a particular confusion factor may be accorded greater or lesser weight; *see, e.g.,* the section on Intent in Chapter 5, *supra.* It must be remembered, also, that the factor tests are only aids in determining the ultimate issue of likelihood of confusion. *See, e.g., Kellogg Co. v. Pack'em Enterprises, Inc.*, 951 F.2d 330 (Fed. Cir. 1991) (single *Du Pont* factor held dispositive); *Eclipse Associates Ltd. v. Data General Corp.*, 894 F.2d 1114, 1118 (9th Cir. 1990) (rejecting defendant's argument that lower court had applied incorrect factor test, noting that such tests are helpful guidelines, not "hoops a district court need jump through"); *Schwinn Bicycle Co. v. Ross Bicycles, Inc.*, 870 F.2d 1176, 1187 (7th Cir. 1989) (criticizing "pedantic" application of the factors without consideration of the totality of the circumstances as a "misapplication of the test" constituting error). *See generally* Faruki, *Litigation Involving Trademarks: Preparing the Trademark Case for Trial*, 16 U. Dayton L. Rev. 85 (1991).

(2) In some cases the Second Circuit has supplemented the *Polaroid* factors with an additional variable: an equitable balancing of the interests of the opposing parties. In *Mushroom Makers, Inc. v. R.G. Barry Corp.*, 580 F.2d 44 (2d Cir. 1978), the court gave this additional variable its greatest possible emphasis. After finding that a likelihood of confusion was established as a matter of law, the court nonetheless denied the injunctive relief requested by plaintiff. It concluded that defendant's "interest in retaining the goodwill developed through concurrent use of an identical trademark far outweighs any conceivable injury of [plaintiff]." Should the public interest in not being misled as to source have any weight in such a balance of interests? *See* Fletcher, *Mushroom Case — A Toadstool By Any Other Name*, 70 Trademark Rep. 314 (1980); Goldberg & Borchard, *Related Goods Trademark Cases in the Second Circuit*, 70 Trademark Rep. 287 (1980); Goldberg, Borchard & Shereff, *Mushroom Revisited: More On Related Goods in the Second Circuit*, 74 Trademark Rep. 207 (1984).

(3) While proof of actual confusion is not requisite to proving likelihood of confusion, when such evidence exists it is often given great weight. As one court has stated, "There can be no more positive or substantial proof of the likelihood of confusion than proof of actual confusion." *World Carpets, Inc. v. Dick Littrell's New World Carpets*, 438 F.2d 482, 489 (5th Cir. 1971). The treatment of actual confusion evidence varies, however, according to the particular circumstances of the case. *See, e.g., Woodsmith Publishing Co. v. Meredith Corp.*, 904 F.2d 1244 (8th Cir. 1990) (summary judgment for defendant affirmed in magazine trade dress case; evidence of confusion of a few inattentive readers held insufficient to create a factual dispute); *Berkshire Fashions, Inc. v. Sara Lee Corp.*, 725 F. Supp. 790 (S.D.N.Y. 1989), *aff'd*, 904 F.2d 33 (2d Cir. 1990) (actual confusion in the trade is highly probative of likely confusion, since the trade is more sophisticated than average consumers); *American International Group, Inc. v. American International Airways, Inc.*, 1990 U.S. Dist. LEXIS 3656 (E.D. Pa. 1990) (evidence of up to one hundred pieces of misdirected mail *de minimis* under the circumstances); *Universal Money Centers, Inc. v. American Telephone & Telegraph Co.*, 17 U.S.P.Q.2d 1435, 1440 (D. Kan. 1990) (approximately one hundred mistaken attempts to use defendant's credit cards in plaintiff's automatic teller machines found "numerically insignificant in light of the four million AT&T cards that are in circulation and in light of the 15,000 daily . . . transactions" in defendant's machines).

Proof of actual confusion is not necessary for injunctive relief; however, some courts require such proof as a basis for awarding monetary damages. *See, e.g., Resource Developers, Inc. v. Statue of Liberty-Ellis Island Foundation, Inc.*, 926 F.2d 134, 139 (2d Cir. 1991).

Might a lack of any actual confusion evidence over a substantial period of time indicate that confusion is *unlikely*? The Restatement (Third) of Unfair Competition (Tentative Draft No. 2, March 23, 1990) provides in Section 23:

(1) A likelihood of confusion may be inferred from proof of actual confusion.

(2) An absence of likelihood of confusion may be inferred from an absence of proof of actual confusion when the actor and the other have made significant use of their respective designations in the same geographic market for a substantial period of time.

See also Pignons S.A. de Mecanique v. Polaroid Corp., 657 F.2d 482, 490 (1st Cir. 1981) (lack of evidence of actual confusion, "when the marks have been side by side, for a substantial period of time, [raises] a strong presumption that there is little likelihood of confusion," quoting Callmann, *The Law of Unfair Competition, Trademarks and Monopolies*, § 82.3(a) (3d ed. 1969)). *Followed: Greentree Laboratories, Inc. v. G.G. Bean, Inc.*, 718 F. Supp. 998, 1000 (D. Me. 1989). *Compare Beer Nuts, Inc. v. Clover Club Foods Co.*, 805 F.2d 920, 928 (10th Cir. 1986) ("Purchasers are unlikely to bother to inform the trademark owner when they are confused about an inexpensive product") *and Chevron Chemical Co. v. Voluntary Purchasing Groups, Inc.*, 659 F.2d 695, 704 (5th Cir. 1981), *cert. denied*, 457 U.S. 1126 (1982) ("it would have been exceedingly difficult to detect instances of actual confusion" so the absence of such evidence did not indicate confusion was unlikely).

(4) A number of courts have recognized likely post-sale nonpurchaser confusion as actionable under the Lanham Act. Originally, § 32(1) of the Lanham Act only proscribed likelihood of confusion, mistake or deception of "purchasers as to the source of origin of such goods and services." In 1962, however, Congress amended the Act to delete the quoted portion from the section. 15 U.S.C. § 1114(1), amended 1962, 76 Stat. 769. The result was a much expanded confusion test encompassing nonpurchasers.

The injury derives in part from the fact that post-sale nonpurchasers may be prospective purchasers, with the confusion potentially affecting their future purchasing decisions. *Lois Sportswear, U.S.A., Inc. v. Levi Strauss & Co.*, 799 F.2d 867, 872–73 (2d Cir. 1986) ("The confusion the Act seeks to prevent in this context is that a consumer seeing [appellant's] familiar stitching pattern will associate the jeans with appellee and that association will influence his buying decisions."). *See also Academy of Motion Picture Arts & Sciences v. Creative House Promotions, Inc.*, 944 F.2d 1446 (9th Cir. 1991) (post-sale confusion likely between corporate award statuette and OSCAR movie award statuette); *Keds Corp. v. Renee International Trading Corp.*, 888 F.2d 215, 222 (1st Cir. 1989) (confusion of prospective consumers); *Polo Fashions, Inc. v. Craftex, Inc.*, 816 F.2d 145, 148 (4th Cir. 1987) (in the after sale context, "it is likely that the observer would identify [defendant's] shirt with the plaintiff, and the plaintiff's reputation would suffer damage if the shirt appeared to be of poor quality"); *Levi Strauss & Co. v. Blue Bell, Inc.*, 632 F.2d 817, 822 (9th Cir. 1980). *See also* Allen, *Who Must Be Confused and When?: The Scope of Confusion Actionable Under Federal Trademark Law*, 26 Wake Forest L. Rev. 321 (1991); Erhlich, *When Should Post-Sale Confusion Prevent Use or Registration of Marks?*, 81 Trademark Rep. 267 (1991).

Post-sale confusion also is an important consideration in trademark counterfeiting cases, as discussed in Chapter 5, *supra*.

(5) Reverse confusion is another type of confusion receiving growing recognition under the Lanham Act. Reverse confusion occurs when the legitimate prior user's goods or services become likely to be perceived as those of the junior user. *Sands, Taylor & Wood Co. v. Quaker Oats Co.*, 978 F.2d 947, 958 (7th Cir. 1992) ("Protecting the trademark owner's interest in capitalizing on the goodwill associated with its mark by moving into new markets is especially compelling in . . . a reverse confusion case, where the junior user so overwhelms the *senior* user's mark that the senior user may come to be seen as the infringer"), *cert. denied*, 113 S. Ct. 1879 (1993); *Banff Ltd. v. Federated Dept. Stores, Inc.*, 841 F.2d 486, 490–91 (2nd Cir. 1988), (reverse confusion held likely between Bloomingdale's use of B-WEAR for women's apparel and plaintiff's prior use of BEE WEAR for similar goods; "Were reverse confusion not a sufficient basis to obtain Lanham Act protection, a larger company could with impunity infringe the senior mark of a smaller one"); *Fuddrucker's Inc. v. Doc's B.R. Others, Inc.*, 826 F.2d 837, 845 (9th Cir. 1987) ("The potential for harm is equally great if the consumers believe that the infringer runs the original user"); *Ameritech, Inc. v. American Information Technologies Corp.*, 811 F.2d 960, 966 (6th Cir. 1987) ("senior user's interest in the trademark can be suffocated by the junior user").

§ 6.03   Surveys and Experts   [Reliability of Surveys]

INTRODUCTION

Survey evidence has been employed increasingly in trademark litigation in proof of issues such as secondary meaning or likelihood of confusion. Properly conducted and presented, a survey can provide valid persuasive evidence of potential or actual consumer reactions. *Ab initio*, however, such evidence is hearsay in nature. There is normally no opportunity for an opposing counsel to cross-examine survey respondents, nor for the trier of fact to observe respondent demeanor and credibility. Accordingly, courts carefully scrutinize the trustworthiness and reliability of the surveying process itself. A poorly designed or sloppily administered survey may be either rejected as evidence or accorded little weight.

Federal Rule of Evidence 703, which allows experts in appropriate circumstances to base their testimony on out of court hearsay information, has also contributed to the increased use of surveys in trademark litigation. "The rule . . . offers a more satisfactory basis for ruling upon the admissibility of public opinion poll evidence. Attention is directed to the validity of the techniques employed rather than to relatively fruitless inquiries into whether hearsay is involved." Notes on Advisory Committee on Proposed Rules, FRE 703. Similarly facilitating the use of survey evidence is Federal Rule of Evidence 803 (3, 5, 6) which liberalizes and codifies what had come to be known as the "shopbook rule" which permitted use of books and records kept in the due course of business. Requisites are that the survey be conducted within a proper *universe* ("that segment of the population whose characteristics are relevant to the proposition in question," Note, 66 Harv. L. Rev. 499 (1953)), and that subjects for the survey constitute a fair and representative *sample* of that universe. Further, the survey must contain unbiased questions, be conducted with proper security so that the interviewers do not know who they represent, and be properly tabulated, verified and interpreted by an expert. These and other factors considered by the courts in assessing the reliability and weight of a survey are illustrated by the cases below. *See also* the *Handbook of Recommended Procedures for the Trial of Protracted Cases*, issued by the Judicial Conference of the United States, 25 F.R.D. 365 (1960).

AMERICAN LUGGAGE WORKS, INC. v. UNITED STATES TRUNK CO.

United States District Court, District of Massachusetts
158 F. Supp. 50 (1957)

WYZANSKI, DISTRICT JUDGE.

Defendant, United States Trunk Co., moved for judgment against plaintiff, American Luggage Works, Inc., at the close of plaintiff's evidence on its cause of action alleging unfair competition. The issue turns to some extent on two questions; first, the admissibility and second, the persuasiveness of experts' testimony relating to a poll they designed and conducted to determine consumer attitudes.

Stated liberally, plaintiff's claim is that it has developed a design for suitcases; that this design has acquired a secondary meaning, so that the public associates the design with a particular source, to wit, the plaintiff; that defendant copied this design; and that customers are likely to be confused by defendant's wares into purchasing them when they intend to purchase plaintiff's products. To succeed plaintiff must establish, among other elements, that its suitcase design had acquired a secondary meaning and that defendant's product would be likely to produce confusion. *General Time Instruments Corp. v. United States Time Corp.*, 2 Cir., 165 F.2d 853. Moreover, plaintiff's burden is to show that this secondary meaning and this risk of confusion exist in the same potential market. This point is of special importance in this case since there is a wholesale market catering to retail dealers in luggage and a retail market catering to ultimate consumers.

To meet its burden of proof, plaintiff offered the goods manufactured by the opposing parties, the testimony of a design expert who showed the marked resemblance of the goods, and the testimony of those who designed and conducted a poll of retail dealers of luggage.

Without the poll, plaintiff clearly cannot prevail. For without the poll there is no evidence whatsoever that plaintiff's design had acquired a secondary meaning in any market. This by itself would be a fatal flaw, *Algren Watch Findings Co. v. Kalinsky*, 2 Cir., 197 F.2d 69, 72. Moreover, without the poll there is on the issue whether there was a likelihood of confusion between plaintiff's and defendant's products only the evidence of the appearance of plaintiff's and defendant's merchandise together with an analysis of that appearance by plaintiff's design expert.

Perhaps because they were not adequately instructed by counsel as to the precise scope of the issues in this litigation, the experts who laid the groundwork for the poll designed a survey directed exclusively at independent retail dealers of luggage. In that "universe" as the statisticians call it, [*see* Note, *Public Opinion Surveys as Evidence: The Pollsters Go to Court*, 66 Harv. L. Rev. 498, 499], the experts took a "sample" from the independent luggage dealers listed in the yellow classified telephone books for Manhattan County, New York and for Metropolitan Boston. For present purposes we may assume that the process of selection from the telephone books was fair and that the division of those selected among the three investigators was also fair. To those selected for the sample, the experts sent one of three investigators, — each of whom came to court prepared to testify. Each investigator would have testified that when he saw a retail dealer he had with him one but only one of these three photographs: one was a photograph of one of plaintiff's bags; another, of one of defendant's bags; and the last, of a third company's bags. Showing the one photograph to the person polled, the investigator asked each selected retail dealer the following questions:

1. Have you ever seen the luggage shown in this photograph?
    Yes _____ No _____ Don't know _____

2. Can you tell me what brand of luggage it is?
    Yes _____ Brand of luggage_____ No _____

3. If "no" on 2, from this list can you identify the brand name of this luggage?
    Tri Taper
    Socialite
    Emerald
    Hartmann
    Skyway
    Samsonite
    Don't know
    Other name

4. What brands of luggage do you carry?

When the investigators had completed the survey, they reported their results to a Boston University professor. He tabulated and analyzed the results. He testified that of the 29 retailers shown the photograph of plaintiff's bag, 23 correctly identified it, 3 thought it was defendant's bag, and 3 made other errors. Of the 51 retailers shown defendant's bag, 16 correctly identified it, 15 thought it was plaintiff's, and 20 made other errors. Of the 35 persons shown the third type of bag, 31 correctly identified it.

In considering the admissibility of this survey, the first point is to note its limited relevance. Those who designed the survey apparently did not fully appreciate the legal consequences of the point that there were at issue in this case two markets, — one wherein retailers were customers and the other wherein ultimate consumers were customers. Of course, the fact that a dealer associates a particular design with a particular source does not tend to show that the same association is made by an ordinary consumer unfamiliar with the intricacies of the trade. Indeed one of the advantages men in a particular business have over the rest of us is that the former are experts in distinguishing the sources from which goods in that field come. The survey, having been limited to retailers, is inadmissible to show that in the market of ultimate consumers the plaintiff's design had acquired a secondary meaning. There being no other evidence that plaintiff's design had in the ultimate consumers' market an established connotation, plaintiff has not borne its burden on that aspect of its case. This conclusion makes it unnecessary for this Court to decide whether plaintiff has borne its burden of proving that ultimate consumers are likely to be confused by the similarity of plaintiff's and defendant's bags. *General Time Instruments Corp. v. United States Time Corp.*, 2 Cir., 165 F.2d 853, 854–855. *Lucien Lelong, Inc. v. Lander Co.*, 2 Cir., 164 F.2d 395, 396.

So far as concerns the retail dealer market, the problem is more sophisticated. We must bear in mind that the result of the poll was offered for two purposes: to show both secondary meaning and likelihood of confusion. It is by no means clear that for these two problems it was appropriate to take the same universe, or to take the same sample. Nor is it clear that in this case the exclusions and inclusions were all defensible. By way of illustration, it may be noted that the universe included retail dealers who never carried plaintiff's bags, or defendant's bags, or any other type of plastic bag; it excluded those who sold luggage at retail in department stores and chains. Put another way, there were included retail dealers whose likelihood of confusion was unimportant because they were not shown to be potential customers, and there were excluded a whole type of potential customers who may do far more than a trivial percentage of the business in the Borough of Manhattan and in the Greater Boston community.

More serious than these objections, the survey was conducted by showing the interviewee not the bags themselves but photographs. The photographs were not true representations of the bags. Two of them entirely failed and one of them partially failed to show the manufacturer's name tags which are prominent in several places on the bags themselves. These distortions are fatal to the proffer of the evidence on the issue of confusion of retail dealers. For the fact that a retail dealer does not recognize an unlabeled bag is no indication that he would not recognize a labeled bag.

Furthermore, another and most significant reason why the evidence of the poll is inadmissible on the issue of confusion is that under the substantive law the issue is not whether the goods would be confused by a casual observer (trained or untrained, professional or lay), but the issue is whether the goods would be confused by a prospective purchaser at the time he considered making the purchase. If the interviewee is not in a buying mood but is just in a friendly mood answering a pollster, his degree of attention is quite different from what it would be had he his wallet in his hand. Many men do not take the same trouble to avoid confusion when they are responding to sociological investigators as when they spend their cash.

There remains the question of the admissibility and value of the results of the poll when offered to show that the design of plaintiff's bag has a secondary meaning among retail dealers. The investigators who conducted the poll are available to testify that a number of persons when shown plaintiff's bag did identify it as coming

(Matthew Bender & Co., Inc.)   (Pub. 725)

from plaintiff. But defendant has argued that the testimony that they are prepared to give, and the tabulations derived therefrom, are excludable under the hearsay rule.

It is, of course, clear that the testimony of the investigators as to what interviewees said is offered to show not the truth of what the interviewees said but to show their state of mind. Some authorities have, therefore, concluded that the testimony is not hearsay. *United States v. 88 Cases, More or Less*, 3 Cir., 187 F.2d 967; 6 Wigmore, *Evidence* (3rd ed.) § 1776; Note, 66 Harv. L. Rev. 498, 501, 503, note 34. Others, however, have noted that the proffered evidence has some of the dangers of hearsay. *See* Note, 66 Harv. L. Rev. 498, 501–502; Morgan, *Hearsay Dangers and the Application of the Hearsay Concept*, 62 Harv. L. Rev. 177, 185, 202–203, 206; McCormick, *The Borderland of Hearsay*, 39 Yale L.J. 489, 491. So long as the interviewees are not cross-examined, there is no testing of their sincerity, narrative ability, perception, and memory. There is no showing whether they were influenced by leading questions, the environment in which questions were asked, or the personality of the investigator. But where a court is persuaded that in a particular case all these risks have been minimized, that the answers given by the interviewees are, on the whole, likely to be reliable indicia of their states of mind, that the absence of cross-examination is not prejudicial, and that other ways of getting evidence on the same point are either impractical or burdensome, the testimony should be admitted. *See* Note, 66 Harv. L. Rev. 498, 503. In this case these conditions have been met. Accordingly, the hearsay objection is overruled and the testimony of the results of the poll is admitted to show whether retail dealers recognized plaintiff as the source of plaintiff's design for suitcases.

The testimony is not only admissible but is to some degree persuasive on the issue that the plaintiff's design has acquired among dealers a secondary meaning. Of course, it is not exceptionally persuasive because there is no evidence as to what fraction of the dealer market does make that identification. Only 29 persons were asked about plaintiff's bag and those 29 not only were a small sample but were selected from a universe designed by experts inadequately informed of the problem and hence arbitrarily making exclusions and inclusions.

This then is the situation: there is some evidence that retail dealers do associate plaintiff's design for a suitcase with plaintiff, but the only evidence that retail dealers are likely to be confused by defendant's product consists first of the very bags manufactured by the parties and second of the testimony of plaintiff's design expert. This evidence of likelihood of confusion on the part of dealers is far from persuasive. Dealers would never be misled by the general design of defendant's bag. They would look at the manufacturer's label on the bag. They would buy only after detailed talk with a manufacturer's salesman or careful inspection of a manufacturer's catalog or both. Presumably they would execute with a particular manufacturer a written contract specifying in minute detail not one but many bags, each of a particular type. Under such conditions the risks of confusion as to source of goods are so small as to be virtually nonexistent. It follows that plaintiff has failed to bear its burden of proof on the unfair competition case and judgment on that count of the complaint . . . must be entered for defendant.

It may be helpful for this Court to make certain additional observations for guidance in future cases. In every case where the results of a poll or similar survey are offered, there arise as preliminary problems the propriety of the universe, the choice of the sample, the qualifications of the experts and investigators, the manner of interviewing, the questions asked by the investigators, and the scope of freedom of the interviewee to frame an answer in his own terms. Ordinarily if the parties have not agreed between themselves as to these matters, it would be desirable to have them discussed at a pre-trial hearing at which the Court can enter appropriate orders. An adversary party, of course, has the right to object to the form, manner, and content of questions put by interrogators to interviewees; and it would usually be more convenient and economical to have the Court rule on such objections before the poll is taken rather than at the full trial. Had this procedure been followed in the case at bar there would have been a considerable saving of money and time, and perhaps plaintiff could have filled gaps in its proof.

THE SCOTCH WHISKEY ASS'N v. CONSOLIDATED DISTILLED PRODUCTS, INC.

United States District Court, Northern District of Illinois
210 U.S.P.Q. 639 (1981)

MAROVITZ, DISTRICT JUDGE.

Plaintiff The Scotch Whiskey Association brings this action against defendant Consolidated Distilled Products, Inc. appealing a decision rendered by the Trademark Trial and Appeal Board (the "Board") of the United States Department of Commerce's Patent and Trademark Office. The jurisdiction of the Court is invoked pursuant to 15 U.S.C. §§ 1071(b) and 1121 and 28 U.S.C. § 1338(a).

Plaintiff, a United Kingdom Corporation, is an association of Scottish whiskey distillers organized for the purpose of promoting the interests of and the trade in whiskey produced in Scotland. Defendant produces and markets alcoholic beverages. Defendant has pending an application to register the mark "Loch-A-Moor" as a trademark for an after-dinner liqueur that it produces and retails in the United States. Plaintiff opposes the registration of "Loch-A-Moor" as a trademark on the ground that the mark is allegedly deceptive as to the geographic origin of defendant's product in violation of 15 U.S.C. §§ 1051(e)(2) and 1125(a), and the Convention of Paris of the Protection of Industrial Property, as implemented by 15 U.S.C. § 1126. Specifically, plaintiff contends that the Loch-A-Moor mark falsely describes the product as having Scotland as its place of origin.

. . . .

Subsequent to the Board's decision in this matter, plaintiff retained the marketing and survey research firm of Elrick & Lavidge to conduct a survey to ascertain what, if any, place of geographic origin the Loch-A-Moor label imparts to consumers. Mr. Robert Lavidge designed the survey used and testified at trial as to its design and the manner in which it was conducted. The survey was conducted in September 1979 by way of face-to-face interviews in New York City, Chicago, and San Francisco metropolitan area shopping centers. No alcoholic beverages were sold within the shopping centers used. The survey population consisted of persons who stated that they had either bought or consumed an after-dinner liqueur within the past year.

At each location, the survey was administered by paid interviewers who were supervised by professionals. The interviewers were never informed for whom the survey was being performed. Once a person replied that he had used or consumed an after-dinner liqueur within the past year, he was shown a bottle of Loch-A-Moor bearing the Loch-A-Moor mark. Interviewers were instructed to permit a respondent to view the bottle as long as he wished, but not to allow a respondent to actually hold the bottle. After viewing the bottle, the respondents were then asked the following two questions: (1) "Where do you think this liqueur comes from?" and (2) "Why do you think it comes from (place mentioned in response to the first question)?" Interviewers were instructed to record all responses verbatim. That the instructions were adhered to by the interviewers in the Chicago area portion of the survey was supported by the testimony of both the supervisor for the Chicago portion of the survey and one of the Chicago interviewers. Validation of all of the survey results was achieved by telephoning approximately 40 percent of the respondents to verify the responses given. This validation technique caused one response to be disregarded when calculating the survey results.

There was a total of 607 persons in the survey population: 201 in the New York City area; 206 in the Chicago area; and 200 in the San Francisco area. Scotland was the most common response given by members of the survey population to the first question. Of the total survey population, 32.7 percent unequivocally gave Scotland as their answer to the first question. Scotland was given as an unequivocal response by 37.3 percent of the New York City area respondents, by 26.7 percent of the Chicago area respondents, and by 34 percent of the San Francisco area respondents. Of those members of the survey population which unequivocally responded Scotland to the first question, the overwhelming majority gave responses to the second question that indicated that that mark's name or label or both caused them to give Scotland as their response to the first question. The second most common response to the first question was Chicago, given by 7.7 percent of the total survey population.

. . . .

Based upon the stipulated facts as to Loch-A-Moor's mark, the Court's own observation of the mark, *see General Foods Corp. v. Borden, Inc.*, 191 U.S.P.Q. 674, 678 (N.D. Ill. 1976), and the survey evidence, the Court finds that the Loch-A-Moor mark is likely to mislead consumers to believe that the geographic origin of the product is Scotland. As stated, "loch" is a Scottish word, "moor" is a British word, and the label displays a castle and refers to a Scottish island. Further, while the Court finds Mr. Klinsky's testimony credible insofar as he testified that the mark was not chosen for the purpose of deceiving the public as to the origin of the product, the Court finds it nonetheless significant that the mark was deliberately chosen because of its Scottish connotation. . . .

In this connection, the Court finds the survey evidence presented by plaintiff to be particularly persuasive. Survey evidence can be helpful in ascertaining the likelihood of confusion for purposes of the trademark laws, *Exxon Corp. v. Texas Motor Exchange of Houston*, 628 F.2d 500, 506, 208 U.S.P.Q. 384, 388–389, (5th Cir. 1980); *James Burrough Ltd. v. Sign of the Beefeater, Inc.*, 540 F.2d 266, 279, 192 U.S.P.Q. 555, 565–566 (7th Cir. 1976); *Union Carbide Corp. v. Ever-Ready, Inc.*, 531 F.2d at 382, 188 U.S.P.Q. at 637–638; *General Foods Corp. v. Borden, Inc.*, 191 U.S.P.Q. at 678. This proposition is also particularly true when a low-cost item is involved. *Union Carbide Corp. v. Ever-Ready, Inc.*, 531 F.2d at 388, 188 U.S.P.Q. at 643–644. The weight accorded survey evidence is determined by examining, inter alia: (1) the sample size; (2) the nature of the universe; (3) the nature of the questions; and (4) by whom the survey was conducted. It is the Court's examination of these factors with regard to plaintiff's survey that causes the Court to accord great weight to the survey evidence.

[handwritten margin note: Survey Criteria]

First, the Court finds that the sample size of 607 persons is easily sufficient to allow the Court to extrapolate the survey responses to the national population of after-dinner liqueur consumers and purchasers. Second, the Court finds that the universe was properly defined as consumers as well as purchasers of after-dinner liqueurs because the universe should include potential purchasers as well as actual purchasers. Third, the questions were properly framed to discover the ultimate question of geographic misdescriptiveness presented to the Court for resolution. They were framed clearly and were not in any fashion leading. Fourth, the survey was scientifically conducted by impartial interviewers and qualified experts. *James Burrough Ltd. v. Sign of the Beefeater, Inc.*, 540 F.2d at 278, 192 U.S.P.Q. at 564–565. The interviewers were not aware of the purpose for which the survey was conducted, were instructed to record responses verbatim, and an effective validation technique was employed. See *id*. While the Court is mindful that the survey was not performed in an actual purchasing situation, it does not deem that fact to significantly undermine the weight of the survey findings because, as discussed above, the universe was properly defined. *See generally General Foods Corp. v. Borden, Inc.*, 191 U.S.P.Q. at 681.

. . . .

Defendant presented evidence at trial that, it argues, casts doubt upon the validity of the 32.6 percent figure as being the percentage of the survey population that unequivocally responded Scotland to the first survey question. Specifically, defendant argues that the disparity between the number of unequivocal Scotland responses by the San Francisco and New York respondents, on the one hand, and the Chicago respondents, on the other, suggests that only the Chicago interviewers strictly adhered to the instruction to record verbatim the responses given. The Court finds unpersuasive the evidence presented in support of this argument. Moreover, the Court is unpersuaded that defendant's argument seeks to establish a significant point. An equivocal Scotland response could in many circumstances be considered evidence of a likelihood of confusion as to geographic origin. In any event, the Court finds that the Chicago portion of the survey would alone be sufficient to demonstrate a violation of § 1125(a). *[handwritten: (20% is enough)]*

. . . .

[Judgement for plaintiff.]

ANHEUSER-BUSCH, INC. v. STROH BREWERY CO.

United States Court of Appeals, Eighth Circuit
750 F.2d 631(1984)

GIBSON, CIRCUIT JUDGE.

For several years Anheuser-Busch had been interested in producing a low alcohol beer both because of its need to develop new markets for growth and because of growing public concern over the health aspects of beer consumption and the problem of drunken driving. Other breweries had similar interests and, in fact, two smaller companies, Hudepohl Brewery and Christian Schmidt Brewing Company, had marketed reduced alcohol beers under the brand names of Pace and Break. Anheuser Busch accelerated its plans in the fall of 1983, obtained approval from the Bureau of Alcohol, Tobacco and Firearms (BATF) for an early version of its LA label on November 21, 1983, and began using the LA mark on beer shipped in interstate commerce on December 5, 1983. On January 20, 1984, Anheuser-Busch issued a press release informing the industry and public of its plans to sell LA beer. On the same date, application was made for registration of the mark LA. In March, Anheuser-Busch commenced marketing the beer. At the time of the commencement of the trial on May 7, 1984, it was marketing the product in ten test markets preparatory to distribution on a national basis.

On March 5, 1984, Stroh issued a press release announcing its plans to introduce a low alcohol beer. On March 7, 1984, Stroh obtained BATF approval of two separate beer labels using LA, one with the product name Schaefer and the other with the product name Old Milwaukee. On March 26, 1984, after receiving objections from Anheuser-Busch, Stroh issued a press release stating that it planned to market Schaefer LA beer. This action, brought on April 18, 1984, against Stroh for trademark infringement, trademark dilution and unfair competition under 15 U.S.C. § 1125(a) (1982), the Lanham Act, and for violation of the Missouri antidilution statute, Mo. Rev.Stat. § 417.061(1978), followed.

. . . .

. . . [In] determining if a term is generic or descriptive, a court is to view the term from the standpoint of the average prospective purchaser. In determining the viewpoint of the prospective purchasers in trademark and unfair competition cases, substantial weight may be accorded the result of a properly conducted survey. . . .

Stroh . . . argues that [Anheuser-Busch's] consumer survey was improperly designed. The survey was designed by Dr. Yoram Wind, Professor of Marketing and Management, Wharton School, University of Pennsylvania.[10] The district court

---

[10]The district court summarized the methodology and results of the survey thus:

The survey was conducted at shopping malls in fifteen cities, eight of which were already test markets for plaintiff's product. Respondents were screened for the proper character-

found that the consumer survey was fairly and scientifically conducted by qualified experts and impartial interviewers, that the study drew responses from a sample of a relevant portion of potential consumers, that the questions, upon which the results relied, did not appear to be misleading or biased, and that the recordation of responses was handled in a completely unbiased manner. These findings were not challenged on appeal. Stroh, however, argues the survey was defective because respondents who were familiar with low alcohol beer were not asked what LA meant.[11]

argues survey was bad

This issue was addressed at trial. On cross-examination Dr. Wind was asked why the question, "What does the designation LA suggest to you?" was not asked. Dr. Wind testified:

> If I will ask them after all these questions what does it mean or what does the designation of this, . . . first of all I'm directing them, I'm leading here, it's a leading question. I am directing them to start scratching their head what does it mean and then they can go into all types of puzzles and games especially in an experimental setting. They will tell me Los Angeles or try to guess what else.

> What I'm trying to do is try to get the true meaning and the best way of getting the true meaning is open ended questions, not directive questions that ask the respondent to tell me. What can be better than asking what it is, describe it, or what type of beer is it, or what is the brand name. Very simple non-biasing type questions.

Dr. Wind also stated that if a student of his had included such a question in "a research design he would have gotten an F in the course." We believe the district court did not err in finding Dr. Wind's defense of his research design persuasive. Further, an opposing expert, Dr. Herbert E. Krugman, testified on direct examination that to ask such a question would be to engage in "a fishing expedition." He further stated that respondents would "start guessing" if so asked and that some might guess "Los Angeles," some "Light Anheuser" and some "low alcohol." That such a variety of answers was posited as probable responses is further indication of the suggestive- ness of the term LA.

see following page

istics and were subsequently divided into two test cells: Those who have not ever seen, heard of, or tried plaintiff's product, and those who have seen, heard of, or tried the product. The researcher's general conclusion was that consumers perceived the LA label to be the brand name of the product and not a generic designation for low alcohol beer. The raw data supports this conclusion. . . . The researcher concluded that the difference between these two sets of data basically measured the effect of advertising on those who *had* ever seen, heard of, or tried the product. Even with the rise of respondents familiar with the product who answered, "low," "less," or "light alcohol," to the question, "what type of beer is it," it is apparent from the study that consumers do not generally recognize the term LA to immediately connote low alcohol when they see such on plaintiff's product.

[11]Responses were gathered from the following statements and questions: Please describe the product. What *type* of beer is it? What is the *brand name* of this new product? What *company produces this brand*?

Dr. Wind was cross-examined at great length. The district court also heard the views of Dr. Krugman. It is clear from the district court's opinion that the Wind surveys were carefully scrutinized before it reached its determination that Stroh's evidence did not contradict the essence of Dr. Wind's research findings. While differing views were expressed, we cannot say that the trial court was clearly in error in reaching its conclusions about the surveys.[12] Stroh also argues that the omission of its proposed question means Anheuser-Busch has not met its burden of proof. Given our conclusions regarding the surveys, we must also conclude that the district court did not clearly err in finding that the weight of credible evidence supported the conclusions it reached and, hence, that Anheuser-Busch's burden of proof was met. *won't overrule the ct*

. . . .

Stroh also argues that LA is descriptive, not suggestive. . . . The district court therefore properly looked to the consumer survey in reaching its conclusion that "LA . . . stands for an idea which requires some operation of the imagination to connect it with the product."

see previous pg

Stroh argues that only when one is unaware that the product is low alcohol beer could any imagination be involved in assessing the nature of the product from the initials LA. However, the survey demonstrated that of those respondents who had seen, heard of, or tried LA beer, when asked "what type of beer is it?" only 24.4% answered "low alcohol," "light alcohol," "half alcohol" or "less alcohol." We cannot say that the trial court was in error in finding, after examining such results, "that consumers do not generally recognize the term LA to immediately connote low alcohol when they see such on plaintiff's product."

Affirmed.

---

[12]Judge Bright in his dissent argues that the market surveys did not deal with the real world and real market, polling only a group of consumers not familiar with low alcohol beer and hence legally irrelevant. First, this criticism overlooks the fact that, with the exception of two reduced alcohol products with low market penetration, this was a new product introduced to a consuming public generally not familiar with low alcohol beer. The Wind surveys were properly concerned in part with just such an audience to whom the new product was being introduced. Second, and crucially, it is clear from the district court's opinion that it carefully compared the responses from consumers who had *not* seen, heard of, or tried the product with those from consumers who *had* seen, heard of, or tried the product before reaching its conclusion that "[e]ven with the rise of respondents familiar with the product who answered, 'low,' 'less,' or 'light alcohol,' to the question, 'what type of beer is it,' it is apparent from the study that consumers do not generally recognize the term LA to immediately connote low alcohol when they see such on plaintiff's product." *See supra* note 10. The argument of the dissent but underscores the fact that the effect of advertising was measured by comparison of the survey responses of the two groups.

NOTES ON SURVEYS AND EXPERTS

(1) Surveys afford a basis for determining likelihood of confusion by ascertaining scientifically the mental associations and reactions of consumers and potential consumers to the marks involved. *See* Gunn & Evans, Jr., *Trademark Surveys*, 20 Texas Tech. L. Rev. 1 (1989); Pattishall, *Reaction Test Evidence in Trade Identity Cases*, 49 Trademark Rep. 145 (1959). Such evidence has also been found probative in determining secondary meaning, *see, e.g., Zatarains, Inc. v. Oak Grove Smokehouse, Inc.*, (698 F.2d 786, 795 (5th Cir. 1983); *Vision Center v. Opticks, Inc.*, 596 F.2d 111, 119 (5th Cir. 1979); *President & Trustees of Colby College v. Colby College-N.H.*, 508 F.2d 804, 809 (1st Cir. 1975) ("The importance of qualified survey evidence in establishing secondary meaning is well recognized"); *Federal Glass Co. v. Corning Glass Works*, 162 U.S.P.Q. 279 (T.T.A.B. 1969); *American Luggage, supra*; and whether a term is generic, *e.g., Anti-Monopoly, Inc. v. General Mills Fun Group, Inc.*, 684 F.2d 1316 (9th Cir. 1982); *King-Seeley Thermos Co. v. Aladdin Indus., Inc.*, 321 F.2d 577 (2d Cir. 1963). Surveys also may properly be used to determine consumer reactions in false advertising cases. *See* Chapter 8, *infra*.

The court's criticisms of the survey evidence offered in *American Luggage, supra*, remain valid today. In *Scotch Whiskey Association, supra*, the confusion survey questions were as follows:

1. First, may I ask, have you bought or consumed any after-dinner liqueur in the past year?
   Yes( )   No ( )
   Don't know, don't remember, not sure ( )

   (IF "NO," OR "DON'T KNOW," THANK
   RESPONDENT AND TERMINATE INTERVIEW)
   IF "YES," SHOW LIQUEUR BOTTLE, AND ASK:

2a. Where do you think this liqueur comes from?
    (RECORD ANSWER VERBATIM)

    IF RESPONDENT MENTIONS A PLACE IN ANSWER TO Q2a, ASK:
 b. Why do you think it comes from (PLACE MENTIONED IN ANSWER TO Q. 2a) (RECORD ANSWER VERBATIM)

3. Thank you. That's all there is to it. So that I may complete this interview, may I please have your name, address and telephone number?

In this sequence, Question 1 is the screen question to obtain the proper universe, Question 2(a) is the key question to determine if there is confusion and Question 2(b) is a probe question to learn why there is confusion. Question 3 is for verification purposes. Note that the *Scotch Whiskey Association* survey was not a probability sample so that the results could not be scientifically projected to a larger universe than those actually interviewed. Nonetheless, the court found it to be persuasive evidence of the deceptively Scottish connotation imparted by the name LOCH-A-MOOR for defendant's liqueur.

In *Union Carbide Corp. v. Ever-Ready, Inc.*, 531 F.2d 366, 385–388 (7th Cir. 1976), the following survey questions were found probative of both secondary meaning and likelihood of confusion where the defendants' EVER-READY lamp was shown as the stimulus (*see* Chapter 2, *supra*):

(2)   Who do you think puts out the lamp shown here?

(3)   What makes you think so?

(4)   Please name any other products put out by the same concern which puts out the lamp shown here.

Ordinarily, of course, secondary meaning would be tested in such a survey by showing the respondent the product for which secondary meaning is claimed. In *Ever-Ready*, however, in excess of 50% of those interviewed associated Union Carbide products, such as batteries and flashlights, with defendants' mark. The court correctly held that these results established secondary meaning, albeit unintentionally.

Similarly, genericness was found based upon the following survey evidence in *E.I. DuPont de Nemours & Co. v. Yoshida International, Inc.*, 393 F. Supp. 502 (E.D.N.Y. 1975):

I'd like to read 8 names to you to get you to tell me whether you think it is a brand name or a common name; by *brand* name, I mean a word like *Chevrolet* which is made by one company; by *common* name, I mean *automobile* which is made by a number of different companies. So if I were to ask you, "Is Chevrolet a brand name or a common name?," what would you say?

[If respondent understands, continue. If not understood, explain again.]

Now, would you say _____ is a brand name or a common name?

[Repeat with each of eight examples]

The results were as follows:

NAME	BRAND %	COMMON %	DON'T KNOW
STP	90	5	5
THERMOS	51	46	3
MARGARINE	9	91	1
TEFLON	68	31	2
JELLO	75	25	1
REFRIGERATOR	6	94	—
ASPIRIN	13	86	—
COKE	76	24	—

The survey caused the court to find that "the public is quite good at sorting out brand names from common names and, for TEFLON, [it] answers the critical question . . . ," demonstrating that TEFLON functions as a brand name. This survey tests the understanding of respondents; does it test usage?

In contrast, in *Anti-monopoly* the court rejected a similar brand name survey for the game Monopoly as irrelevant, stating that, "under the survey definition, 'Monopoly' would have to be a 'brand name' because it is made by only one company. This tells us nothing at all about the *primary* meaning of 'Monopoly' in the minds of consumers." The court endorsed the results of a "motivation" survey, where 65% of the respondents chose, out of two statements, the response "I want a 'Monopoly' game primarily because I am interested in playing 'Monopoly,' I don't much care who makes it," while only 32% chose "I would like Parker Brothers' 'Monopoly' game primarily because I like Parker Brothers' products." The court concluded as a result that the primary significance of "Monopoly" was product, not source, and that the name was therefore generic and the trademark registration for it invalid. What criticisms can be made of the survey designs accepted by each court? Are the two cases reconcilable? *See* Zeisel, *The Surveys That Broke Monopoly*, 50 U. Chi. L. Rev. 896 (1983); R.C. Sorensen, *Survey Research Execution in Trademark Litigation: Does Practice Make Perfection?*; J.P. Reiner, *The Universe and Sample: How Good Is Good Enough?*; A.W. Leiser & C.R. Schwartz, *Techniques for Ascertaining Whether a Trademark is Generic*; V.N. Palladino, *Techniques for Ascertaining If There Is Secondary Meaning*; R.B. Boal, *Techniques for Ascertaining Likelihood of Confusion and the Meaning of Advertising Communications*; Barnaby & Robin, *Trademark Surveys — Heads You Lose, Tails They Win*, 73 Trademark Rep. 349 (1983). In 1984, future use of a purchaser motivation test in trademark cases was legislatively barred by Congress.

(2) What factors should a court consider before accepting a survey into evidence? A number of cases discuss this in depth, including *Brooks Shoe Mfg. Co. v. Suave Shoe Corp.*, 533 F. Supp. 75 (S.D. Fla. 1981), *aff'd*, 716 F.2d 854 (11th Cir. 1983), in which the court enumerates eight elements of a proper survey foundation and discusses how one survey failed to establish those elements while another succeeded. In *American Footwear Corp. v. General Footwear Co.*, 609 F.2d 655 (2d Cir. 1979), the court discusses inappropriate wording of questions, failure to replicate appropriate consumer environment and error in selecting survey universe as justifying the district court's rejection of survey evidence. *See also Mennen Co. v. Gillette Co.*, 220 U.S.P.Q. 354 (S.D.N.Y. 1983); *Amstar Corp. v. Domino's Pizza, Inc.*, 615 F.2d 252 (5th Cir. 1980). Often courts will admit defective surveys, but accord them diminished or minimal weight depending on the perceived magnitude of the imperfections. *McGraw-Edison Co. v. Walt Disney Productions*, 787 F.2d 1163, 1172 (7th Cir. 1986); *Piper Aircraft Corp. v. Way-Aero, Inc.*, 741 F.2d 925, 931(7th Cir. 1984); *Jellibeans, Inc. v. Skating Clubs of Georgia, Inc.*, 716 F.2d 833, 844–45 (11th Cir. 1983); *Inc. Publishing Corp. v. Manhattan Magazine, Inc.*, 616 F. Supp. 370, 390 (S.D.N.Y. 1985), *aff'd without opinion*, 788 F.2d 3 (2d Cir. 1986); *Selchow & Righter Co. v. Decipher, Inc.*, 598 F. Supp. 1489, 1502–03 (E.D. Va. 1984). *See generally* Jacoby & Handlin, *Non-Probability Sampling Designs for Litigation Surveys*, 81 Trademark Rep. 169 (1991); Weiss, *The Use of Survey Evidence in Trademark Litigation: Science, Art or Confidence Game?*, 80 Trademark Rep. 71 (1990); Jones, *Developing and Using Survey Evidence in Trademark Litigation*, 19 Mem. St. U. L. Rev. 471 (1989); Kunin, *Structure and Uses of Survey Evidence in Trademark Cases — Introduction*; Dutka, *A Statistician's Perspective*; Smith,

Strange Bedfellows: Observations of a Psychologist; Lee, *The Legal Aspect — A Trap For the Unwary*, 67 Trademark Rep. 97 (1977).

(3) The relevant universe as to likelihood of confusion is generally defined as "potential customers." *See Rhodes Pharmacal Co. v. FTC*, 208 F.2d 382 (7th Cir. 1953), *modified*, 348 U.S. 940 (1955). Is this correct and sufficient? In *Brooks Shoe*, *supra* Note (2), spectators and participants at running events in the Washington-Baltimore area constituted too narrow a universe to give a fair indication of whether the consuming public associates a "V" design with plaintiff's running shoes. Similarly, in *Vision Sports, Inc. v. Melville Corp.*, 888 F.2d 609, 615 (9th Cir. 1989), the court found the probative value of plaintiff's secondary meaning survey for its logo for clothing for skateboard enthusiasts was decreased where the universe was limited to 10–18-year-olds who attended skateboarding events or read skateboarding magazines, rather than 15–25-year-olds who purchase activewear. In *Universal City Studios, Inc. v. Nintendo Co., Ltd.*, 746 F.2d 112, 118 (2d Cir. 1984), the universe was held improper where the survey was conducted among individuals who had already purchased or leased the DONKEY KONG video game machines at issue. In *Amstar, supra*, 71% of respondents thought the maker of DOMINO pizza also made DOMINO sugar — but the questions were asked of female household members at home, whereas the primary purchasers of defendant's pizza were shown to be single male college students. Also, 8 of 10 cities where the interviews were conducted did not have defendant's pizza outlets and outlets only had just been opened in the remaining two. The court stated "the appropriate universe should include a fair sampling of those purchasers most likely to partake of the alleged infringer's goods or services." This one did not and was therefore fatally defective. In *National Football League Properties v. Wichita Falls Sportswear*, 532 F. Supp. 651 (W.D. Wa. 1982), plaintiff's universe was the entire U.S. population between the ages of 13 and 65. Defendant argued that this was too broad and that the relevant universe was likely purchasers of NFL football jersey replicas. Unfortunately (for defendant) plaintiff's comprehensive survey analysis included a separate data category which contained the suggested universe and accompanying response results. In a similar apparel case, *National Football League Properties, Inc. v. New Jersey Giants, Inc.*, 637 F. Supp. 507 (D.N.J. 1986), the court held proper a universe which consisted of persons 14 years or older who either: (a) in the past year had bought, or (b) within 6 months were likely to buy, a slogan or picture t-shirt, sweatshirt or other clothing.

In *Anheuser-Busch Inc. v. Stroh Brewery Co., supra*, in holding that "LA" for a new low alcohol beer was neither generic nor descriptive, the Eighth Circuit relied on survey responses from a group of respondents who had not seen, heard of or tried plaintiff's product. In *G. Heileman Brewing Co. v. Anheuser-Busch, Inc.*, 873 F.2d 985, 995 (7th Cir. 1989), however, the results of a similar survey were discounted because the survey tested "thoroughly uninformed consumers" regarding their perception of "LA" for beer.

(4) What criteria would you consider in determining whether a survey is biased? *See American Footwear, supra* at 661, in which the court found the question "with whom or what do you associate a product labelled Bionic" too self-serving and

suggested the more relevant inquiry should have been "with whom or what do you associate 'Bionic' boot?" In *Wuv's International, Inc. v. Love's Enterprises, Inc.,* 208 U.S.P.Q. 736 (D. Colo. 1980), the court found the question "do you believe that this restaurant is connected with or related to any other restaurants" to be unnecessarily suggestive because it limited respondent's choices to other restaurant operations, including, *inter alia*, plaintiff's. In *Philip Morris, Inc. v. R.J. Reynolds Tobacco Co.,* 188 U.S.P.Q. 289 (S.D.N.Y. 1975), the court ruled that the survey was tailored to elicit brand identification instead of whether consumers considered the word "lights" to be a descriptive term or a term associated with plaintiff. The court suggested "a neutral question would have been: 'respecting cigarettes, will you tell me what the word Lights means to you?' " It is also possible for a survey to be unbiased but too open-ended and abstract, *Exxon Corp. v. Texas Motor Exchange, Inc.,* 628 F.2d 500, 506 (5th Cir. 1980) ("Surveys that involve nothing more than showing an individual a trademark and asking if it brings anything else to mind are given little weight in this Circuit . . . [they are] little more than word-association tests"), or a survey procedure too rigorous, *Wendy's International, Inc. v. Big Bite, Inc.,* 576 F. Supp. 816, 823 (S.D. Ohio 1983) (instructions to probe respondents until no more answers were forthcoming probably resulted in more sponsorship-confusion answers than would otherwise have resulted). *See generally* 1 Gilson, *Trademark Protection and Practice* § 8.11[3][c] (1993 ed.).

(5) Survey questions and methodology must be designed to determine the actual state of mind of members of the appropriate universe. *Sears, Roebuck & Co. v. All States Life Ins. Co.,* 246 F.2d 161 (5th Cir. 1957), *cert. denied,* 355 U.S. 894 (1957). Can reliable survey responses be induced by flattering letters or offers of prizes in return for prompt replies? *See DuPont Cellophane Co. v. Waxed Prod. Co.,* 85 F.2d 75, 80 (2d Cir. 1936), *cert. denied,* 299 U.S. 601 (1936). Must a survey be conducted in the actual marketing environment to constitute valid evidence of purchaser's state of mind? *See* the *Scotch Whisky Association* case, *supra,* in which the court found that the fact that the survey was not performed in an actual purchasing situation did not significantly undermine the weight of the survey findings because the universe was properly defined. Similarly, in *General Foods Corp. v. Borden, Inc.,* 191 U.S.P.Q. 674 (N.D. Ill. 1976), the court stated that "interviews at respondents' homes are probative of state of mind at the time of purchase. Deviation from the actual purchase situation has been considered in weighing the force of this evidence. . . ." *See also Zippo Mfg. Co. v. Rogers Imports, Inc.,* 216 F. Supp. 670, 685 (S.D.N.Y. 1963); *Inc. Publishing, supra* Note (2), 616 F. Supp. at 392. Surveys taken at a time when market conditions have changed significantly since the alleged infringement occurred may not generate the relevant consumer state of mind. *See, e.g., Zippo Mfg., supra,* 216 F. Supp. at 690; *Calvin Klein Co. v. Farah Mfg. Co.,* 229 U.S.P.Q. 795 (S.D.N.Y. 1985).

(6) Are the problems inherent in survey evidence outweighed by the value of such evidence in ascertaining consumer reaction? In *Levi Strauss & Co. v. Blue Bell, Inc.,* 732 F.2d 676 (9th Cir. 1984), the Court relied heavily on survey evidence indicating minimal actual confusion and no likelihood of confusion in finding that defendant's use of an identifying pocket tab on its shirts did not infringe or unfairly compete with plaintiff's use of the same type of tab. This despite *Levi Strauss & Co. v. Blue*

Bell, Inc., 632 F.2d 817 (9th Cir. 1980), where a similar tab on pants was held to have secondary meaning and Blue Bell was enjoined from use of such a label. Subsequently a rehearing was granted and the opinion withdrawn, *Levi Strauss v. Blue Bell, Inc.*, 734 F.2d 409 (9th Cir. 1984). Should the courts themselves conduct or supervise the obtaining of survey evidence? *See Triangle Publications, Inc. v. Rohrlich*, 167 F.2d 969, 976–977 (2d Cir. 1948) (Frank, J. dissenting); *Piper Aircraft, supra* Note (2), 741 F.2d at 931 ("Plaintiff followed the 'commendable procedure' of submitting the survey questions, along with the results of a preliminary survey, to the district court for a ruling *in limine* on the question of admissibility"). Would a court conducted or supervised survey virtually obviate the necessity of a trial on the issue of likelihood of confusion?

(7) As indicated above, survey evidence has been successfully used to help demonstrate secondary meaning. *See, e.g., Zatarains, Inc. v. Oak Grove Smokehouse, Inc.*, 698 F.2d 786, 795 (5th Cir. 1983) (over 20% of respondents correctly identified plaintiff's brand as a product used for frying fish); *Vision Center v. Opticks, Inc.*, 596 F.2d 111, 119 (5th Cir. 1979), (noting failure to offer an objective survey and finding remaining secondary meaning evidence insufficient), *cert. denied*, 444 U.S. 1016 (1980); *President & Trustees of Colby College v. Colby College-New Hampshire*, 508 F.2d 804, 809 (1st Cir. 1975) ("The importance of qualified survey evidence in establishing secondary meaning is well recognized"); *American Luggage, supra.*

(8) The failure to offer a survey normally will not in and of itself affect the right to relief. *Compare International Kennel Club, Inc. v. Mighty Star, Inc.*, 846 F.2d 1079, 1086 (7th Cir. 1988) (absence of survey evidence does not preclude preliminary injunctive relief) *and Charles Jacquin et Cie, Inc. v. Destileria Serralles, Inc.*, 921 F.2d 467, 476 (3d Cir. 1990) (upholding refusal to give a jury instruction on appellant's failure to offer a confusion survey in a trade dress case) *with Gucci v. Gucci Shops*, 688 F. Supp. 916 (S.D.N.Y. 1988) (absence of rebuttal survey found significant).

(9) What percentage of survey respondent confusion should be sufficient to demonstrate consumer confusion as to product source? In *James Burrough, Ltd. v. Sign of the Beefeater, Inc.*, 540 F.2d 266, 279 (7th Cir. 1976), the Court of Appeals found the district court's characterization of 15% confusion as "small" to be erroneous, finding instead that it "evidences a likelihood of confusion, deception or mistake regarding the sponsorship of [defendant's] services sufficient on this record to establish Distiller's right to relief." In *Henri's Food Products Co., Inc. v. Kraft, Inc.*, 220 U.S.P.Q. 386 (7th Cir. 1983), the Seventh Circuit held that the district court was correct in holding that a 7.6% confusion weighs *against* a finding of infringement. *See also Grotrian, Helfferich, Schulz, Th. Steinway Nachf. v. Steinway & Sons*, 365 F. Supp. 707 (S.D.N.Y. 1973) (8.5% confusion, 7.7% perceived connection between parties held to be strong evidence of confusion; unclear whether percentages were combined).

(10) Expert witnesses can be used in a variety of ways to assist the trier of fact in deciding trademark and unfair competition cases. *See, e.g., WSM Inc. v. Hilton*, 724 F.2d 1320 (8th Cir. 1984) (relying on an expert in the field of regional English

to establish that "opry" was in common use before Grand Ole Opry began using it in 1927); *G.D. Searle & Co. v. Charles Prizer & Co.*, 265 F.2d 385 (7th Cir.), *cert. denied*, 361 U.S. 819 (1959) (relying on the testimony of a Northwestern University professor on the sound similarity of the marks DRAMAMINE and BONAMINE for motion sickness pills in holding confusion likely); *Conagra, Inc. v. Geo. A. Hormel & Co.*, 784 F. Supp. 700 (D. Neb. 1992) (favoring the testimony of defendant's linguist over plaintiff's in holding HEALTHY CHOICE and HEALTHY SELECTIONS for frozen food were not confusingly similar in sound and connotation); *A-Veda Corp. v. Aura, Inc.*, 19 U.S.P.Q.2d 1864 (D. Minn. 1991) (relying on testimony of defendant's graphics expert in holding confusion unlikely between competing shampoo products). In *Sherrell, Inc. v. Revlon, Inc.*, 205 U.S.P.Q. 250 (S.D.N.Y. 1980), defendant made the advertising claim that its copycat perfume was identical to CHANEL NO. 5 perfume, and "only your checkbook will know the difference." Chanel's chief perfumist successfully demonstrated, based on gas chromatograph and "sniff" tests, that the two were not equivalent and that there was "a noticeable difference between genuine Chanel No. 5" and the copy. Sherrell was enjoined from making claims of equivalency, including its claim that "even the most sophisticated perfume expert would have great difficulty in telling 'Ours' from the imported originals." For further discussion of the use of experts in advertising cases, see Chapter 8, *infra*.

(11) In *Daubert v. Merrell Dow Pharmaceuticals, Inc.*, 113 S. Ct. 2783 (1993), the Supreme Court clarified that in the federal courts the standard for admissibility of testimony by expert witnesses is contained in Federal Rule of Evidence 702, and that Rule 702 supplanted the old standard stated in *Frye v. United States*, 293 F. 1013 (D.C. Cir. 1923). Under the old *Frye* test, the judge only had to determine whether the testimony was based on principles generally accepted in the scientific community. Rule 702 provides:

> If scientific, technical or other specialized knowledge will assist the trier of fact to understand the evidence or to determine a fact in issue, a witness qualified as an expert by knowledge, skill, experience, training or education, may testify thereto in the form of an opinion or otherwise.

In *Daubert*, Justice Blackmun found that the terms "scientific" and "knowledge" require that the proposed testimony "rests on a reliable foundation" and that to satisfy Rule 702, a judge will have to make "a preliminary assessment of whether the reasoning or methodology underlying the testimony is scientifically valid and whether that reasoning or methodology properly can be applied to the facts at issue." In his dissent, Chief Justice Rehnquist complained that in focussing on methodology this way, the majority was requiring trial judges "to become amateur scientists" in order to determine the admissibility of such testimony.

It may be that this ruling will make it easier to get novel scientific evidence admitted, since it no longer needs to be generally accepted in the scientific community. In one of the first decisions applying *Daubert*, Judge Zagel in the Northern District of Illinois excluded in a product liability case an expert's testimony that defendant's miter saw was unreasonably dangerous because the expert had done no testing of his theory and had only spent "maybe an hour" thinking about the issue while examining the saw. *Paul Stanczyk v. Black & Decker and DeWalt*, No. 91 C 4054.

CHAPTER 7

SPECIAL DEFENSES AND LIMITATIONS

§ 7.01 Introduction

DEVELOPMENTS IN THE LAW — TRADE-MARKS AND UNFAIR COMPETITION*

68 Harv. L. Rev. 814 (1955)

Since the test of injury to the trade-mark owner is likelihood of public confusion, whatever interest the public may have in the integrity of a symbol it has come to associate with a particular product or source will ordinarily be safeguarded in a private infringement suit. There are cases, however, where a mark which consumers identify exclusively with the plaintiff's product has in fact been infringed, but the plaintiff is precluded by his own conduct from asserting his claim to protection. Thus the doctrine of unclean hands has barred a plaintiff whose mark is misdescriptive of his product, who falsely advertises the trade-marked item, or who has changed the quality of the goods sold under a mark so as to deceive the public. Further, if the plaintiff, with knowledge of the defendant's use, delays an unreasonable time before protesting, or in other ways indicates acquiescence in the adverse use, he may be precluded from complaining if the defendant has relied by investing substantially in the infringing mark. And a contract between the parties allowing for joint use of a mark will be a valid defense against the prior user in an infringement proceeding, as will a release or waiver.

In many estoppel cases it is possible that the public will no longer have an interest in protecting the trade-mark, since through its continued use by more than one person the symbol may have lost distinctiveness in identifying a single source in the public mind. However, when the public is confused by the dual use of the trade-mark, the effect of applying personal defenses against its owner will be only to perpetuate this confusion. Thus in *Proctor & Gamble Co. v. J. L. Prescott Co.*, the court held the plaintiff to be barred by laches and refused an injunction, although there was evidence of substantial confusion among grocers and consumers between the names "Chas-O" and "Chipso," both used on soap. Where the plaintiff's suit is dismissed because of unclean hands, not only is confusion tolerated, but the plaintiff can continue to mislabel or falsely advertise his product. Further, nothing will prevent the defendant from joining the plaintiff in practicing the same deception on the public. Thus where the plaintiff's figless laxative was trade-marked "Syrup of Figs,"

---

* Copyright © 1955 by The Harvard Law Review Association. Reprinted by permission.

(Matthew Bender & Co., Inc.)   (Pub. 725)

the result of the court's refusal to enjoin the defendant was that there might be two misbranded products on the market instead of one.

Strict Limitation of Equitable Defenses, and Conditional or Partial Relief. — Many courts, aware of these possible consequences, have been reluctant to apply rigorously the doctrine of unclean hands in unfair competition and trade-mark cases when the flaws in the plaintiff's action were technical and minor and the danger of public confusion was clear. Similarly, where justification for raising an estoppel is doubtful, some courts, while denying the plaintiff an accounting, will grant him injunctive relief. Furthermore, the traditional discretion of equity in framing decrees has allowed the courts a certain area of maneuver within which they can attempt to lessen this danger. Thus, where the situation causing the plaintiff's unclean hands can be corrected within a short period of time, courts have given conditional decrees; in order to safeguard the public from confusion and deception, the defendant has been enjoined from infringing the mark on condition that the plaintiff cease the undesirable practices. A similar method has been to dismiss the plaintiff's claim without prejudice, so that the plaintiff who "cleans his hands" can return to court and obtain an injunction. And some courts, while allowing the defendant to continue use of the mark, have attempted to lessen the danger of confusion by affording partial relief to a plaintiff barred by laches; defendants have been enjoined from precise imitation of the plaintiff's distinctive script and have been compelled to prefix corporate names.

§ 7.02 Laches and Acquiescence

MENENDEZ v. HOLT

United States Supreme Court
128 U.S. 514 (1888)

[Both parties use the trademark LA FAVORITA for flour. Defendant claimed use of its mark for fourteen years prior to suit and that plaintiff's rights had been forfeited by laches.]

MR. CHIEF JUSTICE FULLER.

. . . .

Counsel in conclusion earnestly contends that whatever rights appellees may have had were lost by *laches*; and the desire is intimated that we should reconsider *McLean v. Fleming*, 96 U.S. 245, so far as it was therein stated that even though a complainant were guilty of such delay in seeking relief upon infringement as to preclude him from obtaining an account of gains and profits, yet, if he were otherwise so entitled, an injunction against future infringement might properly be awarded. We see no reason to modify this general proposition, and we do not find in the facts as disclosed by the record before us anything to justify us in treating this case as an exception.

The intentional use of another's trade-mark is a fraud; and when the excuse is that the owner permitted such use, that excuse is disposed of by affirmative action to put a stop to it. Persistence then in the use is not innocent; and the wrong is a continuing one, demanding restraint by judicial interposition when properly invoked. Mere delay or acquiescence cannot defeat the remedy by injunction in support of the legal right, unless it has been continued so long and under such circumstances as to defeat the right itself. Hence, upon an application to stay waste, relief will not be refused on the ground that, as the defendant had been allowed to cut down half of the trees upon the complainant's land, he had acquired, by that negligence, the right to cut down the remainder, *Attorney General v. Eastlake*, 11 Hare, 205; nor will the issue of an injunction against the infringement of a trademark be denied on the ground that mere procrastination in seeking redress for depredations had deprived the true proprietor of his legal right. *Fullwood v. Fullwood*, 9 Ch. D. 176. Acquiescence to avail must be such as to create a new right in the defendant. *Rodgers v. Norwill*, 3 DeG., M. & G. 614. Where consent by the owner to the use of his trade-mark by another is to be inferred from his knowledge and silence merely, "it lasts no longer than the silence from which it springs; it is, in reality, no more than a revocable license." Duer, J., *Amoskeag Mfg. Co. v. Spear*, 2 Sandford (N.Y.) 599; *Julian v. Hoosier Drill Co.*, 78 Indiana, 408; *Taylor v. Carpenter*, 3 Story, 458; S.C. 2 Woodb. & Min. 1.

So far as the act complained of is completed, acquiescence may defeat the remedy on the principle applicable when action is taken on the strength of encouragement to do it, but so far as the act is in progress and lies in the future, the right to the intervention of equity is not generally lost by previous delay, in respect to which the elements of an estoppel could rarely arise. At the same time, as it is in the exercise of discretionary jurisdiction that the doctrine of reasonable diligence is applied, and those who seek equity must do it, a court might hesitate as to the measure of relief, where the use, by others, for a long period, under assumed permission of the owner, had largely enhanced the reputation of a particular brand.

But there is nothing here in the nature of an estoppel, nothing which renders it inequitable to arrest at this stage any further invasion of complainants' rights. There is no pretense of abandonment. That would require proof of nonuser by the owner or general surrender of the use to the public. The evidence is positive that Holt & Co. continuously used the trade-mark, always asserted their exclusive right to it, and never admitted that of any other firm or person, and, in the instance of every party, including Ryder, who used this brand on flour not of Holt & Co.'s selection, that use, when it came to their knowledge, was objected to by the latter, and personal notice given, while publication was also made in the newspapers, circulating where the flour was usually marketed, containing a statement of Holt & Co.'s rights and warning against imitations. It is idle to talk of acquiescence in view of these facts. Delay in bringing suit there was, and such delay as to preclude recovery of damages for prior infringement; but there was neither conduct nor negligence which could be held to destroy the right to prevention of further injury.

Affirmed.

(Matthew Bender & Co., Inc.)   (Pub. 725)

SEVEN-UP CO. v. O-SO-GRAPE CO.

United States Court of Appeals, Seventh Circuit
283 F.2d 103 (1960)

DUFFY, CIRCUIT JUDGE.

This is a suit for trademark infringement, unfair competition and trademark dilution respecting plaintiff's registered trademark "Seven-Up (7-Up)." Plaintiff complains of defendants' use of the trademark "Bubble Up." Injunctive relief was asked against the "Up" portion of "Bubble Up." Accounting and damages were also asked by plaintiff.

. . . .

On October 2, 1942, plaintiff, Seven-Up Company, filed a suit in the United States District Court at St. Louis, Missouri, against the Cheer Up Sales Company of St. Louis, alleging the registered trademark "Cheer Up" infringed plaintiff's trademark "Seven-Up (7-Up)." On the same day in the same court, plaintiff filed a similar suit charging the registered trademark "Natural Set Up" infringed plaintiff's registered trademark "Seven-Up (7-Up)." About ten months thereafter, in the same court, plaintiff commenced a suit against Leroy O. Schneeberger, doing business as Bubble Up Company, alleging the trademark "Bubble Up" infringed the plaintiff's trademark "Seven-Up (7-Up)."

The case involving the trademark "Cheer Up" was fully tried. The judgment was adverse to plaintiff, the Court deciding that the trademark "Cheer Up" did not infringe the trademark "Seven-Up (7-Up)" and was not confusingly similar thereto. The Seven-Up (7-Up) Company appealed to the Circuit Court of Appeals of the Eighth Circuit, which affirmed. Thereafter, the Seven-Up (7-Up) Company petitioned for certiorari. This was denied. Plaintiff then filed a petition for a bill or review in the Eighth Circuit Court of Appeals. This was denied. A petition for certiorari was again denied.

After this series of reverses, plaintiff voluntarily dismissed its suit against the then owner of the mark "Bubble Up." The order of dismissal was dated March 13, 1946. Plaintiff also dismissed its suit which charged that the mark "Natural Set Up" infringed its mark.

The suit pending in St. Louis involving the trademark "Bubble Up" was fully at issue before it was dismissed. In the thirteen years following such dismissal, plaintiff herein gave no notice and made no claim, orally or in writing, that the trademark "Bubble Up" was invalid or infringed the trademark "Seven-Up (7-Up)."

Between January 14, 1955 and October 18, 1955, the attorneys for the plaintiff and the defendants herein exchanged friendly correspondence which had the objective of cooperation of defendants in the use of its trademark "Bubble Up" to the end that the suffix "Up" would not become generic. During this period, no claim was made by plaintiff that the trademark "Bubble Up" was invalid or infringed plaintiff's trademark.

Defendants filed a motion to dismiss the instant appeal on the ground the judgment sought to be reviewed is essentially the one to which plaintiff consented and which was invited by plaintiff's offer of judgment. We ordered the motion to dismiss to be taken with the case.

We may assume that before the plaintiff agreed to a judgment against it on the issue of laches, plaintiff's attorneys had read the opinion of the trial court on the motion for a separate trial. Among statements appearing in that opinion was: "That estimate of economy in time appeals to the court if it appears likely that a decision on the laches issue in favor of defendants would probably be decisive of all issues in the case. . . . The court is not disposed to order a separate trial of the issues, however, unless it is to be reasonably anticipated that disposition of the laches issue in defendants' favor would place this litigation at rest." *Seven-Up Co. v. 0-So Grape Co.*, D.C., 177 F. Supp. 91, 93. The Court further stated, at page 100: "It appears to the court that the defense of laches, if proved, would act as a bar to essentially all of plaintiff's claims."

When plaintiff's attorneys thereafter offered to permit judgment to be taken against plaintiff on the issue of laches, they knew that after such a judgment was entered, the trial court was likely to regard the litigation as ended. Nevertheless, we reject the argument of defendants that the judgment issued as to laches was necessarily final in the determination of the issues in the case at bar. We deny the motion to dismiss the appeal, and now proceed to consider the case upon the merits.

Mere delay in bringing suit ordinarily does not affect the right to an injunction against further use of an infringed trademark. *Independent Nail & Packing Co., Inc. v. Stronghold Screw Products, Inc.*, 7 Cir., 205 F.2d 921, 927; *Mantle Lamp Co. of America v. Aladdin Mfg. Co.*, 7 Cir., 78 F.2d 426, 429. Laches does not necessarily constitute a conclusive and automatic bar to injunctive relief in trademark actions. However, in many instances, the delay may be so prolonged and inexcusable that it would be inequitable to permit the plaintiff to seek injunctive relief as to future activities.

In *Boris v. Hamilton Mfg. Co.*, 7 Cir., 253 F.2d 526, 529, we said: "Laches is an equitable doctrine, not fixed by any unyielding measure, but to be determined in each case under its factual situation, and allowable 'where the enforcement of the asserted right would work injustice.'"

In the case at bar, much more than mere delay is present. In the thirteen years following the dismissal of its suit charging "Bubble Up" infringed its trademark, plaintiff did more than merely acquiesce in defendant's use of "Bubble Up." It would be highly inequitable to permit plaintiff at this late date, to seriously damage, if not destroy, defendants' business by use of injunctive relief.

In *French Republic v. Saratoga Vichy Spring Co.*, 191 U.S. 427 the Supreme Court ruled that all relief should be denied in a trade-mark case where plaintiff had acquiesced for some thirty years in defendant's use of the word "Vichy" in marking mineral waters. Although a shorter period of time is involved in the case at bar, the equities more strongly demand that injunctive relief be denied. We hold the trial court was correct in dismissing the complaint and action herein.

. . . .

Judgment affirmed.

NOTES ON LACHES AND ACQUIESCENCE

(1) Laches may, and usually does, bar monetary relief, but generally it will not preclude injunctive relief against the continuing tort in trade identity cases. *See McLean v. Fleming*, 96 U.S. 245, 251 (1878); *Standard Oil Co. v. Standard Oil Co.*, 141 F. Supp. 876, 888–889 (D. Wyo. 1956), *aff'd*, 252 F.2d 65 (10th Cir. 1958). In *James Burrough Ltd. v. Sign of the Beefeater, Inc.*, 572 F.2d 574 (7th Cir. 1978), the court held that, upon a showing of laches, plaintiff may lose the right to recover past damages but may be entitled to injunctive relief and post-filing damages. To the same effect are *Ramada Inns, Inc. v. Apple*, 208 U.S.P.Q. 371 (D.S.C. 1980), and *Rolls-Royce Motors Ltd. v. A&A Fiberglass, Inc.*, 428 F. Supp. 689 (N.D. Ga. 1976). In *Houston Sports ass'n., Inc. v. Astro-Card Co.*, 520 F. Supp. 1178 (S.D. Tex. 1981), the court ruled that establishing laches will only bar plaintiff from recovering past damages; establishing *estoppel*, which requires a showing of intentional deception or gross negligence, will bar recovery of post-filing damages and injunctive relief as well. *See also Skippy, Inc. v. CPC International, Inc.*, 674 F.2d 209 (4th Cir. 1982), in which the court stated that if defendant has acted in bad faith, laches may not bar injunctive relief but will bar plaintiff's damages claim; and *University of Pittsburgh v. Champion Products, Inc.*, 686 F.2d 1040, 1044 (3d Cir. 1982), *cert. denied*, 103 S. Ct. 571, 459 U.S. 1088 (1982), in which the court stated that barring a claim for past damages but allowing injunctive relief is "much more common" than "that narrow class of cases where plaintiff's delay has been so outrageous, unreasonable and inexcusable as to constitute a virtual abandonment of its right."

Given the public interest in the elimination of confusion as to product source, should injunctive relief *never* be barred by a demonstration of laches? Senior users generally have not been successful in propounding such a rule. *See Prudential Insurance Co. v. Gibraltar Financial Corp.*, 694 F.2d 1150, 1152 (9th Cir. 1982); *Saratoga Vichy Spring Co., v. Lehman*, 625 F.2d 1037 (2d Cir. 180) ; *Coca-Cola Co. v. Howard Johnson Co.*, 386 F. Supp. 330, 334 (N.D. Ga. 1974). *But see Cuban Cigar Brands N.V. v. Upmann International, Inc.*, 457 F. Supp. 1090 (S.D.N.Y. 1978), *aff'd*, 607 F.2d 995 (2d Cir. 1979).

Compare Underwriters Laboratories v. United Laboratories, 203 U.S.P.Q. 180, 183 (N.D. Ill. 1978), in which the court stated, "application of the defense of laches to these circumstances would ignore the paramount objective of the law of trademark infringement and unfair competition which is protection of the public interest." What if a party delays 20 or 30 years? *See Prudential Insurance, supra*, (28-year delay constituted laches which barred all relief); *Skippy, Inc., supra* (30-year delay barred damages recovery; injunctive relief denied on other grounds); *Borg-Warner Corp. v. York Shipley, Inc.*, 293 F.2d 88, 94 (7th Cir. 1961), *cert. denied*, 368 U.S. 939 (1961); *Seven Up, supra*. Should it make a difference whether the products are non-competitive? *See James Burrough, supra* Note (1); *Polaroid Corp. v. Polarad Electronics Corp.*, 287 F.2d 492 (2d Cir. 1961).

(2) The Trademark Trial and Appeal Board will consider "evidence of laches, estoppel, or acquiescence as a factor in determining the issue of likelihood of confusion or mistake or deception only if there is a reasonable doubt that such a likelihood exists." *White Heather Distillers Ltd. v. American Distilling Co.*, 200 U.S.P.Q. 466, 469 (T.T.A.B. 1978). *Accord: CBS, Inc. v. Man's Day Publishing Co.*, 205 U.S.P.Q. 470, 475 (T.T.A.B. 1980); *Richdel, Inc. v. Mathews Co.*, 190 U.S.P.Q. 37, 41 (T.T.A.B. 1976). Is this an appropriate resolution of the potential conflict created by the public interest in avoiding source confusion and the equitable rights of a trademark user who has relied on the silence of another in building up its business? Should laches and acquiescence begin to run when the opposer or cancellation petitioner first had knowledge of the alleged infringer's *use of the mark*, or knowledge of its attempt to obtain a registration? In 1991, the Federal Circuit held that laches in registration proceedings begins to run from the time of awareness of the *application to register* the mark, since that is the point at which a party begins to acquire rights to which an objection in the Patent and Trademark Office could be made. *National Cable Television Ass'n v. America Cinema Editors, Inc.*, 937 F.2d 1572, 1581 (Fed. Cir. 1991). That may be true for acquiescence as well. *Cf. Coach House Restaurant v. Coach & Six Restaurants, Inc.*, 934 F.2d 1551 (11th Cir. 1991) (distinguishing between acquiescence to use and acquiescence to registration).

(3) The basic elements of laches are (a) that plaintiff had actual or constructive knowledge of defendant's use of its marks, (b) that plaintiff inexcusably delayed in taking action with respect thereto, and (c) that defendant detrimentally relied upon plaintiff's inaction or otherwise would be inequitably prejudiced were plaintiff permitted to assert its rights at the time of filing suit. (*See Cuban Cigar Brands, supra* Note (1) at 198.)

(a) There has been some debate as to the proper standard by which to assess the first element of knowledge. *Compare Armco, Inc. v. Armco Burglar Alarm Co., Inc.*, 693 F.2d 1155, 1161 (5th Cir. 1982) (" 'knew or should have known' is a logical implementation of the duty to police one's mark") *with Georgia-Pacific Corp. v. Great Plains Bag Co.*, 614 F.2d 757 (C.C.P.A. 1980) (actual knowledge of the trademark use must be shown). "Knowledge" may be derived from the constructive notice of another party's actions. For example, a corporation may have imputed to it the knowledge of lower echelon employees. In *Georgia-Pacific, supra*, the court found that while knowledge of mark usage gained by bookkeepers and dock workers would not be so imputed, the knowledge of professional salespersons would be, since they were present in the marketplace and cognizant of sales factors which included the protection of goodwill. *Cf. Plasticolor Molded Products v. Ford Motor Co.*, 698 F. Supp. 199, 202–03 (C.D. Cal. 1988) (ten years of infringement by licensee but no evidence of licensor knowledge). Should a successor in rights to a mark be charged with the knowledge possessed by his predecessor? *Charvet S.A. v. Dominique France, Inc.*, 568 F. Supp. 470 (S.D. N.Y. 1983), *aff'd*, 736 F.2d

846 (2d Cir. 1984). What effect should the constructive notice provision of the Lanham Act have on the issue of laches when the defendant's mark has been registered under the Act? *Compare Carter-Wallace, Inc. v. Proctor & Gamble Co.*, 434 F.2d 794 (9th Cir. 1970) *with Valmor Prods. Co. v. Standard Prods. Corp.*, 464 F.2d 200 (1st Cir. 1972). *See also E-Systems, Inc. v. Monitek, Inc.*, 720 F.2d 604 (9th Cir. 1983), in which plaintiff had constructive notice of the claim of ownership when defendant registered its trademark, but delayed six years in filing suit.

(b) Almost any length of time can constitute inexcusable delay, depending upon the circumstances and the resultant prejudice to the defendant. A mere lapse of time alone will not normally constitute laches, *Jordan K. Rand, Ltd. v. Lazoff Bros., Inc.*, 537 F. Supp. 587, 594 (D.P.R. 1982); *Hank Thorp, Inc. v. Minilite, Inc.*, 474 F. Supp. 228, 239 (D. Del. 1979); *Johanna Farms, Inc. v. Citrus Bowl, Inc.*, 199 U.S.P.Q. 16, 28 (E.D.N.Y. 1978); *Cuban Cigar Brands*, *supra* Note (1), at 199. The other elements must be present. What could constitute *excusable* delay? *See Piper Aircraft Corp. v. Way-Aero, Inc.*, 741 F.2d 925, 932 (7th Cir. 1984) (settlement attempts); *Nabisco Brands Inc. v. Conusa Corp.*, 722 F. Supp. 1287, 1292 (M.D.N.C.) (" 'laches should not necessarily always be measured from defendant's very first use of the contested mark, but from the date that defendant's acts first significantly impacted on plaintiff's goodwill and business reputation' ") (quoting McCarthy, *Trademarks and Unfair Competition* § 31.6 at 570 (2d ed. 1984)), *aff'd*, 14 U.S.P.Q.2d 1324 (4th Cir. 1989); *Coco Rico, Inc. v. Fuertes Pasarell*, 738 F. Supp. 613, 619 (D.P.R. 1990) (no laches where plaintiff sued defendants as soon as defendants' use made an impact on plaintiff's sales); *Varitronics Systems, Inc. v. Merlin Equipment, Inc.*, 682 F. Supp. 1203, 1209 (S.D. Fla. 1988) (delay due to negotiations to avoid litigation did not constitute laches); *Gaston's White River Resort v. Rush*, 701 F. Supp. 1431, 1436 (W.D. Ark. 1988) (inactivity by owner's previous attorneys and delay due to seasonal nature of the business did not constitute laches); *Aluminum Fabricating Co. v. Season-All Window Corp.*, 160 F. Supp. 41 (S.D.N.Y. 1957), *aff'd*, 259 F.2d 314 (2d Cir. 1958) (absence of competition between the parties at the time of knowledge of use); *Haviland & Co. v. Johann Haviland China Corp.*, 269 F. Supp. 928 (S.D.N.Y. 1967) (de minimis sales by defendant). *See also* the discussion on progressive encroachment in Chapter 5, *supra*.

In *NAACP v. NAACP Legal Defense Fund*, 559 F. Supp. 1337 (D.D.C. 1983), the court found that the history of the parties' relationship, the fact that plaintiff never misled defendant as to its objections to the trademark use, and plaintiff's understandable unwillingness to initiate a divisive lawsuit all made the delay excusable. The appellate court reversed, finding that thirteen years of concurrent use without any ongoing settlement negotiations constituted laches, barring plaintiff's suit. *NAACP v. NAACP Legal Defense Fund*, 753 F.2d 131 (D.C. Cir. 1985), *cert. denied*, 105 S. Ct. 3489 (1985). In *Cuban Cigar, supra*, delay was excusable where the Castro takeover in Cuba forced plaintiff to rebuild its business elsewhere, and to litigate its trademark rights for ten years. *See also Hank Thorp, supra*, and *Johanna Farms, supra*. *Compare Saratoga Vichy*

Spring Co., supra Note (1), in which the court found that despite the fact that the mark was not being used by defendant's predecessor during the period of delay, plaintiff knew the mark was in the process of being revived and should have given warning of any objections, *and Charvet, S.A., supra* Note (3)(a), in which the court stated that "it is fatuous to suggest that year in and year out desultory conversations, some occurring during chance meetings, which achieve no result and with each party adhering to its position, excuses [sic] delay."

In *Tandy Corp. v. Malone & Hyde, Inc.*, 769 F.2d 362 (6th Cir. 1985), the court took the unusual position that the "analagous" statute of limitations should be applied to laches claims in trademark cases, raising a presumption that "an action is barred if not brought within the period of the statute of limitations and is alive if brought within the period." 768 F.2d at 365. Applying the three-year Tennessee statute for "tortious injury to property," it then reversed the lower court's denial of all relief based of laches, finding plaintiff's "32-month delay may be evidence of corporate indecision but it is not so unreasonable as to overcome the presumption afforded by the analagous 3-year statute." 769 F.2d at 366. Is there anything wrong with this approach? *Cf. Blue Cross & Blue Shield Assn. v. Group Hospitalization & Medical Services, Inc.*, 744 F. Supp. 700, 717 (E.D. Va.) (Lanham Act claims not barred by the applicable Illinois statute of limitations, since defendant's unlawful conduct was ongoing), *aff'd in part and remanded in part*, 911 F.2d 720 (4th Cir. 1990).

(c) A showing of detrimental reliance by the party asserting the defense of laches is the final requirement. Spending great sums of money on advertising was not enough of a showing of such reliance under the circumstances in *Hank Thorp, supra* Note (3)(b), and *Hurricane Fence Co. v. A-1 Hurricane Fence Co.*, 468 F. Supp. 975 (S.D. Ala. 1979). Increased sales during the period of delay were enough in *Armco, Inc., supra* Note (3)(a), and *Georgia-Pacific, supra* Note (3)(a), but not enough in *Cuban Cigar Brands, supra* Note (1), the court attributing the increase to actions not taken in reliance on plaintiff's silence. The purchasing of parts and equipment to enable the expansion of business and the incurrence of additional potential liability during the period of delay were enough in *Whitaker Corp. v. Execuair Corp.*, 736 F.2d 1341, 1347 (9th Cir. 1984), but expanded use of the allegedly infringing mark was not enough in *Citibank N.A. v. Citibanc Group, Inc.*, 724 F.2d 1540, 1546–47 (11th Cir. 1984); the defendants in *Citibank* were held not to have relied on plaintiff's delay where the expansion was "in the face of plaintiff's constant complaints." *See also American International Group, Inc. v. American International Bank*, 926 F.2d 829, 833 (9th Cir. 1991) (defendant failed to show injury or prejudice). In *Houston Sports Assn., supra* Note (1), at 1181, however, the court observed that a prolonged delay alone may give rise to a presumption of prejudice. One reason for this might be the law's dislike for stale claims; evidence favorable to the defendant may be expected to be lost or destroyed when prolonged delay occurs. *See Charvet S.A., supra* Note (3)(a), at 976.

(4) Are there any other factors which a court should consider in deciding whether laches constitutes a valid defense? *See Carl Zeis Stiftung v. V.E.B. Carl Zeiss, Jena,*

293 F. Supp. 892, 917 (S.D.N.Y. 1968), *aff'd*, 433 F.2d 686 (2d Cir. 1970) *cert. denied*, 403 U.S. 905 (1971), which lists the following among the relevant factors in the determination: (1) strength and value of the trademark rights asserted; (2) plaintiff's diligence in protecting the mark; (3) harm resulting to plaintiff if relief is denied; (4) good or bad faith of the infringer; (5) competitiveness of the uses of the mark; (6) extent of harm suffered by junior user because of the senior user's delay.

Other factors

> Where the owner of the trademark fails to take any action for many years to enforce a relatively weak trademark against a junior user who has proceeded innocently to use the same or similar mark on non-competing goods in which he has invested large sums, so that denial of relief would cause relatively little harm to the senior user in contrast to the serious prejudice that would result to defendant, relief will be denied.

Id. at 917. *See also E-Systems, Inc. v. Monitek, supra* Note (3)(a) (*Carl Zeis Stiftung* factors, on balance, favor defendant; injunctive relief denied). *Conan Properties, Inc. v. Conans Pizza*, 752 F.2d 145, 152 (5th Cir. 1985) (Laches barred relief only in Austin, Texas area). *Compare* Judge Posner's summarization in his concurrence in *Piper Aircraft*, *supra* Note (3)(b), 741 F.2d at 938: "The judge is supposed to balance the impact on the defendant of the plaintiff's delay against the reasonableness of the plaintiff's having waited as long as he did to sue and the strength of the plaintiff's case," *and* Professor McCarthy's statement that "Estoppel by laches = delay × prejudice." McCarthy, *Trademarks and Unfair Competition* § 31.5 at p. 565 (3d ed. 1992).

(5) Delay in assertion of rights also may result in denial of preliminary injunctive relief. In *Citibank, N.A. v. Citytrust*, 756 F.2d 273, 276 (2d Cir. 1985), the court explained:

> Preliminary injunctions are generally granted under the theory that there is an urgent need for speedy action to protect the plaintiffs' rights. Delay in seeking enforcement of those rights, however, tends to indicate at least a re-duced need for such drastic, speedy action. . . . . Significant delay in applying for injunctive relief in a trademark case tends to neutralize any presumption that infringement alone will cause irreparable harm pending trial, and such delay alone may justify denial of a preliminary injunction.

The analysis of delay in the preliminary injunction context is different from that at trial. As the court observed in *Majorica S.A. v. R.H. Macy & Co.*, 762 F.2d 7 (2d Cir. 1985):

> Lack of diligence, standing alone, is insufficient to support a claim of laches; the party asserting the claim also must establish that it was prejudiced by the delay. [Citation]. Lack of diligence, standing alone. may, however, preclude the granting of preliminary injunctive relief, because it goes primarily to the issue of irreparable harm rather than occasional prejudice.

Accord GTE Corp. v. Williams, 731 F.2d 676 (10th Cir. 1984). *See also* Raskopf & Edelman, *Delay in Filing Preliminary Injunction Motions: How Long Is Too Long?*, 80 Trademark Rep. 36 (1990).

(6) Acquiescence constitutes a ground for denial of relief where the plaintiff's conduct amounts to an express or implied assurance that the plaintiff will not assert trademark rights against the defendant. *See, e.g., Carl Zeiss Stiftung, supra* Note (4), at 917. Laches imports a merely passive assent, while acquiescence implies active assent. For what was termed "a classic example of acquiescence," see *CBS, Inc. v. Man's Day Publishing Co.*, 205 U.S.P.Q. 470 (T.T.A.B. 1980). Could the courts correctly imply acquiescence where the plaintiff remains silent with knowledge of defendant's actions for an extended period of time? *See* Calimafde, *Trademarks and Unfair Competition* § 15.10 (1970).

§ 7.03   Unclean Hands

COCA-COLA CO. v. KOKE CO. OF AMERICA

United States Supreme Court
254 U.S. 143 (1920)

HOLMES, J.

This is a bill in equity brought by the Coca-Cola Company to prevent the infringement of its trade-mark Coca-Cola and unfair competition with it in its business of making and selling the beverage for which the trade-mark is used. The District Court gave the plaintiff a decree. 235 Fed. Rep. 408. This was reversed by the Circuit Court of Appeals. 255 Fed. Rep. 894. Subsequently a writ of certiorari was granted by this Court. 250 U.S. 637.

It appears that after the plaintiff's predecessors in title had used the mark for some years it was registered under the Act of Congress of March 3, 1881, c. 138, 21 Stat. 502, and again under the Act of February 20, 1905, c. 592, 33 Stat. 724. Both the Courts below agree that subject to the one question to be considered the plaintiff has a right to equitable relief. Whatever may have been its original weakness, the mark for years has acquired a secondary significance and has indicated the plaintiff's product alone. It is found that defendant's mixture is made and sold in imitation of the plaintiff's and that the word Koke was chosen for the purpose of reaping the benefits of the advertising done by the plaintiff and of selling the imitation as and for the plaintiff's goods. The only obstacle found by the Circuit Court of Appeals in the way of continuing the injunction granted below was its opinion that the trade-mark in itself and the advertisements accompanying it made such fraudulent representations to the public that the plaintiff had lost its claim to any help from the Court. That is the question upon which the writ of certiorari was granted and the main one that we shall discuss.

Of course, a man is not to be protected in the use of a device the very purpose and effect of which is to swindle the public. But the defects of a plaintiff do not offer a very broad ground for allowing another to swindle him. The defense relied on here should be scrutinized with a critical eye. The main point is this: Before 1900 the beginning of the good will was more or less helped by the presence of cocaine, a drug that, like alcohol or caffein or opium, may be described as a deadly poison or as a valuable item of the pharmacopoea according to the rhetorical purposes in view. The amount seems to have been very small, but it may have been enough to begin a bad habit and after the Food and Drug Act of June 30, 1906, c. 3915, 34 Stat. 768, if not earlier, long before this suit was brought, it was eliminated from the plaintiff's compound. Coca leaves still are used, to be sure, but after they have been subjected to a drastic process that removes from them every characteristic substance except a little tannin and still less chlorophyl. The cola nut, at best, on its side furnishes but a very small portion of the caffein, which now is the only element that has appreciable effect. That comes mainly from other sources. It is argued that the continued use of the name imports a representation that has ceased to be true and that the representation is reinforced by a picture of coca leaves and cola nuts upon the label and by advertisements, which however were many years before this suit was brought, that the drink is an "ideal nerve tonic and stimulant," etc., and that thus the very thing sought to be protected is used as a fraud.

The argument does not satisfy us. We are dealing here with a popular drink not with a medicine, and although what has been said might suggest that its attraction lay in producing the expectation of a toxic effect the facts point to a different conclusion. Since 1900 the sales have increased at a very great rate corresponding to a like increase in advertising. The name now characterizes a beverage to be had at almost any soda fountain. It means a single thing coming from a single source, and well known to the community. It hardly would be too much to say that the drink characterizes the name as much as the name the drink. In other words Coca-Cola probably means to most persons the plaintiff's familiar product to be had everywhere rather than a compound of particular substances. Although the fact did not appear in *United States v. Coca Cola Co.*, 241 U.S. 265, 289, we see no reason to doubt that, as we have said, it has acquired a secondary meaning in which perhaps the product is more emphasized than the producer but to which the producer is entitled. The coca leaves and whatever of cola nut is employed may be used to justify the continuance of the name or they may affect the flavor as the plaintiff contends, but before this suit was brought the plaintiff had advertised to the public that it must not expect and would not find cocaine, and had eliminated everything tending to suggest cocaine effects except the name and the picture of the leaves and nuts, which probably conveyed little or nothing to most who saw it. It appears to us that it would be going too far to deny the plaintiff relief against a palpable fraud because possibly here and there an ignorant person might call for the drink with the hope for incipient cocaine intoxication. The plaintiff's position must be judged by the facts as they were when the suit was begun, not by the facts of a different condition and an earlier time.

The decree of the District Court restrains the defendant from using the word Dope. The plaintiff illustrated in a very striking way the fact that the word is one of the most featureless known even to the language of those who are incapable of discriminating speech. In some places it would be used to call for Coca-Cola. It equally would have been used to call for anything else having about it a faint aureole of poison. It does not suggest Coca-Cola by similarity and whatever objections there may be to its use, objections which the plaintiff equally makes to its application to

Coca Cola, we see no ground on which the plaintiff can claim a personal right to exclude the defendant from using it.

The product including the coloring matter is free to all who can make it if no extrinsic deceiving element is present. The injunction should be modified also in this respect.

Decree reversed.

Decree of District Court modified and affirmed.

HÄAGEN-DAZS, INC. v. FRUSEN GLÄDJÉ LTD.

United States District Court, Southern District of New York
493 F. Supp. 73 (1980)

DUFFY, DISTRICT JUDGE.

Successful commercial marketing has many rewards. Most important to the marketer are the financial rewards to be reaped. However, when a manufacturer develops a novel marketing approach — a commercial concept meeting with a receptive consumer — the concept is often imitated. This is precisely what occurred in the case at bar.

Plaintiff, Häagen-Dazs, Inc., is the producer of Häagen-Dazs ice cream. Häagen-Dazs has come to be known as a premium ice cream product. The defendants are the producers and distributors of Frusen Glädjé ice cream which, although a recent entrant into the ice cream market, is advertised as a premium ice cream product.

Plaintiff commenced the instant suit charging defendants with unfair competition in violation of the Lanham Act, 15 U.S.C. § 1125(a), and New York State Law. In addition, plaintiff charges that defendants are attempting to palm their product off as that of the plaintiff.

The essence of plaintiff's claim is that defendants have packaged their product in such a way as to "cash in on the commercial magnetism of the exclusive marketing technique developed . . . by the family which owns and operates Häagen-Dazs." Plaintiff's Memorandum at 2. In particular, plaintiff focuses upon five features on defendants' ice cream container which it charges were taken directly from its ice cream container in an effort to appeal to Häagen-Dazs customers and confuse them into believing that defendants' product is related to the Häagen-Dazs line. These features are: (i) the phraseology used in reciting the ingredients of the product in issue; (ii) a recitation of the artificial ingredients not contained in the product; (iii) the manner in which the product is to be eaten in order to enhance its flavor; (iv) a two-word germanic-sounding name having an umlaut over the letter "a" [ä]; and, (v) a map of Scandinavia.

Plaintiff concludes that defendants have intentionally packaged their product in a manner calculated to trade upon "plaintiff's unique Scandinavian marketing theme." Transcript at 4–5.

Plaintiff has now moved for a preliminary injunction to prevent defendants' continued use of the allegedly infringing container. . . .

. . . .

There is no question that the names in issue, Häagen-Dazs and Frusen Glädjé, are clearly distinguishable. It is true that both names contain two words to identify an ice cream product, but so do the names "Louis Sherry" and "Dolly Madison." Plaintiff cannot hope to base its claim of infringement upon such a fortuitous similarity. It is also true that the names in issue seem to be of Swedish origin and, as is appropriate in that language, an umlaut appears over the letter "a". This, however, is a matter of grammar and not a basis upon which a claim of infringement may hinge.

This suit is grounded in plaintiff's failure to appreciate the difference between an attempt to trade off the good will of another and the legitimate imitation of an admittedly effective marketing technique. In fact, plaintiff attempts by this law suit to significantly broaden its protected "trademark" to include its so-called "unique Scandinavian marketing theme." To do so, however, would work a grave injustice not only upon the defendants in this case, but also upon late entrants into a given product market. For example, when consumers became increasingly aware of the ingredients in food products, producers rushed to extoll the virtues of their "all natural" products. It would be ludicrous, however, to suggest that in our free enterprise system, one producer and not another is permitted to take advantage of the "all natural" marketing approach to enhance consumer reception of its product.

. . . .

I turn finally to consider plaintiff's allegations that defendants' container is intended to deceive the public into believing that their product is made and/or sold in Sweden. In particular, plaintiff charges:

> defendants claim their ice cream is manufactured "under the authority" of a Swedish corporation, although Frusen Glädjé is produced in Pennsylvania by an American company and is not sold in Sweden at all; defendants fail to reveal the actual manufacturer, packer or distributor, all of which are American companies, which violates the applicable statutory labelling requirements; defendants also employ three lines of Swedish language on their container to add to the false impression that their product is sold or made in Sweden; and the English translation appearing beneath the Swedish language states that the recipe for Frusen Glädjé comes "From Old Sweden," whereas, in fact, the recipe is American.

Although defendants dispute the accuracy of these charges, even if true they simply do not advance plaintiff's case at all. On the contrary, since plaintiff itself has attempted to package its product in such a way as to give the impression that it is of Scandinavian origin, although it too is, in fact, of domestic origin, it is guilty of the same deceptive trade practices of which it accuses defendants. In short, since plaintiff's hands are similarly unclean, they may not secure equitable relief simply because defendants' hands may be a shade or two less clean.

Accordingly, plaintiff's motion for a preliminary injunction is denied.

NOTES ON UNCLEAN HANDS

Narrow defense [handwritten marginal note]

(1) As indicated by Mr. Justice Holmes in the *Coca-Cola* case, *supra*, unclean hands is a rather narrow defense in trade identity cases: "But the defects of a plaintiff do not offer a very broad ground for another to swindle him." The effect of the defense is likewise limited by the court's concern that the public not be deceived. *But see Holeproof Hosiery Co. v. Wallach Bros.*, 172 F. 859 (2d Cir. 1909), wherein the court held HOLEPROOF was not so misdescriptive of hosiery as to constitute unclean hands, although holes may appear. *Compare Worden v. California Fig Syrup Co.*, 187 U.S. 516 (1903). What is the correct solution to the dilemma of the courts in this area? Should the courts sustain unclean hands or other equitable defenses and thereby allow confusion as to source to the public's as well as the plaintiff's detriment? In *Bell v. Streetwise Records, Ltd.*, 761 F.2d 67, 75–76 (1st Cir. 1985), rights to the name of the singing group NEW EDITION were in dispute. There the lower court's denial of a preliminary injunction on the ground of unclean hands was reversed, the appellate court stating:

> [T]he court entered a decree that, in effect, left both plaintiffs and defendant free to use the trade name. Even if this result were fair as between the parties, it is not fair in respect to the public. It creates the very "source" confusion that legal trademark, and trade name, doctrine developed to avoid. When arguing parties are, in a sense. both responsible for the success of a name, a court may find it difficult to decide which, in fact, "owns" the name; the temptation may be great to say "both own it" or try to "divide" the name among them. The public interest, however, normally requires an exclusive award. . . . In short, we do not view the "unclean hands" doctrine as sufficient, on the facts of this case, to justify continuation of public confusion.   •

On remand plaintiff's motion for preliminary injunction was granted. *Bell v. Streetwise Records, Ltd.*, 640 F. Supp. 575 (D. Mass. 1986). *See generally* 1 Gilson, *Trademark Protection and Practice* § 8.12[3][a] (1993 ed.); McCarthy, *Trademark Protection and Unfair Competition* § 31:17 (3d ed. 1992); Note, *The Besmirched Plaintiff and the Confused Public: Unclean Hands in Trademark Infringement*, 65 Colum. L. Rev. 109 (1965); Chafee, *Coming Into Equity With Clean Hands*, 47 Mich. L. Rev. 877 (1949).

(2) In *United States Jaycees v. Philadelphia Jaycees*, 639 F.2d 134 (3d Cir. 1981), the lower court's holding that enforcement of plaintiff's trademark rights would unconstitutionally aid the enforcement of its sexually discriminatory membership policy was overturned on appeal because of an insubstantial relationship between the two. However, in *United States Jaycees v. Cedar Rapids Jaycees*, 794 F.2d 379 (8th Cir. 1986), the Eighth Circuit refused to uphold plaintiff's attempt to revoke defendant's license after defendant began admitting women as members. Noting that

plaintiff had subsequently amended its by-laws to allow women members, the court stated, "we agree that USJ normally has a right to choose who uses its trademark, but disagree that the courts must in all instances assist and enforce those choices when the only purpose to be served is punishment of an otherwise productive and conforming member simply because the member was on the prevailing side in a past internal policy dispute." In *Kiwanis International v. Ridgewood Kiwanis Club*, 627 F. Supp. 1381 (D.N.J. 1986), the court was even more adamant in refusing to extend the court's protection to the licensor's "blatant and admitted sexist attitude." "What is truly at issue here is whether Kiwanis can, directly or indirectly, enforce its policy against women with the imprimatur of the court. This opinion concluded that it cannot. Kiwanis' trademark rights are subject to the right of women to be free of discrimination, as indeed they should be." (627 F. Supp. at 1395).

(3) Generally, misconduct that constituted unclean hands has involved either misrepresentations as to the quality and ingredients of the product or service, its source or geographical origin, or its efficacy. In order to be recognized, the basis for the claim of unclean hands normally must be directly related to the trademark rights at issue. *See also* the discussion on Trademark Misuse in the section on Antitrust Violations, *infra. See generally* Derenberg, *Trademark Protection and Unfair Trading* § 60 (1936). Should use of the ® (federal registration) symbol when federal registration has not been granted be grounds for applying the doctrine of unclean hands in infringement cases? *See Shatel Corp. v. Mao Ta Lumber & Yacht Corp.*, 697 F.2d 1352, 1355 (11th Cir. 1983), in which the court stated: "Because misunderstandings about the use of federal registration symbols are common . . . courts have been reluctant to find unclean hands where the misuse of the registration symbol was negligent or immaterial to the litigation." *Compare Ginseng-Up Corp. v. American Ginseng Co.*, 215 U.S.P.Q. 471 (S.D.N.Y. 1981), where the alleged misrepresentations in plaintiff's application for trademark registration were found immaterial since the action was based on common law trademark rights.

§ 7.04 Antitrust Violations

[A] Introduction

The antitrust laws are designed to preserve and promote competition in the marketplace. The resulting benefits from such competition are believed to include higher quality goods and services and lower prices for the consumer. A monopolization, or attempted monopolization, of the market for a product may conflict with the goals the antitrust laws are designed to serve. The applicable statutes provide as follows:

Section 1 of the Sherman Act (15 U.S.C. § 1):

> Every contract, combination, in the form of trust or otherwise, or conspiracy, in restraint of trade or commerce among the several States, or with foreign nations, is declared to be illegal . . .

Section 2 of the Sherman Act (15 U.S.C. § 2):

Every person who shall monopolize, or attempt to monopolize, or combine or conspire with any other person or persons, to monopolize any part of the trade or commerce among the several States, or with foreign nations, shall be deemed guilty of a felony, and, on conviction thereof, shall be punishable by a fine not exceeding $10,000,000 if a corporation, or, if any other person, $350,000, or by imprisonment not exceeding three years, or by both said punishments, in the discretion of the court.

Section 5 of the Federal Trade Commission Act (15 U.S.C. § 45):

(a)(1) Unfair methods of competition in or affecting commerce, and unfair or deceptive acts or practices in or affecting commerce, are declared unlawful.

Section 3 of the Clayton Act (15 U.S.C. § 14):

It shall be unlawful for any person engaged in commerce, in the course of such commerce, to lease or make a sale or contract for sale of goods, wares, merchandise, machinery, supplies or other commodities . . . on the condition, agreement or understanding that the lessee or purchaser thereof shall not use or deal in the goods, wares, merchandise, machinery, supplies or other commodities of a competitor or competitors of the lessor or seller, where the effect . . . may be to substantially lessen competition or tend to create a monopoly in any line of commerce.

Civil damages and injuctive relief are authorized under 15 U.S.C. § 15(a) and § 26.

Normally the objectives of trademark and antitrust law are complementary.

The antitrust laws require competition, not piracy. The essence of competition is the ability of competing products to obtain public recognition based on their own individual merit. A product has not won on its own merit if the real reason the public purchases it is that the public believes it is obtaining the product of another company.

Standard Oil (Ky.) v. Humble Oil & Refining Co., 363 F.2d 945, 954 (5th Cir. 1966). *cert. denied*, 385 U.S. 1007 (1967). In some instances, however, agreements, licenses, distribution controls, and other limitations involving trademark use may be held to be unlawfully anticompetitive restraints of trade. Thus, a familiarity with antitrust concepts is essential in the trade identity field. *See generally* Holmes, *Intellectual Property and Antitrust Law* (1993 ed.).

The fundamental test of antitrust violations is whether the conduct in issue promotes or suppresses competition in the marketplace. The Supreme Court traditionally has used one of two analytical tests to determine whether specific commercial conduct is violative of the antitrust laws.

[T]here are certain agreements or practices which because of their pernicious effect on competition and lack of any redeeming virtue are conclusively presumed to be unreasonable and therefore illegal without elaborate inquiry as to the precise harm they have caused or the business excuse for their use. Such conduct is deemed "illegal *per se*."

Northern Pacific Ry. Co. v. United States, 356 U.S. 1, 5 (1958). The categories of trade restraints considered per se unlawful include horizontal price fixing (agreements among competitors at the same market level to fix prices), market divisions among competitors, and some group boycotts. *See, e.g., United States v. Citizens & Southern National Bank*, 422 U.S. 86, 118 (1975) (market divisions); *Northern Pacific Railway Co. v. United States*, 356 U.S. 1, 5 (1958) (price fixing); *Hahn v. Oregon Physicians' Service*, 868 F.2d 1022 (9th Cir. 1988) (price fixing, market divisions, group boycotts), *cert. denied*, 493 U.S. 846 (1989).

[handwritten: Test ②]

The second test of legality, the "rule of reason," requires more extensive analysis by a court to determine "whether the restraint imposed is such as merely regulates and perhaps thereby promotes competition or whether it is such as may suppress or even destroy competition." *Chicago Board of Trade v. United States*, 246 U.S. 231, 238 (1918). *See* Handler, *Trade-Marks and Anti-Trust Laws*, 38 Trademark Rep. 387 (1948); Timberg, *Trademarks, Monopoly and the Restraint of Competition*, 68 Harv. L. Rev. 814, 898–908 (1955); Hill, *Antitrust Violations as a Defense to Trademark Infringement*, 71 Trademark Rep. 148 (1981); McCarthy, *Trademarks and Unfair Competition*, Ch. 31 (3d ed. 1992).

Many states have state antitrust statutes which authorize both governmental and private enforcement. *See generally* ABA Antitrust Section, *State Antitrust Practice and Statutes* (1991). Many states also have "little FTC Acts" which authorize private causes of action. *See, e.g.,* 85 Ill. Comp. Stat. 510.

[B] Trademark Misuse

[handwritten: Trade identity as monopoly]

Trade identity litigation is occasionally defended on the ground that the plaintiff is trying to monopolize the market for the *product* via misuse of its rights in its trade identity. Like any other unclean hands defense, *see* § 7.03, *supra,* trade identity misuse must be directly related to the trade identity rights in issue for the defense to be recognized. For many years the courts rejected the antitrust defense, reasoning that the trade identity device itself either was not or could not be directly used as the prime instrument to effectuate the antitrust activity. More recently the courts have held that the burden of establishing direct misuse is a heavy but not insuperable one. In *Carl Zeiss Stiftung v. V.E.B. Carl Zeiss, Jena*, 298 F. Supp. 1309 (S.D.N.Y. 1969), defendants in an action for trademark infringement alleged that plaintiffs used their ZEISS camera trademarks in violation of the antitrust laws in a variety of ways, including illegal combinations, territorial restraints, tying, and price discrimination. The court stated that while an antitrust misuse defense may be available, "an essential element of the antitrust misuse defense in a trademark case is proof that the mark itself has been the basic and fundamental vehicle required and used to accomplish the violation." The court concluded that defendants failed to establish that plaintiff had used the ZEISS trademark to violate the antitrust laws. Similarly, in *Coca-Cola Co. v. Howard Johnson Co.*, 386 F. Supp. 330, 335–6 (N.D. Ga. 1974), the court rejected such a defense because an "immediate and necessary relationship" between plaintiff's passing off claim and the alleged antitrust violation was lacking; and in *Rolls-Royce Motors Ltd. v. A & A Fiberglass, Inc.*, 428 F. Supp. 689, 697 (N.D. Ga. 1976), the court summarized its view as follows: "[u]nder this test, based

[handwritten: trademark must be primary vehicle for misuse]

on judicial reluctance to permit every case for trademark infringement to expand into a major antitrust action, the antitrust defenses must fall." *See also Alberto-Culver Co. v. Andrea Dumon, Inc.*, 295 F. Supp. 1155, 1159 (N.D. Ill. 1969).

How can a means for trade identity be more than ancillary to an antitrust violation? In *Domed Stadium Hotel, Inc. v. Holiday Inns, Inc.*, 732 F.2d 480 (5th Cir. 1984), a franchisee alleged that Holiday Inns was attempting to monopolize and restrain trade in the market for Holiday Inn hotel rooms. In granting Holiday Inns summary judgment the court stated that the relevant product market was not Holiday Inn rooms, but hotel rooms generally, and that "absent exceptional market conditions, one brand in a market of competing brands cannot constitute a relevant product market." 732 F.2d at 488. *Compare Kellogg Co. v. National Biscuit Co.*, 71 F.2d 662 (2d Cir. 1934). In that case Nabisco purchased the Shredded Wheat Company and sought to protect shredded wheat as a valid trademark. Plaintiff alleged that Nabisco directed its salesmen to slander plaintiff's product, threatened distributors who carried plaintiff's product, and brought suit against plaintiff to stop plaintiff's manufacture of shredded wheat. The court denied defendant's motion to dismiss the complaint and stated the test as follows, 71 F.2d at 666: "the principal question at trial will be whether the defendant has attempted to monopolize the trade in shredded wheat or only to establish exclusive rights in certain trade names, trademarks and shapes of the manufactured product." In *Drop Dead Co. v. S.C. Johnson & Son, Inc.*, 326 F.2d 87, 96 (9th Cir. 1963), the court rejected appellant's antitrust defense and indicated that appellee's registration of multiple marks for wax products, mass advertising of its trademarks, mass sales, and bringing of infringement suits to protect its trademarks "constitute the sort of aggressive competition and promotion that the antitrust laws seek to protect particularly within the limits of lawful monopolies granted by Congress 'in its wisdom.' " Thus, in *La Maur, Inc. v. Alberto-Culver Co.*, 496 F.2d 618 (8th Cir. 1974), the court stated that the owner of a trademark is entitled to protect its mark even if it strengthens or creates the potential monopoly which a trademark registration affords the registrant. Similarly, in *Procter & Gamble Co. v. Johnson & Johnson, Inc.*, 485 F. Supp. 1185 (S.D.N.Y. 1979), the court found plaintiff's "Minor Brands [token use] Program" was not anticompetitive, and in *Coca-Cola Co. v. Overland, Inc.*, 692 F.2d 1250 (9th Cir. 1982), the court stated that Coca-Cola Company's policy of bringing trademark infringement suits against retailers who substituted other brands for COCA-COLA was not coercive or anticompetitive. In *Professional Real Estate Investors, Inc. v. Columbia Pictures*, 113 S. Ct. 1920 (1993), a copyright infringement action, the Supreme Court held that, regardless of a plaintiff's possible subjective anticompetitive intent, an objectively reasonable effort to litigate cannot constitute a "sham" lawsuit creating antitrust liability.

Compare Phi Delta Theta Fraternity v. J.A. Buchroeder & Co., 251 F. Supp. 968 (W.D. Mo. 1966), where defendants alleged that L.G. Balfour Co., a jewelry manufacturer, had violated the antitrust laws by securing exclusive jeweler licenses from college fraternities and sororities and thereby using federal trademark registrations of their insignia to force local chapters of the fraternities and sororities to honor the exclusive arrangement with Balfour. The court held that the stipulated facts, if proven, showed Balfour had violated the antitrust laws and that the violation was an affirmative defense to allegations of trademark infringement since the trademark itself was the instrument which effectuated the antitrust activity. In *Timken Roller Bearing Co. v. United States*, 341 U.S. 593 (1951), Timken, an Ohio corporation, combined with its British and French subsidiaries to eliminate competition in the manufacture and sale of antifriction bearings. The court rejected appellant's argument that its actions were merely reasonable steps taken to implement a trademark licensing program. The court stated, 341 U.S. at 598: "Furthermore, while a trademark merely affords protection to a name, the agreements in the present case went far beyond protection of the name TIMKEN and provided for control of the manufacture and sale of antifriction bearings whether carrying the mark or not." *See American Aloe Corp. v. Aloe Creme Labs, Inc.*, 420 F.2d 1248 (7th Cir. 1970), *cert. denied*, 398 U.S. 929 (1970) (monopoly); *Radiant Burners, Inc. v. Peoples Gas Light & Coke Co.*, 364 U.S. 656 (1961) (use of a certification mark for an illegal boycott).

See generally Comment, *Use Of A Trademark in Violation of the Antitrust Laws*, 32 N.Y.U. L. Rev. 1002 (1957); Bryan, *Fraud in Trademark Procurement and Maintenance*, 61 Trademark Rep. 1 (1971); Note, *The Besmirched Plaintiff and the Confused Public: Unclean Hands in Trademark Infringement*, 65 Colum. L. Rev. 109, 114–115 (1965); Lunsford, Jr., *Trademarks and the Antitrust Law, Complete Compatibility — No Divorce Needed*, 65 Trademark Rep. 463 (1975); Flinn, *Basic Antitrust Problem Areas and Their Significance for Trademark Owners and Practitioners*, 67 Trademark Rep. 255 (1977); Lavey, *Patents, Copyrights and Trademarks as Sources of Market Power in Antitrust Cases*, 27 Antitrust Bull. 433 (1982).

[C] License and Distribution Controls

[1] Exclusive Dealing

A supplier generally has the right to deal only with those with whom it wishes to deal. As long as it does so independently, it may refuse to deal with anyone. *Monsanto Co. v. Spray-Rite Service Corp.*, 465 U.S. 752 (1984); *H.L. Moore Drug Exchange v. Eli Lilly & Co.*, 662 F.2d 935, 946 (2d Cir. 1981), *cert. denied*, 459 U.S. 880 (1982) ("We need not consider whether Lilly's action was motivated by anticompetitive reasons, since a unilateral decision to terminate, no matter what the reason, does not constitute a violation of the antitrust laws"). Should a supplier of a trademarked product, however, ever be able to prevent its customers from purchasing the product of a competitor? Arrangements which restrict the buyer's ability to purchase similar products from a competitor are termed "exclusive dealing" arrangements. Potentially anticompetitive in their effect, exclusive dealing arrangements are subject to scrutiny under §§ 1 and 2 of the Sherman Act, § 3 of the Clayton Act, and § 5 of the Federal Trade Commission Act. Exclusive dealing arrangements are not *per se* unlawful. The Supreme Court has declared that proper analysis of such arrangements under the Sherman and Clayton Act requires:

> weigh[ing] the probable effect of the contract on the relevant area of effective competition, taking into account the relative strength of the parties, the proportionate volume of commerce involved in relation to the total volume of commerce in the relevant market area, and the probable immediate and future

effects which pre-emption of that share of the market might have on effective competition therein.

Tampa Electric Co. v. Nashville Coal Co., 365 U.S. 320. 329 (1961). "The court [in *Tampa Electric*] further emphasized the significance of the possible economic justification for the accused arrangement in light of the legitimate reasons for employing such a device." *Susser v. Carvel Corp.*, 332 F.2d 505, 516 (2d Cir. 1964). In *Jefferson Parish Hospital District No. 2 v. Hyde*, 466 U.S. 2 (1984), which principally was analyzed as a tying case, the court found no violative exclusive dealing in a hospital's exclusive contract with a group of anesthesiologists. Justice O'Connor stated in her concurrence, "Exclusive dealing is an unreasonable restraint on trade only when a significant fraction of buyers or sellers are frozen out of a market by the exclusive deal." 466 U.S. at 45. There, the contract affected "only a small fraction of the markets in which anesthesiologists may sell their services, and a still smaller fraction of the market in which hospitals may secure anesthesiological services." *Id.* at 46–47. Subsequent decisions have upheld exclusive dealing arrangements where distribution channels were not unduly restricted. *See, e.g., Seagood Trading Corp. v. Jerrico, Inc.*, 924 F.2d 1555 (11th Cir. 1991); *Ryko Mfg. Co. v. Edens Services*, 823 F.2d 1215, 1234–35 (8th Cir. 1987), *cert. denied*, 484 U.S. 1026 (1988). In actions for exclusive dealing brought under § 5 of the Federal Trade Commission Act, the Supreme Court has applied a similar standard. The test is whether the exclusive dealing arrangement effectively forecloses competitors from "a significant number of outlets." *Federal Trade Comm'n v. Brown Shoe Co.*, 384 U.S. 316 (1966).

In *Susser v. Carvel Corp.*, *supra*, plaintiffs claimed that Carvel's franchise agreement violated the Sherman and Clayton Acts by requiring trademark licensees to sell only Carvel products. The Second Circuit held (332 F.2d at 517) that the Carvel franchise agreement was not an unlawfully exclusive dealership and was economically justified:

> The requirement that only Carvel products be sold at Carvel outlets derives from the desirability that the public identify each Carvel outlet as one of a chain which offers identical products at a uniform standard of quality. The antitrust laws certainly do not require that the licensor of a trademark permit his licensees to associate with that trademark other products unrelated to those customarily sold under the mark . . . Carvel was not required to accede to the requests of one or another of the dealers that they be permitted to sell Christmas trees or hamburgers, for example, which would have thrust upon Carvel the obligation to acquaint itself with the production and sale of these items so as to establish reasonable quality controls.

[2] Price Controls

The distributor or manufacturer of a trademarked product does not have the right to fix the price at which wholesalers or retailers resell that product. Such "resale price maintenance" is currently prohibited under the antitrust laws. *See United States v. Bausch & Lomb Optical Co.*, 321 U.S. 707, 721 (1944):

> Soft Lite is the distributor of an unpatented article. It sells to its wholesalers at prices satisfactory to itself. Beyond that point it may not project its power

over the prices of its wholesaler customers by agreement. A distributor of a trademarked article may not lawfully limit by agreement, express or implied, the price at which or the persons to whom its purchasers may resell. . . .

In *Carvel*, *supra*, the plaintiffs alleged that the following language in the Carvel franchise manual was unlawful price fixing: "Whenever Carvel recommends a retail price, such recommendation is based upon Carvel's experience concerning all factors that enter into a proper price, but such recommendation is in no manner binding upon the dealer." The court rejected plaintiff's argument and held that "the mere existence of a means whereby retail price levels are recommended is not sufficient to establish a violation of the Sherman Act, unless there is a showing of an attempt to enforce a price structure upon the retail tradesmen." 332 F.2d at 510. Although the rule against resale price agreements has not been overturned, it has been effectively limited for agreements setting *maximum* resale prices because such agreements do not lessen competition and actually benefit consumers by keeping prices down. Accordingly, courts have found the requisite antitrust injury absent in such cases. *See, e.g., Atlanta Richfield Co. v. USA Petroleum Co.*, 495 U.S. 328 (1990) (no antitrust injury to competitor because inability to raise prices benefitted consumers and did not threaten competition). In *Jack Walters & Sons Corp. v. Morton Building, Inc.*, 737 F.2d 698, 708 (7th Cir. 1984), the court held that a manufacturer can advertise a retail price and "take reasonable measures to make sure the advertised price is not exceeded. These measures include trying to persuade dealers to adhere to the advertised price and checking around to make sure they are adhering." It reasoned that otherwise the advertising would mislead consumers, and, while the manufacturer could not require dealer compliance with minimum prices, a maximum price ceiling based on advertising was justifiable.

From 1937 until 1976, the 1937 Miller-Tydings Act and the 1952 McGuire Act created an exception to the antitrust laws for state "fair trade" laws which permitted resale price maintenance of trademarked products. In 1975, the Consumer Goods Pricing Act repealed both the Miller-Tydings and McGuire Acts. After March 11, 1976, all resale price maintenance agreements fell within the scope of the Sherman Act. *See Continental T.V., Inc. v. GTE Sylvania, Inc.*, 433 U.S. 36 (1977).

[3] Tying Arrangements

When a trademark owner forces a customer to purchase a second "tied" product from the trademark owner or owner-approved source in order to obtain the initial "tying" product that the customer desires, a court may find that an illegal tying arrangement exists. The plaintiff must establish: (1) that the tying product may not be obtained unless the tied product is also purchased; (2) that the tying product and the tied product are separate and distinct; (3) that the tying product possesses sufficient economic power appreciably to restrain competition in the tied market; and (4) that a "not insubstantial" amount of commerce is affected by the arrangement. A defendant in appropriate circumstances may successfully defend against an accusation of illegal tying by showing a special justification for the particular tying arrangement in question.

In *Jack Walters & Sons*, *supra*, 737 F.2d at 704–05, the Seventh Circuit explained the difficulties inherent in a claim of trademark tying:

. . . It is one thing to say that a manufacturer of copying machines who requires his customers to buy from him the copying paper that is used in the machines is conditioning the sale of the machines on the customer's purchase of a distinct product; it is quite another to say that General Motors lets you use the name Buick on condition that you buy the car to which the name is attached. That is a fantastic description of the transaction, and the cases reject the proposition that a tie-in claim can be based on it. . . . To accept it would be to impose in the name of antitrust a regime of compulsory licensing of trademarks — an absurd project. Moreover, since a trademark that denotes a product is rarely licensed apart from the product — and was not in this case — the separate-markets test of *Jefferson Parish* is not satisfied.

However, some cases, including several in this circuit, do treat as tying products trademarks that name not a product manufactured by the trademark's owner but a service which he provides to consumers through a system of franchised retail outlets; the tie-in consists of requiring franchisees, as a condition of being allowed to use the trademark, to buy distinct products supplied by the franchisor.

. . . The trademark is analytically separable from the tied product, so there is not the same absurdity in treating the trademark as a tying product as there is when the trademark is simply the name of the alleged tied product, as in our example of the Buick name and the Buick automobile. "Chicken Delight," in contrast, was the name of a fast-food franchise operation, not the name of a product; and the franchisor, the owner of the "Chicken Delight" mark, manufactured none of the things (which included mixes, fryers, and packaging supplies) that it required its franchisees to buy from it as a condition of their being allowed to use the name. *Siegel v. Chicken Delight, Inc.*, *supra*, 448 F.2d at 48 n. 4. It was a "case of a franchise system set up not to distribute the trade-marked goods of the franchisor, but . . . to conduct a certain business under a common trademark or trade name." *Id.* at 48 (footnote omitted). The name and the tied products thus were separable in a way that the name Buick and the car sold under that name are not. Or so at least it can be argued; for the *Chicken Delight* line of cases is not universally delectated.

Compare the following justification of a tying arrangement in the *Carvel* case which required licensees to purchase directly from Carvel or from a source approved by Carvel, CARVEL ice cream mix made by a secret formula and other products used in either the preparation or sale of the end product offered to the public, 332 F.2d at 519.

. . . The true tying item was . . . the CARVEL trademark, whose growing repute was intended to help the little band of Carvel dealers swim a bit faster than their numerous rivals up the highly competitive stream. There may, of course, be cases where a trademark has acquired such prominence that the coupling of some further item to its license would constitute a *per se* violation; but such a trademark would satisfy the market dominance test of *Times-Picayune* and *Northern Pacific*. The figures show that CARVEL is not such a mark.

Tying arrangements differ from other *per se* violations, such as price-fixing, *United States v. Trenton Potteries Co.*, 273 U.S. 392 (1927), in that they can be justified on occasion, as by proof that "the protection of goodwill may necessitate" their use "where specifications for a substitute would be so detailed that they could not practicably be supplied," *Standard Oil Co. of Calif. and Standard Stations v. United States*, 337 U.S. 293, 306 (1949). Since the value of a trademark depends solely on the public image it conveys, its holder must exercise controls to assure himself that the mark is not shown in a derogatory light. The record affords no sufficient basis for upsetting the finding of the District Judge that "[t]o require Carvel to limit itself to advance specifications of standards for all the various types of accessory products used in connection with the mix would impose an impractical and unreasonable burden of formulation. . . ."

In *Kentucky Fried Chicken Corp. v. Diversified Packaging Corp.*, 549 F.2d 368 (5th Cir. 1977), the court stated that the appellant failed to establish that KFC's system was not a reasonable method of quality control, and in *Phonetele, Inc. v. American Telephone & Telegraph*, 664 F.2d 716, 738–739 (9th Cir. 1981), *cert. denied*, 459 U.S. 1145 (1983), the court ruled that the defendant could offer justifications for undertaking the tie. *See* McCarthy, *Trademark Franchising and Antitrust: The Trouble With Tie-Ins*, 58 Calif. L. Rev. 1085 (1971).

In *Principe v. McDonald's Corp.*, 631 F.2d 303, 309 (4th Cir. 1980), the court stated:

the proper inquiry is not whether the allegedly tied products are associated in the public's mind with the franchisor's trademark, but whether they are integral components of the business method being franchised. Where the challenged aggregation is an essential ingredient of the franchised system's formula for success, there is but a single product and no tie-in exists. . . .

See also Power Test Petroleum Distributors v. Calcu Gas, 754 F.2d 91 (2d Cir. 1985); *California Glazed Products, Inc. v. Burns & Russell Co.*, 708 F.2d 1423 (9th Cir. 1983), *cert. denied*, 464 U.S. 937 (1983); *Krehl v. Baskin-Robbins Ice Cream Co.*, 664 F.2d 1348 (9th Cir. 1982); *Redd v. Shell Oil Co.*, 425 F.2d 1054 (10th Cir. 1975), *cert. denied*, 425 U.S. 912 (1976). *Compare Metrix Warehouse, Inc. v. Daimler-Benz Aktiengesellschaft*, 828 F.2d 1033 (4th Cir. 1987), *cert. denied*, 486 U.S. 1017 (1988) (less restrictive means existed to ensure quality than tying replacement parts to sale of new cars) *with Mozart Co. v. Mercedes-Benz in North America, Inc.*, 833 F.2d 1342 (9th Cir. 1987), *cert. denied*, 488 U.S. 870 (1988) (jury's finding upheld that no less restrictive alternative existed to control quality and protect goodwill than to tie the sale of replacement parts to the sale of new cars). *See also Town Sound & Custom Tops, Inc. v. Chrysler Motors Corp.*, 959 F.2d 468 (3d Cir.) (en banc), *cert. denied*, 113 S. Ct. 196 (1992) (affirming summary judgment that Chrysler had not unlawfully tied the sale of automobile sound systems for Chrysler automobiles to the sale of the automobiles themselves, finding that "competition in the automobile market adequately protects those consumers who consider auto sound systems when buying their cars from having to pay too much").

Does ownership of a trademark confer economic power analogous to ownership of patents or copyrights which are constitutionally sanctioned monopolies? *See Siegel v. Chicken Delight, Inc.*, 448 F.2d 43 (9th Cir. 1971). A number of decisions have required proof of the economic power possessed by the trademark in issue. *See Kentucky Fried Chicken, supra; Capital Temporaries, Inc. v. Olsten Corp.*, 506 F.2d 658 (2d Cir. 1974); *Drop Dead Co. v. S.C. Johnson & Son, Inc.*, 326 F.2d 87 (9th Cir. 1963); *Golden West Insulation, Inc. v. Stardust Invest. Corp.*, 615 P.2d 1048 (Or. App. 1980); Smirti, *Trademarks as Tying Products: The Presumption of Economic Power*, 69 Trademark Rep. 1 (1979).

In *Jefferson Parish Hospital District No. 2 v. Hyde*, 466 U.S. 2, 17–22 (1984), the Supreme Court held that to establish that there are two separate products capable of being tied, there must exist separate markets for each product. Secondly, the owner of the tying product must have sufficient market power to force purchase of the tied product. At issue in *Jefferson Parish* was the requirement that patients at a hospital use the services of one firm of anesthesiologists. While noting that the services unquestionably could be provided separately, the court stated,

> there is nothing inherently anticompetitive about packaged sales. Only if patients are forced to purchase [the firm's] services as a result of the hospital's market power would the arrangement have anticompetitive consequences. If no forcing is present, patients are free to enter a competing hospital and to use another anesthesiologist instead of [the firm].

The existence of numerous competing hospitals employing anesthesiologists resulted in reversal and remand of the Fifth Circuit finding of per se illegal tying.

One court concluded, "the emphasis in the Supreme Court's recent decision in *Jefferson Parish* on proving that the owner of the tying product has real market power may doom the franchise trademark cases, as they mostly involve highly competitive retail industries, such as the fast-food business." *Jack Walters, supra,* 737 F.2d at 705. *See also Will v. Comprehensive Accounting Corp.*, 776 F.2d 665 (7th Cir. 1985) (franchisees failed to establish that franchisor had market power); *cf. Midwestern Waffles, Inc. v. Waffle House, Inc.*, 734 F.2d 705, 712 (11th Cir. 1984) ("if competitors are in some way prevented from offering a franchise comparable to a Waffle House franchise, the court will find that a Waffle House franchise can be a tying product").

A subsequent Supreme Court decision may have given new life to franchise tying cases. In *Eastman Kodak Co. v. Image Technical Services, Inc.*, 112 S. Ct. 2072 (1992), the dispute involved the sale of service and replacement parts for Kodak photocopying and micrographic equipment. Kodak offered separate service contracts for its equipment. Other manufacturers' replacement parts were not compatible with Kodak's equipment. When independent service organizations (ISO's) began offering cheaper and higher quality service for Kodak equipment, with parts, Kodak sought to eliminate them as competition. For example, Kodak pressured Kodak equipment owners and independent parts distributors not to sell Kodak parts to ISO's, and parts manufacturers not to sell Kodak parts to anyone but Kodak. This succeeded in driving a number of ISO's out of business, and forcing unwilling customers to use Kodak service.

In moving for summary judgment, Kodak argued that, as in *Jefferson Parish*, the aggressive competition in the equipment market showed it did not have sufficient market power in the parts and services market to effect a tie. In affirming the Ninth Circuit's denial of summary judgment, the Supreme Court held that a reasonable trier of fact could find that parts and services were distinct products having separate markets, and that Kodak had sufficient power in the parts market to force unwanted purchases of a tied product, service. The majority was influenced by the fact that customers were "locked in" by the equipment purchase, with the cost of switching products high, and by evidence showing that Kodak might be taking advantage of this by raising prices in the service aftermarket above competitive levels. Justice Scalia dissented, stating, "If Kodak set generally supracompetitive prices for either spare parts or repair services without making an offsetting reduction on the price of its machines, national consumers would simply turn to Kodak's competitors for photocopying and micrographic systems." After the *Kodak* decision, franchisees similarly could conceivably claim that they are "locked in" by the franchise agreement, and that unlawful tying has occurred.

[4] Territorial Restrictions

Should a trademark owner be able to impose territorial restraints upon the use of its trademarks? "Territorial restraints" limit the geographical areas in which customers of the trademark owner may market the trademarked product. The courts have distinguished two kinds of territorial restraints: those affecting the relationships in the chain of distribution from manufacturers to the retail customer, called "vertical restraints," and those between competitors, called "horizontal restraints."

In 1977, the Supreme Court held that non-price, vertical restraints should not be considered illegal *per se* but should be analyzed under the "rule of reason." *Continental T.V. Inc. v. GTE Sylvania*, 433 U.S. 36 (1977). Thus, a franchisor ordinarily can validly agree to appoint only one franchisee in a territory (*United States v. Arnold Schwinn & Co.*, 388 U.S. 365 (1967)) and can contractually restrict a franchisee to a territory of primary responsibility, provided the restraint "is likely to promote interbrand competition without overly restricting intrabrand competition." *Continental T.V., Inc. v. GTE Sylvania, Inc.*, 694 F.2d 1132, 1137 (9th Cir. 1982). In that case, on remand from the Supreme Court's *Continental T.V.* decision, *supra*, the Ninth Circuit affirmed a grant of summary judgment to the franchisor, holding the location agreement to be reasonable and lawful. Among the factors it found persuasive were the interchangeability of television products coupled with the presence of viable competitors ready to sell to any retailers in the relevant market, the fact that the agreement was not overly restrictive (e.g., plaintiff was in no way prohibited from selling non-franchise television products in the location in question) and the fact that the agreement was not adopted for the purpose of preventing price discounting.

Post-*Continental T.V.* decisions have upheld territorial restrictions under the rule of reason. *See, e.g., Murrow Furniture Galleries, Inc. v. Thomasville Furniture Industries, Inc.*, 889 F.2d 524 (4th Cir. 1989) (denying preliminary relief against prohibition of orders and advertising outside area of responsibility); *Murphy v. Business Cards Tomorrow, Inc.*, 854 F.2d 1202, 1204 (9th Cir. 1988) (territorial restrictions); *O.S.C. Corp. v. Apple Computer, Inc.*, 792 F.2d 1464 (9th Cir. 1986) (prohibition of mail order sales upheld). Typically, substantial interbrand competition has been the primary factor in court approval. *See, e.g., Mendelovitz v. Adolph Coors Co.*, 693 F.2d 570, 576 n. 10 (5th Cir. 1982); *Muenster Butane, Inc. v. Stewart Co.*, 651 F.2d 292 (5th Cir. 1981) (substantial interbrand competition and lack of market power). *Cf. Midwestern Waffles, supra,* 734 F.2d at 711, where the court reasoned that if the franchisor alone allocated territories a rule of reason analysis would apply to the vertical restriction; whereas if the franchisor and some franchisees agreed among themselves as to the division of territories a horizontal restriction and per se violation would exist. *See also Redd v. Shell Oil,* 524 F.2d at 1058.

[handwritten margin note: Horizontal – per se violation]

Should agreements among competing businesses be accorded similar treatment? In *United States v. Topco Associates, Inc.*, 405 U.S. 596 (1972), the Court held that an agreement by the 25 members of the TOPCO supermarket cooperative association that members would not sell TOPCO brand products outside specifically designated territories was a per se violation of the Sherman Act. Quoting *White Motor Co. v. United States,* 372 U.S. 253, 263 (1963), the Court stated that "horizontal territorial limitations are naked restraints of trade with no purpose except stifling of competition." *Compare Topco with Tripoli Co. v. Wella Corp.*, 425 F.2d 932 (3d Cir. 1970), *cert. denied,* 400 U.S. 831 (1970); *Janel Sales Corp. v. Lanvin Parfums, Inc.*, 396 F.2d 398 (2d Cir. 1968), *cert. denied,* 393 U.S. 938 (1968); *Clairol, Inc. v. Boston Discount Center, Inc.*, 608 F.2d 1114 (6th Cir. 1979). Note also that the 1980 Soft Drink Interbrand Competition Act, 15 U.S.C. §§ 3501–3503 (1980), allows soft drink bottlers or distributors to include territorial restrictions in trademark licenses.

See generally 1 Gilson, *Trademark Protection and Practice* § 6.03(4) (1993 ed.); Altschuler, *Sylvania, Vertical Restraints and Dual Distribution,* 25 Antitrust Bull. 1 (1980); Zelek, Stern & Dunfree, *A Rule of Reason Decision Model After Sylvania,* 68 Cal. L. Rev. 13 (1980); Pitofsky, *The Sylvania Case: Antitrust Analysis of Non-Price Vertical Restrictions,* 78 Colum. L. Rev. 1 (1978); Posner, *The Rule of Reason and the Economic Approach: Reflections on the Sylvania Decision,* 45 U. Chi. L. Rev. 1 (1977).

[D] Price Discrimination *[handwritten: Per Se illegal]*

Section 2(a) of the Robinson-Patman Act [15 U.S.C. § 13(a)], states:

> That it shall be unlawful for any person engaged in commerce . . . to discriminate in price between different purchasers of commodities of like grade and quality . . . where the effect of such discrimination may be substantially to lessen competition or tend to create a monopoly in any line of commerce, or to injure, destroy, or prevent competition. . . .

[handwritten margin note: Diff't labels on Same milk]

In *FTC v. Borden Co.*, 383 U.S. 637 (1966), the Borden Company was selling evaporated milk under both the BORDEN trademark and various private labels. The private label products sold at lower prices. The court found that since the products were identical the price differential was potentially discriminatory in violation of § 2(a) of the Robinson-Patman Act. Justices Stewart and Harlan dissented, arguing that the differences in the products, even if slight, and the consumer preference for

[handwritten margin note: overruled]

the well-known brand justified the differences in price. Might consumer preference for a well-known mark justify a higher price for that product compared to a "generic" product of equal quality, but lower price? *See* McCarthy, *Trademarks and Unfair Competition* § 3:4 (3d ed. 1992); Osgood, *The Borden Litigation — Its Impact Upon the Issues of Like Grade and Quality and Competitive Injury Under the Robinson-Patman Act*, 59 Trademark Rep. 423 (1969); Comment, *The Supreme Court, 1965 Term*, 80 Harv. L. Rev. 91, 236 (1966); Austin, *Product Identity and Branding Under The Robinson-Patman Act*, 12 Vill. L. Rev. 251 (1967). On remand of the *Borden* case, the Court of Appeals set aside the FTC's cease and desist order against Borden's dual distribution practice on various grounds, including that the private label milk was available to all customers of its premium brand. *Borden v. FTC*, 381 F.2d 175 (5th Cir. 1967). In doing so, it stated (381 F.2d at 180):

> It is easily understood why the private label milk is sold at all levels of distribution for substantially less than Borden brand milk. By increased advertising and promotional efforts over the years, Borden has created a decided consumer preference for milk bearing a Borden label. The label has come to represent a value in itself.

[E]   Remedies

What ought to be the remedies for trade identity antitrust violations to redress damage caused by the violations and to restore competition? The successful assertion of civil antitrust claims can result in injunctive relief, treble damages and estoppel for trademark misuse. *See* 15 U.S.C. § 15, and the discussion on Trademark Misuse, *supra*. *Compare United States v. General Elec. Co.*, 115 F. Supp. 835 (D.N.J. 1953) (divestiture) *with Switzer Bros, Inc. v. Locklin*, 297 F.2d 39, 48 (7th Cir. 1961), *cert. denied*, 369 U.S. 851 (1962) ("It seems to us that divestiture of property rights in a trademark, by injunction against the mark's continued use, is a remedy which would seldom commend itself to equity in a private suit under the antitrust laws for injunctive relief and treble damages.") In *Ford Motor Co. v. United States*, 405 U.S. 562 (1972), the court prohibited Ford for five years from using its own trade name on spark plugs. In *United States v. Western Electric Co.*, 569 F. Supp. 1057 (D.D.C. 1983), *aff'd without op.*, 104 S. Ct. 542 (1983), the court in its plan for the reorganization of American Telephone and Telegraph (AT&T), ordered assignment of the BELL trade name and trademark to the new regional telephone operating companies. The court rejected AT&T's argument that AT&T shared a "common heritage" in the BELL trade name and trademark and prohibited AT&T from use of the BELL trade name and trademark after January 1, 1984.

Consider whether compulsory licensing of a trademark should be an alternative remedy to divestiture. In *In re Borden, Inc.*, 92 F.T.C. 669, 672–778 (1976), an FTC Administrative Law Judge ordered the Borden Company to cease activities which monopolized the processed lemon juice market and to grant licenses for a ten-year period for the use of Borden's REALEMON trademark to anyone engaged in or who wished to enter the processed lemon juice market. The FTC set aside the Administrative Law Judge's licensing requirement but noted that it may impose compulsory licensing or suspension of use of a trademark as antitrust relief in an appropriate case. *In re Borden, Inc.*, 92 F.T.C. 669, 807–808 (1978); *order to cease monopolistic activities upheld in Borden, Inc. v. FTC*, 674 F.2d 498 (6th Cir. 1982). Under a compulsory licensing order, would the licensor have to maintain a quality control system in order that the public not be deceived when purchasing a product bearing the licensed trademark? How would compulsory licensing affect consumer perception of the product bearing the licensed trademark? Would restrictions on the amount of money a trademark owner could spend advertising the trademark or restrictions on the size of the trademark on product labels be more appropriate remedies? For additional commentary, see Holmes, *Trademark Licensing As Structural Antitrust Relief: An Analytical Framework*, 71 Trademark Rep. 127 (1981); McCarthy, *Compulsory Licensing of a Trademark: Remedy or Penalty?*, 67 Trademark Rep. 197 (1977); Palladino, *Compulsory Licensing of a Trademark*, 26 Buff. L. Rev. 457 (1977); *Abuse of Trademarks: A Proposal for Compulsory Licensing*, 7 U. Mich. J.L. Ref. 644 (1974); Scherer, *The Posnerian Harvest: Separating Wheat from Chaff* [Book Review], 86 Yale L.J. 974, 999 (1977).

Section 33(b)(7) of the Lanham Act provides that incontestable rights in a trademark are lost if "the mark has been or is being used to violate the antitrust laws of the United States." *See Carl Zeiss Stiftung v. VE.B. Carl Zeiss, Jena*, 298 F. Supp. 1309 (S.D.N.Y. 1969); *Redd v. Shell Oil Co.*, 524 F.2d 1054 (10th Cir. 1975); Smith, *Trademarks and Antitrust: The Misuse Defense Under Section 33(b)(7) of the Lanham Act*, 4 Harv. J.L. & Pub. Pol'y 161 (1981). *But see Phi Delta Theta Fraternity v. J. A. Buchroeder & Company*, 251 F. Supp. 968 (W.D. Mo. 1966), where the court stated that § 33(b)(7) should not be read narrowly; *i.e.*, rights also may be lost in a mark which is not incontestably registered.

§ 7.05 Concurrent Rights (Geographically or unrelated products)

INTRODUCTION

Some of the most perplexing problems of trade identity law arise when conflict develops between two or more confusingly similar marks or trade names which have been used over a period of time in different geographical areas by unrelated companies. Similar problems develop when goods or services previously unrelated have recently become related through technological, marketing, or other socio-economic change. In these situations the rights of each party are exceedingly difficult to evaluate on the basis of existing statutory and case law. Courts are understandably reluctant in such circumstances to deprive the junior user of its valuable goodwill or disturb the public's habits and reasonable expectations, yet they must strive to prevent, or at least minimize, likelihood of confusion. As a consequence of these dilemmas, the courts often accord great weight to considerations such as intent, actual or constructive knowledge, or strained distinctions between marks. The common-law concept which limits the senior user's rights to the areas of actual use persists despite present day patterns of communication, travel, and migration which frequently cause marks to be known beyond such areas. The constructive notice provision of the Lanham Act (15 U.S.C. § 1072), and the courts' application of it, has had great impact upon these problem areas in statutory cases. The cases which follow disclose some of these problems as well as the evolution of the law. A dramatic example of the perplexities generated in this area is found in the territorial division of rights in the trade name and mark STANDARD OIL, and the conflicts spawned thereby (*e.g., Standard Oil Co. (Ky.) v. Humble Oil & Refining Co.*, 363 F.2d 945 (5th Cir. 1966), discussed in the notes in Chapter 5, *supra*).

UNITED DRUG CO. v. THEODORE RECTANUS CO.

United States Supreme Court
248 U.S. 90 (1918)

Mr. Justice Pitney.

. . . .

The essential facts are as follows: About the year 1877 Ellen M. Regis, a resident of Haverhill, Massachusetts, began to compound and distribute in a small way a preparation for medicinal use in cases of dyspepsia and some other ailments, to which she applied as a distinguishing name the word "Rex" — derived from her surname. The word was put upon the boxes and packages in which the medicine was placed upon the market, after the usual manner of a trade-mark. At first alone, and afterwards in partnership with her son under the firm name of "E.M. Regis & Company," she continued the business on a modest scale; in 1898 she recorded the word "Rex" as a trademark under the laws of Massachusetts (Acts 1895, p. 519, c. 462, § 1); in 1900 the firm procured its registration in the United States Patent Office under the Act of March 3, 1881, c. 138, 21 Stat. 502; in 1904 the Supreme Court of Massachusetts sustained their trade-mark right under the state law as against a concern that was selling medicinal preparations of the present petitioner under the designation of "Rex-all remedies" (*Regis v. Jaynes*, 185 Massachusetts, 458); afterwards the firm established priority in the mark as against petitioner in a contested proceeding in the Patent Office; and subsequently, in the year 1911, petitioner purchased the business with the trade-mark right, and has carried it on in connection with its other business, which consists in the manufacture of medicinal preparations, and their distribution and sale through retail drug stores, known as "Rexall stores," situated in the different States of the Union, four of them being in Louisville, Kentucky.

Meanwhile, about the year 1883, Theodore Rectanus, a druggist in Louisville, familiarly known as "Rex," employed this word as a trade-mark for a medicinal preparation known as "a blood purifier." He continued this use to a considerable extent in Louisville and vicinity, spending money in advertising and building up a trade, so that — except for whatever effect might flow from Mrs. Regis' prior adoption of the word in Massachusetts, of which he was entirely ignorant — he was entitled to use the word as his trade-mark. In the year 1906 he sold his business, including the right to the use of the word, to respondent; and the use of the mark by him and afterwards by respondent was continuous from about the year 1883 until the filing of the bill in the year 1912.

Petitioner's first use of the word "Rex" in connection with the sale of drugs in Louisville or vicinity was in April, 1912, when two shipments of "Rex Dyspepsia Tablets," aggregating 150 boxes and valued at $22.50, were sent to one of the "Rexall" stores in that city. Shortly after this the remedy was mentioned by name in local newspaper advertisements published by those stores. In the previous September, petitioner shipped a trifling amount — five boxes — to a drug store in Franklin, Kentucky, approximately 120 miles distant from Louisville. There is nothing to show that before this any customer in or near Kentucky had heard of the Regis remedy, with or without the description "Rex," or that this word ever possessed any meaning to the purchasing public in that State except as pointing to Rectanus and the Rectanus Company and their "blood purifier." That it did and does convey the latter meaning in Louisville and vicinity is proved without dispute. Months before petitioner's first shipment of its remedy to Kentucky, petitioner was distinctly notified (in June, 1911) by one of its Louisville distributors that respondent was using the word "Rex" to designate its medicinal preparations, and that such use had been commenced by Mr. Rectanus as much as 16 or 17 years before that time.

. . . .

The entire argument for the petitioner is summed up on the contention that whenever the first user of a trade-mark has been reasonably diligent in extending the territory of his trade, and as a result of such extension has in good faith come into competition with a later user of the same mark who in equal good faith has extended his trade locally before invasion of his field by the first user, so that finally it comes to pass that the rival traders are offering competitive merchandise in a common market under the same trade-mark, the later user should be enjoined at the suit of the prior adopter, even though the latter be the last to enter the competitive field and the former have already established a trade there. Its application to the case is based upon the hypothesis that the record shows that Mrs. Regis and her firm, during the entire period of limited and local trade in her medicine under the Rex mark, were making efforts to extend their trade so far as they were able to do with the means at their disposal. There is little in the record to support this hypothesis; but, waiving this, we will pass upon the principal contention.

The asserted doctrine is based upon the fundamental error of supposing that a trade-mark right is a right in gross or at large, like a statutory copyright or a patent for an invention, to either of which, in truth, it has little or no analogy. *Canal Co. v. Clark*, 13 Wall. 311, 322; *McLean v. Fleming*, 96 U.S. 245, 254. There is no such thing as property in a trade-mark except as a right appurtenant to an established business or trade in connection with which the mark is employed. The law of trade-marks is but a part of the broader law of unfair competition; the right to a particular mark grows out of its use, not its mere adoption; its function is simply to designate the goods as the product of a particular trader and to protect his good will against the sale of another's product as his; and it is not the subject of property except in connection with an existing business. *Hanover Milling Co. v. Metcalf*, 240 U.S. 403, 412–414.

. . . .

Undoubtedly, the general rule is that, as between conflicting claimants to the right to use the same mark, priority of appropriation determines the question. *See Canal Co. v. Clark*, 13 Wall. 311, 323; *McLean v. Fleming*, 96 U.S. 245, 251; *Manufacturing Co. v. Trainer*, 101 U.S. 51, 53; *Columbia Mill Co. v. Alcorn*, 150 U.S. 460, 463. But the reason is that purchasers have come to understand the mark as indicating the origin of the wares, so that its use by a second producer amounts to an attempt to sell his goods as those of his competitor. The reason for the rule does not extend to a case where the same trade-mark happens to be employed simultaneously by two manufacturers in different markets separate and remote from each other, so that the mark means one thing in one market, an entirely different thing in another. It would be a perversion of the rule of priority to give it such an application in our broadly extended country that an innocent party who had in good faith employed a trade-mark in one State, and by the use of it had built up a trade there, being the first appropriator in that jurisdiction, might afterwards be prevented from using it, with consequent injury to his trade and good-will, at the instance of one who theretofore had employed the same mark but only in other and remote jurisdictions, upon the ground that its first employment happened to antedate that of the first-mentioned trader.

. . . .

The same point was involved in *Hanover Milling Co. v. Metcalf*, 240 U.S. 403, 415, where we said:

> In the ordinary case of parties competing under the same mark in the same market, it is correct to say that prior appropriation settles the question. But where two parties independently are employing the same mark upon goods of the same class, but in separate markets wholly remote the one from the other, the question of prior appropriation is legally insignificant, unless at least it appear that the second adopter has selected the mark with some design inimical to the interests of the first user, such as to take the benefit of the reputation of his goods, to forestall the extension of his trade, or the like.

In this case, as already remarked, there is no suggestion of a sinister purpose on the part of Rectanus or the Rectanus Company; hence the passage quoted correctly defines the status of the parties prior to the time when they came into competition in the Kentucky market. And it results, as a necessary inference from what we have said, that petitioner, being the newcomer in that market, must enter it subject to whatever rights had previously been acquired there in good faith by the Rectanus Company and its predecessor. To hold otherwise — to require Rectanus to retire from the field upon the entry of Mrs. Regis' successor — would be to establish the right of the latter as a right in gross, and to extend it to territory wholly remote from the furthest reach of the trade to which it was annexed, with the effect not merely of depriving Rectanus of the benefit of the good-will resulting from his long-continued use of the mark in Louisville and vicinity, and his substantial expenditures in building up his trade, but of enabling petitioner to reap substantial benefit from the publicity that Rectanus has thus given to the mark in that locality, and of confusing if not misleading the public as to the origin of goods thereafter sold in Louisville under the Rex mark, for, in that market, until petitioner entered, "Rex" meant the Rectanus product, not that of Regis.

. . . .

Here the essential facts are so closely parallel to those that furnished the basis of decision in the *Allen & Wheeler Case*, report *sub nom. Hanover Milling Co. v. Metcalf*, 240 U.S. 403, 419–420, as to render further discussion unnecessary. Mrs. Regis and her firm, having during a long period of years confined their use of the "Rex" mark to a limited territory wholly remote from that in controversy, must be held to have taken the risk that some innocent party might in the meantime hit upon the same mark, apply it to goods of similar character, and, expend money and effort in building up a trade under it; and since it appears that Rectanus in good faith, and without notice of any prior use by others, selected and used the "Rex" mark, and by the expenditure of money and effort succeeded in building up a local but valuable trade under it in Louisville and vicinity before petitioner entered that field, so that "Rex" had come to be recognized there as the "trade signature" of Rectanus and of respondent as his successor, petitioner is estopped to set up their continued use of the mark in that territory as an infringement of the Regis trade-mark. Whatever confusion may have arisen from conflicting use of the mark is attributable to petitioner's entry into the field with notice of the situation; and petitioner cannot complain of this. As already stated, respondent is not complaining of it.

Decree affirmed.

DAWN DONUT CO. v. HART'S FOOD STORES, INC.

United States Court of Appeals, Second Circuit
267 F.2d 358 (1959)

LUMBARD, CIRCUIT JUDGE.

. . . .

Plaintiff, Dawn Donut Co., Inc., of Jackson, Michigan since June 1, 1922 has continuously used the trademark "Dawn" upon 25 to 100 pound bags of doughnut mix which it sells to bakers in various states, including New York, and since 1935 it has similarly marketed a line of sweet dough mixes for use in the baking of coffee cakes, cinnamon rolls and oven goods in general under that mark. In 1950 cake mixes were added to the company's line of products. Dawn's sales representatives call upon bakers to solicit orders for mixes and the orders obtained are filled by shipment to the purchaser either directly from plaintiff's Jackson, Michigan plant, where the mixes are manufactured, or from a local warehouse within the customer's state. For some years plaintiff maintained a warehouse in Jamestown, New York, from which shipments were made, but sometime prior to the commencement of this suit in 1954 it discontinued this warehouse and has since then shipped its mixes to its New York customers directly from Michigan.

Plaintiff furnishes certain buyers of its mixes, principally those who agree to become exclusive Dawn Donut Shops, with advertising and packaging material bearing the trademark "Dawn" and permits these bakers to sell goods made from the mixes to the consuming public under that trademark. These display materials are supplied either as a courtesy or at a moderate price apparently to stimulate and promote the sale of plaintiff's mixes.

The district court found that with the exception of one Dawn Donut Shop operated in the city of Rochester, New York during 1926–27, plaintiff's licensing of its mark in connection with the retail sale of doughnuts in the state of New York has been confined to areas not less than 60 miles from defendant's trading area. The court also found that for the past eighteen years plaintiff's present New York State representative has, without interruption, made regular calls upon bakers in the city of Rochester, N. Y., and in neighboring towns and cities, soliciting orders for plaintiff's mixes and that throughout this period orders have been filled and shipments made of plaintiff's mixes from Jackson, Michigan into the city of Rochester. But it does not appear that any of these purchasers of plaintiff's mixes employed the plaintiff's mark in connection with retail sales.

The defendant, Hart Food Stores, Inc., owns and operates a retail grocery chain within the New York counties of Monroe, Wayne, Livingston, Genesee, Ontario and Wyoming. The products of defendant's bakery, Starhart Bakeries, Inc., a New York corporation of which it is the sole stockholder, are distributed through these stores, thus confining the distribution of defendant's product to an area within a 45 mile radius of Rochester. Its advertising of doughnuts and other baked products over television and radio and in newspapers is also limited to this area. Defendant's bakery corporation was formed on April 13, 1951 and first used the imprint "Dawn" in packaging its products on August 30, 1951. The district court found that the defendant adopted the mark "Dawn" without any actual knowledge of plaintiff's use or federal registration of the mark, selecting it largely because of a slogan "Baked at midnight, delivered at Dawn" which was originated by defendant's president and used by defendant in its bakery operations from 1929 to 1935. Defendant's president testified, however, that no investigation was made prior to the adoption of the mark to see if anyone else was employing it. Plaintiff's marks were registered federally in 1927, and their registration was renewed in 1947. Therefore by virtue of the Lanham Act, 15 U.S.C.A. § 1072, the defendant had constructive notice of plaintiff's marks as of July 5, 1947, the effective date of the Act.

Defendant's principal contention is that because plaintiff has failed to exploit the mark "Dawn" for some thirty years at the retail level in the Rochester trading area, plaintiff should not be accorded the exclusive right to use the mark in this area.

We reject this contention as inconsistent with the scope of protection afforded a federal registrant by the Lanham Act.

Prior to the passage of the Lanham Act courts generally held that the owner of a registered trademark could not sustain an action for infringement against another who, without knowledge of the registration, used the mark in a different trading area from that exploited by the registrant so that public confusion was unlikely. *Hanover Star Milling Co. v. Metcalf*, 1916, 240 U.S. 403; *cf. White Tower System, Inc. v.*

White Castle System of Eating Houses Corporation, 6 Cir., 1937, 90 F.2d 67, *certiorari denied*, 1937, 302 U.S. 720; Note, *Developments in the Law of Trade-Marks and Unfair Competition*, 68 Harv. L. Rev. 814, 857–858 (1955). By being the first to adopt a mark in an area without knowledge of its prior registration, a junior user of a mark could gain the right to exploit the mark exclusively in that market.

But the Lanham Act, 15 U.S.C.A. § 1072, provides that registration of a trademark on the principal register is constructive notice of the registrant's claim of ownership. Thus, by eliminating the defense of good faith and lack of knowledge, § 1072 affords nationwide protection to registered marks, regardless of the areas in which the registrant actually uses the mark.

That such is the purpose of Congress is further evidenced by 15 U.S.C.A. §§ 1115(a) and (b) which make the certificate of registration evidence of the registrant's "exclusive right to use the . . . mark in commerce." "Commerce" is defined in 15 U.S.C.A. § 1127 to include all the commerce which may lawfully be regulated by Congress. These two provisions of the Lanham Act make it plain that the fact that the defendant employed the mark "Dawn," without actual knowledge of plaintiff's registration, at the retail level in a limited geographical area of New York state before the plaintiff used the mark in that market, does not entitle it to exclude the plaintiff from using the mark in that area or to use the mark concurrently once the plaintiff licenses the mark or otherwise exploits it in connection with retail sales in the area.

Plaintiff's failure to license its trademarks in defendant's trading area during the thirty-odd years that have elapsed since it licensed them to a Rochester baker does not work an abandonment of the rights in that area. We hold that 15 U.S.C.A. § 1127, which provides for abandonment in certain cases of non-use, applies only when the registrant fails to use his mark, within the meaning of § 1127, anywhere in the nation. Since the Lanham Act affords a registrant nationwide protection, a contrary holding would create an insoluble problem of measuring the geographical extent of the abandonment. Even prior to the passage of the Lanham Act, when the trade-mark protection flowed from state law and therefore depended on use within the state, no case, as far as we have been able to ascertain, held that a trade-mark owner abandoned his rights within only part of a state because of his failure to use the mark in that part of the state. *Cf. Jacobs v. Iodent Chemical Co.*, 3 Cir., 1930, 41 F.2d 637.

Accordingly, since plaintiff has used its trademark continuously at the retail level, it has not abandoned its federal registration rights even in defendant's trading area.

We reject defendant's further claim that plaintiff is prevented by laches from enjoining defendant's use of the mark "Dawn" upon doughnuts and other baked and fried goods. Defendant argues that plaintiff's New York sales representative, one Jesse Cohn, who also represented several other companies besides plaintiff, called upon defendant on a monthly basis, and that about four years prior to the commencement of this lawsuit he observed boxes bearing the label "Dawn" on the desk of one Jack Solomon, defendant's bakery manager. At the trial Cohn denied that he ever saw any packaging in defendant's bakery for baked and fried goods bearing the label Dawn, although he admitted seeing some packages for other food products in defendant's bakery bearing the mark "Dawn." The district court held that since Cohn's contacts with the defendant were on behalf of companies other than the plaintiff, the knowledge of Cohn would not be imputed. We agree with the district court's conclusion.

. . . .

The Lanham Act, 15 U.S.C.A. § 1114, sets out the standard for awarding a registrant relief against the unauthorized use of his mark by another. It provides that the registrant may enjoin only that concurrent use which creates a likelihood of public confusion as to the origin of the products in connection with which the marks are used. Therefore if the use of the marks by the registrant and the unauthorized user are confined to two sufficiently distinct and geographically separate markets, with no likelihood that the registrant will expand his use into defendant's market, so that no public confusion is possible, then the registrant is not entitled to enjoin the junior user's use of the mark. *See Fairway Foods, Inc. v. Fairway Markets, Inc.*, 9 Cir., 1955, 227 F.2d 193; Note, *Developments in the Law of Trade-Marks and Unfair Competition*, 68 Harv. L. Rev. 814, 857–60 (1955); *cf. Sterling Brewery, Inc. v. Cold Springs Brewing Corp.*, *supra*.

As long as plaintiff and defendant confine their use of the mark "Dawn" in connection with the retail sale of baked goods to their present separate trading areas it is clear that no public confusion is likely.

. . . .

The decisive question then is whether plaintiff's use of the mark "Dawn" at the retail level is likely to be confined to its current area of use or whether in the normal course of its business, it is likely to expand the retail use of the mark into defendant's trading area. If such expansion were probable, then the concurrent use of the marks would give rise to the conclusion that there was a likelihood of confusion.

The district court found that in view of the plaintiff's inactivity for about thirty years in exploiting its trademarks in defendant's trading area at the retail level either by advertising directed at retail purchasers or by retail sales through authorized licensed users, there was no reasonable expectation that plaintiff would extend its retail operations into defendant's trading area. There is ample evidence in the record to support this conclusion and we cannot say that it is clearly erroneous.

We note not only that plaintiff has failed to license its mark at the retail level in defendant's trading area for a substantial period of time, but also that the trend of plaintiff's business manifests a striking decrease in the number of licensees employing its mark at the retail level in New York state and throughout the country. In the 1922-1930 period plaintiff had 75 to 80 licensees across the country with 11 located in New York. At the time of the trial plaintiff listed only 16 active licensees not one of which was located in New York.

The normal likelihood that plaintiff's wholesale operations in the Rochester area would expand to the retail level is fully rebutted and overcome by the decisive fact that plaintiff has in fact not licensed or otherwise exploited its mark at retail in the area for some thirty years.

Accordingly, because plaintiff and defendant use the mark in connection with retail sales in distinct and separate markets and because there is no present prospect that plaintiff will expand its use of the mark at the retail level into defendant's trading area, we conclude that there is no likelihood of public confusion arising from the concurrent use of the marks and therefore the issuance of an injunction is not warranted. *A fortiori* plaintiff is not entitled to any accounting or damages. However, because of the effect we have attributed to the constructive notice provision of the Lanham Act, the plaintiff may later, upon a proper showing of an intent to use the mark at the retail level in defendant's market area, be entitled to enjoin defendant's use of the mark.

. . . .

[*Affirmed.*]

WEINER KING, INC. v. WIENER KING CORP.

Court of Customs and Patent Appeals
615 F.2d 512 (1980)

RICH, J.

. . . .

Weiner King was the first to adopt and use its mark WEINER KING. Later, [Wiener King Corp. of North Carolina] "WKNC" innocently adopt[ed] its mark WIENER KING in a market area remote from that of Weiner King's market area. Under such circumstances, it is settled law that each party has a right to use its mark in its own initial area of use. *United Drug Co. v. Theodore Rectanus Co.*, 248 U.S. 90 (1918); *Hanover Star Milling Co. v. Metcalf*, 240 U.S. 403 (1916). In dispute here are the *registrable rights* to the remainder of the United States possessed by each party.

This case takes on an added dimension of complexity for two reasons: WKNC, the later adopter, was the first to register its mark under the Lanham Act; and, even though an innocent adopter, WKNC underwent a large portion of its expansion after notice of the existence of Weiner King and its use of the WEINER KING mark in the Flemington, New Jersey, area.

Weiner King's major contention on appeal is that any expansion on the part of WKNC which occurred after it learned of Weiner King and the use of the WEINER KING mark was at WKNC's peril and cannot serve as a basis for a right to register as a concurrent user in any of the areas it entered after notice. We do not agree.

It is said that nature abhors a vacuum. The same may be said of equity; it must operate in a factual environment. The TTAB had the task of balancing the equities between a prior user who remained content to operate a small, locally-oriented business with no apparent desire to expand, and who, until recently, declined to seek the benefits of Lanham Act registration, and a subsequent user, whose expressed purpose has been, from its inception, to expand into a nationwide franchising operation, and who has fulfilled its purpose, taking advantage of Lanham Act registration in the process.

"A crucial question brought into issue by Weiner King is the character of WKNC's expansion which occurred subsequent to its learning of Weiner King's existence. If it was in bad faith it cannot support a right to registration for use in those areas.

The District Court found that this expansion was not an attempt to "palm off" or trade on the reputation of Weiner King. "Instead, they [sought] to gain from their own goodwill, founded upon the use of 'Wiener King' throughout a large part of the United States." 407 F. Supp. at 1282. This finding was undisturbed on appeal. It is binding on the parties by stipulation.

The only basis urged by Weiner King for absence of good faith on the part of WKNC is the fact that WKNC expanded out of North Carolina with notice of Weiner King's existence and use of its WEINER KING mark. We hold that this reason is legally insufficient to support a finding of bad faith. In so holding, we caution that such a determination must always be the product of the particular fact pattern involved in each case. While an attempt to "palm off," or a motive to "box in" a prior user by cutting into its probable area of expansion, each necessarily flowing from knowledge of the existence of the prior user, might be sufficient to support a finding of bad faith, *mere knowledge of the existence of the prior user* should not, by itself, constitute bad faith.

Turning to the fundamental question in this case, i.e., who gets what territory, this court has suggested certain criteria which are helpful in resolving this question. In *In re Beatrice Foods, Co.*, 429 F.2d 466, 475 (1970), this court noted that actual use in a territory was not necessary to establish rights in that territory, and that the inquiry should focus on the party's (1) previous business activity; (2) previous expansion or lack thereof; (3) dominance of contiguous areas; (4) presently-planned expansion; and, where applicable (5) possible market penetration by means of products brought in from other areas.

In the present case, reliance on factors 1–4 weighs overwhelmingly in favor of WKNC. This is clear from the stipulated findings in the civil action alone, which demonstrate that Weiner King comes up virtually empty-handed in all of the categories. While we could stop here, there are several other reasons why, in this case, the decision of the TTAB should be affirmed.

In appropriate situations, courts have restricted a prior user to its actual trade territory in favor of a later user who has appeared on the horizon. *See Jacobs v. Iodent Chemical Co.*, 41 F.2d 637 (3d Cir. 1930). In *Zimmerman v. Holiday Inns of America*, 438 Pa. 528, 266 A.2d 87 (1970), *cert. denied*, 400 U.S. 992 (1971), the facts revealed that a local motel operator had unsuccessfully sued a nationwide franchise motel chain which he felt was encroaching on his territory, thus alerting the chain, a later user, to his existence. The later user then opened fifteen additional motels in the state. In a subsequent suit to enjoin the chain, the court, noting a lack of bad faith on the part of the chain, limited injunctive relief to an area within twenty-two miles of the local operator's motel. The Pennsylvania Supreme Court affirmed, thus acknowledging the right of the later user to operate in areas into which it had *Ok to expand.* expanded after notice of the existence of the prior user.

The commentators have not been silent on this issue. Restriction of a prior user to its actual trade territory and zone of probable expansion has been noted. *See* McCarthy, *Trademarks and Unfair Competition*, § 26:8 at 218 & n. 13 (3d ed. 1992). One established authority has stated that the *Hanover* and *Rectanus* cases, *supra*, "are based on the theory that the prior user in each case abandoned its right to expand its trade when it failed to exercise that right." 1 H. Nims, *Unfair Competition and Trade Marks*, § 218(b) at 645 (4th ed. 1947). This is precisely the principle relied upon below by the TTAB. 201 U.S.P.Q. at 916.

We also find it significant that WKNC was the first to register its mark. In *Giant Foods, Inc. v. Malone & Hyde, Inc.*, 522 F.2d at 1396, 187 U.S.P.Q. at 382, a majority of this court stated: *Reward those who register*

> The winner of the race for [virgin territory], according to our system of federal registration, is the senior user at least in those instances where he is also the first to apply for a federal registration.

It was thus implicitly recognized that there is a policy of encouraging prompt registration of marks by rewarding those who first seek registration under the Lanham Act. We restated this policy again in *In re Beatrice Foods Co.*, 429 F.2d at 474 n. 13:

> [W]here the prior user does not apply for a registration before registration is granted to another, *there may be valid grounds, based on a policy of rewarding those who first seek federal registration, and a consideration of the rights created by the existing registration, for limiting his registration to the area of actual use and permitting the prior registrant to retain the nationwide protection of the act restricted only by the territory of the prior user.* [Emphasis ours.]

We deem this to be sound policy when applied in the proper case, as determined *Limit prior user territory* by its facts and circumstances. From our view of the facts and circumstances here, this is a proper case.

Section 2(d) of the Lanham Act (15 U.S.C. § 1052(d)) also supports the decision of the TTAB. One of the stated purposes of the act, to prevent consumer confusion, *see* H.R. Rep. No. 219, 79th Cong., 1st Sess. 2 (1945); S. Rep. No. 1333 (1946), is embodied in § 2(d), which reads in pertinent part:

> No trademark shall be refused registration unless it — (d) Consists of or comprises a mark which so resembles . . . a mark . . . previously used in the United States by another and not abandoned, as to be likely, when applied to the goods of the applicant, to cause confusion, or to cause mistake, or to deceive: *Provided*, That when the Commissioner determines that confusion, mistake, or deception is not likely to result from the continued use by more than one person of the same or similar marks under conditions and limitations as to the mode or place of use of the marks . . . concurrent registrations may be issued to such persons . . . In issuing concurrent registrations, the

Commissioner shall prescribe conditions and limitations as to the mode or place of use of the mark. . . .

Section 2(d) recognizes that, under certain conditions, more than one party may have a right to use, and hence to register, a given mark. The proviso of § 2(d) instructs the Commissioner that, when issuing concurrent registrations, he is to impose conditions and limitations to the use of the mark by the concurrent registrants. It is plain that these conditions and limitations are to be imposed for the purpose of preventing consumer confusion. The proviso exhibits no bias in favor of the prior user.

The TTAB found that "it is an inescapable conclusion that, outside of Weiner King's little enclave, 'WIENER KING' means WKNC's restaurants and to allow Weiner King to step out of its trading area, would cause confusion to the purchasing public." 201 U.S.P.Q. at 916. By finding that Weiner King's reputation zone is a circle with a 15-mile radius, the Third Circuit has made essentially the same finding. It is binding on the parties by stipulation. In light of this fact, the issuance to Weiner King of a concurrent registration which encompasses the entire United States except for the state of North Carolina would serve only to foster the very confusion which the act was meant to prevent.

We do not rely for our decision on § 22 of the Lanham Act (15 U.S.C. § 1072), which provides that a registration serves as constructive notice of the claim of ownership of the registered mark, thus cutting off the defense of subsequent good faith adoption by another party. Although such an approach has been suggested, *see* Schwartz, *Concurrent Registration Under the Lanham Trademark Act of 1946: What is the Impact on Section 2(d) of Section 22?*, 55 T.M. Rep. 413 (1965), we do not believe that a mechanical approach which always defers to the first to register comprehends all of the factors which must be taken into account in order to come to a reasoned decision. The problems of concurrent use issues must ultimately be solved by a comprehensive factual analysis, which the TTAB has both the power and the resources to make.

. . . .

[*Modified.*]

NOTES ON CONCURRENT RIGHTS

(1) At common law, the user of a trademark cannot prevent the good faith use of a confusingly similar mark in a separate geographic market where neither his trade nor his reputation has reached. *See United Drug, supra; Hanover Star Milling Co. v. Metcalf*, 240 U.S. 403 (1916). How much "market penetration" is needed to establish exclusive rights in a particular territory? *See Sweetarts v. Sunline, Inc.*, 436 F.2d 705, 708 (8th Cir. 1971):

> In determining this issue the trial court should weigh all the factors including plaintiff's dollar value of sales at the time defendants entered the market,

number of customers compared to the population of the state, relative and potential growth of sales, and length of time since significant sales. Though the market penetration need not be large to entitle plaintiff to protection, *Sweet Sixteen Co. v. Sweet "16" Shop*, 15 F.2d 920 (8 Cir 1926), it must be significant enough to pose the real likelihood of confusion among the consumers in that area between the products of plaintiff and the products of defendants.

(quoting *Sweetarts v. Sunline, Inc.*, 380 F.2d 923 (8th Cir. 1967)).

In *Wrist-Rocket Mfg. Co. v. Saunders Archery Co.*, 578 F.2d 727 (8th Cir. 1978), in which a prior user confronted a registrant possessing incontestability rights, the court found that the prior user had made "significant sales" (one wrist-rocket per 20-30,000 people in a state) in 25 states, and divided the country between the parties accordingly. *See also Natural Footwear Ltd. v. Hart, Schaffner & Marx*, 760 F.2d 1383 (3d Cir. 1985) (insufficient market penetration outside of New Jersey); *V & V Food Products, Inc. v. Cacique Cheese Co.*, 683 F. Supp. 662, 668 (N.D. Ill. 1988) (market penetration sufficient to establish rights in four states). Should it be possible to lose exclusive rights in some marketing areas while retaining them in others? In *Sheila's Shine Products v. Sheila Shine, Inc.*, 486 F.2d 114 (5th Cir. 1973), the court held that plaintiff had lost its trademark rights either through nonuse and intent to abandon, or, alternatively, through licensing with insufficient control, in all but the seven states in which plaintiff itself continued to use the trademark. As a result, defendant was granted rights to exclusive use of the mark in the remaining forty-three states. *Compare United States Jaycees v. Philadelphia Jaycees*, 639 F.2d 134 (3d Cir. 1981), where, over a strong dissent, the court refused to apply this "regional abandonment" theory to a city-sized area. *See* Gross, *The Territorial Scope of Trademark Rights*, 44 U. Miami L. Rev. 1075 (1990); Alexander & Coil, *Geographical Rights in Trademarks and Service Marks*, 68 Trademark Rep. 101 (1978); Derenberg, *Territorial Scope and Situs of Trademarks and Goodwill*, 47 Va. L. Rev. 73 (1961), 68 Trademark Rep. 387 (1978).

(2) A nondistinctive mark possessing secondary meaning in the territory where it long has been used subsequently may be used by its owner in a new territory where it has not yet acquired secondary meaning. Should the mark's acquired significance in the old territory affect the breadth of protection extended to it in the new? In *beef & brew, inc. v. BEEF & BREW INC.*, 389 F. Supp. 179 (D. Ore. 1974), plaintiff demonstrated secondary meaning for its merely descriptive restaurant name in the Seattle but not the Portland area. The court rejected plaintiff's zone of expansion argument and denied relief. In *A.J. Canfield Co. v. Concord Beverage Co.*, 629 F. Supp. 200, 210 (E.D. Pa. 1985), *aff'd on other grounds*, 808 F.2d 291 (3d Cir. 1986), the court held for defendant, finding plaintiff's mark at most had acquired secondary meaning in the Chicago area, not in defendant's East Coast marketing area. *Compare A.J. Canfield Co. v. Vess Beverages, Inc.*, 612 F. Supp. 1081 (N.D. Ill. 1985) (finding substantial likelihood plaintiff would be able to demonstrate secondary meaning in Chicago area). *See also Bank of Texas v. Commerce Southwest, Inc.*, 741 F.2d 785 (5th Cir. 1984); *Shoppers Fair of Arkansas, Inc. v. Sanders Co.*, 328 F.2d 496 (8th Cir. 1964).

What is the effect of modern communication and travel on trademark rights and likelihood of confusion as to source? In *Chopra v. Kapur*, 185 U.S.P.Q. 195, 200

(N.D. Cal. 1974), the parties' closest restaurants were located in San Francisco and Chicago; nonetheless, the court found likelihood of confusion, in part because "the clientele of plaintiff's restaurants is ambulatory and plaintiff's reputation and good will have extended to the San Francisco area. In these circumstances, geographical proximity is not necessary." *Compare Steak & Brew, Inc. v. Beef & Brew Restaurant, Inc.*, 370 F. Supp. 1030 (S.D. Ill. 1974), in which plaintiff unsuccessfully contended that the *United Drug* principle, which protects the innocent second party in his own market area, does not apply to hotels or restaurants. *See also Maxim's Limited v. Badonsky*, 772 F.2d 388 (7th Cir. 1985) (relief denied where expensive restaurant clientele sophisticated and discriminating); *Stork Restaurant, Inc. v. Sahati*, 166 F.2d 348 (9th Cir. 1948); *Matador Motor Inns, Inc. v. Matador Motel, Inc.*, 376 F. Supp. 385 (D.N.J. 1974); *Travelodge Corp. v. Siragusa*, 228 F. Supp. 238 (N.D. Ala. 1964), *aff'd per curiam*, 352 F.2d 516 (5th Cir. 1965).

Should a prior user's rights extend to areas of natural expansion? In *beef & brew, inc. v. BEEF & BREW INC.*, supra at 185, the court observed that the natural expansion doctrine is imprecise and potentially inconsistent with the objectives of free competition, and that the leading natural expansion cases rest each upon a finding of secondary meaning, or bad faith, or both. *See also Blue Ribbon Feed v. Farmers Union Central Exchange*, 731 F.2d 415, 422 (7th Cir. 1984) (a "mere hope of expansion beyond its trade area is insufficient to support the protection sought"), and *Raxton Corp. v. Anania Assocs., Inc.*, 635 F.2d 924, 930 (1st Cir. 1980), in which the court stated:

A natural expansion doctrine that penalized innocent users of a trademark simply because they occupied what for them would be a largely undiscoverable path of some remote prior user's expansion strikes us as at once unworkable, unfair, and, in the light of statutory protection available today, unnecessary.

Absent a federal registration, why should any "right to natural expansion" be found to exist in trade identity law, if indeed it does? Can such a right be justified under our "protect only against likely confusion" rationale? *See* Marks, *Trademark Protection Under the "Natural Area of Business Expansion" Doctrine*, 53 Notre Dame Law. 869 (1978).

(3) Under the Lanham Act's current interpretation by many courts, a federal registrant acquires rights in his mark even in areas in which he does not conduct his business. *Old Dutch Foods, Inc. v. Dan Dee Pretzel & Potato Chip Co.*, 477 F.2d 150 (6th Cir. 1973); the *Dawn Donut* case, *supra*; 15 U.S.C. § 1072; Lunsford, *Geographic Scope of Registered Rights — Then and Now*, 61 Trademark Rep. 411 (1971). As stated in the *Dawn Donut* case, *supra*, and *American Foods, Inc. v. Golden Flake, Inc.*, 312 F.2d 619 (5th Cir. 1963), once a federal registrant evidences a present prospect or likelihood of expansion, he is entitled to an injunction against a local, junior user. *See Foxtrap, Inc. v. Foxtrap, Inc.*, 671 F.2d 636 (D.C. Cir. 1982) (observing that the Lanham Act constructive notice provision removed the common-law good faith defense of *Hanover* and *Rectanus*). *Cf. Comidas Exquisitos, Inc. v. O'Malley & McGee's, Inc.*, 775 F.2d 260 (8th Cir. 1985) (relief denied where no present likelihood of expansion into defendant's area by registrant); *Pizzeria Uno Corp. v. Temple*, 747 F.2d 1522, 1536 (4th Cir. 1984) (same). *But see Holiday Inns*

of Am., Inc. v. B&B Corp., 409 F.2d 614 (3d Cir. 1969). Is this a sound and fair rule consistent with the basic doctrines of our trade identity law? *See generally* Comment, *The Scope of Territorial Protection of Trademarks*, 65 Nw. U.L. Rev. 781 (1970). Need a federal registrant prove likelihood of expansion if he can show his mark has already established a reputation in a junior user's territory? *Cf. Tisch Hotels, Inc. v. Americana Inn, Inc.*, 350 F.2d 609 (7th Cir. 1965); *Chopra, supra* Note (2); Fletcher, *CHEXTRA Case and Other Spawn of Dawn Donut*, 66 Trademark Rep. 285 (1976).

(4) What territorial rights are acquired by a registrant who is not the first user of the mark? Should the first user's rights be limited to areas of actual use? Should the plans of either to expand business under the mark, e.g., via franchising, be considered in the determination? *See Weiner King, supra; Minute Man Press Int'l, Inc. v. MinuteMen Press, Inc.*, 219 U.S.P.Q. 426 (N.D. Cal. 1983); McCarthy, *Trademarks and Unfair Competition* § 20:23 (3d ed. 1992); Fletcher, *Incontestability and Constructive Notice: A Quarter Century of Adjudication*, 63 Trademark Rep. 71 (1973). Note that § 2(d) of the Lanham Act authorizes concurrent registrations where two or more users are each entitled to use of a mark. *See Noah's, Inc. v. Nark, Inc.*, 560 F. Supp. 1253 (E.D. Mo. 1983), *aff'd*, 728 F.2d 410 (8th Cir. 1984), in which the senior user was granted a registration for the State of Iowa, but held to have abandoned its national trademark rights to an expansionist junior user. *Cf. Holiday Inn v. Holiday Inns, Inc.*, 534 F.2d 312 (C.C.P.A. 1976), in which a prior user of "Holiday Inn" in a small local area was granted a restricted registration for that area despite potential confusion with the famous chain. *See* the section on Concurrent Use Proceedings in Chapter 3, *supra;* Schwartz, *Concurrent Registration Under the Lanham Trademark Act of 1946: What is the Impact on § 2(d) of § 22?*, 55 Trademark Rep. 413 (1965).

(5) Parties also may agree to divide territories of use between them, as long as source confusion remains unlikely. *In re Four Seasons Hotels Ltd.*, 987 F.2d 1565 (Fed. Cir. 1993); *Amalgamated Bank of N.Y. v. Amalgamated Trust & Savings*, 842 F.2d 1270 (Fed. Cir. 1988). *See also Houlihan v. Parliament Import Co.*, 921 F.2d 1258 (Fed. Cir. 1990) (upholding concurrent registration of BAREFOOT BYNUM for wine to two contiguous users who obtained territorial assignments from original owner; the court observed that concurrent registrants need not have products of identical quality).

(6) What determination of rights should result when a mark is registered by the senior user but a junior user innocently adopts the mark prior to the first user's registration and uses it continuously after adoption? The Lanham Act provides such a junior user with a defense to an infringement claim made by a registrant possessing *incontestability* rights in a mark under 15 U.S.C. § 1115, "[p]rovided, however, that this defense . . . shall apply only for the area in which such continuous prior use is proved." 15 U.S.C. § 111 5(b)(5). In *Induct-0-Matic Corp. v. Inductotherm Corp.*, 747 F.2d 358, 366 (6th Cir. 1984), and *Ace Hardware, Co. v. Ace Hardware Corp.*, 218 U.S.P.Q. 240 (N.D.N.Y. 1982), the courts held the junior user entitled to protection in the area of use that predated the registration. *Cf. Casual Corner Assocs., Inc. v. Casual Stores of Nevada, Inc.*, 493 F.2d 709 (9th Cir. 1974), where failure to use

the mark for one year prevented defendant from asserting the defense of *continuous* pre-registration use. For a discussion of the incontestability provisions of the Lanham Act, see Chapter 3, *supra*.

(7) Should innocent adoption by a junior user before registration by the senior user be a defense with regard to *contestable* registered marks? In *Golden Door, Inc. v. Odisho*, 437 F. Supp. 956, 964 (N.D. Cal. 1977), *aff'd*, 646 F.2d 347 (9th Cir. 1980), the court stated:

> [w]hether the enumerated exception constitutes a substantive defense to a claim of infringement, or merely alters the evidentiary weight accorded the presumption of plaintiff's exclusive right to use of the mark established by registration, has been a subject of confusion among the courts and authorities in the field of trademark law,

and reluctantly (*see* 437 F. Supp. at 864, N. 3) following Ninth Circuit precedent, applied the defense to the federal but not the state trademark claim. In *Matador Motor Inns, Inc. v. Matador Motel, Inc.*, 376 F. Supp. 385, 388 (D.N.J. 1974), the court termed "patently absurd" plaintiff's contention that the defense was inapplicable because plaintiff's mark was not yet incontestable.

> An incontestable mark, by definition, enjoys greater procedural protection than one of a lesser status. . . . If this be the case, clearly a defense to an infringement action based on an incontestable service mark must also be applicable to a contestable mark.

Similarly, in *Value House v. Phillips Mercantile Co.*, 523 F.2d 424, 429 (10th Cir. 1975), the court stated "The prior use defense in these circumstances is made available by 15 U.S.C.A. 1115(b)(5) even against a plaintiff whose mark has become incontestable and so the defense is *a fortiori* available here." *See also Wrist-Rocket Mfg. Co., supra* Note(1); *Money Store v. Harriscorp Finance, Inc.*, 689 F.2d 666 (7th Cir. 1982); *T-Shirts Plus v. T-Shirts Plus, Inc.*, 222 U.S.P.Q. 117 (C.D. Cal. 1983); *Allied Telephone Co. v. Allied Telephone Systems Co.*, 218 U.S.P.Q. 817 (S.D. Ohio 1982).

(8) Under the Lanham Act before its 1988 revision, the prior use defense described above had to be based on continuous use begun before the registrant's registration issued. Under the Revision Act, registrants are deemed to have nationwide constructive use as of the application filing date. 15 U.S.C. § 1057(c). Therefore, in actions involving registrations derived from applications filed after the November 16, 1989 effective date of the Revision Act, the prior use must have begun before the registrant's application filing date for the prior use defense to apply. 15 U.S.C. § 1115(b)(5).

§ 7.06 Gray Market Goods

INTRODUCTION

"Parallel imports" or "gray market goods" are goods bearing an authentic trademark which are intended for distribution in foreign countries but which are instead imported and sold to the ultimate consumer in a country where the trademark signifies a domestic source. Typically the manufacturer establishes a distribution system in which it authorizes or licenses the manufacture or sale of its products in specific foreign territories. Parallel importers purchase these products abroad and import them for domestic sale. As a result, these unauthorized goods often compete directly with goods imported and sold by the manufacturer's authorized distributor. In other instances, where the manufacturer has both domestic and foreign production facilities, the parallel imports compete with goods made domestically and intended only for domestic distribution. A number of factors including fluctuations in market conditions and currency exchange rates and disparities in costs, services or wage scales, may enable the sale of gray market goods at a price lower than that of authorized goods.

Historically, trademark law has viewed parallel imports under competing property law concepts: (1) "universal" rights in which a mark has no territorial bounds and ownership is exhausted once the product is sold, and (2) "territorial" rights in which a mark is exclusively owned by the registrant or user within each territory. *See* Hiebert, *Foundations of the Law of Parallel Importation: Duality and Universality in Nineteenth Century Trademark Law*, 80 Trademark Rep. 483 (1990). In the cases which follow, Justice Holmes' *Bourjois* and *Prestonettes* opinions established that in the United States the law of parallel imports is not based upon property law, but upon protection of the public from confusion or deception. If the domestic source has developed a goodwill factually independent from that of the foreign source, confusion may occur. While consideration of the relative benefits to consumers of barring or allowing parallel imports should be part of any analysis of this area of the law, the confusion principle remains fundamental.

A. BOURJOIS & CO. v. KATZEL

United States Supreme Court
260 U.S. 689 (1923)

MR. JUSTICE HOLMES delivered the opinion of the Court.

This is a bill to restrain the infringement of the trade marks "Java" and "Bourjois" registered in the Patent Office of the United States. A preliminary injunction was granted by the District Court, 274 Fed. 856, but the order was reversed by the Circuit Court of Appeals, one Judge dissenting. 275 Fed. 539. A writ of certiorari was granted by this Court. 257 U.S. 630. In 1913 A. Bourjois & Cie., E. Wertheimer & Cie., Successeurs, doing business in France and also in the United States, sold to the plaintiff for a large sum their business in the United States, with their good will and their trade marks registered in the Patent Office. The latter related particularly to face powder, and included the above words. The plaintiff since its purchase has registered them again and goes on with the business that it bought, using substantially the same form of box and label as its predecessors and importing its face powder from France. It uses care in selecting colors suitable for the American market, in packing and in keeping up the standard, and has spent much money in advertising, &c., so that the business has grown very great and the labels have come to be understood by the public here as meaning goods coming from the plaintiff. The boxes have upon their backs: "Trade Marks Reg. U.S. Pat. Off. Made in France — Packed in the U.S.A. by A. Bourjois & Co., Inc., of New York, Succ'rs. in the U.S. to A. Bourjois & Cie., and E. Wertheimer & Cie."

The defendant, finding that the rate of exchange enabled her to do so at a profit, bought a large quantity of the same powder in France and is selling it here in the French boxes which closely resemble those used by the plaintiff except that they have not the last quoted statement on the backs, and that the label reads "Poudre de Riz de Java," whereas the plaintiff has found it advisable to strike out the suggestion of rice powder and has "Poudre Java" instead. There is no question that the defendant infringes the plaintiff's rights unless the fact that her boxes and powder are the genuine product of the French concern gives her a right to sell them in the present form.

We are of opinion that the plaintiff's rights are infringed. After the sale the French manufacturers could not have come to the United States and have used their old marks in competition with the plaintiff. That plainly follows from the statute authorizing assignments. Act of February 20, 1905, c. 592, § 10, 33 Stat. 727. If for the purpose of evading the effect of the transfer, it had arranged with the defendant that she should sell with the old label, we suppose that no one would doubt that the contrivance must fail. There is no such conspiracy here, but, apart from the opening of a door to one, the vendors could not convey their goods free from the restriction to which the vendors were subject. Ownership of the goods does not carry the right to sell them with a specific mark. It does not necessarily carry the right to sell them at all in a given place. If the goods were patented in the United States a dealer who lawfully bought similar goods abroad from one who had a right to make and sell them there could not sell them in the United States. *Boesch v. Graff*, 133 U.S. 697. The monopoly in that case is more extensive, but we see no sufficient reason for holding that the monopoly of a trade mark, so far as it goes, is less complete. It deals with a delicate matter that may be of great value but that easily is destroyed, and therefore should be protected with corresponding care. It is said that the trade mark here is that of the French house and truly indicates the origin of the goods. But that is not accurate. It is the trade mark of the plaintiff only in the United States and indicates in law, and, it is found, by public understanding, that the goods come from the plaintiff although not made by it. It was sold and could only be sold with the good will of the business that the plaintiff bought. *Eiseman v. Schiffer*, 157 Fed. 473. It stakes the reputation of the plaintiff upon the character of the goods. *Menendez v. Holt*, 128 U.S. 514. The injunction granted by the District Court was proper under §§ 17 and 19 of the Trade Mark Act. Act of February 20, 1905, c. 592, 33 Stat. 724, 728, 729.

Decree of Circuit Court of Appeals reversed.

PRESTONETTES, INC. v. COTY

United States Supreme Court
264 U.S. 359 (1924)

MR. JUSTICE HOLMES.

This is a bill in equity brought by the respondent, Coty, a citizen of France, against Prestonettes, a New York corporation, having its principal place of business in the Southern District of New York. It seeks to restrain alleged unlawful uses of the plaintiff's registered trade-marks, "Coty" and "L'Origan" upon toilet powders and perfumes. The defendant purchases the genuine powder, subjects it to pressure, adds a binder to give it coherence and sells the compact in a metal case. It buys the genuine perfume in bottles and sells it in smaller bottles. We need not mention what labels it used before this suit as the defendant is content to abide by the decree of the District Court. That decree allowed the defendant to put upon the rebottled perfume "Prestonettes, Inc., not connected with Coty, states that the contents are Coty's — (giving the name of the article) independently rebottled in New York," every word to be in letters of the same size, color, type and general distinctiveness. It allowed the defendant to make compacts from the genuine loose powder of the plaintiff and to sell them with this label on the container: "Prestonettes, Inc., not connected with Coty, states that the compact of face powder herein was independently compounded by it from Coty's — (giving the name) loose powder and its own binder. Loose powder — per cent, Binder — per cent," every word to be in letters of the same size, color, type and general distinctiveness. The Circuit Court of Appeals, considering the very delicate and volatile nature of the perfume, its easy deterioration, and the opportunities for adulteration, issued an absolute preliminary injunction against the use of the above marks except on the original packages as marked and sold by the plaintiff, thinking that the defendant could not put upon the plaintiff the burden of keeping a constant watch. 285 Fed. 501. *Certiorari granted*, 260 U.S. 720.

The bill does not charge the defendant with adulterating or otherwise deteriorating the plaintiff's product except that it intimates rather than alleges metal containers to be bad, and the Circuit Court of Appeals stated that there were no controverted questions of fact but that the issue was simply one of law. It seemingly assumed that the defendant handled the plaintiff's product without in any way injuring its qualities and made its decree upon that assumption. The decree seems to us to have gone too far.

The defendant of course by virtue of its ownership had a right to compound or change what it bought, to divide either the original or the modified product, and to sell it so divided. The plaintiff could not prevent or complain of its stating the nature of the component parts and the source from which they were derived if it did not use the trade-mark in doing so. For instance, the defendant could state that a certain percentage of its compound was made at a certain place in Paris, however well known as the plaintiff's factory that place might be. If the compound was worse than the constituent, it might be a misfortune to the plaintiff, but the plaintiff would have no cause of action, as the defendant was exercising the rights of ownership and only telling the truth. The existence of a trade-mark would have no bearing on the question. Then what new rights does the trade-mark confer? It does not confer a right to prohibit the use of the word or words. It is not a copyright. The argument drawn from the language of the Trade-Mark Act does not seem to us to need discussion. A trade-mark only gives the right to prohibit the use of it so far as to protect the owner's good will against the sale of another's product as his. *United Drug Co. v. Theodore Rectanus Co.*, 248 U.S. 90, 97. There is nothing to the contrary in *Bourjois & Co. v. Katzel*, 260 U.S. 689. There the trade-mark protected indicated that the goods came from the plaintiff in the United States, although not made by it, and therefore could not be put upon other goods of the same make coming from abroad. When the mark is used in a way that does not deceive the public, we see no such sanctity in the word as to prevent its being used to tell the truth. It is not taboo. *Canal Co. v. Clark*, 13 Wall. 311, 327.

If the name of Coty were allowed to be printed in different letters from the rest of the inscription dictated by the District Court a casual purchaser might look no further and might be deceived. But when it in no way stands out from the statement of facts that unquestionably the defendant has a right to communicate in some form, we see no reason why it should not be used collaterally, not to indicate the goods, but to say that the trade-marked product is a constituent in the article now offered as new and changed. As a general proposition there can be no doubt that the word might be so used. If a man bought a barrel of a certain flour, or a demijohn of Old Crow whiskey, he certainly could sell the flour in smaller packages or in former days could have sold the whiskey in bottles, and tell what it was, if he stated that he did the dividing up or the bottling. And this would not be because of a license implied from the special facts but on the general ground that we have stated. It seems to us that no new right can be evoked from the fact that the perfume or powder is delicate and likely to be spoiled, or from the omnipresent possibility of fraud. If the defendant's rebottling the plaintiff's perfume deteriorates it and the public is adequately informed who does the rebottling, the public, with or without the plaintiff's assistance, is likely to find it out. And so of the powder in its new form.

This is not a suit for unfair competition. It stands upon the plaintiff's rights as owner of a trade-mark registered under the act of Congress. The question therefore is not how far the court would go in aid of a plaintiff who showed ground for suspecting the defendant of making a dishonest use of his opportunities, but is whether the plaintiff has the naked right alleged to prohibit the defendant from making even a collateral reference to the plaintiff's mark. We are of opinion that the decree of the Circuit Court of Appeals must be reversed and that that of the District Court must stand.

OSAWA & COMPANY v. B & H PHOTO

United States District Court, Southern District of New York
589 F. Supp. 1163 (1984)

LEVAL, DISTRICT JUDGE.

. . . .

Plaintiff is the duly registered owner in the United States of the Mamiya marks. . . .

The Mamiya equipment is sophisticated and expensive, designed for use by professional photographers and advanced amateurs. Accordingly it includes a wide range of peripheral equipment designed for special applications. In order to be able to supply promptly the needs of its professional photographer customers, plaintiff maintains at all times a stock of all such peripheral equipment.

Plaintiff purchases advertising and incurs other public relations expenses. To educate users, dealers and potential customers in the advantages and complex capabilities of its equipment, it organizes seminars, which are conducted in various parts of the country. To stimulate sales, it occasionally offers rebates, sometimes consisting of a free piece of peripheral equipment to one who purchases a Mamiya camera during a specified period.

Plaintiff distributes the Mamiya equipment through authorized camera dealers who apply for dealerships. Plaintiff's sales policy is based on its perception of a fundamental difference between equipment of such complexity and a simple amateur's camera. Because of the high cost and complexity of the equipment and because of the sophisticated demands of purchasers, plaintiff foresees a continuing relationship between dealer and customer involving advice, service and the future purchase of specialized peripheral equipment expanding the capabilities of the camera. According to its perception, a purchaser of a Mamiya camera who was unable to obtain such support from his dealer would soon be a dissatisfied customer. Accordingly, plaintiff has been unwilling to distribute its equipment through any camera store but will authorize and sell only to those dealers who demonstrate a willingness to take in an adequate full line stock so that they will be both able and motivated to service future needs of their customers.

Plaintiff also devotes considerable care to handling, including inspection on arrival. It offers free warranty repairs, performed either by its employees or by authorized service representatives, who must receive training in the equipment.

Defendants are discount camera dealers, offering camera equipment often at prices substantially cheaper than are available at other stores. Defendants advertise in national photography magazines. These advertisements characteristically are concerned with price; they set forth, mostly in small print, items of available equipment with prices. They sell by mail and by telephone to credit card purchasers, as well as over the counter. Defendants formerly were authorized Mamiya dealers purchasing from plaintiffs. Their dealerships were terminated as a result of the dispute over gray market merchandising.

Defendants advertise and sell Mamiya equipment that has been imported in violation of the Customs exclusion order. They are found also to have imported such merchandise. They sell this equipment at retail prices far below the prices of authorized dealers. In some cases they sell at prices cheaper than those at which plaintiff offers its merchandise to its dealers.

The reasons for the price disparity have not been fully shown by the evidence. Defendants contend it is because Osawa-Japan, the worldwide distributor, discriminates against the U.S. consumer by selling to plaintiff at arbitrarily higher prices than it charges to distributors in other countries. However, defendants have offered no proof that this is true. Nor have they shown in which countries their equipment is purchased or from whom.

Plaintiffs point to several possible factors explaining price differences. One is currency fluctuation, especially the recent strength of the U.S. dollar as against certain European currencies. Another possible explanation suggested by plaintiff is price differences set by Osawa-Japan that are not arbitrary or discriminatory but are justified by differing cost factors.

Third, plaintiff has convincingly proved that in support of the Mamiya trademarks it incurs substantial costs that defendants do not have. These include the whole range of activities described above in which plaintiff engages in order to create, maintain, protect and enhance the goodwill of the Mamiya marks.

Defendants seek to undercut this proof by showing that they too incur expenses of similar nature. But their contentions miss the point and do not alter the conclusion. For example, defendants point out that they also advertise, contending that this undermines plaintiff's argument as to its advertising expenses. Indeed defendants place ads, but they do not undertake advertising to publicize the quality of the Mamiya products. To the extent their ads mention the Mamiya name, it is only to show, in a one-line-per-item listing, how cheap their prices are. Thus it misses the point to say they have advertising. The expense they do not have is advertising to support the Mamiya marks.

Similar observations are pertinent as to handling expenses. No doubt the defendants incur some handling expenses. But defendants have no incentive to support the goodwill of any mark they sell; their sales are based solely on price advantage. It stands to reason that they conduct their operations as cheaply as possible and do not undertake the same degree of care (equals expense) in inspection and handling as plaintiff does to insure consumer satisfaction with Mamiya products.

Defendants' response is also inadequate on the subject of inventory costs. It was noted above that plaintiff maintains a vast inventory of related peripheral gadgets of special application to be able to satisfy promptly the needs of its professional photographer customers. Plaintiff contends convincingly that this is another cost not incurred by defendants. Defendants try to counter this point by showing that their purchase invoices over a substantial period have included every item in plaintiff's catalogue. This altogether misses the point. Defendants may well have sold every catalogue item at one time or another. That does not show that defendants maintain an inventory. Defendants have no reason to engage in such an expensive practice, and there is no evidence that they have done so.

Warranty expense

Defendants of course have borne no warranty service expense. This is a particularly significant item in several respects. First, plaintiff has not only borne warranty expenses on its own merchandise but has also provided warranty service on gray market equipment sold by defendants. Defendants argue that the latter injury is self-inflicted. Plaintiff has no obligation to warranty defendants' sales and could refuse the service. Defendants also argue that plaintiff could handle the packaging and warranty cards in such a way as to make the purchasing public better aware which cameras were warrantied and which were not. These observations are factually correct but miss the point. Plaintiff gives warranty service on defendants' gray market sales not out of stupidity or neglect but because plaintiff's management perceives that dissatisfied purchasers of Mamiya cameras will damage the reputation of the Mamiya mark, which is the most significant asset on which plaintiff's business is founded. The customers do not know the cameras they purchased are from the gray market because defendants do not tell them. Thus, as to warranty repairs, not only are defendants operating free of a significant cost that plaintiff bears, but their sales increase plaintiff's cost.

Equitable Factors

Similarly, it is all very well for defendants to argue that plaintiff can protect itself to a degree by spending additional money so as to better warn the public which cameras carry, and which do not carry, warranties. It seems to me a significant equitable factor that defendants could also have undertaken to warn their customers that their merchandise was not imported by the authorized U.S. Mamiya distributor and carried no warranty protection. Instead the opposite has been done. B & H has delivered to its customers a notice that falsely advises that the merchandise is protected by the manufacturer's warranty and instructs the customer that "if you bring or send the [defective] item to a manufacturer's authorized service agency, your item will be repaired at no cost to you." *See* Plaintiff's Exhibits 79, 80, 85. This aspect of the defendants' conduct can be properly characterized as bad faith. It deceives the public and conceals the significance to the customer of the double market structure defendants have created. Defendants tell the customers the good news about their cheap prices. But they conceal or affirmatively misrepresent the bad news. Plaintiff is left with the choice of providing free warranty service on defendants' merchandise or suffering damage to the reputation of its marks.

Bad Faith

. . . .

Plaintiff has shown a drastic decline in its sales in 1983 as compared with average levels over the past nine years. Concomitantly, it has laid off a large part of its personnel, including a significant part of the repair force, and has suffered consequent delays in time needed for warranty repairs. The advertising budget for the Mamiya mark has been severely slashed. Competition from gray marketers has caused demoralization, disaffection and misunderstanding among authorized dealers, 40% of whom have dropped the Mamiya line since 1980. There is evidence that some dealers have misunderstood the cause of the problem, believing that plaintiff was granting preferred price treatment to their competitors.

Another aspect of the harm is that plaintiff's advertising expenditures and public relations efforts are incurred largely for the benefit of its competitors, the gray market sellers, who free ride on plaintiff's publicity.

Also in order to avoid consumer confusion, disaffection and resentment, plaintiff has performed warranty repairs and honored rebate offers on gray market cameras, essentially furnishing free service and benefit to support the sales of its competitors.

A number of the circumstances mentioned above as harmful to plaintiff's business also cause damage to its goodwill and to the pubic reputation of its Mamiya marks. Naturally, a reduced advertising budget means reduced opportunity to publicize the marks and consequently further reduced sales. The widespread disaffection among authorized dealers by reason of the gray market price competition creates a substantial risk of loss of enthusiasm or bad-mouthing (where it matters most since buyers are likely to look to dealers for advice on brands and equipment). Delay in performing warranty repairs as a result of staff reductions also creates resentment directed against the brand. Plaintiff's reputation also suffers when defendants perform inadequate inspections of merchandise. For example, gray market cameras have been found to contain instruction manuals written in foreign languages, which causes understandable consumer dissatisfaction.

The issue of warranties, discussed above, is of significant importance on the subject of irreparable harm and confusion. For such an expensive, complicated and sensitive piece of equipment, a prospective purchaser wants assurance that a responsible organization stands behind and guarantees the equipment. The submission to plaintiff of gray market cameras claiming for warranty repairs is significant evidence of consumer confusion. If plaintiff refuses to honor these claims, further confusion will result, coupled with public mistrust of the mark. If it does honor these warranty claims, it is subsidizing its competitors' business. As noted above, B & H's misleading assurance that the goods are warranted by the manufacturer has unnecessarily increased such confusion. Similar confusion arises when gray market customers apply for the benefits of plaintiff's offers of rebates. Again its choice is essentially to risk the confusion and resentment (which defendants have done nothing to obviate) or to subsidize defendants' sales by honoring the claims.

Consumer confusion also arises from the wide price disparities between legitimate and gray imports. Consumers will wonder why the same equipment can be purchased so much more cheaply at one place than at others. Many will no doubt assume the explanation is that plaintiff is gouging, which will engender hostility to the mark.

. . . .

. . . B & H has developed a new strategy in litigation and now undertakes that it will warrant the gray Mamiya merchandise that it sells. (It also offers to parallel all Mamiya rebate offers by similar offers of its own.) This ingenious stratagem, however, offers only a superficial solution. More realistically it can be seen as aggravating the problem. For the warranty is of value to the goodwill of the mark only if offered by one who has the incentive to uphold the reputation of the mark. B & H would have no such incentive. Plaintiff would have no assurance that B & H's warranty repairs would be properly performed or that the obligation would be graciously accepted. It would be constantly subject to the risk that B & H would disavow the obligation or perform inadequate repairs. Disparities between plaintiff's and defendants' performance of warranty work would further confuse the marketplace as to the standing and meaning of the Mamiya mark.

A. *Universality, Territoriality and a Separate Local Goodwill*

A hundred years ago the view was widely held that if a trademark was lawfully affixed to merchandise in one country, the merchandise would carry that mark lawfully wherever it went and could not be deemed an infringer although transported *Rix of* to another country where the exclusive right to the mark was held by someone other *Terretoriality* than the owner of the merchandise.

. . . .

. . . [This] universality principle has faded and been generally supplanted by the principle of "territoriality," upon which the *Bourjois* rulings were based. This *Domestic* principle recognizes that a trademark has a separate legal existence under each *registrant* country's laws, and that its proper lawful function is not necessarily to specify the *over its* origin or manufacture of a good (although it may incidentally do that), but rather *imports* to symbolize the domestic goodwill of the domestic markholder so that the consuming public may rely with an expectation of consistency on the domestic reputation earned for the mark by its owner, and the owner of the mark may be confident that his goodwill and reputation (the value of the mark) will not be injured through use of the mark by others in domestic commerce. . . .

. . . .

The universality decisions were superficially and deceptively consistent with the *Doctrine of Exhaustion* trademark doctrine of "exhaustion." Under this doctrine, as applied within the borders of a sovereignty, a markholder may no longer control branded goods after releasing them into the stream of commerce. After the first sale, the brandholder's control is deemed exhausted. Down-the-line retailers are free to display and advertise the branded goods. Secondhand dealers may advertise the branded merchandise for resale in competition with the sales of the markholder (so long as they do not misrepresent themselves as authorized agents). *See Prestonettes, Inc. v. Coty*, 264 U.S. 359 (1924).

. . . The application of the exhaustion concept to international trade seemed to *applied internationally* suggest that once the original mark owner had lost control of the marked goods by releasing them into commerce, his assignee in a foreign country could not logically own rights superior to those of the assignor. The right of control seemed exhausted.

This reasoning is flawed, however, where the assignee of the mark in the second country has developed a separate, factually independent goodwill. If no such independent goodwill has been developed, then in spite of recognition of territorial limits, arguably there might be no infringement. If the U.S. mark represents nothing more than a foreign outpost of the goodwill associated with the original mark, it might well be argued that exhaustion has taken place with the release into commerce and that no infringement occurs on unauthorized importation . . . .

But where, as here, the U.S. assignee has developed a separate goodwill factually independent from that of the mark originator, whatever exhaustion occurred with the original release into commerce was the exhaustion of a legally distinct and factually different mark. Thus, the development by the assignee of a separate and distinct U.S. goodwill was a crucial finding in *Katzel* , made by the district court, *see* 274 F. 856, 857 (S.D.N.Y 1920), and underlined in Holmes' opinion.

B. *Defendants' Contentions*

Defendants here seek to apply the principles of exhaustion on an international scale, arguing that once the goods bearing the Mamiya mark have been sold in commerce, bringing a profit to the original markholder, neither the original markholder nor his assignees may exert control over them. This position might have substantial force if no independent U.S. goodwill were represented by the Mamiya marks.

However, plaintiff has proved convincingly that, as the result of its efforts, it has developed in the United States marketplace a substantial goodwill separate and distinct from the goodwill emanating from the branded goods themselves. This local goodwill is the product of plaintiff's many U.S. activities (described above) promoting and standing behind the mark, including significantly warranty service, promotional rebates, educational activities and advertising. The Mamiya trademark in the U.S. represents a goodwill generated and importantly influenced by these activities. It is not the same trademark either in law or in fact as the Mamiya trademark at the place of manufacture, where it designates only the goodwill of the manufacturer.

Defendants rely on the turn-of-the-century cases noted above. They argue that both § 526 and the Holmes *Bourjois* decisions should be narrowly limited to situations where the domestic markholder had purchased outright the U.S. mark and goodwill and was not related to the foreign mark originator.

I find no basis for this contention either in fact or in logic. The old universality cases and the theory upon which they rest represent an incorrect analysis that has been repudiated in both statutory and decisional law, at least where the domestic markholder has developed an independent goodwill.

. . . .

Defendants' next arguments are that this interpretation of the trademark laws and of § 526 fosters anticompetitive practices, discriminatory pricing, and violations of antitrust law and policy. Defendants argue that the opportunities for gray marketing are necessarily the consequence of an attempt by Osawa-Japan to discriminate against the U.S. consumer by charging higher prices to its U.S. distributor than it charges to distributors elsewhere. The only way to prevent this, defendants contend, is to construe the trademark laws as they advocate.

There are several sufficient answers to this contention. First, as noted above, there are many possible explanations why a gray market importer can sell cheaper than the exclusive distributor. Although arbitrary price discrimination is one possible explanation, there are many others, as noted above, including particularly fluctuations in international currency markets, differing cost conditions in other countries, and the fact, amply demonstrated here, that the plaintiff-markholder incurs many costs that the gray marketer does not. These include, at a minimum, all the costs incurred for the maintenance and enhancement of the mark's reputation, such as advertising and public relations, consumer and dealer education, warranty service, and maintenance of inventory. No proofs have been adduced by defendants that arbitrary price discrimination was practiced by Osawa-Japan.

But even assuming that it was, and assuming further that those practices violated the antitrust laws or other laws governing fair business practice, it does not follow that the problem should be remedied by an illogical misapplication of the trademark laws. A trademark is, like a patent, a monopoly conferred by law. Unquestionably they are susceptible to abuse and to employment in illegal fashion. When this occurs, the proper remedy is either to deny enforcement in appropriate instances or to impose liability by reason of the finding of unfair competition, violation of the antitrust laws or whatever, and not by distortion of the trademark laws in a fashion that will defeat legitimate trademark expectations.

. . . .

Defendants also ague that plaintiff's position would give plaintiff an unjustifiable monopoly on the U.S. sale of Mamiya equipment. This is simply not so. Nothing in this opinion would bar defendants from importing and selling the equipment manufactured by Mamiya Co. in Japan. What is forbidden is infringing on plaintiff's rights to the Mamiya marks. So long as defendants take steps so as not to infringe on plaintiff's trademark rights, nothing in the reasoning of this opinion would prevent them from dealing in the same equipment. . . .

[*Preliminary Injunction granted*].

LEVER BROTHERS COMPANY v. UNITED STATES

United States Court of Appeals, District of Columbia Circuit
981 F.2d 1330 (1993)

SENTELLE, CIRCUIT JUDGE.

The District Court entered a judgment invalidating the "affiliate exception" of 19 C.F.R. § 133.21(c)(2) (1988) as inconsistent with the statutory mandate of the Lanham Act of 1946, 15 U.S.C. § 1124 (1988), prohibiting importation of goods which copy or simulate the mark of a domestic manufacturer, and issued a nationwide injunction barring enforcement of the regulation with respect to *any* foreign goods bearing a valid United States trademark but materially and physically differing from the United States version of the goods. The United States appeals. We conclude that the District Court, obedient to our limited remand in a prior decision in this same cause, properly determined that the regulation is inconsistent with the statute. However, because we conclude that the remedy the District Court provided is overbroad, we vacate the judgment and remand for entry of an injunction against allowing the importation of the foreign-produced Lever Brothers brand products at issue in this case.

. . . .

Lever Brothers Company ("Lever US" or "Lever"), an American company, and its British affiliate, Lever Brothers Limited ("Lever UK"), both manufacture deodorant soap under the "Shield" trademark and hand dishwashing liquid under the "Sunlight" trademark. The trademarks are registered in each country. The products have evidently been formulated differently to suit local tastes and circumstances. The U.S. version lathers more, the soaps smell different, the colorants used in American "Shield" have been certified by the FDA whereas the colorants in British "Shield" have not, and the U.S. version contains a bacteriostat that enhances the deodorant properties of the soap. The British version of "Sunlight" dishwashing soap produces less suds, and the American version is formulated to work best in the "soft water" available in most American cities, whereas the British version is designed for "hard water" common in Britain.

The packaging of the U.S. and U.K. products is also somewhat different. The British "Shield" logo is written in script form and is packaged in foil wrappings and contains a wave motif, whereas the American "Shield" logo is written in block form, does not come in foil wrappings and contains a grid pattern. There is small print on the packages indicating where they were manufactured. The British "Sunlight" comes in a cylindrical bottle labeled "Sunlight Washing Up Liquid." The American "Sunlight" comes in a yellow, hour-glass-shaped bottle labeled "Sunlight Dishwashing Liquid."

Lever asserts that the unauthorized influx of these foreign products has created substantial consumer confusion and deception in the United States about the nature and origin of this merchandise, and that it has received numerous consumer complaints from American consumers who unknowingly bought the British products and were disappointed.

Lever argues that the importation of the British products was in violation of § 42 of the Lanham Act, 15 U.S.C. § 1124 which provides that with the exception of goods imported for personal use:

> [N]o article of imported merchandise which shall copy or simulate the name of the [sic] any domestic manufacture, or manufacturer . . . or which shall copy or simulate a trademark registered in accordance with the provisions of this chapter . . . shall be admitted to entry at any customhouse of the United States.

Id. The United States Customs Service ("Customs"), however, was allowing importation of the British goods under the "affiliate exception" created by 19 C.F.R. § 133.21(c)(2), which provides that foreign goods bearing United States trademarks are not forbidden when "[t]he foreign and domestic trademark or tradename owners are parent and subsidiary companies or are otherwise subject to common ownership or control."

In *Lever I*, we concluded that "the natural, virtually inevitable reading of § 42 is that it bars foreign goods bearing a trademark identical to the valid U.S. trademark but physically different," without regard to affiliation between the producing firms or the genuine character of the trademark abroad. 877 F.2d 101, 111 (D.C. Cir. 1989).

. . . .

Customs' main argument from the legislative history is that § 42 of the Lanham Act applies only to imports of goods bearing trademarks that "copy or simulate" a registered mark. Customs thus draws a distinction between "genuine" marks and marks that "copy or simulate." A mark applied by a foreign firm subject to ownership and control common to that of the domestic trademark owner is by definition "genuine," Customs urges, regardless of whether or not the goods are identical. Thus, any importation of goods manufactured by an affiliate of a U.S. trademark owner cannot "copy or simulate" a registered mark because those goods are *ipso facto* "genuine."

This argument is fatally flawed. It rests on the false premise that foreign trademarks applied to foreign goods are "genuine" in the United States. Trademarks applied to physically different foreign goods are not genuine from the viewpoint of the American consumer. As we stated in *Lever I*:

> On its fact . . . § [42] appears to aim at deceit and consumer confusion; when identical trademarks have acquired different meanings in different countries, one who imports the foreign version to sell it under that trademark will (in the absence of some specially differentiating feature) cause the confusion Congress sought to avoid. The fact of affiliation between the producers in no way reduces the probability of that confusion; it is certainly not a constructive consent to importation.

877 F.2d at 111.

There is a larger, more fundamental and ultimately fatal weakness in Customs' position in this case. Section 42 on its fact appears to forbid importation of goods that "copy or simulate" a United States trademark. Customs has the burden of adducing evidence from the legislative history of § 42 and its administrative practice of an exception for materially different goods whose similar foreign and domestic trademarks are owned by affiliated companies. At a minimum, this requires that the specific question be addressed in the legislative history or the administrative record. It is not enough to posit that silence implies authorization, when the authorization sought runs counter to the evident meaning of the governing statute. Therefore, we conclude that § 42 of the Lanham Act precludes the application of Customs' affiliate exception with respect to physically, materially different goods.

[*Remanded for modified injunction.*]

NOTES ON GRAY MARKET GOODS

(1) Efforts to bar parallel imports have been criticized as "protectionist." It is argued that "free trade" in parallel imports would promote an effective world-wide division of labor by rewarding those foreign manufacturers or importers who can produce or distribute products less expensively than their United States counterparts. Opponents of parallel imports argue, however, that the issue is not one of free trade versus protectionism if consumers are likely to be confused. This is most obvious where the parallel imports are neither identical to their domestic counterparts nor supported by equal service structures or warranties, but may be equally true where consumers are simply not informed of the non-domestic source of goods. If the

(handwritten margin note: Show diff between domestic & foreign)

domestic owner can show a separate and truly independent domestic goodwill, or material differences between the domestic and foreign products, relief against gray market importation normally will be granted. *See Ferrero U.S.A., Inc. v. Ozak Trading, Inc.*, 21 U.S.P.Q.2d 1215 (3d Cir. 1991) (enjoining gray market importation of materially different TIC TAC breath mints); *PepsiCo Inc. v. Giraud*, 7 U.S.P.Q.2d 1371 (D.P.R. 1988) (material differences in gray market PEPSI created likelihood of confusion); Goldman, *Unfair Competition, False Advertising and Only Two Calories: Will the Tic Tac Case Close the Gray Market for Good?*, 83 Trademark Rep. 495 (1993) (discussing applications of the material differences test).

Some parallel imports are clearly inferior to the authorized product, making exclusion under a confusion standard particularly appropriate. They may also violate U.S. law and regulations such as EPA standards or FDA labeling requirements. *See* Minchan, *The Gray Market: A Call for Greater Protection of Consumers and Trademark Owners*, 12 U. Pa. J. Int'l Bus. L. 457 (1991); Lipner, *Trademarked Goods and Their Gray Market Equivalents: Should Product Differences Result in the Barring of Unauthorized Goods from the U.S. Market?*, 18 Hofstra L. Rev. 1029 (1990); Dorr & Traphegan, *Lurking In The Shadows: The Gray Market Threat To Trademark Owners*, [1984] Merchandising Rep. 33 (Dec-Jan. 1983-1984).

(2) Regardless of whether source confusion is present, many opponents of parallel imports object to parallel importers' free riding on the advertising, warranty, and service efforts of the U.S. company, while selling the same product at a lower price. Should such injury be actionable even absent the basic trademark principle of protecting the public from confusion or deception? *See* Lipner, *The Legality of Parallel Imports: Trademark, Antitrust or Equity?*, 19 Texas Int'l L.J. 553 (1984). In *In the Matter of Certain Alkaline Batteries*, 225 U.S.P.Q. 823 (Int'l Trade Comm'n 1984), DURACELL batteries manufactured by a wholly owned Belgian subsidiary of Duracell Inc. were imported into the United States in competition with DURACELL batteries manufactured by Duracell domestically. The commission majority excluded all Belgian DURACELL batteries stating that the function of trademark law should not be limited only to preventing consumer confusion, but should, *inter alia*, ensure an equal level of quality, assist sellers in advertising and selling their goods, and protect a trademark owner's investment. In a separate opinion, two commissioners disagreed with the legal basis for the majority ruling and urged application of the doctrine established by the *Bourjois* and *Prestonettes* cases, with consequent exclusion only of improperly labelled batteries and of batteries on which use of the DURACELL trademark was likely to cause confusion. On January 4, 1985, President Reagan disapproved the ruling of the Commission in *Duracell* on the ground that "the Commission's interpretation of Section 42 of the Lanham Act (15 U.S.C. § 1124) . . . is at odds with the longstanding regulatory interpretation of the Department of Treasury" which was then under review. *In the Matter of Certain Alkaline Batteries*, 225 U.S.P.Q. 862 (Pres. 1985).

(3) In *Bell & Howell: Mamiya Co. v. Masel Supply Co.*, 548 F. Supp. 1063 (E.D.N.Y. 1982), the plaintiff in *Osawa, supra* under its predecessor name, obtained a preliminary injunction against another gray market dealer, but the injunction was vacated and the case remanded by the Court of Appeals because there was

insufficient proof of likelihood of confusion or deception and of irreparable injury, *Bell & Howell: Mamiya Co. v. Masel Supply Co.*, 719 F.2d 42, 46 (2d Cir. 1983):

> On the basis of the present record, irreparable injury may well not be present herein since there would appear to be little confusion, if any, as to the origin of goods and no significant likelihood of damage to BHMC's reputation since thus far it has not been shown that Masel's goods, which have a common origin of manufacture of BHMC's goods, are inferior to those sold by BHMC and are injuring BHMC's reputation. Further, it does not appear that the lack of warranties accompanying MAMIYA cameras sold by Masel amounts to irreparable injury, since the consumer can be made aware by, among other things, labels on the camera boxes or notices in advertisements as to whether the cameras are sold with or without warranties. Thus, less drastic means would appear to be available to avoid the claimed confusion.

In *Osawa*, 589 F. Supp. at 1165, the court found that the plaintiff had remedied the deficiencies alluded to in *Bell & Howell*, having shown likelihood of confusion and having provided "substantial proof of irreparable harm." *Cf. Model Rectifier Corp. v. Takachiho Int'l, Inc.*, 221 U.S.P.Q. 502 (9th Cir. 1983), where the court affirmed a preliminary injunction against a parallel importer stating that the damages were "by their nature irreparable."

In *Premier Dental Products Co. v. Darby Dental Supply Co.*, 794 F.2d 850 (3d Cir. 1986), the Third Circuit upheld a lower court's preliminary injunction preventing the importation of identical goods under § 526 of the Tariff Act of 1930 where the plaintiff owned the domestic trademark rights and had developed a separate goodwill from that of the foreign trademark owner and manufacturer. The appellate court rejected the lower court's basis for its finding of irreparable harm, finding no immediate danger of a decline in plaintiff's sales which might result in cancellation of its distribution contract. It instead found the requisite irreparable harm in the inevitable injury to the plaintiff's goodwill and mark created by defendant's importations. It stated (at p. 859):

> Purchasers of [plaintiff's] IMPREGUM are confident that they can obtain the same product, service and financial guaranties that they have gotten before. The continued availability of IMPREGUM through sources, like [defendant] not associated with [plaintiff] must inevitably injure [plaintiff's] reputation as the exclusive domestic source of IMPREGUM. This would constitute irreparable injury to the value of the mark because customers would no longer have that same confidence. This is true whether or not the service and financial guaranties are comparable to those offered by [plaintiff].

> . . . [W]e believe that *Bourjois* and Section 526 make it clear that an American distributor's goodwill can be harmed even by the sale of gray market goods that are *identical* to those sold by the distributor.

The court upheld the lower court's requirement that the plaintiff supply the defendant with the trademarked goods on the same terms and conditions the plaintiff supplied its other customers, in order to protect the defendant's interest. *See generally* Supnik, *The Bell and Howell: Mamiya Case — Where Now Parallel Imports?*, 74 Trademark Rep. 1 (1984).

(4) The Customs Service will bar parallel imports under 19 U.S.C. § 1526, except under circumstances identified in 19 C.F.R. § 133.21. 19 U.S.C. § 1526(a) prohibits importing "into the United States any merchandise of foreign manufacture if such merchandise . . . bears a trademark owned by a citizen of, or by a corporation, or association created or organized within, the United States, and registered in the Patent and Trademark Office by a person domiciled in the United States . . ., unless written consent of the owner of such trademark is produced at the time of making entry." Under Customs' implementing regulation, 19 C.F.R. § 133.21, however, Customs did not prohibit parallel imports when (1) both the foreign and domestic trademark were owned by "the same person"; or (2) where the foreign and domestic trademark owners were parent and subsidiary or otherwise subject to common ownership or control; or (3) where use of the trademark by a foreign manufacturer was authorized by the U.S. trademark owner.

In *K Mart Corp. v. Cartier, Inc.*, 486 U.S. 281 (1988), the Supreme Court addressed the validity of 19 C.F.R. § 133.21 and found the third subsection invalid while upholding the validity of the first two. The majority held that given the ambiguities in the statutory terms "foreign manufacture" and "owned by" in 19 U.S.C. § 1526, subsections (1) and (2) were valid regulatory interpretations of that section. The Court found that in the subsection (1) situation either the domestic or foreign entity could be said to "own" the U.S. trademark, and in the subsection (2) situation goods manufactured by a foreign subsidiary of a domestic company could be said to be goods which are not "of foreign manufacture." However, a different majority struck down subsection (3) which had permitted importation of goods manufactured abroad by a company that is merely authorized (i.e. licensed) to use a trademark by the domestic trademark owner. Finding the above ambiguities did not apply to subsection (3), the court stated "Under no reasonable construction of the statutory language can goods made in a foreign country by an independent foreign manufacturer be removed from the purview of the statute." *Id.*, at 1813. Customs subsequently deleted the third subsection from the regulation. 55 Fed. Reg. 52040 (1990) (amending 19 C.F.R. § 133.21).

(5) *K Mart* only addressed the validity of Customs' regulations, and did not address the application of the Lanham Act to gray market issues. Two circuits have held that where the gray goods at issue are materially different from their domestic counterparts, confusion is likely and the Lanham Act is violated regardless of any "common control" or affiliation between the U.S. and foreign trademark owners. *Lever Brothers v. United States, supra*, (Customs enjoined from permitting importation into the U.S. of materially different British SHIELD soap and SUN LIGHT dishwashing detergent); *Societe Des Produits Nestle S.A. v. Casa Helvetia, Inc.*, 25 U.S.P.Q.2d 1256 (1st Cir. 1992) (material differences in Venezuelan PERUGINA chocolates created likely confusion with Italian PERUGINA chocolates distributed in U.S. in violation of §§ 32, 42 and 43(a)). *Cf. Pepsico Inc. v. Nostalgia Products Corp.*, 18 U.S.P.Q.2d 1404, 1406 (N.D. Ill. 1990) (consent judgment entered where third-party importation of unauthorized goods produced by foreign licensee violated Tariff Act, citing *K Mart*); *Duracell, Inc. v. Global Imports, Inc.*, 12 U.S.P.Q.2d 1651, 1653 (S.D.N.Y. 1989) (refusing to vacate injunction entered before *K Mart* decision, noting that although *K Mart* held that Customs' "common control"

regulations were valid, it left open the Lanham Act issues, and that in the Second Circuit goods covered by Customs' "common control" exception still may cause likely confusion in violation of the Lanham Act). *See also* Hahn, *Gray Market Goods: Has A Resolution Been Found?*, 81 Trademark Rep. 58 (1991).

(6) The Ninth Circuit interpreted the Customs Service's common control exception to the exclusion of parallel imports in *United States v. Eighty-Nine (89) Bottles of Eau de Joy*, 797 F.2d 767 (9th Cir. 1986). The defendant had imported perfumes allegedly in violation of the Tariff Act, and the government sought forfeiture of these genuine goods. The defendant argued that the European trademark owner exercised sufficient control over the American trademark owner to bring the parties within the Customs Service's common control exception. The Ninth Circuit held that the exception applied "when the foreign and domestic entity are really the same entity," but not where the relationship between the foreign and domestic trademark owners was essentially that of licensor-licensee, as it was in *Eighty-Nine Bottles.*

In *NEC Electronics v. CAL Circuit Abco*, 810 F.2d 1506 (9th Cir. 1987), *cert. denied*, 484 U.S. 851 (1987), the Ninth Circuit vacated the district court's injunction prohibiting the importation of genuine goods where the plaintiff was the owner of the domestic trademark rights and the wholly-owned subsidiary of the manufacturer, a Japanese computer chip company. The defendant purchased the manufacturer's goods abroad, imported them into the United States and sold the goods. Without an analysis of the plaintiff's efforts to develop a separate domestic goodwill in the trademark for its computer chips, the court observed that plaintiff "cannot look to United States trademark law to insulate the American market or vitiate the effects of international trade." *See also Weil Ceramics & Glass, Inc. v. Dash*, 878 F.2d 659 (3d Cir.), *cert. denied*, 110 S. Ct. 156 (1989), where, without an analysis as to separate goodwill, the Third Circuit denied relief against gray market imports because plaintiff shared in profits from its foreign parent's sales to defendant, the foreign parent could stop selling to defendant, and the domestic and gray goods were identical. To similar effect is *Yamaha Corp. of America v. ABC International Traders, Inc.*, 1991 U.S. App. LEXIS 17882 (9th Cir. 1991), in which the court affirmed summary judgment against plaintiff, holding that federal trademark law affords no protection to a wholly-owned U.S. subsidiary of a foreign manufacturer against a rival company that imports and sells goods made by the foreign parent.

(7) Some courts have found the parallel imports to be genuine goods and held that, as a consequence, there could be no infringement. In *Monte Carlo Shirt, Inc. v. Daewo Int'l (America) Corp.*, 707 F.2d 1054 (9th Cir. 1983), parallel importation of goods ordered but subsequently rejected by the U.S. trademark owner was upheld since the goods were originally produced for the complaining trademark owner on contract for future domestic sale. A similar result was reached in *Parfums Stern, Inc. v. United States Customs Service*, 575 F. Supp. 416 (S.D. Fla. 1983), where the district court distinguished *Bourjois* and *Osawa* on the basis that the U.S. Trademark owner had by its own actions placed the parallel imports into foreign markets in ways which facilitated their importation. *Compare El Greco Leather Products Co. v. Shoe World*, 806 F.2d 392 (2d Cir. 1986), where the court granted relief under the Lanham Act and enjoined importation of foreign goods manufactured for the

trademark owner, finding the goods were not genuine since they had been rejected by the trademark owner. The court stated:

> The mere act of ordering a product to be labeled with a trademark does not deprive its holder of the right to control the product and the trademark. It is true that El Greco did not, at the time it cancelled the last two lots of its order, give instructions on how to dispose of the shoes that had already been manufactured and affixed with the CANDIE'S trademark. But we do not view such a step as necessary on the facts presented here.
>
> Once it cancelled the order, El Greco was entitled to assume that [the manufacturer] would not dispose of the shoes without either removing the CANDIE'S trademark . . . or affording El Greco an opportunity to inspect the goods and certify their quality prior to disposal, or, at the minimum, seeking instructions from El Greco on how to dispose of them.

806 F.2d at 395–96.

(8) Section 602 of the Copyright Act prohibits the importation of unauthorized reproductions of copyrighted works. *CBS, Inc. v. Scorpio Music Distributors*, 569 F. Supp. 47 (E.D. Pa. 1983), *aff'd*, 738 F.2d 421 (3d Cir. 1984) (enjoining unauthorized importation of copyrighted audiorecordings).

(9) Should consumers be able to purchase less expensive parallel imports so long as they are clearly and truthfully informed of the inferiority of the products? California and New York require retailers to inform customers that gray market goods may not be accompanied by the manufacturer's U.S. warranty or may not be eligible for a manufacturer's rebate. (1986 Cal. Rev. Stat. Ch. 1497; N.Y. Gen. Bus. Law § 218aa).

§ 7.07 Permitted Use

INTRODUCTION

The law does not prohibit the use of another's trademark on or in connection with the sale of one's own goods or services as long as such use is not deceptive. The leading decisions on permitted use of another's trademark are still those written by Mr. Justice Holmes in *Bourjois* and *Prestonettes, supra*. More recently, comparative advertising of competing brands has fostered another form of such litigation. In reconciling these decisions, note the courts' emphasis on truthful disclosure. Consider whether a trademark or trade name can truthfully be used on repaired, damaged, deteriorated, or repackaged goods sold by other than the trademark owner if it is made clear that the goods are in fact repaired, damaged, deteriorated, repackaged, unguaranteed or otherwise varying from the trademark owner's standards. The salient principle governing the legal propriety of using another's trademark is simply that of truthfulness and the absence of any likelihood of deception.

CHAMPION SPARK PLUG CO. v. SANDERS

United States Supreme Court
331 U.S. 125 (1947)

MR. JUSTICE DOUGLAS.

Petitioner is a manufacturer of spark plugs which it sells under the trade mark "Champion." Respondents collect the used plugs, repair and recondition them, and resell them. Respondents retain the word "Champion" on the repaired or reconditioned plugs. The outside box or carton in which the plugs are packed has stamped on it the word "Champion" together with the letter and figure denoting the particular style or type. They also have printed on them "Perfect Process Spark Plugs Guaranteed Dependable" and "Perfect Process Renewed Spark Plugs." Each carton contains smaller boxes in which the plugs are individually packed. These inside boxes also carry legends indicating that the plug has been renewed.[1] But respondent company's business name or address is not printed on the cartons. It supplies customers with petitioner's charts containing recommendations for the use of Champion plugs. On each individual plug is stamped in small letters, blue on black, the work "Renewed,"which at times is almost illegible.

Petitioner brought this suit in the District Court, charging infringement of its trade mark and unfair competition. *See* Judicial Code §§ 24 (1), (7), 28 U.S.C. §§ 41(1), , (7). The District Court found that respondents had infringed the trade mark. It enjoined them from offering or selling any of petitioner's plugs which had been repaired or reconditioned unless (a) the trade mark and type and style marks were removed, (b) the plugs were repainted with a durable gray, brown, orange, or green paint, (c) the word "REPAIRED" was stamped into the plug in letters of such size and depth as to retain enough white paint to display distinctly each letter of the word, (d) the cartons in which the plugs were packed carried a legend indicating that they contained used spark plugs originally made by petitioner and repaired and made fit for use up to 10,000 miles by respondent company.[2] The District Court denied an accounting. *See* 56 F. Supp. 782, 61 F. Supp. 247.

The Circuit Court of Appeals held that respondents not only had infringed petitioner's trade mark but also were guilty of unfair competition. It likewise denied

---

[1] "The process used in renewing this plug has been developed through 10 years continuous experience. This Spark Plug has been tested for firing under compression before packing."

"This Spark Plug is guaranteed to be a selected used Spark Plug, thoroughly renewed and in perfect mechanical condition and is guaranteed to give satisfactory service for 10,000 miles."

[2] The prescribed legend read:

> Used spark plug(s) originally made by Champion Spark Plug Company repaired and made fit for use up to 10,000 miles by Perfect Recondition Spark Plug Co., 1133 Bedford Avenue, Brooklyn, N.Y.

The decree also provided: .

> the name and address of the defendants to be larger and more prominent than the legend itself, and the name of plaintiff may be in slightly larger type than the rest of the body of the legend.

an accounting but modified the decree in the following respects: (a) it eliminated the provision requiring the trade mark and type and style marks to be removed from the repaired or reconditioned plugs; (b) it substituted for the requirement that the word "REPAIRED" be stamped into the plug, etc., a provision that the word "REPAIRED" or "USED" be stamped and baked on the plug by an electrical hot press in a contrasting color so as to be clearly and distinctly visible, the plug having been completely covered by permanent aluminum paint or other paint or lacquer; and (c) it eliminated the provision specifying the precise legend to be printed on the cartons and substituted therefor a more general one.[7] 156 F.2d 488. The case is here on a petition for certiorari which we granted because of the apparent conflict between the decision below and *Champion Spark Plug Co. v. Reich*, 121 F.2d 769, decided by the Circuit Court of Appeals for the Eighth Circuit.

There is no challenge here to the findings as to the misleading character of the merchandising methods employed by respondents, nor to the conclusion that they have not only infringed petitioner's trade mark but have also engaged in unfair competition. The controversy here relates to the adequacy of the relief granted, particularly the refusal of the Circuit Court of Appeals to require respondents to remove the word "Champion" from the repaired or reconditioned plugs which they resell.

We put to one side the case of a manufacturer or distributor who markets new or used spark plugs of one make under the trade mark of another. *See Bourjois & Co. v. Katzel*, 260 U.S. 689; *Old Dearborn Co. v. Seagram Corp.*, 299 U.S. 183, 194. Equity then steps in to prohibit defendant's use of the mark which symbolized plaintiff's good will and "stakes the reputation of the plaintiff upon the character of the goods." *Bourjois & Co. v. Katzel, supra* p. 692.

We are dealing here with second-hand goods. The spark plugs, though used, are nevertheless Champion plugs and not those of another make. There is evidence to support what one would suspect, that a used spark plug which has been repaired or reconditioned does not measure up to the specifications of a new one. But the same would be true of a second-hand Ford or Chevrolet car. And we would not suppose that one could be enjoined from selling a car whose valves had been reground and whose piston rings had been replaced unless he removed the name Ford or Chevrolet. . . .

Cases may be imagined where the reconditioning or repair would be so extensive or so basic that it would be a misnomer to call the article by its original name, even though the words "used" or "repaired" were added. *Cf. Ingersoll v. Doyle*, 247 F.620 But no such practice is involved here. The repair or reconditioning of the plugs does not give them a new design. It is no more than a restoration, so far as possible, of their original condition. The type marks attached by the manufacturer are determined by the use to which the plug is to be put. But the thread size and size of the cylinder

---

[7] "The decree shall permit the defendants to state on cartons and containers, selling and advertising material, business records, correspondence and other papers, when published, the original make and type numbers provided it is made clear that any plug referred to therein is used and reconditioned by the defendants, and that such material contains the name and address of defendants."

hole into which the plug is fitted are not affected by the reconditioning. The heat range also has relevance to the type marks. And there is evidence that the reconditioned plugs are inferior so far as heat range and other qualities are concerned. But inferiority is expected in most second-hand articles. Indeed, they generally cost the customer less. That is the case here. Inferiority is immaterial so long as the article is clearly and distinctly sold as repaired or reconditioned rather than as new. The result is, of course, that the second-hand dealer gets some advantage from the trade mark. But under the rule of *Prestonettes, Inc. v. Coty, supra,* that is wholly permissible so long as the manufacturer is not identified with the inferior qualities of the product resulting from wear and tear or the reconditioning by the dealer. Full disclosure gives the manufacturer all the protection to which he is entitled.

The decree as shaped by the Circuit Court of Appeals is fashioned to serve the requirements of full disclosure. We cannot say that of the alternatives available the ones it chose are inadequate for that purpose. We are mindful of the fact that this case, unlike *Prestonettes, Inc. v. Coty, supra,* involves unfair competition as well as trade mark infringement; and that where unfair competition is established, any doubts as to the adequacy of the relief are generally resolved against the transgressor. *Warner & Co. v. Lilly & Co.,* 265 U.S. 526, 532. But there was here no showing of fraud or palming off. Their absence, of course, does not undermine the finding of unfair competition. *Federal Trade Commission v. Winsted Hosiery Co.,* 258 U.S. 483, 493–94; *G. H. Mumm Champagne v. Eastern Wine Corp.,* 142 F.2d 499, 501. But the character of the conduct giving rise to the unfair competition is relevant to the remedy which should be afforded. *See Siegel Co. v. Federal Trade Commission,* 327 U.S. 608. We cannot say that the conduct of respondents in this case, or the nature of the article involved and the characteristics of the merchandising methods used to sell it, called for more stringent controls than the Circuit Court of Appeals provided.

. . . Here, as we have noted, there has been no showing of fraud or palming off. For several years respondents apparently endeavored to comply with a cease and desist order of the Federal Trade Commission requiring them to place on the plugs and on the cartons a label revealing that the plugs were used or second-hand. Moreover, as stated by the Circuit Court of Appeals, the likelihood of damage to petitioner or profit to respondents due to any misrepresentation seems slight. In view of these various circumstances it seems to us that the injunction will satisfy the equities of the case.

Affirmed.

SOCIETE COMPTOIR DE L'INDUSTRIE COTONNIERE ETABLISSEMENTS BOUSSAC v. ALEXANDER'S DEPARTMENT STORES, INC.

United States Court of Appeals, Second Circuit
299 F.2d 33 (1962)

SMITH, CIRCUIT JUDGE.

This is an appeal from denial of two separate motions for preliminary injunction seeking to enjoin the use of the names "Dior" and "Christian Dior" by defendant.

Plaintiff's first application for a preliminary injunction alleging trademark infringement and unfair competition was denied in a reasoned opinion, Dimock, D.J., 190 F. Supp. 594 (S.D.N.Y. 1961) and a subsequent motion made after additional use of the name was likewise denied, Murphy, D. J., May 17, 1961. The two appeals have been considered as one by stipulation of the parties. Affirmed.

Plaintiffs are a group of foreign and domestic corporations who do business under the names of "Dior" and "Christian Dior," which names are registered as trademarks. Defendant is the owner of retail, discount type, department stores in a metropolitan area and is well known for its low cost retailing policies which are made possible by the use of self-service merchandising techniques and a high volume, low mark-up policy. Defendant used the name of "Dior" and "Christian Dior" extensively to promote the sale of garments copied from original creations designed by the house of Dior.

Defendant's representation that the garments being sold by it were copies of plaintiffs' original creations was apparently truthful. We do not understand plaintiffs to claim that the garments were so poorly made or executed as not to constitute copies; but in any event they have certainly failed to establish that to be the case. The merchandise was so described in the newspaper advertisements, on hang tags attached to the garments reading, "Original by Christian Dior—Alexander's Exclusive—Paris—Adaptation"; and on a television fashion show sponsored by defendant which employed a singing commercial.[1]

The District Court concluded that no attempt had been made to deceive the public and that no deception or confusion existed with respect to the garments being sold or as to sponsorship by plaintiffs. While it is possible that plaintiffs may be able to show some confusion in the public mind as to sponsorship, or origin of the goods, at a full trial, there is certainly nothing in the record before us to indicate that the

---

[1] "Dior, Dior, Christian Dior, the latest, latest, Chic-est, sleekest clothing you've been waiting for. That's Christian Dior. — Dior, Dior, Christian you've been waiting for. That's Christian Dior. — Dior, Dior, Christian dresses make you look like a girl. Suits fit floppier, they flatter any form, even if you're just above or just below the norm. Dior, Dior, Christian Dior, the latest, latest, Chic-est, sleekest clothing you've been waiting for. That's Christian Dior."

factual finding that neither the hang tags, the newspaper advertisements nor the television show in fact deceived the public as to origin or sponsorship of the garments, was clearly erroneous.

Plaintiff urges that by virtue of its licensing arrangements with others the public is confused as to sponsorship of the garments. But if it be true that the public associates all dresses referred to as copies of "Dior Originals" with the plaintiff, then plaintiff, the licensor, must be prepared to show that control was maintained, not only of the manner and the price at which the dresses were retailed, but of the manufacture of the garments, for a bare license is a fraud upon the public and unlawful. *E. I. du Pont de Nemours & Co. v. Celanese Corp. of America*, 167 F.2d 484 (C.C.P.A. 1948); *Campbell Soup Co. v. Armour & Co.*, D.C., 81 F. Supp. 114 (1948), *aff'd*, 175 F.2d 795 (3 Cir. 1948). But it is sufficient at this stage of the proceedings to say that neither of the District Judges concluded that a sufficient showing of confusion had been made and we are not persuaded this conclusion was clearly erroneous.

Although the granting or denial of a preliminary injunction is within the discretion of the court to which it is addressed, where it is plain that the disposition was in substantial measure a result of the lower court's view of the law, which is inextricably bound up in the controversy, the appellate court can, and should review such conclusions. *Ring v. Spina*, 148 F.2d 647, 650, 160 A.L.R. 371 (2 Cir. 1945).

In any proceeding under the Lanham Act the gist of the proceeding is a "false description or representation," 15 U.S.C.A. § 1125(a), or a use of the mark which "is likely to cause confusion or mistake or to deceive purchasers as to the source of origin of such goods or services," 15 U.S.C.A. § 1114(1). The registering of a proper noun as a trade-mark does not withdraw it from the language, nor reduce it to the exclusive possession of the registrant which may be jealously guarding against any and all use by others. Registration bestows upon the owner of the mark the limited right to protect his good will from possible harm by those uses of another as may engender a belief in the mind of the public that the product identified by the infringing mark is made or sponsored by the owner of the mark. *Champion Spark Plug Co. v. Sanders*, 331 U.S. 126 (1947), citing with approval, *Prestonettes, Inc. v. Coty*, 264 U.S. 359 (1924). The Lanham Act does not prohibit a commercial rival's truthfully denominating his goods a copy of a design in the public domain, though he uses the name of the designer to do so. Indeed it is difficult to see any other means that might be employed to inform the consuming public of the true origin of the design. *Cf.* Nims, *Unfair Competition and Trade-Marks*, § 130(a) (4th Ed. 1947).

Those cases involving sponsorship, whether trademark infringement or unfair competition, protecting the owner of the mark, are based upon a finding that the defendant's goods are likely to be thought to have originated with, or have been sponsored by, the true owner of the mark. *E.g.*, *Triangle Publications v. Rohrlich*, 167 F.2d 969 (2 Cir. 1948); *Adolph Kastor & Bros., Inc. v. FTC.*, 138 F.2d 824 (2 Cir. 1943).

Common law unfair competition must be grounded in either deception or appropriation of the exclusive property of the plaintiff. The line of cases relied upon by plaintiffs, *e.g., International News Service v. The Associated Press*, 248 U.S. 215 (1911); *Madison Square Garden Corp. v. Universal Pictures Corp.*, 255 App. Div. 459, 7 N.Y.S.2d 845 (1st Dept. 1938); *Dior v. Milton*, 9 Misc. 2d 425, 155 N.Y.S. 2d 443 (Sup. Ct. 1956), *aff'd*, 2 App. Div. 2d 878, 156 N.Y.S.2d 996 (1st Dept.); *Metropolitan Opera Ass'n v. Wagner-Nichols Recorded Corp.*, 199 Misc. 786, 101 N.Y.S.2d 483 (Sup. Ct. 1950), *aff'd,* 279 App. Div. 632, 107 N.Y.S.2d 795 (1st Dept. 1951), did not prohibit the defendant from informing the public as to the source of a product which he was permitted to sell. On the contrary, the defendant in each case was prohibited from pirating the intangible property of complainant. *Norwich Pharmacal Co. v. Sterling Drug, Inc.*, 271 F.2d 569, 571 (2 Cir. 1959); *Continental Casualty Co. v. Beardsley*, 151 F. Supp. 28 (S.D.N.Y. 1957), *aff'd in part*, 253 F.2d 702 (2 Cir.) *cert. den.*, 358 U.S. 816 (1958). *See* Note, 70 Harv. L. Rev. 1117 (1957).

In the case at bar it is conceded that the "pirating" of the design is lawful and proper. *Fashion Originators' Guild of America v. F.T.C.*, 114 F.2d 80 (2 Cir. 1940), *aff'd*, 312 U.S. 457 949 (1941). The only property right alleged to have been invaded is the good will embodied in the trademark. But the right of the complainant in his mark is limited to dilution which is brought about by confusion as to source or affiliation. *Cornell University v. Messing Bakeries*, 285 App. Div. 490, 138 N.Y.S.2d 280 (3rd Dept. 1955), *aff'd per curiam*, 309 N.Y. 722, 128 N.E.2d 421 (1955), *Norwich Pharmacal Co. v. Sterling Drug, Inc., supra; Standard Brands, Inc. v. Smidler*, 2 Cir., 151 F.2d 34 (1945). Involved in the instant case is a conflict of values which necessarily arises in an economy characterized by competition and private property. The courts have come to recognize the true nature of the considerations often involved in efforts to extend protection of common law trade names so as to create a shield against competition. *Standard Brands v. Smidler*, 151 F.2d 34, 41 (2 Cir. 1945) (concurring opinion, Frank, C. J.). The interest of the consumer here in competitive prices of garments using Dior designs without deception as to origin, is at least as great as the interest of plaintiffs in monopolizing the name.

The decision of the District Court is affirmed with respect to both motions.

ZATARAIN'S, INC. v. OAK GROVE SMOKEHOUSE, INC.

United States Court of Appeals, Fifth Circuit
698 F.2d 786 (1983)

GOLDBERG, CIRCUIT JUDGE.

This appeal of a trademark dispute presents us with a menu of edible delights sure to tempt connoisseurs of fish and fowl alike. At issue is the alleged infringement of two trademarks, "Fish-Fri" and "Chick-Fri," held by appellant Zatarain's, Inc. ("Zatarain's"). . . .

Zatarain's "Fish-Fri" consists of 100% corn flour and is used to fry fish and other seafood. "Fish-Fri" is packaged in rectangular cardboard boxes containing twelve or twenty-four ounces of coating mix. The legend "Wonderful FISH-FRI®" is displayed prominently on the front panel, along with the block Z used to identify all Zatarain's products. The term "Fish-Fri" has been used by Zatarain's or its predecessor since 1950 and has been registered as a trademark since 1962.

Zatarain's "Chick-Fri" is a seasoned corn flour batter mix used for frying chicken and other foods. The "Chick-Fri" package, which is very similar to that used for "Fish-Fri," is a rectangular cardboard container labelled "Wonderful CHICK-FRI." Zatarain's began to use the term "Chick-Fri" in 1968 and registered the term as a trademark in 1976.

Zatarain's products are not alone in the marketplace. At least four other companies market coatings for fried foods that are denominated "fish fry" or "chicken fry." Two of these competing companies are the appellees here, and therein hangs this fish tale. Appellee Oak Grove Smokehouse, Inc. ("Oak Grove") began marketing a "fish fry" and a "chicken fry" in March 1979. Both products are packaged in clear glassine packets that contain a quantity of coating mix sufficient to fry enough food for one meal. The packets are labelled with Oak Grove's name and emblem, along with the words "FISH FRY" or "CHICKEN FRY." Oak Grove's "FISH FRY" has a corn flour base seasoned with various spices; Oak Grove's "CHICKEN FRY" is a seasoned coating with a wheat flour base.

Appellee Visko's Fish Fry, Inc. ("Visko's") entered the batter mix market in March 1980 with its "fish fry." Visko's product is packed in a cylindrical eighteen-ounce container with a resealable plastic lid. The words "Visko's FISH FRY" appear on the label along with a photograph of a platter of fried fish. Visko's coating mix contains corn flour and added spices.

. . . .

The district Court found that Zatarain's trademark "Fish-Fri" was a descriptive term with an established secondary meaning [in the New Orleans geographical area], but held that Oak Grove and Visko's had a "fair use" defense to their asserted infringement of the mark. The court further found that Zatarain's trademark "Chick-Fri" was a descriptive term that lacked secondary meaning, and accordingly ordered the trademark registration cancelled. Additionally, the court concluded that Zatarain's had produced no evidence in support of its claims of unfair competition on the part of Oak Grove and Visko's. Finally, the court dismissed Oak Grove's and Visko's counterclaims for antitrust violations, unfair trade practices, misbranding of food products, and miscellaneous damages.

Battered, but not fried, Zatarain's appeals from the adverse judgment on several grounds. First, Zatarain's argues that its trademark "Fish-Fri" is a suggestive term and therefore not subject to the "fair use" defense. Second, Zatarain's asserts that even if the "fair use" defense is applicable in this case, appellees cannot invoke the doctrine because their use of Zatarain's trademarks is not a good faith attempt to describe their products. Third, Zatarain's urges that the district court erred in cancelling the trademark registration for the term "Chick-Fri" because Zatarain's presented sufficient evidence to establish a secondary meaning for the term. For these reasons, Zatarain's argues that the district court should be reversed.

. . .

Even when a descriptive term has acquired a secondary meaning sufficient to warrant trademark protection, others may be entitled to use the mark without incurring liability for trademark infringement. When the allegedly infringing term is "used fairly and in good faith only to describe to users the goods or services of [a] party, or their geographic origin," Lanham Act § 33(b)(4), 15 U.S.C. § 1115(b)(4) (1976), a defendant in a trademark infringement action may assert the "fair use" defense. The defense is available only in actions involving descriptive terms and only when the term is used in its descriptive sense rather than its trademark sense. *Soweco [, Inc. v. Shell Oil Co.]*, 617 F.2d [1178] at 1185; *see Venetianaire Corp. v. A & P Import Co.*, 429 F.2d 1079, 1081–82 (2d Cir. 1970). In essence, the fair use defense prevents a trademark registrant from appropriating a descriptive term for its own use to the exclusion of others, who may be prevented thereby from accurately describing their own goods. *Soweco*, 617 F.2d at 1185. The holder of a protectable descriptive mark has no legal claim to an exclusive right in the primary, descriptive meaning of the term; consequently, anyone is free to use the term in its primary, descriptive sense so long as such use does not lead to customer confusion as to the source of the goods or services. *See* 1 J. McCarthy, *Trademarks and Unfair Competition* § 11.17, at 379 (1973).

. . . .

[Although we affirm the district court's findings that "Fish-Fri" is a descriptive term which has acquired a secondary meaning in the New Orleans geographical area,] Zatarain's does not now prevail automatically on its trademark infringement claim, for it cannot prevent the fair use of the term by Oak Grove and Visko's. The "fair use" defense applies only to descriptive terms and requires that the term be "used fairly and in good faith only to describe to users the goods or services of such party, or their geographic origin." Lanham Act § 33(b), 15 U.S.C. § 1115(b)(4) (1976). The district court determined that Oak Grove and Visko's were entitled to fair use of the term "fish fry" to describe a characteristic of their goods; we affirm that conclusion.

. . . Zatarain's has no legal claim to an exclusive right in the original, descriptive sense of the term; therefore, Oak Grove and Visko's are still free to use the words "fish fry" in their ordinary, descriptive sense, so long as such use will not tend to confuse customers as to the source of the goods. *See* 1 J. McCarthy, *supra*, § 11.17.

The record contains ample evidence to support the district court's determination that Oak Grove's and Visko's use of the words "fish fry" was fair and in good faith. Testimony at trial indicated that the appellees did not intend to use the term in a trademark sense and had never attempted to register the words as a trademark. Record on Appeal, Vol. II at 28, 33, 226–30, 243–47. Oak Grove and Visko's apparently believed "fish fry" was a generic name for the type of coating mix they manufactured. *Id.* at 28, 226, 244. In addition, Oak Grove and Visko's consciously packaged and labelled their products in such a way as to minimize any potential confusion in the minds of consumers. *Id.* at 244–45, 251–52. The dissimilar trade dress of these products prompted the district court to observe that confusion at the point of purchase — the grocery shelves — would be virtually impossible. Our review of the record convinces us that the district court's determinations are correct. We hold, therefore, that Oak Grove and Visko's are entitled to fair use of the term "fish fry" to describe their products; accordingly, Zatarain's claim of trademark infringement must fail.

. . . .

What about Chicken Fri?

Affirmed.

THE NEW KIDS ON THE BLOCK v. NEWS AMERICA PUBLISHING, INC.

United States Court of Appeals, Ninth Circuit
971 F.2d 302 (1992)

KOZINSKI, CIRCUIT JUDGE.

The individual plaintiffs perform professionally as The New Kids on the Block, reputedly one of today's hottest musical acts. This case requires us to weigh their rights in that name against the rights of others to use it in identifying the New Kids as the subjects of public opinion polls.

Background

No longer are entertainers limited to their craft in marketing themselves to the public. This is the age of multi-media publicity blitzkrieg: Trading on their popularity, many entertainers hawk posters, T-shirts, badges, coffee mugs and the like — handsomely supplementing their incomes while boosting their public images. The New Kids are no exception; the record in this case indicates there are more than 500 products or services bearing the New Kids trademark. Among these are services taking advantage of a recent development in telecommunications: 900 area code numbers, where the caller is charged a fee, a portion of which is paid to the call recipient. Fans can call various New Kids 900 numbers to listen to the New Kids talk about themselves, to listen to other fans talk about the New Kids, or to leave messages for the New Kids and other fans.

Δ "infringement"

The defendants, two newspapers of national circulation, conducted separate polls of their readers seeking an answer to a pressing question: Which one of the New Kids is the most popular? *USA Today*'s announcement contained a picture of the New Kids and asked, "Who's the best on the block?" The announcement listed a 900 number for voting, noting that "any USA Today profits from this phone line will go to charity," and closed with the following:

> New Kids on the Block are pop's hottest group. Which of the five is your fave? Or are they a turn off? . . . Each call costs 50 cents. Results in Friday's Life section.

The Star's announcement, under a picture of the New Kids, went to the heart of the matter: "Now which kid is the sexiest?" The announcement, which appeared in the middle of a page containing a story on the New Kids concert, also stated:

Which of the New Kids on the Block would you most like to move next door? STAR wants to know which cool New Kid is the hottest with our readers.

Readers were then directed to a 900 number to register their votes; each call cost 95 cents per minute.[1]

Fearing that the two newspapers were undermining their hegemony over their fans, the New Kids filed a shotgun complaint in federal court raising no fewer than ten claims: (1) common law trademark infringement; (2) Lanham Act false advertising; (3) Lanham Act false designation of origin; (4) Lanham Act unfair competition; (5) state trade name infringement; (6) state false advertising; (7) state unfair competition; (8) commercial misappropriation; (9) common-law misappropriation; and (10) intentional interference with prospective economic advantage. The two papers raised the First Amendment as a defense, on the theory that the polls were part and parcel of their "news-gathering activities." The district court granted summary judgment for defendants. 745 F. Supp. 1540 (C.D. Cal. 1990)

. . . A . . . problem arises when a trademark also describes a person, a place or an attribute of a product. If the trademark holder were allowed exclusive rights in such use, the language would be depleted in much the same way as if generic words were protectable. Thus trademark law recognizes a defense where the mark is used only "to describe the goods or services of [a] party, or their geographic origin." 15 U.S.C. § 115(b)(4). "The 'fair use' defense, in essence, forbids a trademark registrant to appropriate a descriptive term for his exclusive use and so prevent others from accurately describing a characteristic of their goods." *Soweco, Inc. v. Shell Oil Co.*, 617 F.2d 1178, 1185 (5th Cir. 1980). Once again, the courts will hold as a matter of law that the original producer does not sponsor or endorse another product that uses his mark in a descriptive manner. *See, e.g., Schmid Laboratories v. Youngs Drug Products Corp.*, 482 F. Supp. 14 (D.N.J. 1979) ("ribbed" condoms).

With so many well-known trademarks, such as Jell-O, Scotch tape and Kleenex, there are equally informative non-trademark words describing the product (gelatin, cellophane tape and facial tissue). But sometimes there is no descriptive substitute, and a problem closely related to genericity and descriptiveness is presented when many goods and services are effectively identifiable only by their trademarks. For example, one might refer to "the two-time world champions" or "the professional basketball team from Chicago," but it's far simpler (and more likely to be understood) to refer to the Chicago Bulls. In such cases, use of the trademark does not imply sponsorship or endorsement of the product because the mark is used only to describe the thing, rather than to identify its source.

Indeed, it is often virtually impossible to refer to a particular product for purposes of comparison, criticism, point of reference or any other such purpose without using the mark. For example, reference to a large automobile manufacturer based in Michigan would not differentiate among the Big Three; reference to a large Japanese manufacturer of home electronics would narrow the field to a dozen or more

---

[1] The *USA Today* poll generated less than $300 in revenues, all of which the newspaper donated to the Berklee College of Music. *The Star*'s poll generated about $1600.

companies. Much useful social and commercial discourse would be all but impossible if speakers were under threat of an infringement lawsuit every time they made reference to a person, company or product by using its trademark.

A good example of this is *Volkswagenwerk Aktiengesellschaft v. Church*, 411 F.2d 350 (9th Cir. 1969), where we held that Volkswagen could not prevent an automobile repair shop from using its mark. We recognized that in "advertising [the repair of Volkswagens, it] would be difficult, if not impossible, for [Church] to avoid altogether the use of the word 'Volkswagen' or its abbreviation 'VW,' which are the normal terms which, to the public at large, signify appellant's cars." *Id.* at 352. Church did not suggest to customers that he was part of the Volkswagen organization or that his repair shop was sponsored or authorized by VW; he merely used the words, "Volkswagen" and "VW" to convey information about the types of cars he repaired. Therefore, his use of the Volkswagen trademark was not an infringing one.

. . . .

To be sure, this is not the classic fair use case where the defendant has used the plaintiff's mark to describe the defendant's *own* product. Here, the New Kids trademark is used to refer to the New Kids themselves. We therefore do not purport to alter the test applicable in the paradigmatic fair use case. If the defendant's use of the plaintiff's trademark refers to something other than the plaintiff's product, the traditional fair use inquiry will continue to govern. But, where the defendant uses a trademark to describe the plaintiff's product rather than its own, we hold that a commercial user is entitled to a nominative fair use defense provided he meets the following three requirements: First, the product or service in question must be one not readily identifiable without use of the trademark; second, only so much of the mark or marks may be used as is reasonably necessary to identify the product or service; and third, the user must do nothing that would, in conjunction with the mark, suggest sponsorship or endorsement by the trademark holder.

. . . .

The New Kids do not claim there was anything false or misleading about the newspapers' use of their mark. Rather, the first seven causes of action, while purporting to state different claims, all hinge on one key factual allegation: that the newspapers' use of the New Kids name in conducting the unauthorized polls somehow implied that the New Kids were sponsoring the polls. It is no more reasonably possible, however, to refer to the New Kids as an entity than it is to refer to the Chicago Bulls, Volkswagens or the Boston Marathon without using the trademark. Indeed, how could someone not conversant with the proper names of the individual New Kids talk about the group at all? While plaintiffs' trademark certainly deserves protection against copycats and those who falsely claim that the New Kids have endorsed or sponsored them, such protection does not extend to rendering newspaper articles, conversations, polls and comparative advertising impossible. The first nominative use requirement is therefore met.

Also met are the second and third requirements. Both *The Star* and *USA Today* reference the New Kids only to the extent necessary to identify them as the subject of the polls; they do not use the New Kids' distinctive logo or anything else that isn't needed to make the announcements intelligible to readers. First, nothing in the announcements suggests joint sponsorship or endorsement by the New Kids. The *USA Today* announcement implies quite the contrary by asking whether the New Kids might be a "turn off." *The Star*'s poll is more effusive but says nothing that expressly or by fair implication connotes endorsement or joint sponsorship on the part of the New Kids.

The New Kids argue that, even if the newspapers are entitled to a nominative fair use defense for the announcements, they are not entitled to it for the polls themselves, which were money-making enterprises separate and apart from the newspapers' reporting businesses. According to plaintiffs, defendants could have minimized the intrusion into their rights by using an 800 number or asking readers to call in on normal telephone lines which would not have resulted in a profit to the newspapers based on the conduct of the polls themselves.

The New Kids see this as a crucial difference, distinguishing this case from *Volkswagenwerk*, *WCBV-TV* and other nominative use cases. The New Kids' argument in support of this distinction is not entirely implausible: They point out that their fans, like everyone else, have limited resources. Thus a dollar spent calling the newspapers' 900 lines to express loyalty to the New Kids may well be a dollar not spent on New Kids products and services, including the New Kids' own 900 numbers. In short, plaintiffs argue that a nominative fair use defense is inapplicable where the use in question competes directly with that of the trademark holder.

We reject this argument. While the New Kids have a limited property right in their name, that right does not entitle them to control their fans' use of their own money. Where, as here, the use does not imply sponsorship or endorsement, the fact that it is carried on for profit and in competition with the trademark holder's business is beside the point. *See, e.g., Universal City Studios, Inc. v. Ideal Publishing Corp.*, 195 U.S.P.Q. 761 (S.D.N.Y. 1977) (magazine's use of TV program's trademark "Hardy Boys" in connection with photographs of show's stars not infringing). Voting for their favorite New Kid may be, as plaintiffs point out, a way for fans to articulate their loyalty to the group, and this may diminish the resources available for products and services they sponsor. But the trademark laws do not give the New Kids the right to channel their fans' enthusiasm (and dollars) only into items licensed or authorized by them. *See International Order of Job's Daughters v. Lindeburg & Co.*, 633 F.2d 912 (9th Cir. 1990) (no infringement where unauthorized jewelry maker produced rings and pins bearing fraternal organization's trademark). The New Kids could not use the trademark laws to prevent the publication of an unauthorized group biography or to censor all parodies or satires which use their name. We fail to see a material difference between these examples and the use here.

Summary judgment was proper as to the first seven causes of action because they all hinge on a theory of implied endorsement; there was none here as the uses in question were purely nominative.

. . . .

Conclusion

The district court's judgment is

Affirmed.

NOTES ON PERMITTED USE

(1) Repaired, reconditioned, or altered products and product-related services (e.g., automotive repair shops) may display the trademark of the original maker of the product so long as there is full disclosure and the public is not likely to be confused into thinking there is an agency relationship. *See Champion, supra; B.H. Bunn Co. v. AAA Replacement Parts Co.*, 451 F.2d 1254 (5th Cir. 1971); *Volkswagen, A.G. v. Church*, 411 F.2d 350 (9th Cir. 1969); *Bulova, infra* Note (2); *General Signal Corp. v. Donallco, Inc.*, 214 U.S.P.Q. 306 (D. Conn. 1982); *Polaroid Corp. v. Blue Dot Corp.*, 214 U.S.P.Q. 192 (D.N.J. 1981); *Scott & Fetzer Co. v. National Distributors of Saginaw*, 213 U.S.P.Q. 647 (E.D. Mich. 1981). In *Williams v. Curtiss-Wright Corp.*, 691 F.2d 168 (3d Cir. 1982), the court required disclosure that parts were reconditioned where the parts bore numbers which might indicate to members of the industry that the parts were new. The court observed that while part numbers are not trademarks, nonetheless "Section 43(a) would proscribe use of such a designation of origin on used and reconditioned goods without full disclosure." *Id.* at 174. Note that some states have statutes prohibiting use of an original manufacturer's trademark on rebottled or repackaged products. *See, e.g.*, 765 Ill. Comp. Stat. (1992) 1050. Can such statutes be justified if there is full disclosure and confusion is not likely? *See Illinois v. Revlon, Inc.*, 241 N.E.2d 554 (Ill. App. Ct. 1968).

(2) Should a manufacturer be allowed to use on its product another's trademark for an ingredient or component of that product? *See* the *Bourjois* and *Coty* cases, *supra* § 7.06; *Forstmann Woolen Co. v. Murray Sices Corp.*, 144 F. Supp. 283 (S.D.N.Y. 1956). Should one be permitted to sell an altered product bearing another's trademark without the necessity of disclosure if the altered product is of a higher rather than lesser quality than that sold by the trademark's owner (e.g., whiskey purchased in the cask and bottled and sold under the mark of the manufacturer from whom it was purchased)? In some instances the desired higher quality may necessitate such an alteration of the original article that continued use of the original trademark would be inappropriate and misleading. In *Bulova Watch Co. v. Allerton Co.*, 328 F.2d 20 (7th Cir. 1964), the defendant had purchased Bulova watches on the market, then recased the movements, still bearing the "Bulova" trademark, in diamond-decorated cases, which defendant then sold to retail outlets under the trade name "Treasure Mates." Deeming such a significantly altered product to constitute "a new construction," the court stated at p. 23 that "[t]he watch is no longer a Bulova watch." The court allowed proper collateral references to the source of the movement but enjoined any use of the trademark "Bulova" as such. Consequently, the court allowed collateral use with full disclosure as to defendant's

role in the recasing and as the sole guarantor of the watch, for catalog inserts, displays and advertising, but enjoined any use of the "Bulova" trademark on the movement itself.

(3) Should a merchant be allowed to sell to the public "distressed merchandise" comprising defective, damaged, or out of style goods which still bear the trademark of the original manufacturer or supplier? In *J. C. Penney Co. v. Charbeth's Little General Store*, 185 U.S.P.Q. 254 (E.D.N.Y. 1975), defendant represented discontinued or out of style Penney merchandise as new, and sold it at a price lower than that charged by Penney for new merchandise; the court noted several kinds of public deception that might be expected to result and preliminarily enjoined defendant from advertising or selling any merchandise bearing plaintiff's name or trademarks. In *Adolph Coors Co. v. A. Genderson & Sons, Inc.*, 486 F. Supp. 131 (D. Col. 1980), defendant distributed plaintiff's unpasteurized beer without authorization and without following plaintiff's rigid quality control standards; the court compared the case with those where inferior or altered goods were resold under the original trademark, citing *J.C. Penney v. Charbeth's*, *supra*, and enjoined defendant from any further unauthorized distributions. *See also Bill Blass, Ltd. v. SAZ Corp.*, 751 F.2d 152 (3d Cir. 1984) (out of date designer label fashions); *J.C. Penney Co. v. Parrish Co.*, 335 F. Supp. 209 (D. Idaho 1971). *Compare Alfred Dunhill Ltd. v. Interstate Cigar Co.*, 499 F.2d 232 (2d Cir. 1974).

The trademark owner's right to inspect and approve goods sold under its mark was upheld in *Shell Oil Co. v. Commercial Petroleum, Inc.*, 928 F.2d 104, 107 (4th Cir. 1991) in which defendant had purchased bulk oil from plaintiff and resold it under plaintiff's trademarks without adhering to plaintiff's quality control standards, the court holding that this was trademark infringement because the product was not "genuine" if plaintiff's quality control standards were not followed; *C.B. Fleet Co. v. Complete Packaging Corp.*, 739 F. Supp. 393, 398–99 (N.D. Ill. 1990), in which defendant was preliminarily enjoined from selling deodorant products bearing plaintiff's trademark under a "right to inspect and approve" theory; and *Ford Motor Company v. Cook*, 25 U.S.P.Q.2d 1050 (N.D. Ill. 1992), in which defendant was preliminarily enjoined from selling uninspected automotive grilles bearing plaintiff's trademarks that defendant purchased at a supplier's bankruptcy sale.

(4) The use of another's trademark in the advertising or marketing of products or services is permitted provided there is truthful disclosure and no likelihood of confusion. *See* 1 Gilson, *Trademark Protection and Practice* § 5.09[3] (1993 ed.); McCarthy, *Trademarks and Unfair Protection* §§ 25:8–14 (3d ed. 1992); Livermore, *On Uses of a Competitor's Trademark*, 59 Trademark Rep. 30 (1969). As stated in *Societe Comptoir De L'Industrie Cotonniere Etablissements Boussac v. Alexander's Department Stores, Inc.*, *supra*:

> The Lanham Act does not prohibit a commercial rival's truthfully denominating his goods a copy of a design in the public domain, though he uses the name of the designer to do so. Indeed, it is difficult to see any other means that might be employed to inform the consuming public of the true origin of the design.

In essence, is the rule respecting use of another's trademark simply the familiar one that deception or its likelihood will not be permitted but such use is not per se taboo? Does truthful disclosure suffice to avoid the problem of dilution? *See* § 8.01, *infra*.

(5) How may one lawfully use the trademark of another in comparative advertising? *See Smith v. Chanel, Inc.*, 402 F.2d 562 (9th Cir. 1968), wherein one challenge in defendant's advertising was: "We dare you to try to detect any difference between Chanel #5 ($25.00) and Ta'Ron's 2nd Chance. $7.00." *Compare Chanel, Inc. v. Smith*, 178 U.S.P.Q. 630 (N.D. Calif. 1973) *and Saxony Prods., Inc. v. Guerlain, Inc.*, 513 F.2d 716, 722 (9th Cir. 1975), in which the court stated:

> for purposes of comparative advertising Saxony could use Guerlain's trademark SHALIMAR to apprise consumers [truthfully] that Fragrance S is "like" or "similar" to SHALIMAR. The use of Guerlain's trademark, however, constituted a violation of the Lanham Act if Saxony falsely represented that Fragrance S was "like" or "similar" to SHALIMAR or if there was a reasonable likelihood that consumers would be confused as to the source of Fragrance S."

See also the discussion in the Misrepresentation section in Chapter 8, *infra*; Livermore, *On Uses of a Competitor's Trademark*, 59 Trademark Rep. 30 (1969).

(6) The *Zatarain's* case, *supra*, demonstrates that non-deceptive descriptive use of a term that another has claimed as a trademark for a similar product may be permissible under appropriate circumstances. Section 33 of the Lanham Act, 15 U.S.C. § 1115(b)(4) provides that use of a term other than as a trade or service mark is not an infringement if the term is used fairly and in good faith to describe the goods or services of the party. The defense applies at common-law as well as under the statute. *William R. Warner & Co. v. Eli Lilly & Co.*, 265 U.S. 526, 528 (1924). *Venetianaire Corp. of America v. A&P Import Co.*, 429 F.2d 1079, 1081 (2d Cir. 1970) (the statute incorporates the defense previously available at common law).

(7) If plaintiff's mark is suggestive rather than descriptive, should the defense of fair use be precluded? *Compare Seaboard Seed Co. v. Bemis Co.*, 632 F. Supp. 1133, 1138 (N.D. Ill. 1986) (QUICK GREEN for grass seed not descriptive, so defense unavailable) *with Charles of the Ritz Group, Ltd. v. Marcon, Ltd.*, 230 U.S.P.Q. 377 (S.D.N.Y. 1986) (SILK for cosmetics held suggestive, not descriptive, but fair use upheld). In *Kiki Undies Corp. v. Alexander's Department Stores*, 390 F.2d 604 (2d Cir. 1968), the defendant was using the word "Kicky" prominently in advertising its products and was sued by the owner of the trademark "KIKI" for the same products. In affirming a granting of summary judgment to defendant the court cited § 33, attaching greatest significance to "the fact that plaintiff has offered no proof that [defendant] used "Kicky" as a trademark or other than as a descriptive adjective." *Id.* at 606. If the defendant uses the term as a trademark, rather than descriptively, § 33 should not be applicable. *Lindy Pen Co. v. Bic Pen Corp.*, 725 F.2d 1240, 1248 (9th Cir. 1984), *cert. denied*, 469 U.S. 1188 (1985) (mark merely descriptive but used as trademark by defendant; district court's finding of fair use reversed); *Tree Tavern Products, Inc. v. Conagra, Inc.*, 640 F. Supp. 1263, 1268–69 (D. Del. 1986).

(8) Decisions holding that fair use was established include *Soweco, Inc. v. Shell Oil Co.*, 617 F.2d 1178 (5th Cir. 1980) ("Larvacide" on larvae-killer fair use despite plaintiff's registration of "LARVACIDE" for similar products); *Abercrombie & Fitch Co. v. Hunting World, Inc.*, 537 F.2d 4, 12–13 (2d Cir. 1976) ("safari" with respect to boots held fair use); *B & L Sales Associates v. H. Daroff & Sons, Inc.*,

421 F.2d 352 (2d Cir. 1970) ("COME ON STRONG with Botany 500" held not to infringe registered trademark COME ON STRONG for clothing); *Lindy Pen Co. v. Bic Pen Corp.*, 550 F. Supp. 1056 (C.D. Cal. 1982), *aff'd in part and rev'd in part*, 725 F.2d 1240 (9th Cir. 1984) ("Auditor's Fine Point" to refer to a pen type held fair use despite plaintiff's registration of "AUDITORS" for pens). A key factor in such cases often is defendant's prominent use of its own mark. *See B & L Associates, supra.*

In *Sands, Taylor & Wood Co. v. Quaker Oats Co.*, 978 F.2d 947 (7th Cir. 1992), plaintiff, owner of the trademark THIRST-AID, sued defendant for using the advertising slogan "GATORADE is Thirst Aid." Although defendant's GA-TORADE mark was famous and plaintiff's mark was descriptive, the court nonetheless rejected a fair use defense. The court affirmed that defendant used THIRST AID prominently as an "attention-getting symbol," and with its rhyming slogan, created a unique association with defendant's mark that was likely to cause reverse confusion. 978 F.2d at 954. *Compare W.W.W. Pharmaceutical Co. v. Gillette Co.*, 984 F.2d 567 (2d Cir. 1993), where plaintiff owned the mark SPORT STICK for lip balm, and the court found no likelihood of reverse confusion with defendant's RIGHT GUARD SPORT STICK for deodorant, in large part because of the weakness of plaintiff's mark and the renown of defendant's RIGHT GUARD mark.

(9) A well-known trademark may be lawfully referenced as part of a parody or satire, as long as no likelihood of consumer confusion results. In *Cliff's Notes, Inc. v. Bantam Doubleday Dell Pub. Group, Inc.*, 886 F.2d 490 (2d Cir. 1989), for example, defendant's "Spy Notes" was a double parody that poked fun at three modern novels and the well-known Cliff's Notes study aids. The district court found the cover of the publication too closely emulated that of Cliff's Notes, creating likely confusion, and issued a preliminary injunction.

The appellate court vacated the injunction. It recognized that two conflicting principles were at issue: (1) parody is a form of artistic expression protected by the First Amendment; and (2) trademark protection is not lost simply because the allegedly infringing use is made in connection with a work of artistic expression as opposed to a strictly commercial endeavor. *Id.*, at 493. It then reasoned that the Lanham Act "should be construed to apply to artistic works only where the public interest in avoiding consumer confusion outweighs the public interest in free expression." *Id.*, at 494. It concluded that since the covers had some significant differences and defendant's cover repeatedly stated that the piece was "A Satire," a preliminary injunction should not have issued.

In *Jordache Enterprises, Inc. v. Hogg Wyld, Ltd.*, 828 F.2d 1482 (10th Cir. 1987), defendants were permitted to use the mark LARDASHE for oversized jeans with a pig design, despite its obvious similarity and allusion to the well-known JORD-ACHE mark for jeans, the court observing that an intent to parody is not the same as an intent to confuse the public. In *Eveready Battery Co. v. Adolph Coors Co.*, 765 F. Supp. 440, 450 (N.D. Ill. 1991), defendant's advertising use of a well-known actor in a bunny outfit was held a permitted parody of plaintiff's mechanical toy rabbit advertising character: "[t]o the extent the Coors commercial conveys the message 'that it is the original,' it emphatically conveys 'that it is not the original,'" making confusion unlikely.

There are some analytical similarities to copyright parody cases. In *Campbell v. Acuff-Rose Music, Inc.*, 114 S. Ct. 1164, 29 U.S. P.Q.2d 1961 (1994), for example, the Supreme Court considered whether a rap parody of Roy Orbison's song, "Pretty Woman," was fair use. It remanded for determination of whether defendant's copying was excessive, and whether the parody would harm the market for potential rap versions of the original. *Compare Anheuser-Busch, Inc. v. L & L Wings, Inc.*, 962 F.2d 316 (4th Cir.), *cert. denied*, 113 S. Ct. 206 (1992) (Powell, L. dissenting), in which defendant sold t-shirts which closely imitated the famous Budweiser label design, but in place of the beer label references, substituted references to a South Carolina beach resort, e.g., "Contains the Choicest Surf, Sun, and Sand," "King of Beaches," and "This Beach is For You." In reversing the district court's directed verdict for plaintiff and reinstating the jury verdict for defendant, the majority stated, "The purpose of the Lanham Act is to eliminate consumer confusion, not to banish all attempts at poking fun or eliciting amusement." *Id.* at 322. In his dissent, retired Supreme Court Justice Powell, sitting by designation, emphasized that defendant had "borrowed a distinctive mark, without making any discernible changes, and placed that mark on identical products marketed through identical commercial channels" in direct competition with plaintiff, who also sold t-shirts bearing the Budweiser label design. He further observed that the alleged parody lacked any element of ridicule or social commentary. *Id.* at 326–27.

Compare also Mutual of Omaha Insurance Co. v. Novak, 836 F.2d 397 (8th Cir. 1987), *cert. denied*, 488 U.S. 933 (1988), where defendant was enjoined from selling "Mutant of Omaha" t-shirts, coffee mugs, etc., which also bore a depiction of an emaciated Indian head and the words "Nuclear Holocaust Insurance," because the court found confusion likely with the MUTUAL OF OMAHA trademark and logo, and *Schieffelin & Co. v. Jack Co. of Boca, Inc.*, 725 F. Supp. 1314 (S.D.N.Y. 1989), where the court denied a motion to dismiss premised on a parody defense, finding confusion sufficiently likely between defendant's DOM POPIGNON popcorn and plaintiff's DOM PERIGNON champagne. The court in *Schieffelin* observed, "When satire or parody is taken to a certain degree . . . it becomes clear that the owner of the trademark was not involved in the manufacture or sponsorship of the defendant's product. . . . In the case at bar, defendant's product is not a sufficiently strong parody to destroy consumer confusion." 725 F. Supp. at 1324.

To similar effect are *Tin Pan Apple Inc. v. Miller Brewing Co.*, 737 F. Supp. 826, 833–35 (S.D.N.Y. 1990) (parody defense rejected on motion to dismiss, the court noting the closeness of defendant's advertising imitation of the FAT BOYS rap group and defendant's bad faith, having hired look-a-likes only after the FAT BOYS declined to perform in the advertisement); *Gucci Shops, Inc. v. R. H. Macy & Co.*, 446 F. Supp. 838 (S.D.N.Y. 1977) (use of GUCCHI GOO for diaper bags preliminarily enjoined); *Coca-Cola Co. v. Gemini Rising, Inc.*, 346 F. Supp. 1183 (E.D.N.Y. 1972) (defendant enjoined from use of ENJOY COCAINE in famous Coca-Cola script on its posters).

The attempted parody use of a well-known trademark may also be actionable under state anti-dilution law. (Anti-dilution law is discussed more fully in Chapter 8, following). *See, e.g., Coca-Cola Company v. Alma-Leo, U.S.A., Inc.*, 719 F. Supp.

725 (N.D. Ill. 1989) (sale of MAD SCIENTIST MAGIC POWDER bubble gum in container simulating Coca-Cola's bottle enjoined, the court noting that the powder resembled cocaine and sale would injure Coca-Cola's reputation); *American Express Co. v. Vibra Approved Laboratories Corp.*, 10 U.S.P.Q.2d 2006 (S.D.N.Y. 1989) (defendant's marketing of a "condom card," a credit card with condom attached, bearing AMERICA EXPRESS and slogan "Never leave home without it," held likely to dilute plaintiff's AMERICAN EXPRESS mark and slogan "Don't leave home without it"). *Cf. Jordache Enterprises, Inc. v. Hogg Wyld, Ltd., supra*, 828 F.2d 1482, 1490 (10th Cir. 1987) (rejecting state dilution tarnishment claim where defendant's LARDASHE mark "might be considered . . . in poor taste" but was not likely to create "a particularly unwholesome, unsavory or degrading association" with plaintiff's JORDACHE mark); *L.L. Bean, Inc. v. Drake Publishers, Inc.*, 811 F.2d 26 (1st Cir. 1987) (reversing dilution-based summary judgment against defendant's adult magazine sex parody of the L.L. Bean catalog, citing First Amendment concerns and the social value of parody), *cert. denied*, 483 U.S. 1013 (1987). *See generally* Languardt, *Protected Marks and Protected Speech: Establishing First Amendment Boundaries in Trademark Parody Cases*, 82 Trademark Rep. 671 (1992); Smith, *Trademarks, Parody and Consumer Confusion: A Workable Lanham Act Infringement Standard*, 12 Cardozo L. Rev. 1525 (1991); Pattishall, *The Constitutional Foundations of American Trademark Law*, 78 Trademark Rep. 456, 469–475 (1988).

CHAPTER 8

TRADE IDENTITY LAW

§ 8.01 Dilution

INTRODUCTION

Anti-dilution statutes, now law in over half of the states, are a relatively recent and profound development in American trade identity law. They are intended to broaden and supplement the traditional objectives by protecting the distinctive quality of marks and names notwithstanding the absence of classical likelihood of confusion of source or of competition between the parties. Thus, a mark which is or has become distinctive may be protected against the use of a similar mark on totally unrelated products or services. Likewise, it would appear that generic use of a mark in dictionaries, directories, etc., or unauthorized use on reconditioned or otherwise altered products can be restrained under anti-dilution statutes. *See* Hofstetter, *Trademarks in Dictionaries*, 59 Trademark Rep. 735 (1969).

The seminal article on dilution is Schechter, *The Rational Basis of Trademark Protection*, 40 Harv. L. Rev. 813 (1927), although it does not refer to the subject as "dilution." Schechter urged that "The preservation of the uniqueness of a trademark should constitute the only rational basis for its protection." His concept has gradually borne fruit in additional statutory scope of trademark protection through adoption of the now numerous state anti-dilution statutes. Section 12 of the Model State Trademark Act (U.S.T.A. 1965) includes the following anti-dilution provision:

> Likelihood of injury to business reputation or of dilution of the distinctive quality of a mark registered under this Act, or a mark valid at common law, or a trade name valid at common law, shall be a ground for injunctive relief notwithstanding the absence of competition between the parties or the absence of confusion as to the source of goods or services.

In the past, the anti-dilution statutes were afforded exceedingly limited or emasculated application by the courts. It appears, however, that the interpretive law has now developed toward comprehension and support of the concept and that the number of statutes will continue to increase.

POLAROID CORP. v. POLARAID, INC.

United States Court of Appeals, Seventh Circuit
319 F.2d 830 (1963)

MAJOR, CIRCUIT JUDGE.

. . . .

"Polaroid," plaintiff's trademark and its trade name, is a coined or invented word, it has never been used as a trademark or trade name by any other individual or corporation, and it has acquired the status of a famous-brand trademark. It has been used by plaintiff as its trademark on a wide variety of products, including but not limited to, optical devices, such as polarizing materials, lenses, lamps, display filters and other optical elements, photographic products such as cam-apparatus, advertising signs, goggles, sun glasses, molded plastic eras, films, prints, flash guns, processing devices, projectors and the like, television and electrical devices and many other products.

Defendant, Polaraid, Inc., is an Illinois corporation, incorporated September 8, 1953, and has its principal office and place of business in Chicago. It is a general contractor specializing in the designing and installation of refrigeration and heating systems. Many of defendant's installations are, like many of plaintiff's products, electrically powered. It buys equipment from others, assembles, installs and at times maintains it. It does an interstate business in Illinois, Indiana and Iowa, and uses "Polaraid" as its trade name and trademark. It affixes its name plate to the equipment which it installs and uses "Polaraid" as a trade name and trademark on its stationery, in its advertising and promotional literature and on its office window. . . .

[T]he [Anti-dilution] Act furnishes the basis for two causes of action: (1) if there exists a likelihood of injury to business reputation or (2) if there is a dilution of the distinctive quality of the mark or trade name. Moreover, it relieves an aggrieved party of the burden of proving competition between the parties or proving confusion as to the source of goods or services. Unfortunately, we are aware of no Illinois case which has construed this provision, but by its plain, unambiguous language it lays a heavy hand upon one who adopts the trade name or mark of another.

Callmann in *The Law of Unfair Competition and Trademarks*, 2nd edition 1950, at page 1643, defines dilution as follows:

> The gravamen of a dilution complaint is that the continuous use of a mark similar to plaintiff's works an inexorably adverse effect upon the distinctiveness of the plaintiff's mark, and that, if he is powerless to prevent such use, his mark will lose its distinctiveness entirely. This injury differs materially from that arising out of the orthodox confusion. . . . Such confusion leads to immediate injury, while dilution is an infection which, if allowed to spread, will inevitably destroy the advertising value of the mark.

Defendant argues that the Anti-dilution Statute is inapplicable because there is no finding that any representations were made to customers, prospective customers of plaintiff or to the general public that defendant is in any way connected with plaintiff or that any customer or defendant believed he was dealing with plaintiff;

the parties' products are not sold through the same outlets or to the same type of customer; the parties advertise in different media, and there is no showing of an intent on the part of defendant to capitalize on the good will of plaintiff. This is a traditional argument made against a charge of unfair competition and even there, as previously shown, it is without force where a party adopts the invented or coined trademark or trade name of another.

Defendant cites two cases in support of its contention on this point. *HMH Publishing Co., v. Playboy Records, Inc.*, D.C., 161 F. Supp. 540, and *Esquire, Inc. v. Esquire Slipper Mfg. Co.*, 1 Cir., 243 F.2d 540. In the *Playboy* case, the District Court held that the complaint stated a cause of action for trademark infringement and unfair competition. In connection with its discussion of the latter issue, the Court referred to the Anti-dilution Statute as follows (161 F. Supp. page 544):

> The broad language of this provision, together with the holdings of the Lady Esther case and decisions subsequent thereto, makes it clear that under Illinois law a cause of action for unfair competition may be brought even though the products involved in the suit are non-competitive and unrelated.

The *Esquire* case is also of no aid to defendant. There, the Court (243 F.2d page 544) quoted and discussed the Antidilution Statute of Massachusetts, quite similar to that of Illinois. The gist of the holding was that a court was not under a mandatory duty to grant injunctive relief under all circumstances. Even so, the Court approved of an injunction which limited defendant's use of the word, "Esquire." This result flowed from the Court's reasoning that Esquire "is not a coined word but one firmly established in the English vocabulary," that it was "an already diluted name" when the plaintiff selected it, that the protection accorded to such a weak name is not as broad as that which might be accorded to a strong, coined name as " 'Kodak,' for instance," and that plaintiff was entitled only to such a valuable good will as attached to the name "so far as it belongs to the plaintiff." By contrast, in the instant case plaintiff's trademark and trade name was original — it was coined and invented — and was a strong name exclusively appropriated by plaintiff. It was a name which through much effort and the expenditure of large amounts of money had acquired a widespread reputation and much good will, which plaintiff should not be required to share with defendant.

The record discloses there were numerous incidents of confusion as to identity of the parties, but even without proof the conclusion is inescapable that such would be the result, due to the close resemblance of defendant's trade name to that of plaintiff. If the Anti-dilution Statute is not applicable to this situation, it is useless because it adds nothing to the established law on unfair competition and, as heretofore noted, the District Court entered no conclusions in support of its dismissal of the alleged violation of this provision.

We conclude that plaintiff is entitled to injunctive relief against defendant, as prayed for in its complaint, for either unfair competition or for a violation of the Illinois Anti-dilution Statute, or both, without an award of damages or profits. In view of our holding relative to the second and third causes of action, we find no occasion to discuss or decide the issue of trademark infringement as asserted in plaintiff's first cause of action.

The judgment is reversed and the cause remanded, with directions to proceed in accordance with this opinion, each party to pay its own costs.

MEAD DATA CENTRAL, INC. v. TOYOTA MOTOR SALES, U.S.A., INC.

United States Court of Appeals, Second Circuit
875 F.2d 1026 (1989)

VAN GRAAFEILAND, CIRCUIT JUDGE.

. . . .

Toyota Motor Sales, U.S.A., Inc. and its parent, Toyota Motor Corporation, appeal from a judgment of the United States District Court for the Southern District of New York (Edelstein, J.) enjoining them from using LEXUS as the name of their new luxury automobile and the division that manufactures it. The district court held that, under New York's antidilution statute, N.Y. Gen. Bus. Law § 368-d, Toyota's use of LEXUS is likely to dilute the distinctive quality of LEXIS, the mark used by Mead Data Central, Inc. for its computerized legal research service, 702 F. Supp. 1031 (1988). On March 8, 1989, we entered an order of reversal stating that an opinion would follow. This is the opinion.

THE STATUTE

Section 368-d of New York's General Business Law, which has counterparts in at least twenty other states, reads as follows:

> Likelihood of injury to business reputation or of dilution of the distinctive quality of a mark or trade name shall be a ground for injunctive relief in cases of infringement of a mark registered or not registered or in cases of unfair competition, notwithstanding the absence of competition between the parties or the absence of confusion as to the source of goods or services.

THE PARTIES AND THEIR MARKS

Mead and Lexis

Mead is a corporation organized under the laws of Delaware with its principal place of business in Miamisburg, Ohio. Since 1972, Mead has provided a computerized legal research service under the trademark LEXIS. Mead introduced evidence that its president in 1972 "came up with the name LEXIS based on Lex which was Latin for law and I S for information systems." In fact, however, the word "lexis" is centuries old. It is found in the language of ancient Greece, where it had the meaning of "phrase," "word," "speaking," or "diction." Pinkerton, *Word for Word*, 179 (1982). "Lexis" subsequently appeared in the Latin where it had a substantially similar meaning, *i.e.*, "word," "speech," or "language." *Oxford Latin Dictionary*

(1983); Lewis and Short, *A Latin Dictionary* (1980); Lewis, *An Elementary Latin Dictionary* (1979).

Like many other Latin words, "lexis" has been incorporated bodily into the English. It can be found today in at least sixty general dictionaries or other English word books, including *Webster's Ninth New Collegiate Dictionary* and *Webster's New World Dictionary*. Moreover, its meaning has not changed significantly from that of its Latin and Greek predecessors; *e.g.*, "Vocabulary, the total set of words in a language" (*American Heritage Illustrated Encyclopedic Dictionary*); "A vocabulary of a language, a particular subject, occupation, or activity" (Funk & Wagnalls Standard Dictionary). The district court's finding that "to establish that LEXIS is an English word required expert testimony at trial" is clearly erroneous. Anyone with a rudimentary knowledge of English can go to a library or bookstore and find the word in one of the above-mentioned standard dictionaries.

Moreover, the record discloses that numerous other companies had adopted "Lexis" in identifying their business or its product, *e.g.*, Lexis Ltd., Lexis Computer Systems Ltd., Lexis Language and Export Information Service, Lexis Corp., Maxwell Labs Lexis 3. In sum, we reject Mead's argument that LEXIS is a coined mark which originated in the mind of its former president and, as such, is entitled *per se* to the greater protection that a unique mark such as "Kodak" would receive. *See Esquire, Inc. v. Esquire Slipper Mfg. Co.*, 243 F.2d 540, 543 (1st Cir. 1957); *Intercontinental Mfg. Co. v. Continental Motors Corp.*, 230 F.2d 621, 623 (C.C.P.A. 1956).

Nevertheless, through its extensive sales and advertising in the field of computerized legal research, Mead has made LEXIS a strong mark in that field, and the district court so found. In particular, the district court accepted studies proffered by both parties which revealed that 76 percent of attorneys associated LEXIS with specific attributes of the service provided by Mead. However, among the general adult population, LEXIS is recognized by only one percent of those surveyed, half of this one percent being attorneys or accountants. The district court therefore concluded that LEXIS is strong only within its own market.

. . . .

Toyota and Lexus

Toyota Motor Corp. has for many years manufactured automobiles, which it markets in the United States through its subsidiary Toyota Motor Sales, U.S.A. On August 24, 1987 Toyota announced a new line of luxury automobiles to be called LEXUS. The cars will be manufactured by a separate LEXUS division of Toyota, and their marketing pitch will be directed to well-educated professional consumers with annual incomes in excess of $50,000. Toyota had planned to spend $18 million to $20 million for this purpose during the first nine months of 1989.

Before adopting the completely artificial name LEXUS for its new automobile, Toyota secured expert legal advice to the effect that "there is absolutely no conflict between 'LEXIS' and 'LEXUS.'" Accordingly, when Mead subsequently objected to Toyota's use of LEXUS, Toyota rejected Mead's complaints. The district court held correctly that Toyota acted without predatory intent in adopting the LEXUS mark.

> [T]he absence of predatory intent by the junior user is a relevant factor in assessing a claim under the antidilution statute, . . . since relief under the statute is of equitable origin . . . .

Sally Gee, Inc. v. Myra Hogan, Inc., 699 F.2d 621, 626 (2d Cir. 1983) (citations omitted).

However, the district court erred in concluding that Toyota's refusal to acknowledge that its use of LEXUS might harm the LEXIS mark, deprived it of the argument that it acted in good faith. If, as we now hold, Toyota's mark did not dilute Mead's, it would be anomalous indeed to hold Toyota guilty of bad faith in proceeding in reliance on its attorney's correct advice to that effect. *See Sweats Fashions, Inc. v. Stride Rite Corp.*, 656 F. Supp. 484, 490 (S.D.N.Y. 1987); *Inc. Publishing Corp. v. Manhattan Magazine, Inc.*, 616 F. Supp. 370, 394–96 (S.D.N.Y. 1985), *aff'd*, 788 F.2d 3 (2d Cir. 1986); *Procter & Gamble Co. v. Johnson & Johnson, Inc.*, 485 F. Supp. 1185, 1201–02 (S.D.N.Y. 1979), *aff'd*, 636 F.2d 1203 (2d Cir. 1980). Indeed, even if the attorney's professional advice had been wrong, it does not follow that Toyota's reliance on that advice would have constituted bad faith. *Information Clearing House, Inc. v. Find Magazine*, 492 F. Supp. 147, 161–62 (S.D.N.Y. 1980).

. . . .

THE LAW

The brief legislative history accompanying section 368-d describes the purpose of the statute as preventing "the whittling away of an established trade-mark's selling power and value through *its* unauthorized use by others upon dissimilar products." 1954 N.Y. Legis. Ann. 49 (emphasis supplied). If we were to interpret literally the italicized word "its," we would limit statutory violations to the unauthorized use of the identical established mark. This is what Frank Schechter, the father of the dilution theory, intended when he wrote *The Rational Basis of Trademark Protection*, 40 Harv. L. Rev. 813 (1927). *See id.* at 830–33; *see also* Shire, *Dilution Versus Deception — Are State Antidilution Laws an Appropriate Alternative to the Law of Infringement?*, 77 Trademark Rep. 273–76 (1987). However, since the use of obvious simulations or markedly similar marks might have the same diluting effect as would an appropriate of the original mark, the concept of exact identity has been broadened to that of substantial similarity. [Citations omitted]. Nevertheless, in keeping with the original intent of the statute, the similarity must be substantial before the doctrine of dilution may be applied. [Citations omitted].

Indeed some courts have gone so far as to hold that, although violation of an antidilution statute does not require confusion of product or source, the marks in question must be sufficiently similar that confusion may be created as between the marks themselves. *See Holiday Inns, Inc. v. Holiday Out in America*, 481 F.2d 445, 450 (5th Cir. 1973); *King Research, Inc. v. Shulton, Inc.*, 324 F. Supp. 631, 638 (S.D.N.Y. 1971), *aff'd*, 454 F.2d 66 (2d Cir. 1972). We need not go that far. We hold only that the marks must be "very" or "substantially" similar and that, absent such similarity, there can be no viable claim of dilution.

. . . .

[I]f the district court's statement in its Lanham Act discussions that "in everyday spoken English, LEXUS and LEXIS are virtually identical in pronunciation" was intended to be a finding of fact rather than a statement of opinion, we question both its accuracy and its relevance. The word LEXUS is not yet widely enough known that any definitive statement can be made concerning its pronunciation by the American public. However, the two members of this Court who concur in this opinion use "everyday spoken English," and we would not pronounce LEXUS as if it were spelled LEXIS. Although our colleague takes issue with us on this point, he does not contend that if LEXUS and LEXIS are pronounced correctly, they will sound the same. We liken LEXUS to such words as "census," "focus" and "locus," and differentiate it from such words as "axis," "aegis" and "iris." [2] If we were to substitute the letter "i" for the letter "u" in "census," we would not pronounce it as we now do. Likewise, if we were to substitute the letter "u" for the letter "i" in "axis," we would not pronounce it as we now do. In short, we agree with the testimony of Toyota's speech expert, who testified:

> Of course, anyone can pronounce "lexis" and "lexus" the same, either both with an unstressed I or both with an unstressed U, or schwa — or with some other sound in between. But, properly, the distinction between unstressed I and unstressed U, or schwa, is a standard one in English; the distinction is there to be made in ordinary, reasonably careful speech.

In addition, we do not believe that "everyday spoken English" is the proper test to use in deciding the issue of similarity in the instant case. Under the Constitution, there is a " 'commonsense' distinction between speech proposing a commercial transaction, which occurs in an area traditionally subject to government regulation, and other varieties of speech." *Central Hudson Gas & Electric corp. v. Public Service Comm'n*, 447 U.S. 557, 562 (1980) (quoting *Ohralik v. Ohio State Bar Ass'n*, 436 U.S. 447, 455–56 (1978)).

. . . .

"Advertising is the primary means by which the connection between a name and a company is established . . . ," *Beneficial Corp. v. Beneficial Capital Corp.*, 529 F. Supp. 445, 448 (S.D.N.Y. 1982), and oral advertising is done primarily on radio and television. When Mead's speech expert was asked whether there were instances in which LEXUS and LEXIS would be pronounced differently, he replied "Yes, although a deliberate attempt must be made to do so . . . . They can be pronounced distinctly but they are not when they are used in common parlance, in everyday language or speech." We take it as a given that television and radio announcers are more careful and precise in their diction than is the man on the street. Moreover, it is the rare television commercial that does not contain a visual reference to the mark and product, which in the instant case would be the LEXUS automobile. We conclude that in the field of commercial advertising, which is the field subject to regulation, there is no substantial similarity between Mead's mark and Toyota's.

---

[2] Similarly, we liken LEXUS to NEXXUS, a nationally known shampoo, and LEXIS to NEXIS, Mead's trademark for its computerized news service. NEXXUS and NEXIS have co-existed in apparent tranquility for almost a decade.

There are additional factors that militate against a finding of dilution in the instant case. Such a finding must be based on two elements. First, plaintiff's mark must possess a distinctive quality capable of dilution. *Allied Maintenance Corp. v. Allied Mechanical Trades, Inc.*, 369 N.E.2d 1162 (N.Y. 1977). Second, plaintiff must show a likelihood of dilution. *Sally Gee, Inc. v. Myra Hogan, Inc., supra*, 699 F.2d at 625. As section 368-d expressly states, a plaintiff need not show either competition between its product or service and that of the defendant or a likelihood of confusion as to the source of the goods or services. *Allied Maintenance Corp. v. Allied Mechanical Trades, Inc., supra*, 369 N.E.2d 1162.

Distinctiveness for dilution purposes often has been equated with the strength of a mark for infringement purposes. *P.F. Cosmetique, S.A. v. Minnetonka, Inc.*, 605 F. Supp. 662, 672 (S.D.N.Y. 1985); *Allied Maintenance Corp. v. Allied Mechanical Trade, Inc., supra*, 369 N.E.2d 1162. It also has been defined as uniqueness or as having acquired a secondary meaning. *Allied Maintenance, supra*, 369 N.E.2d 1162. A trademark has a secondary meaning if it "has become so associated in the mind of the public with that entity [Allied] or its product that it identifies the goods sold by that entity and distinguishes them from goods sold by others." *Id.* In sum, the statute protects a trademark's "selling power." *Sally Gee, Inc. v. Myra Hogan, Inc., supra*, 699 F.2d at 624–25. However, the fact that a mark has selling power in a limited geographical or commercial area does not endow it with a secondary meaning for the public generally. [Citations omitted].

The strength and distinctiveness of LEXIS is limited to the market for its services — attorneys and accountants. Outside that market, LEXIS has very little selling power. Because only one percent of the general population associates LEXIS with the attributes of Mead's services, it cannot be said that LEXIS identifies that service to the general public and distinguishes it from others. Moreover, the bulk of Mead's advertising budget is devoted to reaching attorneys through professional journals.

This Court has defined dilution as either the blurring of a mark's product identification or the tarnishment of the affirmative associations a mark has come to convey. *Sally Gee, Inc. v. Myra Hogan, Inc., supra*, 699 F.2d at 625 (quoting 3A Callmann, *The Law of Unfair Competition, Trademarks and Monopolies* § 84.2 at 954–55). Mead does not claim that Toyota's use of LEXUS would tarnish affirmative associations engendered by LEXIS. The question that remains, therefore, is whether LEXIS is likely to be blurred by LEXUS.

Very little attention has been given to date to the distinction between the confusion necessary for a claim of infringement and the blurring necessary for a claim of dilution. Shire, *supra*, 77 Trademark Rep. at 293. Although the antidilution statute dispenses with the requirements of competition and confusion, it does not follow that every junior use of a similar mark will dilute the senior mark in the manner contemplated by the New York Legislature.

As already stated, the brief legislative history accompanying section 368-d described the purpose of the statute as preventing "the whittling away of an established trademark's selling power and value through its unauthorized use by others upon dissimilar products." The history disclosed a need for legislation to prevent such "hypothetical anomalies" as "Dupont shoes, Buick aspirin tablets,

Schlitz varnish, Kodak pianos, Bulova gowns, and so forth," and cited cases involving similarly famous marks, *e.g., Tiffany & Co. v. Tiffany Productions, Inc.,* 147 Misc. 679, 264 N.Y.S. 459 (1932), *aff'd,* 237 A.D. 801, 260 N.Y.S. 821, *aff'd,* 262 N.Y. 482, 188 N.E. 30 (1933); *Philadelphia Storage Battery Co. v. Mindlin,* 163 Misc. 52, 296 N.Y.S. 176 (1937). 1954 N.Y. Legis. Ann. 49–50.

It is apparent from these references that there must be some mental association between plaintiff's and defendant's marks.

> [I]f a reasonable buyer is not at all likely to link the two uses of the trademark in his or her own mind, even subtly or subliminally, then there can be no dilution . . . . [D]ilution theory presumes *some kind of mental association* in the reasonable buyer's mind between the two party's [sic] uses of the mark.

McCarthy, *supra,* § 24.13 at 213–14.

This mental association may be created where the plaintiff's mark is very famous and therefore has a distinctive quality for a significant percentage of the defendant's market. *Sally Gee, Inc. v. Myra Hogan, Inc., supra,* 699 F.2d at 625. However, if a mark circulates only in a limited market, it is unlikely to be associated generally with the mark for a dissimilar product circulating elsewhere. *See, e.g., Estee Lauder, Inc. v. Cinnabar 2000 Haircutters, Inc.,* 218 U.S.P.Q. 191 (S.D.N.Y.), *aff'd,* 714 F.2d 112 (2d Cir. 1982); *Markel v. Scovill Mfg. Co.,* 471 F. Supp. 1244 (W.D.N.Y.), *aff'd,* 610 F.2d 807 (2d Cir. 1979). As discussed above, such distinctiveness as LEXIS possesses is limited to the narrow market of attorneys and accountants. Moreover, the process which LEXIS represents is widely disparate from the product represented by LEXUS. For the general public, LEXIS has no distinctive quality that LEXUS will dilute.

The possibility that someday LEXUS may become a famous mark in the mind of the general public has little relevance in the instant dilution analysis since it is quite apparent that the general public associates nothing with LEXIS. On the other hand, the recognized sophistication of attorneys, the principal users of the service, has substantial relevance. *See Sally Gee, Inc. v. Myra Hogan, Inc., supra,* 699 F.2d at 626. Because of this knowledgeable sophistication, it is unlikely that, even in the market where Mead principally operates, there will be any significant amount of blurring between the LEXIS and LEXUS marks.

For all the foregoing reasons, we hold that Toyota did not violate section 368-d. We see no need therefore to discuss Toyota's remaining arguments for reversal.

SWEET, DISTRICT JUDGE, concurring:

. . . .

The only finding that supports a likelihood of dilution is the district court's conclusion that LEXUS eventually may become so famous that members of the general public who now associate LEXIS or LEXUS with nothing at all may associate the terms with Toyota's automobiles and that Mead's customers may think first of Toyota's car when they hear LEXIS. *See* Dist. Ct. Op. at 30–31. This analysis is problematic. First, section 368-d protects a mark's selling power among the consuming public. *Allied Maintenance Corp. v. Allied Mechanical Trades, Inc.,* 369

N.E.2d 1162, 1163–64 (N.Y. 1977); *Sally Gee, Inc. v. Myra Hogan, Inc.*, 699 F.2d 621, 624–25 (2d Cir. 1983). Because the LEXIS mark possesses selling power only among lawyers and accountants, it is irrelevant for dilution analysis that the general public may come to associate LEXIS or LEXUS with Toyota's automobile rather than nothing at all. Second, the district court offered no evidence for its speculation that LEXUS's fame may cause Mead customers to associate "lexis" with Toyota's cars. It seems equally plausible that no blurring will occur — because many lawyers and accountants use Mead's services regularly, their frequent association of LEXIS with those services will enable LEXIS's mark to withstand Toyota's advertising campaign.

Therefore, even if we accept the district court's finding regarding the renown of the LEXUS mark, however, reversal still is required. The differences in the marks and in the products covered by the marks, the sophistication of Mead's consumers, the absence of predatory intent, and the limited renown of the LEXIS mark all indicate that blurring is unlikely.

. . . .

WEDGWOOD HOMES, INC. v. LUND

Oregon Supreme Court
639 P.2d 277 (1983)

ROBERTS, JUSTICE.

. . . .

Plaintiff, Wedgwood Homes of Portland, Inc., and its wholly owned subsidiary, Wedgwood Homes, Inc., sought to enjoin defendant from using "Wedgwood" in its assumed business names, Wedgwood Downs and Wedgwood Place. At trial plaintiff attempted to prove common law unfair competition as well as dilution of its trade name pursuant to ORS 647.107. We accept the facts as found by the trial court and Court of Appeals. Plaintiff has failed to show a likelihood of consumer confusion of the identities of plaintiff and defendant. Its cause of action for unfair competition therefore fails. The trial court nonetheless granted an injunction finding a likelihood of injury to business reputation or dilution of the distinctive quality of plaintiff's name under the statute. The Court of Appeals affirmed. We review to determine if there was "dilution" of the "distinctive quality" of plaintiff's name. The statute does not define either term. . . .

In the context of dilution, the protectable quality of a mark has been defined as the mark's power to evoke images of the product, that is, its favorable associational value in the minds of consumers. This attribute may be developed in a variety of ways: long use, consistent superior quality instilling consumer satisfaction, extensive advertising. Note, *Dilution: Trademark Infringement or Will-O'-The-Wisp?*, 77

Harv. L. Rev. 520, 522 (1963/64); *Recent Developments*, 46 Fordham L. Rev. 1315, 1333–35 (1978).

In application the existence of the mark's distinctive quality must be proven by demonstrating what the mark signifies to the consuming public, *Id.* at 1335. If the mark has come to signify plaintiff's product in the minds of a significant portion of consumers and if the mark evokes favorable images of plaintiff or its product it possesses the distinctive quality of advertising value — consumer recognition, association and acceptance — and will be entitled to protection from dilution.

Plaintiff has been engaged for the past 25 years in the development, construction and marketing of single and multiple family residential real estate in eastern Washington County. Plaintiff's substantial advertising programs seek to promote the quality, styling and flair of plaintiff's residential construction. Defendant has maintained dormitory style housing for the elderly in two retirement apartment complexes in eastern Washington County since 1977.

The trial court found that after 25 years' use plaintiff had established a secondary meaning in its name. Defendant does not dispute this conclusion but argues that the antidilution statute should be limited to marks which are coined, unique or truly famous. Relying on legislative history defendant contends that only the most distinctive marks deserve the enhanced protection afforded by ORS 647.107, and that because plaintiff's name is neither coined, unique nor nationally famous the statute should not be invoked on plaintiff's behalf.

We reject defendant's argument that the protection of the antidilution statute should apply to coined and unique words alone. As we have noted, marks may become distinctive in three ways: by use of coined words, by use of arbitrary words, or by acquisition of secondary meaning.

In light of the nature of the distinctive quality we have defined, there is no reason to assume, as defendant's argument implies, that only coined marks possess advertising value. When first coined a mark will likely have no commercial value at all. Distinctive quality develops over time as consumer recognition and association is instilled. Moreover, defendant cannot dispute that a mark which has become distinctive through the acquisition of secondary meaning could be entitled to protection from dilution. Among examples of marks covered by the statute is Tiffany, a jewelry trademark, which acquired its distinctiveness through secondary meaning. *Tiffany & Co. v. Boston Club, Inc.*, 231 F. Supp. 836, 143 U.S.P.Q. 2 (D. Mass 1964). It is our opinion that protection may be extended regardless of the manner by which a trademark becomes distinctive. *See Ferrara v. Scharf*, 466 F. Supp. 125, 204 U.S.P.Q. 118 (S.D.N.Y 1979); *Great Scott Food Market, Inc. v. Sunderland Wonder, Inc.*, 203 N.E.2d 376, 379, 144 U.S.P.Q. 333 (Mass. 1965); *Skil Corporation v. Barnet*, 150 N.E.2d 551, 117 U.S.P.Q. 461 (Mass. 1958).

Likewise, we reject defendant's suggestion that the statute be limited to nationally famous marks. We see no reason why marks of national renown should enjoy protection while local marks should not. A small local firm may expend efforts and money proportionately as great as those of a large firm in order to establish its mark's distinctive quality. In both situations the interest to be protected and the damage to be prevented are the same. In summary, it is not the manner by which distinctiveness is acquired nor the span of a mark's notoriety but rather the degree of advertising value the mark has gained which determines the applicability of ORS 647.107.

. . . .

Where tradename owners have created a favorable association between their name and their product, they possess a valuable marketing tool. The aura of recognition enhances the value of plaintiff's name. Subsequent use of the name with a nonrelated product broadens the associations linking name and product in the minds of consumers of plaintiff's product and diminishes the specific association plaintiff seeks to foster. "[U]nrelated use erodes selling power by destroying the automatic identification of the trademark with the original product and the favorable images created by advertising." Greiwe, *Antidilution Statutes: A New Attack on Comparative Advertising*, 72 Trademark Rep 178, 186 (1982). A second use may therefore be prevented by means of the antidilution statute.

. . . .

We hold that where a tradename possesses the distinctive quality of favorable associational value a second use may be enjoined under the statute whenever this is proven to be necessary in order to prevent the diminution of plaintiff's name as an advertising tool among consumers of plaintiff's product. In the case before us plaintiff has established that its name possesses the distinctive quality of positive associational value with its product. To a significant percentage of the consuming public of eastern Washington County, Wedgwood connotes homes. Defendant's use of the name in connection with retirement apartments expands the associations consumers are likely to connect with the name and thereby reduces the name's effectiveness in identifying and advertising plaintiff's product. On these facts plaintiff has adequately demonstrated dilution of the distinctive quality of its name.

The decision of the Court of Appeals is affirmed.

NOTES ON DILUTION

(1) The rationale behind the anti-dilution statutes is the protection of the distinctive quality of a mark, even in the absence of likelihood of confusion, against such use by another as may degrade or decrease that distinctiveness. "The essence of dilution is the watering down of the potency of a mark and the gradual debilitation of its selling power." *Toys "R" Us, Inc. v. Canarsie Kiddie Shop, Inc.*, 559 F. Supp. 1189, 1208 (E.D.N.Y. 1983). Even though all of the anti-dilution statutes contain the proviso entitling an injured party to relief "notwithstanding the absence of competition between the parties or the absence of confusion as to the source of goods or services," as interpreted by many courts, however, the anti-dilution statutes have been said to require likelihood of confusion or competition. *See, e.g., Carter-Wallace, Inc. v. Procter & Gamble Co.*, 434 F.2d 794 (9th Cir. 1970); *Beneficial*

Corp. v. Beneficial Capital Corp., 529 F. Supp. 445 (S.D.N.Y. 1982); *Laverne International Ltd. v. American Institute of Interior Designers, Inc.*, 353 F. Supp. 653, 655–666 (S.D.N.Y. 1973). Some courts have gone so far as not to allow claims of dilution because the parties were in competition. *See, e.g., EZ Loader Boat Trailers, Inc. v. Cox Trailers, Inc.*, 746 F.2d 375, 380 (7th Cir. 1984); *Filter Dynamics International, Inc. v. Astron Battery, Inc.*, 311 N.E.2d 386 (Ill. App. Ct. 1974); *Aris-Isotoner Gloves, Inc. v. Townes Brothers & Co.*, 594 F. Supp. 15 (S.D.N.Y. 1983). Note, however, that the Model State Trademark Act, § 12, provides for "injunctive relief notwithstanding the absence of competition between the parties." *Compare LeSportsac, Inc. v. K-Mart Corp.*, 617 F. Supp. 316 (E.D.N.Y. 1985), in which the court stated: "The [anti-dilution] statute affords relief to plaintiff notwithstanding the absence of competition or confusion. That is not the same as saying . . . that such absence is a prerequisite to relief." *See also Vitabiotics, Ltd. v. Kruplea*, 606 F. Supp. 779 (E.D.N.Y. 1984). In *Nikon, Inc. v. Ikon Corp.*, 987 F.2d 91 (2d Cir. 1993), the Second Circuit confirmed that the New York antidilution statute applies to both competitors and noncompetitors.

(2) Is judicial reluctance in applying state dilution statutes warranted? What arguments are there for and against application of the dilution concept? What actually constitutes dilution? In *Ameritech, Inc. v. American Information Technologies*, 811 F.2d 960 (6th Cir. 1987), the court stated that dilution is use that causes a "gradual diminution of the mark's distinctiveness, effectiveness and, hence, value. This kind of infringement corrodes the senior user's interest in the trademark by blurring its product identification or by damaging positive associations that have attached to it." The court then remanded the case for consideration of plaintiff's Ohio common law dilution claim. *See generally* McCarthy, *Trademarks and Unfair Competition* § 24.13(b) (3d ed. 1992); Welkowitz, *Reexamining Trademark Dilution*, 44 Vand. L. Rev. 531 (1991); Leimer, *Trademark Dilution In the United States*, Trademark World (November, 1993); Bronlee, *Mead Data Central v. Toyota and other Contemporary Dilution Cases: High Noon for Trademark Law's Misfit Doctrine?*, 79 Trademark Rep. 471 (1989); Pattishall, *Dawning Acceptance of the Dilution Rationale For Trademark-Trade Identity Protection*, 74 Trademark Rep. 289 (1984); Lunsford, *Trademarks: Dilution and Deception*, 63 Trademark Rep. 41 (1973); Note, *Dilution: Trademark Infringement or Will-o'-The-Wisp?*, 77 Harv. L. Rev. 520 (1964); Derenberg, *The Problem of Trademark Dilution and the Antidilution Statutes*, 44 Cal. L. Rev. 439 (1956); Schechter, *The Rational Basis of Trademark Protection*, 40 Harv. L. Rev. 813 (1927). *Compare* Handler, *Are The State Anti-Dilution Laws Compatible With the National Protection of Trademarks?*, 75 Trademark Rep. 269 (1985). Recent decisions disclose increasing acceptance and application of anti-dilution law and doctrine.

(3) Even prior to Schechter's 1927 promulgation of the dilution rationale, a few courts had rendered opinions implicitly relying on dilution. *Wall v. Rolls-Royce of America*, 4 F.2d 333 (3d Cir. 1925) (ROLLS ROYCE for radio tubes); *Eastman Photographic Materials Co. v. Kodak Cycle Co.*, 15 R.P.C. 105 (1898) (KODAK for bicycles). *See also Stork Restaurant, Inc. v. Sahati*, 166 F.2d 348 (9th Cir. 1948) (remote geographical locations).

(4) The state statutes do not require a "strong" or "celebrated" mark for the dilution doctrine to apply, but some judicial opinions seem to have "read in" such a requirement. *See, e.g., Accuride International, Inc. v. Accuride Corp.*, 871 F.2d 1531 (9th Cir. 1989) (ACCURIDE for drawer slides insufficiently distinctive to be diluted); *Miss Universe, Inc. v. Patricelli*, 753 F.2d 235 (2d Cir. 1985) (Miss U.S.A. not strong enough to be diluted by MISS VENUS U.S.A.); *Freedom Savings & Loan Ass'n. v. Way*, 757 F.2d 1176 (11th Cir. 1985), *cert. denied*, 106 S. Ct. 134 (1985) (FREEDOM for savings and loan, and real estate service); *Astra Pharmaceutical Products, Inc. v. Beckman Instruments, Inc.*, 718 F.2d 1201 (1st Cir. 1983) (ASTRA for local anesthetic, and blood analyzer); *Lindy Pen Co. v. Bic Pen Corp.*, 550 F. Supp. 1056 (C.D. Cal. 1982), *aff'd in part and rev'd in part*, 725 F.2d 1240 (9th Cir. 1984), *cert. denied*, 469 U.S. 1188 (1985); *American Dairy Queen Corp. v. ROT Inc.*, 16 U.S.P.Q.2d 1077 (N.D. Ill. 1990) (slogan WE TREAT YOU RIGHT for fast food restaurants too weak to warrant preliminary relief against defendant's use of slogan for renting television and stereo equipment); *Oxford Industries, Inc. v. JBJ Fabrics, Inc.*, 6 U.S.P.Q.2d 1756 (S.D.N.Y. 1988) (JBJ for wearing apparel not strong enough to be diluted); *Allied Maintenance Corp. v. Allied Mechanical Trades, Inc.*, 369 N.E.2d 1162 (N.Y. 1977) (ALLIED MAINTENANCE for maintenance of large office buildings not diluted by ALLIED MECHANICAL TRADES, INC. for installation and repair of heating, ventilating and air conditioning equipment where "Allied" was used by at least 300 New York City businesses and plaintiff failed to show its name had acquired secondary meaning). *Cf. Dreyfus Fund v. Royal Bank of Canada*, 525 F. Supp. 1108 (S.D.N.Y. 1981) (plaintiffs' "lion" logo strong and diluted by defendant's use in the same financial field). Should the dilution concept be limited in application to so-called "celebrated" marks? Where should the line be drawn as to distinctiveness? Is there a test which would enhance predictability in this area of the law? *See Wedgwood Homes, Inc. v. Lund, supra*.

(5) What relief is appropriate in dilution cases? In most cases where plaintiff prevailed on its dilution claim, the courts have provided only injunctive relief. *See, e.g., Ringling Bros.–Barnum & Bailey Combined Shows, Inc. v. Celozzi-Ettelson Chevrolet, Inc.*, 855 F.2d 480 (7th Cir. 1988) (defendant enjoined from using GREATEST USED CAR SHOW ON EARTH to advertise used cars because the slogan diluted Ringling Bros.' GREATEST SHOW ON EARTH slogan); *Community Federal Savings & Loan Assoc. v. Orondorff*, 678 F.2d 1034 (11th Cir. 1982) (enjoining use of COOKIE JAR on topless bar across the street from bank bearing that name); *Safeway Stores, Inc. v. Safeway Discount Drugs, Inc.*, 675 F.2d 1160 (11th Cir. 1982); *Golden Door, Inc. v. Odisho*, 437 F. Supp. 956 (N.D. Cal. 1977), *aff'd*, 646 F.2d 347 (9th Cir. 1980); *American Express Co. v. Vibra Approved Laboratories Corp.*, 10 U.S.P.Q.2d 2006 (S.D.N.Y. 1989) (defendant enjoined from marketing a "condom card" bearing the name AMERICA EXPRESS and slogan "Never leave home without it," because it was likely to dilute plaintiff's "AMERICAN EXPRESS" credit card mark and its slogan "Don't leave home without it"); *Coca-Cola Company v. Alma-Leo U.S.A., Inc.*, 719 F. Supp. 725 (N.D. Ill. 1989) (defendant enjoined from marketing white powder bubble gum resembling cocaine in a plastic simulation of Coca-Cola's famous bottle); *Eastman Kodak Co. v. Rakow*, 739 F. Supp. 116 (W.D.N.Y. 1989) (nationwide injunction against comedian's use

of stage name "Kodak"). *Cf. Bowmar Instrument Corp. v. Continental Microsystems, Inc.*, 497 F. Supp. 947 (S.D.N.Y. 1980). Although none of the state dilution statutes provides for an award of damages, at least one opinion has suggested that such an award might be appropriate. *See Hyatt Corp., infra* Note (7). Would an award of damages or of the cost of "corrective" advertising ever be warranted in a dilution case?

(6) Dilution as such does not constitute infringement of a federally registered mark under the Lanham Act. *See Jean Patou, Inc. v. Jacqueline Cochran, Inc.*, 201 F. Supp. 861, 867 (S.D.N.Y. 1962), *aff'd*, 312 F.2d 125 (2d Cir. 1963). "Dilution may overlap infringement sometimes, but if infringement were a *sine qua non*, dilution would be a pointless, merely cumulative offense." Fletcher & Weinberg, *U.S.T.A. 1985–86 Trademark Law Handbook* 299 (1986). The inclusion of an anti-dilution provision in the 1988 revision of the Lanham Act was considered and ultimately rejected. *Report of the Trademark Review Commission*, 77 Trademark Rep. 375, 458 (1987). *See also* Gilson, *A Federal Dilution Statute: Is It Time?*, 83 Trademark Rep. 108 (1993). Dilution has been held not to provide a ground upon which to oppose federal registration of a mark. *Tiffany & Co. v. National Gypsum Co.*, 459 F.2d 527 (C.C.P.A. 1972). Is use of a trademark in a generic sense a form of dilution? *See* Robb, *Trademark Misuse in Dictionaries: Inadequacy of Existing Legal Action and a Suggested Cure*, 65 Marq. L. Rev. 179 (1981); Derenberg, *supra*, 44 Cal. L. Rev. 439, 464. Can dilution exist where defendant's reputation and product are held in high esteem? *See Sally Gee, Inc. v. Myra Hogan, Inc.*, 699 F.2d 621 (2d Cir. 1983), where the court held there was no dilution of mass-produced SALLY GEE clothing by handmade SALLY GEE garments.

(7) In *Hyatt Corp. v. Hyatt Legal Services*, 736 F.2d 1153 (7th Cir. 1984), *cert denied*, 469 U.S. 1019 (1985), the well-known Hyatt hotel chain sued the Hyatt Legal Services chain and its principal, Joel Hyatt, for trademark infringement and dilution. Reversing the trial court's denial of injunctive relief, the appellate court relied entirely on the proposition that defendant's use of Hyatt diluted the distinctive quality of plaintiff's HYATT trade name. Among the factors considered by the court in making its determination were "the similarity between the marks used by the parties, and the extent of the marketing effort by the second user." *Id.* at 1158. The court remanded the case to the district court for entry of an injunction. The parties subsequently settled the case, Hyatt Legal Services agreeing to state at the bottom of all advertisements that "Hyatt Legal Services is named after its founder, Joel Z. Hyatt."

(8) Anti-dilution statutes exist in Alabama, Alaska, Arkansas, California, Connecticut, Delaware, Florida, Georgia, Idaho, Illinois, Iowa, Louisiana, Maine, Massachusetts, Missouri, Montana, Nebraska, New Hampshire, New York, Oregon, Pennsylvania, Rhode Island, Tennessee, Texas, and Washington. Additionally, Michigan, New Jersey and Ohio have recognized common law dilution claims.

(9) The Restatement (Third) of Unfair Competition, § 25 (Tentative Draft No. 2, March 23, 1990) provides:

> (1) One who uses the trademark, trade name, collective mark, or certification mark of another may be subject to liability without proof of a likelihood of

confusion only under an applicable antidilution statute. An actor is subject to liability under such a statute if, as a designation to identify its own goods, services, or business, the actor:

(a) uses a designation that resembles the highly distinctive trademark, trade name, collective mark, or certification mark of another in a manner likely to cause a reduction in the distinctiveness of the other's mark; or

(b) uses a designation that resembles the trademark, trade name, collective mark, or certification mark of another and the nature of the actor's goods, services, or business, or the nature of the actor's use, is likely to cause prospective purchasers to associate the actor's and the other's goods, services, businesses, or marks in a manner that disparages the other's goods, services, or business or tarnishes the images associated with the other's mark.

(2) One who uses a designation that resembles the trademark, trade name, collective mark, or certification mark of another, not as a designation to identify the actor's own goods, services, or business, but instead to comment on, criticize, ridicule, parody, or disparage the other or the other's goods, services, business, or mark, is subject to liability without proof of a likelihood of confusion only if the actor's conduct meets the requirements of a cause of action for defamation, or invasion of privacy, or injurious falsehood.

Note that liability for a likely reduction in distinctiveness under part 1(a) requires that the owner's mark be "highly distinctive," while liability for likely disparagement or tarnishment under part 1(b) does not. Why the difference? For an application of the Restatement's part 1(a) distinctiveness standard, see *Tower Publications Inc. v. MTS Inc.*, 21 U.S.P.Q.2d 1303, 1305 (N.D. Ill. 1991), in which the court held that "Tower Records of Illinois" for a company that published decisions and opinions of Illinois government commissions was insufficiently distinctive for dilution protection from defendant's use of TOWER RECORDS for music stores.

How would the parody cases discussed in the notes of the Permitted Use section of Chapter 7, *supra*, fare under part (2) of the Restatement's dilution provision?

§ 8.02 Misrepresentation

INTRODUCTION

The scope of the law, both private and public, respecting misrepresentation and false description of goods or services is in active evolution. The courts increasingly have found a clearly defined "federal law of unfair competition" expressed in § 43(a) of the Lanham Act (15 U.S.C. § 1125(a)), which, as revised by the 1988 Act, provides in part as follows:

Any person who, on or in connection with any goods or services, or any container for goods, uses in commerce any word, term, name, symbol, or device, or any combination thereof, or any false designation of origin, false or misleading description of fact, or false or misleading representation of fact, which —

(1) is likely to cause confusion, or to cause mistake, or to deceive as to the affiliation, connection, or association of such person with another person, or as to the origin, sponsorship, or approval of his or her goods, services, or commercial activities by another person, or

(2) in commercial advertising or promotion, misrepresents the nature, characteristics, qualities, or geographic origin of his or her or another person's goods, services, or commercial activities, shall be liable in a civil action by any person who believes that he or she is or is likely to be damaged by such act.

Section 43(a) was primarily intended by the framers of the Act to provide a remedy for the use of a geographic name, or "appellations of origin" in connection with goods not actually from that locality. Robert, *The New Trade-Mark Manual* 186–188 (1947). Interpretation of the language of the section has evolved, however, to provide a federal cause of action not only against deception as to geographic origin but also against a variety of misrepresentations and false descriptions, and against a variety of acts deceptive as to the identity of the manufacturer, seller, or servicer. It is now also established that such actions can be based on likelihood of damage without the necessity of actual damage. The cases which follow demonstrate the course and current extent of this evolution, but its full scope probably has not yet developed.

likelihood of damage

L'AIGLON APPAREL, INC. v. LANA LOBELL, INC.

United States Court of Appeals, Third Circuit
214 F.2d 649 (1954)

HASTIE, CIRCUIT JUDGE.

. . . .

The present complaint alleges that plaintiff created and alone sold to the retail trade throughout the country a certain distinctively styled dress. To advertise this dress plaintiff published pictures of it, together with its price, $17.95, in advertisements in leading newspapers and in some two million individual mailing pieces distributed through retailers. In this way the picture and price of this dress became associated in the minds of many readers and identified as plaintiff's $17.95 dress.

It is further alleged that, at about the same time, defendant was offering for sale through mail order and otherwise in interstate commerce a dress which in fact was much inferior to plaintiff's in quality and notably different in appearance. In this connection defendant published under its name in a magazine of national circulation a display advertisement worded and designed to promote the mail order sale of its dress at a stated price of $6.95, but showing as the most prominent feature of the advertisement an actual photographic reproduction of plaintiff's dress, thus fraudulently represented as the article defendant was selling for $6.95. Plaintiff alleges that this misrepresentation caused some trade to be diverted from plaintiff to defendant

Put pic of P's dress in Ad?

and caused other trade to be lost by plaintiff as a result of the mistaken impression conveyed to those familiar with the advertising of both parties that plaintiff was offering for $17.95 a dress worth only $6.95.

In relation to the language of Section 43(a) this complaint states about as plain a use of a false representation in the description of goods sold in commerce as could be imagined. And plaintiff's alleged damage as a result of defendant's misrepresentation may well be demonstrable within the normal requirements of legal proof and in such way as to entitle plaintiff to relief authorized by the statute. Thus, Section 43(a) seems to cover this case clearly and without ambiguity.

We quickly dispose of a claim that relevant limitations on liability are to be derived from *Mosler Safe Co. v. Ely-Norris Safe Co.*, 1927, 273 U.S. 132. For that case expresses no more than the Court's judgment as to the inadequacy at common law of a particular pleading of injury as the result of a defendant's misrepresentation that his product contained an important feature of another's product. Here we see no inadequacy in the present plaintiff's statement of such an injury as Section 43(a) explicitly makes the proper subject of redress.

It is also urged that before 1946 a line of cases beginning with *American Washboard Co. v. Saginaw Mfg. Co.*, 6 Cir., 1900, 103 F. 281, established the doctrine that in the area of present concern misrepresentations about goods were actionable only if they had led or were likely to lead customers, through confusion of defendant's and plaintiff's goods, to buy the former under the misapprehension that they were the latter. "Palming off," narrowly conceived, was said to be essential to any recovery. And the view has been expressed judicially that some such limitation is to be read into Section 43(a) of the Lanham Act. *Chamberlain v. Columbia Pictures Corp.*, 9 Cir., 1951, 186 F.2d 923; *Samson Crane Co. v. Union National Sales, Inc.*, D.C. Mass. 1949, 89 F. Supp. 218, 222. But we think it could as plausibly be argued that Section 43(a) reflects the more modern viewpoint of Section 761 of the Restatement of Torts, which provides:

> One who diverts trade from a competitor by fraudulently representing that the goods which he markets have ingredients or qualities which in fact they do not have but which the goods of the competitor do have, is liable to the competitor for the harm so caused, if,
>
> (a) when making the representation he intends that it should, or knows or should know that it is likely to, divert trade from the competitor, ...

However, we reject this entire approach to the statute. We find nothing in the legislative history of the Lanham Act to justify the view that this section is merely declarative of existing law. Indeed, because we find no ambiguity in the relevant language in the statute we would doubt the propriety of resort to legislative history even if that history suggested that Congress intended less than it said. It seems to us that Congress has defined a statutory civil wrong of false representation of goods in commerce and has given a broad class of suitors injured or likely to be injured by such wrong the right to relief in the federal courts. This statutory tort is defined in language which differentiates it in some particulars from similar wrongs which have developed and have become defined in the judge made law of unfair competition. Perhaps this statutory tort bears closest resemblance to the already noted tort of false advertising to the detriment of a competitor, as formulated by the American Law Institute out of materials of the evolving common law of unfair competition. *See Torts Restatement,* Section 761, *supra.* But however similar to or different from pre-existing law, here is a provision of a federal statute which, with clarity and precision adequate for judicial administration, creates and defines rights and duties and provides for their vindication in the federal courts.

. . . .

[*Reversed.*]

MUTATION MINK BREEDERS ASS'N v. LOU NIERENBERG CORP.

United States District Court, Southern District of New York
23 F.R.D. 155 (1959)

FREDERICK VAN PELT BRYAN, DISTRICT JUDGE.

. . . .

The complaint charges that defendants affix the term "Normink" to their synthetic mink garments and that this term is a false description and representation concerning them; that they have described their garments with such words and phrases as "platinum," "hand-tailored by craftsmen furriers," and "the warmth and beauty of mink"; and that they have used words and phrases like "Canadian," "Canadian Fur Corporation" and "Canadian Fur Trappers Corp." in connection with the sale of such garments as well as other words and phrases calculated to create the false impression that the garments are made of mink fur or have the characteristics of mink fur.

It is alleged that in so describing and advertising their garments defendants are likely to deceive the public which is likely to purchase defendants' products in the belief that these products are mink or contain mink . . . .

. . . .

In *Gold Seal Co. v. Weeks,* D.C.D.C., 129 F. Supp. 928, *affirmed sub nom S. C. Johnson & Son, Inc. v. Gold Seal Co.,* 97 U.S. App. D.C. 282, 230 F.2d 832, *cert. denied,* 352 U.S. 829, plaintiff sought a decree authorizing the Commissioner of Patents to register as a lawful trademark the words "Glass Wax" which were used by plaintiff in connection with the sale of a liquid cleaner for glass and metals. S. C. Johnson & Son, Inc., a manufacturer of wax products, intervened, opposing the application for registration and counterclaiming for injunctive relief, profits and damages under § 43(a) of the Lanham Act, on the ground that "Glass Wax" did not contain wax and that the mark was therefore a false representation and description of the goods, causing Johnson damage or the likelihood of damage. While the court held that the evidence adduced at the trial was insufficient to support the counterclaim, its construction of § 43(a) is highly apposite here. The court stated, 129 F. Supp. at page 940:

> . . . Johnson . . . need not prove actual diversion of trade (palming off, so to speak), need not establish a veritable monopoly position in the industry. . . .

> We are satisfied that Johnson had adequate standing to assert its right to recover in a civil action under this section and was entitled to be heard and to present evidence. We are equally satisfied, however, that Johnson has failed to prove that it is entitled to relief in the form of injunction, profits, damages or costs. . . .

The *Gold Seal* case is closely analogous to the case at bar. In that case the defendant was accused of using the word "wax" to describe a product that did not contain wax. Here the defendants are charged with using the word "mink" or words tending to create the impression that their product is made of mink where, in fact, such is not the case. Both in the *Gold Seal* case, and here, the plaintiffs did not monopolize the industry and proof of actual diversion of trade was, therefore, in all practical respects, impossible. The *Gold Seal* case indicates that the "single source" rule is inapplicable to suits under § 43(a) of the Lanham Act and that the "likely to be damaged" provision of § 43(a) obviates the necessity of proving actual diversion of trade. It follows that had such cases as *Mosler Safe Co. v. Ely-Norris Safe Co., supra,* and *California Apparel Creditors v. Wieder of California, supra,* arisen under the Lanham Act, the result might not have been the same. For § 43(a) of the Lanham Act creates a new "federal statutory tort, *sui generis*" and does not merely codify the common law principles of unfair competition. *Gold Seal Co. v. Weeks, supra,* 129 F. Supp. at page 940; *L'Aiglon Apparel Co., Inc. v. Lana Lobell, Inc.,* 3 Cir., 214 F.2d 649.

At the least the complaint at bar states a claim under the Lanham Act.

Defendants also urge that plaintiff Mutation Mink Breeders Association has no standing to sue relying on the *California Apparel* case. However, it appears from the complaint here that plaintiff Association has a pecuniary interest in preventing the diversion of trade from its members to the defendants since in return for its services to its members it receives a percentage of the sales price of the pelts sold by them. Thus, the situation here is different from that in the *California Apparel* case where it was indicated that the plaintiff Association lacked standing to sue only because it did not itself have a direct pecuniary interest which might be affected by defendants' acts. *See* 162 F.2d at page 896. *Cf. Gibbs v. Buck,* 307 U.S. 66.

The defendants' motion to dismiss the Complaint will be denied.

Defendants' motion for summary judgment as to the Lanham Act claim must also be denied. . . .

. . . .

GILLIAM v. AMERICAN BROADCASTING COMPANIES, INC.

United States Court of Appeals, Second Circuit
538 F.2d 14 (1976)

LUMBARD, CIRCUIT JUDGE.

Plaintiffs, a group of British writers and performers known as "Monty Python," appeal from a denial by Judge Lasker in the Southern District of a preliminary injunction to restrain the American Broadcasting Company (ABC) from broadcasting edited versions of three separate programs originally written and performed by Monty Python for broadcast by the British Broadcasting Corporation (BBC).

Since its formation in 1969, the Monty Python group has gained popularity primarily through its thirty-minute television programs created for BBC as part of a comedy series entitled "Monty Python's Flying Circus." . . .

In October 1973, Time-Life Films acquired the right to distribute in the United States certain BBC television programs, including the Monty Python series. . . .

. . . .

ABC broadcast the first of the specials on October 3, 1975. Appellants did not see a tape of the program until late November and were allegedly "appalled" at the discontinuity and "mutilation" that had resulted from the editing done by Time-Life for ABC. Twenty-four minutes of the original 90 minutes of recording had been omitted. Some of the editing had been done in order to make time for commercials; other material had been edited, according to ABC, because the original programs contained offensive or obscene matter.

. . . .

Here, the appellants claim that the editing done for ABC mutilated the original work and that consequently the broadcast of those programs as the creation of Monty Python violated the Lanham Act § 43(a), 15 U.S.C. § 1125(a). This statute, the federal counterpart to state unfair competition laws, has been invoked to prevent misrepresentations that may injure plaintiff's business or personal reputation, even where no registered trademark is concerned. *See Mortellito v. Nina of California,* 335 F. Supp. 1288, 1294 (S.D.N.Y. 1972). It is sufficient to violate the Act that a representation of a product, although technically true, creates a false impression of the product's origin. *See Rich v. RCA Corp.,* 390 F. Supp. 530 (S.D.N.Y. 1975) (recent picture of plaintiff on cover of album containing songs recorded in distant past held to be a false representation that the songs were new); *Geisel v. Poynter Products, Inc.,* 283 F. Supp. 261, 267 (S.D.N.Y. 1968).

These cases cannot be distinguished from the situation in which a television network broadcasts a program properly designated as having been written and performed by a group, but which has been edited, without the writer's consent, into a form that departs substantially from the original work. "To deform his work is to present him to the public as the creator of a work not his own, and thus makes him subject to criticism for work he has not done." *Roeder, supra,* at 569. In such a case, it is the writer or performer, rather than the network. who suffers the consequences of the mutilation, for the public will have only the final product by which to evaluate the work. Thus, an allegation that a defendant has presented to the public a "garbled," *Granz v. Harris, supra* (Frank, J., concurring), distorted version of plaintiff's work seeks to redress the very rights sought to be protected by the Lanham Act, 15 U.S.C. § 1125(a), and should be recognized as stating a cause of action under that statute. *See Autry v. Republic Productions, Inc.*, 213 F.2d 667 (9th Cir. 1954); *Jaeger v. American Int'l Pictures, Inc.*, 330 F. Supp. 274 (S.D.N.Y. 1971), which suggest the violation of such a right if mutilation could be proven.

During the hearing on the preliminary injunction, Judge Lasker viewed the edited version of the Monty Python program broadcast on December 26 and the original, unedited version. After hearing argument of this appeal, this panel also viewed and compared the two versions. We find that the truncated version at times omitted the climax of the skits to which appellants' rare brand of humor was leading and at other times deleted essential elements in the schematic development of a story line. We therefore agree with Judge Lasker's conclusion that the edited version broadcast by ABC impaired the integrity of appellants' work and represented to the public as the product of appellants what was actually a mere caricature of their talents. We believe that a valid cause of action for such distortion exists and that therefore a preliminary injunction may issue to prevent repetition of the broadcast prior to final determination of the issues.

VIDAL SASSOON, INC. v. BRISTOL-MYERS CO.

United States Court of Appeals, Second Circuit
661 F.2d 272 (1981)

IRVING R. KAUFMAN, CIRCUIT JUDGE.

. . . .

. . . In the spring of 1980, appellant Bristol-Myers Co. ("Bristol"), a pharmaceutical manufacturer, decided to wage an aggressive, new advertising campaign on behalf of its shampoo product, "Body on Tap," so named because of its high beer content. Accordingly, Bristol began in June to broadcast on national television a commercial "starring" the high fashion model Cristina Ferrare. The commercial depicts a turbaned Miss Ferrare, apparently fresh from shampooing her hair, holding a bottle of Body on Tap. She claims: "[I]n shampoo tests with over nine hundred women like me, Body on Tap got higher ratings than Prell for body. Higher than Flex for conditioning. Higher than Sassoon for strong, healthy looking hair." As is well known to the consuming public, Prell, Flex, and Sassoon are shampoo competitors of Body on Tap. Sassoon is the product of appellee Vidal Sassoon, Inc. ("Sassoon"). As Miss Ferrare refers in turn to each of the shampoos, the product is flashed on the television screen. The commercial ends as Miss Ferrare, now brushing her dry hair, states: "Now I use Body on Tap for fuller body and for clean, strong, beautifully conditioned hair. Body on Tap. It's great shampoo."

It is undisputed that 900 women did not, after trying both shampoos, make product-to-product comparisons between Body on Tap and Sassoon, or, for that matter, between Body on Tap and any of the other shampoos mentioned in the advertisements. Rather, groups of approximately 200 women, in what the advertising trade terms "blind monadic testing," each tested *one* shampoo and rated it on a qualitative scale ("outstanding," "excellent," "very good," "good," "fair," or "poor") with respect to 27 attributes, such as body and conditioning. Thus, no woman tried more than one shampoo. The data for an attribute of a particular shampoo were combined by category of qualitative rating, so that a percentage figure for each qualitative rating could be derived. The "outstanding" and "excellent" ratings were then added, and the lower four ratings were discarded. Following this procedure, MISI determined that 36% of the women who tested Body on Tap found it "outstanding" or "excellent" with relation to "strong, healthy looking hair," whereas only 24% of the separate group of women who tested Sassoon gave it such ratings. These results are the basis of Bristol's advertising claim that the women preferred Body on Tap to Sassoon. When the "very good" and "good" ratings are combined with the "outstanding" and "excellent" ratings, however, there is only a statistically insignificant difference of 1% between the ratings of the two shampoos respecting "strong, healthy looking hair."

The propriety of blind monadic testing for the purpose of comparative advertising claims is in some doubt. Dr. Edwin N. Berdy, President of MISI, stated by deposition that such testing is typically employed "where one would like an absolute response to the product . . . without reference to another specific product." In his affidavit, Dr. Ben Kajioka, Sassoon's Vice President of Research and Development, stated that blind monadic testing cannot support comparative advertising claims. And indeed, Bristol initially conducted the 1978 tests not with the intention of using their results in comparative advertising, but to determine consumer reaction to the recent national introduction of Body on Tap. On the other hand, Dr. Berdy testified that blind monadic testing had been used in connection with comparative advertising in the past.

The 900 "women like" Cristina Ferrare had tried the shampoos might suggest, at the very least, that 900 adult women participated in the test. In actuality, approximately one-third of the "women" were ages 13-18. This fact is noteworthy in light of the testimony of Alfred Lowman, the advertising executive who created the "Ferrare 900 Women" campaign, that the commercial was designed to attract a larger portion of the adult women's shampoo market to Body on Tap. Sassoon had always fared well among adult women, whereas Body on Tap had appealed disproportionately to teenagers. Bristol's marketing studies have revealed that the advertisements were successful in increasing usage and awareness of Body on Tap among adult women.

There is also some question concerning the methodology of the tests. Dr. Kajioka stated that Bristol instructed the women who tested Sassoon to use it contrary to Sassoon's own instructions. Bristol also allowed the women to use other brands while they were testing Sassoon. Thus, the women's responses may not accurately reflect their reaction to Sassoon as distinct from other shampoos.

In September, 1980 Sassoon commenced this action, claiming that the several "Ferrare-900 Women" advertisements violated the prohibition of § 43(a) of the Lanham Trademark Act, 15 U.S.C. § 1125(a) against false and misleading advertising. . . .

. . . .

Sassoon submitted, together with other evidence, a consumer perception study prepared for it by ASI Market Research, Inc. ("ASI"). Participants in the ASI test were asked to view the "Ferrare-900 Women" commercial twice, following a screening of entertainment and other advertisement materials. Members of the test group were then asked to answer one multiple-choice and three open-ended questions. The multiple-choice question was "How many different brands mentioned in the commercial did *each* of the 900 women try?" (emphasis in original). A choice of five responses followed — "one," "two," "three," "four," or "five or more." Ninety-five percent of those who answered the question said that each of the 900 women had tried two or more brands. Answering the open-ended question, "This commercial described the results of shampoo tests. What did these tests show?", 62% of the participants indicated that the tests showed that Body on Tap was competitively superior, either in a general way (38%), or as specifically compared with one or more other brands (24%). In answer to another question, 53% stated that the primary message of the commercial was Body on Tap's competitive superiority.

On the basis of the evidence submitted to him, Judge Stewart concluded that Sassoon had demonstrated a probability of success on the merits and a possibility of irreparable injury if the dissemination of the advertisements did not cease. Accordingly, he granted Sassoon's motion for a preliminary injunction.

. . . .

We have previously endorsed the ASI format as probative of the meaning consumers derive from commercial advertising. *American Home Products Corp. v. Johnson & Johnson*, 577 F.2d 160, 167–69, 167 n.15 (2d Cir. 1978). The results of the test ASI conducted for Sassoon suggest that most potential purchasers would incorrectly believe that the 900 women in the MISI survey made product-to-product comparisons among two or more shampoos. The study also presents evidence that consumers, after viewing the "Ferrare-900 Women" television commercial, would assume that Body on Tap was competitively superior when a combination of qualitative rating categories different from the one used by Bristol would yield no more than a showing of virtual competitive parity between Body on Tap and Sassoon. Whether or not the statements made in the advertisements are literally true, § 43(a) of the Lanham Act encompasses more than blatant falsehoods. It embraces "innuendo, indirect intimations, and ambiguous suggestions" evidenced by the consuming public's misapprehension of the hard facts underlying an advertisement. *American Home Products Corp. v. Johnson & Johnson, supra*, 577 F.2d at 165. Based largely on his evaluation of the ASI test results, Judge Stewart properly concluded, therefore, that Sassoon had made a showing of a probable § 43(a) violation. We also note that at least one statement made by Bristol, that 900 "women like" Cristina Ferrare tried the shampoo (when in fact only two-thirds of the sample were adult women), appears to be facially false, and may therefore be enjoined without regard to consumer reaction. *Id.*

Bristol asserts that the misrepresentations alleged by Sassoon are only misstatements concerning the test results and the manner in which the tests were conducted, not the "inherent quality," *Fur Information & Fashion Council, Inc. v. E. F. Timme & Son, Inc.,* 501 F.2d 1048, 1051 (2d Cir.), *cert. denied,* 419 U.S. 1022, of Body on Tap. Misleading statements regarding consumer test methodology, Bristol argues, do not fall within § 43(a). We agree that Bristol has not in so many words falsely described the quality of Body on Tap. It has not, to give a hypothetical example, baldly stated that the shampoo smells like roses when it in fact does not. The inaccuracies alleged concern the number and age of the women in the tests, how the comparisons were made, and how the results were tabulated. After a careful review of cases interpreting the Lanham Act and its legislative history, however, we are persuaded that § 43(a) does prohibit the misrepresentations alleged here.

. . . .

[T]he alleged untruths concerning the MISI tests were at least "in connection with" Body on Tap, and, as the ASI study reveals, they quite probably created the impression that Body on Tap was superior. Judge Stewart could appropriately find, moreover, that this view was probably false because, if the qualitative rating categories were combined in a different manner, there would be no significant statistical difference between Sassoon and Body on Tap. While we recognize that § 43(a) encompasses only misrepresentations with reference to the "inherent quality or characteristic" of defendant's product, *see Fur Information & Fashion Council, Inc. v. E. F. Timme & Son, Inc., supra,* 501 F.2d at 1051, we are nevertheless convinced that Judge Stewart was correct in concluding that Sassoon would probably succeed in showing that the intent and total effect of the advertisements were to lead consumers into believing that Body on Tap was competitively superior, surely a representation regarding its "inherent quality." *See R. J. Reynolds Tobacco Co. v. Loew's Theatres, Inc.,* 511 F. Supp. 867 (S.D.N.Y. 1980) (bias in defendant's consumer test caused deception as to the quality of defendant's goods and thereby established action pursuant to § 43(a)).

In a case like this, where many of the qualities of a product (such as "body") are not susceptible to objective measurement, it is difficult to see how the manufacturer can advertise its product's "quality" more effectively than through the dissemination of the results of consumer preference studies. In such instances, the medium of the consumer test truly becomes the message of inherent superiority. We do not hold that every misrepresentation concerning consumer test results or methodology can result in liability pursuant to § 43(a). But where depictions of consumer test results or methodology are so significantly misleading that the reasonably intelligent consumer would be deceived about the product's inherent quality or characteristics, an action under § 43(a) may lie.

Finally, we believe that Sassoon made an adequate showing of the possibility of irreparable injury. Although the likelihood of injury and causation cannot be presumed, *Johnson & Johnson v. Carter-Wallace, Inc.,* 631 F.2d 186, 190 (2d Cir. 1980), Judge Stewart properly concluded that Sassoon had offered "proof providing a reasonable basis for the belief that . . . [it] is likely to be damaged as a result of the false advertising." *Id.* Sassoon and Body on Tap compete in the same market, and it is quite likely that the apparently effective suggestions of competitive superiority, if repeatedly communicated to consumers, would eventually result in loss of sales to Sassoon. *McNeilab, Inc. v. American Home Products Corp.*, 501 F. Supp. 517, 530 (S.D.N.Y. 1980). Although Sassoon offered no evidence of actual sales loss directly traceable to the alleged misrepresentations, proof of diversion of sales is not required for an injunction to issue pursuant to § 43(a). *See Johnson & Johnson v. Carter Wallace, Inc., supra,* 631 F.2d at 192. We also note that Bristol's own "Shampoo Tracking Study" reveals that awareness and purchases of Body on Tap among women ages 18-34 increased significantly shortly after the commencement of the "Ferrare-900 Women" advertising campaign. Judge Stewart properly inferred that Sassoon might be damaged if the advertisements did not cease.

Accordingly, we affirm the order of the district court.

NOTES ON MISREPRESENTATION

(1) The statutory predecessor of § 43(a) of the Lanham Act, 15 U.S.C. § 123 (1920), applied only to "a false designation of origin" affixed to "an article or merchandise . . . willfully and with intent to deceive" and only persons "doing business in the locality falsely indicated as that of origin" had standing to sue under the section. Accordingly, the obstacles presented to a plaintiff attempting to prevent such deception in the marketplace under the old Trademark Act of 1920 often were formidable. *See California Apparel Creators v. Wieder of California, Inc.*, 162 F.2d 893 (2d Cir. 1947). The passage of the Lanham Act dramatically broadened the scope of "false designation of origin" to include "any false or misleading description or representation" use[d] in connection with any goods or services . . . ," such action to be brought "by any person who believes he is or is likely to be damaged by the use of such false description or representation." The goal of Congress was "to modernize the trademark statutes so that they will conform to legitimate present-day business practice." S. Rep. No. 1333, 79th Cong., 2d Sess. (1946), reprinted in 1946 U.S. Code Cong. Service, at 1276.

Response to this Congressional intent, however, was slow in developing. Early decisions limited the scope of § 43(a) to those trademark uses likely to cause confusion as to geographical origin, passing-off cases, and traditional trademark-engendered deception. *Samson Crane Co. v. Union National Sales, Inc.*, 87 F. Supp. 218 (D. Mass. 1949), *aff'd per curiam*, 180 F.2d 896 (1st Cir. 1950). In *Maternally Yours, Inc. v. Your Maternity Shop, Inc.*, 234 F.2d 538, 546 (2d Cir. 1956), Judge Clark, in a concurring opinion, referred to § 43(a), which had not even been cited by the parties, and noted: "Indeed, there is indication here and elsewhere that the bar has not yet realized the potential impact of this statutory provision."

Since that time the application of the section has gradually expanded and courts have relied upon § 43(a) to apply the principles of unfair competition law to the constantly changing and evolving practices in the business world.

Some examples of the broad implementation of § 43(a)'s prohibitions against a "false designation of origin" and "any false or misleading description or representation" are: *Lamoth v. Atlantic Recording Corp.*, 847 F.2d 1403 (9th Cir. 1988) (failure to credit all of song's composers on record album); *PPX Enterprises, Inc. v. Audiofidelity Enterprises*, 818 F.2d 266 (2d Cir. 1987) (misrepresenting that record album featured performances by Jimi Hendrix); *Smith v. Montoro*, 648 F.2d 602 (9th Cir. 1981) (substituting a false name for plaintiff actor's in film credits and advertising); *Boston Professional Hockey Ass'n v. Dallas Cap & Emblem Mfg., Inc.*, 510 F.2d 1004 (5th Cir. 1975) (unlicensed manufacturing for sale of emblems and insignias of professional hockey teams); *Norman M. Morris Corp. v. Weinstein*, 466 F.2d 137 (5th Cir. 1972) (misrepresenting watches as being guaranteed by the manufacturer); *Potato Chip Inst. v. General Mills, Inc.*, 333 F. Supp. 173 (D. Neb. 1971), *aff'd*, 461 F.2d 1088 (8th Cir. 1972) (using the term "potato chips" without explanation for a product made from dried potato granules); *Union Tank Car Co. v. Lindsay Soft Water Corp.*, 257 F. Supp. 510 (D. Neb. 1966), *aff'd*, 387 F.2d 477 (8th Cir. 1967) (falsely claiming authorized dealership); *Manufacturer's Technologies, Inc. v. Cams, Inc.*, 706 F. Supp. 984 (D. Conn. 1989) (use of copyright infringer's own name in copyright notice); *Allen v. National Video, Inc.*, 610 F. Supp. 612 (S.D.N.Y. 1985) (falsely implying through use of look-alike that Woody Allen endorsed video movie rental club); *Nike, Inc. v. Rubber Mfrs. Ass'n, Inc.*, 509 F. Supp. 919 (S.D.N.Y. 1981) (permitting professional athlete shoe endorsers to place sponsor's trademark on competitor's more comfortable shoes); *Bohsei Enterprises Co., U.S.A. v. Porteous Fastener Co.*, 441 F. Supp. 162 (C.D. Cal. 1977) (falsely suggesting product is of domestic manufacture by omission of foreign origin identification); *Cutler-Hammer, Inc. v. Universal Relay Corp.*, 285 F. Supp. 636 (S.D.N.Y. 1968) (mislabeling plaintiff's old products as its new products); *Geisel v. Poynter Prods. Inc.*, 283 F. Supp. 261 (S.D.N.Y. 1968) (misrepresenting toys as authorized by artist-author Dr. Seuss). *Compare*, however, *Norton Tire Co. v. Tire Kingdom Co.*, 858 F.2d 1533 (11th Cir. 1988), where defendant's alleged "bait and switch" advertising techniques did not violate § 43(a) because, with persistence, a customer could obtain the advertised low priced tires instead of the high priced tires promoted in the store by defendant's salespeople; *Nature's Way Products, Inc. v. Nature-Pharma, Inc.*, 736 F. Supp. 245 (D. Utah 1990), where a claim against alleged imitation of plaintiff's marketing techniques such as promoting chaparral as a dietary supplement was dismissed as "frivolous"; *Masdea v. Scholz*, 742 F. Supp. 713 (D. Mass. 1990), where mere imitation of plaintiff's drumming style on a recording did not violate § 43(a); and *Paramount Pictures Corp. v. Video Broadcasting Systems, Inc.*, 1989 U.S. Dist. LEXIS 15684 (D. Kan. 1989), where preliminary relief was denied under § 43(a) even though defendant had recorded advertisements which overlapped or obliterated the original pre-recorded Pepsi commercials and FBI warnings. *See also* McKenney & Long, *Federal Unfair Competition: Lanham Act* § 43(a) (1993 ed.); Pinover, *The Rights of Authors, Artists, and Performers Under Section 43(a) of the Lanham Act*, 83 Trademark Rep. 38

(1993); Bauer, *A Federal Law of Unfair Competition: What Should Be The Reach of Sec. 43(a) of the Lanham Act?*, 31 UCLA L. Rev. 671(1984); *Monty Python (Gilliam v. American Broadcasting Cos., 538 F.2d 14) and the Lanham Act: In Search of the Moral Right*, 30 Rutgers L. Rev. 452 (1977); J.E. Maslow, *Droit Moral and Sections 43(a) and 44(i) of the Lanham Act — A Judicial Shell Game?*, 48 Geo. Wash. L. Rev. 377 (1980). What other possible torts of misrepresentation might fall within the expanding purview of § 43(a)?

(2) As with the other remedial provisions of the Lanham Act (§ 32), it is not necessary under § 43 to prove that a false designation of origin or false description or representation was intentional. *Parkway Baking Co. v. Freihofer Baking Co.*, 255 F.2d 641, 648 (3d Cir. 1958). Neither is it necessary that the representation or description be literally false but only that it convey a false impression. *See American Home Products Corp. v. Johnson & Johnson*, 577 F.2d 160, 165 (2d Cir. 1978) ("Were it otherwise, clever use of innuendo, indirect intimations and ambiguous suggestions could shield the advertisement from scrutiny precisely when protection against such sophisticated deception is most needed"); *followed*: *McNeilab, Inc. v. American Home Products Corp.*, 501 F. Supp. 517 (S.D.N.Y. 1980); *Joshua Meier Co. v. Albany Novelty Mfg. Co.*, 236 F.2d 144 (2d Cir. 1956); *Eastman Kodak Co. v. Royal-Pioneer Paper Box Mfg. Co.*, 197 F. Supp. 132 (E.D. Pa. 1961); *Mutation Mink Breeders Assoc. v. Lou Nierenberg Corp.*, 23 F.R.D. 155 (S.D.N.Y. 1959).

(3) Actual competitive relationship between the parties is not requisite for an action under § 43(a). *National Lampoon, Inc. v. American Broadcasting Co.*, 376 F. Supp. 733 (S.D.N.Y. 1974); *Mortellito v. Nina of Cal., Inc.*, 335 F. Supp. 1288 (S.D.N.Y. 1972). Does a consumer "who believes that he or she is or is likely to be damaged" by acts prohibited under § 43(a) have standing to sue? *Compare Arnesen v. Raymond Lee Organization, Inc.*, 333 F. Supp. 116 (C.D. Cal. 1971), holding that consumers had standing to bring a class action under § 43(a), *with Colligan v. Activities Club of New York, Ltd.*, 442 F.2d 686 (2d Cir.), *cert. denied*, 404 U.S. 1004 (1971), in which the court dismissed a § 43(a) consumer class action, stating at p. 692:

> The Act's purpose, as defined in § 45, is exclusively to protect the interests of a purely commercial class against unscrupulous commercial conduct.

The *Colligan* decision was rejected as contrary to the plain language of § 43(a) by the Third Circuit in *Thorn v. Reliance Van Co.*, 736 F.2d 929, 932 (3d Cir. 1984), which granted standing to an investor in a bankrupt company in a suit against a competitor of that company. *See also In re "Agent Orange" Product Liability Litigation*, 475 F. Supp. 928 (S.D.N.Y. 1979); *Florida, ex rel. Broward County v. Eli Lilly & Co.*, 329 F. Supp. 364 (S.D. Fla. 1971); Keller & Trunko, *Consumer Use of RICO to Challenge False Advertising Claims*, C674 ALI-ABA 51 (1991); Thompson, *Consumer Standing Under Section 43(a): More Legislative History, More Confusion*, 79 Trademark Rep. 341 (1989). Does the *Colligan* view mean that protecting the interests of consumers against deception is not the duty or province of the courts in § 43(a) cases? *See* 1 Gilson, *Trademark Protection and Practice* § 7.02[3][a] (1993 ed.), and *Ames Publishing Co. v. Walker-David Publications, Inc.*, 372 F. Supp. 1 (E.D. Pa. 1974), a § 43(a) case in which the court refused to apply an unclean-hands defense against a plaintiff who was a "vicarious avenger" of a particular class of consumers lacking standing to bring the suit. *But see Stahly v. M.H. Jacobs Co.*, 183 F.2d 914 (7th Cir. 1950).

(4) Unauthorized comparative advertising use of a competitor's trademark will not create liability under § 43(a) in the absence of misrepresentations or likelihood of confusion as to source. In *Diversified Marketing, Inc. v. Estee Lauder, Inc.*, 705 F. Supp. 128 (S.D.N.Y. 1988), the court held that Diversified's BEAUTY USA advertising slogan "If you like ESTEE LAUDER . . . You'll love BEAUTY USA" was permissible comparative advertising. Similarly, in *Smith v. Chanel, Inc.*, 402 F.2d 562 (9th Cir. 1968), defendant was held entitled to advertise "We dare you to detect any difference between Chanel #5 (25.00) and Ta'Ron's 2nd Chance. $7.00." *See also* the discussion in Permitted Use in Chapter 7, *supra. Compare Tyco Industries, Inc. v. Lego Systems, Inc.*, 5 U.S.P.Q.2d 1023 (D.N.J. 1987), in which the court enjoined Tyco's false comparative claim that its toy building block set "looks and feels like Lego."

(5) Prior to the passage of the Revision Act in 1988, some courts limited § 43(a) by recognizing actions under it based on a defendant's misrepresentations about its own products, but holding the section inapplicable to misrepresentations by a defendant about *plaintiff's* products. *See, e.g., Bernard Food Industries, Inc. v. Dietene Co.*, 415 F.2d 1279 (7th Cir. 1969), *cert. denied*, 397 U.S. 912 (1970); *Oil Heat Institute v. Northwest Natural Gas*, 708 F. Supp. 1118 (D. Or. 1988).

The Revision Act now expressly makes misrepresentations about *"another person's* goods, services or commercial activities" actionable under § 43(a). In *U.S. Healthcare, Inc. v. Blue Cross of Greater Philadelphia*, 898 F.2d 914 (3d Cir.), *cert. denied*, 111 S. Ct. 58 (1990), for example, the court found actionable alleged advertising misrepresentations made about one another by two health care competitors. Similarly, in *Holmsten Ice Rinks, Inc. v. Burley's Rink Supply, Inc.*, 14 U.S.P.Q.2d 1492 (D. Minn. 1990), defendant's false representations about plaintiff in defendant's product catalog were preliminarily enjoined.

In *National Artists Management Co. v. Weaving*, 769 F. Supp. 1224 (S.D.N.Y. 1991), plaintiff was a leading theatrical booking agency and defendant was an ex-employee who planned to form her own booking agency. After leaving plaintiff's employ, defendant told a number of plaintiff's clients that "she was forced to terminate her relationship with [plaintiff] because of certain illegal and improper business practices engaged in by [plaintiff's] principals." 769 F. Supp. at 1226. Plaintiff subsequently lost business from some of those she had contacted.

In considering defendant's motion to dismiss, the court set forth a four-prong test for stating a cause of action under § 43(a)(2): (1) "that defendant made false or misleading factual representations of the nature, characteristics, or qualities of plaintiff's services"; (2) "in commerce"; (3) "in the context of commercial advertising or commercial promotion"; and (4) "that defendants' actions made plaintiffs believe that they were likely to be damaged by such false or misleading factual misrepresentations." *Id.*, at 1230. The Court then found that, aside from the truth or falsity of the representations which would have to be determined at trial, the test was satisfied. The "commercial advertising or promotion" prong was satisfied because defendant "had taken sufficient steps toward her new business for the Lanham Act to apply," (769 F. Supp. at 1234), and because her conversations had the commercial purpose of promoting that business.

Plaintiff similarly stated a disparagement cause of action in *Fashion Boutique of Short Hills, Inc. v. Fendi USA, Inc.*, 1992 U.S. Dist. LEXIS 9881 (S.D.N.Y. 1992), alleging that defendant made commercially disparaging remarks about plaintiff's fashion clothing store to potential customers. Noting that both parties relied primarily on word of mouth for promotion, the court held that § 43(a)(2) applied.

(6) Are there any First Amendment constitutional limitations on preventing misrepresentations under § 43(a)? *See Consumers Union of U.S. v. General Signal Corp.*, 724 F.2d 1044, 1051–53 (2d Cir. 1983), where the court refused to preliminarily enjoin a vacuum cleaner manufacturer's television commercials featuring accurate reference to a *Consumer Report's* magazine rating of its product, despite the plaintiff-publisher's longstanding policy against advertising use of its ratings; *Fur Information & Fashion Council, Inc. v. E. F. Timme & Son, Inc.*, 364 F. Supp. 16 (S.D.N.Y. 1973).

In *Wojnarowicz v. American Family Association*, 745 F. Supp. 130, 141–42 (S.D.N.Y. 1990), the court dismissed a § 43(a) claim against dissemination of a pamphlet which disparaged plaintiff's paintings and sculptures as sacrilegious. In doing so, the Court cited the following legislative history:

> [T]he proposed changes in Section 43(a) should not be read in any way to limit political speech, consumer or editorial comment, parodies, satires, or other constitutionally protected material. . . . The section is narrowly drafted to encompass only clearly false and misleading commercial speech. S. 1883, 101st Cong., 1st Sess., 135 Cong. Rec. 1207, 1217 (April 13, 1989).

In *Rogers v. Grimaldi*, 695 F. Supp. 112 (S.D.N.Y. 1988), *aff'd*, 875 F.2d 994 (2d Cir. 1989), Ginger Rogers sued under § 43(a) and state right of publicity law over an Italian film entitled "Ginger and Fred," which was about two cabaret performers who imitated her and Fred Astaire. The district court summarily held for defendant on First Amendment grounds.

In affirming, the Second Circuit for the first time articulated a balancing test for Lanham Act claims involving artistic expression. It stated that enjoining the distribution of artistic works does not violate the First Amendment where the public interest in avoiding consumer confusion outweighs the public interest in free expression. For movie titles using a celebrity's name, the Court held that unless the title had no artistic relevance to the underlying work or was expressly misleading, no injunction should issue. Here the title was artistically relevant to the film, and it was not expressly misleading. The Court also held that the use of Ms. Roger's name in the title was not actionable under Oregon right of publicity law.

Compare the following footnote in *Vidal Sassoon, supra*:

> Bristol argues that, because its advertisements are supposedly protected by the First Amendment to the Constitution, Judge Stewart should have imposed a higher burden on Sassoon. This argument is without merit. Misleading commercial speech is beyond the protective reach of the First Amendment,

Central Hudson Gas & Electric Co. v. Public Service Comm'n., 447 U.S. 557, 566 (1980). The Lanham Act's content-neutral prohibition of false and misleading advertising does not arouse First Amendment concerns that justify alteration of the normal standard for preliminary injunctive relief. *Dallas Cowboys Cheerleaders, Inc. v. Pussycat Cinema, Ltd.*, 604 F.2d 200, 206 (2d Cir. 1979).

(7) Increasingly sophisticated methods of marketing and advertising have in turn made possible more sophisticated methods of misleading the public as to relative qualities of products in the market. When the representation is explicitly or "facially" false, a court may grant injunctive relief under § 43(a) without reference to the advertisement's impact on the buying public. *Coca-Cola Co. v. Tropicana Products, Inc.*, 690 F.2d 312 (2d Cir. 1982) (visual and aural components of television ad suggesting defendant's pasteurized and sometimes frozen orange juice comes fresh-squeezed from the orange held blatantly false). However, when the claims made are literally true but nonetheless have the potential to mislead, confuse or deceive, it becomes necessary for a court to consider evidence of public reaction to the advertisement. "The question in such cases is — what does the person to whom the advertisement is addressed find to be the message?" *American Brands, Inc. v. R.J. Reynolds Tobacco Co.*, 413 F. Supp. 1352, 1357 (S.D.N.Y. 1976). Market research studies have played an increasingly important role in answering that question. *See Vidal Sassoon, supra.*

In *American Home Productsr supra* Note (2), a declaratory judgment action brought under § 43(a), plaintiff's television ads claimed that plaintiff's Anacin aspirin product was superior to defendant's Tylenol pain reliever in reducing inflammation. The district court was unable to reach a definitive conclusion on the truthfulness of this claim, but agreed with defendant that the ads also implicitly and falsely claimed pain-relieving superiority. Relying heavily on consumer reaction test data, the court enjoined the advertisement of such claims. In affirming, the Court of Appeals stated,

> What the ASI test shows, then, is the powerful "subliminal" influence of modern advertisements . . . . The survey reveals that the word "inflammation" triggers pain association, and pain association is what both advertisements are all about. The district court properly relied on these conclusions in finding that the commercial claimed general analgesic superiority.

The Court of Appeals also found that such an implicit claim clearly was intended by plaintiff. *Id.* at 166, n. 12.

In *McNeil-P.C.C., Inc. v. Bristol-Myers Squibb Co.*, 938 F.2d 1544, 1549, 1551 (2d Cir. 1991), the court stated that a plaintiff must show the alleged substantiation for a defendant's advertising claim is "not sufficiently reliable to conclude with reasonable certainty that [it] established the claim made" and, finding plaintiff had done so, enjoined defendant's claim that its pain relieving product "works better" than plaintiff's. In *ALPO Petfoods, Inc. v. Ralston Purina Co.*, 913 F.2d 958 (D.C. Cir. 1990), both defendant's advertising claim that its dog food prevented canine hip dysplasia, and plaintiff's advertising claim that its dog food contained the formula most preferred by veterinarians, were held material and false; the case was remanded for reassessment of each party's damages. *See also Grove Fresh Distributors v. New England Apple Products*, 969 F.2d 552 (7th Cir. 1992) (defendant falsely advertised its orange juice as "100% Florida" when the juice was adulterated with sugar and pulpwash); *Castrol, Inc. v. Quaker State Corp.*, 977 F.2d 57 (2d Cir. 1992) (defendant falsely advertised that tests proved its motor oil provided better protection against engine wear); *U-Haul Int'l, Inc. v. Jartran, Inc.*, 681 F.2d 1159 (9th Cir. 1982) (various advertising claims as to the superiority of defendant's trucks and trailers over those of plaintiff preliminarily enjoined); *American Home Products Corp. v. Abbott Laboratories*, 522 F. Supp. 1035 (S.D.N.Y. 1981) (advertising claims that hemorrhoid preparation was "new" and stopped pain immediately preliminarily enjoined); *Toro Co. v. Textron, Inc.*, 499 F. Supp. 241 (D. Del. 1980) (various advertising claims as to the superiority of defendant's snow thrower over that of plaintiff preliminarily enjoined).

Compare Avis Rent A Car System, Inc. v. Hertz Corp., 782 F.2d 381 (2d Cir. 1986), in which the court held that defendant's advertising claim that "Hertz has more new cars than Avis has cars," while literally false as to car ownership, was not false in context, where the public would perceive it to refer to cars available for rental by the companies, *and Procter & Gamble Co. v. Chesebrough-Pond's, Inc.*, 747 F.2d 114 (2d Cir. 1984), where on cross-motions for preliminary injunction neither party established a likelihood of successfully demonstrating the unreliability of the other's supporting tests for "test-proven" product superiority claims and consequent claim falsity.

See generally BeVier, *Competitor Suits for False Advertising under Section 43(a) of the Lanham Act: A Puzzle in the Law of Deception*, 78 Va. L. Rev. 1 (1992); Tepper, *False Advertising Claims and the Revision of the Lanham Act: A Step in Which Direction?*, 59 U. Cinn. L. Rev. 957 (1991); Singdahlsen, *The Risk of Chill: A Cost of the Standards Governing the Regulation of False Advertising Under Section 43(a) of the Lanham Act*, 77 Va. L. Rev. 339 (1991); Preston, *False or Deceptive Advertising Under the Lanham Act: Analysis of Factual Findings and Types of Evidence*, 79 Trademark Rep. 508 (1989).

(8) In accordance with the broad judicial construction given the rest of the section some courts have stated that for standing under § 43(a) plaintiff need only have "a reasonable interest to be protected against [the alleged] false advertising." *New West Corp. v. NYM Co. of Cal, Inc.*, 595 F.2d 1194, 1198 (9th Cir. 1979); *Quabaug Rubber Co. v. Fabiano Shoe Co.*, 567 F.2d 154, 160 (1st Cir. 1977), citing 1 Callmann, *Unfair Competition, Trademarks and Monopolies* § 18.2(b) at 625 (3d ed. 1967). Because of the difficulty of showing any actual diversion of sales created by allegedly false advertising, courts have also been willing to grant injunctive relief upon a relatively minimal showing of likelihood of damage. Should damage sufficient to satisfy the statute be presumed once a plaintiff shows that the parties compete in a relevant market and that defendant's ads are false? Such an argument was rejected by the court in *Johnson & Johnson v. Carter-Wallace, Inc.*, 631 F.2d 186 (2d Cir. 1980), yet the court found likelihood of damage on very limited evidence.

§ 8.03   Configuration and Trade Dress

INTRODUCTION

The Supreme Court's 1964 decision which begins this section, along with its companion *Compco* decision described in Note (1) *infra*, precipitated an immediate and disturbed reaction within the bar and spawned publication of numerous commentaries, many shedding more heat than light. The decisions did, however, appear to emasculate a particular area which had been the subject of well-developed, although frequently problematical and troublesome, unfair competition common law prohibiting product simulation where secondary meaning had attached to product configuration and likelihood of confusion could be shown. The decisions are likewise notable for their apparent refueling of the monopoly phobias of the New Deal era. *See* Chapter 1, *supra*. To date, most parties entitled to protection have been able to obtain it through registration and subsequent assertion of registered rights (15 U.S.C. § 1091) or through § 43(a)'s broad federal prohibition of unfair competition. Still others may avail themselves of *Compco's* "palming off" exception.

The *Sears* and *Compco* decisions also raised an apparent problem in protecting distinctive packaging and trade dress under unfair competition principles. As stated in *Compco*, "to forbid copying would interfere with the federal policy . . . of allowing free access to copy whatever the federal patent and copyright laws leave in the public domain." *See Spangler Candy Co. v. Crystal Pure Candy Co.*, 353 F.2d 641(7th Cir. 1965). Notwithstanding this pronouncement, the lower courts seem generally to have confined the doctrine of *Sears* and *Compco* to product copying and have not extended it to distinctive packaging or trade dress. Note the following, often neglected, language in *Sears* expressly recognizing a state's right to prohibit the use of labels, trade dress, or packaging likely to cause confusion, 376 U.S. at 232:

> Doubtless a State may, in appropriate circumstances, require that goods, whether patented or unpatented, be labeled or that other precautionary steps be taken to prevent customers from being misled as to the source, just as it may protect businesses in the use of their trademarks, labels, *or distinctive dress in the packaging of goods* so as to prevent others, by imitating such markings, from misleading purchasers as to the source of the goods. [Emphasis added.]

SEARS ROEBUCK & CO. v. STIFFEL CO.

United States Supreme Court
376 U.S. 225 (1964)

Mr. Justice Black.

The question in this case is whether a State's unfair competition law can, consistently with the federal patent laws, impose liability for or prohibit the copying of an article which is protected by neither a federal patent nor a copyright. The respondent, Stiffel Company, secured design and mechanical patents on a "pole lamp" — a vertical tube having lamp fixtures along the outside, the tube being made so that it will stand upright between the floor and ceiling of a room. Pole lamps proved a decided commercial success, and soon after Stiffel brought them on the market Sears, Roebuck & Company put on the market a substantially identical lamp, which it sold more cheaply, Sears' retail price being about the same as Stiffel's wholesale price. Stiffel then brought this action against Sears in the United States District Court for the Northern District of Illinois, claiming in its first count that by copying its design Sears had infringed Stiffel's patents and in its second count that by selling copies of Stiffel's lamp Sears had caused confusion in the trade as to the source of the lamps and had thereby engaged in unfair competition under Illinois law. There was evidence that identifying tags were not attached to the Sears lamps although labels appeared on the cartons in which they were delivered to customers, that customers had asked Stiffel whether its lamps differed from Sears', and that in two cases customers who had bought Stiffel lamps had complained to Stiffel on learning that Sears was selling substantially identical lamps at a much lower price.

The District Court, after holding the patents invalid for want of invention, went on to find as a fact that Sears' lamp was "a substantially exact copy" of Stiffel's and that the two lamps were so much alike, both in appearance and in functional details, "that confusion between them is likely, and some confusion has already occurred." On these findings the court held Sears guilty of unfair competition, enjoined Sears "from unfairly competing with [Stiffel] by selling or attempting to sell pole lamps identical to or confusingly similar to" Stiffel's lamp, and ordered an accounting to fix profits and damages resulting from Sears' "unfair competition."

The Court of Appeals affirmed. 313 F.2d 115, 136 U.S.P.Q. 292. That court held that, to make out a case of unfair competition under Illinois law, there was no need to show that Sears had been "palming off" its lamps as Stiffel lamps; Stiffel had only to prove that there was a "likelihood of confusion as to the source of the products" — that the two articles were sufficiently identical that customers could not tell who had made a particular one. Impressed by the "remarkable sameness of appearance" of the lamps, the Court of Appeals upheld the trial court's findings of likelihood of confusion and some actual confusion, findings which the appellate court construed to mean confusion "as to the source of the lamps." The Court of Appeals thought this enough under Illinois law to sustain the trial court's holding of unfair competition, and thus held Sears liable under Illinois law for doing no more than copying and marketing an unpatented article. We granted certiorari to consider whether this use of a State's law of unfair competition is compatible with the federal patent law. 374 U.S. 826.

. . . .

The grant of a patent is the grant of a statutory monopoly; indeed, the grant of patents in England was an explicit exception to the statute of James I prohibiting monopolies. Patents are not given as favors, as was the case of monopolies given by the Tudor monarchs, *see Case of the Monopolies (Darcy v. Allein)*, 11 Co. 84,

77 Eng. Rep. 1260 (K.B. 1602), but are meant to encourage invention by rewarding the inventor with the right, limited to a term of years fixed by the patent, to exclude others from the use of his invention. . . . [W]hen the patent expires the monopoly created by it expires, too, and the right to make the article — including the right to make it in precisely the shape it carried when patented — passes to the public, *Kellogg Co. v. National Biscuit Co.*, 305 U.S. 111, 120–122, 39 U.S.P.Q. 296, 300–301(1938); *Singer Mfg. Co. v. June Mfg. Co.*, 163 U.S. 169, 185 (1896).

Thus the patent system is one in which uniform federal standards are carefully used to promote invention while at the same time preserving free competition. Obviously a State could not, consistently with a Supremacy Clause of the Constitution, extend the life of a patent beyond its expiration date or give a patent on an article which lacked the level of invention required for federal patents. To do either would run counter to the policy of Congress of granting patents only to true inventions, and then only for a limited time. Just as a State cannot encroach upon the federal patent laws directly, it cannot, under some other law, such as that forbidding unfair competition, give protection of a kind that clashes with the objectives of the federal patent laws.

In the present case the "pole lamp" sold by Stiffel has been held not to be entitled to the protection of either a mechanical or a design patent. An unpatentable article, like an article on which the patent has expired, is in the public domain and may be made and sold by whoever chooses to do so. What Sears did was to copy Stiffel's design and to sell lamps almost identical to those sold by Stiffel. This it had every right to do under the federal patent laws. That Stiffel originated the pole lamp and made it popular is immaterial. "Sharing in the goodwill of an article unprotected by patent or trademark is the exercise of a right possessed by all — and in the free exercise of which the consuming public is deeply interested." *Kellogg Co. v. National Biscuit Co.*, supra, 305 U.S., at 122, 39 U.S.P.Q. at 300–301. To allow a State by use of its law of unfair competition to prevent the copying of an article which represents too slight an advance to be patented would be to permit the State to block off from the public something which federal law has said belongs to the public. The result would be that while federal law grants only 14 to 17 years' protection to genuine inventions, *see* 35 U.S.C. §§ 154, 173, States could allow perpetual protection to articles too lacking in novelty to merit any patent at all under federal constitutional standards. This would be too great an encroachment on the federal patent system to be tolerated.

Sears has been held liable here for unfair competition because of a finding of likelihood of confusion based only on the fact that Sears' lamp was copied from Stiffel's unpatented lamp and that consequently the two looked exactly alike. Of course there could be "confusion" as to who had manufactured these nearly identical articles. But mere inability of the public to tell two identical articles apart is not enough to support an injunction against copying or an award of damages for copying that which the federal patent laws permit to be copied. Doubtless a State may, in appropriate circumstances, require that goods, whether patented or unpatented, be labeled or that other precautionary steps be taken to prevent customers from being misled as to the source, just as it may protect businesses in the use of their trademarks, labels, or distinctive dress in the packaging of goods so as to prevent others, by imitating such markings, from misleading purchasers as to the source of the goods. But because of the federal patent laws a State may not, when the article is unpatented and uncopyrighted, prohibit the copying of the article itself or award damages for such copying. *Cf. G. Ricordi & Co. v. Haendler*, 194 F.2d 914, 916, 92 U.S.P.Q. 340, 341 (C.A. 2d Cir. 1952). The judgment below did both and in so doing gave Stiffel the equivalent of a patent monopoly on its unpatented lamp. That was error, and Sears is entitled to a judgment in its favor.

Reversed.

IN RE MORTON-NORWICH PRODUCTS, INC.

United States Court of Customs and Patent Appeals
671 F.2d 1332 (1982)

RICH, JUDGE.

This appeal is from the ex parte decision of the United States Patent and Trademark Office (PTO) Trademark Trial and Appeal Board (board), 209 U.S.P.Q. 437 (T.T.A.B. 1980), in application serial No. 123,548, filed April 21, 1977, sustaining the examiner's refusal to register appellant's container configuration on the principal register. We reverse the holding on "functionality" and remand for a determination of distinctiveness.

Appellant's application seeks to register the following container configuration as a trademark for spray starch, soil and stain removers, spray cleaners for household use, liquid household cleaners and general grease removers, and insecticides:

Appellant owns U.S. Design Patent 238,655, issued Feb. 3, 1976, on the above configuration, and U.S. Patent 3,749,290, issued July 31, 1973, directed to the mechanism in the spray top.

. . . .

A trademark is defined as "any word, name, symbol, or device or any combination thereof adopted and used by a manufacturer or merchant *to identify his goods* and distinguish them from those manufactured or sold by others" (emphasis ours). 15 U.S.C. § 1127 (1976). Thus, it was long the rule that a trademark must be something other than, and separate from, the merchandise to which it is applied. . . .

Aside from the trademark/product "separateness" rationale for not recognizing the bare design of an article or its container as a trademark, it was theorized that all such designs would soon be appropriated, leaving nothing for use by would-be competitors. One court, for example, feared that "The forms and materials of packages to contain articles of merchandise . . . would be rapidly taken up and appropriated by dealers, until some one, bolder than the others, might go to the very root of things, and claim for his goods the primitive brown paper and tow string, as a peculiar property." *Harrington v. Libby*, 11 F. Cas. 605, 606 (C.C.S.D.N.Y.1877) (No. 6,107). *Accord, Diamond Match Co. v. Saginaw Match Co.*, 142 F. 727, 729–30 (6th Cir. 1906).

This limitation of permissible trademark subject matter later gave way to assertions that one or more features of a product or package design could legally function as a trademark. *E.g., Alan Wood Steel Co. v. Watson*, 150 F. Supp. 861, 863, 113 U.S.P.Q. 311, 312 (D.D.C. 1957); *Capewell Horse Nail Co. v. Mooney, supra.* It was eventually held that the entire design of an article (or its container) could, without other means of identification, function to identify the source of the article and be protected as a trademark. *E.g., In re Minnesota Mining and Manufacturing Co.*, 51 C.C.P.A. 1546, 1547–48, 335 F.2d 836, 837, 142 U.S.P.Q. 366, 367 (1964).

That protection was limited, however, to those designs of articles and containers, or features thereof, which were "nonfunctional." . . . This requirement of "nonfunctionality" is not mandated by statute, but "is deduced entirely from court decisions." *In re Mogen David Wine Corp.*, 51 C.C.P.A. 1260, 1269, 328 F.2d 925, 932, 140 U.S.P.Q. 575, 581 (1964) (Rich, J., concurring). It has as its genesis the judicial theory that there exists a fundamental right to compete through imitation of a competitor's product, which right can only be *temporarily* denied by the patent or copyright laws:

> If one manufacturer should make an advance in effectiveness of operation, or in simplicity of form, or in utility of color; and if that advance did not entitle him to a monopoly by means of a machine or process or a product or a design patent; and if by means of unfair trade suits he could shut out other manufacturers who plainly intended to share in the benefits of unpatented utilities . . . he would be given gratuitously a monopoly more effective than that of the unobtainable patent in the ratio of eternity to seventeen years. [*Pope Automatic Merchandising Co. v. McCrum-Howell Co.*, 191 F. 979, 981–82 (7th Cir. 1911).]

Best Lock Corp. v. Schlage Lock Co., 56 C.C.P.A. 1472, 1476, 413 F.2d 1195, 1199, 162 U.S.P.Q. 552, 555 (1969); *In re Deister Concentrator Co.*, 48 C.C.P.A. 952, 960, 289 F.2d 496, 499, 129 U.S.P.Q. 314, 318 (1961); *Sylvania Electric Products, Inc. v. Dura Electric Lamp Co.*, 247 F.2d 730, 732, 114 U.S.P.Q. 434, 436 (3d Cir. 1957); *Herz v. Loewenstein*, 40 App. D.C. 277, 278 (1913); *Alan Wood Steel Co. v. Watson*, 150 F. Supp. 861, 862, 113 U.S.P.Q. 311, 312 (D.D.C.1957); *Goodyear Tire & Rubber Co. v. Robertson*, 18 F.2d 639, 641 (D. Md. 1927), *aff'd*, 25 F.2d 833 (4th Cir. 1928).

An exception to the right to copy exists, however, where the product or package design under consideration is "nonfunctional" and serves to identify its manufacturer or seller, and the exception exists even though the design is not temporarily protectible through acquisition of patent or copyright. Thus, when a design is "nonfunctional," the right to compete through imitation gives way, presumably upon balance of that right with the originator's right to prevent others from infringing upon an established symbol of trade identification.

This preliminary discussion leads to the heart of the matter — how do we define the concept of "functionality," and what role does the above balancing of interests play in that definitional process?

I. Functionality Defined

. . . .

A. "Functional" means "utilitarian"

From the earliest cases, "functionality" has been expressed in terms of "utility." In 1930, this court stated it to be "well settled that the configuration of *an article having utility* is not the subject of trade-mark protection." (Emphasis ours.) *In re Dennison Mfg. Co.*, 17 C.C.P.A. 987, 988, 39 F.2d 720, 721, 5 U.S.P.Q. 316, 317 (1930) (Arbitrary urn or vase-like shape of reinforcing patch on a tag.). *Accord, Sparklets Corp. v. Walter Kidde Sales Co.*, 26 C.C.P.A. 1342, 1345; 104 F.2d 396, 399; 42 U.S.P.Q. 73, 76 (1939); *In re National Stone-Tile Corp.*, 19 C.C.P.A. 1101, 1102, 57 F.2d 382, 383, 13 U.S.P.Q. 11, 12 (1932). This broad statement of the "law," that the design of an article "having utility" cannot be a trademark, is incorrect and inconsistent with later pronouncements.

We wish to make it clear — in fact, we wish to characterize it as the *first* addition to the *Deister* "truisms" — that a discussion of "functionality" is *always* in reference to the *design* of the thing under consideration (in the sense of its appearance) and *not* the thing itself. One court, for example, paraphrasing Gertrude Stein, commented that "a dish is a dish is a dish." *Hygienic Specialties Co. v. H. G. Salzman, Inc.*, 302 F.2d 614, 621, 133 U.S.P.Q. 96, 103 (2d Cir. 1962). No doubt, by definition, a dish always functions as a dish and has its utility, but it is the appearance of the dish which is important in a case such as this, as will become clear.

Assuming the *Dennison* court intended that its statement reference an article whose *configuration* "has utility," its statement is still too broad. Under that reasoning, the design of a particular article would be protectable as a trademark only where the design was useless, that is, wholly unrelated to the function of the article.

Design only protectable where no utility (handwritten annotation)

For example, where a merchant sought to register on the supplemental register the overall configuration of a triangular chemical cake for use in a process of metal plating, this court stated that the shape was capable of becoming a trademark because it "is entirely arbitrary and, except for its solidity (*all* shapes being solid), has no functional significance whatever." *In re Minnesota Mining and Mfg. Co.*, 51 C.C.P.A. *supra* at 1551, 335 F.2d at 840, 142 U.S.P.Q. at 369.

Most designs, however, result in the production of articles, containers, or features thereof which are indeed utilitarian, and examination into the possibility of trademark protection is not to the mere *existence* of utility, but to the degree of *design* utility. The ore concentrating and coal cleaning table shape in *Deister*, for example, was refused registration as a trademark because its shape was "*in essence* utilitarian," 48 C.C.P.A. *supra* at 968, 289 F.2d at 506, 129 U.S.P.Q. at 322. Likewise, the design of a cast aluminum fitting for joining lengths of tubing together was denied registration because it was held to be "in essence utilitarian or functional." *In re Hollaender Mfg. Co.*, 511 F.2d 1186, 1189, 185 U.S.P.Q. 101, 103 (C.C.P.A. 1975). The configuration of a thermostat cover was also refused registration because a round cover was "probably the most utilitarian" design which could have been selected for a round mechanism. *In re Honeywell, Inc.*, 532 F.2d 180, 182, 189 U.S.P.Q. 343, 344 (C.C.P.A. 1976).

Thus, it is the "utilitarian" *design* of a "utilitarian" *object* with which we are concerned, and the manner of use of the term "utilitarian" must be examined at each occurrence. The latter occurrence is, of course, consistent with the lay meaning of the term. But the former is being used to denote a *legal consequence* (it being synonymous with "functional"), and it therefore requires further explication.

B. *"Utilitarian" means "superior in function (de facto) or economy of manufacture," which "superiority" is determined in light of competitive necessity to copy*

. . . .

. . . [I]t is clear that courts in the past have considered the public policy involved in this area of the law as, not the *right* to slavishly copy articles which are not protected by patent or copyright, but the *need* to copy those articles, which is more properly termed the right to compete *effectively*. Even the earliest cases, which discussed protectability in terms of exhaustion of possible packaging forms, recognized that the real issue was whether "the effect would be to gradually throttle trade." *Harrington v. Libby, supra* at 606.

of hindering competitor (handwritten annotation)

More recent cases also discuss "functionality" in light of competition. One court noted that the "question in each case is whether protection against imitation will hinder the competitor in competition."*Truck Equipment Service Co. v. Fruehauf Corp.*, 536 F.2d 1210, 1218, 191 U.S.P.Q. 79, 85 (8th Cir. 1976). Another court, upon suit for trademark infringement (the alleged trademark being plaintiff's building design), stated that "enjoining others from using the building design [would not] inhibit competition in any way." *Fotomat Corp. v. Cochran*, 437 F. Supp. 1231, 1235, 194 U.S.P.Q. 128, 131 (D. Kan. 1977). This court has also referenced "hinderance of competition" in a number of the "functionality" cases which have been argued before it.

II. Determining "Functionality"

A. In general

Keeping in mind, as shown by the foregoing review, that "functionality" is determined in light of "utility," which is determined in light of "superiority of design," and rests upon the foundation "essential to effective competition," *Ives Laboratories, Inc. v. Darby Drug Co.*, 601 F.2d 631, 643, 202 U.S.P.Q. 548, 558 (2d Cir. 1979), and cases cited *supra*, there exist a number of factors, both positive and negative, which aid in that determination.

Previous opinions of this court have discussed what evidence is useful to demonstrate that a particular design is "superior." In *In re Shenango Ceramics, Inc.*, 53 C.C.P.A. 1268, 1273, 362 F.2d 287, 291, 150 U.S.P.Q. 115, 119 (1966), the court noted that the existence of an expired utility patent which disclosed the *utilitarian advantage of the design* sought to be registered as a trademark was *evidence* that it was "functional." *Accord, Best Lock Corp. v. Schlage Lock Co.*, 56 C.C.P.A. *supra* at 1477, 413 F.2d at 1199, 162 U.S.P.Q. at 556; *Mine Safety Appliances Co. v. Storage Battery Co.*, 56 C.C.P.A. 863, 864, 405 F.2d 901, 902, 160 U.S.P.Q. 413, 414 (1969); *In re Deister Concentrator Co.*, 48 C.C.P.A. *supra* at 962, 289 F.2d at 501, 129 U.S.P.Q. at 319; *Daniel v. Electric Hose & Rubber Co.*, 231 F. 827, 833 (3d Cir. 1916). It may also be significant that the originator of the design touts its utilitarian advantages through advertising. *Shenango, supra*; *Deister, supra*; *Mine Safety Appliances, supra*; *In re Pollak Steel Co.*, 50 C.C.P.A. 1045, 1046–47, 314 F.2d 566, 567, 136 U.S.P.Q. 651, 652 (1963).

Since the effect upon competition "is really the crux of the matter," it is, of course, significant that there are other alternatives available. Nims, *Unfair Competition and Trade-Marks* at 377. *Compare Time Mechanisms, Inc. v. Qonaar Corp.*, 422 F. Supp. 905, 913, 194 U.S.P.Q. 500, 506 (D.N.J. 1976) ("the parking meter mechanism can be contained by housings of many different configurations") *and In re World's Finest Chocolate, Inc.*, 474 F.2d 1012, 1014, 177 U.S.P.Q. 205, 206 (C.C.P.A. 1973) ("We think competitors can readily meet the demand for packaged candy bars by use of other packaging styles, and we find no utilitarian advantages flowing from this package design as opposed to others as was found in the rhomboidally-shaped deck involved in *Deister*.") *and In re Mogen David Wine Corp.*, C.C.P.A. *supra* at 1270, 328 F.2d at 933, 140 U.S.P.Q. at 581 (Rich, J., concurring. "Others can meet any real or imagined demand for wine in decanter-type bottles — assuming there is any such thing — without being in the least hampered in competition by inability to copy the Mogen David bottle design.") *and In re Minnesota Mining and Mfg. Co.*, 51 C.C.P.A. *supra* at 1551, 335 F.2d at 840, 142 U.S.P.Q. at 369 (It was noted to be an undisputed fact of record that the article whose design was sought to be registered "could be formed into almost any shape.") *and Fotomat Corp. v. Cochran*, 437 F. Supp. *supra* at 1235, 194 U.S.P.Q. at 131 (The court noted that the design of plaintiff's building functioned "no better than a myriad of other building designs.") *with In re Honeywell, Inc.*, 532 F.2d at 182, 189 U.S.P.Q. at 344 (A portion of the board opinion which the court adopted noted that there "are only so many basic shapes in which a thermostat or its cover can be made," but then concluded that, "That fact that thermostat covers may be produced in other forms or shapes does not and cannot detract from the functional character of the configuration here involved.").

It is also significant that a particular design results from a comparatively simple or cheap method of manufacturing the article. In *Schwinn Bicycle Co. v. Murray Ohio Mfg. Co.*, 339 F. Supp. 973, 980, 172 U.S.P.Q. 14, 19 (M.D. Tenn. 1971), *aff'd*, 470 F.2d 975, 176 U.S.P.Q. 161 (6th Cir. 1972), the court stated its reason for refusing to recognize the plaintiff's bicycle rim surface design as a trademark:

> The evidence is uncontradicted that the various manufacturers of bicycle rims in the United States consider it commercially necessary to mask, hide or camouflage the roughened and charred appearance resulting from welding the tubular rim sections together. The evidence represented indicates that the only other process used by bicycle rim manufacturers in the United States is the more complex and more expensive process of grinding and polishing.

Accord, In re Pollak Steel Co., 50 C.C.P.A. *supra* at 1050, 314 F.2d at 570, 136 U.S.P.Q. at 654; *Luminous Unit Co. v. R. Williamson & Co.*, *supra* at 269.

B. *The case at bar*

  1. *The evidence of functionality*

We come now to the task of applying to the facts of this case the distilled essence of the body of law on "functionality" above discussed. The question is whether appellant's plastic spray bottle is de jure functional; is it the best or one of a few superior designs available? We hold, on the basis of the evidence before the board, that it is not.

The board thought otherwise but did not state a single supporting reason. In spite of her strong convictions about it, neither did the examiner. Each expressed mere opinions and it is not clear to us what either had in mind in using the terms "functional" and "utilitarian." Of course, the spray bottle is highly useful and performs its intended functions in an admirable way, but that is not enough to render the *design* of the spray bottle — which is all that matters here — functional.

As the examiner appreciated, the spray bottle consists of two major parts, a bottle and a trigger-operated, spray-producing pump mechanism which also serves as a closure. We shall call the latter the spray top. In the first place, a molded plastic bottle can have an infinite variety of forms or designs and still *function* to hold liquid. No one form is *necessary* or appears to be "superior." Many bottles have necks, to be grasped for pouring or holding, and the necks likewise can be in a variety of forms. The PTO has not produced one iota of evidence to show that the shape of appellant's bottle was *required* to be as it is for any de facto functional reason, which might lead to an affirmative determination of de jure functionality. The evidence, consisting of competitor's molded plastic bottles for similar products, demonstrates that the same functions can be performed by a variety of other shapes with no sacrifice of any functional advantage. There is no necessity to copy appellant's trade dress to enjoy any of the functions of a spray-top container.

As to the appearance of the spray top, the evidence of record shows that it too can take a number of diverse forms, all of which are equally suitable as housings for the pump and spray mechanisms. Appellant acquired a patent on the pump mechanism (No. 3,749,290) the drawings of which show it embodied in a structure which bears not the slightest resemblance to the appearance of appellant's spray top. The pictures of the competition's spray bottles further illustrate that no particular housing *design* is necessary to have a pump-type sprayer. Appellant's spray top, seen from the side, is rhomboidal, roughly speaking, a design which bears no relation to the shape of the pump mechanism housed within it and is an arbitrary decoration — no more de jure functional than is the grille of an automobile with respect to its under-the-hood power plant. The evidence shows that even the shapes of pump triggers can and do vary while performing the same function.

What is sought to be registered, however, is no single design feature or component but the overall composite design comprising both bottle and spray top. While that design must be *accommodated* to the functions performed, we see no evidence that it was *dictated* by them and resulted in a functionally or economically superior design of such a container.

Applying the legal principles discussed above, we do not see that allowing appellant to exclude others (upon proof of distinctiveness) from using this trade dress will hinder competition or impinge upon the rights of others to compete effectively in the sale of the goods named in the application, even to the extent of marketing them in *functionally* identical spray containers. The fact is that many others are doing so. Competitors have apparently had no need to simulate appellant's trade dress, in whole or in part, in order to enjoy all of the *functional* aspects of a spray top container. Upon expiration of any patent protection appellant may now be enjoying on its spray and pump mechanism, competitors may even copy and enjoy all of its functions without copying the external appearance of appellant's spray top.

If the functions of appellant's bottle can be performed equally well by containers of innumerable designs and, thus, no one is injured in competition, why did the board state that appellant's *design* is functional and for that reason not registrable?

   2. The relationship between "functionality" and distinctiveness

. . . .

The issues of distinctiveness and functionality may have been somewhat inter-mixed by the board. The design in issue appears to us to be relatively simple and plain, and the board, although not ruling upon appellant's contention that its design has acquired secondary meaning, discussed only distinctiveness before reaching its conclusion that the design was "functional." The unexpressed (and perhaps uncon-scious) thought may have been that if something is not inherently distinctive (appellant admits that its design is not), perhaps even austere, then, since it does not at a particular time function as a legally recognized indication of source, it probably never will. And since it is so plain that one may believe it is not and never will be a trademark, it will be perceived — not that the design is not inherently distinctive — but that it is "functional," without analysis of why it is believed to be "functional." The sole criterion seems to have been that the design is ordinary.

While it is certainly arguable that lack of distinctiveness may, where appropriate, permit an inference that a design was created primarily with an eye toward the utility of the *article*, that fact is by no means conclusive as to the "functionality" of the *design* of that article. Whether in fact the design is "functional" requires closer and more careful scrutiny. We cannot say that there exists an inverse proportional relationship in all cases between distinctiveness of design and functionality (de facto or de jure).

. . . .

[Reversed and remanded on issues of distinctiveness or secondary meaning].

CLAMP MANUFACTURING COMPANY v. ENCO MANUFACTURING COMPANY

United States Court of Appeals, Ninth Circuit
870 F.2d 512 (1989), cert. denied, 493 U.S. 872 (1989)

FARRIS, CIRCUIT JUDGE.

Enco Manufacturing Co. appeals from the district court's judgment against it in favor of Clamp Manufacturing Co. Clamp sued Enco for trademark infringement of its clamps. Following a bench trial, the district court granted injunctive relief and damages to Clamp. We affirm.

BACKGROUND

Clamp, a California corporation principally located in Los Angeles, manufactures and distributes clamps. Clamp and its predecessor, Saxton Manufacturing Co., have manufactured and distributed cantilevered "C" clamps in various sizes and styles since the early 1950's. A patent for the clamp, more precisely described as a "single screw actuated pivoted clamp," was issued in 1955 and expired in 1972. In January 1974, Clamp obtained a trademark registration, valid for twenty years, for the term "KANT-TWIST." No. 977,118, Principal Register, U.S. Patent Office (noting 1954 as date of first use of clamp).

Enco, an Illinois corporation principally located in Chicago, manufactures and distributes machine tools, parts, and accessories.

. . . .

In 1976 or early 1977, Enco began purchasing and distributing a line of cantilevered "C" clamps manufactured in Korea. The clamps were virtually identical to the Kant-twist clamps manufactured by Clamp and were designated as "Enco NO-TWIST clamps" in the Enco sales catalog.

In November 1977, Clamp wrote Enco demanding that Enco cease selling its No-twist clamps because Enco's clamps were confusingly similar to Clamp's Kant-twist clamps. Enco refused, stating that the Clamp patent had expired and the "no-twist" term was used descriptively. In December 1977, Clamp again asked Enco to cease marketing its No-twist clamps; Enco did not respond.

Following the exchange of correspondence, Clamp took several actions in response to Enco's efforts. In May 1978, Clamp filed a complaint with the Federal Trade Commission, alleging the palming off of confusingly similar copies of its clamps by several wholesale distributors, including Enco. Clamp attempted to persuade its customers, through advertising and direct contacts, that its products were superior to those of Enco, and made changes to the appearance of some parts of its clamps.

. . . .

In August 1982, after the FTC decided to take no action on Clamp's complaint, Clamp filed suit.

. . . .

On November 24, 1987, the trial court awarded Clamp $578,689 plus prejudgment interest of $378,077 and issued a permanent injunction prohibiting Enco from using the No-twist name and from promoting or selling confusingly similar cantilevered "C" clamps.

. . . .

B. Validity of the Clamp Configuration Trademark

The physical details and design of a product may be protected under the trademark laws only if they are nonfunctional and have acquired a secondary meaning. *Vuitton Et Fils S.A. v. J. Young Enterprises*, 644 F.2d 769, 772 (9th Cir. 1981). The burden of proving nonfunctionality is on Clamp. *See Rachel v. Banana Republic, Inc.*, 831 F.2d 1503, 1506 (9th Cir. 1987). Evidence of deliberate copying, present in this case, supports a determination of secondary meaning but does not in itself shift the burden of proving secondary meaning from Clamp to Enco. *See Fuddruckers*, 826 F.2d at 844.

1. Functionality

The requirement of nonfunctionality is based "on the judicial theory that there exists a fundamental right to compete through imitation of a competitor's product, which right can only be *temporarily* denied by the patent or copyright laws." *In re Morton-Norwich Products, Inc.*, 671 F.2d 1332, 1336 (C.C.P.A. 1982) (emphasis in original). If the utilitarian aspects of the product are its essence, only patent law protects its configuration from use by competitors. *See Morton-Norwich*, 671 F.2d at 1338–40; *cf. Vuitton*, 644 F.2d at 776–77. *See generally* Annotation, *Application of Functionality Doctrine Under § 43(a) of Lanham Act*, 78 A.L.R. Fed. 712, 736–49 (1986). "Functional features of a product are features 'which constitute the actual benefit that the consumer wishes to purchase, as distinguished from an assurance that a particular entity made, sponsored, or endorsed a product.' " *Vuitton*, 644 F.2d at 774 (quoting *Int'l Order of Job's Daughters v. Lindeburg & Co.*, 633 F.2d 912, 917 (9th Cir. 1980), *cert. denied*, 452 U.S. 941. For an overall product configuration to be recognized as a trademark, the entire design must be nonfunctional. *Textron, Inc. v. U.S. Int'l Trade Comm'n*, 753 F.2d 1019, 1025 (Fed. Cir. 1985). "[T]he right to copy better working designs would, in due course, be stripped of all meaning if overall functional designs were accorded trademark protection because they included a few arbitrary and nonfunctional features." *Id.* To assist in analyzing functionality, several factors may be examined: the existence of an expired utility patent disclosing the utilitarian advantage of the design sought to be protected as a trademark; the extent of advertising touting the utilitarian advantages of the design; the availability of alternative designs; and whether a particular design results from a comparatively simple or cheap method of manufacture. *Morton-Norwich*, 671 F.2d at 1340–41.

The district court found that Kant-twist clamps were distinctive, primarily nonfunctional, and arbitrary, and that commercially feasible alternative configurations exist. Clamp presented evidence of alternative designs and of the arbitrary nature of the clamp arm's shape, including the fact that Clamp made minor design variations in response to the competition from Enco. It also introduced expert testimony concerning a hypothetical design, and evidence of the existence of a non-identical German-made clamp. We therefore cannot find that the district court findings are clearly erroneous, even though another fact-finder could have reached the opposition conclusion.

We recognize that considerable support exists for a determination of functionality. Two of the factors cited in *Morton-Norwich* weigh strongly in Enco's favor. An expired utility patent exists and Clamp's advertising has heavily, if not exclusively, touted the utilitarian aspects of its product. The clamp is not designed in any arbitrary or distinctive manner, with the exception of minor variations in the shape of the clamp arms. Evidence shows that consumers purchased the product on the basis of its function. No evidence was presented that purchasers were aware of Clamp's design variations. Nor does the copying by Enco lessen the necessity for Clamp to prove its configuration nonfunctional. [Citations omitted]. Nonetheless, Clamp presented sufficient evidence to sustain the district court's findings under the clearly erroneous standard. Although the issue is close we are not left with a definite and firm conviction that a mistake has been committed.

2.   Secondary Meaning

A product configuration has secondary meaning if the purchasing public associates that configuration with a particular source. *See Fuddruckers*, 826 F.2d at 843. The factors to be assessed in determining secondary meaning include: whether actual purchasers of cantilevered clamps associate the configuration with Clamp; the degree and manner of Clamp's advertising; the length and manner of Clamp's use of the configuration; and whether Clamp's use of the configuration has been exclusive. *See Transgo v. AJAC Transmission Parts Corp.*, 768 F.2d 1001, 1015 (9th Cir. 1985), *cert. denied*, 474 U.S. 1059 (1986). The district court determined that Clamp satisfied these factors.

Evidence of use and advertising over a substantial period of time is enough to establish secondary meaning. [Citations omitted]. The district court found that Clamp prominently featured the design configuration in its advertising and promotional efforts. This finding is supported by the record. Therefore the district court determination that secondary meaning was established is not clearly erroneous.

We recognize Enco's arguments for overturning the determination of secondary meaning. No evidence concerning the views of actual purchasers was presented. *Cf. Levi Strauss*, 778 F.2d at 1358 ("An expert survey of purchasers can provide the most persuasive evidence of secondary meaning."). Clamp failed to assert trademark rights in its configuration until this litigation was initiated. *See Textron*, 753 F.2d at 1027–28 (evidence of close copying entitled to little weight because trademark in design not asserted prior to litigation; circumstantial evidence of use of design in promotional materials unpersuasive; secondary meaning not shown). However, these arguments do not overcome the findings of the district court on use and advertising.

C. Infringement

1. Likelihood of Confusion

If Clamp is successful in establishing that its product configuration is entitled to trademark protection under 15 U.S.C. §§ 1125(a) by proving nonfunctionality and secondary meaning, it must then prove that Enco's use of a similar configuration is likely to confuse consumers. *See Fuddruckers*, 826 F.2d at 837; 2 McCarthy, *supra* at 42–48.

. . . .

The district court determined that confusion was likely. Its determination is supported by substantial evidence satisfying the factors cited: the similarity of the products, the manner of sale through catalog and telephone orders, and Enco's intentional copying of the Clamp design and promotional materials.

. . . .

Affirmed.

TWO PESOS, INC. v. TACO CABANA, INC.

United States Supreme Court
112 S. Ct. 2753 (1992)

WHITE, JUSTICE

The issue in this case is whether the trade dress [1] of a restaurant may be protected under § 43(a) of the Trademark Act of 1946 (Lanham Act), 60 Stat. 441, 15 U.S.C.

---

[1] The District Court instructed the jury: " '[T]rade dress' is the total image of the business. Taco Cabana's trade dress may include the shape and general appearance of the exterior of the restaurant, the identifying sign, the interior kitchen floor plan, the decor, the menu, the equipment used to serve food, the servers' uniforms and other features reflecting on the total image of the restaurant." 1 App. 83–84. The Court of Appeals accepted this definition and quoted from *Blue Bell Bio-Medical v. Cinbad, Inc.*, 864 F.2d 1253, 1256 (CA 5 1989): "The 'trade dress' of a product is essentially its total image and overall appearance." *See* 932 F.2d

§ 1125(a) (1982 ed.), based on a finding of inherent distinctiveness, without proof that the trade dress has secondary meaning.

I.

Respondent Taco Cabana, Inc., operates a chain of fast-food restaurants in Texas. The restaurants serve Mexican food. The first Taco Cabana restaurant was opened in San Antonio in September 1978, and five more restaurants had been opened in San Antonio by 1985. Taco Cabana describes its Mexican trade dress as

> "a festive eating atmosphere having interior dining and patio areas decorated with artifacts, bright colors, paintings and murals. The patio includes interior and exterior areas with the interior patio capable of being sealed off from the outside patio by overhead garage doors. The stepped exterior of the building is a festive and vivid color scheme using top border paint and neon stripes. Bright awnings and umbrellas continue the theme." 932 F.2d 1113, 1117 (CA 5 1991).

In December 1985, a Two Pesos, Inc. restaurant was opened in Houston. Two Pesos adopted a motif very similar to the foregoing description of Taco Cabana's trade dress. Two Pesos restaurants expanded rapidly in Houston and other markets, but did not enter San Antonio. In 1986, Taco Cabana entered the Houston and Austin markets and expanded into other Texas cities, including Dallas and El Paso where Two Pesos was also doing business.

In 1987, Taco Cabana sued Two Pesos in the United States District Court for the Southern District of Texas for trade dress infringement under § 43(a) of the Lanham Act, 15 U.S.C. § 1125(a) (1982 ed.), and for theft of trade secrets under Texas common law. The case was tried to a jury, which was instructed to return its verdict in the form of answers to five questions propounded by the trial judge. The jury's answers were: Taco Cabana has a trade dress; taken as a whole, the trade dress is nonfunctional; the trade dress is inherently distinctive;[3] the trade dress has not acquired a secondary meaning[4] in the Texas market; and the alleged infringement creates a likelihood of confusion on the part of ordinary customers as to the source or association of the restaurant's goods or services. Because, as the jury was told, Taco Cabana's trade dress was protected if it either was inherently distinctive or had acquired a secondary meaning, judgment was entered awarding damages to Taco

---

1113, 1118 (CA5 1991). It "involves the total image of a product and may include features such as size, shape, color or color combinations, texture, graphics, or even particular sales techniques." *John H. Harland Co. v. Clarke Checks, Inc.*, 711 F.2d 966, 980 (CA11 1983). Restatement (Third) of Unfair Competition § 16, Comment *a* (Tent. Draft No. 2, Mar. 23, 1990).

[3] The instructions were that to be found inherently distinctive, the trade dress must not be descriptive.

[4] Secondary meaning is used generally to indicate that a mark or dress "has come through use to be uniquely associated with a specific source." Restatement (Third) of Unfair Competition § 13, Comment *e* (Tent. Draft No. 2, Mar. 23, 1990). "To establish secondary meaning, a manufacturer must show that, in the minds of the public, the primary significance of a product feature or term is to identify the source of the product rather than the product itself." *Inwood Laboratories, Inc. v. Ives Laboratories, Inc.*, 456 U.S. 844, 851, n. 11 (1982).

Cabana. In the course of calculating damages, the trial court held that Two Pesos had intentionally and deliberately infringed Taco Cabana's trade dress.[5]

The Court of Appeals ruled that the instructions adequately stated the applicable law and that the evidence supported the jury's findings. In particular, the Court of Appeals rejected petitioner's argument that a finding of no secondary meaning contradicted a finding of inherent distinctiveness.

. . . .

We granted certiorari to resolve the conflict among the Courts of Appeals on the question whether trade dress which is inherently distinctive is protectable under § 43(a) without a showing that it has acquired secondary meaning. 502 U.S. — , 112 S. Ct. 964 (1992). We find that it is, and we therefore affirm.

. . . .

Petitioner argues that the jury's finding that the trade dress has not acquired a secondary meaning shows conclusively that the trade dress is not inherently distinctive. Brief for Petitioner 9. The Court of Appeals' disposition of this issue was sound:

> Two Pesos' argument — that the jury finding of inherent distinctiveness contradicts its finding of no secondary meaning in the Texas market — ignores the law in this circuit. While the necessarily imperfect (and often prohibitively difficult) methods for assessing secondary meaning address the empirical question of current consumer association, the legal recognition of an inherently distinctive trademark or trade dress acknowledges the owner's legitimate proprietary interest in its unique and valuable informational device, regardless of whether substantial consumer association yet bestows the additional empirical protection of secondary meaning. 932 F.2d, at 1120, n. 7.

Although petitioner makes the above argument, it appears to concede elsewhere in its briefing that it is possible for a trade dress, even a restaurant trade dress, to be inherently distinctive and thus eligible for protection under § 43(a). Brief for Petitioner 10–11, 17–18; Reply Brief for Petitioner 10–14. Recognizing that a general requirement of secondary meaning imposes "an unfair prospect of theft [or] financial loss" on the developer of fanciful or arbitrary trade dress at the outset of its use, petitioner suggests that such trade dress should receive limited protection without proof of secondary meaning. Reply Brief for Petitioner 10. Petitioner argues that such protection should be only temporary and subject to defeasance when over time the dress has failed to acquire a secondary meaning. This approach is also vulnerable for the reasons given by the Court of Appeals. If temporary protection is available from the earliest use of the trade dress, it must be because it is neither functional nor descriptive but an inherently distinctive dress that is capable of identifying a particular source of the product. Such a trade dress, or mark, is not subject to copying by concerns that have an equal opportunity to choose their own

---

[5] The Court of Appeals agreed: "The weight of the evidence persuades us, as it did Judge Singleton, that Two Pesos brazenly copied Taco Cabana's successful trade dress, and proceeded to expand in a manner that foreclosed several important markets within Taco Cabana's natural zone of expansion." 932 F.2d at 1127, n. 20.

inherently distinctive trade dress. To terminate protection for failure to gain secondary meaning over some unspecified time could not be based on the failure of the dress to retain its fanciful, arbitrary, or suggestive nature, but on the failure of the user of the dress to be successful enough in the marketplace. This is not a valid basis to find a dress or mark ineligible for protection. The user of such a trade dress should be able to maintain what competitive position it has and continue to seek wider identification among potential customers.

. . . .

It would be a different matter if there were textual basis in § 43(a) for treating inherently distinctive verbal or symbolic trademarks differently from inherently distinctive trade dress. But there is none. The section does not mention trademarks or trade dress, whether they be called generic, descriptive, suggestive, arbitrary, fanciful, or functional. Nor does the concept of secondary meaning appear in the text of § 43(a). Where secondary meaning does appear in the statute, 15 U.S.C. § 1052 (1982 ed.), it is a requirement that applies only to merely descriptive marks and not to inherently distinctive ones. We see no basis for requiring secondary meaning for inherently distinctive trade dress protection under § 43(a) but not for other distinctive words, symbols, or devices capable of identifying a producer's product.

Engrafting onto § 43(a) a requirement of secondary meaning for inherently distinctive trade dress also would undermine the purposes of the Lanham Act. Protection of trade dress, no less than of trademarks, serves the Act's purpose to "secure to the owner of the mark the goodwill of his business and to protect the ability of consumers to distinguish among competing producers. National protection of trademarks is desirable, Congress concluded, because trademarks foster competition and the maintenance of quality by securing to the producer the benefits of good reputation." *Park 'N Fly*, 469 U.S., at 198, citing S. Rep. No. 1333, 79th Cong., 2d Sess., 3–5 (1946) (citations omitted). By making more difficult the identification of a producer with its product, a secondary meaning requirement for a nondescriptive trade dress would hinder improving or maintaining the producer's competitive position.

Suggestions that under the Fifth Circuit's law, the initial user of any shape or design would cut off competition from products of like design and shape are not persuasive. Only nonfunctional, distinctive trade dress is protected under § 43(a). The Fifth Circuit holds that a design is legally functional, and thus unprotectable, if it is one of a limited number of equally efficient options available to competitors and free competition would be unduly hindered by according the design trademark protection. *See Sicilia Di R. Blebow & Co. v. Cox*, 732 F.2d 417, 426 (CA 5 1984). This serves to assure that competition will not be stifled by the exhaustion of a limited number of trade dresses.

On the other hand, adding a secondary meaning requirement could have anticompetitive effects, creating particular burdens on the start-up of small companies. It would present special difficulties for a business, such as respondent, that seeks to start a new product in a limited area and then expand into new markets. Denying protection for inherently distinctive nonfunctional trade dress until after secondary meaning has been established would allow a competitor, which has not adopted a distinctive trade dress of its own, to appropriate the originator's dress in other markets and to deter the originator from expanding into and competing in these areas.

As noted above, petitioner concedes that protecting an inherently distinctive trade dress from its inception may be critical to new entrants to the market and that withholding protection until secondary meaning has been established would be contrary to the goals of the Lanham Act. Petitioner specifically suggests, however, that the solution is to dispense with the requirement of secondary meaning for a reasonable, but brief, period at the outset of the use of a trade dress. Reply Brief for Petitioner 11–12. If § 43(a) does not require secondary meaning at the outset of a business' adoption of trade dress, there is no basis in the statute to support the suggestion that such a requirement comes into being after some unspecified time.

III

We agree with the Court of Appeals that proof of secondary meaning is not required to prevail on a claim under § 43(a) of the Lanham Act where the trade dress at issue is inherently distinctive, and accordingly the judgment of that court is affirmed.

NOTES ON CONFIGURATION AND TRADE DRESS

(1) In *Compco Corp. v. Day-Brite Lighting, Inc.*, 376 U.S. 234 (1964), the companion case to *Sears, supra*, the court held that the copier of an unpatented fluorescent lighting fixture design could not be held liable for the copying under state unfair competition law: "To forbid copying would interfere with the federal policy, found in Art. I, § 8, cl. 8, of the Constitution . . . of allowing free access to copy whatever the federal patent and copyright laws leave in the public domain." *Compco* at 237. At page 238 Justice Black went on to observe:

> A State of course has power to impose liability upon those who, knowing the public is relying upon an original manufacturer's reputation for quality and integrity, deceive the public by palming off their copies as the original. That an article copied from an unpatented article could be made in some other way, that the design is "nonfunctional" and not essential to the use of either article, that the configuration of the article copied may have a "secondary meaning" which identifies the maker to the trade, or that there may be "confusion" among purchasers as to which article is which or as to who is the maker, may be relevant evidence in applying a State's law requiring such precautions as labeling; however, neither these facts nor any others can furnish a basis for imposing liability for or prohibiting the actual acts of copying and selling, regardless of the copier's motives.

In *Goldstein v. California*, 412 U.S. 546 (1973), the Supreme Court held that the preemption doctrine expressed in the *Sears* and *Compco* cases does not preclude state action against unauthorized duplication of uncopyrighted recordings by so-called tape pirates. Does the *Goldstein* decision indicate some limitation of the *Sears* and *Compco* rationale? *See* 1 Gilson, *Trademark Protection and Practice* § 7.04 (1993 ed.); McCarthy, *Trademarks and Unfair Competition* § 1:9 (3d ed. 1992); Kaul, *And Now, State Protection of Intellectual Property?*, 60 A.B.A. J. 198 (1974).

(2) If a nonfunctional design acts as a trademark, serving to indicate source to the public, do *Sears* and *Compco* nonetheless preclude its protection from copying under § 43(a)? In *Truck Equipment Service Co. v. Fruehauf Corp.*, 536 F.2d 1210 (8th Cir. 1976), the court rejected such an argument by the defendant, characterizing the cited language from *Compco* (*see* Note (1) *supra*) as dictum and noting at page 1214 that "[t] the law of trademark and the issues of functionality and secondary meaning were not before the Court" in that case. Finding that plaintiff's nonfunctional exterior design for its semitrailer had acquired secondary meaning and that defendant's copying of that design created a likelihood of confusion, the Court awarded injunctive relief and defendant's profits to plaintiff. *Accord: Dallas Cowboys Cheerleaders, Inc. v. Pussycat Cinema, Ltd.*, 604 F.2d 200, 204 (2d Cir. 1979) ("it is clear that *Sears-Compco* did not redefine the permissible scope of the law of trademarks insofar as it applies to origin and sponsorship"); *Rolls-Royce Motors Ltd. v. A&A Fiberglass, Inc.*, 428 F. Supp. 689 (N.D. Ga. 1976). *See also Ideal Toy Corp. v. Plawner Toy Mfg. Corp.*, 685 F.2d 78, 81 (3d Cir. 1982) ("*Sears* and *Compco* do not preclude a court from affording protection from infringement of a design element that has achieved secondary meaning and is non-functional, notwithstanding the absence of a patent"); *Cf. Litton Systems, Inc. v. Whirlpool Corp.*, 728 F.2d 1423 (Fed. Cir. 1984), where noninfringing use of a patented design was held analogous to the uses in *Sears* and *Compco* precluding protection under state law, and *Gemveto Jewelry Co. v. Jeff Cooper, Inc.*, 800 F.2d 256, 230 U.S.P.Q. 876 (Fed. Cir. 1986), where the court held that under *Sears* and *Compco* defendant could be prohibited only from palming off defendant's jewelry as plaintiff's.

In his textbook, *Unfair Competition and Trade-Marks* (4th ed. 1947), Nims explained the difference between the legal protections afforded patents and trademarks:

> The good will of the patentee survives the patent. His popularity as manufacturer or merchant may create a demand for the product as made by him which may be represented by a trade-mark, by non-functional decorative features which have acquired a secondary meaning, or by dress such as a label or wrapper of peculiar design by which the article and its maker have become associated in the public mind. These features have nothing to do with the patent rights. They are property of the patentee which survives the patent. As to them, the general rules with regard to trade-marks and the dress of the goods apply as though no patent were involved. As a manufacturer, one may make any unpatented article, but as a vendor, he may be restricted in the interest of fair competition.

This explanation was cited approvingly by the Court in *In re Mogen David Wine Corp.*, 328 F.2d 925 (C.C.P.A. 1964), in which it held registrable a bottle configuration as a trademark for wines, and further held that use of the configuration during the life of its design patent was valid trademark use. The Court observed:

> In our opinion, trademark rights, or rights under the law of unfair competition, which happen to continue beyond the expiration of a design patent, do not "extend" the patent monopoly. They exist independently of it, under different law and for different reasons. The termination of either has no legal effect on the continuance of the other. When the patent monopoly ends, it ends. The trademark rights do not extend it. We know of no provision of patent law, statutory or otherwise, that guarantees to anyone an absolute right to copy the subject matter of any expired patent. Patent expiration is nothing more than the cessation of the patentee's right to exclude held under the patent law. Conversely, trademarks conceivably could end through non-use during the life of a patent. We doubt it would be argued that the patent rights should also expire so as not to "extend" them.

In his concurrence, Judge Rich found "[w]hether competition would in fact be hindered" to be "the crux of the matter," and concluded, "Others can meet any real or imagined demand for wine in decanter-type bottles — assuming there is any such thing — without being in the least hampered in competition by inability to copy the Mogen David bottle design. They might even excel in competition by producing a more attractive design under the stimulus of a prohibition against copying under the principles of unfair competition law."

(3) Is prevention of product simulation socially or economically desirable in a competitive economy? Can differentiation as to source of copied products satisfactorily be achieved through labeling? *Compare Clamp Mfg. Co. v. Enco Mfg. Co.*, *supra*, in which defendant's product infringed even though it bore defendant's name, *with Litton Systems, Inc. v. Whirlpool Corp.*, *supra*, in which the parties' prominent uses of their respective trademarks dispelled any likely confusion between microwave oven configurations, *and Bristol-Myers Squibb Co. v. McNeil-P.P.C., Inc.*, 973 F.2d 1033 (2d Cir. 1992), in which the prominent presence of defendant's well-known TYLENOL mark on its packaging made confusion with plaintiff's EXCEDRIN PM packaging unlikely.

(4) Can product configuration infringe a word trademark, e.g., can "turtle-shaped" candy infringe the trademark TURTLE for candy? What factors of law and evidence are relevant to such a determination? Should the test in this situation be simply likelihood of confusion? *Compare Laura Secord Candy Shops Ltd. v. Barton's Candy Corp.*, 179 U.S.P.Q. 715 (N.D. Ill. 1973) *with* the discussion on Similarity of Appearance, Sound or Connotation in Chapter 5, *supra*.

(5) The limitations of *Sears* and *Compco* were recognized in a more recent Supreme Court decision, *Bonito Boats, Inc. v. Thunder Craft Boats, Inc.*, 489 U.S. 141 (1989). There, a Florida statute made it unlawful to take a mold of another manufacturer's boat hull and use the mold to build competing boats; the defendant had copied one of plaintiff's hulls in this manner. The Supreme Court held the statute unconstitutional because it prohibited the copying of an unpatented article in contravention of the *Sears* and *Compco* decisions.

In doing so, however, the Court noted that under *Sears*, even in the absence of a patent, the states may protect nonfunctional design aspects that have acquired secondary meaning "where consumer confusion is likely to result." 489 U.S. at 158. The Court also noted that in enacting § 43(a), Congress gave "*federal* recognition to many of the concerns which underlie the state tort of unfair competition." *Id.*, at 166 (emphasis added).

Two district court "lamp" decisions make for an interesting comparison with the *Sears* decision, undertaking the type of analysis that was absent there. In *PAF S.r.l. v. Lisa Lighting Co.*, 712 F. Supp. 394 (S.D.N.Y. 1989), plaintiff's DOVE desk lamp design was held nonfunctional, the court noting the existence of hundreds of other lamp configurations, and was held to possess secondary meaning, based on evidence of extensive sales and advertising, unsolicited media coverage and defendant's intentional copying. Defendant consequently was enjoined under § 43(a) from marketing its SWAN lamp, a low quality Taiwanese imitation. In *Remcraft Lighting Products, Inc. v. Maxim Lighting, Inc.*, 706 F. Supp. 855, 857 (S.D. Fla. 1989), defendant's summary judgment motion was denied because disputed fact issues existed over whether plaintiff's lamp configuration was primarily functional, and, if not, whether the configuration was distinctive, the court noting that it was not the "shades, swivels or canopies which the plaintiff seeks to protect, but the plaintiff's unique *design* of these elements."

(6) The following articles provide particularly valuable insights on the *Sears* and *Compco* cases: Treece, *Patent Policy and Preemption: The Stiffel and Compco Cases*, 32 U. Chi. L. Rev. 80 (1964); Handler & Derenberg, *Product Simulation: A Right or a Wrong?*, 64 Colum. L. Rev. (1964); Lunsford, *The Protection of Packages and Containers*, 56 Trademark Rep. 567 (1966); Damay, *The Sears-Compco Doctrine Today: Trademarks and Unfair Competition*, 67 Trademark Rep. 132 (1977).

(7) Consider the interplay between the law as to simulating the configurations of products themselves and that as to simulating distinctive packages for products. Do the public policy reasons for permitting copying in *Sears* and *Compco* apply to distinctive packages, bottles, containers, and trade or commercial dress generally where presumably no public benefit can result from copying? In *Sicilia Di R. Blebow & Co. v. Cox*, 732 F.2d 417, 426 n.7 (5th Cir. 1984), the court stated, "The need to avoid monopolization of a design lessens . . . in the area of distinctive trade dress. The wide range of available packaging and design options allows a producer to appropriate a distinctive identity without unduly hindering his competitor's ability to compete." In *Johnson & Johnson v. Quality Pure Mfg., Inc.*, 484 F. Supp. 975 (D.N.J. 1979), defendant had copied the trade dress of three different products of plaintiff's for use in the sale of defendant's apparently less expensive products. The court observed (484 F. Supp. at 980–81):

> In and of itself, competition on a price basis is entirely lawful and, in fact, is encouraged. It is what the better mousetrap concept is all about. But it is not fair play to sell a competing product on the basis of a lower price and at the same time use a trade dress designed and calculated to fool the customer into the belief that he is getting someone else's product.

What tests should the courts apply? *See generally* Dorr & Munch, *Protecting Trade Dress* (1992 ed.); Gifford, *The Interplay of Product Definition, Design and Trade Dress*, 75 Minn. L. Rev. 769 (1991); Pegram, *Trademark Protection of Product and Container Configurations*, 81 Trademark Rep. 1 (1991); Comment, *Trade Dress Protection: Inherent Distinctiveness as an Alternative to Secondary Meaning*, 57 Fordham L. Rev. 1123 (1989); Brown, *Design Protection: An Overview*, 34 UCLA L. Rev. 1341 (1987).

(8) In the past, some courts held that if a trade dress was arbitrary and inherently distinctive, its owner was entitled to protection without showing secondary meaning, just as would be the case for word trademarks. As stated in *Chevron Chemical Co. v. Voluntary Purchasing Groups, Inc.*, 659 F.2d 695, 702 (5th Cir. 1981), *cert. denied*, 457 U.S. 1126 (1982):

> [i]f the features of the trade dress sought to be protected are arbitrary and serve no function either to describe the product or assist in its effective packaging, there is no reason to require a plaintiff to show consumer connotations associated with such arbitrarily selected features.

Accord, Blau Plumbing, Inc. v. S.O.S. Fix-It, Inc., 781 F.2d 604, 608 (7th Cir. 1986) (but "location box" in yellow pages advertisement held functional); *Wiley v. American Greetings Corp.*, 762 F.2d 139, 141 (1st Cir. 1985) (but red heart affixed to breast of teddy bear held not inherently distinctive and lacking secondary meaning); *Animal Fair, Inc. v. Amfesco Industries, Inc.*, 620 F. Supp. 175, 190 (D. Minn. 1985), *aff'd*, 794 F.2d 678 (1986) ("bearpaw" slipper design held inherently distinctive). *Cf. Metro Kane Imports, Ltd. v. Rowoco, Inc.*, 618 F. Supp. 273, 276–77 (S.D.N.Y. 1985), *aff'd*, 800 F.2d 1128 (2d Cir. 1986) (showing of secondary meaning in trade dress necessary under Lanham Act but not under New York common law of unfair competition).

The validity of this analysis was confirmed by the Supreme Court in *Two Pesos, Inc. v. Taco Cabana Inc.*, *supra*, which found no reversible error in the district court instruction that allowed the jury to find plaintiff's restaurant trade dress inherently distinctive and protectable without proof of secondary meaning. Cases following *Taco Cabana* include: *Computer Care v. Service Systems Enterprises, Inc.*, 25 U.S.P.Q.2d 1020 (7th Cir. 1992) (trade dress of plaintiff's auto care reminder letters, sales brochure and monthly reports held inherently distinctive and infringed despite presence of some descriptive or generic elements); *George Basch Co. v. Blue Coral, Inc.*, 23 U.S.P.Q.2d 1351 (2d Cir.), *cert. denied*, 113 S. Ct. 510 (1992) (defendant's assertion that plaintiff failed to show secondary meaning in its metal polish trade dress rendered moot by *Taco Cabana*, since jury had found the trade dress inherently distinctive). *Cf. Echo Travel, Inc. v. Travel Associates, Inc.*, 870 F.2d 1264 (7th Cir. 1989) (affirming that plaintiff's promotional poster depicting a beach scene was merely descriptive of its vacation services and lacked secondary meaning), and Dillon, *Two Pesos: More Interesting for What it Did Not Decide*, 83 Trademark Rep. 77 (1993).

(9) Did the Supreme Court in *Taco Cabana*, *supra*, correctly assume that whatever is "inherently distinctive" also indicates source? An inherently distinctive trade dress perhaps may come to indicate source sooner than other subject matter through use

in commerce. But until a trade dress has come to signify source by virtue of use such as has penetrated the consciousness of an appreciable number of relevant persons, there can be no deception. When source signifying awareness has been generated, something exists deserving the law's protection, but not until then. Might the protection of various appearance features, characteristics, combinations or creations as being inherently distinctive amount to the equivalent of a perpetual copyright privilege? "Secondary meaning," in the context of trade identity law, describes a state of mind of persons who have come to perceive or recognize something as signifying a particular (known or unknown by name) source. Secondary meaning is not inherent distinctiveness. Instead, it is a particular acquired distinctiveness.

The words "secondary meaning" were well known and understood in trademark law when the Lanham Trademark Act was being drafted by the late Edward S. Rogers of Chicago. Courts, however, frequently were unfamiliar generally with trademark law, and some had trouble with the arcane term "secondary meaning." The word "distinctive" was substituted for the term "secondary meaning" in the Lanham Act. "Secondary meaning" does not appear anywhere in the Act, which may have contributed to the rationale of *Taco Cabana.*

(10) Where a showing of secondary meaning is necessary, could proof of intentional copying by the defendant be sufficient? See *M. Kramer Mfg. Co. v. Andrews,* 783 F.2d 421, 448 (4th Cir. 1986) ("evidence of intentional, direct copying establishes a *prima facie* case of secondary meaning"); *Osem Food Industries Ltd. v. Sherwood Foods, Inc.,* 917 F.2d 161 (4th Cir. 1990) (defendant's intentional copying of plaintiff's soup packaging raised presumptions of secondary meaning and likely confusion which defendant failed to rebut).

(11) What should be the test of functionality? Must a package or trade dress be essentially or primarily utilitarian to be functional? See *Morton-Norwich, supra; In re World's Finest Chocolate, Inc.,* 474 F.2d 1012 (C.C.P.A. 1973); *In re Deister Concentrator Co.,* 289 F.2d 496 (C.C.P.A. 1961). The Supreme Court in *Inwood Laboratories v. Ives Laboratories,* 454 U.S. 844 n. 10 (1982), defined a functional feature as one that "is essential to the use or purpose of the article or [that] affects the cost or quality of the article." The lower courts also have continued in their efforts to define the elusive concepts of functionality and nonfunctionality. In *Warner Bros., Inc. v. Gay Toys, Inc.,* 724 F.2d 327, 331 (2d Cir. 1983), the court stated:

> The functionality defense . . . was developed to protect advances in functional design from being monopolized. It is designed to encourage competition and the broadest dissemination of useful design features. The question posed is whether by protecting the [plaintiff's] symbols we are creating an eternal monopoly on the shape or form of some useful object, thereby limiting the sharing of utilitarian refinements in useful objects.

Cf. Hartford House Ltd. v. Hallmark Cards, Inc., 846 F.2d 1268, 1273 (10th Cir. 1988) ("the issue of functionality turns on whether protection of the *combination* [of elements] would hinder competition or impinge on the rights of others to compete effectively"); *Truck Equipment Service Co. v. Fruehauf Corp.,* 536 F.2d 1210, 1218

(8th Cir. 1976) ("The question in each case is whether protection against imitation will hinder the competitor in competition"); *Sicilia Di R. Blebow, supra* Note (7), 732 F.2d at 429 ("To achieve the status of "functional" a design or feature must be superior or optimal in terms of engineering, economy or manufacture, or accommodation of utilitarian function or performance"); *Deere & Co. v. Farmhand, Inc.*, 560 F. Supp. 85, 95 (S.D. Iowa 1982), *aff'd*, 721 F.2d 253 (8th Cir. 1983) (distinguishing *Fruehauf* as having found the feature functional because it was "based on sound engineering principles . . . [and chosen for its] utilitarian functionality"). In *W.T. Rogers, Inc. v. Keene*, 778 F.2d 334, 339 (7th Cir. 1985), the court stated:

> [A] functional feature is one which competitors would have to spend money not to copy but to design around, as they would have to do if they wanted to come up with a non-oval substitute for a football. It is something costly to do without (like the hood [of a car] itself), rather than costly to have (like the statue of Mercury [on the hood of a car]).

See also Merchant & Evans v. Roosevelt Building Products, 963 F.2d 628 (3d Cir. 1992) (roofing seam design held functional where it improved watertightness and durability and was one of only two basic designs available on the market); *Woodsmith Pub. Co. v. Meredith Corp.*, 904 F.2d 1244 (8th Cir. 1990) (plaintiff's alleged how-to magazine trade dress, common to many publications in the field, summarily held functional); *Dallas Cowboys Cheerleaders, Inc. v. Pussycat Cinema, Ltd.*, 604 F.2d 200, 204 (2d Cir. 1979) (arbitrary design held to make otherwise functional cheerleading uniform "trademarkable" and protectable under § 43(a)); *John Harland Co. v. Clarke Checks, Inc.*, 711 F.2d 966 (11th Cir. 1983) (some elements of new form of checkbook held functional and unprotectable, others held nonfunctional, protectable and infringed); *In re R.M. Smith, Inc.*, 734 F.2d 1482 (Fed Cir. 1984) (design elements of pistol grip water nozzle held functional and unregistrable); McDonald & Smith, *Proving Non-Functionality of Product Shapes: Honeywell Wins "Round II" on Thermostat Shape*, 79 Trademark Rep. 62 (1989); Zelnick, *Doctrine of Functionality*, 73 Trademark Rep. 128 (1983).

(12) A number of generic drug cases involving the practice of copying the capsule size, shape and color of prescription drugs have also presented a legal forum for addressing trade dress and functionality questions under § 43(a). In *Ives Laboratories, Inc. v. Darby Drug Co.*, 488 F. Supp. 394 (E.D.N.Y. 1980), a generic drug manufacturer was sued under § 43(a) by the brand name manufacturer of a similar drug for copying the capsule colors used by the plaintiff. The plaintiff sued in the alternative for contributory infringement, alleging that the similarity in appearance caused pharmacists to mislabel defendant's generic drug with plaintiff's registered trademark. The district court held there was no § 43(a) violation in the copying of functional drug capsule colors. The functionality was said to lie in the reliance patients, doctors, hospitals, wholesalers and pharmacies placed on colors in determining correct drug and dosage. The court also found that the defendant was not liable for contributory infringement. The Court of Appeals subsequently reversed the latter holding, concluding that the district court had failed to give sufficient weight to plaintiff's evidence of a "pattern of illegal substitution and mislabeling

in New York . . . " *Ives Laboratories, Inc. v. Darby Drug Co.*, 638 F.2d 538, 543 (2d Cir. 1981).

Addressing, on certiorari, the issue of contributory infringement, Justice O'Connor stated the general rule:

> [I]f a manufacturer or distributor intentionally induces another to infringe a trademark, or if it continues to supply its product to one whom it knows or has reason to know is engaging in trademark infringement, the manufacturer or distributor is contributorily responsible for any harm done as a result of the deceit.

Inwood Laboratories, supra Note (11), 456 U.S. at 854. Finding that the Court of Appeals had substituted its own interpretation of the evidence for that of the lower court without adequate justification, and that the trial court's findings on the issues were not clearly erroneous, the Supreme Court reversed the Court of Appeals' holding with directions that the appellate court consider on remand the district court's decision regarding plaintiff's § 43(a) claim. That holding of no § 43(a) violation was later affirmed by the Court of Appeals in an unpublished memorandum, reproduced at 71 Trademark Rep. 117 (1982), the appellate court expressly declining to grant the decision future stare decisis effect. *See also An Analysis of the Ives Case: A TMR Panel* (Kranzow, McCarthy, Palladino, Pattishall, Swann), 72 Trademark Rep. 118 (1982).

In *SK&F Co. v. Premo Pharmaceutical Laboratories*, 625 F.2d 1055 (3d Cir. 1980), the Third Circuit preliminarily enjoined such copying under § 43 (a). The court found (at page 1064) that the copied shape and color scheme had "nothing to do with the purpose or performance of the drug, or with its processing. The only value of the trade dress was in identifying the goods with their source. . . ." It further found that defendant intended that its product would be associated with plaintiff's and that it acted with the awareness that unscrupulous pharmacists would pass off defendant's product as plaintiff's. Similar § 43(a) violations were found in *Ciba-Geigy Corp. v. Balor Pharmaceutical Co.*, 747 F.2d 844 (3d Cir. 1984); *Par Pharmaceutical, Inc. v. Searle Pharmaceuticals, Inc.*, 227 U.S.P.Q. 1024 (N.D. Ill. 1985); *A.H. Robins Co. v. Medicine Chest Corp.*, 206 U.S.P.Q. 1015 (E.D. Mo. 1980), and *Boehringer Ingelhein G.m.b.H. v. Pharmadyne Laboratories*, 532 F. Supp. 1040 (D.N.J. 1980). *See also* McGough, *Reassessing the Protectability of Prescription and OTC Drug Trade Dress*, 81 Trademark Rep. 255 (1991).

(13) Even the shape of a building may possess trademark significance under the proper circumstances. *See* A.L. Fletcher, *Buildings as Trademarks: The Fotomat Cases (Fotomat Corp. v. Photo Drive-Thru, Inc., 425 F. Supp. 693 (D.N.J. 1977); Fotomat Corp. v. Cochran, 437 F. Supp. 1231 (D. Kan. 1977))*, W.B. Whann & J.E. Clevenger, Jr., *A Look Behind The Labels "Functional" and "Nonfunctional" — A Rebuttal*, A.L. Fletcher, *Response*, 69 Trademark Rep. 229–64 (1979). *Compare Prufrock Ltd., Inc. v. Lasater*, 781 F.2d 129 (8th Cir. 1986) (plaintiff's "down home country cooking" trade dress for its restaurant was held functional and unprotectable) *with Taco Cabana Int'l, Inc. v. Two Pesos, Inc.*, 932 F.2d 1113 (5th Cir. 1991), *aff'd*, 112 S. Ct. 2753 (1992) (upholding jury verdict that inherently distinctive Mexican restaurant trade dress was infringed).

(14) Can a feature be functional simply because it is aesthetically appealing? Is aesthetic functionality a valid basis for denying protection? *See Champion Spark Plug Co. v. A.R. Mosler & Co.,* 233 Fed. 112, 116 (S.D.N.Y. 1916) (L. Hand, J.) (spark plugs). *Compare Pagliero v. Wallace China Co.,* 198 F.2d 339 (9th Cir. 1952) (china); *Schwinn Bicycle Co. v. Murray Ohio Mfg. Co.,* 339 F. Supp. 973 (M.D. Tenn. 1971), *aff'd,* 470 F.2d 975 (6th Cir. 1972) (bicycle rim markings). *See generally* Pinover, *Aesthetic Functionality: The Need for a Foreclosure of Competition,* 83 Trademark Rep. 571 (1993); Note, *The Broad Sweep of Aesthetic Functionality: A Threat to Trademark Protection of Aesthetic Product Features,* 51 Fordham L. Rev. 345 (1982); Duft, *"Aesthetic" Functionality,* 73 Trademark Rep. 151 (1983).

The Restatement (Third) of Unfair Competition § 17 (Tentative Draft No. 2, March 23, 1990) defined aesthetic functionality as follows:

> A design is functional because of its aesthetic value only if it confers a significant benefit that cannot be duplicated by the use of alternative designs. Because of the difficulties inherent in evaluating the aesthetic superiority of a particular design, a finding of aesthetic functionality generally will be made only when objective evidence indicates a lack of adequate alternative designs. Such evidence typically exists only when the range of adequate alternative designs is limited by either the nature of the design feature or the basis of its aesthetic appeal. The ultimate test of functionality, as with utilitarian designs, is whether the recognition of trademark rights would significantly hinder competition.

In *Keene Corp. v. Paraflex Industries, Inc.,* 653 F.2d 822, 825 (3d Cir. 1981), the court stated that "The difficulty with . . . a broad view of aesthetic functionality . . . is that it provides a disincentive for development of imaginative and attractive design. The more appealing the design, the less protection it would receive." Nonetheless, the court held the district court was not clearly erroneous in finding that plaintiff's distinctive, source-indicating design for its outdoor wall-mounted luminaire was so architecturally compatible with modern structures that the court could not grant a trademark monopoly without stifling competition. The appellate court referred to the limited number of such designs for a luminaire as distinguishing the factual situation from "the selection of a wine bottle or ashtray design." 653 F.2d at 827. *Followed: Standard Terry Mills, Inc. v. Shen Mfg. Co.,* 803 F.2d 778, 781 (3d Cir. 1986) (weave and check pattern of plaintiff's kitchen towel served to make it "strong, durable and compatible with contemporary kitchen decor" and therefore functional). Some recent cases addressing the issue of aesthetic functionality include: *Schwinn Bicycle Co. v. Ross Bicycles, Inc.,* 870 F.2d 1176, 1191 (7th Cir. 1989) (reversing preliminary injunction grant for failure to properly consider aesthetic functionality defense; "there may come a point where the design feature is so important to the value of the product to consumers that continued trademark protection would deprive them of competitive alternatives"); *Ferrari S.p.A. Esercizio Fabriche Automobile E Corse v. Roberts,* 944 F.2d 1235 (6th Cir. 1991) (rejecting an aesthetic functionality defense regarding plaintiff's classic Ferrari car design), *cert. denied,* 1992 U.S. LEXIS 4603 (1992); *Service Ideas, Inc. v. Traex Corp.,* 846 F.2d 1118, 1123–24 (7th Cir. 1988) (rejecting aesthetic functionality defense in connection with insulated beverage server, noting the alternative designs used by competitors, and that a party developing the product "from scratch" would not necessarily use the design elements of plaintiff's product); and *Deere & Co.*, *supra* Note (11), where, because farmers like to match the color of separately bought loaders with the color of their tractors, plaintiff's "John Deere green" color was found aesthetically functional and copying of it permissible, despite the secondary meaning the color had acquired. *Cf. Sicilia Di R. Blebow v. Cox*, 732 F.2d 417 (5th Cir. 1984), where the case was remanded after the lower court used too broad a definition of aesthetic functionality, i.e., "an important ingredient in the commercial success of" a product, and *Vuitton et Fils S.A. v. J. Young Enterprises, Inc.*, 644 F.2d 769 (9th Cir. 1981), where the appellate court reversed and remanded on the issue of functionality after the district court, citing *Pagliero, supra*, had found a repeated fabric design on plaintiff's luggage to be a factor in the luggage's appeal and salability and therefore functional.

In *Wallace Int'l Silversmiths, Inc. v. Godinger Silver Art*, 916 F.2d 76 (2d Cir. 1990), *cert. denied*, 111 S. Ct. 1622 (1991), the court held that elements such as scrolls and flowers in plaintiff's GRANDE BAROQUE silverware were aesthetically functional and necessary to a competitor in the Baroque silverware market. Only plaintiff's "precise expression" could be protected; otherwise it would obtain an unlawful monopoly on a decorative style. *Id.*, at 80, 81.

(15) Trademarks, configurations and trade dress sometimes acquire a prestige or attractiveness in the public eye which gives them a commercial value of their own, apart from their value to their owner as an indicator of product source. This appeal may create a market for products such as clothing or glassware which feature these source indicators as ornamentation. When such a trade identity is intentionally used by non-owners as ornamentation only, the issue of whether confusion is likely may prove problematic. Should a trade identity owner be able to stop such use by others regardless of source confusion? In *Boston Professional Hockey Ass'n, Inc. v. Dallas Cap & Emblem Mfg., Inc.*, 510 F.2d 1004, 1012 (5th Cir.), *cert. denied*, 423 U.S. 868 (1975), the court held that the sale of replicas of professional hockey team emblems infringed the team's trademarks and, for the one team without registration, violated § 43(a):

> The certain knowledge of the buyer that the source and origin of the trademark symbols were the plaintiffs satisfies the requirement of the Act. The argument that confusion must be as to source of the manufacture of the emblem itself is unpersuasive, where the trademark, originated by the team, is the triggering mechanism for sale of the emblem.

Accord: *University of Georgia Athletic Ass'n v. Laite*, 756 F.2d 1535 (11th Cir. 1985) (representation of school mascot on beer can label violated § 43(a)); *Rolls-Royce Motors, Ltd. v. A & A Fiberglass, Inc.*, 428 F. Supp. 689 (N.D. Ga. 1977) (customizing kits for putting imitation Rolls-Royce front grill and hood ornamentation on a Volkswagen Beetle automobile infringed the registered designs of plaintiff and violated § 43(a)).

Compare International Order of Job's Daughters v. Lindeburg & Co., 633 F.2d 912 (9th Cir. 1980), *cert. denied*, 452 U.S. 941 (1981), in which the court rejected the reasoning of *Boston Hockey* and held that the nontrademark jewelry use of plaintiff fraternal organization's name and emblem did not infringe the organization's trademark rights and did not violate § 43(a): "The name and emblem were functional aesthetic components of the product, not trademarks. There could be, therefore, no infringement." *Id.* at 920. *Cf. WSM, Inc. v. Tennessee Sales Co.*, 709 F.2d 1084, 1087 (6th Cir. 1983) (distinguishing *Job's Daughters*). *See also Application of Penthouse International, Ltd.*, 565 F.2d 679 (C.C.P.A. 1977), where the Trademark Trial and Appeal Board's refusal to register applicant's trademark as a jewelry design was reversed (565 F.2d at 682):

> Depriving the public of the right to copy the Penthouse key logo for jewelry (1) does not hinder competition and (2) does not take from the goods (jewelry) something of substantial value. Moreover, . . . the public is already prevented from making unauthorized copies of the mark in the form of a piece of jewelry.

In *Plasticolor Molded Products v. Ford Motor Co.*, 713 F. Supp. 1329 (C.D. Cal. 1989), the court found Plasticolor's automotive floor mats bearing Ford's trademarks such as MUSTANG were "mixed-use articles," with Ford's trademarks serving both a trademark and a functional purpose on them, the functional purpose being to show the purchaser's allegiance to Ford. The Court held that established trademark principles were inapplicable to claims involving such "mixed-use articles" because total protection "defeats much of the feature's functionality," but that denying any protection "would be decimating a cause of action explicitly provided by Congress." 713 F. Supp. at 1337, 1338. The court therefore sought "a solution that permits trademarks to be copied as functional features, but minimizes the likelihood the public will associate the copied mark with the registrant." *Id.* at 1339.

The Court's proposed solution was to require sufficient disclaimers at the point-of-purchase to avoid likelihood of confusion, but to tolerate some post-sale confusion, by only requiring "all reasonable steps" be taken to eliminate such confusion. The tolerance of some post-purchase confusion was based on the court's conclusion that few customers would be attracted to a "floor‐mat whose upper surface reads 'FORD (not authorized by Ford Motor Company)'." 713 F. Supp. at 1339 (C.D. Cal. 1991). After articulating its new standard for "mixed-use articles," the Court held that it could not dispose of the issue on summary judgment. This decision subsequently was vacated pursuant to an agreement of the parties. 767 F. Supp. 1036 (C.D. Cal. 1991).

§ 8.04 Misappropriation

INTRODUCTION

Another category of unfair competition is "misappropriation." The misappropriation theory recognizes as protectable "quasi-property" values such intangible things as ideas, information, formulas, designs, and artistic creations. It was enunciated by the Supreme Court in the still controversial *INS* case, below. Although rejected by some courts as federal common law obviated by *Erie v. Tompkins* (*see Addressograph-Multigraph Corp. v. American Expansion Bolt & Mfg. Co.*, 124 F.2d 706 (7th

Cir. 1941)), it has shown new vitality in recent years. *Goldstein v. California*, 412 U.S. 546, 569–70 (1973), recognized the power of states to protect such intangibles as performances on tapes and records for the good of important local industries.

INTERNATIONAL NEWS SERVICE v. ASSOCIATED PRESS

United States Supreme Court
248 U.S. 215 (1918)

MR. JUSTICE PITNEY delivered the opinion of the Court.

[The Associated Press (AP), complainant and International News Service (INS), defendant, are competitors in the gathering and distribution of news and its publication for profit in newspapers throughout the United States. AP is a cooperative organization under whose by-laws each member agrees that news received through AP's service is received exclusively for publication in the member's newspaper. The action was brought to restrain INS from pirating AP's news in three ways: (1) bribing employees of AP's members to furnish AP's news prior to publication, (2) inducing AP's members to breach AP's by-laws and permit INS to obtain AP's news prior to publication, and (3) admitted copying of AP news from bulletin boards and early edition newspapers of AP members and selling to INS customers with and without rewriting. The District Court enjoined methods 1 and 2; the Court of Appeals affirmed and remanded to enjoin method 3. The Supreme Court heard argument only as to method 3, and ruled that the case turned upon questions of unfair competition: (1) is there any property right in news, (2) if so, what interest survives first publication, and (3) whether the copying by INS is unfair competition.]

. . . .

[This] case must turn upon the question of unfair competition in business. And, in our opinion, this does not depend upon any general right of property analogous to the common-law right of the proprietor of an unpublished work to prevent its publication without his consent; nor is it foreclosed by showing that the benefits of the Copyright Act have been waived. We are dealing here not with restrictions upon publication but with the very facilities and processes of publication. The peculiar value of news is in the spreading of it while it is fresh; and it is evident that a valuable property interest in the news, as news, cannot be maintained by keeping it secret. Besides, except for matters improperly disclosed, or published in breach of trust or confidence, or in violation of law, none of which is involved in this branch of the case, the news of current events may be regarded as common property. What we are concerned with is the business of making it known to the world, in which both parties to the present suit are engaged. That business consists in maintaining a prompt, sure, steady, and reliable service designed to place the daily events of the world at the breakfast table of the millions at a price that, while of trifling moment to each reader, is sufficient in the aggregate to afford compensation for the cost of gathering and distributing it, with the added profit so necessary as an incentive to effective action in the commercial world. The service thus performed for newspaper readers is not only innocent but extremely useful in itself, and indubitably constitutes a legitimate business. The parties are competitors in this field; and, on fundamental principles applicable here as elsewhere, when the rights or privileges of the one are liable to conflict with those of the other, each party is under a duty so to conduct his own business as not unnecessarily or unfairly to injure that of the other. *Hitchman Coal & Coke Co. v. Mitchell*, 245 U.S. 229, 254.

Obviously, the question of what is unfair competition in business must be determined with particular reference to the character and circumstances of the business. The question here is not so much the rights of either party as against the public but their rights as between themselves. *See Morison v. Moat*, 9 Hare, 241, 258. And although we may and do assume that neither party has any remaining property interest as against the public in uncopyrighted news matter after the moment of its first publication, it by no means follows that there is no remaining property interest in it as between themselves. For, to both of them alike, news matter, however little susceptible of ownership or dominion in the absolute sense, is stock in trade, to be gathered at the cost of enterprise, organization, skill, labor, and money, and to be distributed and sold to those who will pay money for it, as for any other merchandise. Regarding the news, therefore, as but the material out of which both parties are seeking to make profits at the same time and in the same field, we hardly can fail to recognize that for this purpose, and as between them, it must be regarded as *quasi* property, irrespective of the rights of either as against the public.

. . . .

The right of the purchaser of a single newspaper to spread knowledge of its contents gratuitously, for any legitimate purpose not unreasonably interfering with complainant's right to make merchandise of it, may be admitted; but to transmit that news for commercial use, in competition with complainant — which is what defendant has done and seeks to justify — is a very different matter. In doing this, defendant, by its very act, admits that it is taking material that has been acquired by complainant as the result of organization and the expenditure of labor, skill, and money, and which is salable by complainant for money, and that defendant in appropriating it and selling it as its own is endeavoring to reap where it has not sown, and by disposing of it to newspapers that are competitors of complainant's members is appropriating to itself the harvest of those who have sown. Stripped of all disguises, the process amounts to an unauthorized interference with the normal operation of complainant's legitimate business precisely at the point where the profit is to be reaped, in order to divert a material portion of the profit from those who have earned it to those who have not; with special advantage to defendant in the competition because of the fact that it is not burdened with any part of the expense of gathering the news. The transaction speaks for itself, and a court of equity ought not to hesitate long in characterizing it as unfair competition in business.

The underlying principle is much the same as that which lies at the base of the equitable theory of consideration in the law of trusts — that he who has fairly paid the price should have the beneficial use of the property. Pom. Eq. Jur., § 981. It is no answer to say that complainant spends its money for that which is too fugitive or evanescent to be the subject of property. That might, and for the purposes of the discussion we are assuming that it would, furnish an answer in a common-law controversy. But in a court of equity, where the question is one of unfair competition, if that which complainant has acquired fairly at substantial cost may be sold fairly at substantial profit, a competitor who is misappropriating it for the purpose of disposing of it to his own profit and to the disadvantage of complainant cannot be heard to say that it is too fugitive or evanescent to be regarded as property. It has all the attributes of property necessary for determining that a misappropriation of it by a competitor is unfair competition because [it is] contrary to good conscience.

The contention that the news is abandoned to the public for all purposes when published in the first newspaper is untenable. Abandonment is a question of intent, and the entire organization of the Associated Press negatives such a purpose. The cost of the service would be prohibitive if the reward were to be so limited. No single newspaper, no small group of newspapers, could sustain the expenditure. Indeed, it is one of the most obvious results of defendant's theory that, by permitting indiscriminate publication by anybody and everybody for purposes of profit in competition with the news-gatherer, it would render publication profitless, or so little profitable as in effect to cut off the service by rendering the cost prohibitive in comparison with the return. The practical needs and requirements of the business are reflected in complainant's by-laws which have been referred to. Their effect is that publication by each member must be deemed not by any means an abandonment of the news to the world for any and all purposes, but a publication for limited purposes; for the benefit of the readers of the bulletin or the newspaper as such; not for the purpose of making merchandise of it as news, with the result of depriving complainant's other members of their reasonable opportunity to obtain just returns for their expenditures.

. . . .

It is said that the elements of unfair competition are lacking because there is no attempt by defendant to palm off its goods as those of the complainant, characteristic of the most familiar, if not the most typical, cases of unfair competition. *Howe Scale Co. v. Wyckoff Seamans & Benedict*, 198 U.S. 118, 140. But we cannot concede that the right to equitable relief is confined to that class of cases. In the present case the fraud upon complainant's rights is more direct and obvious. Regarding news matter as the mere material from which these two competing parties are endeavoring to make money, and treating it, therefore, as *quasi* property for the purposes of their business because they are both selling it as such, defendant's conduct differs from the ordinary case of unfair competition in trade principally in this that, instead of selling its own goods as those of complainant, it substitutes misappropriation in the place of misrepresentation, and sells complainant's goods as its own.

Besides the misappropriation, there are elements of imitation, of false pretense, in defendant's practices. The device of rewriting complainant's news articles, frequently resorted to, carries its own comment. The habitual failure to give credit to complainant for that which is taken is significant. Indeed, the entire system of appropriating complainant's news and transmitting it as a commercial product to defendant's clients and patrons amounts to a false representation to them and to their newspaper readers that the news transmitted is the result of defendant's own investigation in the field. But these elements, although accentuating the wrong, are not the essence of it. It is something more than the advantage of celebrity of which complainant is being deprived.

The doctrine of unclean hands is invoked as a bar to relief; it being insisted that defendant's practices against which complainant seeks an injunction are not different from the practice attributed to complainant, of utilizing defendant's news published by its subscribers. At this point it becomes necessary to consider a distinction that is drawn by complainant, and, as we understand it, was recognized by defendant also in the submission of proofs in the District Court, between two kinds of use that may be made by one news agency of news taken from the bulletins and newspapers of the other. The first is the bodily appropriation of a statement of fact or a news article, with or without rewriting, but without independent investigation or other expense. This form of pirating was found by both courts to have been pursued by defendant systematically with respect to complainant's news, and against it the Circuit Court of Appeals granted an injunction. This practice complainant denies having pursued, and the denial was sustained by the finding of the District Court. It is not contended by defendant that the finding can be set aside, upon the proofs as they now stand. The other use is to take the news of a rival agency as a "tip" to be investigated, and if verified by independent investigation the news thus gathered is sold. This practice complainant admits that it has pursued and still is willing that defendant shall employ.

. . . .

There is some criticism of the injunction that was directed by the District Court upon the going down of the mandate from the Circuit Court of Appeals. In brief, it restrains any taking or gainfully using of the complainant's news, either bodily or in substance, from bulletins issued by the complainant or any of its members, or from editions of their newspapers, "*until its commercial value as news to the complainant and all of its members has passed away.*" The part complained of is the clause we have italicized; but if this be indefinite, it is no more so than the criticism. Perhaps it would be better that the terms of the injunction be made specific, and so framed as to confine the restraint to an extent consistent with the reasonable protection of complainant's newspapers, each in its own area and for a specified time after its publication, against the competitive use of pirated news by defendant's customers. But the case presents practical difficulties; and we have not the materials, either in the way of a definite suggestion of amendment, or in the way of proofs, upon which to frame a specific injunction; hence while not expressing approval of the form adopted by the District Court, we decline to modify it at this preliminary stage of the case, and will leave that court to deal with the matter upon appropriate application made to it for the purpose.

The decree of the Circuit Court of Appeals will be

Affirmed.

MR. JUSTICE HOLMES, dissenting.

When an uncopyrighted combination of words is published there is no general right to forbid other people repeating them — in other words there is no property in the combination or in the thoughts or facts that the words express. Property, a creation of law, does not arise from value, although exchangeable — a matter of fact. Many exchangeable values may be destroyed intentionally without compensation. Property depends upon exclusion by law from interference, and a person is not excluded from using any combination of words merely because someone has used it before, even if it took labor and genius to make it. If a given person is to be prohibited from making the use of words that his neighbors are free to make, some other ground must be found. One such ground is vaguely expressed in the phrase unfair trade. This means that the words are repeated by a competitor in business in such a way as to convey a misrepresentation that materially injures the person who first used them, by appropriating credit of some kind which the first user has earned. The ordinary case is a representation by device, appearance, or other indirection that the defendant's goods come from the plaintiff. But the only reason why it is actionable to make such a representation is that it tends to give the defendant an advantage in his competition with the plaintiff and that it is thought undesirable that an advantage should be gained in that way. Apart from that the defendant may use such unpatented devices and uncopyrighted combinations of words as he likes. The ordinary case, I say, is palming off the defendant's product as the plaintiff's, but the same evil may follow from the opposite falsehood — from saying, whether in words or by implication, that the plaintiff's product is the defendant's, and that, it seems to me, is what has happened here.

Fresh news is got only by enterprise and expense. To produce such news as it is produced by the defendant represents by implication that it has been acquired by the defendant's enterprise and at its expense. When it comes from one of the great news-collecting agencies like the Associated Press, the source generally is indicated, plainly importing that credit; and that such a representation is implied may be inferred with some confidence from the unwillingness of the defendant to give the credit and tell the truth. If the plaintiff produces the news at the same time that the defendant does, the defendant's presentations impliedly denies to the plaintiff the credit of collecting the facts and assumes that credit to the defendant. If the plaintiff is later in western cities it naturally will be supposed to have obtained its information from the defendant. The falsehood is a little more subtle, the injury a little more indirect, than in ordinary cases of unfair trade, but I think that the principle that condemns the one condemns the other. It is a question of how strong an infusion of fraud is necessary to turn a flavor into a poison. The dose seems to me strong enough here to need a remedy from the law. But as, in my view, the only ground of complaint that can be recognized without legislation is the implied misstatement, it can be corrected by stating the truth; and a suitable acknowledgment of the source is all that the plaintiff can require. I think that within the limits recognized by the decision of the Court the defendant should be enjoined from publishing news obtained from the Associated Press for hours after publication by the plaintiff unless it gives express credit to the Associated Press; the number of hours and the form of acknowledgment to be settled by the District Court.

Mr. Justice McKenna concurs in this opinion.

Mr. Justice Brandeis dissenting.

. . . .

No question of statutory copyright is involved. The sole question for our consideration is this: Was the International News Service properly enjoined from using, or causing to be used gainfully, news of which is acquired knowledge by lawful means (namely, by reading publicly posted bulletins or papers purchased by it in the open market) merely because the news had been originally gathered by the Associated Press and continued to be of value to some of its members, or because it did not reveal the source from which it was acquired?

. . . Plaintiff . . . contended that defendant's practice constitutes unfair competition, because there is "appropriation without cost to itself of values created by" the plaintiff; and it is upon this ground that the decision of this court appears to be based. To appropriate and use for profit, knowledge and ideas produced by other men, without making compensation or even acknowledgment, may be inconsistent with a finer sense of propriety; but, with the exceptions indicated above, the law has heretofore sanctioned the practice. Thus it was held that one may ordinarily make and sell anything in any form, may copy with exactness that which another has produced, or may otherwise use his ideas without his consent and without the payment of compensation, and yet not inflict a legal injury; and that ordinarily one is at perfect liberty to find out, if he can by lawful means, trade secret of another, however valuable, and then use the knowledge so acquired gainfully, although it cost the original owner much in effort and in money to collect or produce.

Such taking and gainful use of a product of another which, for reasons of public policy, the law has refused to endow with the attributes of property, does not become unlawful because the product happens to have been taken from a rival and is used in competition with him. The unfairness in competition which hitherto has been recognized by the law as a basis for relief, lay in the manner or means of conducting the business; and the manner or means held legally unfair, involves either fraud or force or the doing of acts otherwise prohibited by law. In the "passing off" cases (the typical and most common case of unfair competition), the wrong consists in fraudulently representing by word or act that defendant's goods are those of plaintiff. *See Hanover Milling Co. v. Metcalf*, 240 U.S. 403, 41–413. In the other cases, the diversion of trade was effected through physical or moral coercion, or by inducing breaches of contract or of trust or by enticing away employees. In some others, called cases of simulated competition, relief was granted because defendant's purpose was unlawful; namely, not competition but deliberate and wanton destruction of plaintiff's business.

. . . .

It is also suggested, that the fact that defendant does not refer to the Associated Press as the source of the news may furnish a basis for the relief. But the defendant and its subscribers, unlike members of the Associated Press, were under no contractual obligation to disclose the source of the news; and there is no rule of law requiring acknowledgment to be made where uncopyrighted matter is reproduced.

The International News Service is said to mislead its subscribers into believing that the news transmitted was originally gathered by it and that they in turn mislead their readers. There is, in fact, no representation by either of any kind. Sources of information are sometimes given because required by contract; sometimes because naming the source gives authority to an otherwise incredible statement; and sometimes the source is named because the agency does not wish to take the responsibility itself of giving currency to the news. But no representation can properly be implied from omission to mention the source of information except that the International News Service is transmitting news which it believes to be credible.

Nor is the use made by the International News Service of the information taken from papers or bulletins of Associated Press members legally objectionable by reason of the purpose for which it was employed. The acts here complained of were not done for the purpose of injuring the business of the Associated Press. Their purpose was not even to divert its trade, or to put it at a disadvantage by lessening defendant's necessary expenses. The purpose was merely to supply subscribers of the International News Service promptly with all available news.

. . . .

The great development of agencies now furnishing countrywide distribution of news, the vastness of our territory, and improvements in the means of transmitting intelligence, have made it possible for a news agency or newspapers to obtain, without paying compensation, the fruit of another's efforts and to use news so obtained gainfully in competition with the original collector. The injustice of such action is obvious. But to give relief against it would involve more than the application of existing rules of law to new facts. It would require the making of a new rule in analogy to existing ones. The unwritten law possesses capacity for growth; and has often satisfied new demands for justice by invoking analogies or by expanding a rule or principle. This process has been in the main wisely applied and should not be discontinued. Where the problem is relatively simple, as it is apt to be when private interests only are involved, it generally proves adequate. But with the increasing complexity of society, the public interest tends to become omnipresent; and the problems presented by new demands for justice cease to be simple. Then the creation or recognition by courts of a new private right may work serious injury to the general public, unless the boundaries of the right are definitely established and wisely guarded. In order to reconcile the new private right with the public interest, it may be necessary to prescribe limitations and rules for its enjoyment; and also to provide administrative machinery for enforcing the rules. It is largely for this reason that, in the effort to meet the many new demands for justice incident to a rapidly changing civilization, resort to legislation has latterly been had with increasing frequency.

The rule for which the plaintiff contends would effect an important extension of property rights and a corresponding curtailment of the free use of knowledge and of ideas; and the facts of this case admonish us of the danger involved in recognizing such a property right in news, without imposing upon news-gatherers corresponding obligations. . ..

. . . .

Courts are ill-equipped to make the investigations which should precede a determination of the limitations which should be set upon any property right in news or of the circumstances under which news gathered by a private agency should be deemed affected with a public interest. Courts would be powerless to prescribe the detailed regulations essential to full enjoyment of the rights conferred or to introduce the machinery required for enforcement of such regulations. Considerations such as these should lead us to decline to establish a new rule of law in the effort to redress a newly-disclosed wrong, although the propriety of some remedy appears to be clear.

NATIONAL FOOTBALL LEAGUE v. GOVERNOR OF THE STATE OF DELAWARE

United States District Court, District of Delaware
435 F. Supp. 1372 (1977)

STAPLETON, DISTRICT JUDGE.

In August 1976, the Office of the Delaware State Lottery announced a plan to institute a lottery game based on games of the National Football League ("NFL"). Immediately thereafter, the NFL and its twenty-eight member clubs filed suit in this Court against the Governor and the Director of the State Lottery seeking preliminary and permanent injunctive relief barring such a lottery scheme. . ..

. . . .

Plaintiffs have proven that they have invested time, effort, talent and vast sums of money in the organization, development and promotion of the National Football League. They have also convincingly demonstrated the success of that investment. The NFL is now a national institution which enjoys great popularity and a reputation for integrity. It generates substantial revenue from gate receipts, broadcasting rights, film rights, and the licensing of its trademarks.

There also can be no dispute that the NFL popularity and reputation played a major role in defendants' choice of NFL games as the subject matter of its lottery. Defendants concede that in making this election they expected to generate revenue which would not be generated from betting on a less popular pastime.

Based on these facts, plaintiffs assert that defendants are misappropriating the product of plaintiffs' efforts — in the words of the Supreme Court, that the State of Delaware is "endeavoring to reap where it has not sown." *International News Service v. Associated Press*, 248 U.S. 215, 239 211(1918) ("INS"). Thus, plaintiffs maintain the lottery must be halted and the ill-gotten gains disgorged.

This Court has no doubt about the continuing vitality of the *INS* case and the doctrine of misappropriation which it spawned. I conclude, however, that plaintiffs' argument paints with too broad a brush.

. . . The only tangible product of plaintiffs' labor which defendants utilize in the Delaware Lottery are the schedule of NFL games and the scores. These are obtained from public sources and are utilized only after plaintiffs have disseminated them at large and no longer have any expectation of generating revenue from further dissemination. This fact distinguishes the situation in *INS*. In that case the Court recognized the right of INS to protection against misappropriation of the news it had collected for so long as that "product" still retained commercial value to AP. The court was careful to note that the injunction issued by the District Court limited the protection granted only until the time when "[the] commercial value as news to . . . [AP] and all of its . . . [customers had] passed away." 248 U.S., at 245. I do not believe the *INS* case or any other case suggests use of information that another has voluntarily made available to the public at large is an actionable "misappropriation."

Plaintiffs insist, however, that defendants are using more than the schedules and scores to generate revenue for the State. They define their "product" as being the total "end result" of their labors, including the public interest which has been generated.

It is undoubtedly true that defendants seek to profit from the popularity of NFL football. The question, however, is whether this constitutes wrongful misappropriation. I think not.

We live in an age of economic and social interdependence. The NFL undoubtedly would not be in the position it is today if college football and the fan interest that it generated had not preceded the NFL's organization. To that degree it has benefitted from the labor of others. The same, of course, can be said for the mass media networks which the labor of others have developed.

What the Delaware Lottery had done is to offer a service to that portion of plaintiffs' following who wish to bet on NFL games. It is true that Delaware is thus making profits it would not make but for the existence of the NFL, but I find this difficult to distinguish from the multitude of charter bus companies who generate profit from servicing those of plaintiffs' fans who want to go to the stadium or, indeed, the sidewalk popcorn salesman who services the crowd as it surges towards the gate.

While courts have recognized that one has a right to one's own harvest, this proposition has not been construed to preclude others from profiting from demands for collateral services generated by the success of one's business venture. General Motors' cars, for example, enjoy significant popularity and seat cover manufacturers profit from that popularity by making covers to fit General Motors' seats. The same relationship exists between hot dog producers and the bakers of hot dog rolls. But in neither instance, I believe, could it be successfully contended that an actionable misappropriation occurs.

. . . The NFL plaintiffs, however, argue that this case is different because the evidence is said to show "misappropriation" of plaintiffs' "good will" and "reputation" as well as its "popularity." To a large extent, plaintiffs' references to "good will" and "reputation" are simply other ways of stating their complaint that defendants are profiting from a demand plaintiffs' games have generated. To the extent they relate to a claim that defendants' activities have damaged, as opposed to appropriated, plaintiff's good will and reputation, I believe one must look to other lines of authority to determine defendants' culpability. In response to plaintiffs' misappropriation argument, I hold only that defendants' use of the NFL schedules, scores and public popularity in the Delaware Lottery does not constitute a misappropriation of plaintiffs' property.

. . . .

[*Request for relief denied.*]

NOTES ON MISAPPROPRIATION

(1) Mr. Justice Brandeis's dissent in *International News Service (INS)*, *supra* noted that, traditionally, rights were not granted in intangibles such as information and ideas. To be protected against misappropriation, should an intangible be of a unique or exceedingly great value? *See Desclee & Cie., S.A. v. Nemmers*, 190 F. Supp. 381 (E.D. Wis. 1961). Could the *International News Service* decision be interpreted as precluding a party from taking a "free ride" on a competitor's efforts? Note, 46 Harv. L. Rev. 1171 (1933). After the *Sears* and *Compco* decisions were rendered (§ 8.03 *supra*), some courts and commentators contended that the *International News Service* misappropriation theory of relief was inoperative. *See Columbia Broadcasting System, Inc. v. De Costa*, 377 F.2d 315 (1st Cir. 1967); Treece, *Patent Policy and Pre-emption: The Stiffel and Compco Cases*, 32 U. Chi. L. Rev. 80 (1964). Is such a conclusion a necessary or desirable interpretation of those decisions? *See Goldstein v. California*, 412 U.S. 546 (1973); *Capitol Records, Inc. v. Spies*, 264 N.E.2d 874, 876 (Ill. App. Ct. 1970); Comment, *The Misappropriation Doctrine After Sears-Compco*, 2 U.S.F. L. Rev. 292 (1968). *See generally* Baird, *Common Law Intellectual Property and the Legacy of International News Service v. Associated Press*, 50 U. Chi. L. Rev. 411 (1983). Should ideas, concepts, facts, or "hot news" be protectable by state misappropriation law, or preempted by federal law? *Cf. Mayer v. Josiah Wedgwood & Sons, Ltd.*, 601 F. Supp. 1523 (S.D.N.Y. 1985), in which the court ruled there would be no preemption where *prima facie* elements of the state claim contain an "extra element" qualitatively different from federal copyright infringement, and *Harper & Row Publishers, Inc. v. Nation Enterprises*, 723 F.2d 195 (2d Cir. 1983), *rev'd on other grounds*, 471 U.S. 539 (1985), in which the court ruled there would be no preemption if application of the state law requires acts beyond those of copyright infringement.

(2) In analyzing *International News Service*, *supra*, the court in *United States Golf Ass'n v. St. Andrews Systems*, 749 F.2d 1028, 1038 (3d Cir. 1984), characterized INS's activities as potentially destructive of AP's incentive to create the news reports, since INS was directly competing in AP's market — the sale of newspapers. This in turn was against the public interest in having the information created. It found

such direct competition to be essential to a successful misappropriation claim. "[T]he direct competition requirement protects the public interest in free access to information except where protection of the creator's interest is required in order to assure that the information is produced." 749 F.2d at 1038 n. 17. Since the parties in *United States Golf Ass'n* competed only indirectly, the court found that defendant's marketing of a computerized handicapping system using plaintiff's golf handicapping formula was not a disincentive to plaintiff, the governing body of amateur golf in this country, to maintain and update that formula. It accordingly rejected the misappropriation claim. *Cf. Board of Trade v. Dow Jones & Co.*, 456 N.E. 2d 84 (Ill. 1983) (injunction barring Chicago Board of Trade from misappropriating the Dow Jones Industrial Average as the basis for its stock market index commodity futures contract affirmed despite lack of direct competition and unlikelihood of disincentive); *Standard & Poor's Corp., Inc. v. Commodity Exchange, Inc.*, Docket No. 82-2545 (S.D.N.Y. May 13, 1982), *aff'd*, 683 F.2d 704 (2d Cir. 1982) (preliminary injunction against defendant's misappropriation of Standard & Poor's 500 as the basis of its stock index futures contract upheld). Does the lack of direct competition between the parties explain the *National Football League v. Governor of State of Delaware* decision, *supra*?

(3) Could a misappropriation claim be brought under § 43(a) of the Lanham Act as a claim against "reverse palming off," i.e., against a defendant misrepresenting plaintiff's product as emanating from defendant? Is infringement of the right of publicity a type of misappropriation? *See Zacchini v. Scripps-Howard Broadcasting Co.*, 433 U.S. 562 (1977), and the voice misappropriation cases discussed in the section on Right of Publicity, *infra*. Is it possible to misappropriate a trademark? *See Eagle's Eye, Inc. v. Ambler Fashion Shop, Inc.*, 627 F. Supp. 856, 861 (E.D. Pa. 1985) (suggesting it is not); Denicola, *Trademarks as Speech: Constitutional Implications of the Emerging Rationales for the Protection of Trade Symbols*, 1982 Wis. L. Rev. 159, 171 (arguing against recognition of trademark misappropriation). *Compare* Hanson & Walls, *Protecting Trademark Goodwill: The Case for a Federal Standard of Misappropriation*, 81 Trademark Rep. 480 (1991); Winner, *Right of Identity: Right of Publicity and Protection for a Trademark's "Persona"*, 71 Trademark Rep. 193 (1981).

§ 8.05 Distinctive Advertising and Merchandising

INTRODUCTION

Unfair competition cases respecting distinctive advertising and commercial characters basically involve the familiar principles of likelihood of deception as to source or sponsorship. With the development of mass communication, particularly with the advent of television, distinctive advertising motifs, commercial characters, and similar devices have become important mechanisms by which businesses both generate and symbolize goodwill. The trade identity law decisions which follow demonstrate the application of the basic principles to what are often highly ingenious and effectively deceptive means for trading on another's good will.

PREMIER-PABST CORP. v. ELM CITY BREWING CO.

United States District Court, District of Connecticut
9 F. Supp. 754 (1935)

Findings of Fact

. . . .

Plaintiff's Blue Ribbon malt extract since June 2, 1931, and its Pabst Blue Ribbon beer since the legalization of beer on April 7, 1933, have been advertised in weekly radio programs conducted by Ben Bernie, whose soubriquet is "Old Maestro."

The name "Old Maestro" in the mind of the radio public is closely associated with plaintiff and its products, as also with Ben Bernie.

The radio public in New England and generally throughout the country constitutes a substantial part of the consuming public generally, and of the beer-consuming public in particular.

The term "Old Maestro" used in connection with malt beverages is associated with and identifies and distinguishes plaintiff's product.

Since about April 27, 1933, plaintiff has manufactured and sold beer under the trade-mark Old Maestro, but its product thus trademarked has never been merchandised in New England, nor elsewhere, to any substantial extent.

Plaintiff registered said trade-mark in the United States Patent Office on October 24, 1933, No. 307,302, which registration is valid and unexpired.

The defendant was organized in June, 1933, for the manufacture and sale of ale and beer. In August it adopted "Olde Maestro Brew" as the trade-name for its product, and since September, 1933, has distributed its product under that trade-name. It manufactures in New Haven, and sells principally in Connecticut, but also ships into Rhode Island and Massachusetts.

HINCKS, DISTRICT JUDGE.

. . . [E]ven in Blackstone's time the right to reputation was considered as an inherent part of the absolute right of life. He says, 1 Com. 134:

> The security of his reputation or good name from the acts of detraction and slander, are rights to which every man is entitled by reason and natural justice; since without these it is impossible to have the perfect enjoyment of any other advantage or right.

But before one can have a good name, he must have a name; before he can build a reputation, he must have an identity to which that reputation may attach. And so, if indeed reputation is a matter of right, to be known as a particular individual is a right even more fundamental. Conceivably, some alien civilization might exist wherein each member of society was consigned to perpetual anonymity; wherein each was doomed to live and die as one ant in the hill, or as one cog in the machine of the state, without means or right for any identification of personality. But the common law has more nobly appraised the fullness of human life; and in its recognition of a man's right to enjoy the good repute which he has earned, it has from ancient times implicitly recognized his exclusive right to the identity which he has established for himself among his fellows and in the public eye. And this is the right, I think, which has been the subject matter of countless cases of unfair competition, so-called.

In a simpler society, perhaps, the right was seldom differentiated from other human rights because seldom challenged. It had value only to its owner. But as a competitive economy emerged from the guild system, the commercial value, indeed, the necessity, of names as a means of identification came to be recognized; and by use, at first of trade-marks, the right to the exclusive use of a specific means for identification, was extended to include the goods of the individual as well. And later, when the so-called doctrine of secondary meanings was established whereby the law came to recognize the acquisition of rights in the use of geographical and generic names for limited purposes of trade, no new right was born. The law simply recognized that in society as it had developed a man who had come to be identified by the public for specific goods through some specific association was entitled to the exclusive use of such means of identification. Others, to be sure, were free to compete with him; to wrest from him the favorable regard of the public, if they could. But his right to be known as he was known was his right of identity, and against all improper threats the subject-matter of equitable protection.

This tendency of the law has been accelerated by the trend of modern society. The obvious advantages of a system of mass production can only be obtained by a distribution of goods on a national scale. This in turn requires a system of national advertising. To meet this need, every conceivable instrument and method of advertising has been utilized. As a result, it lies within the observation of all that a producer can, with the aid of successful advertising, obtain for himself and his product public recognition of national dimensions, comparatively over night. But the right to establish and enjoy such recognition, as I see it, is nothing but a development of the ancient common-law right of a man to have such an identity in the public eye as he can win by his conduct and personality. And whether this right be classified as an absolute right or as a development of some relative right attaching to the relationship between competitors, is unimportant. It has been recognized as a right by society and has the protection of the law. I think Justice Holmes meant just that in his dictum in *International News Service v. Associated Press,* 248 U.S. at page 247, when he said that:

> The only reason why it is actionable to make such a representation [i.e., a misrepresentation as to the source of goods] is that it tends to give the defendant an advantage in his competition with the plaintiff and that it is thought undesirable that an advantage should be gained in that way.

. . . .

If it is found that the plaintiff has thus established its right, ordinarily it will not be difficult to ascertain whether or not the defendant's conduct has violated that right. On this issue, also, the testimony of individual members of the public, of retailers, salesmen, and experts, is admissible, although, as I have suggested, seldom of controlling weight. Here again the trier will have to apply his knowledge of human nature to the defendant's conduct as proved and determined by inference whether the defendant has done anything tending to sap the virtue of any means of identification found to belong exclusively to the plaintiff. Has the defendant put out goods in such a way as to evoke in the public mind, by word, phrase, or image, an association attaching to the plaintiff or to some means of identification belonging the plaintiff? If so, the tort is complete, and in the proper case enjoinable.

Applying these observations to the case at bar, we see that the primary issue here is not whether the plaintiff has acquired a public recognition of its identity in its own proper name. That fact, I take it, is not disputed; in any event it is amply established. The real question is whether the plaintiff, through its employment of Ben Bernie, has created in the public mind an association with the "Old Maestro" which serves as a means to accentuate the identity of the plaintiff or its products. To be sure, there is no evidence showing what proportion of its sales, if any, is due to the advertising by the "Old Maestro." And the direct evidence is far from sufficient in itself to prove the existence of the association in the public mind. Nevertheless, the evidence relating to the nature, scope and duration of the plaintiff's radio advertising, coupled with the evidence of its popularity, convinces me that the radio public is numerically a substantial part of the beer-purchasing public, and that it necessarily, human nature being what it is, in substantial part has become impregnated with a conscious or subconscious association between "Old Maestro" and the plaintiff's products.

That being so, the defendant's use of "Olde Maestro" as its trade-name necessarily tends to confuse the public and to destroy the effect of a means for identification which, at least in relation to the manufacture and distribution of malt products, belongs exclusively to the plaintiff.

REDDY KILOWATT, INC. v. MID-CAROLINA ELECTRIC COOPERATIVE, INC.

United States Court of Appeals, Fourth Circuit
240 F.2d 282 (1957)

SOPER, CIRCUIT JUDGE.

This suit was brought to secure an injunction against the infringement of the trademark or service mark "Reddy Kilowatt," owned by Reddy Kilowatt, Inc., a Delaware corporation, which was plaintiff in the District Court. The mark is licensed to private electric light and power companies, which use it as a symbol to promote the consumption of electricity. The mark consists of an animated, humanized and fantastic cartoon or figure composed of a body and limbs of jagged lines simulating lighting, a rounded head with a light bulb for a nose and plug-in sockets for ears. It is portrayed in innumerable poses and activities.

The defendants are the National Rural Electric Cooperative Association, a District of Columbia Corporation, which is interested in the development of rural electrification in the United States, and the Mid-Carolina Electric Cooperative, Inc., a rural electric cooperative organized and operated under the State Electric Cooperative Act of South Carolina. The Association is the owner of a trademark or service mark consisting of an animated and fanciful character called "Willie Wirehand" which is alleged to infringe the plaintiff's mark. It was purposely designed to publicize the rural electrification program and is generally used by electric cooperatives including the defendants, Mid-Carolina, to promote their business activities. The figure portrays a little man whose hips and legs are represented by an electric wall plug, the body by an electric wire and the head by a socket with a push button for a nose.

The two characters displayed in their simplest form are shown in the accompanying cuts. Thus shown, they are unquestionably of the same general class and are suggestive of one another, but they are easily distinguishable, and in this form infringement is not claimed. The gist of the accusation is that many postures and situations in which the trademark "Reddy Kilowatt" is used by the plaintiff and its licensees are so closely imitated by the defendants in the portrayal of their mark that the public is confused and infringement occurs. This is the principal issue discussed in the briefs on this appeal. The District Judge who heard voluminous testimony on the point found against the plaintiff and dismissed the suit.

. . . .

Reddy Kilowatt   Willie Wiredhand

. . . "Reddy Kilowatt" is displayed in the plaintiff's material in many different poses associated with the distribution of electricity and the use of electrical appliances, and "Willie Wirehand" is used by the defendants for the same purposes in drawings which, in many instances, closely resemble the drawings which are used by the plaintiff's licensees. The possibility of confusion is increased by the fact that both marks are symbolic of electricity, both are humanized and animated and are engaged in doing the same things in substantially the same manner. The plaintiff produced considerable testimony which tended to show that persons who were well acquainted with the material on which its mark appeared were confused when shown samples of the defendants' mark on similar material, and believed that the character exhibited to them was "Reddy Kilowatt" when, in fact it was the accused mark.

. . . .

. . . This prior use by others of animated characters in advertising goods and services of course did not prevent the plaintiff from entering the field with an original design of its own. Nevertheless, the widespread use of this device has a direct bearing on the charge that members of the public are likely to be confused when "Willie Wirehand" is displayed in a pose or dress or activity in which "Reddy Kilowatt" may also be seen. Whatever property the plaintiff has resides in the figure itself, which it has created, and not in the apparel or activity in which the plaintiff sees fit to place it. The plaintiff has no monopoly on the thousands of situations which it has chosen to depict, for otherwise no other personalized figure in the electrical field would have any validity. In the past thirty years "Reddy Kilowatt" has appeared in a thousand guises, which seem to include almost every imaginable activity, from none of which "Willie Wirehand" may lawfully be excluded; and the resulting confusion, if any there be, is not caused by the similarity of names or of the bare figures alone but by the similarity of the situations to which the plaintiff has no exclusive rights. . . .

The established rule that new and valuable ideas developed in the prosecution of a business do not ordinarily become the exclusive property of the originator is well stated in Nims, *Unfair Competition and Trademarks*, 4th Edition, Vol. 2, § 289, page 947, as follows:

> . . . Generally speaking, there is no protection for new commercial ideas or methods although they may be original and valuable unless they are kept secret or are divulged only by a contract which binds the one to whom they are disclosed to pay for their use if they are adopted. It is not unfair competition to obtain knowledge of or to use a competitor's ideas or methods if such knowledge is obtained in a bona fide way, and such use is fair.

. . . .

. . . When these rules are applied to the circumstances of the pending case it becomes apparent that even if the poses and attitudes of "Willie Wirehand" used by the defendants in their advertising material are strikingly similar to those used by the plaintiff in displaying "Reddy Kilowatt," the plaintiff has no just cause to complain, for it has no right to appropriate as its exclusive property all the situations in which figures may be used to illustrate the manifold uses of electricity.

. . . .

Affirmed.

LONE RANGER, INC. v. COX

United States Court of Appeals, Fourth Circuit
124 F.2d 650 (1942)

PARKER, CIRCUIT JUDGE.

This is an action for damages and for injunction based upon alleged infringement of copyright and unfair competition. The plaintiff is the Lone Ranger, Inc., a Michigan corporation, which since the year 1933 has been broadcasting over the radio copyrighted dramatic serial stories featuring the heroic exploits of a mythical western cowboy, "The Lone Ranger," who rides about masked and on a white horse, called "Silver," championing the cause of the oppressed and redressing the wrongs of the community. Plaintiff has licensed a comic strip, entitled "The Lone Ranger," appearing in a number of newspapers and has licensed the use of the name, "The Lone Ranger,"as a trademark to vendors of various articles. The radio programs of plaintiff are broadcast from one hundred or more radio stations, are very popular and appeal particularly to children. A "Lone Ranger" safety club, promoted in connection with the programs, has attained a membership of between three and four million young people.

The defendant Powell is a motion picture actor, who in 1937 played the part of Alan King as the "Lone Ranger" in a motion picture produced under license from plaintiff. He has been appearing, under contract with the defendant Cox, in a small circus in which he takes the part of the "Lone Ranger," riding masked on a white horse and giving the cry, "Hi yo Silver" or "Hi yo, Silver, away!." . . .

Ct: P entitled to relief

. . . .

. . . [W]e think that plaintiff, under the principles of unfair competition, was entitled to relief. Under the name or title of "The Lone Ranger," plaintiff had built up a radio feature of great value. The exploits of this mythical character, as portrayed in the radio programs, had become of great interest to countless young people throughout the country and were a source of large revenue to plaintiff. Defendants were attempting to avail themselves of the good will created by the broadcasting of the radio programs and the advertising connected therewith, including the "Lone Ranger" safety clubs. Their conduct in advertising Powell as the "Original Lone Ranger" was manifestly calculated and intended to lead the public to believe that he was the "Lone Ranger" of the radio programs and to attract to the circus those who were interested in the programs and particularly the young people who were members of the safety clubs. The fact that the advertisements contained a reference to the talking picture did little, if anything, to minimize the deception of the children to whom they were primarily addressed, and this deception was accentuated by use of the call "Hi, yo, Silver" in some of the advertisements and in Powell's act in the circus. The defendants were in the business of furnishing entertainment, just as was plaintiff, and there can be no doubt but that they were attempting to pass off their show as being identified with the radio programs of plaintiff, or at least as being connected in some manner therewith, and thus to benefit from the good will which had been built up by plaintiff through its broadcasts and advertising.

deception / confusion

. . . .

. . . Even if relief under the principles of unfair competition were confined to cases of palming off of goods or services, we think that the case at bar would be one calling for relief; but we do not understand that relief in this class of cases is so limited. As said by the Supreme Court in *International News Service v. Associated Press, supra:*

> It is said that the elements of unfair competition are lacking because there is no attempt by defendant to palm off its goods as those of the complainant, characteristic of the most familiar, if not the most typical, cases of unfair competition. *Howe Scale Co. v. Wyckoff Seamans [& Benedict]*, 198 U.S. 118, 140. But we cannot concede that the right to equitable relief is confined to that class of cases.

And we are not impressed by the argument that defendants are protected in what they have done because of Powell's connection with the motion pictures licensed by plaintiff. The contention that the advertisement is true is not correct. Powell is not the "Lone Ranger" at all. He is merely a moving picture actor who took the part of the "Lone Ranger" in a motion picture play of that name produced long after the "Lone Ranger" of radio had become widely known. The only reason that defendant's desire to call him the "talking picture Lone Ranger" or the "Lone Ranger of talking picture fame," with "Lone Ranger" emphasized and the qualifying words in smaller lettering, is to attract the patronage of those who will confuse him in some way with the "Lone Ranger" of the radio programs; and the principle is applicable that, not only must one tell the truth, but he must tell it in a truthful way, i.e., so as not to deceive the public. . . .

[*Reversed and remanded.*]

DECOSTA v. COLUMBIA BROADCASTING SYSTEM, INC.

United States Court of Appeals, First Circuit
520 F.2d 499 (1975)
cert. denied, 423 U.S. 1073 (1976)

COFFIN, CHIEF JUDGE.

Plaintiff, a dozen years ago, began this suit against the Columbia Broadcasting System, Inc. and allied corporations (CBS) to seek compensation for their unauthorized use of a character concept he had developed, embodying a costume, slogan, name, and symbol. A mechanic living in Cranston, Rhode Island, his avocation had been to don an all black cowboy suit, with a St. Mary's medal affixed to his flat crowned black hat, a chess symbol to his holster, and an antique derringer secreted under his arm, and make public appearances at rodeos and other events, meeting innumerable children, and passing out his card, inscribed with a chess set knight, proclaiming "Have Gun Will Travel, Wire Paladin, N. Court St., Cranston, R.I.". . .

As every well versed television viewer of the late fifties and early sixties knows, the gestalt conveyed by plaintiff's costume and accessories found its way into defendants' television series, "Have Gun Will Travel," which enjoyed enormous popularity for over eight years in its initial run, grossing in excess of fourteen million dollars.

. . . .

. . . Our first inquiry is whether plaintiff's marks and dress are protectable under either the broad concept of unfair competition or that part of unfair competition dealing with trade and service mark infringement. As to plaintiff's dress, this may have had less claim to protection against infringement than his card. For there is no question but that the photograph of plaintiff in full regalia which he widely distributed was copyrightable. 17 U.S.C. § 5(j), *Burrow-Giles Lithographic Co. v. Sarony*, 111 U.S. 53 (1884). The card is less vulnerable on copyright preemption grounds. Its three components — the slogan, "Have Gun Will Travel," the name in the phrase "Wire Paladin," and the knight chess piece — are in categories protectable as common law trade or service marks. *See, e.g.,* Callmann, *The Law of Trade-marks*, Vol. 3, § 77.4(g) (slogans); § 66.1 (trade names).

What is not clear is whether plaintiff's activities in connection with his marks entitle him to the protection of trade and service mark law. As we said in *DeCosta I*, 377 F.2d at 316, "[t]his was perhaps one of the purest promotions ever staged, for plaintiff did not seek anything but the entertainment of others." Plaintiff testified that he never used the name "Paladin," the slogan or the chess piece for any business use, and never published any advertisements; that he did not even receive his expenses for appearances at horse shows and rodeos; and that the distribution and mailing of pictures and cards was costly to him. . . .

. . . .

. . . It is not a big step in theory to say that an individual who develops and promotes for entertainment purposes a specialty character associated with a distinctive name, costume, slogan, and other marks, but who never charges a fee, is also entitled to protection under the common law doctrine relating to trademarks and unfair competition. But, if the step were taken, what principle should both guide and limit? If plaintiff is recognized as one who performs services in commerce, what about the hobbyist magician, square dance caller, story teller, amateur actor, singer, barbershop quartet, standup comic? How frequent must be the appearances? How prominent the mark? How often must the performer appear in other states to enjoy Lanham Act protection? We know of no logical or obvious line of demarcation. The price of an open-ended extension of protection for some creative activity is, pro tanto, a curtailment of the borrowing, poaching, imitation which underlie so much other innovative activity.

Protection at present has the merits of inherent limitations: the existence of a trade, business, or profession where the "good will" to be protected has been subject to the acid test of the willingness of people to pay for goods or services; or, in the case of nonprofit institutions, the voluntary investment in time, effort, and money of many individuals to create and maintain a program of sufficient interest to consumers, members, and sponsors to warrant protection. We hesitate to take the step of offering common law unfair competition protection to eleemosynary individuals. Whether legislatures are better equipped than courts to deal with this problem, we cannot clearly say, but in our posture of doubt would prefer to see expansion of protection come from that source.

Having exposed our misgivings, we do not rely on a holding that the absence of a profit-oriented enterprise disqualifies plaintiff from protection. We shall assume, therefore, that plaintiff's marks meet the requirements of common law service marks. We also shall assume that they are distinctive enough so that proof of secondary meaning is not essential. In the alternative, we shall accept the finding of the magistrate, adopted by the district court, that, at least among some people, plaintiff's name and card had come to be associated with him.

. . . .

. . . There is another factor, we think, which should guide a judgment as to likelihood of confusion — the time when the evidence is submitted. There is ample reason, at the incipiency of an alleged infringement, in a suit seeking injunctive relief, for a plaintiff to argue and a court to rule that the similarity of marks is such that confusion is all too likely to ensue. Plaintiff should not be expected to stand by and await the dismal proof. Callmann, Vol. 3, § 80.6, pp. 559–560. "[C]onversely," adds Callmann, "after the lapse of substantial time if no one appears to have been actually deceived that fact is strongly probative of the defense that there is no likelihood of deception arising out of the use of the mark in question." *Id.* at 562. Defendants have urged that plaintiff, having delayed for almost the entire limitations period before bringing suit, should be barred by the doctrine of estoppel by laches from further prosecution of this litigation. Plaintiff's rejoinder is that he was, during this period, going from attorney to attorney, seeking assistance before he was able to make progress. We do not find in the authorities sufficient support, where defendants' action was found by the jury to be deliberate and knowing, to invoke this doctrine. Nevertheless, we do say that the delay, for reasons stated, increases the quantum of proof of confusion which the plaintiff has the obligation to supply.

. . . When we examine the magistrate's opinion on this issue, we find only a finding as to the identical nature of the marks used by plaintiff and defendants and the resulting "great likelihood of confusion" therefrom, and another that "At least 6 witnesses testified that they had at first thought, on viewing the television program, that Richard Boone was the plaintiff Mr. DeCosta until they learned the contrary from viewing the credits of the show, or otherwise." The paucity of these findings takes on some significance when we note that after remand of the case to the district court in 1968, following our decision in *DeCosta I*, the plaintiff was given the opportunity to supplement the record in support of his second and third causes of action. The quoted findings are the result.

. . . The magistrate's findings being treated as final, they are here subject to the same standard of review as are district court findings under Fed. R. Civ. Pro. 52(a). They must be accepted unless clearly erroneous. On this issue, however, we see no alternative to saying the finding is not supported. If the identity of the marks settled the question of likelihood of confusion, there was no need for further evidence after

DeCosta I; we had taken some pains to make the point. But, in fact (rather, in law) extrinsic evidence, as we have noted, should be considered. Here, the disparities are substantial. Plaintiff's enterprise was localized; defendants' was nationwide. Plaintiff's appearances were simple happenings, passing out cards and pictures, riding, occasionally walking his horse, and executing a quick draw gun maneuver; defendant's extrinsic television series portrayed an elegant hired gun on manifold missions. Plaintiff's customers were attendees at rodeos and parades, patients at hospitals, etc.; defendants' purchasers were its program's sponsors, who in turn were responsive to the nation's television audience. Moreover, plaintiff's suit was not brought in 1957 when the alleged infringement began; the testimony as to likelihood of confusion was introduced by affidavit eleven years later, when the first run of defendants' series had terminated. After this lapse of time, the testimony of six witnesses that they thought, on first viewing the program, that the television character Paladin was plaintiff, seems to us either no evidence at all or such minimal evidence as not to support a finding of likelihood of confusion requiring an accounting of defendants' profits from a highly successful, 225-episode series grossing over fourteen million dollars. We do not blame plaintiff or counsel; we suspect that the most exacting search for proof would not have produced more.

> *me: Big deal that he waited 11 years.*

. . . We recognize that plaintiff has lost something of value to him. The very success of defendants' series saturated the public consciousness and in time diluted the attractiveness of plaintiff's creation, although he continued his appearances longer than defendants' first run. While he was not injured financially, there can be no doubt that he has felt deprived. As a commentator has observed, "[I]t could be argued that the most appropriate measure of damages would be the emotional harm that he suffered when CBS exploited his character and lured his audience away." 66 Mich. L. Rev. at 1034. But to give any relief, however tailored, we need a predicate of liability. Absent the ultimate fact of confusion, we cannot find a basis for liability for common law service mark infringement or unfair competition.

> *emotional harm is the real harm.*

> *Judgment reversed. Remanded with instructions to enter judgment for defendants.*

NOTES ON DISTINCTIVE ADVERTISING AND MERCHANDISING

(1) Generally, one may protect a distinctive mode of advertising from imitation by others where such imitation is likely to deceive the public. *See, e.g., Premier-Pabst, supra* (radio advertising); *Heuer v. Parkhill*, 114 F. Supp. 665 (W.D. Ark. 1953) (advertising folder); *Hilson Co. v. Foster*, 80 Fed. 896 (S.D.N.Y. 1897) (posters, show-cards, etc.). *Cf. Roux Laboratories, Inc. v. Clairol, Inc.*, 427 F.2d 823, 828–831 (C.C.P.A. 1970) (slogan).

(2) Should trademark significance be accorded to fanciful advertising characters when they are not used on or in immediate connection with the sale of products? *See Premier-Pabst, supra.* Is proof of secondary meaning, i.e., source of goods or

services association, necessary? What is the effect of modern media advertising upon the marketing and economic significance of fanciful advertising characters? *See* Battersby & Grimes, *The Law of Merchandise and Character Licensing* (1993 ed.); Kurtz, *The Independent Legal Lives of Fictional Characters*, 1986 Wis L. Rev. 429 (1986); Coleman, *Character Merchandising*, 4 Eur. Intell. Prop. Rev. 285 (1982); Waldheim, *Characters — May They Be Kidnapped?*, 55 Trademark Rep. 1022 (1965).

(3) Does § 43(a) of the Lanham Act supply a viable basis for protection in this area? *See* the section on Misrepresentation, *supra*, and Proctor, *Distinctive and Unusual Marketing Techniques: Are They Protectable Under Section 43(a) of The Lanham Act? Should They Be?*, 77 Trademark Rep. 4 (1987). The copying or imitation of a distinctive character created by another may result in liability under either unfair competition law or copyright law. Even when such copying does not facilitate the palming off of a particular product as that of the character's creator, § 43(a) of the Lanham Act may apply because the character itself has become associated with plaintiff or its product in the public mind. *See DC Comics, Inc. v. Filmation Associates*, 486 F. Supp 1273 (S.D.N.Y. 1980) (although "plaintiff's remedy more properly lies under the Copyright Act," defendant's animated television series using characters identical to those created by plaintiff infringed plaintiff's Lanham Act and state law rights in its characters; injunctive relief granted and damages awarded); *Frederick Warne & Co. v. Book Sales, Inc.*, 481 F. Supp. 1191, 1196–97 (S.D.N.Y. 1979); *Edgar Rice Burroughs, Inc. v. Manns Theatres*, 195 U.S.P.Q. 159 (C.D. Cal. 1976). In *DC Comics, Inc. v. Powers*, 465 F. Supp. 843 (S.D.N.Y. 1978), the defendant was preliminarily enjoined from titling its newspaper "Daily Planet" on the motion of the plaintiff owner of the rights in the Superman story, a story which includes a newspaper of that title. The court found that although plaintiff had never specifically licensed rights in that element of the Superman story, it had "demonstrated an association of . . . duration and consistency with the Daily Planet sufficient to establish a common law trademark therein." 465 F. Supp. at 847. Defendant's continued use of the title was found likely to cause irreparable injury to plaintiff, making injunctive relief necessary.

(4) The active market in licensing toys and other products based on created characters inevitably has led to attempts to manufacture and sell imitative products without license from, or payment to, the creators of the characters or their assignees. The Second and Seventh Circuit were both called upon to determine whether the sale of toy cars imitative of the distinctive "General Lee" Dodge Charger on the "Dukes of Hazzard" television series infringed the rights of the series' producer under § 43(a). Based in part upon plaintiff's evidence indicating that eight out of every ten children surveyed immediately associated defendant's toy car with the "General Lee" of the television show, the Second Circuit reversed the lower court's denial of plaintiff's motion for a preliminary injunction. The appellate court found that "many of the consumers . . . assumed that the car was sponsored by Warner Bros. This is sufficient to invoke the protection of this Court." *Warner Bros., Inc. v. Gay Toys, Inc.*, 658 F.2d 76, 79 (2d Cir. 1981). In a later decision the Seventh Circuit noted that the Second Circuit's references to consumer perception of direct sponsorship by plaintiff may have overstated the case: "it is sufficient if the public

assumes that the product comes from a single though anonymous, source." *Processed Plastic Co. v. Warner Communications*, 675 F.2d 852, 856 (7th Cir. 1982).

Compare Ideal Toy Corp. v. Kenner Products Div., 443 F. Supp. 291 (S.D.N.Y. 1977), where "Star Team" toys somewhat similar in appearance and theme to characters in the popular "Star Wars" movie were found not to infringe the rights of that movie's producer. On the copyright issue in the declaratory judgment action the court stated,

> The defendants have no more right to a monopoly in the theme of a black robed, helmeted, evil figure in outer space conflict with a humanoid and a smaller nonhumanoid robot than Shakespeare would have in the theme of a "riotous knight who kept wassail to the discomfort of the household," and who had conflicts with "a foppish steward who had become amorous of his mistress."

443 F. Supp. at 304. On the unfair competition issue it stated, "A finding of general 'association' — that the toys 'look like' the movie or remind someone of the movie — does not mean that the prospective purchaser thinks that the toys are derived from the movie or 'sponsored' by the movie." 443 F. Supp. at 308.

(5) The *De Costa* decision, *De Costa v. Columbia Broadcasting System, Inc.*, 520 F.2d 499 (1st Cir. 1975), *cert. denied*, 423 U.S. 1073 (1976) (relief denied creator of "Paladin" character against broadcasting company that based TV series on that character), was roundly criticized after it came down. Mr. DeCosta subsequently persisted in attempting to vindicate his rights. After the 1975 decision, he succeeded in obtaining a federal registration for the Paladin mark over CBS's opposition, the Trademark Trial and Appeal Board stating: "This seems to us to be a bald-face argument that opposer, already branded a pirate, should be allowed to make off with additional plunder unhindered by any inconvenience that might result from the recognition of applicant's lawful rights." *Columbia Broadcasting System, Inc. v. De Costa*, 192 U.S.P.Q. 453, 457 (T.T.A.B. 1976). In *DeCosta v. Viacom International, Inc.*, 758 F. Supp. 807 (D.R.I. 1991), the court found that CBS's assignment of its rights to defendant and De Costa's acquisition of trademark registrations created new "clusters of conduct" and new rights for De Costa justifying a new trial. A jury in the new trial then awarded De Costa $200,000. The First Circuit, however, reversed the district court and dismissed the case, holding De Costa was collaterally estopped by its prior decision. *DeCosta v. Viacom Int'l, Inc.*, 25 U.S.P.Q.2d 1187 (1st Cir. 1992).

§ 8.06   Right of Publicity

INTRODUCTION

The right of publicity is the exclusive right of an individual to the commercial exploitation of his or her identity, including name, likeness and other identity attributes. As the court stated in *Carson v. Here's Johnny Portable Toilets, Inc.*, 698 F.2d 831 (6th Cir. 1983): "A celebrity's right of publicity is invaded whenever his identity is intentionally misappropriated for commercial purposes." The right of publicity developed as an offshoot from the law of the right of privacy, under which a person's feelings and private affairs are afforded protection. *See* J. T. McCarthy, *Rights of Publicity And Privacy* §§ 1.5[D], 1.6 (1987).

Recognition of the right of publicity is a relatively recent legal development. It was first referred to as such in *Haelan Laboratories, Inc. v. Topps Chewing Gum, Inc.*, 202 F.2d 866 (2d Cir.), *cert. denied*, 346 U.S. 816 (1953). There the plaintiff had asserted an exclusive right to use baseball players' photographs in connection with the sales of plaintiffs' chewing gum. In recognizing the right, the court observed that ballplayers "would feel sorely deprived if they no longer received money for authorizing advertisements popularizing their countenances . . . .. This right of publicity would usually yield them no money unless it could be made the subject of an exclusive grant which barred any other advertiser from using their pictures." 202 F.2d at 868. *See also Pavesich v. New England Life Insurance Co.*, 50 S.E. 68 (Ga. 1905) (early case extending individual's right of privacy to the prevention of the unauthorized, nondefamatory advertising use of a name or likeness). *Cf. Roberson v. Rochester Folding Box Co.*, 64 N.E. 442 (N.Y. 1902) (rejecting common law right of privacy claim and permitting nonlibelous use of plaintiff's portrait on advertising posters).

Is the right of publicity more properly viewed as an economic incentive for the type of achievement that brings commercial value to a person's name or likeness, or as a means of preventing unjust enrichment by theft of goodwill? *See Zacchini v. Scripps-Howard Broadcasting Co.*, 433 U.S. 562 (1977). What difference might this make? If a court considers the right to be an economic incentive, and in the particular fact situation there is no deception as to source or sponsorship, a countervailing public interest in having information about the famous personality or in viewing performances or having souvenirs which evoke that personality might be found to outweigh the individual's right of publicity. If, however, the individual was deemed to have created a protectable goodwill subject to the individual's exclusive control, any commercial use by another of that goodwill without permission would be unjust enrichment if not an unlawful theft, presumably making a balancing test inapplicable.

Would the elimination of right of publicity law and the consequent economic benefits to the individual really affect the efforts individuals make to achieve fame, or act to reduce the number of persons willing to make the necessary effort? Should public acclaim result in an individual being protected from *any* unauthorized use of his or her name or likeness when the use has some commercial ramifications (e.g., use of a famous person's name in an novel or movie)? In the material that follows consider the function of, and the basis and necessity for, right of publicity law, and compare it with the law of unfair competition as discussed earlier in this chapter.

WHITE v. SAMSUNG ELECTRONICS AMERICA, INC.

United States Court of Appeals, Ninth Circuit
971 F.2d 1395 (1992)

GOODWIN, SENIOR CIRCUIT JUDGE.

. . . .

This case involves a promotional "fame and fortune" dispute. In running a particular advertisement without Vanna White's permission, defendants Samsung Electronics America, Inc. (Samsung) and David Deutsch Associates, Inc. (Deutsch) attempted to capitalize on White's fame to enhance their fortune. White sued, alleging infringement of various intellectual property rights, but the district court granted summary judgment in favor of the defendants. We affirm in part, reverse in part, and remand.

Plaintiff Vanna White is the hostess of "Wheel of Fortune," one of the most popular game shows in television history. An estimated forty million people watch the program daily. Capitalizing on the fame which her participation in the show has bestowed on her, White markets her identity to various advertisers.

The dispute in this case arose out of a series of advertisements prepared for Samsung by Deutsch. The series ran in an least half a dozen publications with widespread, and in some cases national, circulation. Each of the advertisements in the series followed the same theme. Each depicted a current item from popular culture and a Samsung electronic product. Each was set in the twenty-first century and conveyed the message that the Samsung product would still be in use by that time. By hypothesizing outrageous future outcomes for the cultural items, the ads created humorous effects. For example, one lampooned current popular notions of an unhealthy diet by depicting a raw steak with the caption: "Revealed to be health food. 2010 A.D." Another depicted irreverent "news"-show host Morton Downey Jr. in front of an American flag with the caption: "Presidential candidate. 2008 A.D."

The advertisement which prompted the current dispute was for Samsung videocassette recorders (VCRs). The ad depicted a robot, dressed in a wig, gown, and jewelry which Deutsch consciously selected to resemble White's hair and dress. The robot was posed next to a game board which is instantly recognizable as the Wheel of Fortune game show set, in a stance for which White is famous. The caption of the ad read: "Longest-running game show. 2012 A.D." Defendants referred to the ad as the "Vanna White" ad. Unlike the other celebrities used in the campaign, White neither consented to the ads nor was she paid.

. . .

I.   Section 3344

White first argues that the district court erred in rejecting her claim under [California Civil Code] § 3344. Section 3344(a) provides, in pertinent part, that "[a]ny person who knowingly uses another's name, voice, signature, photograph, or likeness, in any manner, . . . for purposes of advertising or selling, . . . without such person's prior consent . . . shall be liable for any damages sustained by the person or persons injured as a result thereof."

White argues that the Samsung advertisement used her "likeness" in contravention of § 3344. In *Midler v. Ford Motor Co.*, 849 F.2d 460 (9th Cir. 1988), this court rejected Bette Midler's § 3344 claim concerning a Ford television commercial in which a Midler "sound-alike" sang a song which Midler had made famous. In rejecting Midler's claim, this court noted that "[t]he defendants did not use Midler's name or anything else whose use is prohibited by the statute. The voice they used was [another person's], not hers. The term 'likeness' refers to a visual image not a vocal imitation." *Id.* at 463.

In this case, Samsung and Deutsch used a robot with mechanical features, and not, for example, a manikin molded to White's precise features. Without deciding for all purposes when a caricature or impressionistic resemblance might become a "likeness," we agree with the district court that the robot at issue here was not White's "likeness" within the meaning of § 3344. Accordingly, we affirm the court's dismissal of White's § 3344 claim.

II. Right of Publicity

White next argues that the district court erred in granting summary judgment to defendants on White's common law right of publicity claim. In *Eastwood v. Superior Court*, 149 Cal. App. 3d 409, 198 Cal. Rptr. 342 (1983), the California court of appeal stated that the common law right of publicity cause of action "may be pleaded by alleging (1) the defendant's use of the plaintiff's identity; (2) the appropriation of plaintiff's name or likeness to defendant's advantage, commercially or otherwise; (3) lack of consent; and (4) resulting injury." *Id.* at 417 (citing Prosser, *Law of Torts* (4th ed. 1971) § 117 pp. 804–807). The district court dismissed White's claim for failure to satisfy *Eastwood's* second prong, reasoning that defendants had not appropriated White's "name or likeness" with their robot ad. We agree that the robot ad did not make use of White's name or likeness. However, the common law right of publicity is not so confined.

    . . . .

Since Prosser's early formulation, the case law has borne out his insight that the right of publicity is not limited to the appropriation of name or likeness. In *Motschenbacher v. R.J. Reynolds Tobacco Co.*, 498 F.2d 821 (9th Cir. 1974), the defendant had used a photograph of the plaintiff's race car in a television commercial. Although the plaintiff appeared driving the car in the photograph, his features were not visible. Even though the defendant had not appropriated the plaintiff's name or likeness, this court held that plaintiff's California right of publicity claim should reach the jury.

In *Midler*, this court held that, even though the defendants had not used Midler's name or likeness, Midler had stated a claim for violation of her California common law right of publicity because "the defendants . . . for their own profit in selling their product did appropriate part of her identity" by using a Midler sound-alike. *Id.* at 463–64.

In *Carson v. Here's Johnny Portable Toilets, Inc.*, 698 F.2d 831 (6th Cir. 1983), the defendant had marketed portable toilets under the brand name "Here's Johnny" — Johnny Carson's signature "Tonight Show" introduction — without Carson's permission. The district court had dismissed Carson's Michigan common law right of publicity claim because the defendants had not used Carson's "name or likeness." *Id.* at 835. In reversing the district court, the sixth circuit found "the district court's conception of the right of publicity . . . too narrow" and held that the right was implicated because the defendant had appropriated Carson's identity by using, *inter alia*, the phrase "Here's Johnny." *Id.* at 835–37.

. . . .

Although the defendants in these cases avoided the most obvious means of appropriating the plaintiffs' identities, each of their actions directly implicated the commercial interests which the right of publicity is designed to protect. As the *Carson* court explained:

> [t]he right of publicity has developed to protect the commercial interest of celebrities in their identities. The theory of the right is that a celebrity's identity can be valuable in the promotion of products, and the celebrity has an interest that may be protected from the unauthorized commercial exploitation of that identity. . . . If the celebrity's identity is commercially exploited, there has been an invasion of his right whether or not his "name or likeness" is used.

Carson, 698 F.2d at 835. It is not important *how* the defendant has appropriated the plaintiff's identity, but *whether* the defendant has done so. *Motschenbacher*, *Midler*, and *Carson* teach the impossibility of treating the right of publicity as guarding only against a laundry list of specific means of appropriating identity. A rule which says that the right of publicity can be infringed only through the use of nine different methods of appropriating identity merely challenges the clever advertising strategist to come up with the tenth.

. . . .

Consider a hypothetical advertisement which depicts a mechanical robot with male features, an African-American complexion, and a bald head. The robot is wearing black hightop Air Jordan basketball sneakers, and a red basketball uniform with black trim, baggy shorts, and the number 23 (though not revealing "Bulls" or "Jordan" lettering). The ad depicts the robot dunking a basketball one-handed, stiff-armed, legs extended like open scissors, and tongue hanging out. Now envision that this ad is run on television during professional basketball games. Considered individually, the robot's physical attributes, its dress, and its stance tell us little. Taken together, they lead to the only conclusion that any sports viewer who has registered a discernible pulse in the past five years would reach: the ad is about Michael Jordan.

Viewed separately, the individual aspects of the advertisement in the present case say little. Viewed together, they leave little doubt about the celebrity the ad is meant to depict. The female-shaped robot is wearing a long gown, blond wig, and large jewelry. Vanna White dresses exactly like this at times, but so do many other women. The robot is in the process of turning a block letter on a game-board. Vanna

White dresses like this while turning letters on a game-board but perhaps similarly attired Scrabble-playing women do this as well. The robot is standing on what looks to be the Wheel of Fortune game show set. Vanna White dresses like this, turns letters, and does this on the Wheel of Fortune game show. She is the only one. Indeed, defendants themselves referred to their ad as the "Vanna White" ad. We are not surprised.

Television and other media create marketable celebrity identity value. Considerable energy and ingenuity are expended by those who have achieved celebrity value to exploit it for profit. The law protects the celebrity's sole right to exploit this value whether the celebrity has achieved her fame out of rare ability, dumb luck, or a combination thereof. We decline Samsung and Deutsch's invitation to permit the evisceration of the common law right of publicity through means as facile as those in this case. Because White has alleged facts showing that Samsung and Deutsch had appropriated her identity, the district court erred by rejecting, on summary judgment, White's common law right of publicity claim.

III.   The Lanham Act

. . . .

[T]he district court [also] erred in rejecting White's Lanham Act claim at the summary judgment stage. In so concluding, we emphasize two facts, however. First, construing the motion papers in White's favor, as we must, we hold only that White has raised a genuine issue of material fact concerning a likelihood of confusion as to her endorsement. *Cohen v. Paramount Pictures Corp.*, 845 F.2d 851, 852–53 (9th Cir. 1988). Whether White's Lanham Act claim should succeed is a matter for the jury. Second, we stress that we reach this conclusion in light of the peculiar facts of this case. In particular, we note that the robot ad identifies White and was part of a series of ads in which other celebrities participated and were paid for their endorsement of Samsung's products.

IV.   The Parody Defense

In defense, defendants cite of number of cases for the proposition that their robot ad constituted protected speech. The only cases they cite which are even remotely relevant to this case are *Hustler Magazine v. Falwell*, 485 U.S. 46 (1988) and *L.L. Bean, Inc. v. Drake Publishers, Inc.*, 811 F.2d 26 (1st Cir. 1987). Those cases involved parodies of advertisements run for the purpose of poking fun at Jerry Falwell and L.L. Bean, respectively. This case involves a true advertisement run for the purpose of selling Samsung VCRs. The ad's spoof of Vanna White and Wheel of Fortune is subservient and only tangentially related to the ad's primary message: "buy Samsung VCRs." Defendants' parody arguments are better addressed to non-commercial parodies. The difference between a "parody" and a "knock-off" is the difference between fun and profit.

. . . .

[Remanded].

WHITE v. SAMSUNG ELECTRONICS AMERICA, INC.

United States Court of Appeals, Ninth Circuit
989 F.2d 1512 (1993)

KOZINSKI, Circuit Judge, with whom Circuit Judges O'SCANNLAIN and KLEIN-
FELD join, dissenting from the order rejecting the suggestion for rehearing en banc.

I.

Saddam Hussein wants to keep advertisers from using his picture in unflattering
contexts. Clint Eastwood doesn't want tabloids to write about him. Rudolf Valen-
tino's heirs want to control his film biography. The Girl Scouts don't want their
image soiled by association with certain activities. George Lucas wants to keep
Strategic Defense Initiative fans from calling it "Star Wars." Pepsico doesn't want
singers to use the word "Pepsi" in their songs.**6** Guy Lombardo wants an exclusive

---

6 Pepsico Inc. claimed the lyrics and packaging of grunge rocker Tad Doyle's "Jack Pepsi"
song were "offensive to [it] and [. . .] likely to offend [its] customers," in part because they
"associate [Pepsico] and its Pepsi marks with intoxication and drunk driving." Deborah
Russell, *Doyle Leaves Pepsi Thirsty for Compensation*, Billboard, June 15, 1991, at 43.
Conversely, the Hell's Angels recently sued Marvel Comics to keep it from publishing a
comic book called "Hell's Angel," starring a character of the same name. Marvel settled by
paying $35,000 to charity and promising never to use the name "Hell's Angel" again in
connection with any of its publications. *Marvel, Hell's Angels Settle Trademark Suit*, L.A.
Daily J., Feb. 2, 1993, § II, at 1.

Trademarks are often reflected in the mirror of our popular culture. *See* Truman Capote,
Breakfast at Tiffany's (1958); Kurt Vonnegut, Jr., *Breakfast of Champions* (1973); Tom
Wolfe, *The Electric Kool-Aid Acid Test* (1968) (which, incidentally, includes a chapter on
the Hell's Angels); Larry Niven, *Man of Steel, Woman of Kleenex* in *All the Myriad Ways*
(1971); *Looking for Mr. Goodbar* (1977); *The Coca-Cola Kid* (1985) (using Coca-Cola as
a metaphor for American commercialism); *The Kentucky Fried Movie* (1977); *Harley
Davidson and the Marlboro Man* (1991); *The Wonder Years* (ABC 1988-present) ("Wonder
Years" was a slogan of Wonder Bread); Tim Rice and Andrew Lloyd Webber, *Joseph and
the Amazing Technicolor Dream Coat* (musical).

Hear Janis Joplin, *Mercedes Benz*, on *Pearl* (CBS 1971); Paul Simon, *Kodachrome*, on
There Goes Rhymin' Simon (Warner 1973); Leonard Cohen, *Chelsea Hotel*, on *The Best of
Leonard Cohen* (CBS 1975); Bruce Springsteen, *Cadillac Ranch*, on *The River* (CBS 1980);
Prince, *Little Red Corvette*, on *1999* (Warner 1982); dada, *Dizz Knee Land*, on *Puzzle* (IRS
1992) ("I just robbed a grocery store — I'm going to Disneyland/I just flipped off President
George — I'm going to Disneyland"); Monty Python, *Spam*, on *The Final Rip Off* (Virgin
1988); Roy Clark, *Thank God and Greyhound [You're Gone]*, on *Roy Clark's Greatest Hits
Volume I* (MCA 1979); Mel Tillis, *Coca-Cola Cowboy*, on *The Very Best of* (MCA 1981)
("You're just a Coca-Cola cowboy/You've got an Eastwood smile and Robert Redford
hair. . . .").

Dance to Talking Heads, *Popular Favorites 1976–92: Sand in the Vaseline* (Sire 1992);
Talking Heads, *Popsicle*, on *id. Admire* Andy Warhol, *Campbell's Soup Can. Cf.* REO
Speedwagon, 38 Special, and Jello Biafra of the Dead Kennedys.

property right to ads that show big bands playing on New Year's Eve. Uri Geller thinks he should be paid for ads showing psychics bending metal through telekinesis. Paul Prudhomme, that household name, thinks the same about ads featuring corpulent bearded chefs. And scads of copyright holders see purple when their creations are made fun of.

Something very dangerous is going on here. Private property, including intellectual property, is essential to our way of life. It provides an incentive for investment and innovation; it stimulates the flourishing of our culture; it protects the moral entitlements of people to the fruits of their labors. But reducing too much to private property can be bad medicine. Private land, for instance, is far more useful if separated from other private land by public streets, roads and highways. Public parks, utility rights-of-way and sewers reduce the amount of land in private hands, but vastly enhance the value of the property that remains.

So too it is with intellectual property. Overprotecting intellectual property is as harmful as underprotecting it. Creativity is impossible without a rich public domain. Nothing today, likely nothing since we tamed fire, is genuinely new: Culture, like science and technology, grows by accretion, each new creator building on the works of those who came before. Overprotection stifles the very creative forces it's supposed to nurture.

The panel's opinion is a classic case of overprotection. Concerned about what it sees as a wrong done to Vanna White, the panel majority erects a property right of remarkable and dangerous breadth: Under the majority's opinion, it's now a tort for advertisers to *remind* the public of a celebrity. Not to use a celebrity's name, voice, signature or likeness; not to imply the celebrity endorses a product; but simply to evoke the celebrity's image in the public's mind. This Orwellian notion withdraws far more from the public domain than prudence and common sense allow. It conflicts with the Copyright Act and the Copyright Clause. It raises serious First Amendment problems. It's bad law, and it deserves a long, hard second look.

. . . .

The majority isn't, in fact, preventing the "evisceration" of Vanna White's existing rights; it's creating a new and much broader property right, a right unknown in California law. It's replacing the existing balance between the interests of the celebrity and those of the public by a different balance, one substantially more favorable to the celebrity. Instead of having an exclusive right in her name, likeness, signature or voice, every famous person now has an exclusive right to *anything that reminds the viewer of her.* After all, that's all Samsung did. It used an inanimate object to remind people of White, to "evoke [her identity]." 971 F.2d at 1399.

Consider how sweeping this new right is. What is it about the ad that makes people think of White? It's not the robot's wig, clothes or jewelry; there must be ten million blond women (many of them quasi-famous) who wear dresses and jewelry like

---

The creators of some of these works might have gotten permission from the trademark owners, though it's unlikely Kool-Aid relished being connected with LSD, Hershey with homicidal maniacs, Disney with armed robbers, or Coca-Cola with cultural imperialism. Certainly no free society can *demand* that artists get such permission.

White's. It's that the robot is posed near the "Wheel of Fortune" game board. Remove the game board from the ad, and no one would think of Vanna White. *See* Appendix. But once you include the game board, anybody standing beside it — a brunette woman, a man wearing women's clothes, a monkey in a wig and gown — would evoke White's image, precisely the way the robot did. It's the "Wheel of Fortune" set, not the robot's face or dress or jewelry that evokes White's image. The panel is giving White an exclusive right not in what she looks like or who she is, but in what she does for a living.   *right for what she does for a living*

This is entirely the wrong place to strike the balance. Intellectual property rights aren't free: They're imposed at the expense of future creators and of the public at large. Where would we be if Charles Lindbergh had an exclusive right in the concept of a heroic solo aviator? If Arthur Conan Doyle had gotten a copyright in the idea of the detective story, or Albert Einstein had patented the theory of relativity? If every author and celebrity had been given the right to keep people from mocking them or their work? Surely this would have made the world poorer, not richer, culturally as well as economically.

This is why intellectual property law is full of careful balances between what's set aside for the owner and what's left in the public domain for the rest of us. The relatively short life of patents; the longer, but finite, life of copyrights; copyright's idea-expression dichotomy; the fair use doctrine; the prohibition on copyrighting facts; the compulsory license of television broadcasts and musical compositions; federal preemption of overbroad state intellectual property laws; the nominative use doctrine in trademark law; the right to make soundalike recordings. All of these diminish an intellectual property owner's rights. All let the public use something created by someone else. But all are necessary to maintain a free environment in which creative genius can flourish.

The intellectual property right created by the panel here has none of these essential limitations: No fair use exception; no right to parody; no idea-expression dichotomy. It impoverishes the public domain, to the detriment of future creators and the public at large. Instead of well-defined, limited characteristics such as name, likeness or voice, advertisers will now have to cope with vague claims of "appropriation of identity," claims often made by people with a wholly exaggerated sense of their own fame and significance. *See* pp. 1512–13 & notes 1–10 *supra*. Future Vanna Whites might not get the chance to create their personae, because their employers may fear some celebrity will claim the persona is too similar to her own. The public will be robbed of parodies of celebrities, and our culture will be deprived of the valuable safety valve that parody and mockery create.

. . . .

APPENDIX

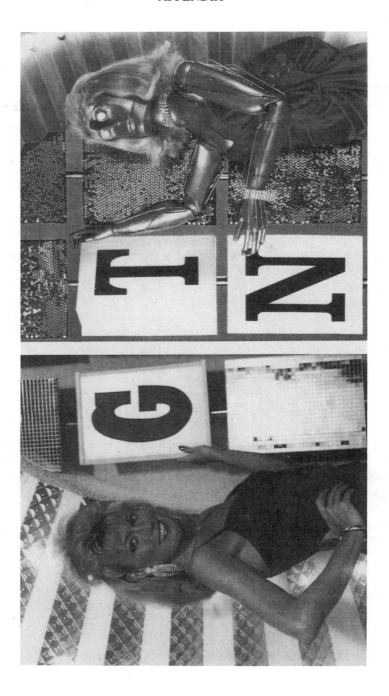

NOTES ON RIGHT OF PUBLICITY

(1) In *Zacchini v. Scripps-Howard Broadcasting Co.*, 433 U.S. 562 (1977), an Ohio television station had shown a film of the entirety of plaintiff's 15-second "human cannonball" circus act on a newscast. In holding that the First and Fourteenth Amendments did not require the state to privilege the press from liability under Ohio's right of publicity law, the Court observed (p. 573) that: "the state's interest in permitting a 'right of publicity', is . . . closely analogous to the goals of patent and copyright law, focusing on the right of the individual to reap the reward of his endeavors and having little to do with protecting feelings or reputation." The Court found that the broadcast went "to the heart of [plaintiff's] ability to earn a living as an entertainer" and therefore constituted "what may be the strongest case for a 'right of publicity' — involving, not the appropriation of an entertainer's reputation to enhance the attractiveness of a commercial product, but the appropriation of the very activity by which the entertainer acquired his reputation in the first place." *Id.* at 576. The Court referred to the prevention of "unjust enrichment by the theft of goodwill" as a rationale for protecting the right of publicity, but rested its decision on the basis of the state's legitimate interest in providing an economic incentive for entertainers "to make the investment required to produce a performance of interest to the public." *Id. See* Note, *Human Cannonballs and the First Amendment: Zacchini v. Scripps-Howard Broadcasting Co.*, 30 Stan. L. Rev. (1978).

(2) If the primary purpose of the unauthorized use is dissemination of ideas or information, the right of publicity may give way to the First Amendment. *Rosemont Enterprises, Inc. V. Random House, Inc.*, 58 Misc. 2d 1, 6 (N.Y. Sup. Ct. 1968), *aff'd*, 301 N.Y.S.2d 948 (App. Div. 1969) ("Just as a public figure's 'right of privacy' must yield to the public interest so too must the 'right of publicity' bow where such conflicts with the free dissemination of thought, ideas, newsworthy events, and matters of public interest"). *See, e.g., Rogers v. Grimaldi*, 875 F.2d 994 (2d Cir. 1989) (right of publicity will not bar use of celebrity's name in a movie title unless it is "wholly unrelated" or simply a disguised advertisement for collateral goods or services); *Hicks v. Casablanca Records*, 464 F. Supp. 426 (S.D.N.Y. 1978) (no liability for novel and movie portrayal of fictionalized account of incident in author Agatha Christie's life). *Compare Elvis Presley Enterprises, Inc. v. Elvisly Yours, Inc.*, 936 F.2d 889 (6th Cir. 1991) (scope of injunction limited to prohibit only unauthorized *commercial* use of Elvis Presley's name, image or likeness, as opposed to *all* use).

The protected informational content, furthermore, need not have great social or political significance. *Ann-Margret v. High Soc. Magazine, Inc.*, 498 F. Supp. 401 (S.D.N.Y. 1980) (no liability for use of semi-nude photograph of actress; First Amendment protection applies even when media is being "trivial or . . . obnoxious"); *Lerman v. Flynt Distributing Co.*, 745 F.2d 123, 128 (2d Cir. 1984), *cert. denied*, 471 U.S. 1054 (1985) (no liability for nude photograph of person misidentified as plaintiff); *Paulsen v. Personality Posters, Inc.*, 299 N.Y.S.2d 501, 506 (N.Y. Sup. Ct. 1968) (no liability for selling unlicensed poster of comedian-presidential candidate Pat Paulsen).

Conversely, where the predominant purpose of the use is commercial, First Amendment rights may give way to a plaintiff's right of publicity. *Tellado v. Time-Life Books, Inc.*, 643 F. Supp. 904, 910, 913 (D.N.J. 1986) (defendant's motion for summary judgment denied; First Amendment claim rejected where defendant's use of a photograph of plaintiff veteran to advertise a book series on the Viet Nam War appeared to be a "predominantly commercial" use designed to "stimulate profits"); *Mendonsa v. Time, Inc.*, 678 F. Supp. 967, 971–72 (D.R.I. 1988) (original magazine publication of famous "kissing sailor" photograph featuring plaintiff on V-J Day was protected by First Amendment, but plaintiff stated a publicity cause of action for the magazine's subsequent offer to sell readers copies of the photograph for $1,600 each).

First Amendment considerations aside, if the commercial benefit from the use is only incidentally or indirectly commercial, then a commercial purpose is not predominant, and the use is lawful. *Benavidez v. Anheuser Busch, Inc.*, 873 F.2d 102 (5th Cir. 1989) (increased goodwill Anheuser-Busch might obtain via war hero documentary with Anheuser-Busch's name at the end of the credits was only incidental and insufficiently commercial to warrant publicity relief); *Faloona v. Hustler Magazine, Inc.*, 607 F. Supp. 1341, 1360 (N.D. Tex. 1985), *aff'd*, 799 F.2d 1000 (5th Cir. 1986), *cert. denied*, 479 U.S. 1088 (1987); *Valentine v. CBS, Inc.*, 698 F.2d 430, 433 (11th Cir. 1983); *Delan v. CBS, Inc.*, 458 N.Y.S.2d 608, 613 (App. Div. 1983).

See generally Coyne, *Toward a Modified Fair Use Defense In Right of Publicity Cases*, 29 Wm. & Mary L. Rev. 781 (1988).

(3) How does right of publicity law differ from unfair competition law and § 43(a) of the Lanham Act? *Compare Carson v. Here's Johnny Portable Toilets, Inc.*, 698 F.2d 831 (6th Cir. 1983) (Johnny Carson's right of publicity held invaded by the intentional appropriation of his identity ("Here's Johnny") for use in connection with defendant's corporate name and product but lower court's holding of no § 43(a) violation affirmed) *with Allen v. National Video, Inc.*, 610 F. Supp. 612 (S.D.N.Y. 1985) (Woody Allen look-alike held liable under § 43(a) without resolving publicity claims under New York's statute). *See also* Goldman, *Elvis Is Alive, But He Shouldn't Be: The Right of Publicity Revisited*, 1992 B.Y.U. L. Rev. 597 (1992) (arguing celebrities should not have their right of publicity protected unless confusion is likely). Should a plaintiff asserting violation of his right of publicity be required to show an identifiable economic loss? *See Estate of Presley v. Russen*, 513 F. Supp. 1339 (D.N.J. 1981) ("Because the doctrine of the right of publicity emphasizes the protection of the commercial value of the celebrity's name or likeness, the plaintiff must demonstrate sufficiently that the defendant's use . . . has or is likely to result in an identifiable economic loss," the court noting in particular the absence of a public deception element in right of publicity claims); *Bi-Rite Enterprises, Inc. v. Button Master*, 555 F. Supp. 1188 (S.D.N.Y. 1983), *Supp. Opinion*, 578 F. Supp. 59 (S.D.N.Y. 1983) (damages).

In *Nurmi v. Peterson*, 10 U.S.P.Q.2d 1775 (C.D. Cal. 1989), plaintiff's publicity claim was dismissed because she did not claim that the actual features of her VAMPIRA character, a 1950's horror movie TV hostess, had been used for commercial purposes, but only that defendant had created a new character that resembled VAMPIRA. *Compare Nurmi* with the *White* decision, *supra*, in which, arguably, a "resemblance" of Vanna White was used for commercial purposes. *See* Gigliotti, *Beyond Name and Likeness: Should California's Expansion of the Right of Publicity Protect Non-Human Identity*, 83 Trademark Rep. 64 (1993) (analyzing the *White* decision).

(4) Should commercial use of an imitation of a professional entertainer's style of vocal delivery create liability for unfair competition or right of publicity infringement? *See Lahr v. Adell Chem. Co.*, 300 F.2d 256 (1st Cir. 1962) (cartoon duck with Bert Lahr's voice enjoined). *Cf. Sinatra v. Goodyear Tire & Rubber Co.*, 435 F.2d 711 (9th Cir. 1970), *cert. denied*, 402 U.S. 906 (1971) (tire advertisement featuring Nancy Sinatra's rendition of "These Boots Are Made For Walking"); *Booth v. Colgate-Palmolive Co.*, 362 F. Supp. 343 (S.D.N.Y. 1973) (voice for "Hazel" cartoon character in a television commercial imitated the voice developed and made famous by plaintiff in the "Hazel" television series). $2.6 million was awarded to singer Tom Waits in *Waits v. Frito-Lay*, 1992 U.S. App. LEXIS 27031 (9th Cir. 1992), *cert. denied*, 113 S. Ct. 1047 (1993), where defendant's use of an imitation of his distinctive voice in a snack food commercial constituted voice misappropriation and also violated § 43(a), and in *Midler v. Ford Motor Co.*, 849 F.2d 460 (9th Cir. 1988), *cert. denied*, 112 S. Ct. 1513 (1992), Bette Midler's unfair competition claims were rejected but use of an imitation of her voice in a car commercial constituted common law misappropriation.

(5) As discussed above, the right of publicity exists only under state statutory and common law. Some states, like New York, statutorily restrict the scope of the right of publicity. *See Stephano v. News Group Publications, Inc.*, 474 N.E.2d 580 (N.Y. 1984) (protection restricted to names and likenesses). Other states, generally through their courts, have been more expansive, so that commercial use of any attribute, characteristic or object associated by the public with the individual may be actionable. *See, e.g., Carson v. Here's Johnny Portable Toilets, Inc.*, 698 F.2d 831 (6th Cir. 1983) (phrase "Here's Johnny" associated with celebrity Johnny Carson). Because the right of publicity exists under state rather than federal law, conflict of law principles often must be applied in publicity cases. *See, e.g., Groucho Marx Productions, Inc. v. Day & Night Co.*, 689 F.2d 317, 319–20 (2d Cir. 1982); *Bi-Rite Enterprises, Inc. v. Bruce Miner Co.*, 757 F.2d 440 (1st Cir. 1985) (considering British and American law).

(6) Is the right of publicity a property right? Should it be assignable? Should the right survive the death of the person originally possessing it? *See Martin Luther King, Jr., Center for Social Change v. American Heritage Products, Inc.*, 694 F.2d 674 (11th Cir. 1983); *Acme Circus Operating Co. v. Kuperstock*, 711 F.2d 1538 (11th Cir. 1983) (applying California law); *Estate of Presley, supra* (New Jersey law); *Price v. Hal Roach Studios, Inc.*, 400 F. Supp. 836, 844 (S.D.N.Y. 1975). *Compare Reeves v. United Artists*, 572 F. Supp. 1231 (N.D. Ohio 1983), *aff'd*, 765 F.2d 79 (6th Cir. 1985); *Lugosi v. Universal Pictures*, 160 Cal. Rptr. 323, 329 (Cal. 1979) ("We hold that the right to exploit name and likeness is personal to the artist and must be exercised, if at all, by him during his lifetime"); *but see* Cal. Civ. Code § 990; 1 Gilson, *Trademark Protection and Practice*, § 2.15 (1984 ed.).

In *Memphis Development Foundation v. Factors Etc., Inc.*, 616 F.2d 956 (6th Cir. 1980), a declaratory judgment action, the plaintiff non-profit foundation had solicited contributions for a large statue of Elvis Presley to be erected in Memphis, and had given contributors small pewter replicas of the statue in exchange for contributions of $25 or more. Defendant licensee of the deceased Presley's right of publicity sought to enjoin distribution of the replicas, claiming that they were actually being sold for $25 a piece. Having to determine the descendibility of the right of publicity under Tennessee law in the absence of precedent in that state, the court reviewed the question in the light of such factors as "policy considerations" and "moral presuppositions." 616 F.2d at 958. It observed (616 F.2d at 959):

> Fame is an incident of . . . strong [psychological] motivation. . . . The desire to exploit fame for the commercial advantage of one's heirs is by contrast a weak principle of motivation. . . .

> On the other hand, there are strong reasons for declining to recognize the inheritability of the right. A whole set of practical problems of judicial line-drawing would arise should the court recognize such an inheritable right. How long would the "property" interest last? Is the right of publicity taxable? At what point does the right collide with the right of free expression guaranteed by the first amendment? Does the right apply to elected officials and military heroes whose fame was gained on the public payroll, as well as to movie stars, singers and athletes?. . . .

> . . . .

> . . . The intangible and shifting nature of fame and celebrity status, the presence of widespread public and press participation in its creation, the unusual psychic rewards and income that often flow from it during life and the fact that it may be created by bad as well as good conduct combine to create serious reservations about making fame the permanent right of a few individuals to the exclusion of the general public. Heretofore, the law has always thought that leaving a good name to one's children is sufficient reward in itself for the individual, whether famous or not. Commercialization of this virtue after death in the hands of heirs is contrary to our legal tradition and somehow seems contrary to the moral presuppositions of our culture.

(7) Should the right of publicity survive after death only *if* the decedent commercially exploited his identity in promoting products or services during his lifetime? Should it only attach, in a manner analogous to trademark use, to those types of products or services actually promoted by the decedent? *See Groucho Marx Productions v. Day and Night Co.*, 689 F.2d 317, 323 (2d Cir. 1982) ("Even if there is a limited descendible right [under California law], applicable to a product or service promoted by the celebrity, the defendants are not using the names or likeness of the Marx brothers in connection with any product or service that the comedians promoted during their lives"; plaintiffs held not protected against production of original play using the Marx Brothers' likenesses and comedic style). *Compare Martin Luther King*, *supra* Note (6), at page 683, where the court stated that,

> The net result of following [such cases] would be to say that celebrities and public figures have the right of publicity during their lifetimes (as others have

the right of publicity), but only those who contract for bubble gum cards, posters and tee shirts have a descendible right of publicity upon their deaths . . . we find no reason to protect after death only those who took commercial advantage of their fame.

See also *Hicks v. Casablanca Records*, 464 F. Supp. 426, 429 (S.D.N.Y. 1978) ("it would appear that a party claiming the right must establish that the decedent acted in such a way as to evidence his or her own recognition of the extrinsic commercial value of his or her name or likeness, and manifested that recognition in some overt manner, e.g., making *inter vivos* transfer of the rights in the name . . . or posing for bubble gum cards. . . ."); Note, *An Assessment of the Commercial Exploitation Requirement as a Limit on the Right of Publicity*, 96 Harv. L. Rev. 1703 (1983).

(8) At least twelve states have statutes which provide protection for the right of publicity: California, Florida, Kentucky, Massachusetts, Nebraska, New York, Oklahoma, Rhode Island, Tennessee, Texas, Virginia and Wisconsin. Additionally, Connecticut, Georgia, Hawaii, Illinois, Michigan, Missouri, New Jersey, Ohio, Pennsylvania, and Utah courts have recognized a common law right of publicity. At least nine states provide by statute that the right may pass to heirs: California, Florida, Kentucky, Nebraska, Nevada, Oklahoma, Tennessee, Texas (recognizing *only* a post-mortem right), and Virginia. *See generally* McCarthy, *Right of Publicity and Privacy*, Chapter 6 (1993 ed.).

(9) Should the right of publicity extend only to natural persons? The determination may rest in part on the privacy/property distinction in the nature of the right. One plaintiff recently was unsuccessful in asserting such a right in its corporate trademark, "Eagle's Eye," for the sale and manufacture of women's clothing. *The Eagle's Eye, Inc. v. Ambler Fashion Shop, Inc.*, 227 U.S.P.Q. 1018, 1022 (E.D. Pa. 1985). It remains to be seen whether the right of publicity might apply to a more famous corporate trademark embodying a more recognizable "persona" than that presented in *Eagle's Eye*. *See* Winner, *Right of Identity: Right of Publicity and Protection for a Trademark's "Persona"*, 71 Trademark Rep. 193(1981).

(10) Could an entertainer's name function as a service mark? This question was answered in the affirmative in *Five Platters, Inc. v. Purdie*, 419 F. Supp. 372 (D. Md. 1976) (entertainment provided by singing group The Platters); *In re Carson*, 197 U.S.P.Q. 554 (T.T.A.B. 1977) (entertainment provided by comedian and talk show host Johnny Carson); and *Estate of Presley v. Russen, supra*. *See also* Heneghan & Wansley, *The Service Mark Alternative to the Right of Publicity: Estate of Presley v. Russen*, 14 Pac. L.J. 181 (1983).

(11) An assertion of publicity rights can come into conflict with the copyright law. In *Baltimore Orioles, Inc. v. Major League Baseball Players Ass'n*, 805 F.2d 663 (7th Cir. 1986), *cert. denied*, 480 U.S 941 (1989), the Seventh Circuit held that the right of publicity claims of professional baseball players concerning their televised on-field performances were preempted by the Copyright Act. *Compare Midler v. Ford Motor Co.*, 849 F.2d 460 (9th Cir. 1988), *cert. denied*, 112 S. Ct. 1513 (1992), in which the Ninth Circuit rejected a copyright preemption argument and granted relief under the common law of misappropriation to a professional

singer whose distinctive and widely known voice was imitated in a television commercial.

(12) Articles discussing the right of publicity include: Bloom, *Preventing the Misappropriation of Identity: Beyond the Right of Publicity*, 13 Hastings Comm. & Ent. L.J. 489 (1991); Armstrong, *The Reification of Celebrity: Persona as Property*, 51 La. L. Rev. 443 (1991); McCarthy, *Public Personas and Private Property: The Commercialization of Human Identity*, 79 Trademark Rep. 681 (1989); Dewey, *The Evolving Doctrine of Right of Publicity: Judicial Protection of A Celebrity's Pecuniary Interest from Commercial Exploitation of His or Her Identity and Theatrical Style*, 22 Creighton L. Rev. 39 (1988); Ropski, *The Right of Publicity and the Celebrity Look-Alike*, 77 Trademark Rep. 31 (1987); Halpern, *The Right of Publicity: Commercial Exploitation of the Associative Value of Personality*, 39 Vand. L. Rev. 1199 (1986); Hoffman, *Limitations on the Right of Publicity*, 28 Bull. Copyright Soc'y 111 (1980); Felcher & Rubin, *Privacy, Publicity and the Portrayal of Real People by the Media*, 88 Yale L.J. 1577 (1979); Gordon, *Right of Property in Name, Likeness, Personality and History*, 55 Nw. U.L. Rev. 553 (1960).

§ 8.07 Passing Off

INTRODUCTION

The term "passing off," as used in Great Britain and in some of the older American cases, is synonymous with trade identity unfair competition. In the United States today the term "passing off" means unexplained substitution of the product of one party on calls for that of another, and it will be enjoined as unfair competition. Although passing off is frequently accomplished with the assistance of deceptive or confusingly similar trade identity devices, it may be, and often is, practiced without benefit of such aids and accessories.

WILLIAM R. WARNER & CO. v. ELI LILLY & CO.

United States Supreme Court
265 U.S. 526 (1924)

MR. JUSTICE SUTHERLAND.

[Respondent manufactured a chocolate-flavored liquid quinine preparation called Coco-Quinine, and sought to enjoin petitioner's manufacture and sale of a similar preparation under the name of Quin-Coco, charging trademark infringement and unfair competition. The Court found no infringement because respondent's mark was merely descriptive, and hereafter treats the remaining issue of unfair competition.]

(Matthew Bender & Co., Inc.)

No infring:
b/c descriptive

The use of chocolate as an ingredient has a three-fold effect: It imparts to the preparation a distinctive color and a distinctive flavor, and, to some extent, operates as a medium to suspend the quinine and prevent its precipitation. It has no therapeutic value; but it supplies the mixture with a quality of palatability for which there is no equally satisfactory substitute. Respondent, by laboratory experiments, first developed the idea of the addition of chocolate to the preparation for the purpose of giving it a characteristic color and an agreeable flavor. There was at the time no liquid preparation of quinine on the market containing chocolate, though there is evidence that it was sometimes so made up by druggists when called for. There is some evidence that petitioner endeavored by experiments to produce a preparation of the exact color and taste of that produced by respondent; and there is evidence in contradiction. We do not, however, regard it as important to determine upon which side lies the greater weight. Petitioner, in fact, did produce a preparation by the use of chocolate so exactly like that of respondent that they were incapable of being distinguished by ordinary sight or taste. By various trade methods an extensive and valuable market for the sale of respondent's preparation already had been established when the preparation of petitioner was put on the market. It is apparent, from a consideration of the testimony, that the efforts of petitioner to create a market for Quin-Coco were directed not so much to showing the merits of that preparation as they were to demonstrating its practical identity with Coco-Quinine, and, since it was sold at a lower price, inducing the purchasing druggist, in his own interest, to substitute, as far as he could, the former for the latter. In other words, petitioner sought to avail itself of the favorable repute which had been established for respondent's preparation in order to sell its own. Petitioner's salesmen appeared more anxious to convince the druggist with whom they were dealing that Quin-Coco was a good substitute for Coco-Quinine and was cheaper, than they were to independently demonstrate its merits. The evidence establishes by a fair preponderance that some of petitioner's salesmen suggested that, without danger of detection, prescriptions and orders for Coco-Quinine could be filled by substituting Quin-Coco. More often, however, the feasibility of such a course was brought to the mind of the druggist by pointing out the identity of the two preparations and the enhanced profit to be made by selling Quin-Coco because of its lower price. There is much conflict in the testimony; but on the whole it fairly appears that petitioner's agents induced the substitution, either in direct terms or by suggestion or insinuation. Sales to druggist are in original bottles bearing clearly distinguishing labels and there is no suggestion of deception in those transactions; but sales to the ultimate purchasers are of the product in its naked form out of the bottle; and the testimony discloses many instances of passing off by retail druggists of petitioner's preparation when respondent's preparation was called for. That no deception was practiced on the retail dealers, and that they knew exactly what they were getting is of no consequence. The wrong was in designedly enabling the dealers to palm off the preparation as that of the respondent. *Coca Cola v. Gay-Ola Co.*, 200 Fed. 720; *N.K. Fairbank Co. v. R. W Bell Manuf'g. Co.*, 77 Fed. 869, 875, 877–878; *Lever v. Goodwin*, L. R. 38 Ch. Div. 1, 3; *Enoch Morgan's Sons Co. v. Whittier-Coburn Co.*, 118 Fed. 657, 661. One who induces another to commit a fraud and furnishes the means of consummating it is equally guilty and liable for the injury. *Hostetter Co. v. Brueggeman-Reinert Distilling Co.*, 46 Fed. 188, 189.

The charge of unfair competition being established, it follows that equity will afford relief by injunction to prevent such unfair competition for the future. . . .

. . . .

Reversed.

THE COCA-COLA CO. v. SCRIVNER

United States District Court, Southern District of California
117 U.S.P.Q. 394 (1958)

CLARKE, DISTRICT JUDGE.

. . . .

In response to calls for Coca-Cola and Coke in their places of business, defendants, and each of them, have sold, substituted, and passed off Pepsi-Cola, a beverage similar in appearance to plaintiff's but which is not plaintiff's beverage, without oral explanation or comment and without taking any other effective action to inform the purchaser at the time of the sale of the identity of the merchandise he was receiving, and unless restrained will continue to do so.

Such substitution and "passing off" was and is likely to deceive the general public and the individual members thereof and has in fact deceived the general public. . . .

. . . .

The defendants did not discharge their duty to deliver Coca-Cola to customers who ordered this product or to give them adequate notice in fact that the various printed signs, decals, menus, described in the evidence, were not sufficient to bring home such notice to the customers with the result that such customers, or many of them, were misled into accepting Pepsi-Cola when they had ordered Coca-Cola and expected to get Coca-Cola.

Defendants introduced evidence to show that their employees had been instructed to explain to customers that they were not selling Coca-Cola, but with minor exception, if any, the employees did not carry out the instructions. After the defendants were warned orally and in writing by plaintiff of the substitutions at defendants' several places of business, the defendants, and each of them, failed to take the necessary, appropriate and effective steps to put an end to the substitution and the practice, of substituting Pepsi-Cola on orders for Coca-Cola and Coke after such warnings continued at the same high rate as prevailed before the warnings.

. . . .

Plaintiff is entitled·to a permanent injunction restraining defendants and each of them, their agents, attorneys, employees, servants, representatives and assigns and against all persons acting by or under their authority, from selling or offering for sale in response for calls or orders for "Coca-Cola" or "Coke," Pepsi-Cola or any product not the plaintiff's without at that time giving the customer actual notice that he is being sold merchandise other than the plaintiff's, and from continuing to rely on the procedures shown to have been followed by the defendants and herein found by the Court to be inadequate to protect the public from passing off. . . .

. . . .

NOTES ON PASSING OFF

Isn't this fraud?

(1) Does passing off constitute trademark infringement? Is it simply an overt act of fraud? *Cf. Singer Mfg. Co. v. Golden*, 171 F.2d 266 (7th Cir. 1948); *Accurate Leather & Novelty Co. v. LTD Commodities*, 18 U.S.P.Q.2d 1327 (N.D. Ill. 1990) (preliminarily enjoining defendant's catalog use of a photograph of plaintiff's handbag to sell defendant's inferior handbag); *L'Aiglon Apparel, Inc. v. Lana Lobell, Inc.*, 214 F.2d 649 (3d Cir. 1954), in the section on Misrepresentation, *supra*. Is wrongful intent a necessary element for a passing off cause of action? *See Venetianaire Corp. v. A&P Import Co.*, 302 F. Supp. 156 (S.D.N.Y. 1969), *aff'd*, 429 F.2d 1079 (2d Cir. 1969); *compare* the *Coca-Cola* case, *supra*. Or is passing off unfair competition in its most elementary form, whether it be simple, unaided substitution (the *Coca-Cola* case), or encouraged and invited substitution (the *Warner* case, *supra*)?

(2) In the *Warner* case, *supra,* the defendant encouraged or enabled passing off by placing the instruments of fraud in the hands of the retailer. *See also Inwood Laboratories v. Ives Laboratories*, 454 U.S. 844 (1982); *Upjohn Co. v. Schwartz*, 246 F.2d 254 (2d Cir. 1957). Must the retailer police the activities of its agents and employees as to passing off when it can be anticipated? *See Scotch Whiskey Ass'n v. Barton Distilling Co.*, 170 U.S.P.Q. 455 (N.D. Ill. 1971), *aff'd*, 179 U.S.P.Q. 712 (7th Cir. 1973). Note that in the *Warner* and *Scotch Whiskey Ass'n* cases, passing off should have been anticipated by the defendants both because of their own enabling acts and the reasonably probable conduct of their distributor customers. What preventive steps by the retailer are necessary once the existence of passing off has been brought to his attention? *See Coca-Cola, supra*.

(3) "Passing off" or "palming off" occurs when one party attempts to sell his goods or services under the trademark or trade dress of another. A different form of unfair competition has been found to occur when there is a resale of purchased goods by the purchaser, after removal of the original trademark and the substitution of a trademark of the purchaser's choosing. Such conduct has been termed "reverse passing [or palming] off." Since the original trademark owner made its profit on the initial sale, the damage to it from such resales is not at once apparent. One court described the injury in this manner:

> in reverse palming off cases, the originator of the misidentified product is involuntarily deprived of the advertising value of its name and of the goodwill that otherwise would stem from public knowledge of the true source of the

satisfactory product. . . . The ultimate purchaser is also deprived of knowing the true source of the product and may even be deceived into believing that it comes from another source.

Smith v. Montoro, 648 F.2d 602 (9th Cir. 1981).

Accordingly, one may not lawfully place one's own trademark on another's product for such deceptive resales, nor may one use such a rebranded product as a sample for sales of one's own product. *FRA S.p.A., v. SURG-O-FLEX of America, Inc.*, 415 F. Supp. 607 (S.D.N.Y. 1976); *Matsushita Electric Corp. v. Solar Sounds Systems, Inc.*, 381 F. Supp. 64, 67 (S.D.N.Y. 1974) ("The use of a misbranded product in soliciting orders for a different product seems as clear a 'false designation of origin' as could be conceived"). *See also F.E.L. Publications, Ltd. v. Catholic Bishop of Chicago*, 214 U.S.P.Q. 409 (7th Cir. 1982); *Nike, Inc. v. Rubber Manufacturers Ass'n*, 509 F. Supp. 919 (S.D.N.Y. 1981); *John Wright, Inc. v. Casper Corp.*, 419 F. Supp. 292, 325 (E.D. Pa. 1976), *aff'd in relevant part sub. nom. Donsco, Inc. v. Casper Corp.*, 587 F.2d 602 (3d Cir. 1978). *Compare Commodore Import Co. v. Hiroka*, 422 F. Supp. 628 (S.D.N.Y. 1976); *PIC Design Corp. v. Sterling Precision Instrument Corp.*, 231 F. Supp. 628 (S.D.N.Y. 1964) (defendant had only removed the original trademark without rebranding the goods, therefore there was no false designation or origin).

(4) Of course, by definition, generic terms normally are not entitled to trademark protection since they have come to signify goods rather than source. Protection may be had, however, from another's deceptive use of the term if the competitor is using it to help pass off his product as that of the generic term user. *See Technical Publishing Co. v. Lebhor-Friedman, Inc.*, 729 F.2d 1136 (7th Cir. 1984); *Miller Brewing Co. v. Joseph Schlitz Brewing Co.*, 605 F.2d 990, 997 (7th Cir. 1979) ("The absence of trademark protection [for LITE for beer] does not mean that Miller must submit to a competitor's palming off of its product as the product of Miller"). Such passing off will typically occur via misleading advertising involving use of the generic term. *See, e.g., Leon Finker, Inc. v. Schlussel*, 469 F. Supp. 674 (S.D.N.Y. 1979), and *Eastern Airlines, Inc. v. New York Airlines, Inc.*, 218 U.S.P.Q. 71 (S.D.N.Y. 1983). Or it may result from the concurrent blatant imitation of the product itself; *see Metric & Multistandard Components v. Metric's Inc.*, 635 F.2d 710 (8th Cir. 1980).

CHAPTER 9

JURISDICTION AND REMEDIES

§ 9.01 Jurisdiction

INTRODUCTION

Trade identity cases usually can be brought in either the federal or state courts. *Dell Publishing Co. v. Stanley Publications, Inc.*, 172 N.E.2d 656 (N.Y. 1961). Most are brought in the federal courts, and those involving the federal trademark statute or diversity plus jurisdictional amount are removable to the federal courts. *Vitarroz Corp. v. Borden, Inc.*, 644 F.2d 960, 964 (2d Cir. 1981); *Deat v. Joseph Swantak, Inc.*, 619 F. Supp. 973, 977 (N.D.N.Y. 1985); *Rossi, Turecamo & Co. v. Best Resume Service, Inc.*, 497 F. Supp. 437, 438 (S.D. Fla. 1980). The federal courts also have supplemental jurisdiction over state law claims "joined with a substantial and related claim" under the Lanham Act. *Quality Chekd Dairy Products Assn. v. Gillette Dairy*, 337 F. Supp. 239 (D. S.D. 1971). Set forth below are controlling statutory provisions affording federal jurisdiction in trade identity unfair competition cases:

15 U.S.C. § 1121

The Lanham Act

(a) The district and territorial courts of the United States shall have original jurisdiction, the circuit courts of appeal of the United States (other than the United States Court of Appeals for the Federal Circuit) shall have appellate jurisdiction, of all actions arising under this Act, without regard to the amount in controversy or to diversity or lack of diversity of the citizenship of the parties.

28 U.S.C. § 1338

Patents, Plant Variety Protection, Mask Works, Trade-marks And Unfair Competition

(a) The district courts shall have original jurisdiction of any civil action arising under any Act of Congress relating to patents, plant variety protection, copyrights and trade-marks. Such jurisdiction shall be exclusive of the courts of the states in patent, plant variety protection and copyright cases.

[handwritten: It does not mention trademarks —]

(b) The district courts shall have original jurisdiction of any civil action asserting a claim of unfair competition when joined with a substantial and related claim under the copyright, patent, plant variety protection or trade-mark laws.

If diversity of citizenship exists between the parties and the matter in controversy exceeds $50,000 in value, federal jurisdiction also may be had under 28 U.S.C. § 1332.

Federal jurisdiction over litigation involving the infringement of a federal trademark registration, unfair competition, dilution, and deceptive trade practices is often based upon all of these statutes. When foreign commerce is involved, 28 U.S.C. § 1331 may also provide a basis for federal jurisdiction.

COCA-COLA CO. v. STEWART

United States Court of Appeals, Eighth Circuit
621 F.2d 287 (1980)

BRIGHT, CIRCUIT JUDGE.

. . . .

Coca-Cola Co. brought suit against the Stewart defendants on September 13, 1972, after its investigators had ordered Coca-Cola or Coke on thirty-five occasions at the Stewarts' restaurants in Riverside, Missouri, and on each occasion had received another product. Coca-Cola Co. filed suit against the Morans on March 12, 1973, after its investigation showed that on twenty-six of twenty-seven occasions when investigators ordered Coca-Cola or Coke at the Morans' Mexican restaurants in Kansas City, another cola product was substituted. On November 22, 1972, and May 4, 1973, final judgments of injunction were entered by consent in these cases.

In order to ascertain whether the appellees were honoring the terms of the injunctions, that is, whether they had ceased passing off substitute products as Coke, the appellant conducted further investigations between 1973 and 1975. These investigations revealed that, in the case of the Stewarts, a product other than Coca-Cola was substituted in response to thirty-one out of thirty-seven orders for Coca-Cola or Coke. In the case of the Morans, another product was substituted in twenty-five out of twenty-seven instances.

On October 14, 1975, appellant filed accusations of civil contempt against appellees. Because appellant sought punitive sanctions, the district court denied its motions and directed that it follow the procedures set forth in Fed. R. Crim. P. 42(b). Appellant then applied for an order directing appellees to show cause why contempt proceedings should not be commenced, filing affidavits in support of its application.

The district court, in a memorandum and order to show cause filed January 6, 1976, found "that there exists reasonable cause to believe that [its] injunctive orders . . . have been violated."

Shortly thereafter, the district court on its own motion directed the parties to brief the issue of the court's subject-matter jurisdiction. On May 9, 1979, the district court issued a memorandum and order dismissing appellant's suits. The court held first that the alleged infringement had not occurred "in commerce," as required by the Lanham Act. *See* 15 U.S.C. § 1114(1)(a) (1976). The court found that there was no evidence that the alleged substitution of some product for Coca-Cola by "purely local" restaurants occurred in commerce, or that it could have any effect on appellant's national operation. The court also held that the amount in controversy was less than the $10,000 required for federal diversity jurisdiction. Citing *Seven-Up Co. v. Blue Note, Inc.*, 260 F.2d 584 (7th Cir. 1958), *cert. denied*, 359 U.S. 966 (1959), the court found that Coca-Cola had failed to establish a nexus between the apparent value of its goodwill and any injury to that goodwill resulting from appellees' acts of substitution.

II. *Jurisdiction Under the Lanham Trade-Mark Act*

The Lanham Act is a comprehensive statute designed to safeguard both the public and the trademark owner. Among other things, the statute prohibits "passing off" by a tradesman — *i.e.*, selling another's goods as those of the trademark owner, by use of the owner's mark. *Franchised Stores of New York, Inc. v. Winter*, 394 F.2d 664, 668 (2d Cir. 1968).

The major issue in this case is the effective reach of this prohibition. Under the terms of the statute, the prohibited act must occur "in commerce." 15 U.S.C. § 1114(1)(a) (1976). 15 U.S.C. § 1127 (1976) explains:

> The word "commerce" means all commerce which may lawfully be regulated by Congress.
>
> . . . .
>
> The intent of this chapter is to regulate commerce within the control of Congress by making actionable the deceptive and misleading use of marks in such commerce[.]

The legislative history of the Lanham Act underlines this intention: "[S]ound public policy requires that trade-marks should receive nationally the greatest protection that can be given them." S. Rep. No. 1333, 79th Cong., 2d Sess., *reprinted in* [1946] U.S. Code Cong. Serv., 1274, 1277.

By consistent interpretation, jurisdiction under the Lanham act encompasses intrastate activity that substantially affects interstate commerce. *See, e.g., Iowa Farmers Union v. Farmers' Educational & Coop. Union*, 247 F.2d 809, 816 (8th Cir. 1957); *Drop Dead Co. v. S. C. Johnson & Son, Inc.*, 326 F.2d 87, 94 (9th Cir. 1963), *cert. denied*, 377 U.S. 907 (1964); *Franchised Stores of New York, Inc. v. Winter, supra*, 394 F.2d at 669. Thus, "in commerce" refers to the impact that infringement has on interstate use of a trademark; it does not mean that an infringer is immune from prosecution under the statute so long as he keeps his infringement entirely within the confines of a state. *World Carpets, Inc. v. Dick Littrell's New World Carpets*, 438 F.2d 482, 488 (5th Cir. 1971). "A substantial effect on interstate commerce is present when the trademark owner's reputation and good will, built up by use of the mark in interstate commerce, are adversely affected by an intrastate infringement." *Franchised Stores of New York, Inc. v. Winter, supra*, 394 F.2d at 669 (citations omitted).

This broad focus comports fully with the modern scope of the commerce clause. The Supreme Court has many times upheld the application of national legislation to purely local activities. For example, in *Wickard v. Filburn*, 317 U.S. 111 (1942), a small farmer challenged federal limitations on the amount of wheat that he could grow for consumption on his farm. The Supreme Court observed:

> That appellee's own contribution to the demand for wheat may be trivial by itself is not enough to remove him from the scope of federal regulation where, as here, his contribution, taken together with that of many others similarly situated, is far from trivial. [*Id.* at 127–128 (citations omitted).]

Generally speaking, if a class of activities is within the reach of federal regulation, the courts have no power to excise individual instances as trivial. *See, e. g., Perez v. United States*, 402 U.S. 146, 154 (1971). In this case, however, the district court found that Coca-Cola Co. had failed to show that appellees' passing off "could have had *any* direct and material effect on [its] national operation; not to mention 'a substantially adverse effect.'. . . ". Yet, the affidavits submitted to the district court indicated that over one million gallons of fountain syrup a year were sold by Coca-Cola Co. in metropolitan Kansas City between 1969 and 1972. Coke was widely advertised in the area, and appellant sought to maintain its reputation for high quality products. On a national level, appellant spent over $45,000,000 a year in advertising and marketing of its product. The annual budget of the Trade Research Department in these same years exceeded $350,000.

We believe that these allegations, which are not disputed, support an inference that appellees' acts of passing off substantially affected appellant's interstate operations. The appropriate vantage point is that of the trademark holder. So viewed, appellees' actions jeopardized appellant's carefully nurtured reputation and undermined its claim to a distinctive (*i. e.,* nongeneric) trademark. That appellees' acts of infringement, standing alone, may not have cost Coca-Cola Co. a great deal in terms of lost sales does not detract from the fact that they served to misappropriate appellant's valuable goodwill, which rests on the distinctiveness of its federally protected trademark. The acts of these local retailers must be deemed, in the circumstances of this case, to have had substantial effect on interstate commerce. *See Maier Brewing Co. v. Fleischmann Distilling Corp.*, 390 F.2d 117, 120 (9th Cir.), *cert. denied*, 391 U.S. 966 (1968).

Appellees rely chiefly on *Application of Bookbinder's Restaurant*, 240 F.2d 365, 44 C.C.P.A. 731 (1957), and *Peter Pan Restaurants v. Peter Pan Diner*, 150 F. Supp. 534 (D.R.I. 1957), in support of the district court's holding. Both cases determined that activities of purely local restaurants lie outside the Lanham Act. The *Bookbinder's* decision, however, reflects the Patent Office's once-narrow view of federal trademark registrability, a view never adopted by the federal courts with respect to infringement actions and one since rejected by the Patent Office itself. *See* 1 Gilson, *Trademark Protection and Practice* §§ 8.03[3] and 3.02[5] (1976). The *Peter Pan* case can be distinguished on its facts; moreover, it and the cases it cites reflect a minority position that has been widely criticized. *See, e.g.,* 1 Gilson, *supra,* at § 8.03[3].

In our view, this case is governed by the holdings in *Franchised Stores of New York, Inc. v. Winter, supra; Maier Brewing Co. v. Fleischmann Distilling Corp., supra;* and *Pure Foods v. Minute Maid Corp.,* 214 F.2d 792 (5th Cir.), *cert. denied,* 348 U.S. 888 (1954). In all three cases the courts found that the potentially adverse effects of infringement on the plaintiff's reputation and goodwill satisfied the "substantial effect" test. Coca-Cola similarly satisfied the jurisdictional test in the present case. Apart from the clear authority supporting this conclusion, we believe that a contrary holding would seriously undermine the congressional intent behind the Lanham Act — namely, to protect the holders of federally registered trademarks. It would imply that local infringers could pirate a national mark with virtual impunity from federal restrictions, inflicting "death by a thousand cuts" upon the trademark holder.

Accordingly, we reverse the judgment of the district court. The cases will be remanded to that court for further proceedings consistent with this opinion.

SCOTCH WHISKY ASS'N v. BARTON DISTILLING CO.

United States Court of Appeals, Seventh Circuit
489 F.2d 809 (1973)

FAIRCHILD, CIRCUIT JUDGE.

Two of plaintiffs are producers of Scotch whisky in Scotland, marketed throughout much of the world, including Panama and the Canal Zone. Plaintiff Association was formed to promote the interests of distillers and merchants in Scotland. Defendant Barton is a Delaware corporation which produces and markets alcoholic beverages in the United States and elsewhere. One of defendant's products is Scotch whisky sold under the trademark House of Stuart. This action concerns a product distributed under the "House of Stuart Blended Scotch Whisky" label in Panama, which reached the Canal Zone as well.

In 1964, as amended in 1965, defendant made an agreement appointing a Panamanian corporation, Diers & Ullrich, its exclusive distributor in Panama. Defendant supplied Diers & Ullrich with House of Stuart labels and bottles, shipped from the United States, and vatted Scotch malts, shipped from Scotland. Diers & Ullrich mixed the Scotch malts with locally produced spirits and sold the product under the House of Stuart label. It appears without dispute that the House of Stuart label indicates that the product has its origin in Scotland, and that when applied to the Diers & Ullrich product there was a false designation of origin.

. . . .

. . . . The district court concluded that the use of the label was a false designation of the place of origin in violation of 15 U.S.C. § 1125(a) and certain provisions of the International Convention of Paris for the Protection of Industrial Property; and that defendant was responsible for the use of the label. Judgment was entered enjoining defendant from using the words "Scotch whisky" or its House of Stuart trademark or otherwise indicating origin in Scotland in connection with a product similar to the one involved. . . .

. . . .

The essence of defendant's position is that the goods bearing the challenged label were produced in Panama and caused to enter into the commerce of Panama, not the interstate or foreign commerce "which may lawfully be regulated by Congress." *See* 15 U.S.C. § 1127, so defining "commerce" and providing "The intent of this chapter is to regulate commerce within the control of Congress by making actionable the deceptive and misleading use of marks in such commerce. . . ."

It is true that it was the labels and bottles supplied by defendant which were transported from within the United States to Panama. Although defendant's agreement gave it the power to control the ingredients of the product, and thus defendant was properly charged with responsibility for the blending and labeling, this process did not happen within the United States. We think, however, that so literal a concept of entering into commerce is untenable. No principle of international law bars the United States from governing the conduct of its own citizens upon the high seas or even in foreign countries when the rights of other nations or their nationals are not infringed. Congress has the power to prevent unfair trade practices in foreign commerce by citizens of the United States, although some of the acts are done outside the territorial limits. The question is whether Congress intended the Act to apply to a situation of this type. *Steele v. Bulova Watch Co.*, 344 U.S. 280, 285–6, 95 U.S.P.Q. 391, 393–394 (1952).

In *Steele*, the Supreme Court construed another section of the Act, 15 U.S.C. § 1114(1), which creates a civil cause of action against one who uses an infringing mark "in commerce." The Court upheld a broad concept of "commerce."

Steele was a United States citizen who registered the trademark "Bulova" in Mexico. He imported parts from the United States and assembled and sold watches in Mexico. Plaintiff Bulova Watch company manufactured, advertised, and sold watches in the United States and elsewhere, using a trademark registered in the United States. Defective spurious Bulova watches filtered back to the United States and were brought to jewelers for repair by dissatisfied owners. In deciding that the Act applied, the Court considered both the purchase of parts in the United States, and the advent of some watches in the United States, as well as the adverse reflection Steele's goods could have on plaintiff's reputation both in the United States and elsewhere.

Defendant correctly points out that there are factual differences between *Steele* and the case at bar. Steele personally sold watches in Mexico under an infringing mark while defendant sold mislabeled whisky in Panama only vicariously; Steele's

Bulova trademark was ultimately nullified by Mexican decree while here it has not been demonstrated that Diers & Ullrich violated any Panamanian law; some of Steele's watches did come into the United States and damage the American owner of the trademark in this country while the Diers & Ullrich product appears to have reached only Panama and the Canal Zone, and damaged the Scotch plaintiffs only in those markets. None the less, viewing the entire course of business and the responsibility found on the part of defendant, we think the "commerce" involved began with defendant's acts in the United States and continued to the ultimate distribution of the whisky.

In *Steele*, the Supreme Court emphasized the invalidation of the Mexican trademark registration because of the danger otherwise of affront to Mexican sovereignty: the extraterritorial application of the United States trademark laws would nullify the affirmative grant of trademark protection within Mexico by the Mexican government. However, in the case at bar no such conflict is present. First, although the Panamanian government has apparently not prohibited the sale of local spirits under the designation of "Scotch whisky," it has taken no affirmative action to protect either the United States licensor or the Panamanian distributor in doing so. Moreover, the injunction is directed only against the United States licensor which acts only vicariously in Panama where Diers & Ullrich is not prohibited by the injunction from continuing to manufacture and market adulterated whisky.

Although there is no evidence that the adulterated Scotch whisky filtered into the United States, defendant concedes that sales of the product (though few) were made in the Canal Zone. Section 471 of the Canal Zone Code provides that the trademark laws of the United States have the same force and effect in the Canal Zone as in the continental United States.

We note that had the defendant made the same arrangements with an American licensee who packaged the mislabeled House of Stuart Scotch Whisky in the United States and shipped it to Panama, there would be no question but that the defendant caused the mislabeled goods to enter commerce. The purpose underlying the Lanham Act, to make actionable the deceptive use of false designations of origin, should not be evaded by the simple device of selecting a foreign licensee. *Steele*, p. 287, 95 U.S.P.Q. at 394.

Defendant argues that *Vanity Fair Mills, Inc. v. T. Eaton*, 234 F.2d 633, 109 U.S.P.Q. 438 (2d Cir., 1956), *cert. denied*, 352 U.S. 871, Ill U.S.P.Q. 468 (1956), *reh. denied*, 352 U.S. 913 (1956), precludes extra-territorial application of the Lanham Act here. However, in *Vanity Fair* the defendant was a foreign national who acted in his home country under a presumably valid trademark registration in that country. *Vanity Fair*, *supra*, at p. 642, 109 U.S.P.Q. at 443–444. Defendant also cites *George W. Luft Company v. Zande Cosmetic Company*, 142 F.2d 536, 61 U.S.P.Q. 424 (2d Cir. 1944), *cert. denied*, 323 U.S. 756, 63 U.S.P.Q. 358 (1944); however, in *Luft*, the defendants had obtained a registered and valid trademark from a foreign country and the decision in Luft preceded enactment of the Lanham Trademark act as well as the interpretation of it in *Steele*.

We conclude that a cause of action was established under the Lanham Act and that the district court had jurisdiction. . . .

    · · · ·

NOTES ON JURISDICTION

(1) Under what circumstances, if any, should an American plaintiff be able to successfully sue in a U.S. court against a party's infringing activities which occur in another country? What countervailing principles and factors come into play? *See Scotch Whisky Ass'n, supra*; *J. Walker & Sons, Ltd. v. Demert & Dougherty, Inc.*, 821 F.2d 399, 407–408 (7th Cir. 1987) (infringing artwork placed on deodorant cans in Illinois, which were shipped first to Florida and then sold to consumers in Panama and Columbia); *American Rice, Inc. v. Arkansas Rice Growers*, 701 F.2d 408 (5th Cir. 1983) (injunction granted though defendant's infringing products sold only in Saudi Arabia); *Purolator, Inc. v. EFRA Distributors, Inc.*, 687 F.2d 554 (1st Cir. 1982) (injunction granted against sales in Puerto Rico); *Calvin Klein v. BFK Hong Kong*, 714 F. Supp. 78 (S.D.N.Y. 1989) (defendant enjoined from selling rejected, defective CALVIN KLEIN sportswear anywhere in world where plaintiff had a presence, jurisdiction for the order deriving from the effect defendant's sales would have on U.S. commerce, including the exclusive rights of plaintiff's licensees and plaintiff's goodwill and reputation); Dabney, *On The Territorial Reach of the Lanham Act*, 83 Trademark Rep. 465 (1993).

(2) 28 U.S.C. § 1338(b) was intended to codify the "related action" doctrine of pendent federal jurisdiction enunciated in *Hurn v. Oursler*, 289 U.S. (1933). In *United Mine Workers v. Gibbs*, 383 U.S. 715 (1966), the Supreme Court held that a claim is related if "the state and federal claims . . . derive from a common nucleus of operative fact." Does this test affect the joinder of federal statutory trademark infringement and state common law unfair competition claims? *See Armstrong Paint & Varnish Works v. Nu-Enamel Corp.*, 305 U.S. 315 (1938); *Astor-Honor, Inc. v. Grosset & Dunlap, Inc.*, 441 F.2d 627 (2d Cir. 1971) (copyright infringement and unfair competition). Absent diversity, jurisdictional amount, or federal statutory bases, can a federal court continue to hear and decide what were pendent common-law trade identity unfair competition claims after all claims of statutory trademark infringement have been dismissed? *Compare Koufakis v. Carvel*, 425 F.2d 892 (2d Cir. 1970) *with Seven-Up Bottling Co. v. Seven-Up Co.*, 420 F. Supp. 1246 (E.D. Mo. 1976), *aff'd*, 561 F.2d 1275 (8th Cir. 1977).

(3) Should subject matter jurisdiction exist in the federal courts where the plaintiff is an intent to use applicant for federal registration who has yet to make use of the mark in commerce? *See Fila Sport, S.p.A. v. Diadora America, Inc.*, 21 U.S.P.Q.2d 1063 (N.D. Ill. 1991) (motion to dismiss granted). What if the activities at issue only occur intrastate? *Compare Coca-Cola v. Stewart, supra, with Fitzgerald v. J&R Chicken & Ribs, Inc.*, 11 U.S.P.Q.2d 384 (D.N.J. 1989), in which the case was dismissed because plaintiff failed to allege any connection with interstate commerce: "On the contrary, plaintiff appears to acknowledge that both his take-out chicken business as well as that of the alleged infringer . . . are local in nature."

(4) Establishing personal jurisdiction over a non-resident defendant is a matter of satisfying the long-arm statute of the particular situs state and demonstrating sufficient minimum contacts to satisfy due process. *See* Swann, *Bringing Home The Nonresident Infringer: How Long Or Short Should The Jurisdictional Arm Be?*, 62 Trademark Rep. 267 (1972). Typically a court looks for the transaction of business by the defendant within the state, with the cause of action relating to that transaction of business. *See, e.g., Sales Service, Inc. v. Daewoo Int'l (America) Corp.*, 719 F.2d 971, 972 (8th Cir. 1983).

The absence of physical entry into the state by the defendant will not preclude personal jurisdiction, as explained by the Supreme Court in *Burger King Corp. v. Rudzewicz*, 471 U.S. 462, 475 (1985):

> Jurisdiction in these circumstances may not be avoided merely because the defendant did not *physically* enter the forum state. — [I]t is an inescapable fact of modern commercial life that a substantial amount of business is transacted solely by mail and wire communications across state lines, thus obviating the need for physical presence within the state in which business is conducted. So long as a commercial actor's efforts are "purposefully directed" toward residents of another state, we have consistently rejected the notion that an absence of physical contacts can defeat personal jurisdiction there. [Citations omitted].
>
> . . . .
>
> [W]here a defendant who purposefully has directed his activities at forum residents seeks to defeat jurisdiction, he must present a compelling case that the presence of some other considerations would render jurisdiction unreasonable. Most such considerations usually may be accommodated through means short of finding jurisdiction unconstitutional.

This reasoning has been followed in trade identity cases. *See, e.g., Dakota Industries, Inc. v. Dakota Sportswear, Inc.*, 946 F.2d 1384 (8th Cir. 1991) (dismissal reversed where, although infringement defendant had no offices in the state, never advertised there and never directly shipped goods there, it knew that the major impact of the injury would be in that state); *J. Walker & Sons, Ltd. v. Demert & Dougherty, Inc.*, 821 F.2d 399, 404 (7th Cir. 1987) (ongoing business contacts with the state sufficient).

For an unusual use of a court's discretion in this area, see *Curtis Management Group, Inc. v. Academy of Motion Picture Arts & Sciences*, 717 F. Supp. 1362 (S.D. Ind. 1989), in which the court struck defendant's motion to dismiss and allowed the action to proceed even though there was no personal jurisdiction or venue, because defendant's affidavits supporting its motion contained false statements.

(5) Even though a trademark plaintiff establishes personal jurisdiction over the defendant, the suit still may be subject to dismissal on the basis of improper venue. As stated in *Johnson Creative Arts, Inc. v. Wool Masters, Inc.*, 743 F.2d 947, 949 (1st Cir. 1984):

> The minimum contacts test for personal jurisdiction is based on the *minimum* amount of "fairness" required in order to comport with due process. Venue

limitations are generally added by Congress to insure a defendant a fair location for trial and to protect him from inconvenient litigation."

In federal question cases, including those brought under the Lanham Act, Congress has authorized suit "only in the judicial district where all defendants reside, or in which the claim arose." 28 U.S.C. § 1391(b). In trademark infringement suits, where the allegedly infringing activities may occur in a number of different forms, venue arguably could exist in each of those forums as a location where "the claim arose." In *Leroy v. Great Western Corp.*, 443 U.S. 173, 185 (1979), the Supreme Court addressed this type of problem, stating:

> In our view . . . the broadest interpretation of the language of § 1391(b) that is even arguably acceptable is that in the unusual case in which it is not clear that the claim arose in only one specific district, a plaintiff may choose between those two (or conceivably even more) districts that with approximately equal plausibility — in terms of the availability of witnesses, the accessibility of other relevant evidence, and the convenience of the defendant (but *not* of the plaintiff) — may be assigned as the locus of the claim.

See J. Walker & Sons v. Demert & Dougherty, Inc., 821 F.2d 399, 406–407 (7th Cir. 1987), in which the *Leroy* factors such as accessibility of evidence and availability of witnesses weighed in favor of plaintiff, and *Noxell Corp. v. Firehouse No. 1 Barbecue Restaurant*, 760 F.2d 312 (D.C. Cir. 1985), in which the court dismissed a trademark case brought in Maryland where defendant made approximately 1.5% of its allegedly infringing sales, saying:

> [I]n terms of accessibility of relevant evidence (including witness testimony) and the convenience of the [California] defendants, the Northern District of California and the District of Columbia plainly are not places [plaintiff] could choose "with approximately equal plausibility. . . ." Defending a trademark infringement action some 3000 miles from where all employees and corporate records are located would exceed inconvenience — it would occasion a hardship for [defendant] and his current business.

A federal court also has discretion under 28 U.S.C. § 1404(a) to transfer a civil action for "the convenience of parties and witnesses, in the interest of justice." *US LIFE Corp. v. American Republic Insurance Corp.*, 218 U.S.P.Q. 298, 309 (D.D.C. 1982).

Under a 1988 amendment to the venue statute, for a corporation, residency for venue purposes now exists where it is subject to personal jurisdiction. 28 U.S.C. § 1391.

(6) To establish standing under the Lanham Act, a plaintiff normally need only show that it has a legitimate commercial interest in the proceeding's outcome. *See, e.g., Jewelers Vigilance Committee, Inc. v. Ullenberg Corp.*, 853 F.2d 888 (Fed. Cir. 1988) (diamond trade association had standing to oppose an application to register FOREVER YOURS/DEBEERS DIA. LTD. since DeBeers Consolidated Mines is the world's major source of diamonds).

But see Dovenmuehle v. Gilldorn Mortgage Midwest Corp., 871 F.2d 697 (7th Cir. 1989) (members of family surnamed "Dovenmuehle," lacked standing under

§ 43(a) to challenge defendant's use of the trade name DOVENMUEHLE, where they had failed to show any interest in the trade name after the sale of their family business, and had only an emotional desire to prevent others from using it); *Berni v. International Gourmet Restaurants, Inc.*, 838 F.2d 642 (2d Cir. 1988) (ex-shareholders had no standing to sue under § 43(a) over the alleged improper transferral of rights in a mark because they could not show that they would sustain commercial or competitive injury); *Jackson v. Lynley Designs, Inc.*, 729 F. Supp. 498 (E.D. La. 1990) (suit alleging plaintiff's name LISA JACKSON was fraudulently used in obtaining registration of that name for clothing dismissed for lack of standing where plaintiff had never engaged in business or attempted to exploit her name commercially).

Consumers also have been held to lack standing under the Lanham Act. *See, e.g., Serbin v. Ziebart International Corp.*, 28 U.S.P.Q.2d 1881 (3d Cir. 1992) (consumers lack standing to bring action for false advertising under § 43(a)), and the discussion on consumer standing in the Misrepresentation section notes in Chapter 8, *supra.*

§ 9.02   Remedies

INTRODUCTION

The traditional remedies in trade identity cases are injunctions, damages, profits and attorneys' fees. *See Developments in the Law — Trade-Marks and Unfair Competition*, 68 Harv. L. Rev. 814, 863–867 (1955); 15 U.S.C. §§ 1116–1118. Injunctive relief is ordinarily the principal remedy, and its terms are tailored to the facts of each case. Injunctions may include qualified prohibitions or requirements respecting trade dress, explanatory language, geographical and other limitations, and provisions as the court may deem just and equitable in the particular circumstances (*see, e.g.,* the sections on Geographical Terms and Surnames in Chapter 2 and on Permitted Use in Chapter 7). Usually, however, an unqualified injunction is needed to abate the wrong. Occasionally, the serious and immediately damaging consequences of the defendant's activities warrant preliminary injunctive relief. *See Warner Bros., infra.*

At common law and under the Lanham Act, monetary relief may also be awarded to compensate for harm to the plaintiff ("damages") and to reallocate any wrongful gains by the defendant ("profits"). Recovery of damages ordinarily encompasses injury to the plaintiff's goodwill, plaintiff's expenses in counteracting confusion, and plaintiff's lost profits caused by defendant's wrongful acts. In actions arising under the Lanham Act the court may, in its discretion, award treble damages. 15 U.S.C. § 1117.

In 1975, the Lanham Act was amended to provide that "the court in exceptional cases may award attorney's fees to the prevailing party." *Id.*

Award of an accounting of profits entitles the plaintiff to the defendant's profits from sales resulting from the wrongful use of an infringing mark. The defendant's sales are presumed to result from the wrongful use unless the defendant proves otherwise, and the gross revenue from sales is considered profit except for the actual costs of materials, production, and direct marketing expenses proved by defendant. *Id*. The Lanham Act provides that "In assessing profits the plaintiff shall be required to prove defendant's sales only; defendant must prove all elements of cost or deduction claimed." 15 U.S.C. § 1117. Profits are often awarded on a theory of unjust enrichment. *See* the *Monsanto* case, *infra*. Both damages and profits may be awarded, but the courts have usually avoided the potential for double recovery by excluding lost sales from the calculation of damages where profits are recovered. *Harper House, Inc. v. Thomas Nelson Publishers, Inc.*, 4 U.S.P.Q.2d 1897, 1910–1911 (C.D. Cal. 1987); *Polo Fashions, Inc. v. Extra Special Products, Inc.*, 208 U.S.P.Q. 421, 427 (S.D.N.Y. 1980).

An injunction prohibiting further use of a mark will prevent the damage of future confusion, but it will neither compensate for the damages caused by the infringement nor achieve the worthy end of destroying the incentive of infringers for such unjust enrichment. *Cf*. the relief afforded in FTC cases discussed in Chapter 10, *infra*.

[A] Injunction

WILLIAM R. WARNER & CO. v. ELI LILLY & CO.

United States Supreme Court
265 U.S. 526 (1924)

SUTHERLAND, JUSTICE.

[*See* facts, *supra* at § 8.07.]

. . . . [T]he right to which respondent is entitled is that of being protected against unfair competition, not having the aid of a decree to create or support, or assist in creating or supporting, a monopoly of the sale of a preparation which everyone, including petitioner, is free to make and vend. The legal wrong does not consist in the mere use of chocolate as an ingredient, but in the unfair and fraudulent advantage which is taken of such use to pass off the product as that of respondent. The use dissociated from the fraud is entirely lawful, and it is against the fraud that the injunction lies. But respondent being entitled to relief, is entitled to effective relief; and any doubt in respect of the extent thereof must be resolved in its favor as the innocent producer and against the petitioner, which has shown by its conduct that it is not to be trusted. Clearly, the relief should extend far enough to enjoin petitioner and its various agents, from, directly or indirectly, representing or suggesting to its customers any feasibility or possibility of passing off Quin-Coco for Coco-Quinine. The Court of Appeals held that petitioner should be unconditionally enjoined from the use of chocolate. We think this goes too far; but having regard to the past conduct of petitioner, the practices of some druggists to which it has led, and the right of respondent to an effective remedy, we think the decree fairly may require that the original packages sold to druggists shall not only bear labels clearly distinguishing petitioner's bottled product from the bottled product of respondent, but that these labels shall state affirmatively that the preparation is not to be sold or dispensed as

Coco-Quinine or be used in filling prescriptions or orders calling for the latter. With these general suggestions, the details and form of the injunction can be more satisfactorily determined by the District Court. The decree of the Court of Appeals is reversed and the cause remanded to the District Court for further proceedings in conformity with this opinion.

WARNER BROS., INC. v. GAY TOYS, INC.

United States Court of Appeals, Second Circuit
658 F.2d 76 (1981)

RE, CHIEF JUDGE.

[Action under § 43(a) of the Lanham Act for preliminary injunction against defendant's manufacture and sale of its "Dixie Racer" toy car which copied the bright orange color, confederate flag decal and other symbols of the "General Lee" car featured on the "Dukes of Hazzard" television show.]

[T]he legal standard which must be met by appellant, Warner Bros., is clear. There must be a showing of (A) irreparable harm and (B) either (1) likelihood of success on the merits or (2) sufficiently serious questions going to the merits to make them a fair ground for litigation and a balance of hardships tipping decidedly toward the party requesting the preliminary relief. *Jackson Dairy, Inc. v. H. P. Hood & Sons*, 596 F.2d 70 (2d Cir. 1979). This standard applies where a preliminary injunction is sought as relief for alleged trademark infringement. *Dallas Cowboys Cheerleaders, Inc. v. Pussycat Cinema, Ltd.*, 604 F.2d at 206–207.

In examining Warner Bros.' substantive position, the District Court properly held that "the basic inquiry in an unfair competition action is whether the public is likely to be misled into believing that the defendant is distributing products manufactured or vouched for by the plaintiff." At 1068. *See American Marietta Co. v. Krigsman*, 275 F.2d 287 (2d Cir. 1960).

. . . .

The District Court properly inferred that "many children buy the car (or induce their parents to buy it for them) as a prop for play in which they pretend they are 'the Duke Boys' of television fame". It is clear that many of the consumers did confuse the "Dixie Racer" with the "General Lee" and assumed that the car was sponsored by Warner Bros. This is sufficient to invoke the protection of this Court. *Scarves By Vera, Inc. v. Todo Imports Ltd. (Inc.)*, 544 F.2d 1167 (2d Cir. 1976).

Warner Bros. has licensed other toy manufacturers to produce authorized replicas of the "General Lee" through its subsidiary, Licensing Corporation of America. The undisputed facts demonstrate that this was not only the custom and practice of the industry, but also that product licensing arrangements were ultimately more profitable than the T.V. series itself.

On the question of competition and the likelihood of confusion, it is not necessary that Warner Bros. actually manufacture the toy cars, but merely that a confusion as to manufacture or sponsorship result. This Court has previously held in *Dallas Cowboys Cheerleaders, Inc. v. Pussycat Cinema, Ltd., supra,* that "[i]n order to be confused, a consumer need not believe that the owner of the mark actually produced the item and placed it on the market. The public's belief that the mark's owner sponsored or otherwise approved the use of the trademark satisfies the confusion requirement." *Id.* at 204, 205 (citations omitted).

We have no doubt that Warner Bros. has met its burden of proof of the likelihood of confusion as to the sponsorship of the "Dixie Racer."

We find that Warner Bros. has made a showing of irreparable harm as well as a showing of likelihood of success on the merits. It has a substantial financial interest at stake, and a history of first use of the symbols in this context. Warner Bros. also incurred great expense to publicize the symbols which identify the "General Lee." If the injunction is denied, Warner Bros. and its licensees will suffer substantial lost sales, and its licensing program will lose much of the confidence reposed in it by the licensees, who also made substantial investments based upon the exclusivity of their licenses.

. . . .

The Order of the District Court denying the preliminary injunction is reversed.

[B] Damages

ALADDIN MFG. CO. v. MANTLE LAMP CO.

United States Court of Appeals, Seventh Circuit
116 F.2d 708 (1941)

LINDLEY, DISTRICT JUDGE.

. . . .

Under the act covering trademarks, Title 15 U.S.C.A. Section 99, plaintiff was "entitled to recover, in addition to the profits to be accounted for by the defendant, the damages. . . ." The procedure is analogous to that in patent cases. *Hamilton-Brown Shoe Co. v. Wolf Bros. & Co.,* 240 U.S. 251. Before passage of the act of 1870, 16 Stat. 270, two remedies were open to the owner of a patent whose rights had been infringed, and he had his election between the two. He might proceed in equity and recover the profits which the infringer had made by the unlawful use of his invention, the infringer in such a suit being regarded as trustee of the owner of the patent as respects such gains and profits; or he might sue at law, in which case he would be entitled to recover, as damages, compensation for the pecuniary injury suffered by the infringement; the measure of damages in such case being not what the defendants had gained but what the plaintiff had lost. When the suit is at law, the measure of damages remains unchanged to the present time, the rule still being that the verdict must be for the actual damages sustained by the plaintiff. Damages of a compensatory character may also be allowed in equity where the gains and profits made by the respondent are not sufficient to compensate for the injury sustained. Gains and profits are still the proper measure of damages in equity suits, except in cases where the injury sustained by the infringement is plainly more than the aggregate of what was made by the respondent, in which event the provision is that the complainant shall be entitled to recover, in addition to the profits to be accounted for by the respondent, the damages he has sustained thereby. *Birdsall v. Collidge*, 93 U.S. 64; *Tilghman v. Proctor*, 125 U.S. 136, at pages 144, 145.

In law the infringer "is regarded as a mere wrong-doer compelled to make compensation for the injury he has inflicted." In equity he has a double character, being first treated as a species of agent or trustee practising the invention for the benefit of its true owner and obliged to pay to him the profits of the enterprise, and then, if, in the judgment of the court, the interests of the plaintiff so require, mulcted as a tort-feasor in a sum sufficient to redress the injury which the plaintiff has sustained." 3 Robinson on Patents, § 1050. In *Hamilton-Brown Shoe Co. v. Wolf Bros. & Co.*, 240 U.S. 251, at page 259, the court, dealing with unfair competition and infringement of a trademark, said: "In the courts of England, the rule seems to be that a party aggrieved must elect between damages and profits, and cannot have both. In this country, it is generally held that in a proper case both damages and profits may be awarded." *See also Child v. Boston & Fairhaven Iron Works, C.C.*, 19 F. 258, at page 259.

. . . .

A tort feasor is liable for all consequences naturally resulting, all injuries actually flowing from his wrongful act, whether in fact anticipated or contemplated by him when his tortious act was committed. Recoverable damages, therefore, include compensation for all injury to appellant's business arising from wrongful acts committed by appellee, provided such injury was the natural and proximate result of the wrongful acts. *Fidelity & D. Co. v. Bucki & Son Lumber*, 189 U.S. 135. This includes injury to business standing or good will, loss of business, additional expenses incurred because of the tort and all other elements of injury to the business. 15 Amer.Jur. §§ 133, 134, 135, 136 and 138. These are the governing principles applying to compensatory damages.

Exemplary damages are allowed against a tort feasor whose acts are intentionally fraudulent, malicious, wilful or wanton. They have always been recoverable at common law. . . . [S]uch damages are allowed, as sometimes said, in the interest of society, not as compensatory damages but rather in addition thereto, or as elsewhere said, as compensation to the injured party for the wrong suffered, though incidentally they may operate by way of punishment. *Cairo & St. L. R. Co. v. Peoples*, 92 Ill. 97, 34 Am. Rep. 112. They are not a favorite in law, however, *Post v. Buck's Stove & Range Co.*, 8 Cir., 200 F. 918, 43 L.R.A.,N.S., 498; and are, therefore, to be allowed only with caution and confined within narrow limits. Whether damages be compensatory or exemplary, if unliquidated, when determined by the trier of facts, their propriety cannot be governed or measured by any precise yardstick. They must bear some reasonable relationship to the injury inflicted and the amount must rest largely in the discretion of the trier of facts, a discretion not to be arbitrarily exercised. Ordinarily this court will interfere only where it appears that an injustice has been done or it is clear that there has been error in law.

In the present case, there was direct proof that because of the fraudulent and wilful infringement and unfair competition of appellee, appellant incurred legal expenses aggregating $18,515.03. Counsel's fees necessitated by the tort have been said in some instances to be recoverable as a part of the compensatory damages and in other cases as a part of exemplary damages. As the master's finding of wilful and fraudulent conduct is sustained by the evidence, this sum was recoverable as compensatory damages had hence properly included in the amount recommended by him.

. . . .

. . . . Accordingly the master's report should be approved in the allowance of damages in the sum of $18,515.03 for costs and expenses incurred and in the reduced amount of $25,000 for all other damages. The total recovery should be: Gains and profits $56,626.08; Damages $43,515.03, or a total of $100,141.11.

BIG O TIRE DEALERS, INC. v. GOODYEAR TIRE & RUBBER COMPANY

United States Court of Appeals, Tenth Circuit
561 F.2d 1365 (1977)

LEWIS, CHIEF JUDGE.

This civil action was brought by Big O Tire Dealers, Inc. ("Big O") asserting claims of unfair competition against The Goodyear Tire & Rubber Co. ("Goodyear") based upon false designation of origin under 15 U.S.C. § 1125(a) and common law trademark infringement. . . .

. . . .

In the fall of 1973 Big O decided to identify two of its lines of private brand tires as "Big O Big Foot 60" and "Big O Big Foot 70." These names were placed on the sidewall of the respective tires in raised white letters. The first interstate shipment of these tires occurred in February 1974. Big O dealers began selling these tires to the public in April 1974. Big O did not succeed in registering "Big Foot" as a trademark with the United States Patent and Trademark Office.

In the last three months of 1973 Goodyear began making snowmobile replacement tracks using the trademark "Bigfoot." From October 1973 to August 1975 Goodyear made only 671 "Bigfoot" snowmobile tracks and sold only 411 tracks. In December 1973 Goodyear filed an application to register "Bigfoot" as a trademark for snowmobile tracks with the United States Patent and Trademark Office; the registration was granted on October 15, 1974.

In July 1974 Goodyear decided to use the term "Bigfoot" in a nationwide advertising campaign to promote the sale of its new "Custom Polysteel Radial" tire. The name "Custom Polysteel Radial" was molded into the tire's sidewall. Goodyear employed a trademark search firm to conduct a search for "Bigfoot" in connection with tires and related products. This search did not uncover any conflicting trademarks. After this suit was filed, Goodyear filed an application to register "Bigfoot" as a trademark for tires but withdrew it in 1975. Goodyear planned to launch its massive, nationwide "Bigfoot" advertising campaign on September 16, 1974.

On August 24, 1974, Goodyear first learned of Big 0's "Big Foot" tires. Goodyear informed Big 0's president, Norman Affleck, on August 26 of Goodyear's impending "Bigfoot" advertising campaign. . . .

. . . On September 10, Affleck and two Big O directors met in New Orleans, with Kelley and Goodyear's manager of consumer market planning to discuss the problem further. At this time the Big O representatives objected to Goodyear using "Bigfoot" in connection with tires because they believed any such use would severely damage Big O. They made it clear they were not interested in money in exchange for granting Goodyear the right to use the "Bigfoot" trademark, and asked Goodyear to wind down the campaign as soon as possible. Goodyear's response to this request was indefinite and uncertain.

During the trial several Goodyear employees conceded it was technically possible for Goodyear to have deleted the term "Bigfoot" from its television advertising as late as early September. However, on September 16, 1974, Goodyear launched its nationwide "Bigfoot" promotion on ABC's Monday Night Football telecast. By August 31, 1975, Goodyear had spent $9,690,029 on its massive, saturation campaign.

On September 17 Affleck wrote Kelley a letter setting forth his understanding of the New Orleans meeting that Goodyear would wind up its "Bigfoot" campaign as soon as possible. Kelley replied on September 20, denying any commitment to discontinue use of "Bigfoot" and declaring Goodyear intended to use "Bigfoot" as long as it continued to be a helpful advertising device.

On October 9 Kelley told Affleck he did not have the authority to make the final decision for Goodyear and suggested that Affleck call Charles Eaves, Goodyear's executive vice-president. On October 10 Affleck called Eaves and Eaves indicated the possibility of paying Big O for the use of the term "Bigfoot." When Affleck stated no interest in the possibility Eaves told him Goodyear wished to avoid litigation but that if Big O did sue, the case would be in litigation long enough that Goodyear might obtain all the benefits it desired from the term "Bigfoot."

. . . .

. . . Goodyear challenges the jury's verdict awarding Big 0 $2.8 million in compensatory damages and $16.8 million in punitive damages. Goodyear contends Big 0 failed to prove either the fact or the amount of damages. Big 0 asserts the evidence supporting the fact of damages falls into two categories: (1) Goodyear's enormous effort to adopt, use, and absorb Big 0's trademark virtually destroyed Big 0's ability to make any effective use of its "Big Foot" trademark and (2) Goodyear's false statements that "Bigfoot" was available only from Goodyear created the appearance of dishonesty and wrongful conduct by Big 0, thereby harming its reputation within the trade and with the public. We agree with the district court that there is sufficient evidence to support the jury's finding of the fact of damages.

. . . .

The purpose of general compensatory damages is to make the plaintiff whole. Big O concedes it was unable to prove with precision the amount necessary to make itself whole. However, the district court concluded "[t]he damages awarded by the jury would enable Big O to do an equivalent volume of advertising in the states in which there are Big O dealers to inform their customers, potential customers, and the public as a whole about the true facts in this dispute or anything else necessary to eliminate the confusion." 408 F. Supp. 1232. Moreover, the Supreme Court has pointed out that a plaintiff's inability to prove with precision that amount necessary to make itself whole does not preclude recovery since

> [t]he most elementary conceptions of justice and public policy require that the wrongdoer shall bear the risk of the uncertainty which his own wrong has created.

Bigelow v. RKO Radio Pictures, Inc., 327 U.S. 251, 265.

There is precedent for the recovery of corrective advertising expenses incurred by a plaintiff to counteract the public confusion resulting from a defendant's wrongful conduct. . . . Goodyear contends the recovery of advertising expenses should be limited to those actually incurred prior to trial. In this case the effect of such a rule would be to recognize that Big O has a right to the exclusive use of its trademark but has no remedy to be put in the position it was in prior to September 16, 1974, before Goodyear effectively usurped Big O's trademark. The impact of Goodyear's "Big-foot" campaign was devastating. The infringing mark was seen repeatedly by millions of consumers. It is clear from the record that Goodyear deeply penetrated the public consciousness. Thus, Big O is entitled to recover a reasonable amount equivalent to that of a concurrent corrective advertising campaign.

As the district court pointed out, the jury's verdict of $2.8 million corresponds to 28 percent of the approximately $10 million Goodyear spent infringing Big O's mark. Big O has dealers in 14 states which equal 28 percent of the 50 states. Big O also points out the jury's award is close to 25 percent of the amount Goodyear spent infringing on Big O's mark. Big O emphasizes that the Federal Trade Commission often requires businesses who engage in misleading advertising to spend 25 percent of their advertising budget on corrective advertising.

Taking cognizance of these two alternative rationales for the jury's award for compensatory damages we are convinced the award is not capable of support as to any amount in excess of $678,302. As the district court implied in attempting to explain the jury's verdict, Big O is not entitled to the total amount Goodyear spent on its nationwide campaign since Big O only has dealers in 14 states, thus making it unnecessary for Big O to run a nationwide advertising campaign. Furthermore, implicit in the FTC's 25 percent rule in corrective advertising cases is the fact that dispelling confusion and deception in the consuming public's mind does not require a dollar-for-dollar expenditure. In keeping with "[t]he constant tendency of the courts . . . to find some way in which damages can be awarded where a wrong has been done," we hold that the maximum amount which a jury could reasonably find necessary to place Big O in the position it was in before September 16, 1974, vis-a-vis its "Big Foot" trademark, is $678,302. We arrive at this amount by taking 28 percent of the $9,690,029 it was stipulated Goodyear spent on its "Bigfoot" campaign, and then reducing that figure by 75 percent in accordance with the FTC rule, since we agree with that agency's determination that a dollar-for-dollar expenditure for corrective advertising is unnecessary to dispel the effects of confusing and misleading advertising.

Under Colorado law exemplary damages must bear some relation to the compensatory award. *Barnes v. Lehman*, 118 Colo. 161, 163, 193 P.2d 273, 274. The district court in its post-trial opinion upheld the jury's punitive damage award of $16.8 million as not being disproportionate under Colorado law. We find the district court's determination of the reasonableness of a six-to-one exemplary to compensatory ratio to be persuasive, and thus we defer to the district court's interpretation of Colorado law. Therefore, in light of the reduction in compensatory damages proved, the punitive damage award is similarly reduced to $4,069,812, thus maintaining the jury's and district court's six-to-one exemplary to compensatory ratio.

. . . .

[*Remanded*]

[C]   Profits

HAMILTON-BROWN SHOE CO. v. WOLF BROTHERS & CO.

United States Supreme Court
240 U.S. 251 (1961)

PITNEY, JUSTICE.

. . . .

Having reached the conclusion that complainant is entitled to the use of the words "The American Girl" as a trade-mark, it results that it is entitled to the profits acquired by defendant from the manifestly infringing sales under the label "American Lady," at least to the extent that such profits are awarded in the decree under review. The right to use a trade-mark is recognized as a kind of property, of which the owner is entitled to the exclusive enjoyment to the extent that it has been actually used. *McLean v. Fleming*, 96 U.S. 245, 252; *Manhattan Medicine Co. v. Wood*, 108 U.S. 218, 224. The infringer is required in equity to account for and yield up his gains to the true owner, upon a principle analogous to that which charges a trustee with the profits acquired by wrongful use of the property of the *cestui que trust*. Not that equity assumes jurisdiction upon the ground that a trust exists. As pointed out in *Root v. Railway*, 105 U.S. 189, 214, and *Tilghman v. Proctor*, 125 U.S. 136, 148 (patent cases), the jurisdiction must be rested upon some other equitable ground — in ordinary cases, as in the present, the right to an injunction — but the court of equity having acquired jurisdiction upon such a ground, retains it for the purpose of administering complete relief, rather than send the inquired party to a court of law for his damages. And profits are then allowed as an equitable measure of compensation, on the theory of a trust *ex maleficio*. In the courts of England, the rule seems to be that a party aggrieved must elect between damages and profits, and cannot have both. In this country, it is generally held that in a proper case both damages and profits may be awarded. . . .

It is, however, insisted by defendant (petitioner) that whether the recovery be based upon the theory of trademark, or upon that of unfair competition, the profits recoverable should be limited to such amount as may be shown by direct and positive evidence to be the increment to defendant's income by reason of the infringement, and that the burden of proof is upon complainant to show what part of defendant's profits were attributable to the use of the infringing mark. . . . But, as pointed out in the *Westinghouse Case* (p. 618), there is a recognized exception where the plaintiff carries the burden of proof to the extent of showing the entire profits, but is unable to apportion them, either because of the action of the wrongdoer in confusing his own gains with those which belong to plaintiff, or because of the inherent impossibility of making an approximate apportionment. There, "on established principles of equity, and on the plainest principles of justice, the guilty trustee cannot take advantage of his own wrong."

. . . [A] sufficient reason for not requiring complainant in the present case to make an apportionment between the profits attributable to defendant's use of the offending mark and those attributable to the intrinsic merit of defendant's shoes is that such an apportionment is inherently impossible. Certainly, no formula is suggested by which it could be accomplished. The result of acceding to defendant's contention, therefore, would be to deny all compensation to complainant. And it is to be remembered that defendant does not stand as an innocent infringer. Not only do the findings of the Court of Appeals, supported by abundant evidence, show that the imitation of complainant's mark was fraudulent, but the profits included in the decree are confined to such as accrued to defendant through its persistence in the unlawful simulation in the face of the very plain notice of complainant's rights that is contained in its bill. As was said by the Supreme Court of California in a similar case, *Graham v. Plate*, 40 Cal. 593, 598; 6 Am. Rep. 639, 640:

> In sales made under a simulated trade mark it is impossible to decide how much of the profit resulted from the intrinsic value of the commodity in the market, and how much from the credit given to it by the trade-mark. In the very nature of the case it would be impossible to ascertain to what extent he could have effected sales and at what prices except for the use of the trade-mark. No one will deny that on every principle of reason and justice the owner of the trade-mark is entitled to so much of the profit as resulted from the use of the trade-mark. The difficulty lies in ascertaining what proportion of the profit is due to the trade-mark, and what to the intrinsic value of the commodity; and as this cannot be ascertained with any reasonably certainty, it is more consonant with reason and justice that the owner of the trade-mark should have the whole profit than that he should be deprived of any part of it by the fraudulent act of the defendant. . . .

. . . .

Decree affirmed.

MONSANTO CHEMICAL CO. v. PERFECT FIT PRODS. MFG. CO.

United States Court of Appeals, Second Circuit
349 F.2d 389 (1965)

LUMBARD, CHIEF JUDGE.

The issue on this appeal is whether the district court erred in refusing to allow an accounting of the profits gained by the defendant through its deliberate infringement of the plaintiff's trademark on the ground that the parties were not in direct competition. We conclude that the public interest in deterring fraudulent sales practices requires that such an accounting be allowed, and we therefore remand the case for such accounting.

The facts, as found by Judge McLean after a trial at which the defendant adduced no evidence, are undisputed. The plaintiff, Monsanto Chemical Co., produces an acrylic fiber, which it markets under the registered trademark "Acrilan." This mark was registered under the Lanham Trademark Act of 1947, 15 U.S.C. § 1051 et seq. The defendant, Perfect Fit, deliberately infringed this mark by selling mattress pads falsely labeled as Acrilan-filled. . . .

. . . .

Consideration of the principles which we think should govern the award of an accounting in the present case must begin with § 35 of the Lanham Act, 15 U.S.C. § 1117, which provides for the award of damages and accounts for the infringement of marks registered under the Act. The trademark plaintiff is entitled under § 35 to recover, "subject to the principles of equity,"

> (1) defendant's profits, (2) any damages sustained by the plaintiff, and (3) the costs of the action. . . . In assessing profits the plaintiff shall be required to prove defendant's sales only; defendant must prove all elements of cost or deduction claimed. In assessing damages the court may enter judgment, according to the circumstances of the case, for any sum above the amount found as actual damages, not exceeding three times such amount. If the court shall find that the amount of the recovery based on profits is either inadequate or excessive the court may in its discretion enter judgment for such sum as the court shall find to be just, according to the circumstances of the case. Such sum in either of the above circumstances shall constitute compensation and not a penalty.

On its face, § 35 would seem to give to district court the broadest kind of discretion in tailoring the plaintiff's recovery, whether in damages or by way of an accounting, to the facts of the particular case. *Compare* Trade-Mark Act of 1905, § 19, 33 Stat. 729. So far as accountings are concerned, however, recourse to this broad discretion has been considered by a number of courts, including this one, to be limited by the nature of the right asserted by the trade-mark plaintiff.

The more narrow view of the right has been that it is merely a means of protecting a businessman from injury resulting from another's use of his mark. *Durable Toy & Novelty Corp. v. J. Chein & Co.*, 133 F.2d 853 (2 Cir.), *cert. denied*, 320 U.S. 211 (1943). Injunctive relief may be warranted by the mere possibility of such injury, but a monetary award, whether in the form of damages or an accounting, is justified only to the extent that injury is shown already to have been suffered. This has been the conventional view, *see* Note, 1963 Wash. U.L.Q. 243, and it is the view underlying the decisions of this court relied on by Judge McLean in this case.

There is nothing in this view of the trademark right which entitles the plaintiff to the infringer's profits as such. An accounting has been thought proper only as an indirect measure of the plaintiff's injury, that is, only if some relationship between the infringer's profits and the plaintiff's injury can be inferred. As a result accountings have been limited to cases in which the parties are competing for trade and the defendant's trade may thus be presumed to have been diverted from the plaintiff. This is the rule adopted by the Restatement of Torts, § 747.

An alternative view of the trademark right is that it is a form of property, similar in this respect to a copyright or patent right. Taking this view, the justification for an accounting is found in the principles of unjust enrichment traditionally applicable where property is used for profit without the owner's permission, and, if the view is carried to its logical conclusion, an accounting should be awarded automatically in most cases. In particular, since the accounting is not dependent upon presumed injury to the plaintiff, it is irrelevant that the plaintiff was not selling in the market exploited by the infringer. . . .

. . . .

In enacting the Lanham Act, Congress observed that any trademark statute had a two-fold purpose:

> One is to protect the public so it may be confident that, in purchasing a product bearing a particular trade-mark which it favorably knows, it will get the product which it asks for and wants to get. Secondly, where the owner of a trade-mark has spent energy, time, and money in presenting to the public the product, he is protected in his investment from its misappropriation by pirates and cheats.

S. Rep. No. 1333, 79th Cong., 2d Sess. 1–2 (1946), in U.S. Code Cong. Serv. 1274 (1946).

We think it doubtful whether even the second of these purposes, protection of the trademark owner, is adequately served by a rule which would allow accountings only where the parties directly compete. To have proved directly that the reputation of its Acrilan trademark was injured by Perfect Fit's activities, Monsanto would have been required first to trace the pads from Perfect Fit through the retailer to their ultimate purchasers and then to introduce, in some manner or another, the testimony of a sampling of these purchasers in court. *Cf. Zippo Mfg. Co. v. Rogers Imports, Inc.*, 216 F. Supp. 670 (S.D.N.Y. 1963) (use of opinion poll). Whether Monsanto tried to obtain such evidence and failed or simply did not try does not appear. However, it seems obvious that there must have been some economic injury to Monsanto, such as loss of sales to legitimate producers and the loss of the goodwill of some of the retail purchasers of Perfect Fit's inferior "Acrilan" mattress pads.

In any event, whatever may be the merit of the narrow rule regarding accountings so far as the trademark owner is concerned, the narrow rule is entirely inadequate to protect the interest of the public. Because the amount involved in a single purchaser may be small — here $3.98 for a mattress pad — the ultimate purchaser almost never brings suit even in so blatant a case of deception as here, and the public must depend for protection on the private actions brought by trademark owners. While private actions such as this do not compensate those who purchased the infringer's product, they can deter future infringements by imposing a money judgment on the defendant. The principal defect of the § 747 rule is that it does nothing to render infringement unprofitable in cases such as this. The plaintiff is unable to offer satisfactory proof of its injury, and, so long as the defendant does not infringe the trademark of a direct competitor, it can retain its profits.

We do not hold that it is irrelevant whether the parties are in direct competition; compensation for diverted trade is one important purpose which an accounting may serve. To restrict accountings to this single purpose, however, fails to take account of the other purposes served by the trademark law. Under the circumstances of this case, a judgment limited to an injunction is clearly inadequate to deter those who deliberately engage in commercial piracy which defrauds thousands of consumers and injures a trade name built up at considerable cost by legitimate means.

The judgment of the district court is reversed and the case is remanded for an accounting.

ALPO PETFOODS, INC. v. RALSTON PURINA COMPANY

United States Court of Appeals, District of Columbia Circuit
913 F.2d 958 (1990)

CLARENCE THOMAS, CIRCUIT JUDGE:

In this case, Ralston Purina Co. and ALPO Petfoods, Inc., two of the leading dog food producers in the United States, have sued each other under § 43(a) of the Lanham Act, 15 U.S.C. § 1125(a) (1982) (amended 1988), alleging false advertising. ALPO asserts that Ralston has violated § 43(a) by claiming that its Puppy Chow can lessen the severity of canine hip dysplasia (CHD), a crippling joint condition. Ralston, for its part, attacks ALPO's claims that ALPO Puppy Food contains "the formula preferred by responding vets two to one over the leading puppy food."

After a sixty-one-day bench trial, the district court decided that Ralston's CHD-related advertising and ALPO's veterinarian preference advertising both violated § 43(a). *ALPO Petfoods, Inc. v. Ralston Purina Co.*, 720 F. Supp. 194, 209–11 (D.D.C. 1989). The court permanently enjoined both companies from making "advertising or other related claims" similar to those held false, and ordered both parties to disseminate corrective statements. *Id.* at 216–17. Applying § 35(a) of the Lanham Act, 15 U.S.C. § 1117(a) (1982 & Supp. V 1987) (amended 1988), the court also awarded ALPO $10.4 million (plus costs and attorneys' fees). The court reached this figure by determining the amount that Ralston spent on its CHD-related advertising, using that amount as a measure of Ralston's benefit from the advertising, and then doubling the amount to capture the full harm that the advertising caused ALPO. *ALPO*, 720 F. Supp. at 215 (citing *U-Haul Int'l, Inc. v. Jartran, Inc.*, 793 F.2d 1034, 1037 (9th Cir. 1986)). Ralston, in contrast, was awarded only its costs and attorneys' fees. *Id.* at 215, 216.

Ralston appeals the district court's judgment, focusing on the court's determination that the CHD-related advertising claims were false, as well as the court's monetary award to ALPO, its refusal to award similar relief to Ralston, and its broad and expansively implemented injunction.

. . . .

Section 35(a) authorizes courts to award to an aggrieved plaintiff both plaintiff's damages and defendant's profits, but, as this court noted in *Foxtrap*, 671 F.2d at 641, courts' discretion to award these remedies has limits. Just as "any award based on plaintiff's damages requires some showing of actual loss," *id.* at 642; *see also infra* p. 969 (discussing actual damages under § 35(a)), an award based on a defendant's profits requires proof that the defendant acted willfully or in bad faith, *see Foxtrap*, 671 F.2d at 641; *Frisch's Restaurants, Inc. v. Elby's Big Boy*, 849 F.2d 1012, 1015 (6th Cir. 1988). Proof of this sort is lacking. Ralston's decision to run CHD-related advertising that lacked solid empirical support does not, without more, reflect willfulness or bad faith. *See supra* pp. 965–66; *cf. U-Haul, Int'l, Inc. v. Jartran, Inc.*, 601 F. Supp. 1140, 1147–48 (D. Ariz. 1984) (describing *U-Haul* defendant's targeted comparative advertising, which misrepresented plaintiff's and defendant's prices), *aff'd in part and rev'd in part*, 793 F.2d 1034 (9th Cir. 1986).

In *Conservative Digest* we "left open the possibility that a court could properly award damages to a plaintiff when the defendant has been unjustly enriched." 821 F.2d at 807–08 (citing *Foxtrap*, 671 F.2d at 641 & n. 9). The unjust-enrichment theory, which emerged in trademark cases in which the infringer and the infringed were not competitors, holds that courts should divest an infringer of his profits, regardless of whether the infringer's actions have harmed the owner of the infringed trademark. Awards of profits are justified under the theory because they deter infringement in general and thereby vindicate consumers' interests. *See, e.g., Monsanto Chemical Co. v. Perfect Fit Prods. Mfg. Co.*, 349 F.2d 389, 392, 395–97 (2d Cir. 1965), *cert. denied*, 383 U.S. 942 (1966); *see also* 2 J.T. McCarthy, [*Trademarks and Unfair Competiton, 2d Ed., 1984*], p. 14 § 30:25(B) (citing cases). As we state below, however, we doubt the wisdom of an approach to damages that permits courts to award profits for their sheer deterrent effect.

. . . .

[T]his court in *Foxtrap* advised a district court to make an award that would "deter the defendant, *yet not be a windfall to plaintiff nor amount to punitive damages.*" *Id.* at 642 n. 11 (emphasis added). Based on *Foxtrap*, as well as our concern that deterrence is too weak and too easily invoked a justification for the severe and often cumbersome remedy of a profits award, *see* Koelemay, *Monetary Relief for*

Trademark Infringement Under the Lanham Act, 72 Trademark Rep. 458, 493–94, 536–37 (1982), we hold that deterrence alone cannot justify such an award.

Since this case lacks the elements required to support the court's award of Ralston's profits, we vacate the $10.4 million judgment in favor of ALPO. We do not mean, however, to deny ALPO all monetary relief for Ralston's false advertising. Because the district court has so far focused on awarding Ralston's profits, it has not yet decided what actual damages ALPO has proved. On remand, the court should award ALPO its actual damages, bearing in mind the requirement that any amount awarded have support in the record, *see Foxtrap,* 671 F.2d at 642; *Gold Seal,* 129 F. Supp. at 940, as well as the following points about the governing law.

In a false-advertising case such as this one, actual damages under § 35(a) can include:

— profits lost by the plaintiff on sales actually diverted to the false advertiser, *see, e.g., Foxtrap,* 671 F.2d at 642 (trademark case);

— profits lost by the plaintiff on sales made at prices reduced as a demonstrated result of the false advertising, *see, e.g., Burndy Corp. v. Teledyne Indus.,* 748 F.2d 767, 773 (2d Cir. 1984);

— the costs of any completed advertising that actually and reasonably responds to the defendant's offending ads, *see, e.g., Cuisinarts, Inc. v. Robot-Coupe Int'l Corp.,* 580 F. Supp. 634, 640–41 (S.D.N.Y. 1984); and

— quantifiable harm to the plaintiff's good will, to the extent that completed corrective advertising has not repaired that harm, *see, e.g., Engineered Mech. Servs., Inc. v. Applied Mech. Technology, Inc.,* 591 F. Supp. 962, 966 (M.D. La. 1984); *see also* Comment, 55 U. Chi. L. Rev. at 650–57 (discussing how courts might directly measure good will).

See generally Koelemay, [*Monetary Relief for Trademark Infringement Under the Lanham Act,*] 72 Trademark Rep. [458] at 505–07.

When assessing these actual damages, the district court may take into account the difficulty of proving an exact amount of damages from false advertising, as well as the maxim that "the wrongdoer shall bear the risk of the uncertainty which his own wrong has created." *Otis Clapp & Son v. Filmore Vitamin Co.,* 754 F.2d 738, 745 (7th Cir. 1985) (quoting *Bigelow v. RKO Radio Pictures, Inc.,* 327 U.S. 251, 265 (1946). At the same time, the court must ensure that the record adequately supports all items of damages claimed and establishes a causal link between the damages and the defendant's conduct, lest the award become speculative or violate § 35(a)'s prohibition against punishment. *See, e.g., Bigelow,* 327 U.S. at 264 (stating, in antitrust case, that "speculation or guesswork" cannot sustain an award of damages); *Burndy Corp.,* 748 F.2d at 773 (asserted causal connection between defendant's conduct and plaintiff's reduced-price sales lacked support in record; denial of reduced-price sales damages affirmed); *Foxtrap,* 671 F.2d at 642 (same problem with respect to lost sales; damages award vacated and case remanded for detailed findings).

Section 35(a) also authorizes the court to "enter judgment, according to the circumstances of the case, for any sum above the amount found as actual damages, not exceeding three times such amount." Lanham Act § 35(a), 15 U.S.C. § 1117(a) (1982 & Supp. V 1987) (amended 1988). This provision gives the court discretion to enhance damages, as long as the ultimate award qualifies as "compensation and not [as] a penalty." *Id.*; *see* Koelemay, 72 Trademark Rep. at 516–19, 521–25 (discussing interplay of damages enhancement provision and antipenalty clause); *see also Getty Petroleum Corp. v. Bartco Petroleum Corp.*, 858 F.2d 103, 112–13 (2d Cir. 1988) (in trademark infringement case, interpreting § 35(a) to ban any awards of punitive damages), *cert. denied*, 109 S. Ct. 1642 (1989). Given this express statutory restriction, if the district court decides to enhance damages under § 35(a), it should explain why the enhanced award is compensatory and not punitive.

C.   Denial of Monetary Relief in Favor of Ralston

The foregoing comments on actual damages apply as well to the monetary remedy for ALPO's false advertising. As noted above, the district court held that ALPO's veterinarian preference advertising violated § 43(a). *ALPO*, 720 F. Supp. at 209–11. Despite this decision, the court did not award Ralston any damages or profits under § 35(a) because "[t]he magnitude of the wrongdoing by Ralston in comparison to that of ALPO is so much greater than a damage award would not be justified," because ALPO, but not Ralston, had shown remorse, and because the court considered Ralston's counterclaim "an afterthought." *Id.* at 216; *see also id.* at 212 (finding an injunction the most appropriate redress for ALPO's false advertising).

The Lanham Act does not authorize courts to deny monetary relief for these reasons. Once a party establishes a violation of § 43(a), § 35(a) "entitle[s]" that party to monetary relief, subject only to the statutes referred to in the section and to the principles of equity. Lanham Act § 35(a), 15 U.S.C. § 1117(a); *cf. ALPO*, 720 F. Supp. at 214 (rejecting both parties' "unclean hands" defenses, a ruling that neither party appeals). Since § 35(a) expressly provides for compensation, rather than punishment, courts dealing with offsetting meritorious claims must let the degree of injury that each party proves, rather than the degree of opprobrium that the court attaches to each party's conduct, determine the monetary relief.

At more than one point in this case, Ralston came close to admitting that it cannot prove lost profits. *See* Brief of appellee at 47 & app. B (citing Ralston's statement, in a proposed finding of fact, that none of its regression analyses proved diverted sales); Reply Brief of Appellant at 18–19 ("Ralston's position . . . is that under a *proper* construction of the Lanham Act, *neither* party can quantify lost profits sufficiently to recover damages."). In this appeal, however, Ralston has shown that it still considers its lost profits a live issue. *See id.* at 18 & n. 40 (citing evidence, other than regressions, of lost sales). Since Ralston has some evidence of lost sales, and since, more importantly, § 35(a) entitles Ralston to damages other than lost profits, *see supra* p. 969, the district court should on remand award Ralston whatever actual damages it has proved. In this connection, as with ALPO's damages, the court should decide whether the parties have already had a sufficient opportunity to prove the types of damages outlined above, or whether further hearings are necessary.

D.   Attorneys' Fees

The court awarded each company the attorneys' fees associated with its successful false-advertising claim. *ALPO*, 720 F. Supp. at 216. Only Ralston has appealed.

Section 35(a) entitles prevailing parties to attorneys' fees "in exceptional cases." This court's decision in *Conservative Digest*, 821 F.2d at 808, establishes an abuse-of-discretion standard for review of attorneys' fees awards. That same decision, however, holds that a court can award a plaintiff her attorneys' fees only in cases involving willful or bad-faith conduct by the defendant; applying that standard, the *Conservative Digest* court affirmed a denial of fees to a plaintiff who had proved trade dress infringement, but not willfulness or bad faith on the part of the infringer. *Id.* Seeing no relevant distinction between fee awards in trade dress infringement actions and fee awards in false-advertising actions, we apply *Conservative Digest* here. *See id.* at 803 (§ 43(a) covers trade dress infringement).

In announcing its fee awards, the district court did not expressly find that Ralston had acted willfully or in bad faith. Indeed, it made no finding that this case is "exceptional" in any respect. *See ALPO*, 720 F. Supp. at 216, 216; *supra* p. 963. During a postjudgment hearing, the court explained that since, in its view, federal agencies are not sufficiently enforcing the laws against false advertising, it had awarded fees "to encourage private attorneys general in this case." Transcript of Motions Hearing at 7 (Sept. 18, 1989). Since neither the court's opinion nor its later statements support the award with a finding of willfulness or bad faith, and since we have decided that any such finding would be clearly erroneous, *see supra* pp. 965–66, we reverse the district court's decision to award attorneys' fees to ALPO.[14]

. . . .

NOTES ON REMEDIES

(1) Injunctive relief can take a variety of forms. A defendant simply may be enjoined from any further infringing or deceptive activity, or may be asked to take affirmative steps to prevent further deception. *See, e.g., Perfect Fit Industries, Inc. v. Acme Quilting Co.*, 646 F.2d 800 (2d Cir. 1981), *later app.*, 673 F.2d 53 (2d Cir. 1982), *cert. denied*, 459 U.S. 832 (1982), in which the lower court's order that defendant recall, at its expense, the offending materials was found to be a proper

---

[14] Because ALPO has failed to challenge the district court's award of attorneys' fees to Ralston, we do not disturb the award. *See, e.g., Smith v. Nixon*, 807 F.2d 197, 204 n. 4 (D.C. Cir. 1986) (plaintiffs waived potential claims by neglecting to press them on appeal). Although, in some cases, we might forgive a party's waiver and reverse a district court's determination as plain error, we decline to do so here. This court typically reviews a district court's ruling for plain error only when a party has objected to the ruling on appeal. *See, e.g., Anderson v. Group Hosp., Inc.*, 820 F.2d 465, 469 n. 1 (D.C. Cir. 1987); *Hobson v. Wilson*, 737 F.2d 1, 31–31, 32 n. 96 (D.C. Cir. 1984), *cert. denied*, 470 U.S. 1084(1985).

exercise of that court's discretion, and *Moore Business Forms, Inc. v. Seidenberg*, 229 U.S.P.Q. 821 (W.D. La. 1985), where defendant was ordered to establish a telephone intercept operator to answer defendant's telephone and advise callers of plaintiff's telephone number. *See also Playskool, Inc. v. Product Development Group, Inc.*, 699 F. Supp. 1056, 1063 (E.D.N.Y. 1988) (defendant that falsely advertised its toy construction set "attaches to" plaintiff's set ordered to recall its products because they might cause structures unsafe for children); *Tripledge Products, Inc. v. Whitney Resources, Ltd.*, 735 F. Supp. 1154, 1166–1167 (E.D.N.Y. 1988) (defendant ordered to refund money to customers who ordered falsely advertised windshield wipers); *Shen Mfg. Co. v. Suncrest Mills, Inc.*, 673 F. Supp. 1199, 1207 (S.D.N.Y. 1987) (defendants ordered to recall and destroy infringing dishcloths).

(2) If a defendant attempts to evade the effect of an injunction, a contempt proceeding may then be necessary. *See, e.g., Howard Johnson Co. v. Khimani*, 892 F.2d 1512, 1515 (11th Cir. 1990) (ex-franchisee who had been enjoined from using HOWARD JOHNSON'S service marks held in contempt for using name H. J. INNS, a name they admittedly chose to "get as close to Howard Johnson as you could without infringing"); *Manhattan Industries, Inc. v. Sweater Bee by Banff, Ltd.*, 885 F.2d 1 (2d Cir. 1989) (failure to use additional distinguishing source reference as required by order), *cert. denied*, 494 U.S. 1029 (1990). *See also Service Ideas Inc. v. Traex Corp.*, 846 F.2d 1118, 1124 (7th Cir. 1988) (defendant's post-injunction design for its beverage server held "too close to the boundary"). *See also Young v. United States*, 481 U.S. 787 (1987) (plaintiff's counsel in counterfeiting civil action cannot be appointed special prosecutor in subsequent related criminal contempt proceeding due to bias concerns). The difficulties of bringing recalcitrant defendants within the scope of an effective injunction are discussed in *Scandia Down Corp. v. Euroquilt, Ltd.*, 772 F.2d 1423 (7th Cir. 1985), and *Taylor Wine Co., Inc. v. Bully Hill Vineyards, Inc.*, 590 F.2d 701 (2d Cir. 1978).

(3) It is within the discretion of the court to decide that voluntary discontinuance will render the need for an injunction moot. *Schutt Mfg. Co. v. Riddell, Inc.*, 673 F.2d 202, 207 (7th Cir. 1982); *Camel Hair & Cashmere Institute, Inc. v. Associated Dry Goods Corp.*, 799 F.2d 6 (1st Cir. 1986) (preliminary injunction motion denied). This is true whether discontinuance occurred before or after suit, although the discretion will usually be resolved against the infringer if discontinuance came after suit. *Scotch Whiskey Ass'n v. Barton Distilling Co.*, 489 F.2d 809 (7th Cir. 1973). *See Menendez v. Saks & Co.*, 485 F.2d 1355, 1375 (2d Cir. 1973), in which the court ruled: "It is elementary that a court of equity will not enjoin one from doing what he is not attempting and does not intend to do"; and *Johnny Carson Apparel, Inc. v. Zeeman Manufacturing Co.*, 203 U.S.P.Q. 585, 591 (N.D. Ga. 1978), in which the court states that "[a]s the acts and practices complained of by plaintiff have been stopped, and the defendants have made clear that they do not intend to resume such, it appears to the court that there is not basis upon which an injunction could issue." *Compare John T. Lloyd Laboratories, Inc. v. Lloyd Brothers Pharmacists*, 131 F.2d 703 (6th Cir. 1942), in which the court ruled: "The mere fact . . . use was discontinued by them before the commencement of this action is no guarantee that they may not resume its use should the injunction be dissolved. If appellants have

no such wrongful intent, no injury ensues to them from maintenance of the bar." To similar effect is *Polo Fashions, Inc. v. Dick Bruhn, Inc.*, 793 F.2d 1132 (9th Cir. 1986). The decision generally turns on the court's belief as to the likelihood of repeated misconduct in the future. What factors should influence a court in determining whether an injunction should issue after voluntary discontinuance by an infringer? Should a distinction be made between an isolated instance of unfair competition and a case where several acts are established? Is an infringer's good faith adoption significant?

(4) What bases might there be for modifying an injunction after a passage of years? *Compare Humble Oil & Refining Co. v. American Oil Co.*, 405 F.2d 803 (8th Cir. 1969), *cert. denied*, 395 U.S. 905 (1969) (where a claim of substantial and unforeseeable change of circumstances or oppressive hardship was rejected) *with King-Seeley Thermos Co. v. Aladdin Industries, Inc.*, 418 F.2d 31, 35 (2d Cir. 1969) ("While changes in fact or in law afford the clearest bases for altering an injunction, the power of equity has repeatedly been recognized as extending also to cases where a better appreciation of the facts in light of experience indicates that the decree is not properly adapted to accomplishing its purposes.")

(5) Courts sometimes favor the use of disclaimers in close cases. *See R.J. Toomey Co. v. Toomey*, 683 F. Supp. 873 (D. Mass. 1988) (son was required to disclaim association with his father's competing business); *Gucci v. Gucci Shops, Inc.*, 688 F. Supp. 916 (S.D.N.Y. 1988) (Paolo Gucci required to disclaim association from the Gucci leather goods empire).

Consumer studies, however, have indicated that disclaimers are often ineffective in reducing the likelihood of confusion. *See* the discussion in *Home Box Office, Inc. v. Showtime/Movie Channel, Inc.*, 832 F.2d 1311, 1315–16 (2d Cir. 1987) (placing the burden on the infringer to produce evidence that the proposed disclaimer would significantly reduce the likelihood of confusion). *Cf. Soltex Polymer Corp. v. Fortex Industries*, 832 F.2d 1325, 1330 (2d Cir. 1987) (citing *Home Box Office*, but noting it is within the discretion of the district court to permit use with a disclaimer where likelihood of confusion is "far less than substantial").

In *International Kennel Club, Inc. v. Mighty Star, Inc.*, 846 F.2d 1079, 1093 (7th Cir. 1988), the court affirmed the lower court's refusal to order a disclaimer remedy, stating "plaintiff's reputation and good will should not be forever dependent on the effectiveness of fine print disclaimers often ignored by consumers." In *Basile S.p.A. v. Basile*, 899 F.2d 35, 37 (D.C. Cir. 1990), the district court had ordered that the following disclaimer be used on defendant's watches:

> BASILE watches emanate exclusively from Diffusione Basile de Francesco Basile & Co., S.A.S. in Venice, Italy. Diffusione Basile is devoted solely to the manufacture and sale of fine watches throughout the world.

In vacating, the Appellate Court found that "common sense" dictated that the watches will still be known as "Basile watches" under the lower court's injunction. *Id.*, at 37. "The disclaimer is inadequate because it uses the appellant's protected name: Basile. The inclusion of 'Venezia' in the court's order would not help American consumers disassociate the watch with appellant's watch manufactured in Milan." *Id.*, at 38. *See also* the *Dobbs* case in Chapter 2, *supra*; *University of Georgia Athletic Ass'n v. Laite*, 756 F.2d 1535, 1547 (11th Cir. 1985) (rejecting disclaimer defense); *Charles of Ritz Group, Ltd. v. Quality King Distributors*, 832 F.2d 1317, 1324 (2d Cir. 1987) (following *Home Box Office, supra*, in rejecting disclaimer remedy); Palladino, *Disclaimers Before and After HBO v. Showtime*, 82 Trademark Rep. 203 (1992); Comment, *Injunctive Relief for Trademark Infringement — The Second Circuit Misses The Mark: Home Box Office v. Showtime/The Movie Channel*, 62 St. John's L. Rev. 286 (1988).

(6) What are the criteria for granting or denying a preliminary injunction? Should the public interest be considered? *See Warner Bros., Inc. v. Gay Toys, Inc., supra*; *International Kennel Club, Inc. v. Mighty Star, Inc.*, 846 F.2d 1079, 1084 (7th Cir. 1988); *California Cedar Products Co. v. Pine Mountain Corp.*, 724 F.2d 827 (9th Cir. 1984); Kessler, Sterne & Dillon, *Preliminary Injunctions in Patent and Trademark Cases*, 26 Trial 42 (1990).

(7) Should monetary relief be granted in addition to injunctive relief where the defendant has acted without knowledge or intent? What factors should the court consider in awarding treble damages under the Lanham Act? *See* Barber, *Recovery of Profits Under the Lanham Act: Are The District Courts Doing Their Job?*, 82 Trademark Rep. 141 (1992); Bussert & Davis, *Calculating Profits Under Section 35 of The Lanham Act: A Practitioner's Guide*, 82 Trademark Rep. 182 (1992); Note, *Trademark Law: Equity's Role in Unfair Competition Cases*, 13 U. Hawaii L. Rev. 137 (1991); Comment, *Money Damages and Corrective Advertising: An Economic Analysis*, 55 U. Chicago L. Rev. 629 (1988); Keating, *Damages Standards for False Advertising Under the Lanham Act: A New Trend Emerges*, 20 Rutgers L.J. 125 (1988); Comment, *Monetary Relief for False Advertising Claims Arising Under Section 43(a) of the Lanham Act*, 34 UCLA L. Rev. 953 (1987); Koelemay, *Monetary Relief for Trademark Infringement Under The Lanham Act*, 72 Trademark Rep. 458 (1982); Pattishall, *The Impact of Intent in Trade Identity Cases*, 65 Nw. U.L. Rev. 421 (1970).

(8) A variety of legal theories have provided the basis for monetary awards in Lanham Act cases. *See, e.g., Taco Cabana Int'l, Inc. v. Two Pesos, Inc.*, 932 F.2d 1113, 1127 (5th Cir. 1991), *aff'd*, 112 S. Ct. 2753 (1992) (plaintiff entitled to profits lost due to foreclosure of a geographic market by defendant's prior infringing entry); *Broan Mfg. Co. v. Associated Distributors, Inc.*, 923 F.2d 1232, 1240–41 (6th Cir. 1991) (plaintiff entitled to profits lost from discontinued relationship with defendant and compensatory damages for potential erroneous product liability claims against plaintiff caused by defendant's hazardous infringing product); *U-Haul International, Inc. v. Jartran, Inc.*, 793 F.2d 1034 (9th Cir. 1986), ($40 million award based on doubling the amount of plaintiff's actual corrective advertising expenditures when combined with defendant's advertising expenditures); *Transgo, Inc. v. Ajac Transmission Corp.*, 768 F.2d 1001 (9th Cir. 1985) (awarding compensatory, punitive (state law) damages and attorney fees); *Otis Clapp & Son, Inc. v. Filmore Vitamin Co.*, 754 F.2d 738 (7th Cir. 1985), (plaintiff awarded an amount equivalent to defendant's "profits" even though defendant lost money, and attorney's fees, but the fees award reduced because plaintiff was "overly aggressive" under the

circumstances). *See also Schroeder v. Lotito*, 747 F.2d 801 (1st Cir. 1984) (profits and attorneys' fees); *West Des Moines State Bank v. Hawkeye Bancorporation*, 722 F.2d 411 (8th Cir. 1983) (projected corrective advertising expenses, following *Big O, supra*). In *Boston Professional Hockey Ass'n v. Dallas Cap Mfg.*, 597 F.2d 71 (5th Cir. 1979), and *Deering, Milliken & Co. v. Gilbert*, 269 F.2d 191 (2d Cir. 1959), the courts calculated the damages amounts based on constructive license royalties. This approach was rejected under the circumstances of *Bandag, Inc. v. Al Bolser's Tire Stores*, 750 F.2d 903 (Fed. Cir. 1984), where the court found such a measure "grossly out of proportion" to the rights appropriated, and *Playboy Enterprises, Inc. v. Baccarate Clothing Co.*, 692 F.2d 1272 (9th Cir. 1982), where the court observed that constructive royalties do not adequately take the economic incentive out of trademark infringement. *See also Universal City Studios, Inc. v. Nintendo Co., Ltd.*, 797 F.2d 70, 77 (2d Cir. 1986), where defendant was awarded over $1 million in attorneys' fees incurred in defending against a suit brought in bad faith.

(9) Punitive damages are not authorized under the Lanham Act, 15 U.S.C. § 1117, but may be awarded under state law. *Getty Petroleum Corp. v. Bartco Petroleum Corp.*, 858 F.2d 103, 106, 113 (2d Cir. 1988) ($2 million dollar punitive damage award under Lanham Act vacated), *cert. denied*, 490 U.S. 1006 (1989); *Getty Petroleum Corp. v. Island Transportation Corp.*, 878 F.2d 650 (2d Cir. 1989) ($250,000 punitive damage award under New York law affirmed).

(10) Proving a case to be "exceptional" so as to warrant an award of attorneys' fees under the Lanham Act often requires showing defendant acted in bad faith. 15 U.S.C. § 1117. *Compare TakeCare Corp. v. Takecare of Oklahoma, Inc.*, 889 F.2d 955, 958 (10th Cir. 1989) (affirming attorneys' fee award in "exceptional case" where reliance on counsel's advice not shown to be reasonable) *and Universal City Studios, Inc. v. Nintendo Co.*, 797 F.2d 70, 77 (2d Cir.), *cert. denied*, 479 U.S. 987 (1986) (defendant awarded over $1 million in attorneys' fees incurred in defending against suit brought in bad faith) *with Ferrero U.S.A., Inc. v. Ozak Trading, Inc.*, 21 U.S.P.Q.2d 1215 (3d Cir. 1991) (reversing award of attorneys' fees where no bad faith conduct shown in a close case).

(11) Section 37 of the Lanham Act, 15 U.S.C. § 1119, provides that in any civil action involving a registered trade mark the court may order the cancellation of registrations. This power in the courts to "rectify the register" provides an important additional remedy in a trademark infringement action.

(12) The Lanham Act's § 42 (15 U.S.C. § 1124) provides for deposit of copies of one's trademark registration with the Bureau of Customs which will then take steps to prohibit importation of merchandise bearing copies or simulations of the mark. *See* Chapter 3, *supra*; Kuhn, *Remedies Available at Customs for Infringement of A Registered Trademark*, 70 Trademark Rep. 387 (1980); Atwood, *Import Restrictions on Trademarked Merchandise — The Role of the United States Bureau Of Customs*, 59 Trademark Rep. 301 (1969).

(13) The Trademark Counterfeiting Act of 1984 provides that the court shall award successful plaintiffs in counterfeiting cases treble damages or profits and reasonable attorneys' fees "unless the court finds extenuating circumstances." 15 U.S.C. § 1117. *See* the section on Counterfeiting in Chapter 5, *supra*.

CHAPTER 10

GOVERNMENTAL REGULATION

§ 10.01 The Federal Trade Commission

INTRODUCTION

The Federal Trade Commission is the leading federal administrative agency protecting consumers and competitors against deceptive advertising. As originally conceived in 1914, the FTC was primarily intended to bolster what was widely believed to be ineffective enforcement of the antitrust laws, rather than to be the watchdog of advertising. *See* MacIntyre & Volhard, *The Federal Trade Commission*, 11 B.C. Ind. & Com. L. Rev. 723 (1970); Note, *Developments in the Law, Deceptive Advertising*, 80 Harv. L. Rev. 1005 (1967). In order to arm the FTC for unbridled antitrust enforcement, § 5 of the original Federal Trade Commission Act broadly declared all "unfair methods of competition in commerce" to be unlawful and "empowered and directed" the FTC to prevent such practices. 15 U.S.C. § 45(a) (1914). *See generally* Kanwit, *Federal Trade Commission* (1993).

Notwithstanding this original intent of Congress, over 90 percent of the actions initiated by the FTC during its first two decades were directed against deceptive trade practices rather than antitrust violations. *See* Posner, *The Federal Trade Commission*, 37 U. Chi. L. Rev. 47 (1969). Moreover, the FTC's power to prevent deceptive advertising was upheld at the very outset in *Sears, Roebuck & Co. v. FTC*, 258 F. 307 (7th Cir. 1919), and later confirmed in *FTC v. Winsted Hosiery Co.*, 258 U.S. 483 (1922).

Until 1938, however, the FTC's latitude in challenging deceptive practices was severely limited. In *FTC v. Gratz*, 253 U.S. 421 (1920), the Supreme Court held that § 5 of the FTC Act prohibited only those unfair trade practices which were proscribed either by other statutes or by the common law as it was in 1914. In *FTC v. Raladam Co.*, 283 U.S. 643 (1931), the Supreme Court held the FTC could proceed only against those practices which harmed competitors, regardless of their effect on consumers. It was not until the decision in *FTC v. R. F. Keppel & Bros., Inc.*, 291 U.S. 304 (1934), and the passage of the Wheeler-Lea Act of 1938 (52 Stat. 111 (1938)) that the FTC Act became a potentially effective weapon to protect consumer interests. In *Keppel*, the Court reversed its decision in *Gratz* on the types of practices prohibited by § 5, stating, 291 U.S. at 310:

> Neither the language nor the history of the Act suggests that Congress intended to confine the forbidden methods to fixed and unyielding categories. The

common law afforded a definition of unfair competition and, before the enactment of the Federal Trade Commission Act, the Sherman Act had laid its inhibition upon combinations to restrain or monopolize interstate commerce which the courts had construed to include restraints upon competition in interstate commerce. It would not have been a difficult feat of draftsmanship to have restricted the operation of the Trade Commission Act to those methods of competition in interstate commerce which are forbidden at common law or which are likely to grow into violations of the Sherman Act, if that had been the purpose of the legislation.

The Wheeler-Lea Act, a reaction to the decision in *Raladam*, amended § 5 of the FTC Act by adding a prohibition against "unfair or deceptive acts or practices in commerce." The purpose of the Amendment was expressed by a Senate Committee member as follows:

> Section 5 of the present act declares unlawful unfair methods of competition in commerce, and the pending bill amends that section by also declaring unlawful, unfair or deceptive acts and practices in commerce. Under the present act it has been intimated in court decisions that the Commission may lose jurisdiction of a case of deceptive and similar unfair practices if it should develop in the proceeding that all competitors in the industry practiced the same methods, and the Commission may be ousted of its jurisdiction, no matter how badly the public may be in need of protection from said deceptive and unfair acts. Under the proposed amendment, the Commission would have jurisdiction to stop the exploitation or deception of the public, even though the competition of the respondent are themselves entitled to no protection because of their engaging in similar practices.

S. Rep. No. 221, 75th Cong. 1st Sess. 3 (1937).

The Wheeler-Lea Amendment also assigned to the FTC jurisdiction over the advertising of foods, drugs, cosmetics, and devices (15 U.S.C. § 52), leaving the regulation of their labeling and packaging to the Food and Drug Administration, 21 U.S.C. §§ 301–394. In subsequent years, the FTC has also been given either total or partial responsibility for enforcing a number of other statutes, many of which are designed to protect the consumer. These acts include the Fair Packaging and Labeling Act, 15 U.S.C. § 1451 *et seq.*; Consumer Credit Protection Act, 15 U.S.C. §§ 1601–1615, 1631–1641, 16, 71–77; Federal Cigarette Labeling and Advertising Act, 15 U.S.C. § 1331 *et seq.*; Trademark Act, 15 U.S.C. § 1064; McCarran-Ferguson Insurance Act, 15 U.S.C. § 1011 *et seq.*; and the Emergency Petroleum Allocation Act, 15 U.S.C. § 751 *et seq.*

In 1973, the FTC's potential effectiveness was supplemented through amendment of the FTC Act to empower it to seek relief pendente lite against unfair or deceptive practices. 15 U.S.C. § 53. Previously, the FTC had such power in some areas, such as the false advertising of foods, drugs, cosmetics or devices (15 U.S.C. § 52); Wool Products Labeling Act (15 U.S.C. §§ 68–68j); Fur Product Labeling Act (15 U.S.C. §§ 69–69j); and Textile Fiber Product Identification Act (15 U.S.C. §§ 70–70k). It could not, however, stop most unfair or deceptive acts or practices during the often lengthy pendency of FTC proceedings. The amendment also gave the FTC authority to apply directly to the courts for enforcement of its orders and for subpoenas, avoiding the delay or obstruction formerly caused by the FTC's dependency on the Justice Department to bring such actions. 15 U.S.C. §§ 49, 53.

In 1975, the Magnuson-Moss Warranty-Federal Trade Commission Improvement Act extended the jurisdiction to matters "affecting commerce." Pub. L. No. 93-637 § 201, 15 U.S.C. §§ 45, 52 (1975), *see* H.R. REP. No. 93-1107, 93 Cong. 2d. Sess. 45 (1974). Section 5, as amended, states:

> Unfair methods of competition in or affecting commerce, and unfair or deceptive acts or practices in or affecting commerce, are declared unlawful.

15 U.S.C. § 45(a)(1). In addition, the Act established standards for warranties and conferred upon the FTC the authority to (1) issue trade regulation rules defining unfair or deceptive acts or practices, (2) seek civil penalties in federal district court for violations of FTC orders prohibiting unfair acts or practices by individuals already subject to an FTC order as well as by any person, partnership, or corporation which knowingly violates an FTC rule or order, and (3) impose civil penalties of up to $10,000 for each such violation. Pub. L. No. 93-637 §§ 202(a), 204(b), 205(a), 15 U.S.C. §§ 57(a)(1), 45(m) (1975). The Act also permits the FTC to institute civil actions in either federal or state court seeking consumer redress for injuries caused by rule violations or practices resulting in a cease and desist order. Pub. L. No. 93-637, § 206(a), 15 U.S.C. § 57(b) (1975). Remedies available for such injuries include damages, rescission or reformation of contracts, refund of money or return of property. For additional commentary, see *Empirical Study of the Magnuson-Moss Warranty Act*, 31 Stan. L. Rev. 1117 (1979); Schroeder, *Private Actions Under the Magnuson-Moss Warranty Act*, 66 Cal. L. Rev. 1 (1978).

In 1980, however, in response to criticism that the FTC abused its extensive powers, Congress passed the Federal Trade Commission Improvements Act of 1980, Pub. L. No. 96-252, 94 Stat. 374. The Act, as amended, limits FTC powers affecting insurance, children's advertising, agricultural cooperatives, the funeral industry, private standard-setting and certification, and trademarks asserted by the FTC to have become generic. Pub. L. No. 96-252 §§ 5, 7, 11, 18–20, 94 Stat. 374.

[A] Organization and Procedures

[1] Membership and Staff

One of the Congressional purposes in establishing the Federal Trade Commission was to create an administrative agency free from executive and political control. This legislative intent is reflected in the membership requirements of the Commission (15 U.S.C. § 41): (1) the five commissioners are to be appointed by the President with the confirmation by the Senate for staggered seven-year terms; (2) no more than three of the commissioners may belong to the same political party; and (3) the President may remove a commissioner only for "inefficiency, neglect of duty or malfeasance in office." In *Humphrey's Ex'r v. United States*, 295 U.S. 602 (1935), the Supreme Court held that this last provision prevented President Roosevelt from removing a commissioner simply because they had different points of view.

The FTC is organized into four primary components: (1) the Bureau of Consumer Protection, which enforces all consumer laws within the Commission's jurisdiction; (2) the Bureau of Competition, which enforces the Clayton Act and restraints of trade violating Section 5 of the FTC Act; (3) the Bureau of Economics, which furnishes the enforcement bureaus with economic and statistical information, and (4) the regional offices, which also conduct investigations and litigation and provide guidance to business in their respective regions.

[2] Investigatory Powers

Section 6 of the Federal Trade Commission Act provides the Commission with the power to "gather and compile information concerning and to investigate" the conduct and practices affecting commerce of any person, partnership or corporation and to require them to file reports or answer specific questions concerning such matters. 15 U.S.C. § 46. The FTC Improvements Act of 1980 added § 20 to the Act, requiring the FTC in its investigations to use "civil investigative demands" which state the nature of the conduct alleged to be unfair or deceptive. 15 U.S.C. § 57b-1. Civil investigative demands are the only form of compulsory process available in investigations of unfair or deceptive acts or practices. *See* 16 C.F.R. § 2.7(b) (1983), amended 48 Fed. Reg. 41,375 (Sept. 15, 1983); and S. Rep. No. 96-500 at 23–24. The use of subpoenas (§§ 9 and 10 of the Act empower the Commission to subpoena witnesses and documents) is now limited to investigations of unfair methods of competition and to adjudicative proceedings. FTC Act §§ 9–10, 15 U.S.C. §§ 49–50; FTC Act § 20, 15 U.S.C. § 57b-1. In addition, the 1980 Act requires that all forms of compulsory process must be signed by a Commissioner acting pursuant to a Commission resolution. FTC Act § 20, 15 U.S.C. § 57b-1(i).

Investigatorial powers have long been available to the FTC in assembling information for possible new Rules or legislation. For many years, however, the courts viewed these powers as a grant apart from the FTC's role as an adjudicative body and therefore not available for prelitigation inquiries concerning possible violations of § 5. *FTC v. American Tobacco Co.*, 264 U.S. 298 (1924). More recent decisions have upheld the FTC's authority to use these broad powers prior to issuing a complaint, *e.g., FTC v. Invention Submission Corp.*, 965 F.2d 1086 (D.C. Cir. 1992), *cert. denied*, 113 S. Ct. 1255 (1993); and to determine compliance with § 5 cease and desist orders. *See United States v. Morton Salt Co.*, 338 U.S. 632 (1950).

[3] Nonadjudicative Authority and Functions

[a] Industry Guides

Soon after its inception, the FTC was faced with the prospect of prosecuting numerous individual complaints against members of the same industry committing the same offense. With the agreement of industry, which strenuously pleaded ignorance of the meaning of the phrase, "unfair methods of competition" in § 5 of the FTC Act, the Trade Practice Conference Program was adopted as an alternative to case-by-case adjudication. At these conferences, proposed Trade Practice Conference Rules (later called Trade Practice Rules) prepared by FTC attorneys were discussed with representatives of the subject industry and sometimes modified.

Once the Commission approved and promulgated the Rules, industry members were asked to indicate their acceptance and proposed compliance with them. Acceptance of the Trade Practice Rules usually resulted in the cessation of a proceeding against an industry member based on a practice covered in the Rules, unless the good faith of the member was considered doubtful.

Trade Practice Rules no longer exist as such. The majority of the rules were rescinded by the FTC in 1978, 43 Fed. Reg. 44,483 and the remaining rules were reclassified as Industry Guides. A Guide is essentially the FTC's interpretation of what constitutes a violation of a statute that it enforces and may apply to a practice which is prevalent in more than one industry. 16 C.F.R. §§ 1.5, 1.6. They are promulgated on the FTC's own initiative or at the request of any interested party or group, when it appears to the FTC that they "would be beneficial in the public interest" and "bring about more widespread and equitable observance of laws administered by the Commission." 16 C.F.R. § 1.6. These Guides have no substantive legal effect.

[b]   Trade Regulation Rules

The FTC also promulgates Trade Regulation Rules. Proceedings to issue these Rules may be initiated by the FTC itself or at the request of any interested party and may include investigations, conferences and hearings following notice of the proposed Rule in the Federal Register. 16 C.F.R. §§ 1.9–1.13. After considering all relevant matters including those presented by interested persons, the Rules are published in the Federal Register. 16 C.F.R. § 1.14. The Rules become effective four days after publication. 16 C.F.R. § 1.14(c). Unlike Industry Guides, Trade Regulation Rules constitute substantive rules of law. 16 C.F.R. § 1.8(a). Thus, the FTC may establish a statutory violation merely by proving that the challenged conduct is prohibited by such a Rule. *National Petroleum Refiners Ass'n v. FTC*, 482 F.2d 672 (D.C. Cir. 1973), *cert. denied*, 415 U.S. 951 (1974). As a result, the FTC can foreclose the defenses that the particular practice is not prohibited by § 5 or that prior adjudications are inapposite or should be overruled.

In 1975, the Magnuson-Moss Act codified the FTC's rule-making powers (15 U.S.C. § 57a(a)(1) (1975)) and provided that notice of proposed rule-making must be given and interested persons must be permitted to testify before the FTC. 15 U.S.C. § 57a(c)(2). Rules promulgated under the Act may be challenged by appeal to a court of appeals within 60 days after promulgation. 15 U.S.C. § 57a(e)(1)(A). *See American Optometric Ass'n v. FTC*, 626 F.2d 896 (D.C. Cir. 1980), in which the portion of a Rule curtailing state and professional restrictions on the advertising of ophthalmic goods and services remanded to the FTC for reconsideration after *Bates v. State Bar of Arizona*, 433 U.S. 350 (1977).

[c]   Advisory Opinions

In 1962, the FTC also began giving Advisory Opinions as to whether proposed conduct is legal or complies with an outstanding Commission order. These Opinions are usually rendered and published after a conference with the FTC staff and their certification to the Commission. 16 C.F.R. § 1.2. The FTC has, however, placed certain limitations upon the availability of such Opinions:

A request ordinarily will be considered inappropriate for such advice: (a) where the course of action is already being followed by the requesting party; (b) where the same or substantially the same course of action is under investigation or is or has been the subject of a current proceeding, order, or decree initiated or obtained by the Commission or another governmental agency; or (c) where the proposed course of action or its effects may be such that an informed decision thereon cannot be made or could be made only after extensive investigation, clinical study, testing, or collateral inquiry.

16 C.F.R. § 1.1. While an Advisory Opinion is outstanding, a party will not be prosecuted by the FTC for acting in good faith reliance upon it, but an Opinion may be revoked at any time and a proceeding initiated unless the practice is promptly discontinued. 16 C.F.R. § 1.3.

[4] Adjudicative Procedures

FTC adjudicative proceedings are instituted by issuance of an administrative complaint stating the charges and giving notice of a hearing. The FTC institutes proceedings whenever it has "reason to believe" that § 5, or a provision of any other act that it administers, is being violated and that an adjudicative proceeding would be in the "interest of the public." 15 U.S.C. § 45(b). In nearly all cases, however, the FTC has accorded the alleged offender the opportunity to agree to a consent order during the investigational stage. 16 C.F.R. § 2.31(a).

The FTC generally sends the party a proposed complaint and consent order, together with notice of its intention to institute proceedings. 16 C.F.R. § 2.31(a). If a consent order is accepted, it is placed on public record for sixty days for comment, after which the FTC must either withdraw its acceptance of the order or issue a decision in disposition of the proceeding. 16 C.F.R. §§ 2.32, 2.34. Consent orders are entered in the great majority of cases docketed by the FTC and have the same effect as orders entered after an administrative adjudication. 16 C.F.R. § 2.32. *See* Wald, *FTC Settlement Procedures*, 5 Litigation 8 (1979). If a consent order is not agreed upon or accepted by the FTC, a formal complaint is issued and the availability of the consent procedure usually is foreclosed. 16 C.F.R. § 2.31(b). After the formal complaint issues, pretrial conferences are held and limited discovery is conducted. 16 C.F.R. §§ 3.21, 3.31.

Thereafter, the matter is heard by an administrative law judge who issues an Initial Opinion. 16 C.F.R. § 3.51. The proceedings are conducted according to evidentiary rules similar to, but less rigid than, the rules ordinarily used in court proceedings. The administrative law judge's decision becomes final unless (1) a party appeals to the Commission, (2) the Commission stays the decision, or (3) the Commission dockets it for review. 16 C.F.R. §§ 3.51–3.52. On review, the Commission accepts briefs, hears oral arguments, and can make findings of fact in deciding whether to modify, accept or set aside the examiner's decision. 16 C.F.R. §§ 3.52, 3.54.

If a cease and desist order is issued, the respondent may then appeal to a Circuit Court of Appeals within sixty days from the date of service of the order. 15 U.S.C. § 45(c). The appellate court's scope of review is limited to determining whether the Commission's findings of fact are supported by substantial evidence and whether the choice of remedy is within the FTC's powers. The reviewing court is also empowered to issue injunctions enforcing the cease and desist orders. 15 U.S.C. § 45(c). Once the order has become final, the respondent must submit one report within sixty days and further reports if requested by the FTC, setting forth the manner of compliance with the order. 16 C.F.R. § 2.41.

Each separate violation of a final cease and desist order is punishable by a fine of up to $10,000, except that for violations occurring "through continuing failure or neglect of a final order" each day constitutes a separate offense. 15 U.S.C. § 45(1). This penalty is recovered through a civil action in federal district court. 15 U.S.C. § 45(m).

Under the 1973 Amendment to the FTC Act, district courts also are expressly authorized to issue injunctions in civil actions to enforce the Commission's orders. 15 U.S.C. § 45(1). In addition, once an order has been affirmed on appeal, the Commission may seek to enforce it through an action for criminal contempt of the court's enforcement order. *FTC v. Gladstone*, 450 F.2d 913 (5th Cir. 1971); *In re Holland Furnace Co.*, 341 F.2d 548 (7th Cir. 1965), *aff'd sub nom.*, *Cheff v. Schnackenberg*, 384 U.S. 373 (1966).

[B] Constitutionality

INTRODUCTION

The First Amendment to the U.S. Constitution provides that "Congress shall make no law . . . abridging the freedom of speech, or of the press . . . ." In *Valentine v. Chrestensen*, 316 U.S. 52 (1942), the Supreme Court stated without any explanation that "purely commercial advertising" is not protected by the First Amendment. For years the lower courts almost unquestioningly adhered to that principle despite the lack of explanation for it. This omission was commented on by Mr. Justice Douglas in a concurring opinion in *Cammarano v. United States*, 358 U.S. 498, 514 (1959): "Those who make their living through exercise of First Amendment rights are no less entitled to its protection than those whose advocacy or promotion is not hitched to a profit motive. . . ."

In *New York Times Co. v. Sullivan*, 376 U.S. 254 (1964), the Supreme Court bypassed an opportunity to explain why "purely commercial speech" was undeserving of First Amendment protection. The issue there was whether a paid advertisement by a civil rights group criticizing police actions deserved protection. The Court ignored the commercial motivation of the *Times* and instead examined the content of the speech, stating that "the publication here was not a 'commercial' advertisement [in that it] communicated information, expressed opinion, recited grievances . . . ." This set the stage for the Court's decision in *Bigelow v. Virginia*, 421 U.S. 809, 826 (1975), striking down a Virginia statute prohibiting the advertising of abortions, in which the Court stated that "commercial speech is not stripped of all First Amendment protection. The relationship of speech to the marketplace does not make it valueless in the marketplace of ideas."

In 1976, in *Virginia State Board of Pharmacy v. Virginia Citizens Consumer Council, Inc.*, 425 U.S. 748, 763 (1976), the Court held invalid a Virginia statute which prohibited pharmacists from advertising prices for prescription drugs, stating that "speech which does no more than propose a commercial transaction is not so removed from truth, science, morality and acts in general, in its diffusion of sentiment on the administration of Government that it lacks all protection." *See also Linmark Associates v. Township of Willingboro*, 431 U.S. 85 (1977) (township ordinance prohibiting the display of "For Sale" signs in an attempt to stem "white flight" held to be in violation of First Amendment); *Carey v. Population Services International*, 431 U.S. 678 (1977) (New York law prohibiting the advertising of contraceptives held unconstitutional); *Bates v. State Bar of Arizona*, 433 U.S. 350 (1977) (Arizona prohibition on attorney advertising held unconstitutional).

After the *Bates* decision, the Court seemed to retreat somewhat in its protection of commercial speech. *Ohralik v. Ohio State Bar Association*, 436 U.S. 447 (1978) (commercial speech should be afforded only a limited measure of protection); *Friedman v. Rodgers*, 440 U.S. 1 (1979) (Texas act which prohibited the practice of optometry under an assumed trade name held constitutional). In *Central Hudson Gas & Electric Corp. v. Public Service Commission*, 447 U.S. 557 (1980), the Court set forth a four-part test for commercial speech: (1) the speech must concern lawful activity and not be misleading; if so, a restriction on it will be held valid only if it (2) seeks to implement a substantial governmental interest; (3) directly advances that interest; and (4) reaches no further than necessary to accomplish the given objective. Further, the Court stated that "the Constitution therefore accords a lesser protection to commercial speech than to other constitutionally guaranteed expression." *Id.* at 563. *See Board of Trustees v. Fox*, 492 U.S. 469 (1989), in which the Court affirmed the test for commercial speech set forth in *Central Hudson*, and clarified that the fourth prong does not require that restrictions on commercial speech be the absolutely least restrictive means of achieving the governmental interests asserted, but only requires a reasonable "fit" between the ends and the means. The Court has thus shifted — from according commercial speech no First Amendment protection, to according protection almost equal to that of other forms of speech, then moving back again to a middle ground seemingly still in the process of definition.

SCIENTIFIC MANUFACTURING CO. v. FEDERAL TRADE COMMISSION

United States Court of Appeals, Third Circuit
124 F.2d 640 (1941)

JONES, CIRCUIT JUDGE:

. . . .

Scientific Manufacturing Company, Inc., is a Pennsylvania corporation having its place of business in Scranton, Pennsylvania, which is also the place of residence of Force, the other petitioner, who, with members of his immediate family, owns all of the capital stock of the company. Force, as president of the company, controls and directs its activities and practices. Among the latter, are the publication and sale of pamphlets containing two articles written by Force in intended exposition of alleged dangers to health from poisoning which, according to him, attend the use of aluminum utensils in the preparation or storage of food for human consumption.

The Commission found that Force and his company sold and distributed many of the pamphlets throughout the United States "to the public and to various manufacturers, distributors, dealers and salesmen of cooking and storage utensils made of materials other than and competitive with utensils made of aluminum." Neither Force nor his company was engaged in any way or interested materially in the manufacture, sale or distribution of cooking utensils of any sort. As indicated by the Commission's findings, the petitioner's course of trade in interstate commerce was limited to the sale and distribution of the pamphlets. This activity was motivated by a zeal on the part of Force, who is a graduate pharmacist and chemist of some twenty-odd years experience, to propagate his own unorthodox ideas and theories by independently disseminating what, unquestionably, he believes to be the truth concerning the effect of aluminum metals upon foods. The Commission further found that the statements and representations respecting aluminum utensils, as contained in the pamphlets were "false, misleading and disparaging"; that they serve to "mislead and deceive a substantial portion of the purchasing public with the false and erroneous belief that cooking utensils made from aluminum are . . . harmful and are dangerous to the consumers of food prepared or stored" therein; and that the present petitioners through their sale and distribution of the pamphlets supply an "instrumentality by means of which uninformed or unscrupulous manufacturers, distributors, dealers and salesmen may deceive or mislead members of the purchasing public and induce them to purchase utensils made from materials other than aluminum."

On this factual basis, the Commission concluded that the acts and practices of the present petitioners were "to the prejudice and injury of the public and constitute unfair and deceptive acts and practices in commerce within the intent and meaning of the Federal Trade Commission Act." The cease and desist order thereupon ensued.

. . . .

It was for the purpose of clothing the Commission with jurisdiction to act in respect of unfair acts or practices in commerce regardless of their effect upon competition that the [Wheeler-Lea Amendment] was offered and enacted. True enough, as the Commission argues, the effect of the amendment was to so broaden the Commission's jurisdiction as to enable it to act where only the public interest was adversely affected by the unfair practices. Nonetheless, it was still the unfair acts of traders in the affected commerce that the Commission was empowered to enjoin. The public interest to be served is no different under the amendment than it was under the original Act. The change effected by the amendment lay in the fact that the Commission could thenceforth prevent unfair or deceptive acts or practices in commerce which injuriously affected the public interest alone, while under the original Act the Commission's power to safeguard the public against unfair trade practices depended upon whether the objectionable acts or practices affected competition. But the restrainable acts or practices in commerce continued to be such as are performed or perpetrated in the trade affected by the offenses, whether or not there is competition. In short, the Commission's intervention is limited to acts or practices in the affected trade. If the amendment were given any broader scope, the Act would relate to far more than trade practices, and the Commission would become the absolute arbiter of the truth of all printed matter moving in interstate commerce, even where scholars in the particular field of knowledge were in wide disagreement. "The findings of the commission as to facts, if supported by testimony, shall be conclusive." The courts are bound to accept them as such. *Federal Trade Commission v. Standard Education Society*, 302 U.S. 112, 117; *Federal Trade Commission v. Algoma Lumber Co.*, 291 U.S. 67, 73.

It follows from what we have said that, the present petitioners not being engaged or materially interested in the cooking utensil trade, the Commission was without power to enjoin their sale and distribution of the pamphlets which they published concerning the use of aluminum cooking utensils and, further, that the publication, sale and distribution of matter concerning an article of trade by a person not engaged or financial interested in commerce in that trade is not an unfair or deceptive act or practice within the contemplation of the Federal Trade Commission Act, as amended, if the published matter, even though unfounded or untrue, represents the publisher's honest opinion or belief.

In the view we thus take of the intent of the Federal Trade Commission Act as amended, no question of abridgement of the petitioner's freedom of speech or of press arises. However, we may say that the constitutional inhibition of any such abridgement which the Commission's interpretation of the amendment to the statute at once involves, would so seriously threaten its validity as to justify rejection of the Commission's contention. *Blodgett v. Holden*, 275 U.S. 142, 148, 276 U.S. 594; *United States v. Standard Brewery*, 251 U.S. 210, 220; *United States v. Delaware & Hudson Co.*, 213 U.S. 366, 407, 408; and *United States v. Jin Fuey Moy*, 241 U.S. 394, 401.

The petitioner Force dealt in opinions and no more. Nor does the Commission alter their category by tabulating their statements of fact. They are theories or ideas, false, it may well be, but sincerely held none the less, and that, too, in a field of knowledge where even experts at times must be content with approximations to verity. To the situation here presented the words of Mr. Justice Holmes are apposite, — "Certitude is not the test of certainty. We have been cocksure of many things that were not so. . . . But while one's experience thus makes certain preferences dogmatic for oneself, recognition of how they came to be so leaves one able to see that others, poor souls, may be equally dogmatic about something else." Surely Congress did not intend to authorize the Federal Trade Commission to foreclose expression of honest opinion in the course of one's business of voicing opinion. The same opinion, however, may become material to the jurisdiction of the Federal Trade Commission and enjoinable by it if, wanting in proof or basis in fact, it is utilized in the trade to mislead or deceive the public or to harm a competitor. *Cf. Perma Maid Co., Inc. v. Federal Trade Commission*, 6 Cir., 121 F.2d 282.

The order of the Federal Trade Commission is set aside.

ANDREWS MORTUARY, INC. v. FEDERAL TRADE COMMISSION

Unites States Court of Appeals, Fourth Circuit
726 F.2d 994 (1984)

K.K. HALL, CIRCUIT JUDGE.

. . . .

THE RULEMAKING PROCEEDING

In 1972, the FTC began an investigation of funeral practices across the nation. As a result of this investigation, the Commission initiated a rulemaking proceeding to regulate the funeral industry. The Commission published a notice containing the text of a proposed rule, a statement of the Commission's reasons for issuing it, and an invitation for public comment. Hearings were scheduled to take place in six cities during 1976.

In response to the FTC's notice, more than 9,000 documents, comprising in excess of 20,000 pages, were submitted by interested parties, including consumers and industry representatives. During the fifty-two days of hearings, 315 witnesses testified. The witnesses also presented exhibits and underwent cross-examination by participating parties or the FTC's Presiding Officer. The hearings generated 14,719 pages of transcripts and approximately 4,000 additional pages of exhibits. Thereafter, another comment period was held for rebuttal of any materials previously admitted into evidence. Forty-seven rebuttal submissions were received.

Following these hearings, the Presiding Officer and commission staff concluded that existing funeral practices left the consumer vulnerable to unfair and deceptive practices, and that state regulation against deceptive funeral practices was dominated by industry interests. These conclusions were published in 1978, and the Commission allowed ninety days for public comment.

Over 1,300 separate comments were received. In February, 1979, the staff and the Bureau Director forwarded to the Commission their final recommendations that a rule be promulgated, but with numerous modifications in response to the comments received. In 1980, the Commission voted to publish for public comment a revised version of the Funeral Rule.

A notice containing the revised rule was published in the *Federal Register* on January 22, 1981, and provided for a sixty-day written comment period, followed by a rebuttal period in which parties could respond to the initial round of comments. After expiration of the comment period and following several public hearings in 1981, the Commission made final revisions to the Funeral Rule and submitted it to both Houses of Congress. When Congressional review expired with no resolution of disapproval, the Commission set January 1, 1984, as the effective date of the Funeral Rule. This appeal followed.

. . . .

The rule promulgated by the Commission . . . requires that before any discussion of arrangements, funeral providers: (1) give consumers a written list containing prices of funeral goods and services on an itemized basis (although providers may also quote prices on combinations of goods and services); (2) offer price information to consumers who request it over the telephone; (3) obtain permission from a family member before embalming (except under certain designated circumstances); (4) refrain from requiring use of a casket for cremation; (5) refrain from making specified misrepresentations; and (6) include several short disclosures on the price list informing consumers of their legal rights and purchase options.

. . . .

V.   THE IMPROVEMENTS ACT AND THE FIRST AMENDMENT

[P]etitioners argue that, even if there is substantial evidence supporting the Commission's conclusions regarding pre-purchase disclosures, the remedy of itemized price lists exceeds the Commission's power under the Improvements Act, and violates petitioners' First Amendment rights of commercial free speech. We disagree.

Section 19(c)(1)(B)(i) of the Improvements Act expressly prohibits the FTC from promulgating a regulation except to the extent that it prohibits funeral providers from "engaging in any misrepresentation." The remedy of price itemization is not inconsistent with this limitation. The Commission's conclusion that itemized pricing is necessary to prevent unwanted and unnecessary purchasing is a judgment that is specifically allowed by Section 19(c)(1)(B)(iii). This section stipulates that the Commission may promulgate rules designed to "prevent [funeral] providers from conditioning the furnishing of any such goods or services." Section 19(c)(1)(A) also supports the Commission's authority to require the remedy of itemized pricing by establishing that the Commission may require funeral providers "to disclose the fees or prices for such goods and services *in a manner prescribed by the Commission*." (Emphasis added).

Nor do we agree that the First Amendment prevents the Commission from remedying deception by means of an affirmative disclosure requirement. Assuming that the sales practices in question are commercial "speech," the First Amendment gives that speech no protection when it is misleading, *Central Hudson Gas & Electric Corp. v. Public Serv. Comm'n*, 447 U.S. 557, 566 (1980), and poses no barrier to any remedy formulated by the Commission reasonably necessary to the prevention of future deception. *American Home Products Corp. v. FTC*, 695 F.2d 681, 713 (3d Cir. 1982). The practices that the Commission sought to remedy by promulgation of the Funeral Rule were unfair and misleading and thus are not "speech" entitled to First Amendment protection.

. . . .

Rule affirmed.

NOTES ON CONSTITUTIONALITY

(1) For examples of how the FTC has regulated commercial speech since *Central Hudson*, 447 U.S. 557 (1980), see *American Medical Ass'n v. FTC*, 638 F.2d 443, 452 (2d Cir. 1980), *aff'd per curiam by an equally divided court*, 455 U.S. 676 (1982), modifying an FTC order requiring the AMA to cease and desist from promulgating, implementing and enforcing restraints on advertising, solicitation and contract practices by physicians; *United States v. Reader's Digest Ass'n*, 662 F.2d 955, 965 (3d Cir. 1981), *cert. denied*, 455 U.S. 908 (1982), affirming a district court order penalizing Reader's Digest for violating an FTC Consent Order which had required Reader's Digest to cease and desist from using or distributing simulated checks, currency or "new car certificates" in the company's sweepstakes promotions, and enjoining Reader's Digest from further violations of the Consent Order; *Removatron Int'l Corp. v. FTC*, 884 F.2d 1489 (1st Cir. 1989), upholding an FTC order enjoining petitioners from representing that their hair removal system achieved long-term efficacy without possession of and reliance upon a well-controlled, scientific study; *Litton Industries, Inc. v. FTC*, 676 F.2d 364, 373 (9th Cir. 1982), modifying and enforcing an FTC order requiring Litton to cease and desist from making inadequately substantiated claims with respect to its microwave ovens; and *Bristol-Myers Co. v. Federal Trade Commission*, 102 F.T.C. 21 (1983), enforcing an FTC order requiring Bristol-Myers not to make any performance or freedom-from-side-effects claims for its Bufferin or Excedrin products unless it had a "reasonable basis" for making that claim. *See also Board of Trustees of the State University of New York v. Fox*, 492 U.S. 469 (1989), in which a SUNY regulation barred a tupperware party in a student dormitory. The Court, in an opinion by Justice Scalia, held that application of the least-restrictive-means test of *Central Hudson, supra*, need not require "the least restrictive means but . . . a means narrowly tailored to achieve the desired objective," and remanded for a determination of whether some means other than a complete bar would meet the regulatory objective.

In *Jay Norris Inc. v. FTC*, 598 F.2d 1244 (2d Cir. 1979), the petitioners challenged a similar order requiring a substantiated "reasonable basis" for any claims regarding the safety and performance of petitioner's gift and novelty products. They argued the Order suppressed even truthful speech and amounted to a prior restraint. Petitioners previously had made deceptive claims as to numerous and various products such as flame guns that would "dissolve the heaviest snow drifts, whip right through the thickest ice" and "completely safe" roach powder which "never loses its killing power — even after years." Noting that the First Amendment does not protect deceptive and misleading speech, the court held that the FTC's remedy was reasonable and constitutional and observed that the doctrine of prior restraint may be inapplicable to commercial speech.

In *FTC v. Brown and Williamson Tobacco Corp.*, 778 F.2d 35 (D.C. Cir. 1985), the court scaled back the lower court's order intended to prevent deceptive claims about a cigarette's tar and nicotine content, on the grounds that the injunction as written would have effectively enshrined the FTC's system of measuring tar and nicotine as the only legitimate testing method, thereby potentially suppressing truthful, non-confusing claims about tar and nicotine content as measured by other systems. *Cf. Kraft, Inc. v. FTC*, 970 F.2d 311 (7th Cir. 1992), upholding the FTC's order enjoining certain Kraft advertising claims, emphasizing that "no First Amendment concerns are raised when facially apparent [false] implied claims are found without resort to extrinsic evidence."

(2) Should the FTC be able to prevent the advertising of false statements concerning a product which are also contained in a book? *See Koch v. FTC*, 206 F.2d 311 (6th Cir. 1953), in which the court held that the FTC could regulate the advertising but not the book. Would the fact that the advertising was for the book itself affect this decision? *See Witkower Press, Inc.*, 57 FTC 145 (1960); *Rodale Press, Inc.*, 71 F.T.C. 1184, 1247–1253 (1967) (Comm'r Elman, dissenting), *quoted with approval in Rodale Press, Inc. v. FTC*, 407 F.2d 1252, 1258 (D.C. Cir. 1968) (Robinson, J., concurring).

(3) Whether a given advertisement constitutes commercial speech may depend on its content as well as the "means, messages and motives" of its sponsor. In *In re R.J. Reynolds, Inc.*, 5 (CCH) Trade Reg. Rep. (CCH) ¶ 22,522 (April 11, 1988), the FTC challenged an editorial/advertisement sponsored by R.J. Reynolds, describing the results of a health study measuring the effects of smoking cigarettes. The Administrative Law Judge dismissed the case on the grounds that the advertisement was an editorial, not commercial speech, and therefore lay outside the jurisdiction of the FTC. A divided Commission remanded the case to the ALJ for reconsideration of the issue of whether the advertisement was commercial speech, explaining that an important consideration on remand would be the subjective motivation of the sponsor. *Id.*, at 22,184. In remanding the case, the FTC explained that the ad could constitute commercial speech, despite the absence of express promotional language, because the ad referred to a specific product, targeted consumers of the product, discussed the health effects of that product, and was published by means of a paid-for advertisement. *See also Bolger v. Youngs Drug Products*, 463 U.S. 60, 66–67 (1983), in which the Court classified a pamphlet analyzing facts about venereal disease as commercial speech because: (1) the pamphlet was a paid-for advertisement, (2) it referred to a specific product, and (3) the advertisement was motivated by economic gain; and *Peel v. Attorney Registration and Disciplinary Commission of Illinois*, 496 U.S. 91 (1990), in which the Court held that a State may not "completely ban statements that are not actually or inherently misleading, such as certification [of a lawyer] as a specialist by bona fide organizations such as the [National Board of Trial Advocacy]."

(4) There are various Constitutional limits on relief which may affect Governmental regulation of unfair or deceptive acts or practices. In *Lucas v. South Carolina Coastal Council*, 112 S. Ct. 2886, 2894–5 (1992), in holding that a developer had to be compensated where a state regulatory commission barred development of his beachfront property, the Supreme Court, in an opinion by Justice Scalia, ruled that state "regulations that leave the owner of land without economically beneficial or productive options for its use . . . carry with them a heightened risk that private property is being pressed into some form of public service under the guise of mitigating serious public harm." *See* R. Epstein, *Bargaining with the State* (1993).

(5) *See generally* Westen, *First Amendment: Barrier or Impetus to FTC Advertising Remedies*, 46 Brooklyn L. Rev. 487 (1980); Note, *Corrective Advertising and*

the Limits of Virginia Pharmacy, 32 Stanford L. Rev. 121 (1979); Note, *First Amendment Restrictions on the FTC's Regulation of Advertising*, 31 Vand. L. Rev. 349 (1978).

[C]   Tests of Deceptiveness

INTRODUCTION

The Supreme Court has held that the FTC cannot take action against deceptive practices unless the public interest involved is specific and substantial. *FTC v. Royal Milling Co.*, 288 U.S. 212 (1933). If the controversy is private in character and any public interest only incidental, a reviewing court may dismiss the suit without inquiry into the merits. *FTC v. Klesner*, 280 U.S. 19 (1929).

The FTC's articulation of the test for measuring deception under § 5 of the FTC Act has evolved over the years. Historically, acts or practices were found deceptive if their net impression had the capacity to deceive the public as to a material factor in its purchasing decisions. *See Charles of the Ritz Distributors Corp. v. FTC*, 143 F.2d 676 (2d Cir. 1944). The application of this test was construed as affording protection to even the gullible or credulous. *See Charles of the Ritz, supra; FTC v. Standard Education Soc'y*, 302 U.S. 112 (1937); *Aronberg v. FTC*, 132 F.2d 165 (7th Cir. 1942). *Cf. Standard Oil Co. of California v. FTC*, 577 F.2d 653, 657 (9th Cir. 1978). However, in 1983 the FTC issued a policy statement which indicated that the FTC will only find acts or practices deceptive if there is a representation, omission or practice likely to mislead a consumer acting reasonably under the circumstances, to the consumer's detriment. FTC, *Policy Statement on Deception, reprinted in* Trade Reg. Rep. (CCH) ¶ 50,455 (October 14, 1983).

The absence of evidence of actual deception, intent to deceive or actual injury to the public, consumers, or competitors, continues to be irrelevant in evaluating whether a material misrepresentation violates § 5. *See Beneficial Corp. v. FTC*, 542 F.2d 611, 617 (3d Cir. 1976), *cert. denied*, 430 U.S. 983 (1977); *FTC v. World Travel Vacation Brokers, Inc.*, 861 F.2d 1020, 1029 (7th Cir. 1988). Furthermore, the fact that a representation is literally true, or deceptive only by omission, does not constitute a defense. *See Kraft, infra*; Alexander, *Federal Regulation of False Advertising*, 17 U. Kan. L. Rev. 573 (1969); Millstein, *The Federal Trade Commission and False Advertising*, 64 Colum. L. Rev. 439 (1964).

FTC v. COLGATE-PALMOLIVE CO.

United States Supreme Court
380 U.S. 374 (1965)

Mr. Chief Justice Warren

The basic question before us is whether it is a deceptive trade practice, prohibited by § 5 of the Federal Trade Commission Act, to represent falsely that a televised test, experiment, or demonstration provides a viewer with visual proof of a product claim, regardless of whether the product claim is itself true.

The case arises out of an attempt by respondent Colgate-Palmolive Company to prove to the television public that its shaving cream, "Rapid Shave," outshaves them all. Respondent Ted Bates & Company, Inc., an advertising agency, prepared for Colgate three one-minute commercials designed to show that Rapid Shave could soften even the toughness of sandpaper. Each of the commercials contained the same "sandpaper test." The announcer informed the audience that, "To prove RAPID SHAVE'S super-moisturizing power, we put it right from the can onto this tough, dry sandpaper. It was apply . . . soak . . . and off in a stroke." While the announcer was speaking, Rapid Shave was applied to a substance that appeared to be sandpaper, and immediately thereafter a razor was shown shaving the substance clean.

The Federal Trade Commission issued a complaint against respondents Colgate and Bates charging that the commercials were false and deceptive. The evidence before the hearing examiner disclosed that sandpaper of the type depicted in the commercials could not be shaved immediately following the application of Rapid Shave, but required a substantial soaking period of approximately 80 minutes. The evidence also showed that the substance resembling sandpaper was in fact a simulated prop, or "mock-up," made of plexiglass to which sand had been applied. However, the examiner found that Rapid Shave could shave sandpaper, even though not in the short time represented by the commercials, and that if real sandpaper had been used in the commercials the inadequacies of television transmission would have made it appear to viewers to be nothing more than plain, colored paper. The examiner dismissed the complaint because neither misrepresentation — concerning the actual moistening time or the identity of the shaved substance — was in his opinion a material one that would mislead the public.

The Commission, in an opinion dated December 29, 1961, reversed the hearing examiner. It found that since Rapid Shave could not shave sandpaper within the time depicted in the commercials, respondents had misrepresented the product's moisturizing power. Moreover, the Commission found that the undisclosed use of a plexiglass substitute for sandpaper was an additional material misrepresentation that was a deceptive act separate and distinct from the misrepresentation concerning Rapid Shave's underlying qualities. Even if the sandpaper could be shaved just as depicted in the commercials, the Commission found that viewers had been misled into believing they had seen it done with their own eyes. As a result of these findings the Commission entered a cease-and-desist order against the respondents.

An appeal was taken to the Court of Appeals for the First Circuit which rendered an opinion on November 20, 1962, 310 F.2d 89. That court sustained the Commission's conclusion that respondents had misrepresented the qualities of Rapid Shave, but it would not accept the Commission's order forbidding the future use of undisclosed simulations in television commercials. It set aside the Commission's order and directed that a new order be entered. On May 7, 1963, the Commission, over the protest of respondents, issued a new order narrowing and clarifying its original order to comply with the court's mandate. The Court of Appeals again found unsatisfactory that portion of the order dealing with simulated props and refused to enforce it, 326 F.2d 517. We granted certiorari, 377 U.S. 942, to consider this aspect of the case and do not have before us any question concerning the misrepresentation that Rapid Shave could shave sandpaper immediately after application, that being conceded.

. . . .

II.

In reviewing the substantive issues in the case, it is well to remember the respective roles of the Commission and the courts in the administration of the Federal Trade Commission Act. When the Commission was created by Congress in 1914, it was directed by § 5 to prevent "[u]nfair methods of competition in commerce." Congress amended the Act of 1938 to extend the Commission's jurisdiction to include "unfair or deceptive acts or practices in commerce" a significant amendment showing Congress' concern for consumers as well as for competitors. It is important to note the generality of these standards of illegality; the proscriptions in § 5 are flexible, "to be defined with particularity by the myriad of cases from the field of business." *Federal Trade Comm. v. Motion Picture Advertising Service Co.*, 344 U.S. 392, 394.

This statutory scheme necessarily gives the Commission an influential role in interpreting § 5 and in applying it to the facts of particular cases arising out of unprecedented situations. Moreover, as an administrative agency which deals continually with cases in the area, the Commission is often in a better position than are courts to determine when a practice is "deceptive" within the meaning of the Act. This Court has frequently stated that the Commission's judgment is to be given great weight by reviewing courts. This admonition is especially true with respect to allegedly deceptive advertising since the finding of a § 5 violation in this field rests so heavily on inference and pragmatic judgment. Nevertheless, while informed judicial determination is dependent upon enlightenment gained from administrative experience, in the last analysis the words "deceptive practices" set forth a legal standard and they must get their final meaning from judicial construction. *Cf. Federal Trade Comm. v. R.F. Keppel & Bro., Inc.*, 291 U.S. 304, 314.

We are not concerned in this case with the clear misrepresentation in the commercials concerning the speed with which Rapid Shave could shave sandpaper, since the Court of Appeals upheld the Commission's finding on that matter and the respondents have not challenged the finding here. We granted certiorari to consider the Commission's conclusion that even if an advertiser has himself conducted a test, experiment or demonstration which he honestly believes will prove a certain product claim, he may not convey to television viewers the false impression that they are seeing the test, experiment or demonstration for themselves, when they are not because of the undisclosed use of mock-ups.

We accept the Commission's determination that the commercials involved in this case contained three representations to the public: (1) that sandpaper could be shaved by Rapid Shave; (2) that an experiment had been conducted which verified his claim; and (3) that the viewer was seeing this experiment for himself. Respondents admit that the first two representations were made, but deny that the third was. The

Commission, however, found to the contrary, and, since this is a matter of fact resting on an inference that could reasonably be drawn from the commercials themselves, the Commission's finding should be sustained. For the purposes of our review, we can assume that the first two representations were true; the focus of our consideration is on the third which was clearly false. The parties agree that § 5 prohibits the intentional misrepresentation of any fact which would constitute a material factor in a purchaser's decision whether to buy. They differ, however, in their conception of what "facts" constitute a "material factor" in a purchaser's decision to buy. Respondents submit, in effect, that the only material facts are those which deal with the substantive qualities of a product. The Commission, on the other hand, submits that the misrepresentations of *any* fact so long as it materially induces a purchaser's decision to buy is a deception prohibited by § 5.

The Commission's interpretation of what is a deceptive practice seems more in line with the decided cases than that of respondents. This Court said in *Federal Trade Comm. v. Algoma Lumber Co.*, 291 U.S. 67, 78: "[T]he public is entitled to get what it chooses, though the choice may be dictated by caprice or by fashion or perhaps by ignorance." It has long been considered a deceptive practice to state falsely that a product ordinarily sells for an inflated price but that it is being offered at a special reduced price, even if the offered price represents the actual value of the product and the purchaser is receiving his money's worth. Applying respondents' arguments to these cases, it would appear that so long as buyers paid no more than the product was actually worth and the product contained the qualities advertised, the misstatement of an inflated original price was immaterial.

It has also been held a violation of § 5 for a seller to misrepresent to the public that he is in a certain line of business, even though the misstatement in no way affects the qualities of the product. As was said in *Federal Trade Comm. v. Royal Milling Co.*, 288 U.S. 212, 216:

> If consumers or dealers prefer to purchase a given article because it was made by a particular manufacturer or class of manufacturers, they have a right to do so, and this right cannot be satisfied by imposing upon them an exactly similar article, or one equally as good, but having a different origin.

The court of appeals have applied this reasoning to the merchandising of reprocessed products that are as good as new, without a disclosure that they are in fact reprocessed. And it has also been held that it is a deceptive practice to misappropriate the trade name of another.

Respondents claim that all these cases are irrelevant to our decision because they involve misrepresentations related to the product itself and not merely to the manner in which an advertising message is communicated. This distinction misses the mark for two reasons. In the first place, the present case is not concerned with a mode of communications, but with a misrepresentation that viewers have objective proof of a seller's product claim over and above the seller's word. Secondly, all of the above cases, like the present case, deal with methods designed to get a consumer to purchase a product, not with whether the product, when purchased, will perform up to expectations. We find an especially strong similarity between the present case and those cases in which a seller induces the public to purchase an arguably good product by misrepresenting his line of business, by concealing the fact that the product is reprocessed, or by misappropriating another's trademark. In each case the seller has used a misrepresentation to break down what he regards to be an annoying or irrational habit of the buying public — the preference for particular manufacturers or known brands regardless of a product's actual qualities, the prejudice against reprocessed goods, and the desire for verification of a product claim. In each case the seller reasons that when the habit is broken the buyer will be satisfied with the performance of the product he receives. Yet, a misrepresentation has been used to break the habit and, as was stated in *Algoma Lumber*, a misrepresentation for such an end is not permitted.

We need not limit ourselves to the cases already mentioned because there are other situations which also illustrate the correctness of the Commission's finding in the present case. It is generally accepted that it is a deceptive practice to state falsely that a product has received a testimonial from a respected source. In addition, the Commission has consistently acted to prevent sellers from falsely stating that their product claims have been "certified." We find these situations to be indistinguishable from the present case. We can assume that in each the underlying product claim is true and in each the seller actually conducted an experiment sufficient to prove to himself the truth of the claim. But in each the seller has told the public that it could rely on something other than his word concerning both the truth of the claim and the validity of his experiment. We find it an immaterial difference that in one case the viewer is told to rely on the word of a celebrity or authority he respects, in another on the word of a testing agency, and in the present case on his own perception of an undisclosed simulation.

Respondents again insist that the present case is not like any of the above, but is more like a case in which a celebrity or independent testing agency has in fact submitted a written verification of an experiment actually observed, but, because of the inability of the camera to transmit accurately an impression of the paper on which the testimonial is written, the seller reproduces it on another substance so that it can be seen by the viewing audience. This analogy ignores the finding of the Commission that in the present case the seller misrepresented to the public that it was being given objective proof of a product claim. In respondents' hypothetical the objective proof of the product claim that is offered, the word of the celebrity or agency that the experiment was actually conducted, does exist; while in the case before us the objective proof offered, the viewer's own perception of an actual experiment, does not exist. Thus, in respondents' hypothetical, unlike the present case, the use of the undisclosed mockup does not conflict with the seller's claim that there is objective proof.

We agree with the Commission, therefore, that the undisclosed use of plexiglass in the present commercials was a material deceptive practice, independent and separate from the other misrepresentation found. We find unpersuasive respondents' other objections to this conclusion. Respondents claim that it will be impractical to inform the viewing public that it is not seeing an actual test, experiment or demonstration, but we think it inconceivable that the ingenious advertising world will be unable, if it so desires, to conform to the Commission's insistence that the public be not misinformed. If, however, it becomes impossible or impractical to show simulated demonstrations on television in a truthful manner, this indicates that television is not a medium that lends itself to this type of commercial, not that the commercial must survive at all costs. Similarly unpersuasive is respondents' objection that the Commission's decision discriminates against sellers whose product claims cannot be "verified" on television without the use of simulations. All methods of advertising do not equally favor every seller. If the inherent limitations of a method do not permit its use in the way a seller desires, the seller cannot by material misrepresentation compensate for those limitations.

. . . .

III.

We turn our attention now to the order issued by the Commission. It has been repeatedly held that the Commission has wide discretion in determining the type of order that is necessary to cope with the unfair practices found, *e.g., Jacob Siegel Co. v. Federal Trade Comm.*, 327 U.S. 608, 611, and that Congress has placed the primary responsibility for fashioning orders upon the Commission, *Federal Trade Comm. v. National Lead Co.*, 352 U.S. 419, 429. For these reasons the court should not "lightly modify" the Commission's orders. *Federal Trade Comm. v. Cement Institute*, 333 U.S. 683, 726. However, this Court has also warned that an order's prohibitions "should be clear and precise in order that they may be understood by those against whom they are directed," *Federal Trade Comm. v. Cement Institute*, *supra*, at 726, and that "[t]he severity of possible penalties prescribed . . . for violations of orders which have become final underlines the necessity for fashioned orders which are, at the outset, sufficiently clear and precise to avoid raising serious questions as to their meaning and application." *Federal Trade Comm. v. Henry Broch & Co.*, 368 U.S. 360, 367–368.

The Court of Appeals has criticized the references in the Commission's order to "test, experiment or demonstration" as not capable of practical interpretation. It could find no difference between the Rapid Shave commercial and a commercial which extolled the goodness of ice cream while giving viewers a picture of a scoop of mashed potatoes appearing to be ice cream. We do not understand this difficulty. In the ice cream case the mashed potato prop is not being used for additional proof of the product claim, while the purpose of the Rapid Shave commercial is to give the viewer objective proof of the claims made. If in the ice cream hypothetical the focus of the commercial becomes the undisclosed potato prop and the viewer is invited, explicitly or by implication, to see for himself about the ice cream's rich texture and full color, and perhaps compare it to a "rival product," then the commercial has become similar to the one now before us. Clearly, however, a commercial which depicts happy actors delightedly eating ice cream that is in fact mashed potatoes or drinking a product appearing to be coffee but which is in fact some other substance is not covered by the present order.

The crucial terms of the present order — "test, experiment or demonstration . . . represented . . . as actual proof of a claim" — are as specific as the circumstances will permit. If respondents in their subsequent commercials attempt to come as close to the line of misrepresentation as the Commission's order permits, they may without specifically intending to do so cross into the area proscribed by this order. However, it does not seem "unfair to require that one who deliberately goes perilously close to an area of proscribed conduct shall take the risk that he may cross the line." *Boyce Motor Lines, Inc. v. United States*, 342 U.S. 337, 340. In commercials where the emphasis is on the seller's word, and not on the viewer's own perception, the respondents need not fear that an undisclosed use of props is prohibited by the present order. On the other hand, when the commercial not only makes a claim, but also invites the viewer to rely on his own perception, for demonstrative proof of the claim, the respondents will be aware that the use of undisclosed props in strategic places might be a material deception. We believe that respondents will have no difficulty applying the Commission's order to the vast majority of their contemplated future commercials. If, however, a situation arises in which respondents are sincerely unable to determine whether a proposed course of action would violate the present order, they can, by complying with the Commission's rules, oblige the Commission to give them definitive advice as to whether their proposed action, if pursued, would constitute compliance with the order.

Finally, we find no defect in the provision of the order which prohibits respondents from engaging in similar practices with respect to "any product" they advertise. The propriety of a broad order depends upon the specific circumstances of the case, but the courts will not interfere except where the remedy selected has no reasonable relation to the unlawful practices found to exist. In this case the respondents produced three different commercials which employed the same deceptive practice. This we believe gave the Commission a sufficient basis for believing that the respondents would be inclined to use similar commercials with respect to the other products they advertise. We think it reasonable for the Commission to frame its order broadly enough to prevent respondents from engaging in similarly illegal practices in future advertisements. As was said in *Federal Trade Comm. v. Ruberoid Co.*, 343 U.S. 470, 473: "[T]he Commission is not limited to prohibiting the illegal practice in the precise form in which it is found to have existed in the past." Having been caught violating the Act, respondents "must expect some fencing in." *Federal Trade Comm. v. National Lead Co.*, 352 U.S. 419, 431.

The judgment of the Court of Appeals is reversed and the case remanded for the entry of a judgment enforcing the Commission's order.

Reversed and remanded.

MR. JUSTICE HARLAN, whom MR. JUSTICE STEWART joins, dissenting in part.

. . . .

The faulty prop in the Court's reasoning is that it focuses entirely on what is taking place in the studio rather than on what the viewer is seeing on his screen. That which the viewer sees with his own eyes is not, however, what is taking place in the studio, but an electronic image. If the image he sees on the screen is an accurate reproduction of what he would see with the naked eyes were the experiment performed before him with sandpaper in his home or in the studio, there can hardly be a misrepresentation in any legally significant sense. While the Commission undoubtedly possesses broad authority to give content to the proscriptions of the Act, its discretion, as the Court recognizes, is not unbridled, and "in the last analysis the words 'deceptive practices' set forth a legal standard and they must get their final meaning from judicial construction" (*ante*, p. 1043). In this case, assuming that Rapid Shave could soften sandpaper as quickly as it does sand-covered plexiglass, a viewer who wants to entertain his friends by duplicating the actual experiment could do so by buying a can of Rapid Shave and some sandpaper. If he wished to shave himself, and his beard were really as tough as sandpaper, he could perform this part of his morning ablutions with Rapid Shave in the same way as he saw the plexiglass shaved on television.

I do not see how such a commercial can be said to be "deceptive" in any legally acceptable use of that term. The Court attempts to distinguish the case where a "celebrity" has written a testimonial endorsing some product, but the original testimonial cannot be seen over television and a copy is shown over the air by the manufacturer. The Court states of this "hypothetical": "In respondents' hypothetical the objective proof of the product claim that is offered, the word of the celebrity or agency that the experiment was actually conducted, does exist; while in the case before us the objective proof offered, the viewer's own perception of an actual experiment, does not exist." But in both cases the viewer is told to "see for himself," in the one case that the celebrity has endorsed the product; in the other, that the product can shave sandpaper; in neither case is the viewer actually seeing the proof; and in both cases the objective proof does exist, be it the original testimonial or the sandpaper test actually conducted by the manufacturer. In neither case, however, is there a material misrepresentation, because what the viewer sees *is* an accurate image of the objective proof.

Nor can I readily understand how the accurate portrayal of an experiment by means of a mock-up can be considered more deceptive than the use of mashed potatoes to convey the glamorous qualities of a particular ice cream; indeed, to a potato-lover "the smile on the face of the tiger" might come more naturally than if he were actually being served ice cream.

It is commonly known that television presents certain distortions in transmission for which the broadcasting industry must compensate. Thus, a white towel will look dingy gray over television, but a blue towel will look a sparkling white. On the Court's analysis, an advertiser must achieve accuracy in the studio even though it results in an inaccurate image being projected on the home screen. This led the Court of Appeals to question whether it would be proper for an advertiser to show a product on television that somehow, because of the medium, looks better on the screen than it does in real life. 310 F.2d 89, 94; 326 F.2d 517, 523, n.16.

A perhaps more commonplace example suggests itself: Would it be proper for respondent Colgate, in advertising a laundry detergent, to "demonstrate" the effectiveness of a major competitor's detergent in washing white sheets; and then "before the viewer's eyes," to wash a white (not a blue) sheet with the competitor's detergent? The studio test would accurately show the quality of the product, but the image on the screen would look as though the sheet had been washed with an ineffective detergent. All that has happened here is the converse: a demonstration has been altered in the studio to compensate for the distortions of the television medium, but in this instance in order to present an accurate picture to the television viewer.

In short, it seems to me that the proper legal test in cases of this kind concerns not what goes on in the broadcasting studio, but whether what is shown on the television screen is an accurate representation of the advertised product and of the claims made for it.

. . . .

KRAFT v. FEDERAL TRADE COMMISSION

Unites States Court of Appeals, Seventh Circuit
970 F.2d 311 (1992)

FLAUM, CIRCUIT JUDGE.

. . . .

Kraft Singles are process cheese food slices. In the early 1980s, Kraft began losing market share to an increasing number of imitation slices that were advertised as both less expensive [than] and equally nutritious as dairy slices like Singles. Kraft responded with a series of advertisements, collectively known as the "Five Ounces of Milk" campaign, designed to inform consumers that Kraft Singles cost more than imitation slices because they are made from five ounces of milk rather than less expensive ingredients. The ads also focused on the calcium content of Kraft Singles in an effort to capitalize on growing consumer interest in adequate calcium consumption.

The FTC filed a complaint against Kraft charging that this advertising campaign materially misrepresented the calcium content and relative calcium benefit of Kraft Singles. The FTC Act makes it unlawful to engage in unfair or deceptive commercial practices, 15 U.S.C. § 45, or to induce consumers to purchase certain products through advertising that is misleading in a material respect. *Id.* at §§ 52, 55. Thus, an advertisement is deceptive under the Act if it is likely to mislead consumers, acting reasonably under the circumstances, in a material respect.

. . . .

In implementing this standard, the Commission examines the overall net impression of an ad and engages in a three-part inquiry: (1) what claims are conveyed in this ad; (2) are those claims false or misleading; and (3) are those claims material to prospective consumers.

Two facts are critical to understanding the allegations against Kraft. First, although Kraft does use five ounces of milk in making each Kraft Single, roughly 30% of the calcium contained in the milk is lost during processing. Second, the vast majority of imitation slices sold in the United States contain 15% of the U.S.

Recommended Daily Allowance (RDA) of calcium per ounce, roughly the same amount contained in Kraft Singles. Specifically then, the FTC complaint alleged that the challenged advertisements made two implied claims, neither of which was true: (1) that a slice of Kraft Singles contains the same amount of calcium as five ounces of milk (the "milk equivalency" claim); and (2) that Kraft Singles contain more calcium than do most imitation cheese slices (the "imitation superiority" claim).[1]

The two sets of ads at issue in this case, referred to as the "Skimp" ads and the "Class Picture" ads, ran nationally in print and broadcast media between 1985 and 1987. The Skimp ads were designed to communicate the nutritional benefit of Kraft Singles by referring expressly to their milk and calcium content. The broadcast version of this ad on which the FTC focused contained the following audio copy:

> *Lady (voice over):* I admit it. I thought of skimping. Could you look into those big blue eyes and skimp on her? so I buy Kraft Singles. Imitation slices use hardly any milk. But Kraft has five ounces per slice. Five ounces. So her little bones get calcium they need to grow. No, she doesn't know what that big Kraft means. Good thing I do.
>
> *Singers:* Kraft Singles. More milk makes 'em . . . more milk makes 'em good.
>
> *Lady (voice over):* Skimp on her? No way.

. . . .

The visual image corresponding to this copy shows, among other things, milk pouring into a glass until it reaches a mark on the glass denoted "five ounces." The commercial also shows milk pouring into a glass which bears the phrase "5 oz. milk slice" and which gradually becomes part of the label on a package of Singles. In January 1986, Kraft revised this ad, changing "Kraft *has* five ounces per slice" to "Kraft is *made from* five ounces per slice," IDF 28; *see* CX 276F, CX 106 (emphasis added), and in March 1987, Kraft added the disclosure, "one 3/4 ounce slice has 70% of the calcium of five ounces of milk" as a subscript in the television commercial and as a footnote in the print ads.

The Class Picture ads also emphasized the milk and calcium content of Kraft Singles but, unlike the Skimp ads, did not make an express comparison to imitation slices. The version of this ad examined by the FTC depicts a group of school children having their class picture taken, and contains the following audio copy:

> *Announcer (voice over):* Can you see what's missing in this picture?
>
> Well, a government study says that half the school kids in America don't get all the calcium recommended for growing kids. That's why Kraft Singles are important. Kraft is made from five ounces of milk per slice. So they're concentrated with calcium. Calcium the government recommends for strong bones and healthy teeth!
>
> *Photographer:* Say Cheese!
>
> *Kids:* Cheese!

---

[1] Because Kraft concedes that these claims, if made, are false, the second step of the aforementioned inquiry — whether the alleged claims are false — is not before us on appeal.

Announcer (voice over): Say Kraft Singles. 'Cause kids love Kraft Singles, right down to their bones.

. . . . The Class Picture ads also included the subscript disclaimer mentioned above.

. . . .

As to the Skimp ads, the Commission found that four elements conveyed the milk equivalency claim: (1) the use of the word "has" in the phrase "Kraft has five ounces per slice"; (2) repetition of the precise amount of milk in a Kraft Single (five ounces); (3) the use of the word "so" to link the reference to milk with the reference to calcium; and (4) the visual image of milk being poured into a glass up to a five-ounce mark, and the superimposition of that image onto a package of Singles. It also found two additional elements that conveyed the imitation superiority claim: (1) the express reference to imitation slices combined with the use of comparative language ("hardly any," "but") and (2) the image of a glass containing very little milk during the reference to imitation slices, followed by the image of a glass being filled to the five-ounce mark during the reference to Kraft Singles. The Commission based all of these findings on its own impression of the advertisements and found it unnecessary to resort to extrinsic evidence; it did note, however, that the available extrinsic evidence was consistent with its determinations.

The Commission then examined the Class Picture ads — once again, without resorting to extrinsic evidence — and found that they contained copy substantially similar to the copy in the Skimp ads that conveyed the impression of milk equivalency. It rejected, however, the ALJ's finding that the Class Picture ads made an imitation superiority claim, determining that the ads neither expressly compared Singles to imitation slices, nor contained any visual images to prompt such a comparison, and that available extrinsic evidence did not support the ALJ's finding.

The FTC next found that the claims were material to consumers. It concluded that the milk equivalency claim is a health-related claim that reasonable consumers would find important and that Kraft believed that the claim induced consumers to purchase Singles. The FTC presumed that the imitation superiority claim was material because it found that Kraft intended to make that claim. It also found that the materiality of that claim was demonstrated by evidence that the challenged ads led to increased sales despite a substantially higher price for Singles than for imitation slices.

Finally, the FTC modified the ALJ's cease and desist order by extending its coverage from "individually wrapped slices of cheese, imitation cheese, and substitute cheese" to "any product that is a cheese, cheese related product, imitation cheese, or substitute cheese." The Commission found that the serious, deliberate nature of the violation, combined with the transferability of the violations to other cheese products, justified a broader order. Kraft filed this petition to set-aside the Commission's order or, alternatively, to modify its scope.

. . . .

We find substantial evidence in the record to support the FTC's finding. Although Kraft downplays the nexus in the ads between milk and calcium, the ads emphasize visually and verbally that five ounces of milk go into a slice of Kraft Singles; this image is linked to calcium content, strongly implying that the consumer gets the calcium found in five ounces of milk. The fact that the Commission listed four elements in finding an implied claim in the Skimp ads does not mean that those same elements must all be present in the Class Picture ad to reach that same conclusion. Furthermore, the Class Picture ads contained one other element reinforcing the milk equivalency claim, the phrase "5 oz. milk slice" inside the image of a glass superimposed on the Singles package, and it was reasonable for the Commission to conclude that there were important similarities between these two ads. Finally, to support its own interpretation of the ads, the Commission examined available extrinsic evidence and this evidence, in the Commission's view, bolstered its findings.

Kraft asserts that the literal truth of the Class Picture ads — they *are* made from five ounces of milk and they *do* have a high concentration of calcium — makes it illogical to render a finding of consumer deception. The difficulty with this argument is that even literally true statements can have misleading implications.

. . . .

Here, the average consumer is not likely to know that much of the calcium in five ounces of milk (30%) is lost in processing, which leaves consumers with a misleading impression about calcium content. The critical fact is not that reasonable consumers might believe that a 3/4 ounce slice of cheese actually contains five ounces of *milk*, but that reasonable consumers might believe that a 3/4 ounce slice actually contains the *calcium* in five ounces of milk.

. . . .

In determining that the milk equivalency claim was material to consumers, the FTC cited Kraft surveys showing that 71% of respondents rated calcium content an extremely or very important factor in their decision to buy Kraft Singles, and that 52% of female, and 40% of all respondents, reported significant personal concerns about adequate calcium consumption. The FTC further noted that the ads were targeted to female homemakers with children and that the 60 milligram difference between the calcium contained in five ounces of milk and that contained in a Kraft Single would make up for most of the RDA calcium deficiency shown in girls aged 9–11. Finally, the FTC found evidence in the record that Kraft designed the ads with the intent to capitalize on consumer calcium deficiency concerns.

Significantly, the FTC found further evidence of materiality in Kraft's conduct: despite repeated warnings, Kraft persisted in running the challenged ads.

. . . .

With regard to the imitation superiority claim, the Commission applied a presumption of materiality after finding evidence that Kraft intended the challenged ads to convey this message. (Recall that intent to convey a claim is one of three categories qualifying for a presumption of materiality. *See, e.g., Thompson Medical*, 104 F.T.C. at 816–17.) It found this presumption buttressed by the fact that the challenged ad copy led to increased sales of Singles, even though they cost 40 percent more than imitation slices. Finally, the FTC determined that Kraft's consumer surveys were insufficient to rebut this inference and in particular criticized

Kraft's survey methodology because it offered limited response options to consumers.

. . . .

To reiterate, the FTC's order does two things: it prohibits the Skimp ads and the Class Picture ads (as *currently* designed) and it requires Kraft to base future nutrient and calcium claims on reliable scientific evidence. Kraft mischaracterizes the decision as a categorical ban on commercial speech when in fact it identifies with particularity two nutrient claims that the Commission found actually misleading and prohibits only those claims. It further places on Kraft the (minor) burden of supporting future nutrient claims with reliable data. This leaves Kraft free to use any advertisement it chooses, including the Skimp and Class Picture ads, so long as it either eliminates the elements specifically identified by the FTC as contributing to consumer deception or corrects this inaccurate impression by adding prominent, unambiguous disclosures. *See, e.g., Removatron,* 884 F.2d at 1497. We note one additional consideration further alleviating first amendment concerns; Kraft, like any party to an FTC order, may seek an advisory opinion from the Commission as to whether any future advertisements comply with its order, 16 C.F.R. § 2.41(d), and this procedure has been specifically cited by courts as one method of reducing advertiser uncertainty.

. . . .

For these reasons, we hold that the specific prohibitions imposed on Kraft in the FTC's cease and desist order are not broader than reasonably necessary to prevent deception and hence not violative of the First Amendment.

. . . .

For the foregoing reasons, Kraft's petition to set-aside the order is DENIED and the Commission's order is ENFORCED.

NOTES ON TESTS OF DECEPTIVENESS

(1) Acts or practices which are likely to mislead violate § 5 of the FTC Act. *See Kraft, supra.* In determining whether an act, omission or representation is likely to mislead, each phrase is not technically interpreted. *Ward Laboratories, Inc. v. FTC,* 276 F.2d 952 (2d Cir. 1960), *cert. denied,* 364 U.S. 827 (1960). Rather, it is the overall impression created, with ambiguities construed against the advertiser. *Kraft, supra; American Home Products Corp. v. FTC,* 695 F.2d 681, 687, (3d Cir. 1983); *Murray Space Shoe Corp. v. FTC,* 304 F.2d 270, 272 (2d Cir. 1962). Literal truth is not a defense when a § 5 violation is alleged. *See Kalwajtys v. FTC,* 237 F.2d 654 (7th Cir. 1956), *cert. denied,* 352 U.S. 1025 (1957); *Kraft, supra; L.G. Balfour Co. v. FTC,* 442 F.2d 1, 17 (7th Cir. 1971).

(2) The courts have held that misrepresentations violating Section 5 must be "material" to a decision to make a purchase. *See Colgate-Palmolive, supra; Kraft,*

supra; *Exposition Press, Inc. v. FTC*, 295 F.2d 869 (2d Cir. 1961). Does the requirement of materiality insure public interest? *See Pep Boys — Manny, Moe & Jack, Inc. v. FTC*, 122 F.2d 158 (3d Cir. 1941). In the *Colgate* case, the court held that "within reasonable bounds" the FTC may infer that a misrepresentation will be a material factor in the purchase decision. Can the FTC make such an inference if there is contradictory evidence? *See Kerran v. FTC*, 265 F.2d 246 (10th Cir. 1959), *cert. denied*, 361 U.S. 818 (1959). Should the FTC be required to explain the basis for such an inference? *See* Justice Harlan's dissent in *FTC v. Mary Carter Paint Co.*, 382 U.S. 46, 49 (1965). Why is a failure to disclose that a product demonstration is simulated a material deception? What other types of nondisclosures might constitute deception? *See FTC v. Figgie Int'l, Inc.*, 994 F.2d 595, 599–600 (9th Cir. 1993); *Keele Hair & Scalp Specialists, Inc. v. FTC*, 275 F.2d 18 (5th Cir. 1960). Is a label misrepresentation more likely to deceive than an advertising misrepresentation? *See Korber Hats, Inc. v. FTC*, 311 F.2d 358 (1st Cir. 1962).

(3) In addition to immateriality, there are other defenses to a charge of deception which will be sustained if proven. *See FTC v. Winsted Hosiery Co.*, 258 U.S. 483 (1922) (no deception if term achieves secondary meaning such that consumers are not deceived by manufacturer's representation); *Kidder Oil Co. v. FTC*, 117 F.2d 892 (7th Cir. 1941) (representation merely constitutes puffing); *Waltham Precision Instrument Co., Inc.*, FTC Dkt. 6914, *aff'd on other grounds, Waltham Precision Instrument Co. v. FTC*, 327 F.2d 427 (7th Cir. 1964), *cert. denied*, 377 U.S. 992 (1964) (all persons receiving advertisement aware of deceptiveness). Should it be a defense to a charge of deception that consumers received products identical or equal to those they ordered? *See FTC v. Royal Milling*, 288 U.S. 212 (1933). In *FTC v. Algoma Lumber Co.*, 291 U.S. 67, 78 (1934) Justice Cardozo stated: "The consumer is prejudiced if upon giving an order for one thing, he is supplied with something else. . . . In such matters, the public is entitled to get what it chooses, though the choice may be dictated by caprice or by fashion or perhaps by ignorance." Other defenses which have been rejected in FTC cases include *FTC v. Kay*, 35 F.2d 160 (7th Cir. 1929), *cert. denied*, 281 U.S. 764 (1930) (registration of deceptive term as a trademark affords no protection against proceedings under FTC Act); *Gimbel Bros., Inc. v. FTC*, 116 F.2d 578 (2d Cir. 1941) (acting on customers' instructions); *National Silver Co. v. FTC*, 88 F.2d 425 (2d Cir. 1937) (product defect visible to naked eye).

(4) Does the requirement of a "specific and substantial" public interest merely mean that the FTC should not decide private quarrels between competitors? *Cf. Hershey Chocolate Corp. v. FTC*, 121 F.2d 968 (3d Cir. 1941). Could the number of competitors affected be a factor in determining whether a proceeding is in the public interest? *See Branch v. FTC*, 141 F.2d 31 (7th Cir. 1944). What standard should courts use in reviewing the FTC's determination that a proceeding is in the public interest? *See Slough v. FTC*, 396 F.2d 870 (5th Cir. 1968), *cert. denied*, 393 U.S. 980 (1968). *Compare* the discussion on § 43(a) of the Lanham Act in the Misrepresentation section of Chapter 8, *supra*.

(5) Should the question whether the FTC has "reason to believe" an illegal practice is occurring also be a jurisdictional issue? *See Miles Laboratories, Inc. v. FTC*, 140

F.2d 683 (D.C. Cir. 1944), *cert. denied*, 322 U.S. 752 (1944). Note that this is a threshold question for the court's determination in granting relief pendente lite. 15 U.S.C. §§ 52, 53; *cf. FTC v. Sterling Drug, Inc.*, 317 F.2d 669 (2d Cir. 1963).

(6) A number of decisions prohibit the use of deceptive initial offers ("first contact") despite the fact that they are rectified before any purchase is made in reliance upon them. *See FTC v. Standard Educ. Society*, 302 U.S. 112 (1937); *Exposition Press, Inc. v. FTC*, 295 F.2d 869 (2d Cir. 1961). Could the false promising of leads to prospective salesmen constitute a deceptive first contact? *See Goodman v. FTC*, 244 F.2d 584 (9th Cir. 1957). Is the *Colgate-Palmolive* case also a first contact case? *See Developments in the Law — Deceptive Advertising*, 80 Harv. L. Rev. 1005 (1967).

(7) Should the FTC protect even gullible consumers? In *In re Cliffdale Associates, Inc.*, [1983-1987 Transfer Binder] Trade Reg. Rep. (CCH) ¶ 22,137 (March 23, 1984), Chairman Miller, writing for the majority, endorsed the "consumer acting reasonably" standard. He stated that the standard was not new, and that it only emphasized long standing Commission policy "that the law should not be applied in such a way as to find that honest representations are deceptive simply because they are misunderstood by a few." While concurring with the majority that respondent's value and performance claims for its Gas Save Valve automobile engine attachment were deceptive, Commissioner Pertschuk dissented as to the endorsement of the new standard. He stated:

> The new deception analysis has a more serious effect that is clearly not unintentional. That is to withdraw the protection of Section 5 from consumers who do not act "reasonably."
>
>   . . . .
>
> How will the Commission judge the conduct of consumers who succumb to sales pitches for worthless or grossly over-valued investments? Do "reasonable consumers" buy diamonds or real estate, sight unseen, from total strangers? Is a consumer "acting reasonably" when he or she falls for a hard-sell telephone solicitation to buy "valuable" oil or gas leases from an unknown corporation? Can a consumer "reasonably" rely on oral promises that are expressly repudiated in a written sales contract?
>
> The sad fact is that a small segment of our society makes its livelihood preying upon consumers who are very trusting and unsophisticated. Others specialize in weakening the defenses of especially vulnerable, but normally cautious, consumers. Through skillful exploitation of such common desires as the wish to get rich quick or to provide some measure of security for one's old age, professional con men can prompt conduct that many of their victims will readily admit — in hindsight — is patently unreasonable.
>
> Of course, what strikes me as "unreasonable" consumer behavior may not seem so to other commissioners. The very subjective nature of the "reasonable consumer" standard is cause for concern. How can consumer conduct be measured for reasonableness? I know of no test for it, and I am fearful of the *ad hoc* determination that will be made in the future.

Since the enunciation of the "reasonable consumer" standard in *Cliffdale, supra,* at least one court, in reviewing the application of this adjudicative standard, has found that the FTC bears a greater evidentiary burden in showing a § 5 violation than under the previous "tendency and capacity to deceive" standard. *Southwest Sunsites, Inc. v. FTC,* 785 F.2d 1431, 1436 (9th Cir. 1986). However, courts and commentators are undecided as to whether the "new standard" has actually had any practical effect on FTC enforcement activity. *See* Schecter, *The Death of the Gullible Consumer: Towards a More Sensible Definition of Deception at the FTC,* 1989 U. Ill. L. Rev. 571, 592–593 (1989); Pridgen, *Consumer Protection and the Law,* § 10.04 (1991).

(8) "Bait and switch" selling is initiated by the advertising of a bargain buy which is intended to lure customers into a store. The deception is carried out when the customers who appear are actively discouraged by sales personnel from purchasing the advertised product, or are told it is unavailable, or when the product upon actual inspection proves to be intrinsically undesirable. The perpetrator of such a scheme expects to sell profitable "switched" merchandise in place of the "bait" merchandise advertised. *See Tashof v. FTC,* 437 F.2d 707 (D.C. Cir. 1970), and the FTC position set forth at 16 C.F.R. §§ 238.0 and 238.1 (1977). Would it be any defense to a "bait and switch" charge that advertising gave notice of limited quantity of cheaper articles? *See United States v. George's Radio & Television Co.,* 1962 Trade Cas. ¶ 70,281 (D.C. Cir. 1962). Is the rationale for illegality similar in "bait and switch" and "first contact" cases? *Compare All-State Indus., Inc. v. FTC,* 423 F.2d 423 (4th Cir. 1970), *cert. denied,* 400 U.S. 828 (1970) *with FTC v. Standard Educ. Society,* 302 U.S. 112 (1937). What other types of pricing practices might be deceptive?

[D] Tests of Unfairness

INTRODUCTION

Section 5 of the FTC Act prohibits "unfair" acts or practices, as well as those that are deceptive. Despite the fact that "unfairness" is a broader concept than deceptiveness, most § 5 proceedings, excluding those involving antitrust violations, have been brought on the ground that the challenged conduct is deceptive. Even when the FTC has attacked certain types of practices on the grounds of unfairness alone, it traditionally avoided applying this standard to advertising. It now appears, however, that the FTC will consider unfairness as an additional standard to regulate advertising. At least part of the impetus for this development must be attributed to the *Sperry & Hutchinson* case, 405 U.S. 233 (1972). In that case, the Supreme Court held that § 5 empowers the FTC to proscribe "unfair" acts or practices regardless of whether they violate the spirit or letter of the antitrust laws. Subsequently, the FTC relied heavily upon *Sperry & Hutchinson* in applying unfairness as a standard for regulating advertising in order to protect consumer interests. *See Orkin, below; FTC v. Pfizer, Inc.,* 81 F.T.C. 23 (1972).

ORKIN EXTERMINATING CO. v. FEDERAL TRADE COMMISSION

United States Court of Appeals, Eleventh Circuit
849 F.2d 1354 (1988)

CLARK, CIRCUIT JUDGE:

. . . .

According to its officers, Orkin [a wholly owned subsidiary of Rollins, Inc.] is the largest termite and pest control company in the world. Among the services which Orkin offers to its customers is the treatment of houses, buildings and other structures for the destruction of and protection against termites and other wood infesting organisms. Orkin's agreements with its customers to provide these services are typically embodied in standard printed forms which are not subject to modification by Orkin's agents or customers.

Prior to 1966, Orkin's customers could purchase guarantees for continued protection of a treated structure by paying a specified fee. These guarantees lasted for a stated period, typically between five and fifteen years. In 1966, Orkin began to offer similar guarantees that were, by the terms of its contracts, to last the "lifetime" of a treated structure. Between January 1966, when Orkin started to offer these "lifetime" guarantees, and February 1, 1975, Orkin's contracts for termite protection and control ("pre-1975 contracts") provided that a customer could renew the coverage of its "lifetime" guarantee by paying an annual renewal fee, the amount of which was specified in the contract. The contracts state that as long as a customer continues to pay this annual fee, the guarantee remains in effect for the lifetime of the treated structure, unless the structure is structurally modified after the initial treatment date.

. . . .

[A]ll of the contracts stated specifically that Orkin could adjust the annual renewal fee in the event of a structural modification to the treated premises. No other provision in the contract indicates that these fees are subject to increases.

. . . .

In 1978, Orkin began to consider increasing the annual fees contained in the pre-1975 contracts. Rollins's general counsel concluded initially that there was no contractual basis for an increase. Yet convinced that Orkin could not have intended to lock the company into a perpetually fixed contract, he sought the advice of the company's law firm. A memorandum produced by the law firm considered the question whether "there [are] any grounds for the claim that a contract which may be renewed or extended from year to year, indefinitely, is unenforceable." It concluded that one unidentified Orkin contract appeared "to be of *indefinite* duration" and would therefore be "terminable by Orkin after a reasonable period of time."

. . . .

In August 1980, Orkin began notifying customers who were parties to pre-1975 contracts that the company was going to increase its annual renewal fees. Increase notices were sent to approximately 207,000 pre-1975 customers.

. . . .

Many of Orkin's customers complained about the increase in their annual renewal fees. In addition, various officials in seventeen states questioned the lawfulness of Orkin's actions. But customers did not have any real alternative to paying the increased renewal fees. Although some of Orkin's competitors were willing to assume Orkin's obligations of the pre-1975 contracts, they apparently would not have done so "without imposing conditions that would have resulted in additional charges to Orkin's customers or subsequently raising the renewal fees as expressly permitted in their own contracts." 108 F.T.C. at 347 (footnote omitted).

. . . .

In May 1984, the FTC issued an administrative complaint charging that Orkin had committed an unfair act or practice in violation of § 5. The complaint alleged that Orkin's pre-1975 contracts provided for a fixed annual renewal fee and that Orkin had violated the terms of these contracts by unilaterally raising the fees specified therein.

After conducting some pretrial discovery, counsel for the FTC supporting the complaint . . . moved for a summary decision.

. . . .

Orkin filed a cross-motion for summary decision on the ground that conduct which is not alleged to be deceptive cannot constitute an "unfair act or practice" within the meaning of section 5. The Administrative Law Judge responsible for the case ruled in favor of the Commission. The ALJ found specifically that (1) Orkin's pre-1975 contracts did provide for a fixed renewal fee and that Orkin had breached these contracts by attempting to raise the renewal fees; (2) these breaches of contract could constitute a violation of § 5; (3) there was substantial consumer injury; (4) consumers could not reasonably have avoided this injury; and (5) there were no countervailing benefits to consumers or competition. The ALJ entered an order requiring Orkin to roll back all fees in pre-1975 contracts to the levels specified in those contracts.

Orkin appealed the ALJ's decision to the Commission. The Commission affirmed all aspects of the ALJ's decision.

. . . .

IV

. . . .

Orkin contends that a "mere breach of contract," which does not involve some sort of deceptive or fraudulent behavior, is outside the ambit of § 5. In support of this proposition, Orkin cites cases that have interpreted state statutes similar to the FTCA, commonly referred to as a "little" § 5 laws, to require "something more" than a simple breach of contract before a given course of conduct can be found "unfair or deceptive." *See United Roasters, Inc. v. Colgate-Palmolive Co.*, 649 F.2d 985 (4th Cir.), *cert. denied*, 454 U.S. 1054 (1981).

. . . .

Orkin's argument is clearly inconsistent with the ways in which the FTC's unfairness authority has developed, as a result of both legislation and judicial interpretation. *See American Financial Services v. F.T.C.*, 767 F.2d 957, 965–72 (D.C. Cir. 1985) ("A.F.S."), *cert. denied*, 475 U.S. 1011, (1986). The Supreme Court, for example, has "put its stamp of approval on the Commission's evolving use of a consumer unfairness doctrine not moored in the traditional rationales of anticompetitiveness or *deception*." *Id.* at 971 (emphasis added) (citing *FTC v. Sperry & Hutchinson Co.*, 405 U.S. 233 (1972). Moreover, as the Commission noted, there is nothing which constrains it to follow judicial interpretations of state statutes in construing the agency's § 5 authority. *See* 108 F.T.C. at 361. Orkin's suggestion that we should rely on these cases overlooks the fact that it is the Commission itself which is charged, by statute, with the duty of prescribing "interpretative rules and general statements of policy with respect to unfair or deceptive acts or practices (within the meaning of section [5])." 15 U.S.C. § 57(a)(1).

In 1980, the Commission promulgated a policy statement containing an abstract definition of "unfairness" which focuses upon unjustified customer injury. *See A.F.S.*, 767 F.2d at 971. Under the standard enunciated in this policy statement,

> [t]o justify a finding of unfairness the injury must satisfy three tests. It must be substantial; it must not be outweighed by any countervailing benefits to consumers or competition that the practice produces; and it must be an injury that consumers themselves could not reasonably have avoided.

It is true that the emphasis placed by the Commission on consumer unfairness is "of comparatively recent origin."

. . . .

But Orkin has not argued that the Commission's definition of what constitutes an unfair practice is itself outside the scope of the Commission's § 5 authority. Indeed, the courts reviewing applications of the Commission's unfairness standard have assumed, necessarily, that it is a valid standard. *See, e.g., A.F.S.*, 767 F.2d at 972.

. . . .

In deciding whether Orkin's conduct was "unfair," we owe "some deference" to the Commission's judgment on the issue. *F.T.C. v. Indiana Federation of Dentists*, 476 U.S. 447, (1986).

We must therefore decide whether the Commission exceeded its authority in deciding that one company's unilateral breach of 207,000 consumer contracts could meet the Commission's definition of unfairness.

. . . .

B

The first prong of the unfairness standard requires a finding of substantial injury to consumers.

. . . .

The Commission's finding of "substantial" injury is supported by the undisputed fact that Orkin's breach of its pre-1975 contracts generated, during a four-year period, more than $7,000,000 in revenues from renewal fees to which the Company was not entitled. As the Commission noted, although the actual injury to individual customers may be small on an annual basis, this does not mean that such injury is not "substantial." 108 F.T.C. at 362 (citing *In re International Harvester, Co.*, 104 F.T.C. 949, 1064 n. 55 (1984); *see also A.F.S.*, 767 F.2d at 972 (Commission's Policy Statement makes clear that injury may be sufficiently substantial if it causes small harm to a large class of people); Averitt, 70 Geo. L.J. at 246.

As for the second prong of the unfairness standard, the Commission noted that "conduct can create a mixture of both beneficial and adverse consequences." 108 F.T.C. at 364 (citing *International Harvester* 104 F.T.C. at 1061). But because "[t]he increase in the fee was not accompanied in an increase in the level of service provided or an enhancement of its quality," the Commission concluded that no consumer benefit had resulted from Orkin's conduct. 108 F.T.C. at 364. The Commission also rejected various arguments that an order requiring Orkin to roll back its fee increases "would have adverse effects on its entire customer base and on many of its competitors." 108 F.T.C. at 365.

. . . .

With regard to the third prong of the unfairness standard, the Commission concluded that consumers could not have reasonably avoided the harm caused by Orkin's conduct. The Commission's focus on a consumer's ability to reasonably avoid injury "stems from the Commission's general reliance on free and informed consumer choice as the best regulator of the market." *A.F.S.*, 767 F.2d at 976.

. . . .

As the Commission explained, "Consumers may act to avoid injury before it occurs if they have reason to anticipate the impending harm and the means to avoid it, or they may seek to mitigate the damage afterward if they are aware of potential avenues toward that end." 108 F.T.C. at 366.

The Commission determined that "neither anticipatory avoidance nor subsequent mitigation was reasonably possible for Orkin's pre-1975 customers." *Id.* at 366. Anticipatory avoidance through consumer choice was impossible because these contracts gave no indication that the company would raise the renewal fee as a result of inflation, or for any other reason.

. . . .

C

. . . .

There remains, however, the question whether this case represents a significant departure from prior Commission precedent.

. . . .

We think it important to remember . . . that § 5 by its very terms makes deceptive and unfair practices distinct lines of inquiry which the Commission may pursue. As is suggested above, while a practice may be both deceptive and unfair, it may be unfair without being deceptive. *See A.F.S.*, 767 F.2d at 967; *cf.* Averitt, 70 Geo. L.J. at 265 (deception "is really just one specific form of unfair consumer practice"). Furthermore, the Commission has explained in its Policy Statement that it operates under the assumption that the unfairness doctrine "differs from, and supplements, the prohibition against consumer deception." H.R. Rep. 156, Pt. 1, 98th Cong., 1st Sess. 34 (1983); Trade Reg. Rep. (CCH) ¶ 50,421 at 55,946.

An adoption of Orkin's position would mean that the Commission could never proscribe widespread breaches of retail consumer contracts unless there was evidence of deception or fraud. The Supreme Court has, on more than one occasion, recognized that the standard of unfairness is "by necessity, an elusive one," which defies such a limitation. *See Indiana Federation of Dentists*, 106 S. Ct. at 2016 (citing *Sperry & Hutchinson*, 405 U.S. at 244). The statutory scheme at issue here "necessarily gives the Commission an influential role in interpreting section 5 and in applying to it facts of particular cases arising out of *unprecedented situations*." *F.T.C. v. Colgate-Palmolive Co.*, 380 U.S. 374, 385 (1965) (emphasis added).

. . . .

This case may be "unprecedented" to the extent it concerns non-deceptive contract breaches. But given the extraordinary level of consumer injury which Orkin has caused and the fact that deceptiveness is often not a component of the unfairness inquiry, we think the limitation of the Commission's § 5 authority urged by Orkin would be inconsistent with the broad mandate conferred upon the Commission by Congress. Thus, because the Commission's decision fully and clearly comports with the standard set forth in its Policy Statement, we conclude that the Commission acted within its § 5 authority.

. . . .

NOTES ON TESTS OF UNFAIRNESS

(1) In *FTC v. Keppel*, 291 U.S. 304 (1934), the Supreme Court held that selling candy by lottery was an "unfair" practice prohibited by § 5 of the FTC Act because it was "contrary to public policy" and considered "unscrupulous" in the industry. *See also Carter Carburetor Corp. v. FTC*, 112 F.2d 722 (8th Cir. 1940); *Chamber of Commerce of Minneapolis v. FTC*, 13 F.2d 673 (8th Cir. 1926). Do the following factors, considered by the FTC in determining unfairness, and quoted with apparent approval by the Supreme Court in *Sperry & Hutchinson*, 405 U.S. 233 (1972), constitute a broader test?

(1) whether the practice, without necessarily having been considered unlawful, offends public policy as it has been established by statute, the common law, or otherwise . . . ;

(2) whether it was immoral, unethical, oppressive or unscrupulous;

(3) whether it causes substantial injury to consumers (or competitors or other businessmen).

What additional factors might be considered in determining whether advertising is unfair? *See* FTC Chairman Engman's dissent in *ITT Continental Baking Co. and Ted Bates & Co.*, 83 F.T.C. 865, 90 F.T.C. 181 (1973); Hobbs, *Unfairness at the FTC — The Legacy of S&H*, 47 ABA Antitrust L.J. 1023 (1978); Averitt, *Meaning of "Unfair Acts or Practices" in Section 5 of the Federal Trade Commission Act*, 70 Geo. L.J. 225 (1981). In *Pfizer*, the Commission ruled a manufacturer must have a "reasonable basis" for all affirmative product claims. Will requiring advertisers to substantiate claims before making them make it easier for the FTC to enforce § 5 of the FTC Act? *See* Note, *Unfairness in Advertising: Pfizer, Inc.*, 59 Va. L. Rev. 324 (1973); Note, *Fairness and Unfairness in Television Product Advertising*, 76 Mich. L. Rev. 498 (1978).

(2) In 1980, in a letter to the Consumer Subcommittee of the Senate Committee on Commerce, Science and Transportation, the FTC discussed how it interpreted the *Sperry & Hutchinson* test, *supra*. FTC, *Policy Statement on Unfairness*, [1969-1983 Transfer Binder] Trade Reg. Rep. (CCH) ¶ 50,421 (December 17, 1980). The Commission indicated that consumer injury is the "primary focus" of the FTC Act and the most important of the three *Sperry & Hutchinson* criteria. As stated in *Orkin*, *supra*, to justify a finding of unfairness, the consumer injury must satisfy three tests: (a) It must be substantial; (b) it must not be outweighed by any countervailing benefits to consumers or competition that the practice produces; and (c) it must be an injury that consumers themselves could not reasonably have avoided. The "public policy" test was viewed by the Commission not as a separate consideration, but as a means of providing additional evidence on the degree of consumer injury caused by a specific practice. "Unethical or unscrupulous" conduct was viewed as largely duplicative of the first two criteria and not a basis for Commission action.

(3) There are endless varieties of "unfair" and "deceptive" acts and practices within the ambit of § 5 of the FTC Act. Some of the most important of these offenses in terms of FTC enforcement activity are as follows:

(a) Misrepresentations of facts concerning the business, product or service, *i.e.*, its origin, composition or effectiveness. *See FTC v. Algoma Lumber Co.*, 291 U.S. 67, 68 (1934) (Justice Cardozo stating that "the public is entitled to get what it chooses, though the choice may be dictated by caprice or by fashion or perhaps by ignorance"); *Carter's Products, Inc. v. FTC*, 268 F.2d 461 (9th Cir. 1959) (holding that "Carter's Little Liver Pills" product name and advertisements deceptively represented that the pills had a therapeutic action on the liver); *FTC v. Thompson Medical Co.*, 791 F.2d 189 (D.C. Cir. 1986), *cert. denied*, 479 U.S. 1085 (1987) (upholding FTC's ruling that "Aspercreme" for arthritis rub falsely implied that the product contained aspirin and its requirement of a disclaimer); *See also In re Campbell Soup*, 56 Antitrust & Trade Reg. Rep. (BNA) 783 (May 25, 1989) (FTC complaint issued charging that soup company's advertisement falsely represented health benefits of consumption of its products).

(b) Misrepresentations respecting guarantees, endorsements, and testimonials. *See Orkin Exterminating Co., supra; National Comm'n on Egg Nutrition v. FTC*, 570 F.2d 157 (7th Cir. 1977), *cert. denied*, 439 U.S. 821 (1978) (prohibiting advertisements misrepresenting existence of scientific evidence indicating that eating eggs increases risk of heart disease); *Warner-Lambert Co. v. FTC*, 562 F.2d 749 (D.C. Cir. 1977) (enjoining petitioner's representations that its mouthwash cured cold symptoms); *Montgomery Ward & Co. v. FTC*, 379 F.2d 666 (7th Cir. 1967) (enjoining representations as to an "unconditional" guarantee where the actual written guarantee was limited notwithstanding the company's policy of honoring its guarantee as advertised); *Goodman v. FTC*, 244 F.2d 584 (9th Cir. 1957) (holding that "Weaver's Guild" falsely implied an association for men for mutual aid and protection); *Adolph Kastor & Bros., Inc. v. FTC*, 138 F.2d 824 (2d Cir. 1943) (Judge Learned Hand ruling that "Scout" on a boy's knife implied endorsement by the Boy Scouts of America). What guarantees besides those concerning product characteristics might be deceptive? *See All-State Indus., Inc. v. FTC*, 423 F.2d 423 (4th Cir. 1970), *cert. denied*, 400 U.S. 828 (1970) (manufacturing output 100 percent guaranteed); *cf. Goodman v. FTC*, 244 F.2d 584 (9th Cir. 1957) (full refund if purchaser not able to complete course).

(c) False disparagement and comparison. *Compare Carter Products, Inc. v. FTC*, 323 F.2d 523 (5th Cir. 1963), in which it was held that television use of simulated shaving lather did not provide a valid comparison of the qualities of "Rise" shaving cream and tended to disparage competing lathers, *with FTC v. Sterling Drug, Inc.*, 317 F.2d 669 (2d Cir. 1963), in which an advertisement summarizing the results of a scientific investigation of five leading analgesic products was held *not* to be false or misleading.

(d) Deceptive pricing, sales, and credit practices. *See FTC v. Standard Education Society*, 302 U.S. 112 (1937), in which fictitious testimonials and representations that the encyclopedia was free and the customer only paid for a loose-leaf service were held deceptive; *Charnita v. FTC*, 479 F.2d 684 (3d Cir. 1973) in which a "judgment note" enabling the holder to enter judgment in state court without notice was held to be a "security interest" within scope of the Truth In Lending Act so that purchasers had to be notified of their right to rescind.

(e) Deceptive promises and omissions regarding the nature, risk and anticipated performance of an investment. *See FTC v. Atlantex Assoc.*, 1989-1 Trade Cas. (CCH) ¶ 68,585 (11th Cir. 1989) (defendant misrepresented oil and gas ventures); *FTC v. Kaplan*, 55 Antitrust & Trade Reg. Rep. (BNA) 938 (December 1, 1988) (defendant misrepresented earning capacity of prospective distributors of burglar alarms); *Southwest Sunsites, Inc. v. FTC*, 785 F.2d 1431 (9th Cir. 1986) (petitioners misrepresented financial risk and nature of investment in parcels of land).

(f) Misrepresentation by omission of material information. *See Theodore Kagen Corp. v. FTC*, 283 F.2d 371 (D.C. Cir. 1960) (per curiam), *cert. denied*, 365 U.S. 843 (1961) (base metal simulating gold); *FTC v. World Travel Vacation*

Brokers, Inc., 861 F.2d 1020, 1023 (7th Cir. 1988) (advertisement for $29 airfare certificates failed to disclose that full costs were added to "hotel cost" determination); *Libbey-Owens-Ford Glass Co. v. FTC*, 352 F.2d 415 (6th Cir. 1965) (per curiam) (television advertisement for automotive window glass failed to disclose use of automobile with windows rolled down); *Royal Oil Corp. v. FTC*, 262 F.2d 741 (4th Cir. 1959) (nondisclosure that oil is reprocessed); *Royal Baking Powder Co. v. FTC*, 281 F. 744 (2d Cir. 1922) (nondisclosure of change of ingredients).

An exhaustive list of unfair and deceptive trade practices is contained in the C.C.H. Trade Regulation Reporter, which includes the FTC's Industry Guides and Trade Regulation Rules. For a generally comprehensive approach to the problem of categorizing these offenses, see Kanwit, *Federal Trade Commission* (1993); Von Kalinowski, *Business Organizations — Antitrust Laws and Trade Regulations* (1983); Craswell, *The Identification of Unfair Acts and Practices By the Federal Trade Commission*, 1981 Wis. L. Rev. 107.

(4) An important piece of consumer legislation is the Consumer Credit Protection Act, 15 U.S.C. § 1601 *et seq.* Its two major parts are known as the Truth in Lending Act, 15 U.S.C. § 1601 *et seq.* and the Fair Credit Reporting Act, 15 U.S.C. § 1681 *et seq.* The purposes of the Act are to: (1) "assure a meaningful disclosure of credit terms so that the consumer will be able to compare more readily the various credit terms available to him and avoid the uninformed use of credit"; (2) discourage the use of unrestricted garnishment as a basis for the making of predatory extensions of credit; and (3) insure that consumer credit reporting agencies exercise their responsibilities "with fairness, impartiality and a respect for the consumers' right of privacy." 15 U.S.C. §§ 1601, 1671, 1681. The Truth in Lending Act, the Fair Credit Reporting Act and their implementing regulations are largely enforced by the FTC. The Act also provides for a private right of action for damages where a creditor fails to make, or inaccurately makes, a required disclosure or where there is willful or negligent noncompliance by a credit reporting agency. *See generally* CCH Consumer Credit Guide (4 Vols.); Halverson, *Consumer Credit Regulation by the FTC*, 90 Banking L.J. 479 (1973); Weisart, *Consumer Protection in the Credit Card Industry, Federal Legislative Controls*, 70 Mich. L. Rev. 1475 (1972); Warren & Larmore, *Truth in Lending: Problems of Coverage*, 24 Stan. L. Rev. 793 (1972); Feldman, *The Fair Credit Reporting Act — Provisions and Problems*, 61 Ill. B.J. 314 (1973); Klasky, LeValley, & Taylor, *Truth In Lending, Fair Credit Billing and Fair Credit Reporting*, 33 Bus. Law. 981 (1978); Raleigh, *What You Should Know About Revised Regulation Z*, 70 Ill. B.J. 506 (1982); Camden, *Fair Credit Reporting Act: What You Don't Know May Hurt You*, 57 U. Cin. L. Rev. 267 (1988).

(5) In 1992, the FTC promulgated extensive guidelines regarding so-called "green" marketing claims. The regulations, set forth at 16 C.F.R. § 260.6 *et seq.*, provide a uniform national standard for advertising claims regarding the environmental merits of particular products. The "green" guidelines contain general principles applicable to all environmental marketing claims, as well as specific examples of approved and disapproved usages of particular claims regarding the environmental attributes or benefits of a product, *e.g.*, "biodegradable," "recyclable," "refillable," "ozone friendly."

[E]　Scope of Remedies

INTRODUCTION

[1]　Administrative Remedies

The traditional FTC remedy in false advertising cases has been a cease and desist order requiring either the prohibition of the conduct or the disclosure of information necessary to prevent the conduct from being unfair or deceptive. 15 U.S.C. § 45. Within this framework, the FTC has traditionally been given wide latitude in fashioning remedial orders. *See Jacob Siegel Co. v. FTC*, 327 U.S. 608 (1946). In order to meet the demand for greater consumer protection, however, the FTC has initiated several innovative remedial programs. A principal remedial technique is corrective advertising. One form of this remedy requires the advertiser to devote a substantial portion of its future advertising directly to rectifying past deceptions. *ITT Continental Baking Co.*, 79 F.T.C. 248 (1971) ("PROFILE bread is not effective for weight reduction, contrary to possible interpretations of prior advertising"). A more drastic form of this remedy requires a portion of future advertising to include a confession of wrongdoing. *Wasem's Inc.*, 84 F.T.C. 209 (1974) ("This advertisement is run pursuant to an order of the Federal Trade Commission. I have . . . made various claims which are erroneous or misleading. . . ."). While not a remedy as such, the FTC has also inaugurated an advertising substantiation program requiring that advertisers, on demand, furnish the FTC with documentation substantiating advertising claims. These materials are then placed on the public record for examination.

Additional remedies under various other statutes are also available to the FTC but are used relatively infrequently. The Wool Products Labeling Act, 15 U.S.C. §§ 68–68(j); and Fur Products Labeling Act, 15 U.S.C. §§ 69–69(j), empower the FTC to seek condemnation orders from the courts. Under the Lanham Act, the FTC may apply to the Patent Office for cancellation of trademark registrations. 15 U.S.C. § 1064.

[2]　Remedies in the Federal Courts

In conjunction with the issuance of a cease and desist order, the FTC may file suit in the federal courts requesting injunctive as well as monetary equitable relief. Section 19 of the FTC Act states, in part, that

> [i]f the Commission satisfies the court that the act or practice to which [a] cease and desist order relates is one which a reasonable man would have known under the circumstances was dishonest or fraudulent, the court may . . . grant such relief as the court finds necessary to redress injury to consumers or other persons . . . resulting from the rule violation or the unfair or deceptive act or practice. . . .

15 U.S.C. §§ 57b(a)–(b). Accordingly, under § 19, the Commission may seek restitution or other redress for consumers who made purchases during a period in which the violator reasonably should have known the dishonest or fraudulent nature of the

objectionable practice. *See FTC v. Figgie Int'l, Inc., infra; Windsor Distributing Co. v. FTC*, 77 F.T.C. 204, *aff'd*, 437 F.2d 443 (3d Cir. 1971).

Additionally, Section 13(b) of the FTC Act provides, in part, that

> [u]pon a proper showing . . . a temporary restraining order or a preliminary injunction may be granted without bond. . . . Provided further, [t]hat in proper cases the Commission may seek, and after proper proof, the court may issue, a permanent injunction.

15 U.S.C. § 53(b). When read in conjunction with the 1975 amendments to the FTC Act, courts have construed § 13(b) as enabling the FTC to seek preliminary and permanent injunctive relief, as well as "any ancillary relief necessary to effectuate the exercise of the granted powers." *FTC v. Amy Travel Service, Inc.*, 875 F.2d 564, 572 (7th Cir.), *cert. denied*, 493 U.S. 954 (1989) (district court had power to order monetary equitable relief, such as rescission and restitution, and to enter temporary restraining order freezing defendant's assets in a § 13(b) proceeding); *see also FTC v. Elders Grain, Inc.*, 868 F.2d 901 (7th Cir. 1989) (district court could order rescission in a § 13(b) proceeding); *FTC v. World Travel Vacation Brokers, Inc.*, 861 F.2d 1020 (7th Cir. 1988) (district court had authority under § 13(b) to grant interlocutory relief).

In addition to the FTC's ability to pursue various forms of consumer redress in the federal courts, the 1973 Amendment to the FTC Act and the Magnuson-Moss Act empower the Commission to seek civil penalties of up to $10,000 per day for violations of FTC orders or trade regulation rules. 15 U.S.C. §§ 45(l), (m). *See United States v. Reader's Digest Ass'n*, 1981-2 Trade Cas. (CCH) ¶ 64,247 (3d Cir. 1981), in the first section of this Chapter, *supra*.

WARNER-LAMBERT CO. v. FEDERAL TRADE COMMISSION

United States Court of Appeals, District of Columbia Circuit
562 F.2d 749 (1977)

WRIGHT, CIRCUIT JUDGE

. . . .

Listerine has been on the market since 1879. Its formula has never changed. Ever since its introduction it has been represented as being beneficial in certain respects for colds, cold symptoms, and sore throats. Direct advertising to the consumer, including the cold claims as well as others, began in 1921.

Following the 1972 complaint, hearings were held before an administrative law judge (ALJ). . . . In 1974 the ALJ issued an initial decision sustaining the allegations of the complaint. Petitioner appealed this decision to the Commission. On December 9, 1975 the Commission issued its decision essentially affirming the ALJ's findings. It concluded that petitioner had made the challenged representations that Listerine will ameliorate, prevent, and cure colds and sore throats, and that these representations were false. Therefore the Commission ordered petitioner to:

(1) cease and desist from representing that Listerine will cure colds or sore throats, prevent colds or sore throats, or that users of Listerine will have fewer colds than non-users;

(2) cease and desist from representing that Listerine is a treatment for, or will lessen the severity of, colds or sore throats; that it will have any significant beneficial effect on the symptoms of sore throats or any beneficial effect on symptoms of colds; or that the ability of Listerine to kill germs is of medical significance in the treatment of colds or sore throats or their symptoms;

(3) cease and desist from disseminating any advertisement for Listerine unless it is clearly and conspicuously disclosed in each such advertisement, in the exact language below, that: "Contrary to prior advertising, Listerine will not help prevent colds or sore throats or lessen their severity." This requirement extends only to the next ten million dollars of Listerine advertising.

. . . .

Petitioner relies on the legislative history of the 1914 Federal Trade Commission Act and the Wheeler-Lea amendments to it in 1938 for the proposition that corrective advertising was not contemplated. In 1914 and in 1938 Congress chose not to authorize such remedies as criminal penalties, treble damages, or civil penalties, but that fact does not dispose of the question of corrective advertising.

Petitioner's reliance on the legislative history of the 1975 amendment to the Act is also misplaced. The amendments added a new Section 19 to the Act, authorizing the Commission to bring suits in federal District Courts to redress injury to consumers resulting from a deceptive practice. The section authorizes the court to grant such relief as it "finds necessary to redress injury to consumers or other persons, partnerships, and corporations resulting from the rule violation or the unfair or deceptive act or practice," including, but not limited to,

recission or reformation of contracts, the refund of money or return of property, the payment of damages, and public notification respecting the rule violation of the unfair or deceptive act or practice.

Petitioner and *amici* contend that this congressional grant *to a court* of power to order public notification of a violation establishes that the Commission by itself does not have that power.

We note first that "public notification" is not synonymous with corrective advertising; public notification is a much broader term and may take any one of many forms. Second, the "public notification" contemplated by the amendment is directed at *past* consumers of the product ("to redress injury"), whereas the type of corrective advertising currently before us is directed at *future* consumers. Third, petitioner's construction of the section runs directly contrary to the congressional intent as expressed in a later subsection: "Nothing in this section shall be construed to affect any authority of the Commission under any other provision of law." [15 U.S.C. § 57b(e) (Supp. V 1975)].

. . . .

According to petitioner, "The first reference to corrective advertising in Commission decisions occurred in 1970, nearly fifty years and untold numbers of false advertising cases after passage of the Act." In petitioner's view, the late emergence of this "newly discovered" remedy is itself evidence that it is beyond the Commission's authority. This argument fails on two counts. First the fact that an agency has not asserted a power over a period of years is not proof that the agency lacks such power. Second, and more importantly, we are not convinced that the corrective advertising remedy is really such an innovation. This label may be newly coined, but the concept is well established. It is simply that under certain circumstances an advertiser may be required to make affirmative disclosure of unfavorable facts.

One such circumstance is when an advertisement that did not contain the disclosure would be misleading. For example, the Commission has ordered the sellers of treatments for baldness to disclose that the vast majority of cases of thinning hair and baldness are attributable to heredity, age, and endocrine balance (so-called "male pattern baldness") and that their treatment would have no effect whatever on this type of baldness. It has ordered the promoters of a device for stopping bedwetting to disclose that the device would not be of value in cases caused by organic defects or diseases. And it has ordered the makers of Geritol, an iron supplement, to disclose that Geritol will relieve symptoms of tiredness only in persons who suffer from iron deficiency anemia, and that the vast majority of people who experience such symptoms do not have such a deficiency.

Each of these orders was approved on appeal over objections that it exceeded the Commission's statutory authority. The decisions reflect a recognition that, as the Supreme Court has stated,

> If the Commission is to attain the objectives Congress envisioned, it cannot be required to confine its road block to the narrow lane the transgressor has traveled; it must be allowed effectively to close all roads to the prohibited goal, so that its order may not be by-passed with impunity.

[*FTC v. Ruberoid Co.*, 343 U.S. 470, 473 (1952).]

Affirmative disclosure has also been required when an advertisement, although not misleading if taken alone, becomes misleading considered in light of past advertisements. For example, for 60 years Royal Baking Powder Company had stressed in its advertising that its product was superior because it was made with cream of tartar, not phosphate. But, faced with rising costs of cream of tartar, the time came when it changed its ingredients and became a phosphate baking powder. . . .

The Commission held, and the Second Circuit agreed, . . . that it was proper to require the company to take affirmative steps to advise the public. . . .

In another case the Waltham Watch Company of Massachusetts had become renowned for the manufacture of fine clocks since 1849. Soon after it stopped manufacturing clocks in the 1950's, it transferred its trademarks, good will and the trade name "Waltham" to a successor corporation, which began importing clocks from Europe for resale in the United States. The imported clocks were advertised as "product of Waltham Watch Company since 1850," "a famous 150-year-old company."

The Commission found that the advertisements caused consumers to believe they were buying the same fine Massachusetts clocks of which they had heard for many years. To correct this impression the Commission ordered the company to disclose in all advertisements and on the product that the clock was not made by the old Waltham company and that it was imported. The Seventh Circuit affirmed, relying on "the well-established general principle that the Commission may require affirmative disclosure for the purpose of preventing future deception."

. . . .

Here, as in *Royal* and *Waltham*, it is the accumulated impact of *past* advertising that necessitates disclosure in *future* advertising. To allow consumers to continue to buy the product on the strength of the impression built up by prior advertising — an impression which is now known to be false — would be unfair and deceptive.

. . . .

The Commission has adopted the following standard for the imposition of corrective advertising:

> [I]f a deceptive advertisement has played a substantial role in creating or reinforcing in the public's mind a false and material belief which lives on after the false advertising ceases, there is clear and continuing injury to competition and to the consuming public as consumers continue to make purchasing decisions based on the false belief. Since this injury cannot be averted by merely requiring respondent to cease disseminating the advertisement, we may appropriately order respondent to take affirmative action designed to terminate the otherwise continuing ill effects of the advertisement.

We think this standard is entirely reasonable. It dictates two factual inquiries: (1) did Listerine's advertisements play a substantial role in creating or reinforcing in the public's mind a false belief about the product? and (2) would this belief linger on after the false advertising ceases? It strikes us that if the answer to both questions is not yes, companies everywhere may be wasting their massive advertising budgets. Indeed, it is more than a little peculiar to hear petitioner assert that its commercials really have no effect on consumer belief.

For these reasons it might be appropriate in some cases to presume the existence of the two factual predicates for corrective advertising. But we need not decide that question, or rely on presumptions here, because the Commission adduced survey evidence to support both propositions. We find that the "Product Q" survey data and the expert testimony interpreting them constitute substantial evidence in support of the need for corrective advertising in this case.

We turn next to the specific disclosure required: "Contrary to prior advertising, Listerine will not help prevent colds or sore throats or lessen their severity." Petitioner is ordered to include this statement in every future advertisement for Listerine for a defined period. In printed advertisements it must be displayed in type size at least as large as that in which the principal portion of the text of the advertisement appears and it must be separated from the text so that it can be readily noticed.

In television commercials the disclosure must be presented simultaneously in both audio and visual portions. During the audio portion of the disclosure in television and radio advertisements, no other sounds, including music, may occur.

These specifications are well calculated to assure that the disclosure will reach the public. It will necessarily attract the notice of readers, viewers, and listeners, and be plainly conveyed. Given these safeguards, we believe the preamble "Contrary to prior advertising" is not necessary. It can serve only two purposes: either to attract attention that a correction follows or to humiliate the advertiser. The Commission claims only the first purpose for it, and this we think is obviated by the other terms of the order. The second purpose, if it were intended, might be called for in an egregious case of deliberate deception, but this is not one. While we do not decide whether petitioner proffered its cold claims in good faith or bad, the record compiled could support a finding of good faith. On these facts, the confessional preamble to the disclosure is not warranted.

Finally, petitioner challenges the duration of the disclosure requirement. By its terms it continues until respondent has expended on Listerine advertising a sum equal to the average annual Listerine advertising budget for the period April 1962 to March 1972. That is approximately ten million dollars. Thus if petitioner continues to advertise normally the corrective advertising will be required for about one year. We cannot say that is an unreasonably long time in which to correct a hundred years of cold claims. But, to petitioner's distress, the requirement will not expire by mere passage of time. If petitioner cuts back its Listerine advertising, or ceases it altogether, it can only postpone the duty to disclose. The Commission concluded that correction was required and that a duration of a fixed period of time might not accomplish that task, since petitioner could evade the order by choosing not to advertise at all. The formula settled upon by the Commission is reasonably related to the violation it found.

Accordingly, the order, as modified, is

Affirmed.

FEDERAL TRADE COMMISSION v. FIGGIE INTERNATIONAL, INC.

United States Court of Appeals, Ninth Circuit
994 F.2d 595 (1993)

PER CURIAM:

. . . .

Figgie manufactures and markets heat detectors for home use under the brand name "Vanguard." Unlike smoke detectors, heat detectors are mechanically operated devices requiring no electricity. . . . Until the 1970's heat alarms were considered efficacious. Thereafter fire safety experts modified their views and recommended smoke detectors over heat detectors as the preferred safety device for most locations, recognizing that there were several problems with heat detectors as a household fire alarm system. . . .

These limitations were demonstrated in a series of test fires conducted by fire-prevention experts in the mid 1970's. In almost all test fires, heat detectors sounded their alarms several minutes later than smoke detectors did. Furthermore, heat detectors usually did not sound until after "tenability limits" (levels of smoke, fumes, heat or other hazardous conditions making escape difficult) had been reached. . . .

The Vanguard heat detector first came on the market in 1959. For many years, the National Fire Prevention Association recommended both smoke and heat detectors as part of a household fire warning system. However, following the tests just described, the NFPA changed its standards. The standard adopted in 1978 required at a minimum that smoke detectors be installed on each level of the home and outside each sleeping area. ALJ ¶ 172. . . .

Figgie knew of the results of the Indiana Dunes and Cal Chiefs tests and knew of the changes in the NFPA standards. However, its representations to consumers during the 1980's did not reflect them. The crux of Figgie's message was that heat detectors could be relied on as life-saving fire warning devices, and that the best protection for one's home is a combination of four or five heat detectors to one smoke detector. . . .

Figgie sold its products to the public through at-home sales visits by distributors. This sales technique "heightened the impact of the materials because the captive consumer's attention is focussed for the duration of the sales presentation." ALJ ¶ 84. In addition to the slide-tape shows, a sales presentation would often include a demonstration using a cardboard house with a tissue paper roof. The salesperson would place a lit candle inside the house while holding a heat detector directly over the tissue. The heat detector would alarm before the paper scorched. ALJ ¶ 62. This dramatic and seemingly informative demonstration was in fact misleading. The cardboard house channelled hot air from the candle directly to the fuse, a situation that would be "completely fortuitous" under actual fire conditions. Also, given that the ignition temperature of paper is 450, the demonstration proved only that a heat detector held inches above a flame will activate sometime before the fuse reaches 450. ALJ ¶ 183. Other forms of sales pressure could also be exerted in the home. Customers who bought less than the recommended number of the more expensive heat detectors were asked to sign a release acknowledging that only "partial fire detection protection" had been purchased. ALJ ¶ 65. Figgie's promotional techniques were very successful: its customers bought four or five heat detectors for every smoke detector. ALJ ¶ 18.

The ALJ concluded that Figgie's representations were misleading and deceptive in the absence of an explanation of the limits of heat detectors and the comparative superiority of smoke detectors. ALJ ¶ 187–88. The ALJ issued an order requiring that Figgie make appropriate disclosures to its customers and avoid all misrepresentations. Specifically, all promotional materials for heat detectors were required to carry the following notice: "CAUTION: In most residential fires dangerous levels of smoke, heat and carbon monoxide gas will build up before the heat detector alarm goes off."

On appeal, the Commission upheld most of the ALJ's findings and conclusions. . . .

. . . .

The Commission's cease and desist order was upheld on appeal. *Figgie Int'l, Inc. v. FTC*, 817 F.2d 102 (4th Cir. 1987). . . . FTC then brought the current suit for consumer redress under § 19 for the period between May 18, 1980 and July 20, 1987. . . . On February 9, 1990, the district court concluded that:

> A reasonable man under the circumstances would have known that Figgie's representations that a) Vanguard heat detectors provide the necessary warning to allow safe escape in most residential fires, and b) a combined system of heat detectors and smoke detectors provides significantly greater warning than smoke detectors alone because heat detectors give earlier warning of hot, flaming fires were dishonest or fraudulent.

Summary judgment was therefore granted to FTC on the issue of liability.

On January 14, 1991, the district court granted summary judgment on the amount of redress. The court found that Figgie received $7.59 million in gross revenues from sale of Vanguard heat detectors between the relevant dates, and that consumers paid $49.95 million for them (293,824 units @ $170). The court further concluded that "The Vanguard heat detector's value, given the misrepresentations recommended by Figgie and made by distributors to consumers, is de minimis." Therefore, the court ordered that Figgie pay $7.59 million into a fund which would refund the full purchase price of Vanguard heat detectors to customers. If aggrieved customers claim less than that amount, the balance is to be used for "indirect redress" in the form of corrective advertising or donations to non-profit fire safety organizations. If customers claim more, Figgie is to continue to add to the fund as necessary, to a maximum of $49.95 million.

Figgie timely appeals both summary judgment orders.

. . . .

The Federal Trade Commission has two powers relevant to this case, to deal with deceptive trade practices. If satisfied that a firm has been or is using a deceptive practice affecting commerce, the FTC may, after satisfying procedural requirements, order it to cease and desist from the violation. 15 U.S.C. § 45(b). In addition, under 15 U.S.C. § 57b(a)(2),

> If any person, partnership, or corporation engages in any unfair or deceptive act or practice (within the meaning of section 45(a)(1) of this title) with respect to which the Commission has issued a final cease and desist order which is applicable to such person, partnership, or corporation, then *the Commission may commence a civil action against such person, partnership, or corporation in a United States district court or in any court of competent jurisdiction of a State*. If the Commission satisfies the court that the act or practice to which the cease and desist order relates is one which a reasonable man would have known under the circumstances was dishonest or fraudulent, the court may grant relief under subsection (b) of this section.

15 U.S.C. § 57b(a)(2).

The case before us involves only the redress remedy, not the cease and desist remedy. The latter affects only future conduct. The redress remedy relates to past conduct and requires proof of the extra element that a reasonable person would have known under the circumstances that the practice was dishonest or fraudulent. In this case liability for past conduct would be imposed on Figgie if a reasonable person would have known in the circumstances that it was dishonest or fraudulent for Figgie to use the practices it did to sell heat detectors.

Figgie would have us construe "reasonable person would have known" to require actual knowledge. Although Figgie's argument finds some support in *FTC v. AMREP Corp.*, 705 F. Supp. 119, 127 (S.D.N.Y. 1988), that court's construction does not fit the words and grammar of the statute. Congress unambiguously referred the district court to the state of mind of a hypothetical reasonable person, not the knowledge of the defendant. The standard is objective, not subjective. That Figgie's Vice President-Marketing was innocent of any dishonest intentions, as his declarations establish for purposes of summary judgment, may be probative as to whether a reasonable person would also have been innocent of such intentions, but the issue of law is what a reasonable person would have known, not what Figgie's executive knew. The statute is unambiguous.

C.　Dishonest or Fraudulent Practices

Figgie correctly argues that the Commission's findings describing an "unfair or deceptive" trade practice under § 5 do not necessarily describe a "dishonest or fraudulent" one under § 19. Section 19 liability must not be a rubber stamp of § 5 liability. Figgie appears to argue, however, that the Commission's findings alone can never be the basis of § 19 liability. We disagree. When the findings of the Commission in respect to the defendant's practices are such that a reasonable person would know that the defendant's practices were dishonest or fraudulent, the district need not engage in further fact finding other than to make the ultimate determination that a reasonable person would know. This is such a case.

Figgie sold its product to the public on the basis of misrepresentations as to its effectiveness as a fire safety device. Specifically, Figgie misled customers about "the single most useful piece of information" they could have used: that smoke detectors provide earlier warnings for almost all residential fires. . . . Further, it failed to warn that in most instances the warning from heat detectors would come too late to save lives. There is ample evidence in the Commission's findings to satisfy a court that a reasonable person with Figgie's access to the scientific data establishing the relative inferiority of heat detectors would have known that Figgie's vigorous misrepresentations on their behalf were dishonest and fraudulent.

. . . .

Figgie argues that it was reasonable to act on its own interpretation of the test results until the time the Commission's cease and desist order became final. We disagree. *The Commission found that Figgie's marketing practices were deceptive in light of the test fires and the NFPA's rule changes. Once that information became available in the late 1970's, it was unreasonable for Figgie to ignore it.* If Figgie's practices were "dishonest or fraudulent," it is because of their relationship to the known facts of fire safety, not their relationship to the history of this litigation.

. . . .

Figgie argues that because its liability is premised on certain misrepresentations or misleading statements, only those consumers that can prove that they purchased a Vanguard heat detector in reliance on those statements should be entitled to redress. . . .

. . . .

. . . It is well established with regard to § 13 of the FTC Act (which gives district courts the power to order equitable relief) that proof of individual reliance by each purchasing customer is not needed. . . . A presumption of actual reliance arises once the Commission has proved that the defendant made material misrepresentations, that they were widely disseminated, and that consumers purchased the defendant's product. . . . Because Figgie has presented no evidence to rebut the presumption of reliance, injury to consumers has been established.

. . . .

The district court's order creates no windfall for Figgie's customers. Refunds are available to those buyers "who can make a valid claim for such redress." Those who paid less than the $170 figure challenged by Figgie (and discussed *infra*) will therefore obtain redress based on the lesser figure. Those consumers who decide, after advertising which corrects the deceptions by which Figgie sold them the heat detectors, that nevertheless the heat detectors serve their needs, may then make the informed choice to keep their heat detectors instead of returning them for refunds.

. . . .

The district court's order provides that any unrefunded money be distributed by "donation to one or more nonprofit entities, at the discretion of the Commission, for the support of research, fellowships or consumer education in the field of fire safety." This extraordinary provision cannot be characterized as "redress." The word connotes making amends to someone who has been wronged. The nonprofit organizations, recipients of fellowships, researchers, and educators who might receive the money under this portion of the order were not wronged by Figgie's deceptive sales methods. Calling a fine "indirect redress" does not make it redress. An adjective, such as "indirect," cannot be used to exceed the statutory limitation on the remedy. Congress expressly prohibited exemplary or punitive damages under § 57b(b), so we know that its intent was not to punish deceptive trade practices, only to authorize redress to consumers and others for "injury resulting" from the trade practice. This portion of the award was outside the boundaries of the discretion given to the district court by the statute. The FTC cites cases under other statutes in which similar remedies have been upheld, but in none of these does the statute limit recovery to redress and expressly prohibit exemplary or punitive damages. The district court should modify its order to provide for refund to Figgie of any funds not expended for authorized purposes.

. . . .

Accordingly, the summary judgment on liability is AFFIRMED, but the summary judgment on damage is MODIFIED and the order VACATED for modification consistent with this opinion.

NOTES ON SCOPE OF REMEDIES

(1) The FTC is not limited to proscribing illegal conduct in the precise form in which it existed in the past but may also restrain like or related unlawful acts. *FTC v. Mandel Bros., Inc.*, 359 U.S. 385 (1959). Its remedy, however, must bear a reasonable relationship to the adjudicated illegal conduct. *Jacob Siegel Co. v. FTC*, 327 U.S. 608 (1946). Can the FTC prohibit the false advertising of products not previously misrepresented? *Compare American Home Prod. Corp. v. FTC*, 402 F.2d 232 (6th Cir. 1968) *with Niresk Indus., Inc. v. FTC*, 278 F.2d 337 (7th Cir. 1960), *cert. denied*, 364 U.S. 883 (1960). Can the FTC even prohibit conduct in which the respondent has never engaged? *See Slough v. FTC*, 396 F.2d 870 (5th Cir. 1968), *cert. denied*, 393 U.S. 980 (1968).

(2) What factors should be considered in determining whether an order is too broad? *See Beneficial Corp. v. FTC*, 542 F.2d 611 (3d Cir. 1976); *Bankers Securities Corp. v. FTC*, 297 F.2d 403 (3d Cir. 1961). In *FTC v. National Lead Co.*, 352 U.S. 419 (1957), the Supreme Court affirmed the prohibition of lawful practices to prevent the recurrence of unlawful ones, reasoning that violators must "expect some fencing in." Is this what the FTC did in *Colgate-Palmolive, supra*? *See also Kraft, supra*, in which the FTC was held to have the discretion to issue a multi-product, "fencing-in" order extending beyond the violation involving one Kraft cheese product to advertising for all of Kraft's cheese-related products so as to prevent similar deceptive practices in the future; *Sears, Roebuck & Co. v. FTC*, 676 F.2d 385 (9th Cir. 1982) (affirming FTC's order preventing performance misrepresentations regarding any major home appliance, where Sears had previously misrepresented the performance of a dishwasher); *American Home Products Corp. v. FTC*, 695 F.2d 681 (3d Cir. 1982) (upholding FTC's order prohibiting deception extending to all of offending company's non-prescription drugs, not merely the drug for which deception had been found); *Jay Norris v. FTC*, 598 F.2d 1244 (2d Cir.), *cert. denied*, 444 U.S. 980 (1979) (upholding FTC's "all-products" order despite having found deception with regard to only six products); *J.B. Williams v. FTC*, 381 F.2d 883 (6th Cir. 1967) (Commission's order forbidding petitioner from representing that iron deficiency anemia can be self-diagnosed and medicated with Geritol was overbroad as Congressional policy encourages self-help where the consumer is fully informed and the product is safe).

(3) Who can be made subject to an FTC order? *See Colgate-Palmolive, supra* (advertising agency); *FTC v. Amy Travel Services, Inc.*, 1989-1 Trade Cas. (CCH) ¶ 68,549 (7th Cir. 1989) (principal shareholders and officers of travel agencies who

were involved in various levels of direction in regard to operation of the businesses); *FTC v. Austin Galleries of Illinois*, 1988-2 Trade Cas. (CCH) ¶ 68,341 (N.D. Ill. 1988) (corporate officers liable if they occupied positions of control, knew or should have known that company engaged in deceptive practices and failed to stop those practices); *New York Times*, Aug. 22, 1991, Section D, p. 19 (Volvo's advertising agency paid $150,000 to the FTC to settle allegations that Volvo advertisements, highlighting safety features, used cars with reinforced roofs); McLaughlin & White, *Advertising Agencies: Their Legal Liability Under the Federal Trade Commission Act*, 17 U. Kan. L. Rev. 587 (1967). *But see Computer Searching Service Corp. v. Ryan*, 439 F.2d 6 (2d Cir. 1971) (subsidiary corporation); *P.F. Collier & Son Corp. v. FTC*, 427 F.2d 261 (6th Cir. 1970), *cert. denied*, 400 U.S. 926 (1970) (parent corporation); *Coro, Inc. v. FTC*, 338 F.2d 149 (1st Cir. 1964), *cert. denied*, 380 U.S. 954 (1965) (unaware chairman of the board who was also president and largest stockholder); *Benrus Watch Co. v. FTC*, 352 F.2d 313 (8th Cir. 1965), *cert. denied*, 384 U.S. 939 (1966) (disaffiliated personnel).

(4) Appellate courts have the authority to modify or set aside FTC orders. 15 U.S.C. § 5(c). Their scope of review, however, is essentially limited to determining whether substantial evidence supports the FTC's findings of fact and an allowable judgment was made in its choice of remedy. *Jacob Siegel Co., supra. See also FTC v. National Lead Co.*, 352 U.S. 419 (1957); *FTC v. Ruberoid Co.*, 343 U.S. 470 (1952). Moreover, courts will not interfere with a remedy if it has a "reasonable relation" to the proscribed conduct. *Jacob Siegel Co. v. FTC*, 327 U.S. 608 (1946). On occasion FTC orders have not been upheld because a less drastic remedy would be sufficient. *See FTC v. Royal Milling Co.*, 288 U.S. 212 (1933); *Beneficial Corp. v. FTC*, 542 F.2d 611 (3d Cir. 1976), *cert. denied*, 430 U.S. 983 (1977); *Elliot Knitwear, Inc. v. FTC*, 266 F.2d 787 (2d Cir. 1959). Does this limit the FTC's discretion to fashion orders in "reasonable relation" to the proscribed conduct? *See* Millstein, *The Federal Trade Commission on False Advertising*, 64 Colum. L. Rev. 439 (1964). Should the Court refuse to uphold an FTC order if it would have fashioned a different remedy? *See Waltham Watch Co. v. FTC*, 318 F.2d 28 (7th Cir. 1963), *cert. denied*, 375 U.S. 944 (1963); *Encyclopedia Britannica, Inc. v. FTC*, 605 F.2d 964 (7th Cir. 1979).

(5) The FTC is empowered to stop and prevent the future recurrence of unlawful practices, but not to punish past offenses. *FTC v. Figgie Int'l, Inc., supra; Coro, Inc. v. FTC*, 338 F.2d 149 (1st Cir. 1964), *cert. denied*, 380 U.S. 954 (1965). *But see Fedders Corp. v. FTC*, 529 F.2d 1398 (2d Cir. 1976) (requiring the disclosure of information to prevent future claims from being deceptive does not exceed this remedial power); *J.B. Williams v. FTC*, 381 F.2d 884 (6th Cir. 1967) (upholding FTC's requirement that Geritol advertisements affirmatively disclose the negative fact that a majority of persons who experience symptoms of "tiredness" do not experience them because of a vitamin or iron deficiency, and that for those people, Geritol will be of no benefit). *See also American Home Products Corp. v. FTC*, 695 F.2d 681 (3d Cir. 1983); *National Commission on Egg Nutrition v. FTC*, 570 F.2d 157 (7th Cir. 1977), *cert. denied*, 439 U.S. 821 (1978); *Feil v. FTC*, 285 F.2d 879 (9th Cir. 1960). Do corrective advertising orders exceed these powers and constitute punishment? *See Removatron Int'l v. FTC*, 884 F.2d 1489, 1500–1501 (1st Cir.

1989) (upholding an FTC order requiring petitioners to include in any advertisement regarding their hair removal system a prominent disclaimer stating that such removal is only temporary, and to send a copy of the order and a notice to all past purchasers of their machine); Note, *Warner Lambert Co. v. FTC: Corrective Advertising Gives Listerine A Taste of Its Own Medicine*, 73 Nw. U. L. Rev. 957 (1978); Note, *Corrective Advertising Orders of the Federal Trade Commission*, 85 Harv. L. Rev. 477 (1971); Note, *Corrective Advertising and the FTC: No Virginia, Wonder Bread Doesn't Help Build Bodies Twelve Ways*, 70 Mich. L. Rev. 374 (1970).

What is the line between orders that merely deter and those that punish? *See FTC v. Ruberoid*, 343 U.S. 470 (1952). In 1974, the Ninth Circuit Court of Appeals flatly rejected the argument that the cease and desist power of the FTC Act impliedly permitted the Commission to seek monetary consumer redress as an ancillary form of equitable relief. *Heater v. FTC*, 503 F.2d 321 (9th Cir. 1974). With the enactment of § 19 of the FTC Act, Congress effectively overruled the *Heater* decision by expressly authorizing the Commission to seek monetary relief in courts for rule violations or unfair or deceptive trade practices resulting in cease and desist orders. Pub. L. No. 93-637, Title II, § 206(a), 88 Stat. 2201, 15 U.S.C. § 57(b) (1975). Accordingly, following the 1975 amendments, the Commission has successfully pursued consumer monetary redress under § 19, as well as under § 13(b), of the FTC Act. *See, e.g., FTC v. H.N. Singer, Inc.*, 668 F.2d 1107 (9th Cir. 1982).

(6) Courts have consistently rejected an implied private cause of action under the FTC Act. In *Holloway v. Bristol-Myers Corp.*, 485 F.2d 986 (D.C. Cir. 1973), in which consumers alleged that Bristol-Myers had deceptively advertised its pain reliever Excedrin, the court found that private plaintiffs could not sue under the Act, since neither the legislative history nor the statute indicated Congress' intention to grant such a right, and the FTC's ability to develop a cohesive body of law would be compromised, contrary to legislative design. *See also American Airlines v. Christensen*, 967 F.2d 410 (10th Cir. 1992); *but compare Guernsey v. Rich Plan of the Midwest*, 408 F. Supp. 582 (N.D. Ind. 1976) (allowing action by consumers attempting to compel defendant to comply with an FTC order because the private action did not interfere with FTC's function of defining "unfair or deceptive practices," and would permit the FTC Act to make good on its promise to consumers), *criticized in ABA Distributors, Inc. v. Adolph Coors Co.*, 496 F. Supp. 1194 (W.D. Mo. 1980).

§ 10.02   Food, Drug and Cosmetic Act

The basic purposes of the FDC Act are to prevent the manufacture, distribution and sales of adulterated and misbranded foods, drugs, devices and cosmetics. A "device" means an instrument, apparatus, implement, machine, contrivance, implant, in vitro reagent, or other similar or related article, including any component, part, or accessory, which is —

(1) recognized in the official National Formulary, or the United States Pharmacopeia, or any supplement to them,

(2) intended for use in the diagnosis of disease or other conditions, or in the cure, mitigation, treatment, or prevention of disease, in man or other animals, or

(3) intended to affect the structure or any function of the body of man or other animals, and which does not achieve its primary intended purposes through chemical action within or on the body of man or other animals and which is not dependent upon being metabolized for the achievement of its primary intended purposes. 21 U.S.C. § 321(h).

Products are "adulterated" under the Act if they (1) contain specific categories of harmful or objectionable substances, (2) contain unnecessary substances, (3) lack a specified quantity or quality of specific categories of substances, (4) are packaged in containers consisting in whole or in part of harmful or dangerous substances, or (5) are prepared, packaged or stored under unsanitary or technically inadequate conditions. 21 U.S.C. §§ 342, 351, 361. Physical adulteration is the use of harmful, objectionable or, in the case of drugs, impure substances; economic adulteration of food is the omission of ingredients, the substituting of cheaper ingredients for valuable ones, or the concealing of defects. A product is "misbranded" under the Act if its labeling is "false or misleading in any particular" or violates any of the numerous specific branding requirements of the Act. 15 U.S.C. §§ 343, 352, 362.

The Secretary of Health and Human Services has primary responsibility for achieving the purposes of the FDC Act and delegates enforcement to the Food and Drug Administration (FDA). The FDA interprets and implements the Act through regulations establishing (1) definitions and standards for foods when needed to "promote honesty and fair dealing in the interest of the consumers," 21 U.S.C. § 341; (2) lists of safe color additives for food, drugs and cosmetics, 21 U.S.C. § 379e; and (3) tolerances for certain pesticide chemicals in raw agricultural commodities and poisonous or deleterious substances in food, §§ 346, 346a. For an explanation of the administrative procedures followed by the FDA in promulgating regulations, see CCH, *Food Drug and Cosmetic Law Reporter* ¶ 2617. Failure to comply with these regulations may cause a product to be deemed adulterated, misbranded or both under the provisions of the Act. In addition, the FDA has a large testing and investigative staff for determining when food, drugs, devices and cosmetics are adulterated or misbranded within the meaning of the Act and these regulations.

Additional regulatory controls exercised by the FDA include: (1) requiring emergency permits for shipping food from contaminated areas, 21 U.S.C. § 344; (2) certifying certain drugs before their shipment, 21 U.S.C. §§ 356, 357; and (3) approving new drugs as being safe and effective before being marketed, 21 U.S.C. § 355. The FDA also promulgates regulations for packaging and labeling under The Fair Packaging and Labeling Act. 15 U.S.C. §§ 1451–61. *See* Merrill, *FDA And The Effects of Substantive Rules*, 35 Food Drug Cosm. L.J. 270 (1980); Stimson, *FDA's Standards Policy*, 35 Food Drug Cosm. L.J. 300 (1980).

The FDA has broad discretion in determining whether the general misbranding prohibition of the Act has been violated by labeling which is "false or misleading in any particular." In contrast to the FTC's standards, the misbranding need not be "materially" false or misleading. 21 U.S.C. § 321(n). *Compare* § 9.01, *supra*. The term "misbranding" applies only to labels and labeling, however, with the FTC regulating almost all advertising for these products. Sachs, *Health Claims in the Marketplace: The Future of the FDA and the FTC's Regulatory Split*, 48 Food & Drug L.J. 263 (1993). Labeling is defined by the Act as "all labels and other written, printed or graphic matter (1) upon any article or any of its containers or wrappers, or (2) accompanying such article." 21 U.S.C. § 321(m). "The term 'label' means a display of written, printed or graphic matter upon the immediate container of any article." 15 U.S.C. § 321(k). This definition has been construed to encompass materials which supplement a label, such as a pamphlet or directions, even though they are given to the consumer or shipped in interstate commerce separate from the product. *United States v. Urbuteit*, 335 U.S. 355 (1948); *Kordel v. United States*, 335 U.S. 345 (1948). In addition, the FDA indirectly regulates advertising by enforcing the FDC Act's requirements that directions be stated on the labeling for each use claimed for a drug. In *Alberty Food Products Co. v. United States*, 185 F.2d 321 (9th Cir. 1950), a drug was held to be misbranded because its label did not give directions for a use claimed in a newspaper advertisement.

Pursuant to the Nutrition Labeling and Education Act of 1990, Pub. L. No. 101-535, 104 Stat. 2353 (1990), the FDA promulgated sweeping new regulations requiring standardized nutrition labeling for almost all processed foods regulated by the FDA and authorizing appropriate health claims on the labels of such products. 21 C.F.R. § 101.1 *et seq.* The regulations, promulgated in 1993 ensure that: (1) nutrition information will be virtually universal in the marketplace; (2) information will be up-to-date with the dietary needs of Americans in the 1990s; (3) labels will show how each food fits into an overall healthy diet, nutrient by nutrient; and (4) credibility will be restored to the often hyperbolic marketing claims such as "light," "fat-free," "low-calorie," and "high fiber." FDA, *Taking the Guesswork Out of Good Nutrition*, *FDA Consumer, Special Report: Focus on Food Labeling*, May, 1993. *See also* 21 C.F.R. §§ 101.54, 101.56, covering specific requirements for nutrient content claims for "good source," "high," "more," "light," and "lite." The FDA has been particularly diligent in prohibiting the use of "heart marks" on labels. In *G.F.A. Brands, Inc. v. Canbra Foods, Ltd.*, 16 U.S.P.Q.2d 1734 (N.D. Cal. 1990), the private litigants disputed whether plaintiff's trademark "Heart Beat" for canola oil was confusingly similar to defendant's "Heartlight" mark for the same product. The court found no likelihood of confusion. However, the FDA subsequently barred the use of *both* names as well as the use of a depiction of a heart on the labels, reasoning that such representations suggested that the products had health benefits, without saying that other dietary factors were necessary to achieve a healthy heart. *See* "P&G Drops No-Cholesterol Labels," *Supermarket News*, Vol. 41, No. 20 (May 20, 1991); "December Trends," *New Product News*, (Jan. 7, 1992). *See also* 21 C.F.R. § 101.14, (referring to the use of a brand name including the term "heart," or use of a heart symbol on a label, as constituting an implied health claim subject to regulation); Levitt, *FDA Enforcement Under the Nutrition Labeling and Education Act*, 48 Food & Drug L.J. 119 (1993).

In the past, the FDC Act was interpreted by some courts as protecting even gullible purchasers from deception. *See* Forte, *The Ordinary Purchaser and the Federal Food, Drug and Cosmetic Act*, 52 Va. L. Rev. 1467 (1966). The Act was similarly held to prohibit labels and labeling which merely had a tendency to mislead due to their net impression, ambiguity or contradictions. *See generally* Toulmin, *The Law of Food, Drugs and Cosmetics*, §§ 15, 23–26, 31 (1963). *Compare* the FTC "reasonable purchaser" standard discussed in the Tests of Deceptiveness section of this Chapter, *supra.*

The FDA's enforcement of misleading and false claims under these standards was frequently attacked for being "*ad hoc*, arbitrary, and confusing." Levitt, *FDA Enforcement Under the Nutrition Labeling and Education Act*, 48 Food & Drug L.J. 119 (1993). The new guidelines issued by the FDA are intended to eliminate these criticisms. FDA labeling enforcement will be confined to the circumstances and wording expressly set forth in the promulgated regulations, with the intention of rendering moot the questions of what is false or misleading and what is the proper purchaser protection standard. One commentator has noted that compliance under the new standards "could be envisioned as a matter of holding the label next to the law and the regulations — if they match, the labeling is acceptable; if they do not, the product is misbranded." Levitt, 48 Food & Drug L.J. at 119. Any deviation from the FDA's regulations will, by definition, render the product liable to a charge of misbranding under 21 U.S.C. § 343. The meaning of claims such as "light," "fat free," and "reduced" have been expressly defined by the FDA, for example, eliminating the need to demonstrate the misleading or false nature of such claims; nutrient content claims that have yet to be defined by the FDA are simply not permissible labeling claims. 21 U.S.C. § 343(r).

Both civil and criminal remedies are available to prevent violations of the FDC Act, but the FDA must rely upon the Justice Department to bring court actions seeking such relief. 21 U.S.C. § 337(a). The FDA also gains compliance with the Act through its powers to publicize (1) judgments under the FDA Act, (2) its own determinations that a product is dangerous to health or grossly deceptive to consumers, and (3) the results of its investigations. 21 U.S.C. § 375. The Justice Department has discretion both as to the bringing of an action and the relief sought, but generally follows the FDA's recommendations. 1990 Amendments to the Act permit individual states to bring court actions within their jurisdictions for specified violations regarding misbranded food if the food at issue is located in the state. 21 U.S.C. § 337(b).

Although there is no private cause of action under the FDC Act, private litigants sometimes use FDA rules and regulations to help demonstrate that a particular claim is misleading. In *Kraft General Foods, Inc. v. Del Monte Corp.*, 28 U.S.P.Q.2d 1457, 1459, 1461 (S.D.N.Y. 1993), for example, the court relied upon the FDA's definition of "gelatin" as an animal by-product in enjoining as misleading Del Monte's use of "Gelatin Snacks" for a product made from seaweed. *Cf. Mylan Laboratories, Inc. v. Matkari*, 28 U.S.P.Q.2d 1533, 1539–40 (4th Cir. 1993), in which plaintiff's claims that by placing their drugs on the market, defendants falsely represented that their drugs had been "properly approved by the FDA" was held to constitute an improper attempt to use the Lanham Act as a vehicle by which to enforce the FDC Act; and *Sandoz Pharmaceutical Corp. v. Richardson-Vicks, Inc.*, 902 F.2d 222, 232 (3d Cir. 1990), in which the court stated, "[T]he issue of whether an ingredient is properly labeled 'active' or 'inactive' under FDA standards is not properly decided as an original matter by a district court in a Lanham Act case."

The civil remedies available under the Act are seizure, 21 U.S.C. § 334, and injunction, 21 U.S.C. § 332. Seizure is the more commonly employed and is an *in rem* action against the misbranded or adulterated article itself initiated by the seizure of the article pursuant to an administrative writ of attachment. There are two basic statutory limitations upon seizure. First, the article must be introduced into, or shipped in, interstate commerce, or held for sale thereafter. 21 U.S.C. § 334(a)(1). The courts have interpreted this as also allowing the seizure of products purchased for transportation to another state. *National Confectioners Ass'n v. Califano*, 569 F.2d 690, 693 (D.C. Cir. 1978). Second, multiple seizures cannot be instituted for the same misbranding unless (1) a prior judgment was entered against the misbranding, or (2) it is administratively determined, without a hearing, that the article is dangerous to health or that its label is fraudulent or materially misleading to the injury or damage of the consumer. 21 U.S.C. § 334(a)(1). After seizure, the article is held by the government until final disposition of the case, including appeals. If a condemnation decree is entered at the conclusion of the case, the articles may be destroyed or sold for the benefit of the government. If the claimant wishes to obtain the article to correct the violations, a penal bond may be required which will be forfeited if the violations continue. 21 U.S.C. § 334(d)(1); *Stinson Canning Co. v. United States*, 170 F.2d 764 (4th Cir. 1948), *cert. denied*, 336 U.S. 951 (1949).

Injunctive relief has two major advantages under the FDC Act. It may be obtained (1) prior to the introduction of an article into interstate commerce and (2) where the FDC Act is violated, but the product is not subject to seizure because it is neither misbranded nor adulterated. *See generally* 21 U.S.C. § 332. A defendant violating an injunction also may be held in criminal contempt. 21 U.S.C. § 332(b). For a comparison of these two civil remedies in FDA cases, see Note *Developments In The Law — Deceptive Advertising*, 80 Harv. L. Rev. 1005, 1111–1112 (1967).

The criminal remedies under the FDC Act provide for the imposition of fines or imprisonment with varying degrees of severity depending on the substance of the violation, and the existence of any prior violations of the Act by the offender. 21 U.S.C. § 333. Before the FDA can recommend a criminal action, however, it must afford the accused an opportunity to "present his views" on the alleged violation. 21 U.S.C. § 335. Such hearings both avoid unwarranted litigation and offer the accused an opportunity to correct the violation.

Good faith and lack of knowledge of a violation are not defenses to prosecution under the FDC Act except in specific situations. *See* 21 U.S.C. § 333(c). There are conflicting decisions respecting the effect of an acquittal in a criminal prosecution under the FDC Act on a subsequent civil action under the Act. *See* Dickerman, *Res Judicata — An Acquittal in a Criminal Case Does Not Bar Subsequent Seizure Action*, 7 Food Drug Cosm. L.J. 293 (1952). It is well settled, however, that a decision under either the FTC Act or the FDC Act will constitute res judicata barring a later action on the same issues under the other Act. *United States v. An Article of Drug Consisting of 4,680 Pails*, 725 F.2d 976, 984 (5th Cir. 1984). *See generally* Note, *Res Judicata and Two Co-ordinate Federal Agencies*, 95 U. Pa. L. Rev. 388 (1947).

Another remedy available is "recall" which is the removal or correction of consumer products which violate the FDC Act. Recall is a voluntary action. The FDA may request a recall by the manufacturer, but it may not order a recall. 21 C.F.R. § 7.40 *et seq.*; *see National Confectioners Ass'n v. Califano*, 569 F.2d 690, 694 (D.C. 1978); *United States v. Superpharm Corp.*, 530 F. Supp. 408, 410 (E.D.N.Y. 1981). A request by the FDA for recall is reserved for urgent situations where (1) a product presents a risk of illness or injury or gross consumer deception; (2) a firm has not initiated a recall of the product; (3) agency action is necessary to protect the public health and welfare, 21 C.F.R. § 7.40 *et seq.*, (1984). Recall generally affords the consumer greater protection than seizure in cases where many lots of the product in question have been distributed. A seizure, however, may be initiated by the FDA when a firm refuses to comply with the FDA request for a recall or when the FDA has reason to believe a recall would be ineffective or when it discovers a violation is continuing, 21 C.F.R. § 7.40 *et seq.* (1984). *See* Weeda, *FDA Seizure and Injunction Actions: Judicial Means of Protecting the Public Health*, 35 Food Drug Cosm. L.J. 112 (1980); Note, *Mandatory Food and Drug Recalls: An Analysis of a Developing FDC Enforcement Tool*, 36 Food Drug Cosm. L.J. 669 (1981); *Recalls: Legal and Corporate Responses to FDA, CPSC, NHTSA and Product Liability Considerations — A Program*, 39 Bus. Law. 757 (1984).

A majority of the states have also enacted laws patterned after the FDC Act. These state statutes often provide their administering agencies with significant powers not possessed by the FDA, such as the regulation of advertising and the administrative prevention of intrastate commerce in the accused food product pending a court's determination of legality under the Act. *See generally* 4 Food Drug Cosm. L. Rep. (CCH); Rosden, *The Law of Advertising*, § 16.01 *et seq.* (1993).

§ 10.03   The Fair Packaging and Labeling Act

The policy of the Fair Packaging and Labeling Act, 15 U.S.C. § 1451 *et seq.*, is set forth in the Act as follows:

> Informed consumers are essential to the fair and efficient functioning of a free market economy. Packages and their labels should enable consumers to obtain accurate information as to the quantity of the contents and should facilitate value comparisons.

15 U.S.C. § 1451. The Act seeks to achieve these goals by requiring that the following information appear on the labels of all consumer commodities: the identity and source of the product; the net quantity of the contents in specified measures and prominence and, if applicable, the net quantity of the servings represented as being contained in the product. 15 U.S.C. § 1453. Detailed regulations for these labelling requirements are set forth at 16 C.F.R. § 500.1 *et seq.* To the extent that any state or local laws provide more lenient standards for labeling as to the net quantity of contents, they are superseded. 15 U.S.C. § 1461. Expressly excluded from the Act's definition of consumer commodities are meats, pesticides, tobacco, poultry, prescription drugs, alcoholic beverages and seeds. 15 U.S.C. §§ 1459(a)(1)–(5).

In addition to these mandatory labeling requirements, the Act's administering agencies, the FTC and the Department of Health and Human Services, are empowered to issue regulations on a product-by-product basis as necessary to prevent consumer confusion and facilitate value comparison. 15 U.S.C. § 1454. The FTC administers the Act and issues regulations under it for all consumer products, except food, drugs, devices and cosmetics which are under the jurisdiction of the Department of Health and Human Services. These regulations may (1) define standards for characterizing package sizes, i.e., "giant," "family size," "jumbo"; (2) control the use of price savings claims, i.e., "cents off"; (3) require label disclosures of the common names of non-food products and their ingredients; and (4) prevent the marketing of packages less than full, i.e., slack-filling. 15 U.S.C. §§ 1454(c)(1)–(4). Foods are covered by this type of requirement under the FTC Act. These agencies also are empowered to issue regulations, exempting consumer commodities from the mandatory labeling requirements of the Act when compliance is impractical or unnecessary to protect consumers. 15 U.S.C. § 1454(b).

The Act applies only to packagers and labelers of consumer commodities distributed in interstate commerce and to distributors of such commodities in interstate commerce. 15 U.S.C. § 1452(a). It excludes retailers and wholesalers unless they are involved in the packaging or labeling of commodities distributed in interstate commerce. 15 U.S.C. § 1452(b).

Violations of the Act respecting foods, drugs, cosmetics and devices are deemed misbrandings and enforced in accordance with the FDC Act. 15 U.S.C. § 1456(a). Violations respecting other consumer commodities constitute unfair or deceptive acts or practices in commerce and are enforced under the FTC Act. 15 U.S.C. § 1456(b). In addition, the Secretary of the Treasury may refuse to admit any import not complying with the Fair Packaging and Labeling Act. 15 U.S.C. § 1456(c).

§ 10.04 The Consumer Product Safety Act

The Consumer Product Safety Act of 1972, 15 U.S.C. § 2051 *et seq.*, constitutes a Congressional effort to fashion a comprehensive consumer protection statute. The Act resulted from the work of the National Commission on Product Safety which summarized the need for consumer protection from dangerous products as described in the Forward to *National Commission on Product Safety, Final Report* (1976):

> When it authorized the Commission, Congress recognized that modern technology poses a threat to the physical security of consumers. We find the threat to be bona fide and menacing. Moreover, we believe that, without effective governmental intervention, the abundance and variety of unreasonable hazards associated with consumer products cannot be reduced to a level befitting a just and civilized society.
>
> Rhetoric, educational campaigns, piecemeal legislation, and appeals to conscience serve the useful function of mitigating the fallout of injuries induced by our complex technology. But we believe, on the basis of the evidence presented to us, that a concerned government can and should provide a

continuing system to assure that our great technological resources are used to protect consumers from unreasonable product risks.

Perhaps a case can be made for the acceptability of willful personal risk-taking by an occasional well-informed consumer, but there is no justification for exposing an entire populace to risks of injury or death which are not necessary and which are not apparent to all. Such hazards must be controlled and limited not at the option of the producer but as a matter of right to the consumer. Many hazards described in this report are unnecessary and can be eliminated without substantially affecting the price to the consumer.

Unfortunately, in the absence of external compulsion it is predictable that there will continue to be an indecent time lag between exposure to a hazard and its elimination. Other advanced nations apparently have discovered this flaw in the output of competitive free enterprise and have made safe products an ongoing governmental objective.

The purposes of the Consumer Product Safety Act are to: "(1) protect the public against unreasonable risks of injury associated with consumer products; (2) assist consumers in evaluating the comparative safety of consumer products; (3) develop uniform safety standards for consumer products and minimize conflicting State and local regulations; and (4) promote research and investigation into the causes and prevention of product-related deaths, illnesses, and injuries." 15 U.S.C. § 2051(b). The Act defines consumer products as products and parts thereof produced or distributed for personal rather than work related consumer use and certain specific products, including tobacco products, firearms, motor vehicles, boats, aircraft, food, drugs, devices and cosmetics. 15 U.S.C. § 2052(a)(1).

To implement the Act and centralize the administration of various other safety laws, Congress created a new administrative agency, the Consumer Product Safety Commission (CPSC). 15 U.S.C. § 2053. The CPSC is also responsible for enforcing the Federal Hazardous Substances Act, Poison Prevention Packaging Act, Flammable Fabrics Act and Refrigerator Safety Act and is required to follow the procedures of those statutes to the extent that the risk from a consumer product is without authority to regulate risks from consumer products which "could be eliminated or reduced to a sufficient extent" under the Occupational Safety and Health Act, The Atomic Energy Act and the Clean Air Act. 15 U.S.C. §§ 2079, 2080. The most important functions of this agency are the promulgation of product safety standards reasonably necessary to prevent or reduce unreasonable risks of injuries to consumers and the banning of products for which no feasible standards could be established to prevent such unreasonable risks. 15 U.S.C. § 2056. The Act provides that these standards should be stated in terms of performance requirements when feasible but that they may also include requirements (1) as to composition, contents, design, construction, finish, or packaging, (2) that a consumer product be marked with or accompanied by clear and adequate warnings or instructions, and (3) as to the form of warnings or instructions. 15 U.S.C. § 2056(a).

The Commission is also empowered to (1) require manufacturers to furnish consumer product performance and safety information, 15 U.S.C. § 2076(e), (2) inspect consumer product factories, warehouses and transportation, 15 U.S.C.

§ 2065, (3) prescribe testing programs, which can be conducted by third parties, for products subject to consumer standards, 15 U.S.C. § 2063(b), and (4) require the use of labeling containing information as to the manufacturer and private labeler of the product and the safety standards applicable to the product, 15 U.S.C. § 2063(c).

The major thrust of the CPS Act is to prohibit the manufacture, offering for sale, or distribution in commerce of any consumer product which does not conform to established safety standards or has been banned under the Act. 15 U.S.C. § 2068(a). These prohibitions, however, do not apply to persons without actual knowledge of the violation who (1) have a manufacturer's or private labeler's certificate of conformance with the safety rules which has been issued in accordance with the Act, or (2) relied in good faith on the manufacturer's or distributor's representation that the product was not subject to any safety rule. 15 U.S.C. § 2068(b).

The Act provides for a variety of enforcement methods, including public and private civil actions, criminal prosecutions and administrative actions. 15 U.S.C. §§ 2069–74. The remedies available to the government through civil actions are fines, injunctions and seizures; however, the Commission does not have authority to proceed administratively in assessing civil penalties. 15 U.S.C. §§ 2069, 2071(a).

Fines can be imposed only against persons who have actual knowledge of a violation of the Act or are presumed to have knowledge because a reasonable man exercising due care would have knowledge under the circumstances. 15 U.S.C. § 2069(a)(1),(d). Such persons are subject to fines of up to $5,000 for each offending product or violation with a maximum penalty of $1,250,000 for related violations. 15 U.S.C. § 2069(a)(1). The maximum penalty amounts are adjusted for inflation every five years in accordance with the Consumer Price Index published by the Department of Labor. 15 U.S.C. § 2069(a)(3). A person who is not the manufacturer, private labeler, or distributor of the product must have actual knowledge of the violation to be fined. 15 U.S.C. § 2069(a)(2). As with the FDC Act, seizures can only be made for violations involving the consumer product itself after its entry into interstate commerce. 15 U.S.C. § 2071(b). Similarly, injunctive relief is available against violations not involving a product and to prevent the introduction of an illegal product into interstate commerce. 15 U.S.C. § 2071(a). In addition, persons and corporations and their directors, officers and agents, who willfully and knowingly violate the Act after being notified of their noncompliance by the Commission, may be fined up to $50,000, imprisoned for one year or both. 15 U.S.C. § 2070.

One of the major innovations of the CPS Act is its provision for private civil actions for the enforcement of CPSC safety rules, remedial orders or injunctions. "Any interested person" may bring such an action thirty days after giving notice of the substance of the claim to the Commission, Justice Department and proposed defendant unless a government action is pending against the same alleged violation. 15 U.S.C. § 2073. If such plaintiff also seeks attorney's fees, such fees and costs will be awarded to the prevailing party. 15 U.S.C. § 2073. The Act also creates a private right of action for injuries caused by knowing violations of any rule or order issued by the Commission. 15 U.S.C. § 2072. See Baas v. Hoye, 766 F.2d 1190 (8th Cir. 1989), in which the parents of a deceased infant who had ingested prescription drugs succeeded in their action against pharmacists who had dispensed the drugs in a non-childproof container in violation of a consumer product safety rule. Under this provision of the CPS Act, a plaintiff may recover actual damages in addition to any remedies provided under State or common laws. *See Butcher v. Robertshaw Controls Co.*, 550 F. Supp. 692, 706 (D. Md. 1981) ("15 U.S.C. § 2072(b) preserves any additional remedies that may be available under common law or under Federal or State law"). Although § 2072 of the CPS Act clearly permits a private cause of action for injuries caused by knowing violations of rules issued by the CPSC pursuant to explicit legislative authority, there is disagreement as to whether a private right of action also exists for violations of disclosure or reporting rules. *Compare Drake v. Honeywell, Inc.*, 797 F.2d 603 (8th Cir. 1986) (failure to comply with product hazard reporting rules issued by CPSC does not give rise to private cause of action under the CPS Act) *and Klinger v. Yamaha Motor Corp., U.S.A.*, 738 F. Supp. 898 (E.D. Pa. 1990) (no private cause of action to enforce reporting requirements of Consumer Products Safety Act) *with Wilson v. Robertshaw Controls Co.*, 600 F. Supp. 671 (N.D. Ind. 1985) (private right of action exists for the violation of administrative disclosure provisions of the CPS Act) *and Young v. Robertshaw Controls Co.*, 560 F. Supp. 288 (N.D.N.Y. 1983) (manufacturer's failure to disclose information with respect to a product defect in accordance with CPSC reporting regulations entitled a widow to maintain a private action under the Act for injuries to her decedent).

The Commission itself has certain remedial powers to protect consumers against a substantial product hazard. 15 U.S.C. § 2064. Manufacturers, distributors and retailers of consumer products are required by the Act to notify the Commission upon discovering information which reasonably supports the conclusion that a product presents a substantial product hazard. 15 U.S.C. § 2064(b). After conducting a hearing open to interested persons and determining that a product distributed in commerce presents a substantial product hazard, the Commission may order the manufacturer, distributor or retailer of the product to (1) give a specified public notice of the defect or non-compliance, (2) mail such notice to each manufacturer, distributor or retailer of the product, or (3) mail such notice to every person whom the mailer knows received or was sold the product. 15 U.S.C. § 2064(c). In addition, the Commission may, in the public interest, order the party subject to the order to perform one of the following actions in a manner approved by the Commission: (1) to repair or conform the product to applicable safety standards, (2) to replace the product with a conforming non-defective product, or (3) to refund the purchase price less a reasonable allowance for use. 15 U.S.C. § 2064(d). Such orders may also require a party to reimburse other distributors, manufacturers or retailers of the product for their expenses in carrying out the order. 15 U.S.C. § 2064(e).

§ 10.05 State and Municipal Regulation

The first comprehensive legislative effort to curb unfair trade practices at the state level was the "Printer's Ink" model penal statute which made the use of advertisements containing an "untrue, deceptive or misleading statement" a misdemeanor. Although eventually adopted in some form in almost every state, this statute never proved effective, largely because penal statutes are narrowly construed and state amendments often require proof of negligence or scienter. More recent civil legislation in this area has proved effective, including the Uniform Deceptive Trade Practices Act ("UDTPA"), drafted in 1964, and the Unfair Trade Practices and Consumer Protection Law ("UTPCPL"), which was drafted in 1967 by the FTC in collaboration with state officials and has been enacted in various forms by 49 states and the District of Columbia. *See* Goldstein, Kitch & Perlman, *Selected Statutes and International Agreements on Unfair Competition, Trademark, Copyright and Patent* (1993), and USTA, *State Trademark and Unfair Competition Law* (1993), for summaries of state statutes modeled on these two proposed acts. These Consumer Protection Acts are often characterized as "little FTC Acts" because most of them prohibit "deceptive acts or practices," and confer upon State Attorneys General a jurisdiction analogous to that of a regional Federal Trade Commission. The definition of illegal conduct is included in most states' Consumer Protection Acts in one of the following three forms:

Alternative Form No. 1:

Unfair methods of competition and unfair or deceptive acts or practices in the conduct of any trade or commerce are hereby declared unlawful.

See Fla. Stat. ch. 501.201 *et seq.*

Alternative Form No. 2:

False, misleading or deceptive acts or practices in the conduct of any trade or commerce are hereby declared unlawful.

See N.Y. Gen. Bus. L. §§ 349 *et seq.*

Alternative Form No. 3:

The following unfair methods of competition and unfair or deceptive acts or practices in the conduct of any trade or commerce are hereby declared to be unlawful:

(1) passing off goods or services as those of another;

(2) causing likelihood of confusion or of misunderstanding as to the source, sponsorship, approval, or certification of goods or services;

(3) causing likelihood of confusion or of misunderstanding as to affiliation, connection, or association with, or certification by, another;

(4) using deceptive representations or designations of geographic origin in connection with goods or services;

(5) representing that goods or services have sponsorship, approval, characteristics, ingredients, uses, benefits, or quantities that they do not have or that a person has a sponsorship, approval, status, affiliation, or connection that he does not have;

(6) representing that goods are original or new if they are deteriorated, altered, reconditioned, reclaimed, used, or secondhand;

(7) representing that goods or services are of a particular standard, quality, or grade, or that goods are of a particular style or model, if they are of another;

(8) disparaging the goods, services, or business of another by false or misleading representation of fact;

(9) advertising goods or services with intent not to sell them as advertised;

(10) advertising goods or services with intent not to supply reasonably expectable public demand, unless the advertisement discloses a limitation of quantity;

(11) making false or misleading statements of fact concerning the reasons for, existence of, or amounts of price reductions;

(12) engaging in any other conduct which similarly creates a likelihood of confusion or of misunderstanding; or

(13) engaging in any act or practice which is unfair or deceptive to the consumer.

See Tex. Bus. & Com. Code §§ 17.41 *et seq.*

In addition, the UTPCPL includes a number of modes of enforcement which have been adopted in various forms by many states. Under these provisions, the attorney-general is usually empowered to promulgate rules and regulations to administer and interpret the Act, and to issue precomplaint "civil investigative demands" for the examination of documents, witnesses and other matters.

Unlike the FTC Act which does not expressly provide for the voluntary compliance procedures employed by the FTC, many of these state statutes contain such provisions. Many also provide for innovative and sometimes drastic remedies in addition to the traditional forms of injunctive relief provided for in all of them. Among the types of remedies which enforcement officials may obtain are: (1) civil penalties for initial violations; (2) suspension or forfeiture of state corporate franchises or licenses to do business; and (3) appointment of receivers for distribution of a violator's assets to aggrieved parties.

The "little FTC Acts" commonly are used to stop deceptive activities akin to those attacked by the Federal Trade Commission. In *Mother & Unborn Baby Care of North Texas, Inc. v. Texas*, 749 S.W.2d 533 (Tex. App. 1988), for example, the defendants advertised their pro-life-oriented center in the *Yellow Pages* under "Abortion Services," when, in fact, the facility did not perform abortions but instead attempted to persuade the women who arrived at the center against having an abortion. Finding that defendants violated the Texas Deceptive Trade Practices Consumer Protection Act, Tex. Bus. & Com. Code Ann. §§ 17.41–17.50, by "purposefully attract[ing] pregnant women to their facility by disseminating information which could lead women to believe that abortions were available there," the court affirmed an order enjoining the deceptive conduct and mandating disclosure in advertising. *Id.* at 544. In *Southwest Starving Artists Group, Inc. v. Mississippi*, 364 So. 2d 1128 (Miss. 1978), under a similar statute, advertising for the sale of paintings from Hong Kong (and other non-U.S. countries) under the name

"Southwest Starving Artists Group" was held deceptive. The trial court had found that it was "entirely possible" that the advertising would lead a reasonable person to believe that the paintings were being sold by needy local artists willing to sell at low prices. The imposition of a $1,500 civil penalty and the issuance of a broad injunction against the defendants, as modified, were affirmed.

In addition, many of these statutes provide for private causes of action and empower enforcement officials to obtain restitution for consumers. *See State v. Andrews*, 533 A.2d 282 (Md. Ct. Spec. App. 1987). Often the state legislature will specifically provide that FTC and federal court decisions interpreting § 5 of the FTC Act should be relied on by the state courts in determining whether an act or practice is deceptive or unfair. *See V.S.H. Realty, Inc. v. Texaco, Inc.*, 757 F.2d 411, 416 (1st Cir. 1985), and Mass. Gen. Laws. Ann. ch. 93A (Massachusetts Consumer Protection Law "provides no definition of an unfair or deceptive act or practice, and instead directs [the court's] attention to interpretations of unfair acts and practices under the Federal Trade Commission Act. . . ."); *State of Washington v. Readers Digest Ass'n*, 81 Wash. 2d 259 (1972) (looking to federal court interpretations of § 5 of the FTC Act for guidance in applying Washington's Consumer Protection Act). *Cf. City of New York v. Toby's Electronics, Inc.*, 110 Misc. 2d 848, 443 N.Y.S.2d 561 (1981) (applying New York City's Consumer Protection Laws, which required consistency with the rules, regulations and decisions of the FTC and the federal courts in interpreting § 5 of the FTC Act). *See generally* Leaffer & Lipson, *Consumer Actions Against Unfair or Deceptive Acts or Practices: The Private Uses of Federal Trade Commission Jurisprudence*, 48 Geo. Wash. L. Rev. 521 (1980).

While the variety of unfair or deceptive trade practices to be encountered in the marketplace is limited only by the imagination of the unscrupulous, some forms of deception have demonstrated an enduring and unfortunate popularity.

Automobile, heating, air conditioning and appliance repairs, home renovation, door-to-door sales, training schools, real estate and mobile home sales, employment agencies and lending services are some of the areas in which consumers frequently claim to be victimized. *See Maryland v. Cottman Transmission Systems, Inc.*, 587 A.2d 1190 (Md. Ct. Spec. App.), *cert. denied*, 596 A.2d 627 (Md. 1991) (auto repair); *Meshinsky v. Nichols Yacht Sales, Inc.*, 541 A.2d 1063 (N.J. 1988) (boat repair); *Gabriel v. O'Hara*, 534 A.2d 488 (Pa. Super. 1987) (real estate); *Scott v. Assoc. for Childbirth at Home, Int'l*, 430 N.E.2d 1012 (Ill. 1982) (childbirth education and training services); *State v. Grogan*, 628 P.2d 570 (Alaska 1981) (aircraft repair); Sebert, *Enforcement of State Deceptive Trade Practice Statutes*, 42 Tenn. L. Rev. 689 (1975); Lovett, *State Deceptive Trade Practice Legislation*, 46 Tul. L. Rev. 724 (1972).

The "chain referral" or "pyramid" scheme is a recurring consumer protection problem. Characteristically, victims are lured into such schemes via spirited introductory "opportunity" meetings in which they are bombarded with affirmations of the great wealth attainable through enlistment in the instigator's marketing plan. The product to be marketed, *e.g.*, cosmetics, is actually of secondary significance. The real objective is to make money through the recruitment of new participants in the plan. Each initiate pays in a large sum of money, either as an entry fee or for a substantial amount of non-returnable inventory. The paid-in money is then distributed among those already participating in the plan. A person desiring a larger percentage normally must make an additional payment into the plan or supply some requisite number of new recruits.

The deception is said to lie in the law of diminishing returns that operates against later initiates. As stated in *Kugler v. Koscot Interplanetary, Inc.*, 120 N.J. Super. 216, 232 (1972):

> A pyramid type practice is similar to a chain letter operation. Such a program is inherently deceptive for the seemingly endless chain must come to a halt inasmuch as growth cannot be perpetual and the market becomes saturated by the number of participants. *See, e.g., State by Lefkowitz v. ITM, Inc.*, 275 N.Y.S.2d 303 (N.Y. Sup. Ct. 1966). Thus many participants are mathematically barred from ever recouping their original investments.

These practices have been enjoined in state courts under state statutes which specifically refer to such pyramid schemes, or under the general statutory prohibitions against unfair or deceptive trade practices. *See, e.g., Watkins v. Alvey*, 549 N.E.2d 74 (Ind. Ct. App. 1990); *Webster v. Membership Marketing, Inc.*, 766 S.W.2d 654 (Mo. Ct. App. 1989); *People ex rel. Hartigan v. Unimax, Inc.*, 523 N.E.2d 26 (Ill. App. Ct. 1988); *Bell v. Commonwealth*, 374 S.E.2d 13 (Va. 1988). They have also been the subject of action by the Federal Trade Commission. *See, e.g., In re Koscot Interplanetary, Inc.*, 86 F.T.C. 1106 (1975), *aff'd sub nom. Turner v. FTC*, 580 F.2d 701 (D.C. Cir. 1978); *In re Ger-Ro-Mar*, 84 F.T.C. 95 (1974), *aff'd in part, rev'd in part*, 513 F.2d 33 (2d Cir. 1975); *In re Holiday Magic, Inc.*, 84 F.T.C. 748 (1974). *Compare In re Amway Corporation*, Trade Reg. Rep. (CCH) ¶ 21,574 (1979).

Criminal as well as civil remedies against perpetrators of unfair or deceptive trade practices may be available to state law enforcement officials. The common law of larceny by false pretenses may be applicable if the practices do not fall within specific statutory provisions. However, apparently little use is given to this enforcement tool. Various suggestions have been made by commentators as to why this is so, among them the greater burden of proof required in criminal cases and the necessity of proving intent to defraud under the common law. *See* Ebert, *Enforcement of State Deceptive Trade Practice Statutes, supra*, Note (1), at 745–46; Gold & Cohan, *State Protection of the Consumer: Integration of Civil and Criminal Remedies*, 12 New Eng. L. Rev. 933 (1977). For additional commentary, see Geis & Edelhertz, *Criminal Law and Consumer Fraud: A Sociological View*, 11 Am. Crim. L. Rev. 989 (1975).

Most of the recently enacted state consumer protection statutes provide that media such as newspapers, radio, and television are generally not liable for the deceptive nature of advertisements which they disseminate on behalf of others.

Deceptive practices also may be redressed on the municipal level. Among the obvious advantages in such local enforcement are the accessibility of the enforcement agency to consumers and the attention given problems too small in magnitude to warrant state or federal involvement. However, it may be that the resources necessary to redress consumer grievances effectively under such a code are available realistically only in large metropolitan areas. *See, e.g., City of New York v. Toby's Electronics, Inc.,* 110 Misc. 2d 848, 443 N.Y.S.2d 561 (1981), which implements New York City's civil code. That municipal code is reviewed in Note, *New York City's Alternative to the Consumer Class Action: The Government as Robin Hood,* 9 Harv. J. on Legis. 301 (1972). One way to avoid potential conflicts with state law and questions of preemption would be to empower local agencies to enforce the state's unfair and deceptive trade practice law. This also might enable municipalities with limited resources to provide aid to local consumers. *See* Sebert, *Enforcement of State Deceptive Trade Practice Statutes,* 42 Tenn. L. Rev. 689, 754–55 (1975).

For discussions of various state consumer protection laws, see United States Trademark Association, *State Trademark and Unfair Competition Law* (1993 ed.); Pridgen, *Consumer Protection and the Law* (1993); Batt, *Litigation Under the Idaho Consumer Protection Act,* 20 Idaho L. Rev. 63 (1984); Aycock, *North Carolina Law on Antitrust and Consumer Protection: Sleeping Giant or Illusive Panacea?,* 60 N.C. L. Rev. 205 (1982); Benedetto, *Illinois Consumer Protection Act,* 69 Ill. B.J. 350 (1981); Langer & Ormstedt, *Connecticut Unfair Trade Practices Act,* 54 Conn. B.J. 388 (1980); Jenkins, *Attempting a Balance: The 1979 Amendments to the Deceptive Trade Practices — Consumer Protection Act,* 11 Tex. Tech. L. Rev. 1 (1979); Kemper, *Misrepresentations and Deception under Section 480-2 of the Hawaii Revised Statute,* 10 Hawaii B.J. 69 (1973); Note, *Consumer Fraud — New Jersey Consumer Fraud Act Bars Pyramid Sales Schemes,* 27 Rutgers L. Rev. 220 (1973); and Comment, *Kentucky Consumer Act — True Happiness?* 61 Ky. L.J. 793 (1973).

Although many state consumer protection statutes differ from the FTC Act in that they provide for private causes of action, there have been relatively few reported private consumer actions to date. Plaintiffs typically face strong economic disincentives in bringing such suits, as exemplified by the nominal rescissionary relief awarded to the defrauded consumers in *American Buyers Club of Mt. Vernon, Illinois, Inc. v. Honecker,* 361 N.E.2d 1370 (Ill. App. Ct. 1977) (seller of memberships in retail club who misrepresented that $39 fee would permit members to receive 50% discount on selected items was ordered to rescind members' contract and to return the $39 fee). *See also Kentucky ex rel. Beshear v. ABAC Pest Control,* 621 S.W.2d 705, 707 (Ky. Ct. App. 1981), in which the court found that the economic disincentives to private actions and the legislature's intent to provide a strong consumer protection program required the court to recognize the Attorney General's right to seek restitution on behalf of victims of consumer fraud. Yet, state enforcement officials, due to limited personnel and financial resources, cannot adequately handle all the complaints which they receive. *See Slaney v. Westwood Auto, Inc.,* 322 N.E.2d 768, 776 (Mass. 1975). *See also* Sebert, *Enforcement of State Deceptive Trade Practice Statutes,* 42 Tenn. L. Rev. 689 (1975); Comment, *Consumer Protection: The Practical Effectiveness of State Deceptive Trade Practices Legislation,* 59 Tul. L. Rev. 427, 449 (1984). The enactment of statutory provisions for multiple damages recoveries and attorney's fees in private actions is one way state legislators have sought to encourage greater use of consumer protection law by private individuals. *See* Leaffer & Lipson, *Consumer Actions Against Unfair Deceptive Acts or Practices: The Private Uses of Federal Trade*

Commission Jurisprudence, 48 Geo. Wash. L. Rev. 521 (1980); Roberts, *Consumerism Comes of Age: Treble Damages and Attorneys Fees in Consumer Transactions — The Ohio Consumer Sales Practices Act*, 42 Ohio St. L.J. 927 (1981). *See generally* Waxman, *Private Enforcement of Consumer Laws in Wisconsin*, 56 Wis. B. Bull. 22 (May, 1983); Note, *New York Creates a Private Right of Action to Combat Consumer Fraud: Caveat Venditor*, 48 Brooklyn L. Rev. 509 (1982); Comment, *Maryland's Consumer Protection Act: A Private Cause of Action for Unfair or Deceptive Trade Practices*, 38 Md. L. Rev. 733 (1979); Comment, *The Private Remedy under Oregon's Unlawful Trade Practices Act*, 56 Or. L. Rev. 490 (1977).

Common law actions for fraud and deceit require proof of such elements as actual reliance by the plaintiff upon the misrepresentation, and defendant's knowledge of the representation's falsity, elements a plaintiff normally need not prove in an action brought under a Consumer Protection Act. *See V.S.H. Realty, Inc. v. Texaco, Inc.*, 757 F.2d 411, 414–15 (1st Cir. 1985); *Slaney v. Westwood Auto, Inc.*, 322 N.E.2d 768, 776 (Mass. 1975). Additional remedies such as attorney fee awards also may be available under statutory but not common law. Given the social goal of eradicating fraud and deceptive dealing by encouraging private actions, should the legislated Acts supercede the common law in this area in all instances? Some courts have sought to limit the application of such statutes, imposing a "public interest" requirement on private actions brought under them. In *Anhold v. Daniels*, 614 P.2d 184, 188 (Wash. 1984), the plaintiff allegedly had been conned into investing in an ill-fated restaurant business. The court held that a private individual must demonstrate that the allegedly unfair or deceptive act affects the public interest in order to bring an action under the Washington Act. That effect could be demonstrated by showing "the defendant's deceptive acts or practices have the potential for repetition." The court remanded the case for consideration of whether defendant's alleged use of the same ploy on another victim demonstrated this potential for repetition. In *Newman-Green, Inc. v. Alfonzo-Larrain*, 590 F. Supp. 1083, 1088 (N.D. Ill. 1984), the court, applying Illinois law to a contract controversy between businessmen, dismissed the count brought under that state's Act for lack of the requisite public injury element, stating "a scheme to defraud a single entity in a single course of dealing does not amount to a 'pattern' of deceptive activities." Is such a requirement valid or advisable? *See* Comment, *Private Suits Under Washington's Consumer Protection Act: The Public Interest Requirement*, 54 Wash. L. Rev. 795 (1979).

For some examples of state private action decisions in this area, see *Sellinger v. Freeway Mobile Home Sales*, 521 P.2d 1119 (Ariz. 1974) (fraud in mobil home sale; damages award held inadequate and case remanded); *Gour v. Daray Motor Co.*, 373 So. 2d 571 (La. Ct. App. 1979) (manufacturer of automobile engine misrepresented; restitution and attorneys fees awarded); *Moore v. Goodyear Tire and Rubber Co.*, 364 So. 2d 630 (La. Ct. App. 1978) (oppressive debt collecting harassment; actual and general damages and attorney's fees awarded); *Neveroski v. Blair*, 358 A.2d 473 (N.J. Super. 1976) (false certification of termite absence by exterminator; actual and punitive damages and attorney's fees awarded); *Allen v. Morgan Drive Away*,

542 P.2d 896 (Or. 1975) (punitive damages award affirmed for calculated misrepresentations by mover); *Bennett v. Bailey*, 597 S.W.2d 532 (Tex. Ct. Civ. App. 1980) (unconscionable actions by dance instructors; treble damages and attorney's fees awarded).

The Uniform Deceptive Trade Practices Act, adopted in a number of states (*see, e.g.*, 815 Ill. Comp. Stat. 510) is a state statute which is essentially identical to the Alternative Form No. 3 of the little FTC Acts noted above. Summarized, the UDPTA affords a statutory basis for injunctive relief for (1) passing off or likelihood of confusion as to source, sponsorship, approval or certification; (2) false or misleading advertising or other representation of fact; (3) commercial disparagement; or (4) "any other conduct which similarly creates a likelihood of confusion or of misunderstanding." Its application can be very similar to that of § 43(a), 15 U.S.C. § 1125(a), of the Lanham Act. In *Bonner v. Westbound Records*, 49 364 N.E.2d 570 (Ill. App. Ct. 1977), for example, the defendants had substantially altered unedited and unfinished taped musical performances by the plaintiffs and then released the newly edited result as being performed by the plaintiffs. Finding the public would likely be deceived as to the nature of the recording in violation of the Illinois Act, the court affirmed the grant of a preliminary injunction against defendants. *Compare Gilliam v. American Broadcasting Cos., Inc.*, and the notes in the Misrepresentation section in Chapter 8, *supra*.

TITLE 15, UNITED STATES CODE
COMMERCE AND TRADE

CHAPTER 22
TRADEMARKS

SUBCHAPTER I
The Principal Register

§ 1051. Registration; application; payment of fees; designation of agent for service of process. *Sec 1 Lanham Act (1946)*

Actual application

(a) The owner of a trademark used in commerce may apply to register his or her trademark under this Act on the principal register hereby established:

(1) By filing in the Patent and Trademark Office—

(A) a written application, in such form as may be prescribed by the Commissioner, verified by the applicant, or by a member of the firm or an officer of the corporation or association applying, specifying applicant's domicile and citizenship, the date of applicant's first use of the mark, the date of applicant's first use of the mark in commerce, the goods on or in connection with which the mark is used and the mode or manner in which the mark is used in connection with such goods, and including a statement to the effect that the person making the verification believes himself, or the firm, corporation, or association in whose behalf he makes the verification, to be the owner of the mark sought to be registered, that the mark is in use in commerce, and that no other person, firm, corporation, or association, to the best of his knowledge and belief, has the right to use such mark in commerce either in the identical form thereof or in such near resemblance thereto as to be likely, when used on or in connection with the goods of such other person, to cause confusion, or to cause mistake, or to deceive: *Provided,* That in the case of every application claiming concurrent use the applicant shall state exceptions to his claim of exclusive use, in which he shall specify, to the extent of his knowledge, any concurrent use by others, the goods on or in connection with which and the areas in which each concurrent use exists, the periods of each use, and the goods and area for which the applicant desires registration;

(B) a drawing of the mark; and

(C) such number of specimens or facsimiles of the mark as used as may be required by the Commissioner.

(2) By paying into the Patent and Trademark Office the prescribed fee.

(3) By complying with such rules or regulations, not inconsistent with law, as may be prescribed by the Commissioner.

(b) A person who has a bona fide intention, under circumstances showing the good faith of such person, to use a trademark in commerce may apply to register the trademark under this Act on the principal register hereby established:

(1) By filing in the Patent and Trademark Office—

(A) a written application, in such form as may be prescribed by the Commissioner, verified by the applicant, or by a member of the firm or an officer of the corporation or association applying, specifying applicant's domicile and citizenship, applicant's bona fide intention to use the mark in commerce, the goods on or in connection with which the applicant has a bona fide intention to use the mark and the mode or manner in which the mark is intended to be used on or in connection with such goods, including a statement to the effect that the person making the verification believes himself or herself, or the firm, corporation, or association in whose behalf he or she makes the verification, to be entitled to use the mark in commerce, and that no other person, firm, corporation, or association, to the best of his or her knowledge and belief, has the right to use such mark in commerce either in the identical form of the mark or in such near resemblance to the mark as to be likely, when used on or in connection with the goods of such other person, to cause confusion, or to cause mistake, or to deceive; however, except for applications filed pursuant to section 1126, no mark shall be registered until the applicant has met the requirements of subsection (d) of this section; and

(B) a drawing of the mark.

(2) By paying in the Patent and Trademark Office the prescribed fee.

(3) By complying with such rules or regulations, not inconsistent with law, as may be prescribed by the Commissioner.

(c) At any time during examination of an application filed under subsection (b) of this section, an applicant who has made use of the mark in commerce may claim the benefits of such use for purposes of this Act, by amending his or her application to bring it into conformity with the requirements of subsection (a).

(d) (1) Within six months after the date on which the notice of allowance with respect to a mark is issued under section 1063(b)(2) to an applicant under subsection (b) of this section, the applicant shall file in the Patent and Trademark Office, together with such number of specimens or facsimiles of the mark as used in commerce as may be required by the Commissioner and payment of the prescribed fee, a verified statement that the mark is in use in commerce and specifying the date of the applicant's first use of the mark in commerce, those goods or services specified in the notice of allowance on or in connection with which the mark is used in commerce, and the mode or manner in which the mark is used on or in connection with such goods or services. Subject to examination and acceptance of the statement of use, the mark shall be registered in the Patent and Trademark Office, a certificate of registration shall be issued for those goods or services recited in the statement of use for which the mark is entitled to registration, and notice of registration shall be published in the Official Gazette of the Patent and Trademark Office. Such examination may include an examination of the factors set forth in subsections (a) through (e) of section 1052. The notice of registration shall specify the goods or services for which the mark is registered.

(2) The Commissioner shall extend, for one additional 6-month period, the time for filing the statement of use under paragraph (1), upon written request of the applicant before the expiration of the 6-month period provided in paragraph (1). In addition to an extension under the preceding sentence, the Commissioner may, upon a showing of good cause by the applicant, further extend the time for filing the statement of use under paragraph (1) for periods aggregating not more than 24 months, pursuant to written request of the applicant made before the expiration of the last extension granted under this paragraph. Any request for an extension under this paragraph shall be accompanied by a verified statement that the applicant has a continued bona fide intention to use the mark in commerce and specifying those goods or services identified in the notice of allowance on or in connection with which the applicant has a continued bona fide intention to use the mark in commerce. Any request for an extension under this paragraph shall be accompanied by payment of the prescribed fee. The Commissioner shall issue regulations setting forth guidelines for determining what constitutes good cause for purposes of this paragraph.

(3) The Commissioner shall notify any applicant who files a statement of use of the acceptance or refusal thereof and, if the statement of use is refused, the reasons for the refusal. An applicant may amend the statement of use.

(4) The failure to timely file a verified statement of use under this subsection shall result in abandonment of the application.

(e) If the applicant is not domiciled in the United States he shall designate by a written document filed in the Patent and Trademark Office the name and address of some person resident in the United States on whom may be served notices or process in proceedings affecting the mark. Such notices or process may be served upon the person so designated by leaving with him or mailing to him a copy thereof at the address specified in the last designation so filed. If the person so designated cannot be found at the address given in the last designation, such notice or process may be served upon the Commissioner. **Leg.H.** July 5, 1946, ch. 540, § 1, 60 Stat. 427; October 9, 1962, P.L. 87-772 § 1, 76 Stat. 769; January 2, 1975, P.L. 93-596 § 1, 88 Stat. 1949; November 16, 1988, P.L. 100-667 § 103, 102 Stat. 3935.

§ 1052.   Trademarks Registrable on the Principal Register; Concurrent Registration.

No trademark by which the goods of the applicant may be distinguished from the goods of others shall be refused registration on the principal register on account of its nature unless it—

(a) Consists of or comprises immoral, deceptive, or scandalous matter; or matter which may disparage or falsely suggest a connection with persons, living or dead, institutions, beliefs, or national symbols, or bring them into contempt, or disrepute.

(b) Consists of or comprises the flag or coat of arms or other insignia of the United States, or of any State or municipality, or of any foreign nation, or any simulation thereof.

(c) Consists of or comprises a name, portrait, or signature identifying a particular living individual except by his written consent, or the name, signature, or portrait of a deceased President of the United States during the life of his widow, if any, except by the written consent of the widow.

(d) Consists of or comprises a mark which so resembles a mark registered in the Patent and Trademark Office, or a mark or trade name previously used in the United States by another and not abandoned, as to be likely, when used on or in connection with the goods of the applicant, to cause confusion, or to cause mistake, or to deceive: *Provided*, That if the Commissioner determines that confusion, mistake, or deception is not likely to result from the continued use by more than one person of the same or similar marks under conditions and limitations as to the mode or place of use of the marks or the goods on or in connection with which such marks are used, concurrent registrations may be issued to such persons when they have become entitled to use such marks as a result of their concurrent lawful use in commerce prior to (1) the earliest of the filing dates of the applications pending or of any registration issued under this Act; (2) July 5, 1947, in the case of registrations previously issued under the Act of March 3, 1881, or February 20, 1905, and continuing in full force and effect on that date; or (3) July 5, 1947, in the case of applications filed under the Act of February 20, 1905, and registered after July 5, 1947. Use prior to the filing date of any pending application or a registration shall not be required when the owner of such application or registration consents to the grant of a concurrent registration to the applicant. Concurrent registrations may also be issued by the Commissioner when a court of competent jurisdiction has finally determined that more than one person is entitled to use the same or similar marks in commerce. In issuing concurrent registrations, the Commissioner shall prescribe conditions and limitations as to the mode or place of use of the mark or the goods on or in connection with which such mark is registered to the respective persons.

(e) Consists of a mark which, (1) when used on or in connection with the goods of the applicant is merely descriptive or deceptively misdescriptive of them, or (2) when used on or in connection with the goods of the applicant is primarily geographically descriptive of them, except as indications of regional origin may be registrable under section 1054, (3) when used on or in connection with the goods of the applicant is primarily geographically deceptively misdescriptive of them, or (4) is primarily merely a surname.

(f) Except as expressly excluded in paragraphs (a), (b), (c), (d), and (e)(3) of this section, nothing herein shall prevent the registration of a mark used by the applicant which has become distinctive of the applicant's goods in commerce. The Commissioner may accept as prima facie evidence that the mark has become distinctive, as used on or in connection with the applicant's goods in commerce, proof of substantially exclusive and continuous use thereof as a mark by the applicant in commerce for the five years before the date on which the claim of distinctiveness is made. Nothing in this section shall prevent the registration of a mark which, when used on or in connection with the goods of the applicant, is primarily geographically deceptively misdescriptive of them, and which became distinctive of the applicant's goods in commerce before the date of the enactment of the North American Free Trade Agreement Implementation Act. **Leg.H.** July 5, 1946, ch. 540, § 2, 60 Stat. 428; October 9, 1962, P.L. 87-772 § 2, 76 Stat. 769; January 2, 1975, P.L. 93-596 § 1, 88 Stat. 1949; November 16, 1988, P.L. 100-667 § 104, 102 Stat. 3937.

§ 1053. Service marks registrable.

Subject to the provisions relating to the registration of trademarks, so far as they are applicable, service marks shall be registrable, in the same manner and with the same effect as are trademarks, and when registered they shall be entitled to the protection provided herein in the case of trademarks. Applications and procedure under this section shall conform as nearly as practicable to those prescribed for the registration of trademarks. **Leg.H.** July 5, 1946, ch. 540, § 3, 60 Stat. 429; November 16, 1988, P.L. 100-667 § 105, 102 Stat. 3938.

§ 1054. Collective marks and certification marks registrable.

Subject to the provisions relating to the registration of trademarks, so far as they are applicable, collective and certification marks, including indications of regional origin, shall be registrable under this Act, in the same manner and with the same effect as are trademarks, by persons, and nations, States, municipalities, and the like, exercising legitimate control over the use of the marks sought to be registered, even though not possessing an industrial or commercial establishment, and when registered they shall be entitled to the protection provided herein in the case of trademarks, except in the case of certification marks when used so as to represent falsely that the owner or a user thereof makes or sells the goods or performs the services on or in connection with which such mark is used. Applications and procedure under this section shall conform as nearly as practicable to those prescribed for the registration of trademarks. **Leg.H.** July 5, 1946, ch. 540, § 4, 60 Stat. 429; November 16, 1988, P.L. 100-667 § 106, 102 Stat. 3938.

§ 1055. Use by related companies.

Where a registered mark or a mark sought to be registered is or may be used legitimately by related companies, such use shall inure to the benefit of the registrant or applicant for registration, and such use shall not affect the validity of such mark or of its registration, provided such mark is not used in such manner as to deceive the public. If first use of a mark by a person is controlled by the registrant or applicant for registration of the mark with respect to the nature and quality of the goods or services, such first use shall inure to the benefit of the registrant or applicant, as the case may be. **Leg.H.** July 5, 1946, ch. 540 § 5, 60 Stat. 429; November 16, 1988, P.L. 100-667 § 107, 102 Stat. 3938.

§ 1056. Disclaimers

(a) The Commissioner may require the applicant to disclaim an unregistrable component of a mark otherwise registrable. An applicant may voluntarily disclaim a component of a mark sought to be registered.

(b) No disclaimer, including those made under subsection (e) of section 1057 of this Act, shall prejudice or affect the applicant's or registrant's rights then existing or thereafter arising in the disclaimed matter, or his right of registration on another application if the disclaimed matter be or shall have become distinctive of his goods or services. **Leg.H.** July 5, 1946, ch. 540 § 6, 60 Stat. 429; October 9, 1962, P.L. 87-772 § 3, 76 Stat. 769; November 16, 1988, P.L. 100-667 § 108, 102 Stat. 3938.

✳ § 1057. Certificates of registration.

(a) Form. Certificates of registration of marks registered upon the principal register shall be issued in the name of the United States of America, under the seal of the Patent and Trademark Office, and shall be signed by the Commissioner or have his signature placed thereon, and a record thereof shall be kept in the Patent and Trademark Office. The registration shall reproduce the mark, and state that the mark is registered on the principal register under this Act, the date of the first use of the mark, the date of the first use of the mark in commerce, the particular goods or services for which it is registered, the number and date of the registration, the term thereof, the date on which the application for registration was received in the Patent and Trademark Office, and any conditions and limitations that may be imposed in the registration.

(b) Effect; prima facie evidence. A certificate of registration of a mark upon the principal register provided by this Act shall be prima facie evidence of the validity of the registered mark and of the registration of the mark, of the registrant's ownership of the mark, and of the registrant's exclusive right to use the registered mark in commerce on or in connection with the goods or services specified in the certificate, subject to any conditions or limitations stated in the certificate.

(c) Filing as constructive use of mark. Contingent on the registration of a mark on the principal register provided by this Act, the filing of the application to register such mark shall constitute constructive use of the mark, conferring a right of priority, nationwide in effect, on or in connection with the goods or services specified in the registration against any other person except for a person whose mark has not been abandoned and who, prior to such filing—

(1) has used the mark;

(2) has filed an application to register the mark which is pending or has resulted in registration of the mark; or

(3) has filed a foreign application to register the mark on the basis of which he or she has acquired a right of priority, and timely files an application under section 1126(d) to register the mark which is pending or has resulted in registration of the mark.

(Matthew Bender & Co., Inc.)

(d) Issuance to Assignee. A certificate of registration of a mark may be issued *Assignee* to the assignee of the applicant, but the assignment must first be recorded in the Patent and Trademark Office. In case of change of ownership the Commissioner shall, at the request of the owner and upon a proper showing and the payment of the prescribed fee, issue to such assignee a new certificate of registration of the said mark in the name of such assignee, and for the unexpired part of the original period.

(e) Cancellation upon application by registrant; amendment or disclaimer of registration. Upon application of the registrant the Commissioner may permit any registration to be surrendered for cancellation, and upon cancellation appropriate entry shall be made in the records of the Patent and Trademark Office. Upon application of the registrant and payment of the prescribed fee, the Commissioner for good cause may permit any registration to be amended or to be disclaimed in part: *Provided*, That the amendment or disclaimer does not alter materially the character of the mark. Appropriate entry shall be made in the records of the Patent and Trademark Office and upon the certificate of registration or, if said certificate is lost or destroyed, upon a certified copy thereof.

(f) Sealed and certified copies as evidence. Copies of any records, books, papers, or drawings belonging to the Patent and Trademark Office relating to marks, and copies of registrations, when authenticated by the seal of the Patent and Trademark Office and certified by the Commissioner, or in his name by an employee of the Office duly designated by the Commissioner, shall be evidence in all cases wherein the originals would be evidence; and any person making application therefor and paying the prescribed fee shall have such copies.

(g) Correction of mistakes made by Patent and Trademark Office. Whenever a material mistake in a registration, incurred through the fault of the Patent and Trademark Office, is clearly disclosed by the records of the Office a certificate stating the fact and nature of such mistake, shall be issued without charge and recorded and a printed copy thereof shall be attached to each printed copy of the registration certificate and such corrected registration shall thereafter have the same effect as if the same had been originally issued in such corrected form, or in the discretion of the Commissioner a new certificate of registration may be issued without charge. All certificates of correction heretofore issued in accordance with the rules of the Patent and Trademark Office and the registrations to which they are attached shall have the same force and effect as if such certificates and their issue had been specifically authorized by statute.

(h) Correction of mistakes made by applicant. Whenever a mistake has been made in a registration and a showing has been made that such mistake occurred in good faith through the fault of the applicant, the Commissioner is authorized to issue a certificate of correction or, in his discretion, a new certificate upon the payment of the prescribed fee: *Provided*, That the correction does not involve such changes in the registration as to require republication of the mark. **Leg.H.** July 5, 1946, ch. 540 § 7, 60 Stat. 430; August 17, 1950, ch. 733, 64 Stat. 459; October 9, 1962, P.L. 87-772 § 4, 76 Stat. 770; January 2, 1975, P.L. 93-596 § 1, 88 Stat. 1949; November 16, 1988, P.L. 100-667 § 109, 102 Stat. 3938.

§ 1058. Duration 10 years *Provided, registration yrs.*   §8

(a) Each certificate of registration shall remain in force for ten years: *Provided,* That the registration of any mark under the provisions of this Act shall be canceled by the Commissioner at the end of six years following its date, unless within one year next preceding the expiration of such six years the registrant shall file in the Patent and Trademark Office an affidavit setting forth those goods or services recited in the registration on or in connection with which the mark is in use in commerce and attaching to the affidavit a specimen or facsimile showing current use of the mark, or showing that any nonuse is due to special circumstances which excuse such nonuse and is not due to any intention to abandon the mark. Special notice of the requirement for such affidavit shall be attached to each certificate of registration.

(b) Any registration published under the provisions of subsection (c) of section 1062 of this Act shall be canceled by the Commissioner at the end of six years after the date of such publication unless within one year next preceding the expiration of such six years the registrant shall file in the Patent and Trademark Office an affidavit showing that said mark is in use in commerce or showing that its nonuse is due to special circumstances which excuse such nonuse and is not due to any intention to abandon the mark.

(c) The Commissioner shall notify any registrant who files either of the above-prescribed affidavits of his acceptance or refusal thereof and, if a refusal, the reasons therefor. **Leg.H.** July 5, 1946, ch. 540 § 8, 60 Stat. 431; January 2, 1975, P.L. 93-596 § 1, 88 Stat. 1949; August 27, 1982, P.L. 97-247 § 8, 96 Stat. 320; November 16, 1988, P.L. 100-667 § 110, 102 Stat. 3939.

§ 1059. Renewal Every 10 years   §9

(a) Each registration may be renewed for periods of ten years from the end of the expiring period upon payment of the prescribed fee and the filing of a verified application therefor, setting forth those goods or services recited in the registration on or in connection with which the mark is still in use in commerce and having attached thereto, a specimen or facsimile showing current use of the mark, or showing that any nonuse is due to special circumstances which excuse such nonuse and it is not due to any intention to abandon the mark. Such application may be made at any time within six months before the expiration of the period for which the registration was issued or renewed, or it may be made within three months after such expiration on payment of the additional fee herein prescribed.

(b) If the Commissioner refuses to renew the registration, he shall notify the registrant of his refusal and the reasons therefor.

(c) An applicant for renewal not domiciled in the United States shall be subject to and comply with the provisions of section 1051(e) of this Act. **Leg.H.** July 5, 1946, ch. 540 § 9, 60 Stat. 431; October 9, 1962, P.L. 87-772 § 5, 76 Stat. 770; November 16, 1988, P.L. 100-667 § 111, 102 Stat. 3939.

§ 1060. Assignment.

[handwritten: § 10   Assignable w/ goodwill.]

A registered mark or a mark for which application to register has been filed shall
be assignable with the goodwill of the business in which the mark is used, or with *[handwritten: (i)]*
that part of the goodwill of the business connected with the use of and symbolized
by the mark. However, no application to register a mark under section 1051(b) shall *[handwritten: intent @ to use]*
be assignable prior to the filing of the verified statement of use under section
1051(d), except to a successor to the business of the applicant, or portion thereof, *[handwritten: Can't register, then assign w/out use.]*
to which the mark pertains, if that business is ongoing and existing. In any assign-
ment authorized by this section it shall not be necessary to include the goodwill of
the business connected with the use of and symbolized by any other mark used in
the business or by the name or style under which the business is conducted. *[handwritten: (2)]*
Assignments shall be by instruments in writing duly executed. Acknowledgment
shall be prima facie evidence of the execution of an assignment and when recorded
in the Patent and Trademark Office the record shall be prima facie evidence of
execution. An assignment shall be void as against any subsequent purchaser for a *[handwritten: (4)]*
valuable consideration without notice, unless it is recorded in the Patent and
Trademark Office within three months after the date thereof or prior to such
subsequent purchase. A separate record of assignments submitted for recording
hereunder shall be maintained in the Patent and Trademark Office.

An assignee not domiciled in the United States shall be subject to and comply
with the provisions of section 1051(e) hereof. **Leg.H.** July 5, 1946, ch. 540 § 10,
60 Stat. 431; October 9, 1962, P.L. 87-772, § 6, 76 Stat. 770; January 2, 1975, P.L.
93-596 § 1, 88 Stat. 1949; November 16, 1988, P.L. 100-667 § 112, 102 Stat. 3939.

§ 1061. Acknowledgments and verifications.

[handwritten: § (1)]

Acknowledgments and verifications required hereunder may be made before any
person within the United States authorized by law to administer oaths, or, when made
in a foreign country, before any diplomatic or consular officer of the United States
or before any official authorized to administer oaths in the foreign country concerned
whose authority is proved by a certificate of a diplomatic or consular officer of the
United States, or apostille of an official designated by a foreign country which, by
treaty or convention, accords like effect to apostilles of designated officials in the
United States, and shall be valid if they comply with the laws of the state or country
where made. **Leg.H.** July 5, 1946, ch. 540 § 11, 60 Stat. 431; August 27, 1982, P.L.
97-247 § 14(c), 96 Stat. 321. **Related Regs.** 37 C.F.R. §§ 2, 4.

§ 1062. Publication.

[handwritten: § 12]

(a) Upon the filing of an application for registration and payment of the prescribed
fee, the Commissioner shall refer the application to the examiner in charge of the
registration of marks, who shall cause an examination to be made and, if on such
examination it shall appear that the applicant is entitled to registration, or would be
entitled to registration upon the acceptance of the statement of use required by

section 1051(d) of this Act, the Commissioner shall cause the mark to be published in the Official Gazette of the Patent and Trademark Office: *Provided*, That in the case of an applicant claiming concurrent use, or in the case of an application to be placed in an interference as provided for in section 1066 of this Act, the mark, if otherwise registrable, may be published subject to the determination of the rights of the parties to such proceedings.

(b) If the applicant is found not entitled to registration, the examiner shall advise the applicant thereof and of the reasons therefor. The applicant shall have a period of six months in which to reply or amend his application, which shall then be reexamined. This procedure may be repeated until (1) the examiner finally refuses registration of the mark or (2) the applicant fails for a period of six months to reply or amend or appeal, whereupon the application shall be deemed to have been abandoned, unless it can be shown to the satisfaction of the Commissioner that the delay in responding was unavoidable, whereupon such time may be extended.

(c) A registrant of a mark registered under the provisions of the Act of March 3, 1881, or the Act of February 20, 1905, may, at any time prior to the expiration of the registration thereof, upon the payment of the prescribed fee file with the Commissioner an affidavit setting forth those goods stated in the registration on which said mark is in use in commerce and that the registrant claims the benefits of this Act for said mark. The Commissioner shall publish notice thereof with a reproduction of said mark in the Official Gazette, and notify the registrant of such publication and of the requirement for the affidavit of use or nonuse as provided for in subsection (b) of section 1058 of this Act. Marks published under this subsection shall not be subject to the provisions of section 1063 of this Act. **Leg.H.** July 5, 1946, ch. 540 § 12, 60 Stat. 432; October 9, 1962, P.L. 87-772 § 7, 76 Stat. 770; January 2, 1975, P.L. 93-596 § 1, 88 Stat. 1949; November 16, 1988, P.L. 100-667 § 113, 102 Stat. 3940. **Related Regs.** 37 C.F.R. §§ 2, 4.

§ 1063. Opposition

(a) Any person who believes that he would be damaged by the registration of a mark upon the principal register may, upon payment of the prescribed fee, file an opposition in the Patent and Trademark Office, stating the grounds therefor, within thirty days after the publication under subsection (a) of section 1062 of this Act of the mark sought to be registered. Upon written request prior to the expiration of the thirty-day period, the time for filing opposition shall be extended for an additional thirty days, and further extensions of time for filing opposition may be granted by the Commissioner for good cause when requested prior to the expiration of an extension. The Commissioner shall notify the applicant of each extension of the time for filing opposition. An opposition may be amended under such conditions as may be prescribed by the Commissioner.

(b) Unless registration is successfully opposed—

(1) a mark entitled to registration on the principal register based on an application filed under section 1051(a) or pursuant to section 1126 shall be registered in the

Patent and Trademark Office, a certificate of registration shall be issued, and notice of the registration shall be published in the Official Gazette of the Patent and Trademark Office; or

(2) a notice of allowance shall be issued to the applicant if the applicant applied for registration under section 1051(b). **Leg.H.** July 5, 1946, ch. 540 § 13, 60 Stat. 433; October 9, 1962, P.L. 87-772 § 8, 76 Stat. 771; January 2, 1975, P.L. 93-596 § 1, 88 Stat. 1949; January 2, 1975, P.L. 93-600 § 1, 88 Stat. 1955; August 27, 1982, P.L. 97-247 § 9(a), 96 Stat. 320; November 16, 1988, P.L. 100-667 § 114, 102 Stat. 3940. **Related Regs.** 37 C.F.R. §§ 2, 4.

§ 1064. Cancellation   w/in 5 years   §14

A petition to cancel a registration of a mark, stating the grounds relied upon, may, upon payment of the prescribed fee, be filed as follows by any person who believes that he is or will be damaged by the registration of a mark on the principal register established by this Act, or under the Act of March 3, 1881, or the Act of February 20, 1905:

(1) Within five years from the date of the registration of the mark under this Act.

(2) Within five years from the date of publication under section 1062(c) hereof of a mark registered under the Act of March 3, 1881, or the Act of February 20, 1905.

(3) At any time if the registered mark becomes the generic name for the goods or services, or a portion thereof, for which it is registered, or has been abandoned, or its registration was obtained fraudulently or contrary to the provisions of section 1054 or of subsection (a), (b), or (c) of section 1052 for a registration under this Act, or contrary to similar prohibitory provisions of such prior Acts for a registration under such Acts, or if the registered mark is being used by, or with the permission of, the registrant so as to misrepresent the source of the goods or services on or in connection with which the mark is used. If the registered mark becomes the generic name for less than all of the goods or services for which it is registered, a petition to cancel the registration for only those goods or services may be filed. A registered mark shall not be deemed to be the generic name of goods or services solely because such mark is also used as a name of or to identify a unique product or service. The primary significance of the registered mark to the relevant public rather than purchaser motivation shall be the test for determining whether the registered mark has become the generic name of goods or services on or in connection with which it has been used.

(4) At any time if the mark is registered under the Act of March 3, 1881, or the Act of February 20, 1905, and has not been published under the provisions of subsection (c) of section 1062 of this Act.

(5) At any time in the case of a certification mark on the ground that the registrant (A) does not control, or is not able legitimately to exercise control over, the use of such mark, or (B) engages in the production or marketing of any goods or services to which the certification mark is applied, or (C) permits the use of the certification

mark for purposes other than to certify, or (D) discriminately refuses to certify or to continue to certify the goods or services of any person who maintains the standards or conditions which such mark certifies:

Provided, That the Federal Trade Commission may apply to cancel on the grounds specified in paragraphs (3) and (5) of this section any mark registered on the principal register established by this Act, and the prescribed fee shall not be required. **Leg.H.** July 5, 1946, ch. 540 § 14, 60 Stat. 433; October 9, 1962, P.L. 87-772 § 9, 76 Stat. 771; August 27, 1982, P.L. 97-247 § 9(b), 96 Stat. 320; November 8, 1984, P.L. 98-620 § 102, 98 Stat. 3335; November 16, 1988, P.L. 100-667 § 115, 102 Stat. 3940. **Related Regs.** 37 C.F.R. §§ 2, 4.

After 5 years,
affidavit
§ **1065.   Incontestability of right to use mark.**   § 15

Except on a ground for which application to cancel may be filed at any time under paragraphs (3) and (5) of section 1064 of this Act, and except to the extent, if any, to which the use of a mark registered on the principal register infringes a valid right acquired under the law of any State or Territory by use of a mark or trade name continuing from a date prior to the date of registration under this Act of such registered mark, the right of the registrant to use such registered mark in commerce for the goods or services on or in connection with which such registered mark has been in continuous use for five consecutive years subsequent to the date of such registration and is still in use in commerce, shall be incontestable: *Provided,* That—

(1) there has been no final decision adverse to registrant's claim of ownership of such mark for such goods or services, or to registrant's right to register the same or to keep the same on the register; and

(2) there is no proceeding involving said rights pending in the Patent and Trademark Office or in a court and not finally disposed of; and

(3) an affidavit is filed with the Commissioner within one year after the expiration of any such five-year period setting forth those goods or services stated in the registration on or in connection with which such mark has been in continuous use for such five consecutive years and is still in use in commerce, and other matters specified in paragraphs (1) and (2) of this section; and

(4) no incontestable right shall be acquired in a mark which is the generic name for the goods or services or a portion thereof, for which it is registered.

Subject to the conditions above specified in this section, the incontestable right with reference to a mark registered under this Act shall apply to a mark registered under the Act of March 3, 1881, or the Act of February 20, 1905, upon the filing of the required affidavit with the Commissioner within one year after the expiration of any period of five consecutive years after the date of publication of a mark under the provisions of subsection (c) of section 1062 of this Act.

The Commissioner shall notify any registrant who files the above-prescribed affidavit of the filing thereof. **Leg.H.** July 5, 1946, ch. 540 § 15, 60 Stat. 433; October 9, 1962, P.L. 87-772 § 10, 76 Stat. 771; January 2, 1975, P.L. 93-596 § 1,

88 Stat. 1949; August 27, 1982, P.L. 97-247 § 10, 96 Stat. 320; November 16, 1988, P.L. 100-667 § 116, 102 Stat. 3941. **Related Regs.** 37 C.F.R. §§ 2, 4.

§ 1066.   Interference

Upon petition showing extraordinary circumstances, the Commissioner may declare that an interference exists when application is made for the registration of a mark which so resembles a mark previously registered by another, or for the registration of which another has previously made application, as to be likely when used on or in connection with the goods or services of the applicant to cause confusion or mistake or to deceive. No interference shall be declared between an application and the registration of a mark the right to the use of which has become incontestable. **Leg.H.** July 5, 1946, ch. 540 § 16, 60 Stat. 434; October 9, 1962, P.L. 87-772 § 11, 76 Stat. 771; August 27, 1982, P.L. 97-247 § 11, 96 Stat. 321; November 16, 1988, P.L. 100-667 § 117, 102 Stat. 3941. **Related Regs.** 37 C.F.R. §§ 2, 4.

§ 1067.   Notice of inter partes proceedings; bearing by Trademark Trial and Appeal Board.

In every case of interference, opposition to registration, application to register as a lawful concurrent user, or application to cancel the registration of a mark, the Commissioner shall give notice to all parties and shall direct a Trademark Trial and Appeal Board to determine and decide the respective rights of registration.

The Trademark Trial and Appeal Board shall include the Commissioner, the Deputy Commissioner, the Assistant Commissioners, and members appointed by the Commissioner. Employees of the Patent and Trademark Office and other persons, all of whom shall be competent in trademark law, shall be eligible for appointment as members. Each case shall be heard by at least three members of the Board, the members hearing such case to be designated by the Commissioner. **Leg.H.** July 5, 1946, ch. 540 § 17, 60 Stat. 434; August 8, 1958, P.L. 85-609 § 1(a), 72 Stat. 540; January 2, 1975, P.L. 93-596 § 1, 88 Stat. 1949; October 15, 1980, P.L. 96-455 § 1, 94 Stat. 2024; November 16, 1988, P.L. 100-667 § 117, 102 Stat. 3941. **Related Regs.** 37 C.F.R. §§ 2, 4.

§ 1068.   Refusal, cancellation, or restriction of registration; concurrent use.

In such proceedings the Commissioner may refuse to register the opposed mark, may cancel the registration, in whole or in part, may modify the application or registration by limiting the goods or services specified therein, may otherwise restrict or rectify with respect to the register the registration of a registered mark, may refuse to register any or all of several interfering marks, or may register the mark or marks for the person or persons entitled thereto, as the rights of the parties hereunder may be established in the proceedings: *Provided,* That in the case of the registration of any mark based on concurrent use, the Commissioner shall determine and fix the conditions and limitations provided for in subsection (d) of section 1052 of this Act. However, no final judgment shall be entered in favor of an applicant under section 1051(b) before the mark is registered, if such applicant cannot prevail without establishing constructive use pursuant to section 1057(c). **Leg.H.** July 5, 1946, ch. 540 § 18, 60 Stat. 435; November 16, 1988, P.L. 100-667 § 118, 102 Stat. 3941. **Related Regs.** 37 C.F.R. §§ 2, 4.

§ 1069.   Applicability, in inter partes proceeding, of equitable principles of laches, estoppel and acquiescence.

In all inter partes proceedings equitable principles of laches, estoppel, and acquiescence, where applicable may be considered and applied. **Leg.H.** July 5, 1946, ch. 540 § 19, 60 Stat. 435; January 2, 1975, P.L. 93-594 § 1, 88 Stat. 1949; November 16, 1988, P.L. 100-667 § 119, 102 Stat. 3941. **Related Regs.** 37 C.F.R. §§ 2, 4.

§ 1070.   Appeal from examiner to Trademark Trial and Appeal Board.

An appeal may be taken to the Trademark Trial and Appeal Board from any final decision of the examiner in charge of the registration of marks upon the payment of the prescribed fee. **Leg.H.** July 5, 1946, ch. 540 § 20, 60 Stat. 435; August 8, 1958, P.L. 85-609 § 1(b), 72 Stat. 540. **Related Regs.** 37 C.F.R. §§ 2, 4.

§ 1071.   Review of Commissioner's or Trademark Trial and Appeal Board's decision.

(a) (1) An applicant for registration of a mark, party to an interference proceeding, party to an opposition proceeding, party to an application to register as a lawful concurrent user, party to a cancellation proceeding, a registrant who has filed an affidavit as provided in section 1058, or an applicant for renewal, who is dissatisfied with the decision of the Commissioner or Trademark Trial and Appeal Board, may appeal to the United States Court of Appeals for the Federal Circuit thereby waiving his right to proceed under subsection (b) of this section: *Provided,* That such appeal shall be dismissed if any adverse party to the proceeding, other than the Commissioner, shall, within twenty days after the appellant has filed notice of appeal according to paragraph (2) of this subsection, files notice with the Commissioner that he elects to have all further proceedings conducted as provided in subsection (b) of this section. Thereupon the appellant shall have thirty days thereafter within which to file a civil action under subsection (b) of this section, in default of which the decision appealed from shall govern the further proceedings in the case.

(2) When an appeal is taken to the United States Court of Appeals for the Federal Circuit, the appellant shall file in the Patent and Trademark Office a written notice of appeal directed to the Commissioner, within such time after the date of the decision from which the appeal is taken as the Commissioner prescribes, but in no case less than 60 days after that date.

(3) The Commissioner shall transmit to the United States Court of Appeals for the Federal Circuit a certified list of the documents comprising the record in the Patent and Trademark Office. The court may request that the Commissioner forward the original or certified copies of such documents during pendency of the appeal. In an ex parte case, the Commissioner shall submit to that court a brief explaining the grounds for the decision of the Patent and Trademark Office, addressing all the issues involved in the appeal. The court shall, before hearing an appeal, give notice of the time and place of the hearing to the Commissioner and the parties in the appeal.

(4) The United States Court of Appeals for the Federal Circuit shall review the decision from which the appeal is taken on the record before the Patent and Trademark Office. Upon its determination the court shall issue its mandate and opinion to the Commissioner, which shall be entered of record in the Patent and Trademark Office and shall govern the further proceedings in the case. However, no final judgment shall be entered in favor of an applicant under section 1051(b) before the mark is registered, if such applicant cannot prevail without establishing constructive use pursuant to section 1057(c).

(b) (1) Whenever a person authorized by subsection (a) of this section to appeal to the United States Court of Appeals for the Federal Circuit is dissatisfied with the decision of the Commissioner or Trademark Trial and Appeal Board, said person may, unless appeal has been taken to said United States Court of Appeals for the Federal Circuit, have remedy by a civil action if commenced within such time after such decision, not less than sixty days, as the Commissioner appoints or as provided in subsection (a) of this section. The court may adjudge that an applicant is entitled to a registration upon the application involved, that a registration involved should be canceled, or such other matter as the issues in the proceeding require, as the facts in the case may appear. Such adjudication shall authorize the Commissioner to take any necessary action, upon compliance with the requirements of law. However, no final judgment shall be entered in favor of an applicant under section 1051(b) before the mark is registered, if such applicant cannot prevail without establishing constructive use pursuant to section 1057(c).

(2) The Commissioner shall not be made a party to an inter partes proceeding under this subsection, but he shall be notified of the filing of the complaint by the clerk of the court in which it is filed and shall have the right to intervene in the action.

(3) In any case where there is no adverse party, a copy of the complaint shall be served on the Commissioner, and, unless the court finds the expenses to be unreasonable, all the expenses of the proceeding shall be paid by the party bringing the case, whether the final decision is in favor of such party or not. In suits brought hereunder, the record in the Patent and Trademark Office shall be admitted on motion of any party, upon such terms and conditions as to costs, expenses, and the

further cross-examination of the witnesses as the court imposes, without prejudice to the right of any party to take further testimony. The testimony and exhibits of the record in the Patent and Trademark Office, when admitted, shall have the same effect as if originally taken and produced in the suit.

(4) Where there is an adverse party, such suit may be instituted against the party in interest as shown by the records of the Patent and Trademark Office at the time of the decision complained of, but any party in interest may become a party to the action. If there be adverse parties residing in a plurality of districts not embraced within the same State, or an adverse party residing in a foreign country, the United States District Court for the District of Columbia shall have jurisdiction and may issue summons against the adverse parties directed to the marshal of any district in which any adverse party resides. Summons against adverse parties residing in foreign countries may be served by publication or otherwise as the court directs. **Leg.H.** July 5, 1946, ch. 540 § 21, 60 Stat. 435; July 19, 1952, ch. 950 § 2, 66 Stat. 814; August 8, 1958, P.L. 85-609 § 1(c), 72 Stat. 540; October 9, 1962, P.L. 87-772 § 12, 76 Stat. 771; January 2, 1975, P.L. 93-596 § 1, 88 Stat. 1949; January 2, 1975, P.L. 93-600 § 2, 88 Stat. 1955; April 2, 1982, P.L. 97-164 § 162(1), 96 Stat. 49; November 8, 1984, P.L. 98-620 § 414(b), 98 Stat. 3363; November 16, 1988, P.L. 100-667 § 120, 102 Stat. 3942. **Related Regs.** 37 C.F.R. §§ 2, 4.

§ 1072. **Registration as notice.**   Sec 22 [Lanham]

Registration of a mark on the principal register provided by this Act or under the Act of March 3, 1881, or the Act of February 20, 1905, shall be constructive notice of the registrant's claim of ownership thereof. **Leg.H.** July 5, 1946, ch. 540 § 22, 60 Stat. 435.

SUBCHAPTER II
The Supplemental Register

§ 1091. **Supplemental Register.**   Sec 23 [Lanham]

(a) In addition to the principal register, the Commissioner shall keep a continuation of the register provided in paragraph (b) of section 1 of the Act of March 19, 1920, entitled "An Act to give effect to certain provisions of the convention for the protection of trademarks and commercial names, made and signed in the city of Buenos Aires, in the Argentine Republic, August 20, 1910, and for other purposes," to be called the supplemental register. All marks capable of distinguishing applicant's goods or services and not registrable on the principal register herein provided, except those declared to be unregistrable under subsections (a), (b), (c), (d), and (e)(3) of section 1052 of this Act, which are in lawful use in commerce by the owner thereof, on or in connection with any goods or services may be registered on the supplemental register upon the payment of the prescribed fee and compliance with the provisions of subsections (a) and (e) of section 1051 so far as they are applicable. Nothing in this section shall prevent the registration on the supplemental register of a mark, capable of distinguishing the applicant's goods or services and not registrable on the principal register under this Act, that is declared to be unregistrable under section 1052(e)(3), if such mark has been in lawful use in commerce by the owner therof, on or in connection with any goods or services, since before the date of the enactment of the North American Free Trade Agreement Implementation Act.

(b) Upon the filing of an application for registration on the supplemental register and payment of the prescribed fee the Commissioner shall refer the application to the examiner in charge of the registration of marks, who shall cause an examination to be made and if on such examination it shall appear that the applicant is entitled to registration, the registration shall be granted. If the applicant is found not entitled to registration the provisions of subsection (b) of section 1062 of this Act shall apply.

(c) For the purposes of registration on the supplemental register, a mark may consist of any trademark, symbol, label, package, configuration of goods, name, word, slogan, phrase, surname, geographical name, numeral, or device or any combination of any of the foregoing, but such mark must be capable of distinguishing the applicant's goods or services. **Leg.H.** July 5, 1946, ch. 540 § 23, 60 Stat. 435; October 9, 1962, P.L. 87-772 § 13, 76 Stat. 773; November 16, 1988, P.L. 100-667 § 121, 102 Stat. 3942. **Related Regs.** 37 C.F.R. §§ 2, 4.

§ 1092.   Cancellation.

Marks for the supplemental register shall not be published for or be subject to opposition, but shall be published on registration in the Official Gazette of the Patent and Trademark Office. Whenever any person believes that he is or will be damaged by the registration of a mark on this register he may at any time, upon payment of the prescribed fee and the filing of a petition stating the ground therefor, apply to the Commissioner to cancel such registration. The Commissioner shall refer such application to the Trademark Trial and Appeal Board which shall give notice thereof to the registrant. If it is found after a hearing before the Board that the registrant is not entitled to registration, or that the mark has been abandoned, the registration shall be canceled by the Commissioner. However, no final judgment shall be entered in favor of an applicant under section 1051(b) before the mark is registered, if such applicant cannot prevail without establishing constructive use pursuant to section 1057(c). **Leg.H.** July 5, 1946, ch. 540 § 24, 60 Stat. 436; August 8, 1958, P.L. 85-609 § 1(d), 72 Stat. 540; October 9, 1962, P.L. 87-772 § 14, 76 Stat. 773; January 2, 1975, P.L. 93-596 § 1, 88 Stat. 1949; November 16, 1988, P.L. 100-667 § 122, 102 Stat. 3943. **Related Regs.** 37 C.F.R. §§ 2, 4.

§ 1093.   Supplemental registration certificate.

The certificates of registration for marks registered on the supplemental register shall be conspicuously different from certificates issued for marks registered on the principal register. **Leg.H.** July 5, 1946, ch. 540 § 25, 60 Stat. 436. **Related Regs.** 37 C.F.R. §§ 2, 4.

§ 1094.　General provisions.　§26

The provisions of this Act shall govern so far as applicable applications for registration and registrations on the supplemental register as well as those on the principal register, but applications for and registrations on the supplemental register shall not be subject to or receive the advantages of sections 1051(b), 1052(e), 1052(f), 1057(b), 1057(c), 1062(a), 1063 to 1068, inclusive, 1072, 1115 and 1124 of this Act. **Leg.H.** July 5, 1946, ch. 540 § 26, 60 Stat. 436; November 16, 1988, P.L. 100-667 § 123, 102 Stat. 3943. **Related Regs.** 37 C.F.R. §§ 2, 4.

§27

§ 1095.　Principal registration not precluded by supplemental registration.

Registration of a mark on the supplemental register, or under the Act of March 19, 1920, shall not preclude registration by the registrant on the principal register established by this Act. Registration of a mark on the supplemental register shall not constitute an admission that the mark has not acquired distinctiveness. **Leg.H.** July 5, 1946, ch. 540 § 27, 60 Stat. 436; November 16, 1988, P.L. 100-667 § 124, 102 Stat. 3943. **Related Regs.** 37 C.F.R. §§ 2, 4.

§28

§ 1096.　Department of Treasury; supplemental registration not filed.

Registration on the supplemental register or under the Act of March 19, 1920, shall not be filed in the Department of the Treasury or be used to stop importations. **Leg.H.** July 5, 1946, ch. 540 § 28, 60 Stat. 436. **Related Regs.** 19 C.F.R. § 133.

SUBCHAPTER III
General Provisions

Both Sections

§29

§ 1111.　Notice of Registration; display with mark; actual notice.

Notwithstanding the provisions of section 1072 hereof, a registrant of a mark registered in the Patent and Trademark Office, may give notice that his mark is registered by displaying with the mark the words "Registered in U.S. Patent and Trademark Office" or "Reg. U.S. Pat. & Tm. Off." or the letter R enclosed within a circle, thus ® ; and in any suit for infringement under this Act by such a registrant failing to give such notice of registration, no profits and no damages shall be recovered under the provisions of this Act unless the defendant had actual notice of the registration. **Leg.H.** July 5, 1946, ch. 540 § 29, 60 Stat. 436; October 9, 1962, P.L. 87-772 § 15, 76 Stat. 773; January 2, 1975, P.L. 93-596 §§ 1, 2, 88 Stat. 1949; November 16, 1988, P.L. 100-667 § 125, 102 Stat. 3943. **Related Regs.** 37 C.F.R. §§ 2, 4.

§ 1112.   Classification of goods and services; registration in plurality of classes.

The Commissioner may establish a classification of goods and services, for convenience of Patent and Trademark Office administration, but not to limit or extend the applicant's or registrant's rights. The applicant may apply to register a mark for any or all of the goods or services on or in connection with which he or she is using or has a bona fide intention to use the mark in commerce: *Provided,* That if the Commissioner by regulation permits the filing of an application for the registration of a mark for goods or services which fall within a plurality of classes, a fee equaling the sum of the fees for filing an application in each class shall be paid, and the Commissioner may issue a single certificate of registration for such mark. **Leg.H.** July 5, 1946, ch. 540 § 30, 60 Stat. 436; October 9, 1962, P.L. 87-772 § 16, 76 Stat. 773; January 2, 1975, P.L. 93-596 § 1, 88 Stat. 1949; November 16, 1988, P.L. 100-667 § 126, 102 Stat. 3943. **Related Regs.** 37 C.F.R. §§ 2, 4, 6.

§ 1113.   Fees.

(a) The Commissioner will establish fees for the filing and processing of an application for the registration of a trademark or other mark and for all other services performed by and materials furnished by the Patent and Trademark Office related to trademarks and other marks. However, no fee for the filing or processing of an application for the registration of a trademark or other mark or for the renewal or assignment of a trademark or other mark will be adjusted more than once every three years. No fee established under this section will take effect prior to sixty days following notice in the Federal Register.

(b) The Commissioner may waive the payment of any fee for any service or material related to trademarks or other marks in connection with an occasional request made by a department or agency of the Government, or any officer thereof. The Indian Arts and Crafts Board will not be charged any fee to register Government trademarks of genuineness and quality for Indian products or for products of particular Indian tribes and groups. **Leg.H.** July 5, 1946, ch. 540 § 31, 60 Stat. 437; August 8, 1958, P.L. 85-609 § 1(e), 72 Stat. 540; July 24, 1965, P.L. 89-83 § 3, 79 Stat. 260; January 2, 1975, P.L. 93-596 § 1, 88 Stat. 1949; December 12, 1980, P.L. 96-517 § 5, 94 Stat. 3018; August 27, 1982, P.L. 97-247 § 3(f), 96 Stat. 319; September 8, 1982, P.L. 97-256 § 103, 96 Stat. 816; December 10, 1991, P.L. 102-204 § 5(f)(1), 105 Stat. 1640. **Related Regs.** 37 C.F.R. §§ 2, 4.

§ 1114.   Remedies; infringement; innocent infringers

(1) Any person who shall, without the consent of the registrant—

(a) use in commerce any reproduction, counterfeit, copy, or colorable imitation of a registered mark in connection with the sale, offering for sale, distribution, or advertising of any goods or services on or in connection with which such use is likely to cause confusion, or to cause mistake, or to deceive; or

(b) reproduce, counterfeit, copy, or colorably imitate a registered mark and apply such reproduction, counterfeit, copy, or colorable imitation to labels, signs, prints, packages, wrappers, receptacles or advertisements intended to be used in commerce upon or in connection with the sale, offering for sale, distribution, or advertising of goods or services on or in connection with which such use is likely to cause confusion, or to cause mistake, or to deceive,

shall be liable in a civil action by the registrant for the remedies hereinafter provided. Under subsection (b) hereof, the registrant shall not be entitled to recover profits or damages unless the acts have been committed with knowledge that such imitation is intended to be used to cause confusion, or to cause mistake, or to deceive. As used in this subsection, the term ~any person~ includes any State, any instrumentality of a State, and any officer or employee of a State or instrumentality of a State acting in his or her official capacity. Any State, and any such instrumentality, officer, or employee, shall be subject to the provisions of this Act in the same manner and to the same extent as any nongovernmental entity.

(2) Notwithstanding any other provision of this Act, the remedies given to the owner of a right infringed under this Act or to a person bringing an action under section 1125(a) shall be limited as follows:

(A) Where an infringer or violator is engaged solely in the business of printing the mark or violating matter for others and establishes that he or she was an innocent infringer or innocent violator, the owner of the right infringed or person bringing the action under section 1125(a) shall be entitled as against such infringer or violator only to an injunction against future printing.

(B) Where the infringement or violation complained of is contained in or is part of paid advertising matter in a newspaper, magazine, or other similar periodical or in an electronic communication as defined in section 2510(12) of Title 18, the remedies of the owner of the right infringed or person bringing the action under section 1125(a) as against the publisher or distributor of such newspaper, magazine, or other similar periodical or electronic communication shall be limited to an injunction against the presentation of such advertising matter in future issues of such newspapers, magazines, or other similar periodicals or in future transmissions of such electronic communications. The limitations of this subparagraph shall apply only to innocent infringers and innocent violators.

(C) Injunctive relief shall not be available to the owner of the right infringed or person bringing the action under section 1125(a) with respect to an issue of a newspaper, magazine, or other similar periodical or an electronic communication containing infringing matter or violating matter where restraining the dissemination of such infringing matter or violating matter in any particular issue of such periodical or in an electronic communication would delay the delivery of such issue or transmission of such electronic communication after the regular time for such delivery or transmission, and such delay would be due to the method by which publication and distribution of such periodical or transmission of such electronic communication is customarily conducted in accordance with sound business practice, and not due to any method or device adopted to evade this section or to prevent or delay the issuance of an injunction or restraining order with respect to such infringing matter or violating matter.

(D) As used in this paragraph—

(i) the term "violator" means a person who violates section 1125(a); and

(ii) the term "violating matter" means matter that is the subject of a violation under section 1125(a). **Leg.H.** July 5, 1946, ch. 540 § 32, 60 Stat. 437; October 9, 1962, P.L. 87-772 § 17, 76 Stat. 773; November 16, 1988, P.L. 100-667 § 127, 102 Stat. 3943; October 27, 1992, P.L. 102-542 § 3, 106 Stat. 3567.

§ 1115. Registration as evidence of right to exclusive use; defenses. §33

(a) Any registration issued under the Act of March 3, 1881, or the Act of February 20, 1905, or of a mark registered on the principal register provided by this Act and owned by a party to an action shall be admissible in evidence and shall be prima facie evidence of the validity of the registered mark and of the registration of the mark, of the registrant's ownership of the mark, and of the registrant's exclusive right to use the registered mark in commerce on or in connection with the goods or services specified in the registration subject to any conditions or limitations stated therein, but shall not preclude another person from proving any legal or equitable defense or defect, including those set forth in subsection (b) of this section which might have been asserted if such mark had not been registered.

(b) To the extent that the right to use the registered mark has become incontestable under section 1065, the registration shall be conclusive evidence of the validity of the registered mark and of the registration of the mark, of the registrant's ownership of the mark, and of the registrant's exclusive right to use the registered mark in commerce. Such conclusive evidence shall relate to the exclusive right to use the mark on or in connection with the goods or services specified in the affidavit filed under the provisions of section 1065, or in the renewal application filed under the provisions of section 1059 if the goods or services specified in the renewal are fewer in number, subject to any conditions or limitations in the registration or in such affidavit or renewal application. Such conclusive evidence of the right to use the registered mark shall be subject to proof of infringement as defined in section 1114, and shall be subject to the following defenses or defects:

(1) That the registration or the incontestable right to use the mark was obtained fraudulently; or

(2) That the mark has been abandoned by the registrant; or

(3) That the registered mark is being used by or with the permission of the registrant or a person in privity with the registrant, so as to misrepresent the source of the goods or services on or in connection with which the mark is used; or

(4) That the use of the name, term, or device charged to be an infringement is a use, otherwise than as a mark, of the party's individual name in his own business, or of the individual name of anyone in privity with such party, or of a term or device

which is descriptive of and used fairly and in good faith only to describe the goods or services of such party, or their geographic origin; or

(5) That the mark whose use by a party is charged as an infringement was adopted without knowledge of the registrant's prior use and has been continuously used by such party or those in privity with him from a date prior to (A) the date of constructive use of the mark established pursuant to section 1057(c), (B) the registration of the mark under this Act if the application for registration is filed before the effective date of the Trademark Law Revision Act of 1988, or (C) publication of the registered mark under subsection (c) of section 1062 of this Act: *Provided, however,* That this defense or defect shall apply only for the area in which such continuous prior use is proved; or

(6) That the mark whose use is charged as an infringement was registered and used prior to the registration under this Act or publication under subsection (c) of section 1062 of this Act of the registered mark of the registrant, and not abandoned: *Provided, however,* That this defense or defect shall apply only for the area in which the mark was used prior to such registration or such publication of the registrant's mark; or

(7) That the mark has been or is being used to violate the antitrust laws of the United States; or

(8) That equitable principles, including laches, estoppel, and acquiescence, are applicable. **Leg.H.** July 5, 1946, ch. 540 § 33, 60 Stat. 438; October 9, 1962, P.L. 87-772 § 18, 76 Stat. 774; November 16, 1988, P.L. 100-667 § 128(a), (b), 102 Stat. 3944.

§ 1116. Injunctions; enforcement; notice of filing suit given Commissioner.

(a) The several courts vested with jurisdiction of civil actions arising under this Act shall have power to grant injunctions, according to the principles of equity and upon such terms as the court may deem reasonable, to prevent the violation of any right of the registrant of a mark registered in the Patent and Trademark Office or to prevent a violation under section 1125(a). Any such injunction may include a provision directing the defendant to file with the court and serve on the plaintiff within thirty days after the service on the defendant of such injunction, or such extended period as the court may direct, a report in writing under oath setting forth in detail the manner and form in which the defendant has complied with the injunction. Any such injunction granted upon hearing, after notice to the defendant, by any district court of the United States, may be served on the parties against whom such injunction is granted anywhere in the United States where they may be found, and shall be operative and may be enforced by proceedings to punish for contempt, or otherwise, by the court by which such injunction was granted, or by any other United States district court in whose jurisdiction the defendant may be found.

(b) The said courts shall have jurisdiction to enforce said injunction, as herein provided, as fully as if the injunction had been granted by the district court in which it is sought to be enforced. The clerk of the court or judge granting the injunction shall, when required to do so by the court before which application to enforce said injunction is made, transfer without delay to said court a certified copy of all papers on file in his office upon which said injunction was granted.

(c) It shall be the duty of the clerks of such courts within one month after the filing of any action, suit, or proceeding involving a mark registered under the provisions of this Act to give notice thereof in writing to the Commissioner setting forth in order so far as known the names and addresses of the litigants and the designating number or numbers of the registration or registrations upon which the action, suit, or proceeding has been brought, and in the event any other registration be subsequently included in the action, suit, or proceeding by amendment, answer, or other pleading, the clerk shall give like notice thereof to the Commissioner, and within one month after the judgement is entered or an appeal is taken the clerk of the court shall give notice thereof to the Commissioner, and it shall be the duty of the Commissioner on receipt of such notice forthwith to endorse the same upon the file wrapper of the said registration or registrations and to incorporate the same as a part of the contents of said file wrapper.

(d) (1)(A) In the case of a civil action arising under section 1114(1)(a) of this Act entitled ~An Act to incorporate the United States Olympic Association~, approved September 21, 1950 (36 U.S.C. 380) with respect to a violation that consists of using a counterfeit mark in connection with the sale, offering for sale, or distribution of goods or services, the court may, upon ex parte application, grant an order under subsection (a) of this section pursuant to this subsection providing for the seizure of goods and counterfeit marks involved in such violation and the means of making such marks, and records documenting the manufacture, sale, or receipt of things involved in such violation.

(B) As used in this subsection the term "counterfeit mark" means—

(i) a counterfeit of a mark that is registered on the principal register in the United States Patent and Trademark Office for such goods or services sold, offered for sale, or distributed and that is in use, whether or not the person against whom relief is sought knew such mark was so registered; or

(ii) a spurious designation that is identical with, or substantially indistinguishable from, a designation as to which the remedies of this Act are made available by reason of section 110 of the Act entitled ~An Act to incorporate the United States Olympic Association~, approved September 21, 1950 (36 U.S.C. 380);

but such term does not include any mark or designation used on or in connection with goods or services of which the manufacture or producer was, at the time of the manufacture or production in question authorized to use the mark or designation for the type of goods or services so manufactured or produced, by the holder of the right to use such mark or designation.

(2) The court shall not receive an application under this subsection unless the applicant has given such notice of the application as is reasonable under the circumstances to the United States attorney for the judicial district in which such order is sought. Such attorney may participate in the proceedings arising under such

application if such proceedings may affect evidence of an offense against the United States. The court may deny such application if the court determines that the public interest in a potential prosecution so requires.

(3) The application for an order under this subsection shall—

(A) be based on an affidavit or the verified complaint establishing facts sufficient to support the findings of fact and conclusions of law required for such order; and

(B) contain the additional information required by paragraph (5) of this subsection to be set forth in such order.

(4) The court shall not grant such an application unless—

(A) the person obtaining an order under this subsection provides the security determined adequate by the court for the payment of such damages as any person may be entitled to recover as a result of a wrongful seizure or wrongful attempted seizure under this subsection; and

(B) the court finds that it clearly appears from specific facts that—

(i) an order other than an ex parte seizure order is not adequate to achieve the purposes of section 1114 of this Act;

(ii) the applicant has not publicized the requested seizure;

(iii) the applicant is likely to succeed in showing that the person against whom seizure would be ordered used a counterfeit mark in connection with the sale, offering for sale, or distribution of goods or services;

(iv) an immediate and irreparable injury will occur if such seizure is not ordered;

(v) the matter to be seized will be located at the place identified in the application;

(vi) the harm to the applicant of denying the application outweighs the harm to the legitimate interests of the person against whom seizure would be ordered of granting the application; and

(vii) the person against whom seizure would be ordered, or persons acting in concert with such person, would destroy, move, hide, or otherwise make such matter inaccessible to the court, if the applicant were to proceed on notice to such person.

(5) An order under this subsection shall set forth—

(A) the findings of fact and conclusions of law required for the order;

(B) a particular description of the matter to be seized, and a description of each place at which such matter is to be seized;

(C) the time period, which shall end not later than seven days after the date on which such order is issued, during which the seizure is to be made;

(D) the amount of security required to be provided under this subsection; and

(E) a date for the hearing required under paragraph (10) of this subsection.

(6) The court shall take appropriate action to protect the person against whom an order under this subsection is directed from publicity, by or at the behest of the plaintiff, about such order and any seizure under such order.

(7) Any materials seized under this subsection shall be taken into the custody of the court. The court shall enter an appropriate protective order with respect to discovery by the applicant of any records that have been seized. The protective order shall provide for appropriate procedures to assure that confidential information contained in such records is not improperly disclosed to the applicant.

(8) An order under this subsection, together with the supporting documents, shall be sealed until the person against whom the order is directed has an opportunity to contest such order, except that any person against whom such order is issued shall have access to such order and supporting documents after the seizure has been carried out.

(9) The court shall order that a United States marshal or other law enforcement officer is to serve a copy of the order under this subsection and then is to carry out the seizure under such order. The court shall issue orders, when appropriate, to protect the defendant from undue damage from the disclosure of trade secrets or other confidential information during the course of the seizure, including, when appropriate, orders restricting the access of the applicant (or any agent or employee of the applicant) to such secrets or information.

(10)(A) The court shall hold a hearing, unless waived by all the parties, on the date set by the court in the order of seizure. That date shall be not sooner than ten days after the order is issued and not later than fifteen days after the order is issued, unless the applicant for the order shows good cause for another date or unless the party against whom such order is directed consents to another date for such hearing. At such hearing the party obtaining the order shall have the burden to prove that the facts supporting findings of fact and conclusions of law necessary to support such order are still in effect. If that party fails to meet that burden, the seizure order shall be dissolved or modified appropriately.

(B) In connection with a hearing under this paragraph, the court may make such orders modifying the time limits for discovery under the Rules of Civil Procedure as may be necessary to prevent the frustration of the purposes of such hearing.

(11) A person who suffers damage by reason of a wrongful seizure under this subsection has a cause of action against the applicant for the order under which such seizure was made, and shall be entitled to recover such relief as may be appropriate, including damages for lost profits, cost of materials, loss of good will, and punitive damages in instances where the seizure was sought in bad faith, and, unless the court finds extenuating circumstances, to recover a reasonable attorney's fee. The court in its discretion may award prejudgment interest on relief recovered under this paragraph, at an annual interest rate established under section 6621 of the Internal Revenue Code of 1954, commencing on the date of service of the claimant's pleading setting forth the claim under this paragraph and ending on the date such recovery is granted, or for such shorter time as the court deems appropriate. **Leg.H.** July 5, 1946, ch. 540 § 34, 60 Stat. 439; January 2, 1975, P.L. 93-596 § 1, 88 Stat. 1949; October 12, 1984, P.L. 98-473 § 1503(1), 98 Stat. 2179; October 22, 1986, P.L. 99-514 § 2, 100 Stat. 2095; November 16, 1988, P.L. 100-667 § 128(c)-(e), 102 Stat. 3945.

§ 1117.   Recovery of profits, damages, and costs.

(a) When a violation of any right of the registrant of a mark registered in the Patent and Trademark Office, or a violation under section 1125(a), shall have been established in any civil action arising under this Act, the plaintiff shall be entitled, subject to the provisions of sections 1111 and 1114, and subject to the principles of equity, to recover (1) defendant's profits, (2) any damages sustained by the plaintiff, and (3) the costs of the action. The court shall assess such profits and damages or cause the same to be assessed under its direction. In assessing profits the plaintiff shall be required to prove defendant's sales only; defendant must prove all elements of cost or deduction claimed. In assessing damages the court may enter judgment, according to the circumstances of the case, for any sum above the amount found as actual damages, not exceeding three times such amount. If the court shall find that the amount of the recovery based on profits is either inadequate or excessive the court may in its discretion enter judgment for such sum as the court shall find to be just, according to the circumstances of the case. Such sum in either of the above circumstances shall constitute compensation and not a penalty. The court in exceptional cases may award reasonable attorney fees to the prevailing party.

(b) In assessing damages under subsection (a), the court shall, unless the court finds extenuating circumstances, enter judgment for three times such profits or damages, whichever is greater, together with a reasonable attorney's fee, in the case of any violation of section 1114(1)(a) of this Act or section 110 of the Act entitled ~An Act to incorporate the United States Olympic Association~, approved September 21, 1950 (36 U.S.C. 380) that consists of intentionally using a mark or designation, knowing such mark or designation is a counterfeit mark (as defined in section 1116(d) of this Act, in connection with the sale, offering for sale, or distribution of goods or services. In such cases, the court may in its discretion award prejudgment interest on such amount at an annual interest rate established under section 6621 of the Internal Revenue Code of 1954, commencing on the date of the service of the claimant's pleadings setting forth the claim for such entry and ending on the date such entry is made, or for such shorter time as the court deems appropriate. **Leg.H.** July 5, 1946, ch. 540 § 35, 60 Stat. 439; October 9, 1962, P.L. 87-772 § 19, 76 Stat. 774; January 2, 1975, P.L. 93-596 § 1, 88 Stat. 1949; January 2, 1975, P.L. 93-600 § 3, 88 Stat. 1955; October 12, 1984, P.L. 98-473 § 1503(2), 98 Stat. 2182; October 22, 1986, P.L. 99-514 § 2, 100 Stat. 2095; November 16, 1988, P.L. 100-667 § 129, 102 Stat. 3945.

§ 1118.   Destruction of infringing articles.

In any action arising under this Act, in which a violation of any right of the registrant of a mark registered in the Patent and Trademark Office, or a violation under section 1125(a), shall have been established, the court may order that all labels, signs, prints, packages, wrappers, receptacles, and advertisements in the possession of the defendant, bearing the registered mark or, in the case of a violation of section 1125(a), the word, term, name, symbol, device, combination thereof, designation, description, or representation that is the subject of the violation, or any reproduction, counterfeit, copy, or colorable imitation thereof, and all plates, molds, matrices, and other means of making the same, shall be delivered up and destroyed. The party seeking an order under this section for destruction of articles seized under section 1116(d) shall give ten days' notice to the United States attorney for the judicial district in which such order is sought (unless good cause is shown for lesser notice) and such United States attorney may, if such destruction may affect evidence of an offense against the United States, seek a hearing on such destruction or participate in any hearing otherwise to be held with respect to such destruction. **Leg.H.** July 5, 1946, ch. 540 § 36, 60 Stat. 440; January 2, 1975, P.L. 93-596 § 1, 88 Stat. 1949; October 12, 1984, P.L. 98-473 § 1503(3), 98 Stat. 2182; November 16, 1988, P.L. 100-667 § 130, 102 Stat. 3945.

§ 1119. Power of court over registration; certification of decrees and §37 orders.

In any action involving a registered mark the court may determine the right to registration, order the cancelation of registrations, in whole or in part, restore canceled registrations, and otherwise rectify the register with respect to the registrations of any party to the action. Decrees and orders shall be certified by the court to the Commissioner, who shall make appropriate entry upon the records of the Patent and Trademark Office, and shall be controlled thereby. **Leg.H.** July 5, 1946, ch. 540 § 37, 60 Stat. 440; January 2, 1975, P.L. 93-596 § 1, 88 Stat. 1949.

§ 1120. Fraud; civil liability.   § 38

Any person who shall procure registration in the Patent and Trademark Office of a mark by a false or fraudulent declaration or representation, oral or in writing, or by any false means, shall be liable in a civil action by any person injured thereby for any damages sustained in consequence thereof. **Leg.H.** July 5, 1946, ch. 540 § 38, 60 Stat. 440; January 2, 1975, P.L. 93-596 § 1, 88 Stat. 1949.

§ 1121. Jurisdiction of federal courts; State, local, and other agency requirements.   Sec 39   Lanham

(a) The district and territorial courts of the United States shall have original jurisdiction and the courts of appeal of the United States (other than the United States Court of Appeals for the Federal Circuit) and the United States Court of Appeals for the District of Columbia shall have appellate jurisdiction, of all actions arising under this Act, without regard to the amount in controversy or to diversity or lack of diversity of the citizenship of the parties.

(b) No State or other jurisdiction of the United States or any political subdivision or any agency thereof may require alteration of a registered mark, or require that additional trademarks, service marks, trade names, or corporate names that may be associated with or incorporated into the registered mark be displayed in the mark in a manner differing from the display of such additional trademarks, service marks, trade names, or corporate names contemplated by the registered mark as exhibited in the certificate of registration issued by the United States Patent and Trademark Office. **Leg.H.** July 5, 1946, ch. 540 § 39, 60 Stat. 440; June 25, 1948, ch. 646 §§ 1, 32(a), 62 Stat. 870, 991; May 24, 1949, ch. 139 § 127, 63 Stat. 107; April 2, 1982, P.L. 97-164 § 148, 96 Stat. 46; October 12, 1982, P.L. 97-296, 96 Stat. 1316; November 16, 1988, P.L. 100-667 § 131, 102 Stat. 3946.

§ 1122. Liability of States, instrumentalities of States and State officials. *Sec 40 [repealed]*

(a) Any state, instrumentality of a State or any officer or employee of a State or instrumentality of a State acting in his or her official capacity, shall not be immune, under the eleventh amendment of the Constitution of the United States or under any other doctrine of sovereign immunity, from suit in Federal court by any person, including any governmental or nongovernmental entity for any violation under this Act.

(b) In a suit described in subsection (a) for a violation described in that subsection, remedies (including remedies both at law and in equity) are available for the violation to the same extent as such remedies are available for such a violation in a suit against any person other than a State, instrumentality of a State, or officer or employee of a State or instrumentality of a State acting in his or her official capacity. Such remedies include injunctive relief under section 1116, actual damages, profits, costs and attorney's fees under section 1117, destruction of infringing articles under section 1118, the remedies provided for under sections 1114, 1119, 1120, 1124, and 1125, and for any other remedies provided under this Act. **Leg.H.** October 27, 1992, P.L. 102-542 § 3, 106 Stat. 3567.

§ 1123. Rules and regulations. *Sec 41*

The Commissioner shall make rules and regulations, not inconsistent with law, for the conduct of proceedings in the Patent and Trademark Office under this cAct. **Leg.H.** July 5, 1946, ch. 540 § 41, 60 Stat. 440; January 2, 1975, P.L. 93-596 § 1, 88 Stat. 1949.

§ 1124. Importation of goods bearing infringing marks or names forbidden. *Sec 42*

Except as provided in subsection (d) of section 526 of the Tariff Act of 1930, no article of imported merchandise which shall copy or simulate the name of the any domestic manufacture, or manufacturer, or trader, or of any manufacturer or trader located in any foreign country which, by treaty, convention, or law affords similar privileges to citizens of the United States, or which shall copy or simulate a trademark registered in accordance with the provisions of this Act or shall bear a name or mark calculated to induce the public to believe that the article is manufactured in the United States, or that it is manufactured in any foreign country or locality other than the country or locality in which it is in fact manufactured, shall be admitted to entry at any customhouse of the United States; and, in order to aid the officers of the customs in enforcing this prohibition, any domestic manufacturer or trader, and any foreign manufacturer or trader, who is entitled under the provisions of a treaty, convention, declaration, or agreement between the United States and any foreign country to the advantages afforded by law to citizens of the United States in respect to trademarks and commercial names, may require his name and residence, and the name of the locality in which his goods are manufactured, and a copy of the certificate of registration of his trademark, issued in accordance with the provisions of this Act, to be recorded in books which shall be kept for this purpose in the Department of the Treasury, under such regulations as the Secretary of the Treasury shall prescribe, and may furnish to the Department facsimiles of his name, the name of the locality in which his goods are manufactured, or of his registered trademark, and thereupon the Secretary of the Treasury shall cause one or more copies of the same to be transmitted to each collector or other proper officer of customs. **Leg.H.** July 5, 1946, ch. 540 § 42, 60 Stat. 440; October 3, 1978, P.L. 95-410 § 211(b), 92 Stat. 903.

Sec 43

§ 1125.   False designations of origin and false descriptions forbidden.

(a) (1) Any person who, on or in connection with any goods or services, or any container for goods, uses in commerce any word, term, name, symbol, or device, or any combination thereof, or any false designation of origin, false or misleading description of fact, or false or misleading representation of fact, which—

(A) is likely to cause confusion, or to cause mistake, or to deceive as to the affiliation, connection, or association of such person with another person, or as to the origin, sponsorship, or approval of his or her goods, services, or commercial activities by another person, or

(B) in commercial advertising or promotion, misrepresents the nature, characteristics, qualities, or geographic origin of his or her or another person's goods, services, or commercial activities,

shall be liable in a civil action by any person who believes that he or she is or is likely to be damaged by such act.

(2) As used in this subsection, the term "any person" includes any State, instrumentality of a State or employee of a State or instrumentality of a State acting in his or her official capacity. Any State, and any such instrumentality, officer, or employee, shall be subject to the provisions of this Act in the same manner and to the same extent as any nongovernmental entity.

(b) Any goods marked or labeled in contravention of the provisions of this section shall not be imported into the United States or admitted to entry at any customhouse of the United States. The owner, importer, or consignee of goods refused entry at any customhouse under this section may have any recourse by protest or appeal that is given under the customs revenue laws or may have the remedy given by this Act in cases involving goods refused entry or seized. **Leg.H.** July 5, 1946, ch. 540 § 43, 60 Stat. 441; November 16, 1988, P.L. 100-667 § 132, 102 Stat. 3946; October 27, 1992, P.L. 102-542 § 3, 106 Stat. 3567.

§ 1126.   International conventions. § 44

(a) Register of Marks Communicated by international Bureaus. The Commissioner shall keep a register of all marks communicated to him by the international bureaus provided for by the conventions for the protection of industrial property, trademarks, trade and commercial names, and the repression of unfair competition to which the United States is or may become a party, and upon the payment of the fees required by such conventions and the fees herein prescribed may place the marks so communicated upon such register. This register shall show a facsimile of the mark or trade or commercial name; the name, citizenship, and address of the registrant; the number, date, and place of the first registration of the mark, including the dates on which application for such registration was filed and granted and the term of such registration; a list of goods or services to which the mark is applied as shown by the registration in the country of origin, and such other data as may be useful concerning the mark. This register shall be a continuation of the register provided in section 1(a) of the Act of March 19, 1920.

(b) Rights of foreign owner of trademark. Any person whose country of origin is a party to any convention or treaty relating to trademarks, trade or commercial names, or the repression of unfair competition, to which the United States is also a party, or extends reciprocal rights to nationals of the United States by law, shall be entitled to the benefits of this section under the conditions expressed herein to the extent necessary to give effect to any provision of such convention, treaty or reciprocal law, in addition to the rights to which any owner of a mark is otherwise entitled by this Act.

(c) Registration of mark in country of origin. No registration of a mark in the United States by a person described in subsection (b) of this section shall be granted until such mark has been registered in the country of origin of the applicant, unless the applicant alleges use in commerce. For the purposes of this section, the country of origin of the applicant is the country in which he has a bona fide and effective industrial or commercial establishment, or if he has not such an establishment the country in which he is domiciled, or if he has not a domicile in any of the countries described in subsection (b) of this section, the country of which he is a national.

(d) Effect of foreign application. An application for registration of a mark under sections 1051, 1053, 1054, 1091 or 1126(e) of this Act filed by a person described in subsection (b) of this section who has previously duly filed an application for registration of the same mark in one of the countries described in subsection (b) shall be accorded the same force and effect as would be accorded to the same application if filed in the United States on the same date on which the application was first filed in such foreign country: *Provided,* That—

(1) the application in the United States is filed within 6 months from the date on which the application was first filed in the foreign country;

(2) the application conforms as nearly as practicable to the requirements of this Act, inclusing a statement that the applicant has a bona fide intention to use the mark in commerce.

(3) the rights acquired by third parties before the date of the filing of the first application in the foreign country shall in no way be affected by a registration obtained on an application filed under this subsection (d);

(4) nothing in this subsection (d) shall entitle the owner of a registration granted under this section to sue for acts committed prior to the date on which his mark was registered in this country unless the registration is based on use in commerce.

In like manner and subject to the same conditions and requirements, the right provided in this section may be based upon a subsequent regularly filed application in the same foreign country, instead of the first filed foreign application: *Provided*, That any foreign application filed prior to such subsequent application has been withdrawn, abandoned, or otherwise disposed of, without having been laid open to public inspection and without leaving any rights outstanding, and has not served, nor thereafter shall serve, as a basis for claiming a right of priority.

(e) Registration of foregn-registered mark on principal or supplemental register. A mark duly registered in the country of origin of the foreign applicant may be registered on the principal register if eligible, otherwise on the supplemental register herein provided. The application therefor shall be accompanied by a certification or a certified copy of the registration in the country of origin of the applicant. The application must state the applicant's bona fide intention to use the mark in commerce, but use in commerce shall not be required prior to registration.

(f) Duration, validity, transfer or mark to be determined under this Act. The registration of a mark under the provisions of subsections (c), (d), and (e) of this section by a person described in subsection (b) of this section shall be independent of the registration in the country of origin and the duration, validity, or transfer in the United States of such registration shall be governed by the provisions of this Act.

(g) Trade names or commercial names. Trade names or commercial names of persons described in subsection (b) of this section shall be protected without the obligation of filing or registration whether or not they form parts of marks.

(h) Protection from unfair competition. Any person designated in subsection (b) of this section as entitled to the benefits and subject to the provisions of this Act shall be entitled to effective protection against unfair competition, and the remedies provided herein for infringement of marks shall be available so far as they may be appropriate in repressing acts of unfair competition.

(i) Benefits to citizens or residents of United States. Citizens or residents of the United States shall have the same benefits as are granted by this section to persons described in subsection (b) of this section. **Leg.H.** July 5, 1946, ch. 540 § 44, 60 Stat. 441; October 3, 1961, P.L. 87-333 § 2, 75 Stat. 748; October 9, 1962, P.L. 87-772 § 20, 76 Stat. 774; November 16, 1988, P.L. 100-667 § 133, 102 Stat. 3946.

§ 1127. Definition of terms; construction; intent.

In the construction of this Act, unless the contrary is plainly apparent from the context—

United States. The United States includes and embraces all territory which is under its jurisdiction and control.

Commerce. The word "commerce" means all commerce which may lawfully be regulated by Congress.

Principal Register, Supplemental Register. The term "principal register" refers to the register provided for by sections 1051 through 1072 hereof, and the term "supplemental register" refers to the register provided for by sections 1091 through 1096 thereof.

Person, juristic person. The term "person" and any other word or term used to designate the applicant or other entitled to a benefit or privilege or rendered liable under the provisions of this Act includes a juristic person as well as a natural person. The term "juristic person" includes a firm, corporation, union, association, or other organization capable of suing and being sued in a court of law. The term "person" also includes any State, any instrumentality of a State, and any officer or employee of a State or instrumentality of a State acting in his or her official capacity. Any State, and any such instrumentality, officer, or employee, shall be subject to the provisions of this Act in the same manner and to the same extent as any nongovernmental entity.

Applicant, registrant. The terms "applicant" and "registrant" embrace the legal representatives, predecessors, successors and assigns of such applicant or registrant.

Commissioner. The term "Commissioner" means the Commissioner of Patents and Trademarks.

Related company. The term "related company" means any person whose use of a mark is controlled by the owner of the mark with respect to the nature and quality of the goods or services on or in connection with which the mark is used.

Trade name, commercial name. The terms "trade name" and "commercial name" mean any name used by a person to identify his or her business or vocation.

Trademark. The term "trademark" includes any word, name, symbol, or device, or any combination thereof—

(1) used by a person, or

(2) which a person has a bona fide intention to use in commerce and applies to register on the principal register established by this Act,

to identify and distinguish his or her goods, including a unique product, from those manufactured or sold by others and to indicate the source of the goods, even if that source is unknown.

Service mark. The term "service mark" means any word, name, symbol, or device, or any combination thereof—

(1) used by a person, or

(2) which a person has a bona fide intention to use in commerce and applies to register on the principal register established by this Act,

to identify and distinguish the services of one person, including a unique service, from the services of others and to indicate the source of the services, even if that source is unknown. Titles, character names, and other distinctive features of radio or television programs may be registered as service marks notwithstanding that they, or the programs, may advertise the goods of the sponsor.

Certification mark. The term "certification mark" means any word, name, symbol, or device, or any combination thereof—

(1) used by a person other than its owner, or

(2) which its owner has a bona fide intention to permit a person other than the owner to use in commerce and files an application to register on the principal register established by this Act,

to certify regional or other origin, material, mode of manufacture, quality, accuracy, or other characteristics of such person's goods or services or that the work or labor on the goods or services was performed by members of a union or other organization.

Collective mark. The term "collective mark" means a trademark or service mark—

(1) used by the members of a cooperative, an association, or other collective group or organization, or

(2) which such cooperative, association, or other collective group or organization has a bona fide intention to use in commerce and applies to register on the principal register established by this Act, and includes marks indicating membership in a union, an association, or other organization.

Mark. The term "mark" includes any trademark, service mark, collective mark, or certification mark.

Use in commerce. The term "use in commerce" means the bona fide use of a mark in the ordinary course of trade, and not made merely to reserve a right in a mark. For purposes of this Act, a mark shall be deemed to be in use in commerce—

(1) on goods when—

(A) it is placed in any manner on the goods or their containers or the displays associated therewith or on the tags or labels affixed thereto, or if the nature of the goods makes such placement impracticable, then on documents associated with the goods or their sale, and

(B) the goods are sold or transported in commerce, and

(2) on services when it is used or displayed in the sale or advertising of services and the services are rendered in commerce, or the services are rendered in more than one State or in the United States and a foreign country and the person rendering the services is engaged in commerce in connection with the services.

Abandonment of mark. A mark shall be deemed to be "abandoned" when either of the following occurs:

(1) When its use has been discontinued with intent not to resume such use. Intent not to resume may be inferred from circumstances. Nonuse for two consecutive years shall be prima facie evidence of abandonment. "Use" of a mark means the bona fide use of that mark made in the ordinary course of trade, and not made merely to reserve a right in a mark.

(2) When any course of conduct of the owner, including acts of omission as well as commission, causes the mark to become the generic name for the goods or services on or in connection with which it is used or otherwise to lose its significance as a mark. Purchaser motivation shall not be a test for determining abandonment under this paragraph.

Colorable imitation. The term "colorable imitation" includes any mark which so resembles a registered mark as to be likely to cause confusion or mistake or to deceive.

Registered mark The term "registered mark" means a mark registered in the United States Patent and Trademark Office under this Act or under the Act of March 3, 1881, or the Act of February 20, 1905, or the Act of March 19, 1920. The phrase "marks registered in the Patent and Trademark Office" means registered marks.

Prior acts. The term "Act of March 3, 1881," "Act of February 20, 1905," or "Act of March 19, 1920," means the respective Act as amended.

Counterfeit. A "counterfeit" is a spurious mark which is identical with, or substantially indistinguishable from, a registered mark.

Singular and plural. Words used in the singular include the plural and vice versa.

Intent of Act. The intent of this Act is to regulate commerce within the control of Congress by making actionable the deceptive and misleading use of marks in such commerce; to protect registered marks; and to provide rights and remedies stipulated by treaties and conventions respecting trademarks, tradenames, and unfair competition entered into between the United States and foreign nations. **Leg.H.** July 5, 1946, ch. 540 § 45, 60 Stat. 443; October 9, 1962, P.L. 87-772 § 21, 76 Stat. 774; January 2, 1975, P.L. 93-596 § 1, 88 Stat. 1949; November 8, 1984, P.L. 98-620 § 103, 98 Stat. 3335; November 16, 1988, P.L. 100-667 § 134, 102 Stat. 3946; October 27, 1992, P.L. 102-542, 106 Stat. 3567.

TABLE OF CASES

[References are to pages. Principal cases capitalized/pages italicized.]

[References are to pages. Principal cases capitalized/pages italicized.]

[References are to pages. Principal cases capitalized/pages italicized.]

[References are to pages. Principal cases capitalized/pages italicized.]

[References are to pages. Principal cases capitalized/pages italicized.]

[References are to pages. Principal cases capitalized/pages italicized.]

[References are to pages. Principal cases capitalized/pages italicized.]

[References are to pages. Principal cases capitalized/pages italicized.]

[References are to pages. Principal cases capitalized/pages italicized.]

[References are to pages. Principal cases capitalized/pages italicized.]

Q

R

[References are to pages. Principal cases capitalized/pages italicized.]

[References are to pages. Principal cases capitalized/pages italicized.]

[References are to pages. Principal cases capitalized/pages italicized.]

[References are to pages. Principal cases capitalized/pages italicized.]

U

[References are to pages. Principal cases capitalized/pages italicized.]

INDEX

[References are to pages.]

A

[References are to pages.]

[References are to pages.]

[References are to pages.]

D

[References are to pages.]

[References are to pages.]

(Matthew Bender & Co., Inc.)

[References are to pages.]

[References are to pages.]

J

L

[References are to pages.]

[References are to pages.]

Q

QUALITY CONTROL (See LICENSING)

R

REGIONAL ORIGIN (See GEOGRAPHICAL TERMS)

REGISTRATION

[References are to pages.]

S

[References are to pages.]

[References are to pages.]

TRADE NAMES
Definition of term; Lanham Act 19
Dilution of distinctiveness 337–352
Registration 103
Rights (See TRADE IDENTITY RIGHTS)

TTAB (See TRADEMARK TRIAL AND APPEAL BOARD)

TYING ARRANGEMENTS
Antitrust violations 278–282

U

UNCLEAN HANDS DOCTRINE
Judicial application 267–372
Trademark rights 257–258, 267–372

UNFAIR COMPETITION
(See also specific subject headings)
Advertising misrepresentations 352–368
Antitrust violations 272–285
Configuration of product 369–396
Confusion as to source (See CONFUSION; SIMILARITY)
Disparagement 337–352
False designation/description of product; misrepresentation 352–368
False/misleading labeling (See MISREPRESENTATION)
Federal Trade Commission regulation 471–521
Food and Drug Administration regulation 521–526
Imitation of professional entertainer; commercials 419–434
Imitative products 212–226
Intent as factor 199–212
International Trade Commission regulation 112–116
Misappropriation doctrine 396–407
Misbranding (See MISREPRESENTATION)
Trade dress 369–396
Trademark infringement compared 3–5

UNIFORM DECEPTIVE TRADE PRACTICES ACT
Generally 530–537

USE (See TRADE IDENTITY RIGHTS and specific subject headings, *e.g.,* PERMITTED USE)

V

VENUE
Infringement actions 447–448

(Matthew Bender & Co., Inc.)